Educational
Administration

Educational

An Introduction

SECOND EDITION

Administration

Ralph B. Kimbrough
Michael Y. Nunnery
University of Florida

MACMILLAN PUBLISHING CO., INC.
New York
COLLIER MACMILLAN PUBLISHERS
London

Macmillan Publishing Co., Inc.
866 Third Avenue, New York, New York 10022

Collier Macmillan Canada, Inc.

Library of Congress Cataloging in Publication Data

Kimbrough, Ralph B.
  Educational administration.

  Includes bibliographies and indexes.
  1. School management and organization. I. Nunnery,
Michael Y. II. Title.
LB2805.K5165   1983   371.2   82-15168
ISBN 0-02-363980-6   AACR2

Printing: 1 2 3 4 5 6 7 8   Year: 3 4 5 6 7 8 9 0 1

ISBN 0-02-363980-6

Preface

ALTHOUGH the first edition of *Educational Administration: An Introduction* was well received as a beginning textbook in the field, professors and students have suggested changes that we believe will greatly improve its utility in preparation programs. These have been incorporated in this edition. Through reorganization of the sections, the student may read an overview of educational administration and an extensive discussion of how educational functions are organized before the more abstract conceptual foundations of administration are presented. Numerous professors using the book felt that this arrangement would help students to comprehend better and make application of the material included in the part concerning the conceptual milieu of the educational administrator. Thus material in the first edition about job perspectives and educational administration as a profession has been reorganized as Chapter 1. This is followed by a rewritten discussion of the tasks of educational administration and then by Part II, which explains how formal educational activities are organized at the federal, state, and local levels. The result is a textbook that is appropriate for use with a wider range of graduate students.

In our first edition we noted the almost universal agreement among professors that one of the principal attributes of a profession is a systematic body of theory that people must learn in college before they are licensed to practice. Thus we incorporated in the textbook, along with the knowledge about administration, a rather extensive discussion of the conceptual bases of the profession. This has been strengthened and incorporated as Part III. In addition to some reorganization and extensive rewriting of these chapters, the chapter on ethics of educational administration was moved to this part. Also, the discussion about the application of management theories to educational administration is included as a part of each chapter in which the theories are discussed. This is intended to improve the understandability and the conceptual application of the theories.

The focus of the final part of the book is on the socioeconomic and political forces that influence how education is organized and administered. The internal arrangement of the first edition has been maintained; however, the material has been updated.

Those using the textbook will find that, although some of the material is reorganized and all chapters are brought up to date, we have not deleted any of the subject matter used in the first edition. Thus we believe we have retained those qualitative aspects included in the first edition and improved the readability and usefulness of the textbook.

In summary, Part I provides an overview of professional development, career patterns, professional opportunities, educational preparation, and the basic tasks of educational administration. How education is organized and administered, including discussion of some basic issues, is contained in the four chapters included as Part II. Part III is a rather comprehensive discussion of the basic concepts of educational administration, including basic management theories, the cultural perspectives of formal education, administrative functions or processes, values, and administrative ethics. Part IV describes the social and political forces that influence educational administration, including the collective-bargaining process.

Finally, readers will note more reference to the administration of colleges and universities in this edition than was included in the first edition. This is intended to improve the usefulness of the textbook for those colleges in which the preparation programs for higher education administration and the administration of K–12 schools are integrated into one department. Moreover, we believe that educational administration is becoming an increasingly generalized function in which administrators of K–12 schools should understand higher education administration, and higher education administrators need greater knowledge and understanding of school administration. From this beginning, and depending on the reception of this idea by professors and students, future editions may offer greater integrated discussion of all levels of educational administration.

R. B. K.
M. Y. N.

Contents

ix

PART ONE
An Overview of Educational Administration

PERSONS *pondering a career choice are understandably interested in the opportunities that particular professions may offer them for personal advancement. But what a profession offers may depend upon the personal contributions one is willing and able to make to it. Sir Francis Bacon once observed, "I hold every man a debtor to his profession." Success may be greatly determined by how effectively one pays these debts in improving the profession.*

Each year many persons prepare to enter the practice of educational administration. Their success depends upon many factors, such as professional training, ability, professional opportunities, career planning, and so on. Persons planning to enter educational administration should make careful plans and think seriously about their personal responsibilities to the profession, such as being well prepared, working toward improving the profession, and understanding the tasks of educational administration.

In Chapter 1 the discussion centers upon the importance of selecting a career and opportunities in

1

educational administration. Persons will seldom be successful if they do not enjoy their work. Another aspect of professional success is educational preparation, which is also discussed here. An overview discussion of the tasks of educational administration is presented in Chapter 2. These tasks must be accomplished if the mission of an educational organization is to be achieved. Here the prospective educational leader can gain comprehension of the complex work that educational administration entails.

1

Educational Administration: A Perspective on Development, Preparation, and Opportunities

THIS chapter and the one following are based on the assumption that many readers have made a tentative choice of educational administration as a career or are considering such a choice and that relevant information is important in the choice process. The process is complex and one can choose from a plethora of theories related to career choice and development.[1] The theories appear to have several common elements, including the significance of information about career opportunities and about oneself as a basis for more intelligent career choices. Therefore, we urge that an effort be made to understand the status of educational administration as a field of work, the nature of the preparation required to enter the field, the available opportunities, and the tasks associated with various administrative positions. With such information, an assessment should be made of personal assets, liabilities, desires, and circumstances. The result should be a more rational decision about a career in educational administration. If the choice is to enter the field, a career plan should be implemented that gives attention to the type and level of prepa-

[1] For those interested in a review of the several prevailing theories of career choice and development, see: Samuel H. Osipow, *Theories of Career Development,* 2nd ed. (New York: Appleton, 1973).

3

ration needed, timing of the preparation in relation to experience, types of experience, and length of such experience.

Educational Administration As an Evolving Profession

In comparison to such professions as law, medicine, and theology and the fields of business, hospital, and public administration, educational administration is a relatively new field of study. As schooling became separated from the home and church, local communities "provided what minor finance was necessary, and elected a teacher, usually through a special committee of which the clergyman was a member."[2] This practice, which began in Massachusetts, was the basis for what was to continue for many years—direct management of public schools by lay persons. Only as the need for more schooling and more complex arrangements arose (e.g., multiteacher schools, high schools, partial state financing of schools, the creation of local school districts) was there a felt need to employ "school administrators."

The first state school superintendent was appointed in New York in 1812, as Brubacher observed, "largely out of the need to have someone administer the state common school fund."[3] The first school district superintendencies were created in the cities, with Buffalo and Louisville appointing superintendents in 1837 and Providence and St. Louis in 1839.[4] At the local school level, the "head" or "principal" teacher position emerged in the 1830s and 1840s with cities, such as Cincinnati and Detroit, appointing principal teachers for each of their "schoolhouses." The role of the principal teacher essentially was to handle clerical chores and look after the school building, in addition to his or her teaching duties. By 1870, in some large cities (e.g., Cincinnati, New York) the principal teacher had evolved into a full-time "supervising principal."[5]

By the late 1800s, school administrator positions were firmly established in the urban areas of the nation. However, in the small towns and rural areas, where one- and two-room schools remained the norm for several decades, full-time school administrator positions continued to evolve throughout much of the first half of this century. Thus it seems appropriate to characterize educational administration as an "evolving profession."

---

[2] Arthur B. Moehlman, *School Administration* (Boston: Houghton, 1940), p. 233.
[3] John S. Brubacher, *A History of the Problems of Education* (New York: McGraw-Hill, 1947), p. 576.
[4] Moehlman, op. cit., pp. 241–242.
[5] Ibid., pp. 237–238.

Significant Influences for Professionalization

The term *profession* is used loosely by the members of many occupational groups. On this point Goode stated, "An inclusive list of the occupations whose claims to professional status have been announced very likely would total as many as one hundred."[6] The U.S. Census Bureau lists numerous occupational pursuits as professions (e.g., accountant, architect, artist, attorney, clergyman, college professor, dentist, engineer, journalist, judge, librarian, natural scientist, optometrist, pharmacist, physician, social worker, teacher). Etzioni used the term *semiprofessions* in reference to many of these occupational pursuits.[7]

From their review of the development of professions, Carr-Saunders and Wilson concluded, "there can be no doubt that with the progress of science and the complexity of social organization, new intellectual techniques will evolve round which new professions will grow up."[8] Thus in their view there is progress in the growth of professionalism. How to achieve high professional status, however, is very complex. Goode saw the process as a competition among occupational groups for money, power, and prestige.[9] He pointed to the fact that raising the educational standards in medicine during the 1910–1920 decade "required the expenditure of power, money, and friendship."[10] Yet by virtue of their characteristics and status, many occupational groups may never achieve professional status. There are important traditions involved as well as great differences in the complexity of occupations.

Some writers have defined the sequential steps involved in the emergence of professions. Caplow identified four steps as follows: (1) establish a professional association with criteria for membership to keep out those unqualified; (2) change the name of the occupation to sever association with previous occupation; (3) develop and promulgate a code of ethics; and (4) prolong political agitation.[11] Wilensky offered eight steps to professionalization: (1) full-time pursuit of professional status; (2) university training established; (3) an organized national association; (4) redefinition of the work of the occupa-

---

[6] William J. Goode, "The Theoretical Limits of Professionalization," in Amitai Etzioni (ed.), *The Semi-Professions and Their Organization* (New York: The Free Press, 1969), p. 276.

[7] In Etzioni, ibid.

[8] Alexander M. Carr-Saunders and Paul A. Wilson, "The Emergence of Professions" in Sigmund Nosow and William H. Form (eds.), *Man, Work, and Society* (New York: Basic Books, 1962), p. 206.

[9] Goode, op. cit., p. 267.

[10] Ibid., p. 268.

[11] Theodore Caplow, *The Sociology of Work* (Minneapolis: University of Minnesota Press, 1954), pp. 139–140.

tion; (5) internal conflict between the old-guard leaders and new persons desiring to upgrade the occupation; (6) competition with closely allied occupations; (7) political agitation to gain legal protection; and (8) adoption of a code of ethics.[12]

Goode objected to defining the rise of professions through sequential steps. He expressed the view that, "Most of these social processes are going on simultaneously, so that it is difficult to state whether one actually began before another."[13] He felt, for example, that a code of ethics may be written very early.

Goode amplified the condition observed by others concerning the professional–client relationship in professions such as medicine, law, and theology. This is the need for the professional to have knowledge of private information about the client that is potentially dangerous to the client.[14] Goode contended that this access to the privacy of individuals heightens the need for the profession to enforce a code of ethics to protect its members thus producing cohesion within the profession. Moreover, there is the need for autonomy of the profession to protect the professional–client relationship. This is well-established in the legal and medical professions.[15]

As the development of educational administration is reviewed, many of the professionalization processes identified have obviously been given attention. As educational administration became a full-time activity, preparation programs were being established in some of the large universities, and by the onset of World War II these programs were moving toward maturity. Yet the number of programs and underlying knowledge base that focused on scientific management concepts (see Chapter 8) was inadequate. (We make no distinction between *administration* and *management*. Administration has often been used in connection with governmental and other nonprofit organizations and management with profit-making organizations; yet both have come to be defined essentially in terms of the coordination and integration of people and material to accomplish objectives.) Following World War II there was a significant expansion in the number of preparation programs, yet the concern for their quality remained. Under the leadership of some veteran practitioners, especially large-city superintendents, and some persons associated with educational administration degree programs, efforts were made to deal with some of the preparation program concerns and other problems seen as critical in developing a profession of educational administration. The principal mechanism used was organizational activity.

[12] Harold Wilensky, "The Professionalization of Everyone," *American Journal of Sociology,* 70 (September 1964), 142–146.
[13] Goode, op. cit., p. 275.
[14] Ibid., p. 297.
[15] Ibid., pp. 297–304.

In the forefront was the American Association of School Administrators (AASA), whose major concern was the superintendency and whose leadership during the late 1940s demonstrated much interest in the improvement of preparation programs. Also significant was the first national meeting of professors of educational administration held at Endicott, New York, in 1947. The result was the formation of the National Conference of Professors of Educational Administration (NCPEA), which has since met annually. This event was significant because, for the first time, college professors were talking to each other on a national basis, and fresh concepts were being developed about the training of educational administrators.

During this same period important conversations were also being held among leaders of the AASA, the W. K. Kellogg Foundation, and persons associated with the academic preparation of educational administrators. Moore described the activities that eventually led to the development of the W. K. Kellogg Foundation-supported Cooperative Program in Educational Administration (CPEA).[16] In his description of the discussions concerning the best way to proceed in improving the professional status of the field, Moore included some points that the student of educational administration today may well ponder. Some of the leaders thought that what would best accomplish professionalization in the field would be a strategy consistent with the Flexner Report. Flexner's analysis of the poor state of affairs in the schools preparing physicians was instrumental in upgrading the professional status of that field.[17] The W. K. Kellogg Foundation CPEA centers were visualized by many of the leaders in educational administration as a means of reaching the same objectives as those achieved in the movement headed by Flexner.

As a result of five regional conferences during 1948 and 1949, the W. K. Kellogg Foundation funded the CPEA with eight regional centers. The centers were funded initially as five-year programs, and funding was continued for some programs at reduced amounts for four more years. These regional programs provided stimulation for research and development of training programs and influenced knowledge development in the field. The programs provided an opportunity for professors, practitioners, and advanced-level graduate students to examine the conditions under which school aministrators practice and the programs that should be developed to prepare persons for practice.

The AASA created the Committee for the Advancement of School Administration in 1955 to seek improvement of the preparation and

---

[16] Hollis A. Moore, Jr., *Studies in School Administration* (Washington, D.C.: American Association of School Administrators, 1957).

[17] Abraham Flexner, *Medical Education in the United States and Canada*, Bulletin No. 4 (New York: Carnegie Foundation, 1910).

in-service assistance of administrators. The committee also worked with those associated with CPEA centers and provided advice and assistance in these programs. The interest of AASA in the in-service needs of educational administrators has continued. Its numerous publications and conferences provide the opportunities for practitioners to keep abreast of knowledge developments in the field. In 1968, AASA brought into existence the National Academy for School Executives, which serves the continuing education needs of practitioners through the many programs it sponsors each year at various locations around the nation.

In 1956 the leaders in the CPEA center at Teachers College, Columbia University, proposed the organization of the University Council for Educational Administration (UCEA). This proposed organization was to include in its membership the universities with larger programs in educational administration. The functions envisioned for the UCEA were (1) to seek improvement in programs for the preparation of school administrators, (2) to stimulate research and knowledge development, and (3) to provide for dissemination of ideas and practices. The work of the UCEA in program development has been noteworthy. Of particular merit has been the development of instructional materials. The UCEA became, for example, the primary producer and distribution agent for simulation materials for programs in educational administration. Through its research seminars, other conference activities, and its several journals, the UCEA has been active in knowledge development and its use in professional development. In the late 1970s, the UCEA created a university–school system partnership in a further effort to enhance linkages with practitioners in the dissemination of knowledge in educational administration.

The foregoing account of organizations and their efforts at professionalizing the field is by no means exhaustive. For example, the National Association of Secondary School Principals and National Elementary Principals Association have long maintained interests in the development of the principalship; AASA has developed a code of ethics for school administrators; and the federal government, through its financing of research and providing fellowships for those desiring to be educational administrators (e.g., Education Professions Development Act of 1967), has made a contribution to the professionalization of the field.

From the end of World War II through the 1970s there were many activities that were intended to enhance the professional status of the field, yet there were some counteractive forces. For the most part those interested in higher professional status did not have a political strategy. Professional maturity comes through the exercise of political influence to legitimize the monopolistic rights of the profession to control those who enter and to provide criminal prosecution for the "quacks" who attempt to practice without qualification. Other countervailing problems also existed. Even though the efforts of AASA to establish higher standards were laudable, there were serious divisions among administrative groups, which worked against cohesiveness and solidarity of effort.

Professional Attributes and Educational Administration

The body of literature about the attributes of a profession is considerable.[18] With the assistance of his students, Greenwood reviewed available sociological literature concerning these attributes and distilled them into five categories. According to Greenwood, "all professions seem to possess: (1) systematic theory, (2) authority, (3) community sanction, (4) ethical codes, and (5) culture."[19] Let us examine these attributes in terms of their meaning for educational administration.

Systematic Body of Theory. According to Greenwood, one differentiating factor in professions is that the "skills that characterize a profession flow from and are supported by a fund of knowledge that has been organized into an internally consistent system, called a *body of theory*."[20] Amplifying this point Greenwood observed, "And so treatises are written on legal theory, music theory, social work theory, the theory of the drama, and so on; but no books appear on the theory of punch-pressing or pipe-fitting or bricklaying."[21] The abstract nature of this theory requires a formal educational program to gain the conceptual knowledge as a basis for task performance or skill development. According to Greenwood, this suggests a program of preparation involving both intellectual achievement (learning the theory) and apprenticeship (learning the skills of the profession). (The nature and functions of theory are detailed in Chapter 8.)

To what extent has a body of theory been developed and disseminated through formal educational programs in educational administration? From the previous discussion on significant influences for professionalization there obviously has been much effort in this area. Numerous theories have been developed that borrow heavily from relevant basic disciplines and other fields of administration. However,

---

[18]Illustrative literature includes the following: Alexander M. Carr-Saunders and Paul A. Wilson, *The Professions* (Oxford: Clarendon, 1933); Everett C. Hughes, *Men and Their Work* (New York: The Free Press, 1958); John A. Jackson (ed.), *Professions and Professionalization* (London: Cambridge University Press, 1970); Philip Elliott, *The Sociology of Professions* (New York: Herder, 1972).

[19]Ernest Greenwood, "Attributes of a Profession," in Nosow and Form, op. cit., p. 207.

[20]Ibid., p. 208.

[21]Ibid.

the utility of many of the theories is questionable, and in the minds of many there is real doubt as to whether the theories constitute a *systematized* body of conceptual knowledge. (As discussed in Chapter 10, there is the possibility that "systems theory" might serve as a systemizing framework.) Furthermore, there are wide variations among the preparation programs for educational administrators concerning what conceptual knowledge is taught and how it is related to practice by means of clinical experiences.

Professional Authority. In explaining the concept of professional authority, Greenwood suggested the difference between customers and clients. Nonprofessional occupations have customers. In this relationship the customers are the authorities about the services desired. However, in the professional–client relationship, the professional is the authority for what the client needs relative to the professional's area of specialization.

The client derives a sense of security from the professional's assumption of authority. It is this authoritative air that is the principal source of the client's faith that the relationship he or she is about to enter contains the potential for meeting his or her needs.[22]

Numerous writers have observed that achieving this attribute presents problems for educational administrators, particularly of public schools, because the concept runs counter to the idea that educational policies (or what the clients need) should be determined through democratic participation. Superintendents are expected to recommend or suggest policies to the board of education. Should the community and the board not have enough confidence to follow any of the suggestions of the superintendent, the relationship is soon severed either through the purchase of or nonrenewal of contract.

There has been a tendency to admire those individuals who achieve an authoritative relationship with the board of education and the community. These are often referred to as "the true professionals." In other words, their superior achievements in influencing communities in the adoption of educational policies consistent with the norms of their admirers have won them a special place. The important question is whether the influence of the professional can be generalized.

Sanction of the Community. Sanction is an attribute that has given educators great concern. Sanction of the community relates to the formal or informal control of a profession over its training centers, licensure, confidentiality of client–professional relationships, and

---

[22]Ibid., p. 210.

powers to police the profession. As Greenwood noted, "By granting or withholding accreditation, a profession can, ideally, regulate its schools as to their number, location, curriculum content, and caliber of instruction."[23] Admission to practice is controlled by the profession through required graduation from an accredited school and through a screening process controlled by the profession. Attempts to practice the profession without a license make one subject to criminal charges and punishment.

Persons in the field of education have for many years recognized that they were weak in achieving this professional attribute. Consequently, there has been much interest in professional control over licensure, particularly among organizations for classroom teachers. The National Council for Accreditation of Teacher Education (NCATE) was formed to serve as a national accrediting agency for colleges of education. The accreditation of departments of educational administration is included as a part of this process. However, the influence of NCATE has not come close to the status the American Medical Association has achieved in influencing the education of physicians.

The licensing process for public school administrators in most of the states is not controlled by those in educational administration. A review of the certification requirements among the states, as compiled by Woellner, reveals much consistency.[24] In nearly all the states the person must have experience as a teacher, hold a master's degree with certain courses in educational administration, and hold a valid certificate as a teacher. Some of the states require administrative experience and additional graduate work beyond the master's degree (e.g., Minnesota) for the superintendent's certificate, and in isolated instances there is no special certification for administrators (e.g., Michigan).[25] The usual experience requirement for the principalship certificate is three years' experience as a teacher, although some states specify two years. There is some variation among the states. For example, in some states the person must have the endorsement of a college that offers an approved program.

In sum, even though there are efforts in most of the states to provide formal controls relative to those who practice as public school administrators and there is a mechanism to accredit preparation programs, the power of those in the field over such regulatory machinery is limited. Furthermore, control by those in the field over persons who practice in settings other than K–12 public schools (e.g., in higher education) is almost nonexistent.

[23] Ibid., p. 211.
[24] Elizabeth H. Woellner, *Requirements for Certification,* 45th ed. (Chicago: University of Chicago Press, 1980).
[25] Ibid., pp. 117–119.

Regulative Code of Ethics. A code of ethics does not of itself distinguish professional from nonprofessional occupations. In the case of professionals, Greenwood observed, "a professional code is perhaps more explicit, systematic, and binding; it certainly possesses more altruistic overtones, and is more public service-oriented."[26] The Hippocratic Oath in the medical profession is, of course, exemplary of written codes. The code of a profession goes much further than its formal aspects. There are unwritten norms that control the behavior of those in the profession. For example, some professions exercise guidance over the fees that should be charged.

The American Association of School Administrators has a code of ethics and a process for administering it. Knezevich noted that the code of ethics, first published in 1966, "represents the first time in the more than 100-year history of AASA when a written statement on the ethical concerns of the professional prevailed."[27] The 1976 version of the code (see Chapter 13) includes ten standards for governing the behavior of educational administrators.[28] However, the AASA code of ethics for educational administrators has not been taken as seriously as it deserves. In our opinion, too many educational administrators lack knowledge of the code, it is not emphasized in preparation programs, and the consequences of violating the code are practically nil.

The Professional Culture. Greenwood included in the professional culture all the norms, symbols, values, and expressions that are unique to the profession. Members of the profession are expected to subscribe to this culture. "Every profession entertains a stereotype of the ideal colleague; and, of course, it is always one who is thoroughly adjusted to the professional culture."[29] Greenwood went on to say that the professional training schools have the responsibility to admit only those who are acceptable to this culture.

Those in educational administration have learned this culture by observation of others, from professors, and from personal experience on the job. Much of what is learned is incidental to direct instruction, and often those who follow such a culture are not readily aware of it. Presumably one of the responsibilities of the preparation programs is to screen out those who do not subscribe to the professional culture; how well this responsibility has been assumed is open

[26] Greenwood, op. cit., p. 212.
[27] Stephen J. Knezevich, "The Ethical Concerns of Professional School Administrators," in Glenn L. Immegart and John Burroughs (eds.), *Ethics and the School Administrator* (Danville, Ill.: Interstate, 1970), p. 18.
[28] AASA Ethics Committee, *AASA Statement of Ethics for School Administrators and Procedural Guidelines* (Arlington, Va.: American Association of School Administrators, 1976), pp. 12–13.
[29] Greenwood, op. cit., p. 216.

to debate. Another alternative is to leave such screening to employers, but again, the effectiveness of this step is open to question.

Preparation Programs for Educational Administrators

As suggested previously, college preparation programs are central to the development of a profession, and in most of the states a minimum of a master's degree or the equivalent with an emphasis in educational administration is required to practice in public K–12 schools. Furthermore, it is estimated that well over 300 colleges and universities offer at least one graduate degree in educational administration. (Some institutions offer a master's degree, specialist or sixth-year certificate, and doctorate degree; others may offer the master's only or the master's and specialist.) Given the centrality of preparation programs to the development of the field, it is important, even for the beginning student, to understand the status of these programs and the issues related to them.

Preparation Program Trends

From a survey of educational administration preparation programs conducted over a decade ago, four major trends were identified.[30] First was the emphasis on "theory based substance drawn from social science disciplines" rather than the previously emphasized "technique-oriented subjects based on practical experience."[31] Second, a variety of field experiences in several differing settings was being used in the preparation of administrators. Third, a variety of instructional materials and methods (e.g., case method, multimedia simulation) was being employed. Fourth, in comparison to previous practice, there was greater specialization among the faculties, and the institutions were "employing fewer generalists with administration experience and more young scholars with social science backgrounds. . . ."[32]

With the possible exception of the fourth trend, the trends identified are still fairly descriptive of preparation programs, and are likely to remain so for the immediate future, even though the ferment and change-oriented mentality of that period are no longer as apparent. The emphasis on conceptual content drawn from the social sciences has continued. This is a reflection of the employment in the late 1960s

[30] Robin H. Farquhar and Michael Martin, "New Developments in the Preparation of Educational Leaders," *Phi Delta Kappan,* LIV (September 1972), 26–30.
[31] Ibid., 26.
[32] Ibid., 27.

and early 1970s of "young scholars with social science backgrounds." There is still an emphasis on individually designed clinical experiences and variety in instructional approaches. Support for our contention of the continuance of such trends may be found in a survey of 258 preparation programs, which was reported in 1978.[33] In this survey a heavy emphasis was found on "conceptual skills" and on three topics—administrative theory, leadership, and decision making.[34] There was also wide use of group processes, case studies, simulation, and role playing.[35]

During the 1970s, full-time enrollments in many programs dropped significantly, and the proportion of part-time students increased. As a result, fewer new professors were being employed and competition for the available professorships increased. Therefore, we believe that institutions, while continuing to desire persons with social science backgrounds, began to place more emphasis on administrative experience and to expect those persons employed to be broader in their teaching, research, and service responsibilities. This increase in breadth of expectations is a reflection of smaller faculties because of decreased full-time equivalent students.

Data from the 1978 survey and our own observations suggest four other program trends. First, there has been an increase in the proportion of women and minorities enrolled in educational administration preparation programs. Minorities made up about one-fifth of the enrollments and women were about one-third of the master's and about one-fourth of the doctoral enrollments.[36] If this trend is to continue, the graduates must succeed in securing appropriate employment in a rather competitive market. Second, there is an interest in competency-based programs where the emphasis is on student acquisition of identified competencies and the demonstration of their mastery (e.g., through an internship or state examinations) rather than the mere completion of required courses and the fulfillment of a teaching experience requirement. Third, there is a broadening of the scope of programs by adding specializations, such as special education administration and community education administration.[37] Also, it has been suggested that this broadened scope thrust is a reflection of efforts to maintain programs because there has been a decreased demand for educational administrators in conventional positions such as principals and superintendents. Fourth, there is increased flexibility in meeting the "residence" requirements. Historically, a fairly

[33] Dennis W. Spuck, William J. Davis, and Paula Silver, "A Descriptive Study of Administrator Training Programs," *UCEA Review,* XX (Fall 1978), 14–19.
[34] Ibid., 16.
[35] Ibid., 17.
[36] Ibid., 16.
[37] Ibid., 18.

common practice for institutions had been to require a period of "concentrated full-time study" as a part of degree programs (e.g., a year of residency in doctoral programs and a shorter period for nondoctoral programs). Some colleges are making alternative arrangements for residency, particularly for those students who are already practicing administrators.

Issues and Problems Relating to Preparation Programs

In view of the evolving nature of educational administration as a profession, some problems related to preparation for practice are to be expected. These range from the general, such as the low esteem in which these programs are held by the universities—an example of the status of education generally—to specific program substance and processes. Following is a brief discussion of four major program-related concerns.

Is a national strategy aimed at confining educational administrator preparation to a few very high-quality programs, thus limiting admissions, defensible? As noted earlier, one of the means by which medicine achieved high professional status was by limiting and upgrading the preparation programs. Some leaders in educational administration feel this is a necessary step if "true" professional status is to be achieved. They note the number of programs in existence is excessive, and there is great variation among the available programs relative to size, staff, admission standards, fiscal resources, and so on. Given that there is no predicted shortage of educational administrators, one may argue that resources should be concentrated in a few places where the emphasis would be on producing fewer but much more highly qualified educational administrators.

There is general agreement that no real need exists for the present number of programs and that they vary greatly on most quality measures; yet, is the concentrated preparation strategy the appropriate response? March suggested another alternative arguing that because educational organizations consist of a large number of relatively small autonomous units and that there is rapid turnover among administrators, educational administration could be "improved more rapidly by increasing the density of good administrators through the system than by focusing on a relatively small elite."[38] Accordingly, the concern should be for "the average quality of the top 50–75 percent" of the programs.[39]

What should be taught in educational administrator preparation programs? Previously the authors noted that the knowledge base for

---

[38]James G. March, "American Public School Administration: A Short Analysis," *School Review*, 86 (February 1978), 234.
[39]Ibid., 236.

educational administration needs to be strengthened. As such, what knowledge is necessary for practice is at the base of controversies about what should be taught and in what proportions. According to the 1978 survey of practice in 258 college and university departments, eight topics constituted the "core of educational administrator training programs." These were administrative theory, leadership, decision making, educational law, curriculum development, instructional supervision, district administration, and finance/budgeting.[40] A delphi panel (see Chapter 11) of fifteen superintendents and thirteen professors, as part of a projection of the future in educational administration, suggested the need for greater study of communication, economics of education, law, group dynamics, human relations, collective bargaining, and greater emphasis on internships.[41] In a report prepared for the AASA Committee for the Advancement of School Administration (CASA), a distinguished twelve-member committee recommended that administrator preparation (1) be interdisciplinary, including knowledge from law, business and economics, science, and the humanities; (2) include study of the processes of leadership, forms of communication, relationships with a board of education, and the tools of research and planning; (3) be performance based and field oriented, including a year-long, individually designed internship; and (4) provide a core of common knowledge and special knowledge for the several specializations within educational administration.[42] Given the trend to increase the scope of specializations in departments, common versus specialized knowledge probably will be of even greater concern in the future. To complicate the issue even further, March, assuming a high level of ambiguity in educational administration, suggested that "skills in intelligent foolishness, constructive aesthetics, and nonexperiential forms of learning are likely to be of greater importance than conventional wisdom suggests."[43]

To what extent should educational administrator preparation programs reflect the requirements and traditions of such time-honored degrees as the Master of Science and the Doctor of Philosophy? The time-honored degrees generally reflect study in a single academic discipline, base student admission on such academic criteria as previous grades and Graduate Record Examiniation (GRE) or other test scores, include a period of full-time study, require that mastery of subject matter be demonstrated in written and oral examinations, and re-

[40]Spuck, Davis, and Silver, op. cit., 16.

[41]Kenneth W. Brooks, Donald L. Martin, and Denny R. Vincent, "Educational Administration: Some Projections 1979–1984," *UCEA Review*, XXI (Winter 1980), 18–19.

[42]Committee for the Advancement of School Administration, *Guidelines for the Preparation of School Administrators* (Arlington, Va.: American Association of School Administrators, 1979), pp. 6–9.

[43]March, op. cit., 236.

quire completion of a thesis or dissertation. The CASA group recommended that programs be performance based and field oriented and
said further that the preparation "should have the characteristics of
a professional school rather than the qualities of graduate study in a
single academic discipline."[44] Conventional admissions criteria, the
usual examinations for a degree, the thesis or dissertation, and full-
time study requirements have been questioned regarding their relevance in preparing a person to practice as an educational administrator. The result is that some exceptions to the traditional admissions
criteria and examinations are sought and many institutions no longer
demand a master's or specialist's thesis. In some schools a "field project" has replaced the doctoral dissertation, and, as already noted, alternatives to full-time residence study are being offered by a number
of institutions. Perhaps the most radical departure from the traditional programs is the development of "external" degree programs,
which came into existence in the 1970s. These programs generally
provide study opportunities at a geographically convenient location
(i.e., no extended campus study is required) for the practicing administrators, use the student's workplace as a laboratory for research,
employ faculty on a part-time basis, and focus on projects designed to
solve actual problems in lieu of the traditional thesis or dissertation.
Such programs are very controversial with the critics arguing that
they lack the needed campus instructional resources, a "critical mass"
of students and faculty who interchange ideas, and the rigor of the
more traditional programs.[45]

*What should be the role of professors and practitioners in prepar-
ing persons for educational administration positions?* Historically, the
primary control of educational administrator preparation programs
has been vested with the college and university-based professors who,
within the requirements of accreditation agencies and state certification demands, determined program content, decided on means of delivery of instruction, directed student research, and provided most of
the instruction. State certification requirements reinforced this control in that a college or university graduate degree was mandated.
Practitioners were involved in that they sometimes served as adjunct
professors and taught an occasional course and/or supervised internships and served on special committees for advising a program staff,
program accreditation, or determining administrator certification requirements. In the late 1970s, with an increasing concern about the
relevance of the program content being provided by the professors,
some states set up practitioner-controlled academies, patterned some-

---

[44]Committee for the Advancement of School Administration, op. cit., p. 6.

[45]For the several viewpoints about the external doctorate see "Continuing the
Debate on External Degrees," *Phi Delta Kappan,* 60 (April 1979), 559–574.

what after AASA's National Academy for School Executives, to serve the continuing education needs of those already employed as educational administrators. The question in the minds of some is why not use these academies as an alternative for college or university-based preparation. Since they are "free" from the traditional institutional degree requirements, they can provide more relevant instruction. Two guidelines for preparing educational administrators, offered by the CASA group, tend to reinforce the notion of more practitioner involvement and control of preparation. Specifically, they suggested that colleges and universities should involve practitioners in designing, developing, operating, and evaluating programs and that the preparation should be under the jurisdiction of a school district *or* higher education institution.[46]

Educational Administration Opportunities in School Districts

Considered collectively, the public school districts of the nation employ the large majority of persons prepared as educational administrators. In the paragraphs that follow, the types of positions available are identified and described in terms of qualifications, demands, and rewards. In this instance both local school districts and regional units of various types are considered as districts.

Types of Jobs

Defining the jobs as those for which a certificate is required or thought desirable by school boards, opportunities available in school centers include the positions of principal; assistant, associate, and vice principals; administrative assistants; and deans. In some instances administrator preparation may be seen as desirable for department heads and/or team leaders. Because this is not usual, these positions are not included among the opportunities available. However, experience in such a position may be of value as a steppingstone or in helping a person to reach a decision about a career in educational administration. Beyond the local school, in area offices and central offices of districts there are administrative assistants, coordinators, supervisors, directors, and area, assistant, associate, and deputy superintendents. At the apex is the chief executive—the superintendent. (The foregoing titles are most frequently used, but some districts use other titles.)

There is a tendency to think in terms of being a superintendent when preparing to be a school administrator. This is a very restricted

[46] Committee for the Advancement of School Administration, op. cit., pp. 6–7.

view—there are fewer opportunities at the top. We estimate that fewer than 15,000 persons are employed as local district superintendents. Generally speaking, working with the school board, the superintendent develops policy, clarifies district goals, establishes and maintains an organizational structure, assumes leadership in the procurement of human and fiscal resources, ensures appropriate allocation of resources, and establishes and maintains an appraisal system to determine the extent of achievement toward organizational goals.

Where the title of deputy superintendent is used for the "number two" position in a school district, the incumbent acts for the superintendent and has broad responsibilities. In other districts, a deputy superintendent may be charged with a large part of the activities of the district, such as support services or instruction. Assistant and associate superintendents are usually given leadership in some specific aspect of the district's operation; however, in smaller districts the title may be used to designate the "number two" position.

As we discuss in Chapter 5, many large districts have been subdivided into geographic areas. In such cases the usual procedure is for each area to be headed by an area superintendent, with subordinate administrators consistent with the functions assigned to the area office.

The task areas of educational administration are described in Chapter 2. These include tasks associated with organization, curriculum and instruction, finance, business management, support services, staff personnel, student personnel, school buildings, school–community relations, and research and evaluation. As a general rule there are administrative positions in the central office of school districts associated with each of these areas of activity. In larger, more complex districts it is not unusual to find an assistant or associate superintendent in charge of one of these areas—for example, an associate superintendent for instruction, or some combination, such as assistant superintendent for finance and business management. Furthermore, depending upon the complexity of the district, the person in charge of a task area(s) may need assistance from a variety of directors, supervisors, coordinators, specialists, and/or administrative assistants. For example, in the area of instruction, the major responsibilities may include the following programs: elementary, secondary, exceptional child, vocational and technical, adult and community, and instructional services. The unit head may be an assistant superintendent, and he or she may be assisted by several subordinates, such as a director of elementary programs, a coordinator of instructional media, and a specialist in language arts.

During the 1970s, because of a variety of forces, the nature and scope of responsibilities in some task areas changed dramatically. Specifically, in many school districts, the construction of new school facilities shifted to the renovation of existing facilities. There was also significant expansion in the negotiation and administration of collectively bargained contracts; the provision of services for exceptional pupils; the institution and maintenance of management information systems for research, planning, and reporting activities; the provision of adult, vocational, and technical programs; and the taking of steps to ensure equal access for women and minorities to available jobs. These changes resulted in new or modified jobs—for example, coordinator of energy management, supervisor of management information systems, director of community education, and affirmative action specialist.

Central office job opportunities vary from district to district because of the size, complexity, and internal organization. Furthermore, job opportunities will change in relation to educational and support services demanded, changes in pupil enrollment, and changes in financial support. For these reasons there are no very meaningful estimates of the number of central and area office positions below the level of superintendent. Taking into account projections regarding pupil enrollments and teacher demand, we offer the rough estimate that during the 1980s the number of such positions will be in the 50,000 to 60,000 range.

The position of principal probably needs little description. Even though the nature of the job will vary with school size and type (i.e., elementary, middle, junior high, senior high, adult-vocational), as executive head of an attendance unit the principal is expected to work with the central office personnel to secure the needed human and fiscal resources to operate the school, deploy the staff in such a way as to enhance educational opportunities for pupils, serve as a link between the school and community, supervise the instructional program, and perform several business related duties. If the school is of sufficient size, the principal may be assisted by one or more assistant, associate, or vice principals. For example, in a fairly large school there might be an assistant principal for instruction and one for administration. In some schools there also are administrative assistants and/or deans. With the revival of the community education movement, many schools also employ community education coordinators. In numerous instances the administrative positions in an attendence unit are filled by persons who devote part of their time to teaching. It is not unusual to find assistant principals and/or deans who also teach. Again, estimates of the number of principals, assistant principals, administrative assistants, deans, and so on are not very meaningful. Considering pupil and teacher projections, our crude guess is that the number of public school principal and assistant principal positions during the 1980s will be in the 85,000 to 95,000 range.

Qualifying for the Jobs

As has been noted, the basic qualifications for an administrative position in school districts most often include a master's degree and a state administrative certificate. However, to suggest that a master's degree and a state-issued certificate are universally required is to overstate the case because such credentials are not required for a number of central office administrative positions. For example, not many states require certificates for administrative positions in fiscal affairs, research, planning, data processing, transportation, food services, and school facilities. Thus it is not unusual for persons to qualify for these support positions without educational administration and/or supervision preparation and an administrative or supervisory certificate. To cite one example, an AASA study noted that numerous school business affairs administrators had been trained in such areas as business administration, engineering, architecture, accounting, and law, and that only about 75 percent of the persons employed in the administration of school business affairs had educational experience before assuming their positions.[47]

There is considerable evidence that far more persons hold or are eligible to hold some type of administrative/supervisory certificate than there are available positions, and this situation will probably continue for the foreseeable future. Therefore, it is logical to ask what qualities are sought by school district employers. Even though employment practices have become more open and formalized due to legal requirements for equal access to jobs, there is still much variation among school districts. Thus, the query about what qualities are sought cannot be answered fully. A partial answer may be found in examining the characteristics of those who have been employed in such positions.

Surveys of the characteristics of public school administrators on a national basis by such organizations as AASA and the more local studies, often done by doctoral students, show much consistency in the findings. Excluding those central office positions for which an administrative certificate is seldom required, most administrators have been classroom teachers, most achieve their first administrative post by the age of thirty, the vast majority are "locals" (i.e., they confine their careers to a single state and often to a single district), and for those in the higher status positions an increasing proportion have earned a doctorate. Those who become superintendents tend to achieve their first superintendency before the age of forty. The great majority are white males. Despite efforts to provide women and minorities

[47] American Association of School Administrators, *Profiles of the Administrative Team* (Washington, D.C.: The Association, 1971), p. 69.

with equal access to such jobs, the surveys show that females hold less than 1 percent of the superintendent positions, less than one-third of the central office administrative posts, less than 5 percent of the high school principalships, and about 20 percent of the elementary principalships. Minorities hold less than 20 percent of the administrative positions. Women and minorities are better represented in the lower-level central office positions, the elementary principalships, and assistant principalships. Finally, one may safely assume that those selected for administrative positions have performed successfully, as measured by local norms, in their previous positions and possessed those personal qualities that were deemed acceptable.

We would emphasize that there is a difference in possessing characteristics such as the foregoing and securing an administrative post. There has been a general lack of definitive qualitative measures of performance and/or knowledge used in educational administrator selection. As such, there has been a tendency to rely on formal education, certification, experience, and interview performance. Where there is a large pool of applicants who appear to possess the requisite education, certification, and experience, heavy reliance is often placed on screening committee interview performance. With the increased competition for administrative posts in school districts, the type and quality of previous experience are becoming more significant. For example, if the opening is for an assistant principal for instruction in an inner-city elementary school, the selection process will center on those persons who have demonstrated their ability to perform in an instructional leadership role in such settings (e.g., as head of a school curriculum development council, as a team leader in a similar school).

In an effort to improve the methods used to select persons for administrative positions, in the late 1970s some school districts established assessment centers.

> The assessment center process consists of having participants engage in a set of management exercises, administrative discussions, interviews, writing assignments and personnel situations that are specifically designed to highlight the presence or absence of certain behaviors that have been determined to be necessary for successful leadership.[48]

The process is time consuming (two full days for a participant) and costly. Thus the process may not become commonplace. However, if it does, more emphasis will be placed on behaviors and less on characteristics, such as those identified, in choosing school district administrators.

[48]Edward Deluzain and Barry M. Cohen, "An Application of the Assessment Center in Education," *Planning and Changing,* 7 (Spring 1976), 31.

Job Demands and Rewards

Two significant dimensions of job demand are time and stress. The available evidence suggests that district administration demands more than an 8:00 A.M. to 5:00 P.M. five-day week. Even though definitive broad-scale studies have not been conducted on all types of positions, those available indicate that a district administrator would be likely to devote fifty or more hours per week to the job and this would include some evenings and weekends. To illustrate, based on a synthesis of prior studies, March posited that the higher the prestige of the job the longer the workweek. He estimated that assistant principals work about forty-five hours per week, principals about fifty to fifty-five hours, and superintendents about sixty hours, with those in large districts working more hours than those in small districts.[49] Long hours and exhaustive expenditure of energy have also been noted as being associated with various central office positions.[50]

District administrative positions have numerous problems associated with them, which create much pressure and stress for the occupants. Consider the position of principal: In many cases the person in this position carries the burden for enforcing collective bargaining agreements, which may restrict and reduce the prerogatives of the position. Teachers may have negotiated relief from duties they consider noninstructional or nonprofessional which results in added duties for the principal without a corresponding increase in paraprofessional personnel to provide assistance. Often the principal is the first step in the grievance process. Also in many districts the principal has no legal tenure rights in the principalship. The school principal must cope with a variety of new management and instructional concepts at the operational level often with little forewarning.[51]

Even though the majority of central and area office administrators are in a staff role, the demands of these positions often create stress. Administrators may be asked to support positions or represent the superintendent's position when they do not agree with the position, yet as members of the superintendent's team their support is expected. Also, many assignments are "handed down" and expected to be completed regardless of the time demands. Central office staff persons often find themselves with heavy responsibilities but without final authority. For example, those whose primary responsibility is instruction must work through and with the teachers and others who work directly with the pupils to achieve success. Business affairs ad-

[49] March, op. cit., 225.

[50] American Association of School Administrators, op. cit., pp. 40, 71.

[51] National Association of Secondary School Principals, *Principals: An Organized Force for Leadership* (Reston, Va.: The Association, 1974), pp. 1–15.

ministrators carry heavy responsibilities in the decision-making process when money is involved. In many instances they also work against externally imposed deadlines. Negotiated contracts, due process proceedings, and affirmative action programs can add to these pressures.

The crises and issues facing a superintendent are many. A survey of AASA members identified inadequate school financing, cost reduction, dismissal of incompetent staff, completion of state and federal reporting forms, curriculum planning and renewal, and the level of public confidence in education as important concerns of district administrators.[52] These concerns are central to the activities of the superintendent.

Even though the demands of district administrative positions are considerable, so too are the rewards, both in financial earnings and in personal satisfaction. In 1980–81, based on a survey of 1,094 school districts, the estimated average annual salaries for selected administrative positions were as follows: superintendents, $43,001; deputy/associate superintendents, $41,117; assistant superintendents, $36,633; subject area supervisors, $26,640; senior high principals, $32,231; junior high/middle school principals, $30,401; elementary principals, $27,923; senior high assistant principals, $27,285; junior high/middle school assistant principals, $26,045; and elementary assistant principals, $23,118.[53] Salary figures such as the foregoing in and of themselves are not very useful in considering a career choice; economic conditions tend to render them obsolete before they are published. What is perhaps more meaningful is the relation between administrative salaries and teaching salaries. Following are indexes showing the relative value of each of the above positions indexed to the teacher's estimated average salary ($17,678) determined from the same survey.

Classroom Teacher	1.00
Elementary Assistant Principal	1.31
Junior High/Middle School Assistant Principal	1.47
Senior High Assistant Principal	1.54
Elementary Principal	1.58
Junior High/Middle School Principal	1.72
Senior High Principal	1.82
Subject Matter Supervisor	1.51
Assistant Superintendent	2.07
Deputy/Associate Superintendent	2.33
Superintendent	2.43

[52]*The School Administrator,* 37 (February 1980), 2.

[53]Educational Research Service, *ERS Composite Indicator of Changes in Average Salaries and Wages Paid in Public Schools: Update 1980–81* (Arlington, Va.: The Service, 1981), pp. 6–7.

Assuming the relationships remained constant—which is highly unlikely, although the yearly fluctuations tend to be modest—if the teacher's average salary rose to $20,000, the average for an elementary school principal would be $31,600 ($20,000 × 1.58). However, the foregoing deals with averages, and the range among the school districts of the United States is considerable. Higher salaries are to be found in the larger school districts, those that have higher per pupil expenditures, and those located in the Far West.

Comprehensive surveys of personal satisfaction derived from school district administrative employment are limited, but the available evidence suggests that incumbents do derive considerable personal satisfaction from their jobs. Surveys conducted among such administrator groups show that job satisfaction tends to be related to job level with those in the higher level positions reporting higher job satisfaction than those at lower levels.[54] Furthermore, the majority of administrators reaffirm their career choice. If one is to accept the proposition, supported by considerable research in a wide variety of settings, that financial reward alone is insufficient to induce job satisfaction, then the conclusion must be that incumbent administrators find intrinsic rewards in their jobs.

Based on the available survey data, the sources of intrinsic rewards for central office administrators include status, being a key member of the administrative team, participating in districtwide decision making, being respected as an expert in one's field, and performing a useful service for the district. Principals appear to derive satisfaction from working with central office personnel and teachers, particularly the able ones. They like the autonomy that the job can afford (i.e., "being able to run one's own ship"). Considerable satisfaction is also derived from working with parents on school problems and concerns.

In sum, the available data show that administrative positions in school districts are demanding both in time and on the psyche. However, the rewards, which outweigh the demands for most incumbents, are several: the work itself, recognition, and not least, financial gain.

Opportunities in Other Settings

There are many settings other than school districts in which persons prepared as educational administrators may expect to find employment opportunities, including nonpublic schools, state departments of education, federal education agencies, community colleges, area vocational-technical schools, and colleges and universities. There

[54]See, for example, Frank Brown, "Job Satisfaction of Educational Administrators: A Replication," *Planning and Changing*, 7 (Summer 1976), 45–53.

are opportunities in nonconventional settings, such as legislative staffs, private corporations, private foundations, and health services agencies. Even though the descriptive information about school district opportunities is incomplete, it is far more detailed than information about the number of jobs, qualifications, demands, rewards, and the like, in these other settings. Given this limitation, the discussion that follows is lacking in specific details and tends in places to be speculative.

Types of Jobs

Numerous nonpublic groups operate elementary and secondary schoools. From a national perspective, the Roman Catholic Church with its diocesan system is the only group to build a fairly extensive administrative hierarchy. Elsewhere in the nonpublic sector a school will typically have an executive head who works directly with the school's policy-making body. The school's executive head will be assisted by subordinate administrators within the school. Even though we know of no reliable national estimates, it is our belief that the nonpublic schools employ proportionally fewer administrators than do public schools. Certainly given the prevailing structure, they employ proportionally fewer "central office" administrators. A crude estimate is that the nonpublic elementary and secondary schools employ 12,000 to 15,000 administrators. As a proportion of the national K–12 enrollment, the nonpublic schools are projected to increase from about 10 percent to 11 percent by 1989;[55] thus, there should be some modest growth in job opportunities in such schools.

There exists within each of the states a department of education that is organized into divisions, such as administrative services, facilities, finance, instruction, and planning and research. With professional staffs in the central headquarters and regional offices averaging 250 to 300 persons per state, there are numerous administrative positions available with state education departments. There are opportunities below the chief school officer for general administrators (e.g., deputy state superintendent, administrative assistants), as well as administrators with special knowledge in specific areas, such as finance, personnel, and planning and research. Furthermore, these positions are at various levels—division, bureau, program—in the hierarchy. The dominant federal agency for education is the Department of Education, which maintains an extensive staff in Washington, D.C., and in the several regional offices. Administrator job opportunities within this agency are roughly parallel to those available in a state agency.

[55] National Center for Educational Statistics, *The Condition of Education* (Washington, D.C.: U.S. Government Printing Office, 1980), p. 56.

Postsecondary schools in the form of community junior colleges and vocational-technical schools grew rapidly in the 1960s. In some states the pattern was for comprehensive community colleges to be established, which provide for both vocational-technical training and the first two years of collegial academic preparation; in other states two different institutions emerged. In some instances these institutions are controlled by local or regional districts while in other instances they are controlled by state-level agencies. There are also nonpublic junior colleges and vocational-technical schools. Regardless of the governance structure, administrative opportunities are available within these institutions. At the department-head level the administrative responsibilities are in most cases assigned to a person whose basic preparation and commitment are to his or her discipline or field (e.g., mathematics, medical technology). Above the department-head level, these schools generally employ academic administrators, pupil personnel administrators, general and business affairs administrators, and, of course, chief executives. The total number of such positions in the nation is unknown. However, the 1980 edition of the *Community, Junior, and Technical College Directory* listed 1,230 public and nonpublic community and junior colleges, technical institutes, and two-year branch campuses of four-year institutions. The total number of administrators (defined as those who devote at least 50 percent of their time to administration) employed was reported as 16,170 of which 31.5 percent were female.[56] Assuming that such institutions average six to seven administrators each above the department-head level, one may estimate about 7,000 to 8,000 administrative positions above that level.

Within colleges and universities there are two basic types of opportunities for persons prepared in the field of educational administration. First, like junior colleges, the four-year institutions employ numerous administrators above the department-head level. However, most frequently persons in administrative positions in colleges and universities are selected on the basis of factors other than formal preparation in educational administration. Second, as was mentioned previously, well over 300 institutions offer at least one degree in educational administration. These institutions afford opportunities to be a professor (in the generic sense) of educational administration. In 1973 it was estimated that about 2,000 persons were employed as professors of educational administration.[57] Since 1973, however, we estimate that there has been a 10 to 20 percent decline in such posi-

[56] American Association of Community and Junior Colleges, *Community, Junior, and Technical College Directory* (Washington, D.C.: The Association, 1980), pp. 2–3.

[57] Roald F. Campbell and L. Jackson Newell, *A Study of Professors of Educational Administration* (Columbus, Ohio: University Council for Educational Administration, 1973), p. 2.

tions. These jobs involve teaching in the field, conducting relevant research, writing for publication, and engaging in field activities (working with practitioners to improve existing administrative practices).

Our experience assisting in the placement of persons who have degrees in educational administration leads us to the conclusion that there is an increasing number of opportunities for people prepared in educational administration in what might be called nonconventional settings. For example, as state legislative bodies have broadened the scope of their activities, there has been a corresponding increase in legislative staff employees. In most legislative bodies there are education committees that employ staff members to handle the myriad activities associated with proposing, drafting, and passing legislation related to education. Numerous private corporations run extensive in-house, job-related educational programs for their employees, and these programs must be administered.[58]

Qualifying for the Jobs

Generally speaking, positions such as the foregoing do not require a certificate. The possible exceptions are in community junior college and vocational-technical school settings. Thus qualifying for such positions means gaining the requisite preparation and experience. However, what constitutes appropriate preparation and experience varies widely by type of position and among employing agencies. In some instances graduate preparation in educational administration is not a significant factor (e.g., university administration). In many cases persons employed in such administrative positions hold doctorates, but this is not always a requisite. Our observation plus some empirical evidence suggests that qualifying for higher-level administrative positions in nonpublic schools, state education agencies, community junior colleges, vocational-technical schools, and federal education agencies involves working up through the ranks; that is, an extensive apprenticeship in lower-level jobs in such settings is a requisite. However, we do not believe this pattern always follows, nor is it the norm in corporate and legislative settings.

Descriptive studies of persons occupying such positions are limited; however, some support for the foregoing generalizations can be found in the available survey data. To illustrate, as a part of a larger study of twelve state education agencies, the data showed that the chief state school officers and a sample of their subordinates tended to be middle-aged, white males (over 90 percent), "locals," and expe-

---

[58] For more detail see "Education/Training in Business and Industry," *Phi Delta Kappan,* 6 (January 1980), 311–337.

rienced as teachers and/or administrators in local school districts.[59] Similarly, a study of over 1,300 professors of educational administration showed that the mean age was forty-eight, 98 percent were male, 97 percent were white, and 89 percent had held three or more educational appointments.[60] These surveys are somewhat out of date, but since in 1980 31.5 percent of the administrators employed in the community, junior, and technical colleges were reported to be female, we trust that the proportion of women and minorities being employed by state educational agencies, and so on, is increasing. However, we believe that qualifying will continue to require preparation, successful experience as judged by norms of the employing agency, and the skills necessary to impress interviewing/screening committees.

Demands and Rewards

The time devoted to the job by line administrators in nonpublic schools, community junior colleges, and vocational-technical schools probably does not vary greatly from the time devoted to the job by public school principals and superintendents. Also, those persons occupying professorships and administrative positions in state and federal agencies, with legislative staffs, corporations, and so on, who are seen as successful, are likely to work long and irregular hours. However, the occupants of certain positions (e.g., a professor) may be more in control of their time than the school district practitioner. In sum, like school district administrators, persons who practice educational administration in other settings or who are professors generally find the time demands extensive—particularly if they are going to be successful.

Positions such as the foregoing have numerous problems that create stress for the occupant. The line administrator in a nonpublic school, in a community junior college, or in a vocational-technical school is confronted with a variety of personnel and fiscal problems and must cope with numerous new management and instructional techniques. Administrators in federal and state agencies frequently find themselves in the position of supporting programs or concepts with which they do not agree. Further, in attempting to assist with the implementation of legislated programs, they find their influence limited and may be often frustrated because, like their district central office counterparts, they are at least two steps removed from the classroom. Perceived intrarole conflicts may be another source of stress. A program director in a state education agency may perceive

[59] Roald F. Campbell and Tim L. Mazzoni, Jr., *State Governance Models for the Public Schools* (Columbus, Ohio: The Educational Governance Project, Ohio State University, 1974), pp. 18–22.

[60] Campbell and Newell, op. cit., pp. 17–32.

one set of expectancies from the local district administrators with whom he or she is working and quite another set from superiors and/or powerful legislators whose acts set the program in motion.

Based on our observations, discussions with the occupants of various positions, and some limited survey data, we believe the rewards outweigh the demands and that these occupants do, by and large, receive considerable satisfaction from their jobs despite the stress and demands of time. To illustrate, in the previously referred to survey of professors of educational administration, 89 percent of the responding professors indicated that if they could do it over again they would still choose to be professors of educational administration.[61]

In terms of monetary rewards, historically the nonpublic schools have not paid as well for comparable positions as local public school districts. Because close to 90 percent of these schools are church-affiliated, it is presumed that they have relied, in part, on religious commitment to secure administrative personnel. Because in several states community junior college and/or vocational-technical schools are controlled by local districts or regional units, administrative salaries in these settings tend to be competitive with administrative salaries in the school districts. Administrative positions with federal agencies are assigned federal civil service grades and as such, to the extent that salaries of federal government employees keep pace with the economy, the salaries are competitive. State education agencies have, in the past, not been competitive with local districts and federal agencies for positions demanding comparable skills. Harris, in his 1973 report of state agencies, cited the relatively low levels of compensation as a continuing problem.[62] However, salaries in these agencies have improved in recent years.

Salaries paid to professors of educational administration have tended to vary widely. For example, in 1981–82 many institutions were offering $15,000 to $17,000 for an academic-year appointment for beginning assistant professors, yet some senior full professors of educational administration were earning more than $45,000 for the same academic year. Corporations keep pace with the marketplace and offer competitive salaries for available positions in these settings.

It seems reasonable to assume that general administrators, those in finance, instruction, personnel, and so on, in community junior colleges, vocational-technical schools, state education agencies, federal education agencies, and nonpublic schools derive the same personal satisfactions from their job as do their public school district counter-

---

[61] Ibid., pp. 141–142.
[62] Sam P. Harris, *State Departments of Education, State Boards of Education, and Chief State School Officers,* DHEW Publication No. (OE) 73-07400 (Washington, D.C.: U.S. Government Printing Office, 1973), p. 44.

parts. The nature of the task, the contributions being made to the larger effort, the associations, and the recognition afforded are all sources of personal satisfaction.

Self-assessment and Career Choice

As implied in the chapter introduction, many persons do not evaluate the alternatives they have in regard to preparation or specific jobs in terms of the impact on their total career. An important ingredient for vocational success is to have some basic understanding of career movement, one's abilities and needs, and a definitive career plan.

Some Basic Concepts About Careers

Many scholars of vocational choice have conceived of a career as progressing through stages. Super has identified four such stages. First, a person explores various alternatives, makes a vocational choice, and implements this choice. This involves an awareness of the need to make a choice, making a choice, planning to implement the choice, qualifying for entry, and obtaining an entry-level job. This stage is usually complete by about age twenty-five. The second stage is occupational establishment and stabilization, which usually occurs roughly between the ages ages of twenty-five and forty-five. In this stage a person is expected to change jobs but rarely the chosen vocation. Also it is during this stage that occupational advancement occurs and status is acquired. The third stage, occurring roughly between the ages of forty-five and sixty-five, is the maintenance stage. This involves maintaining one's status and position through the application of competencies, seniority, and so on. The fourth stage involves reduced work involvement and then exit.[63]

Even though the foregoing may be criticized as an oversimplification, applicable only to "normal" careers, of which there are fewer and fewer, and as not accounting for the frequent changes in vocation that may be necessitated by advances in technology, it does suggest three important points for persons seeking careers in educational administration. First, a person's career—moving from one stage to another—makes different demands at different points in life. Second, the earlier one makes a choice and implements it, the sooner one is able to begin the establishment and advancement process. As an example, classroom teaching is an important requisite for many educational administration positions. As such, it is a part of qualifying for entry. However, to spend ten to fifteen years as a teacher before seek-

---

[63] Donald E. Super, *The Psychology of Careers* (New York: Harper & Row, 1957).

ing entry serves in most instances only to delay one's stablization in educational administration. The third point relates to the maintenance stage. Most persons reach a stage in their career where they are no longer upward mobile; they have acquired the job and status they are going to acquire. Thus advancement is no longer a motivation. For emotional health at this stage, one is motivated to high-level commitment and performance because of the inner satisfaction derived.

This last point leads to the notion of the dimensions of career movement. Schein, conceptualizing an organization as a "cone" as it pertains to an individual's career within the organization, identified three dimensions of career movement. He posited that one could move vertically, meaning increasing or decreasing one's rank within the organization; radially, meaning an increase or decrease in inclusion or centrality; and circumferentially, meaning a lateral change in function or area within the organization. From the perspective of an individual a given move may represent a change in all of these dimensions. As an illustration, a coordinator in the personnel division of a large school district might seek a job change to an equivalent position within the finance division (a lateral move), because the person feels the change will provide an opportunity to become more centrally involved in the major decisions of the district (an increase in inclusion) and, as such, serve as a steppingstone to the career goal of superintendent (vertical movement). Schein also suggested that these movements represent crossing "boundaries" within the organization, which vary in number, permeability, and filtering properties. The nature of these boundaries will determine the degree of difficulty an individual will have in achieving the within-organization career goal. To illustrate, some organizations have many levels in the hierarchy; others have few. Where there are many levels, vertical movement may be fairly easy (it is a long way to the top), whereas in a "flat" organization the hierarchical boundaries may be much less permeable. In some organizations movement from one function area to another may stress specific skills and competencies, whereas in other organizations little emphasis may be placed on such skills and competencies. Some organizations may be relatively easy to enter but the boundaries to the inner circle (interior inclusion) may be relatively impenetrable, depending upon adherence to organizational norms, acceptance of approved goals, and the like. In other situations, where there is an emphasis on careful selection, initial entry is difficult but it is relatively easy to move to the inner circle.[64]

[64]Edgar H. Schein, "The Individual, the Organization, and the Career: A Conceptual Scheme," *Journal of Applied Behavioral Science,* 7, (July/August 1971), 401–426.

Even though the Schein model relates to movement within an organization, and survey data suggest that many persons do not confine themselves to a single educational organization, it does emphasize an often overlooked point. Career movement cannot be adequately defined in terms of vertical movement alone. Further, the model suggests that in making a decision about entering a given educational organization, attention should be given to the nature of the subsystem boundaries in relation to the career movement desired.

Two other problems relative to career development need to be considered. First, should career commitment be focused on a given organization or a given specialization? Second, for those who desire upward career movement, what career management strategies are possible and acceptable?

Several writers have given attention to the nature of career commitment.[65] Those whose commitment is to a given organization, often called "locals," will seek advancement within that setting, identify with the goals of the organization, and seek recognition primarily from their superiors. Those whose commitment is to their specialty, often called "cosmopolitans," will seek status within their professional group and recognition of those outside the organization as well as those in it. There are recognized weaknesses in such simple classifications; yet, they seem to make the essential point—one must try to define his or her personal career commitment and consider this in relation to career options available.

Porter and associates, citing research involving executives in corporate settings, identified several strategies that were employed by upward-mobile persons. Among the more frequently identified strategies were improving qualifications, choosing jobs that are steppingstones, avoiding dead-end jobs, doing the job well, improving interpersonal relations, selecting the right sponsor, taking on risky assignments, solving major crises, and developing special competencies that are revealed at the appropriate time. They commented that getting the right sponsor is a demonstrated effective strategy, provided the sponsor is promoted and can carry along the protégés. They also noted that even though available research in business organization does not necessarily support the strategy, many individuals follow the nimble and safe strategy; that is, they place emphasis on getting along, avoiding controversial positions and risks, and presenting the "correct" outward appearance.[66]

[65] See, for example, Campbell and Newell, op. cit., p. 142; Richard O. Carlson, *School Superintendents: Careers and Performance* (Columbus, Ohio: Merrill, 1972); Frank W. Lutz, "Executive Succession in Higher Education: Cosmopolitan-Local and Outsider-Insider," *Planning and Changing*, 6 (Fall and Winter 1975–76), 165–175.

[66] Lyman W. Porter, Edward E. Lawler III, and J. Richard Hackman, *Behavior in Organizations* (New York: McGraw-Hill, 1975), pp. 201–202.

Persons who want to be upward mobile in educational administration, like executives in other settings, will employ some combination of these strategies in an effort to further their careers, even though they may not be conscious of doing so. It appears that intelligent planning demands that one make a conscious effort to identify and use those strategies that are acceptable in terms of personal values and that have a high likelihood of success.

Assessment of Self

Even though according to the personality theorists we all have in common basic psychological needs—the need for social interaction, ego satisfaction, and so on—as individuals we differ greatly in our psychological make-up. We are each unique in how we satisfy our higher-order needs, in our desires, in our abilities, and in our liabilities. Persons considering careers in educational administration need to take stock of themselves in relation to the demands of the field in general and in relation to specific jobs within the field. This self-appraisal also should occur when one is considering a job change.

As discussed previously, we all seek rewards from our work. These rewards take on meaning in terms of the relative importance we as individuals place on them. How important is money—both in terms of what it will buy and as a symbol of success? Even though most of us consider money to be important, it has a higher priority for some than for others. If a person has a strong need for a large salary, it may be that a career in another field should be chosen. Even though in recent years the monetary rewards of educational administration have improved, it lags behind many other fields and will probably continue to do so. Within the field there are differences in salaries that most persons can expect. Line administrative positions, particularly in large urban school districts, tend to be more financially rewarding than staff positions, particularly in state agencies, and professorships.

How important is personal autonomy? To some persons it is very important to be relatively free to choose their own hours of work, to feel free to accept or reject civic obligations as they see fit, to be responsible for their own actions and not answerable for the actions of others, and to be independent in setting their own priorities. Persons in leadership positions in school districts, state agencies, community junior colleges, and so on, often find the demands placed on them by the bureaucracy provide little choice in terms of hours of work; the leadership position seems to carry with it a number of civic obligations (e.g., chairman of the united fund, member of the local human relations council), which cannot be freely accepted or rejected; and inherent in the practice of administration is the responsibility for others and the necessity of setting work priorities in terms of organizational needs.

Closely related to autonomy is the degree of public recognition or visibility that one finds desirable. As frequently emphasized, we all seek recognition but we find this need satisfied in different forms. For some, recognition among colleagues is most important, and recognition among the public at large is of little significance. For others, public recognition fills an important need. Even though educational administrators do not achieve the public visibility of actors, athletes, and the like, school principals, superintendents, and college presidents are often in the public eye; whereas staff administrators in educational bureaucracies and professors are virtually anonymous. High public visibility may ensure numerous courtesies from the public, but it may also ensure public inspection of activities that one might consider personal.

How important is it to be in direct contact with pupils? Seemingly, many persons enter education because of their desire to teach or otherwise work rather directly with pupils. Even though assistant principals, principals, professors of educational administration, and student personnel administrators in colleges have frequent contact with pupils, many educational administrators do not. In general, the higher within the educational hierarchy a person goes, the less frequent is meaningful contact with pupils. If a person finds association with pupils most important, consideration should be given to remaining in the classroom or setting one's goal in terms of positions such as those just mentioned.

Is it important to be directly involved in the consideration of major policy issues? Many of us find a sense of exhilaration in being at the center of power; others have a greater need to pursue their own special project. Those near the top of the hierarchy and line administrators are most frequently key figures in the resolution of major policy issues. The specialist may be on call only for his or her particular expertise.

Each person has limitations in terms of abilities. Further, even though one may have the abilities, there may be no desire to do the task. Thus another aspect of self-assessment is to consider what you are best able to do and what you are most willing to do.

How do you react to conflict, confrontation, and crises? Most educational leadership positions, particularly line positions in schools serving a heterogeneous population, have inherent in them frequent crises. Conflict and confrontation are a way of life. The successful administrator is one who can approach and deal with such situations with a contagious calmness. Furthermore, such a person has the capacity to contain his or her own level of emotional involvement.

People differ in terms of the amount of structure they desire. Some perform best when the job ends and means are carefully defined and find this high degree of definition desirable. Others are bored by detailed job definition; they find a challenge in uncertainty. Even though educational administration jobs usually have job descriptions attached, the jobs most often depend upon the individual for full definition, particularly in regard to means. Also, given the frequent crises confronting administrators, there is considerable uncertainty involved.

How do you feel about making decisions that affect directly the lives of many people? Most educational administrators face a number of personnel decisions. Which person gets employed? Transferred? Promoted? Dismissed? Is this pupil to be retained? Disciplined? Honored? Some persons have difficulty in making firm decisions where the alternative selected will have a profound impact. Also, some who are able to act as necessary have difficulty in living with their decisions.

Some jobs in educational administration require considerable time and effort to be devoted to long-range planning, research, and writing (e.g., professorial positions and certain administrative staff jobs). Such activities are detailed and time-consuming, and require a high level of personal discipline. Persons who see themselves as doers, people-oriented, and so on, may find it difficult to meet this demand of such jobs.

The matter of geographic mobility needs to be confronted directly. As previously pointed out, to achieve career goals it is frequently necessary to relocate. Relocation may involve a spouse and children who have their own goals. It also involves gaining insight into the formal and informal structures of a new organization.

We are not suggesting that persons engage in such self-appraisal alone. Assistance is needed. This can be in the form of perceptions of peers, subordinates, and superiors. It might well include results from various standardized psychological measures (e.g., critical thinking appraisals, needs inventories, interest inventories) and a review of past performance (seemingly, past achievement is still one of the more accurate predictors of expected achievement). If you are a teacher considering administration, talk to your colleagues, your principal, and others who know you as a professional; consider what you have been able to do in the past and how you felt about what was done; consider your willingness to make the personal sacrifices that may be involved.

Illustrative Career Routes

Describing feasible career routes in any field is difficult. In a relatively new and rapidly changing field such as educational administration, with the vast difference in types and sizes of organizations having educational missions, the task is particularly hazardous. However, based on the conviction that the neophyte can be aided in the career choice process by the examination of illustrative models (even though they are not perfect portrayals of reality), we now present three illustrative career routes. These have been developed from an examination of demographic data about successful persons, discussions with knowledgeable individuals, and our own observations. The illustrations assume the requisite teaching experience, a master's de-

Figure 1-1. An illustrative career pattern for a superintendent.

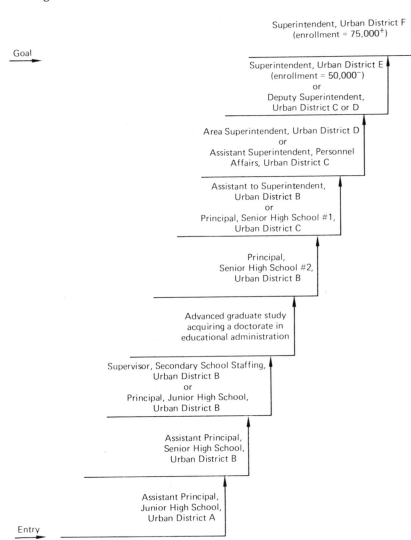

gree, and the needed certificates as a basis for entry into the initial administrative position.

Figure 1-1 is an *example* of the career steps for a person seeking the superintendent's position in a large urban school district. The alternatives at various stages show district mobility is involved, and provisions are made for advanced graduate study. As stated previously, one can become a superintendent of a large district without occupying all the steppingstones or a significant portion of them; however, this is the exception rather than the rule.

An *illustrative* route to achieving the career goal of chief educational finance administrator within a state department of education is shown in Figure 1-2. Even though no alternative assignments at various levels are shown, many are possible. The essential point is that they be closely related to the finance function. Because study of state education agency personnel shows that the majority tend to confine themselves to a single state and have a background in local districts, those features are shown in the illustration. However, state agency employees do move from one state to another (and in instances back into local districts, to federal agencies, and to institu-

Figure 1-2. An illustrative career pattern for a state department administrator in finance.

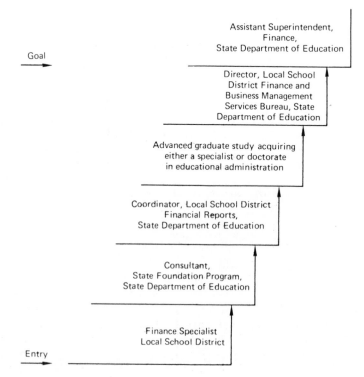

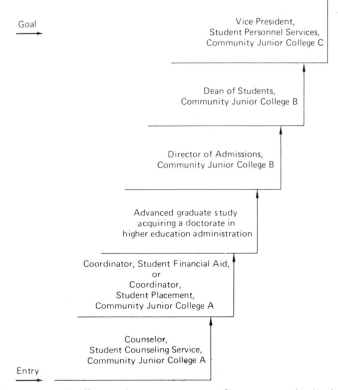

Goal →

Vice-President,
Student Personnel Services,
Community Junior College C

Dean of Students,
Community Junior College B

Director of Admissions,
Community Junior College B

Advanced graduate study
acquiring a doctorate in
higher education administration

Coordinator, Student Financial Aid,
or
Coordinator,
Student Placement,
Community Junior College A

Counselor,
Student Counseling Service,
Community Junior College A

Entry →

Figure 1-3. An illustrative career pattern for a community junior college administrator in student personnel.

tions of higher education) and local district experience is not an absolute requirement. Also, persons following careers in a specific area, such as finance, may find a master's degree related to the area (e.g., in business administration or in educational administration with a finance emphasis) most helpful for entry.

Figure 1-3 is a *possible* route for a person interested in community junior college administration, with a specific goal in the student personnel services area. Such a person would probably find that a strong emphasis in counseling, psychological foundations, and the like, would be an essential part of graduate preparation. Further, it is expected such a person would have a higher education emphasis in the doctorate. Even though teaching experience in a community junior college is not required, such experience or experience in a service role is frequently expected. In the 1960s it was not unusual for persons to move directly from local school administration into community junior college administration. However, in the 1970s this rapidly growing sector of education developed its own norms. As such, moving into administrative posts without some prior experience in community junior colleges has become far less frequent.

Two comments need to be offered about the foregoing illustrations. First, career movement in terms of the inclusion dimension is not shown. If a person achieves the upward mobility desired it will be necessary to achieve inner-circle status by application of one or more of the strategies previously identified. Second, the illustrations tend to show movement vertically within the major sectors of the educational enterprise (e.g., school districts, community junior colleges, state agencies). We recognize that for a few persons movement among these sectors may occur. However, our observation suggests that these different sectors have developed their own norms and rites of passage, and movement among the sectors has become less frequent except for short-term special assignments.

ACTIVITIES/QUESTIONS FOR FURTHER STUDY

1. Prepare a list of national organizations that have a direct concern for the professionalization of educational administration. For each, determine the location of its national headquarters, major purposes, membership requirements, whether there are state and local affiliates, and major activities. In terms of your own career interests, select one of the organizations with a local affiliate and interview one or more of the leaders to determine the organization's interests and activities.
2. Discuss what conditions are necessary to achieve professional status. What practical steps can educational administrators take during the next two decades to achieve a higher level of professionalization?
3. Review the preparation program trends and issues; then, with the assistance of your colleagues and professors, study the program in which you are enrolled in terms of these trends and issues. What major changes, if any, are anticipated?
4. Identify an educational administration position. Using documents and interviews with informed persons, determine the qualifications, state certification requirements (if any), responsibilities, rewards, and employment outlook for the position. Prepare a letter of application and supporting résumé for the position and have these criticized by an experienced administrator.

SUGGESTED READINGS

CAMPBELL, ROALD F., EDWIN M. BRIDGES, and RAPHAEL O. NYSTRAND. *Introduction to Educational Administration,* 5th ed. Boston: Allyn & Bacon, Inc., 1977, Chapters 11–13.

CARR-SAUNDERS, ALEXANDER M., and PAUL A. WILSON. *The Professions.* Oxford: Clarendon Press, 1933.

Committee for the Advancement of School Administration. *Guidelines for the Preparation of School Administrators.* Arlington, Va.: American Association of School Administrators, 1979.

CUNNINGHAM, LUVERN L., WALTER G. HACK, and RAPHAEL O. NYSTRAND (eds.). *Educational Administration: The Developing Decades.* Berkeley: McCutchan Publishing Corp., 1977.

"Education/Training in Business and Industry," *Phi Delta Kappan,* 61 (January 1980), 311–337.

ETZIONI, AMITAI (ed.). *The Semi-Professions and Their Organization.* New York: The Free Press, 1969.

JACKSON, JOHN A. (ed.). *Professions and Professionalization.* London: Cambridge University Press, 1970.

MARCH, JAMES G. "American Public School Administration: A Short Analysis," *School Review,* 86 (February 1978), 217–250.

OSIPOW, SAMUEL H. *Theories of Career Development,* 2nd ed. New York: Appleton-Century-Crofts, Inc., 1973.

SCHEIN, EDGAR H. "The Individual, the Organization, and the Career: A Conceptual Scheme," *Journal of Applied Behavioral Science,* 7 (July/August 1971), 401–426.

SERGIOVANNI, THOMAS J., et al. *Educational Governance and Administration.* Englewood Cliffs, N.J.: Prentice-Hall, Inc., 1980, Chapter 1.

SILVER, PAULA F., and DENNIS W. SPUCK (eds.). *Preparatory Programs for Educational Administrators in the United States.* Columbus, Ohio: The University Council for Educational Administration, 1978.

WOELLNER, ELIZABETH H. *Requirements for Certification.* Chicago: University of Chicago Press, revised annually.

2

The Tasks of Educational Administration

CONTINUING our overview of the field of educational administration, we now focus attention on what administrators do. To keep the presentation within reasonable bounds, the discussion is restricted to illustrative kinds of tasks that must be performed in the operation of a school, school system, or higher education organization. Although the task areas may be presented in slightly different form by different authors, there is substantive agreement concerning the tasks. Within these task areas the student will find the fundamental subject-matter fields of educational administration. The material published about the performance of the many tasks in these areas runs into volumes—journal articles, books, and pamphlets too numerous to record. Consequently, our discussion in this chapter is primarily an introduction to the tasks of educational administration.

A comprehensive study of the task areas of educational administration was completed as a part of the W. K. Kellogg-sponsored Southern States Cooperative Program in Educational Administration. The critical task areas included in this taxonomy were as follows: (1) instruction and curriculum development, (2) pupil personnel, (3) community–school leadership, (4) staff personnel, (5) school plant, (6) school transportation, (7) organization and structure, and (8) school finance and business management.[1] Other comprehensive analyses of task areas usually include those represented in the SSCPEA scheme; however, they may be organized differently. For example, in some classifications, tasks in transportation may be discussed under plant facilities, finance may be presented as a separate category from business management, and so on.

Although there is considerable stability in the task areas of educational administration, change is evident in the specific tasks performed and also in the significance of tasks. For example, before 1960 tasks relative to collective bargaining and the administration of collectively bargained contracts would not have been discussed in most, if any, textbooks about educational administration. The performance of specific tasks may vary in significance; witness the present critical nature of tasks related to fuel conservation compared to the frivolous way the conservation of fuel was viewed during the decades of cheap energy. These changes in the nature of tasks may be the result of socioeconomic, cultural changes discussed in other chapters of this textbook.

There are many specific tasks to be performed in a complex organization, and no one administrator could possibly have the expertise or the time to perform all of the tasks. In fact, one would need a team of highly educated, technically skilled persons to accomplish the specific tasks in only one of the task areas, such as business management. A person holding a given position, say, the principal, may perform *some* tasks in several task areas but not *all* tasks in these areas. For example, the principal in a large, urban school system would not usually make purchases; this would be accomplished on the basis of an approved requisition by an administrator in the business office. On the other hand, the principal would supervise the performance of some tasks related to business management, such as accounting for internal school funds.

Organizational Structure

A comprehensive discussion of the task areas of educational administration must include tasks related to the initiation and maintenance of a well-functioning organizational structure. Concurrent with the heavy emphasis upon group process during the human relations era of the 1950s (see Chapter 9), scholarly interest waned in how best to organize to perform the work of educational systems. However, this overemphasis on group process resulted in renewed interest in how

[1] Southern States Cooperative Program in Educational Administration, *Better Teaching in School Administration* (Nashville, Tenn.: McQuiddy, 1955), pp. 125–177.

best to structure the staff and faculty. Because of this renewed interest, much of the material in Chapters 3–6 and 8–11 is devoted to a conceptual discussion of organizational arrangements, theories, and processes. Some of the tasks critical to organizational structure are discussed in the following sections.

The Need for Goal Focus and Structure in Organizations

One of the basic concepts for organizing is that structure should be based on the purposes of the enterprise. No organization representing several conflicting purposes ever accomplished much.

When most of our educational organizations were initiated, those involved probably had a general idea of their goals. Persons were assigned various roles to perform in carrying out the mission. As the organization grew in complexity and changes in personnel occurred, the perceptions of organizational mission became blurred and numerous problems emerged (e.g., problems of communication, decision making, value conflicts). Moreover, as Miringoff observed, the operative goals of an organization (what it is actually doing) may in time become very different from the officially stated goals. This leads to goal displacement—the process in which the means established to achieve the official goals become ends in themselves and all energies are directed to maintaining the organization instead of achieving the official aims.[2]

Unless a means exists for organizational renewal, the members of an organization may in time lose sight of purpose. In this situation the organization may feed upon its own inadequacies rather than focus on goals. Parkinson presented a humorously critical analysis of how grotesquely ineffective a bureaucratic organization can become when people in it lose sight of purpose.[3] Consequently, one of the main functions of those engaged in organizational development is to help the personnel achieve a sense of mission—to come to terms with their objectives.

Options in Structuring Organizations to Achieve Goals

Regardless of the type of organizational model educators use, the structure must provide for (1) a way in which tasks can be divided among personnel; (2) a means through which decisions can be made; (3) the establishment of communication channels so that work can be coordinated; (4) the maintenance of organizational effectiveness to meet unforeseen problems; (5) an effective climate of flexibility, cooperativeness, personal security, creativity, and organizational re-

---

[2] Marc L. Miringoff, *Management in Human Service Organizations* (New York: Macmillan, 1980), pp. 51–57.

[3] C. N. Parkinson, *Parkinson's Law* (Boston: Houghton, 1957).

newal; and (6) the establishment of appropriate operational units (e.g., elementary, middle, junior high, senior high schools).

The bureaucratic model is the most prevalent concept guiding the structuring of educational organizations. However, most people have a stereotyped idea of the nature of bureaucratic organization, which Woodring has so well expressed:

> Bureaucracy, though an accepted part of modern life, is rarely defended. Even the meaning of the word is unclear. It is generally assumed that it has something to do with red tape, petty rules, and massive confusion. In a bureaucracy there is a piling up of layer on layer of administrative authority, which makes it necessary to submit all reports with seven carbon copies in order that one may be filed at each of the various echelons. A typical bureaucrat is thought to be a stupidly determined little man who always gets to work on time and likes order. His purpose in life is to see that all rules are followed to the letter and that fresh ideas are frustrated. His ultimate horror is to find an IBM card that has been bent, folded, spindled, or mutilated.[4]

The real meaning of bureaucracy is much different from this popular concept of the term. Nevertheless, when enough of the principles advanced by Weber become corrupted in practice, the worst consequences of bureaucratic organizations emerge to make Woodring's statement a regrettable reality. (The structural nature of bureaucracy, as conceived by Weber, is discussed in Chapter 8.)

Recognizing the tendency of the bureaucratic organization toward autocracy, many educational administrators have made major structural alterations. Most of these are in the form of committee structures for participative planning and decision making and attempted decentralization of control in the interest of greater democracy. Thus the bureaucracy is used for the execution of policies, and not for policy decision making. Democratic processes for planning and policy development are substituted for top executive control.

Some believe that bureaucratic organization should be completely abandoned in favor of some form of pluralistic or collegial type of organization. Thompson, Argyris, and Bennis are among many who have directed strong criticism at the bureaucratic type.[5] The term *collegial organization* is taken from the traditional illustration of the college, where there are provisions for academic freedom and faculty control of academic matters. Those in the administrative hierarchy provide leadership and services to make the system function well,

---

[4] Paul Woodring, "The Editors Bookshelf," *Saturday Review*, XLV (August 20, 1966), 64.

[5] Illustrative of this criticism are Victor A. Thompson, *Modern Organization* (New York: Knopf, 1961); Warren G. Bennis, *Changing Organizations* (New York: McGraw-Hill, 1966); Chris Argyris, *Personality and Organization* (New York: Harper & Row, 1957).

rather than functioning as all-directing industrial tycoons. In the collegial organization professors may have higher salaries than administrators, which is very different from the typical bureaucratic structure.

The differentiated-staff concept has some of the elements of the collegial model. For instance, teachers are assigned professional functions and greater control over program development, not unlike those of professors in a college. Caldwell pointed to the increased decision making of teachers in differentiated staffing.[6]

Because the collegial concept provides for the abandonment of monocratic control and provision is made for democratic processes of decision making on educational policies, communication in the organization flowing downward is no longer necessarily greater than that flowing upward. Those concerned with the development of programs are better characterized as a community of equal scholars than as management over labor.

As stated previously, most educational organizations resemble bureaucratic organizations. This is especially true of the very large school systems. The growth of collective bargaining may enhance the bureaucratization of large educational organizations so that they come to resemble big industrial companies. If education continues to follow private industry, administrators may have much control over the purposes of education, and teachers will bargain over wages and working conditions, thus giving up the collegial model and firmly establishing the bureaucratic model.

Many different structures are possible within the collegial and bureaucratic types of organizations. For example, a bureaucratic type of organization may be described as a tall structure, a flat structure, a line-and-staff structure, a centralized organization, a decentralized organization, and so on. The terminologies relate to such elements as the vertical divisions in the hierarchy, the style of decision making and leadership, different ways of delegating authority, and the like. The tall organization, for example, has more hierarchical layers from the top to bottom than the flat structure. In a centralized structure all of the administrative and supervisory services are provided from a central office, whereas in the decentralized organization many of these services may be located in several regional offices of a school district or in several colleges of a university. (These organizational models are defined and discussed in some detail in Chapter 6.)

A decision concerning the best structure for an educational program depends upon an assessment of several factors, among which are the purposes and objectives to be accomplished, the size of the

---

[6] Bruce G. Caldwell, *Differentiated Staffing: The Key to Effective School Organization* (New York: Center for Applied Research, 1973).

organization, the technical nature of the tasks, and the demands of the environment.

A Structure for Decision Making

Administrators are responsible for the establishment of a structure for organizational decision making that is clearly understood by the faculty, other administrators, and members of the noninstructional staff. Having confusion in this important area is deadening to organizational effectiveness. The structure for decision making varies much among organizations. In some the decision-making structure is hierarchical, and all important decisions are made by the single executive at the top. In other organizations decision making is decentralized to allow important decisions to be made nearer the scene of educational activity. Cooperative structures and processes for decision making consistent with the concept of participative management are also found. Unfortunately, the avoidance of decisions may also be the norm; consequently, the structure for decision making is difficult to trace. These laissez-faire organizations are probably among the least effective types.

A Structure for Planning

Decision making and planning are permeating processes engaged in by all of the administrative staff and faculty. However, to assure that the activities associated with this important process are carried out satisfactorily, the professional planning process must be included in the structure of the organization. Most universities, for example, have an office of institutional planning that provides professional assistance in the cooperative process through which the goals are identified, objectives detailed, and strategies are adopted for the accomplishment of the institutional mission. In a like manner, school districts make provisions for professional assistance in the planning function. Banghart and Trull explained:

> The need for planning arose with the intensified complexities of modern technological society. Problems such as population, manpower needs, ecology, decreasing natural resources and haphazard applications of scientific developments—all place demands on educational institutions for solution. If educational organizations are to meet these problems, then planning becomes a necessity and planning competence becomes mandatory.[7]

Among the specific activities involved in planning are assessing educational needs, establishing educational goals, identifying re-

[7]Frank W. Banghart and Albert Trull, Jr., *Educational Planning* (New York: Macmillan, 1973), p. 5.

sources and restraints, generating and evaluating alternative choices, making and implementing decisions, and monitoring and revising processes. Thus, contrary to what some presume, the entire process involves literally hundreds and possibly thousands of persons.

Planning may also involve the use of many theoretical formulations, and the process includes decision making. Planning may be approached as the management of change or as a part of organizational renewal. Application of the management-by-objectives concept, PERT, and various future-forecasting techniques may be a part of the process (see Chapter 11).

A Structure for Initiating and Maintaining Communication

One of the most challenging functions in the management of a large, complex educational organization is the establishment and maintenance of an effective network of communication. Barnard emphasized the critical importance of this area by observing that the structure of organizations is almost completely determined by the communication techniques.[8] Moreover, a structure for communication is an area in which most organizations are deficient.

Communication in organizations may be structured into two classifications: formal and informal. The formal structure for communication includes all official communication upward, downward, and horizontally through written (i.e., memos, letters, reports, bulletin boards, handbooks, procedural statements, etc.), oral (e.g., verbal communication between superior and subordinate), and nonverbal forms (e.g., the frown of a boss to a secretary). Informal communication is structured through unofficial "grapevines" and usually is heavily dependent on verbal exchanges between persons but also includes written messages (e.g., scribbled notes passed between officials) and nonverbal forms.

However, the primary task of educational administrators is to structure an offical communication network that provides all persons in the organization the information they need when they want it. The members of the organization should be reasonably well-informed and know where and how they can get needed information. In addition is the task of developing a structure for effective communication with the local publics, state educational officials, and federal agencies.

A Structure for Relating with Local, State, and Federal Agencies

The task of establishing a means for effective relations with state and federal agencies has grown in importance as their funding of ed-

---

[8]Chester Barnard, *The Functions of the Executive* (Cambridge, Mass.: Harvard University Press, 1938), p. 91.

ucation has increased, and because this trend is likely to continue, administration of this task will be of growing importance. Also involved is the establishment of cooperative relations with noneducational agencies on the local, state, and national levels. This may take the form of formal "educational linkage" mechanisms or it may be less formal. In any event, some means must be developed to ensure that the needed linkages are established between educational organizations and other agencies.

A Structure for Citizen Participation in Planning and Decision Making

Public school administrators must always remember that the schools are subject to public control. Likewise, administrators of private schools are accountable to their governing board and to parents. Establishing effective working relations with the alumni, the governing board, and other constituent groups is especially critical in the administration of programs in higher education. Therefore, mechanisms should be included for the appropriate participation of parents and other citizens in planning activities and establishing goals. This has usually been attempted through citizens' committees, parent–teacher organizations, cooperative school studies, and so on.

Administration of Curriculum and Instruction

The instructional program of an educational organization consists of the curricular opportunities offered students and the instructional methods through which these opportunities are delivered. Once the educational goals of the organization are known, leadership in the development of the instructional program becomes of primary importance.

Decision making about the school curriculum is frequently supercharged with conflicting philosophies of education. Some very troublesome questions must be answered, and each of these may have several answers, depending upon one's values. Finding answers to these questions is the greatest conceptual problem faced by educational administrators. What is the function of the institution in the society? What is the nature of the culture in which the institution functions? What is the nature of the learning process? How do students grow and develop? What is the nature of knowledge? What is the nature of the physical environment for learning? What are developments in the future that will influence educational programs?

Although all these questions must be satisfactorily answered, the knowledge to be taught, experiences to be offered, and methods to be used become the focus of conflicts. Persons with a traditional view emphasize the three R's and traditional college-preparatory subjects, whereas some "modernists" may not even indicate a specific body of knowledge to be taught. Agreeing on a theory of learning as the basis for the delivery system is again a value choice. Theories of learning must be examined in relation to goals.

Stating Clearly Understood Educational Purposes

As emphasized throughout this section, goals are the basis for all responsible administrative activity. Little can be accomplished in the classroom unless teachers focus upon tasks related to clearly understood and personally appreciated goals, and all administrative activity must be consistent with this goal—task focus. The goals of the educational organizations should be attainable: They should be socially relevant, individually challenging, and meet the compelling needs of the culture.

The educational goals must be meaningful to the educators directly concerned with program development. The test of meaningfulness is how useful the goals are in developing programs. Translating goals into specific programs is immensely important because this is where educators can determine whether they know what they want and need.

Numerous statements of the goals of education have been produced by various groups. In 1918 the Commission on the Reorganization of Secondary Education propounded the Seven Cardinal Principles as follows: health, command of the fundamental processes, worthy home membership, vocation, citizenship, worthy use of leisure time, and ethical character.[9] Some attempts to establish goals in recent decades have been made by the Educational Policies Commission, National Committee for the Project on Instruction, and American Association of School Administrators.[10]

The establishment of goals for colleges and universities has been as difficult as it has been in the public schools. Frequently involved in the discussion of goals for higher education are conflicts about the nature of general education, liberal education versus professional aims, the nature of the university as an agent of social change, the pro-

[9]*Cardinal Principles of Secondary Education,* Commission on the Reorganization of Secondary Education, Bulletin 35 (Washington, D.C.: Bureau of Education, 1918).

[10]See, for example, Project on the Instructional Program in the Public Schools, *Deciding What to Teach* (Washington, D.C.: National Education Association, 1963); John W. Gardner, "National Goals for Education," in The President's Commission on National Goals, *Goals for Americans* (New York: The American Assembly, Columbia University, 1960), pp. 81–102; Educational Policies Commission, *The Central Purposes of American Education* (Washington, D.C.: National Education Association, 1961); American Association of School Administrators, *Imperatives in Education* (Washington, D.C.: The Association, 1966).

grams that should be given preferential emphasis, and so on. Commenting on the establishment and maintenance of appropriate programs for university undergraduate programs, Sandeen observed:

> Undergraduate education in the United States today is badly fragmented; it lacks a coherent overall philosophy, it needs a strong and enlightened leadership, and it affects too little the people it is meant for—the students. The agendum for many colleges and universities has been so sidetracked by problems and crises during the past fifteen years that too often the undergraduate curriculum and the students themselves have been ignored, or "put off until later."[11]

To be meaningful, the statement of purposes must be thoroughly legitimized and internalized intellectually by administrators, teachers, and most of the clients of the educational organization. Moreover, it must be spelled out in detailed objectives. This means that processes must be established to encourage as many persons as possible to participate in the development of educational goals.

Translation of Goals into Instructional Systems

The process of translating the goals of the school into a school curriculum is a difficult one. There is the problem of selecting from available knowledge and the problem of how to structure this knowledge to facilitate attainment of objectives. The presentation of what is to be taught involves a concept of how human beings grow and develop. There are conflicting views on the subject, all of which seem to have academic respectability.

An illustration of this point is the subject curriculum linked with the principles of behavioral psychology. In relation to the educational goals, one structures (or packages) what needs to be learned in various subject areas (or disciplines). The principles of behavioral psychology (e.g., operant conditioning) may be followed in structuring the instructional materials. Behavioral psychology may also undergird the delivery system (e.g., methods of teaching, media).

The subject curriculum, which was based on this conceptual design, is not acceptable to many parents and educators who hold different beliefs about the nature of learning. For example, those believing in experimentalist views of knowledge and accepting Gestalt principles of psychology believe that pupils should be more active in what and when they learn. The experimentalists are concerned about persons learning how to think through real-life situations.

The point of this discussion is that numerous alternative choices of curriculum designs are available, and a value choice must be made.

---

[11] Arthur Sandeen, *Undergraduate Education: Conflict and Change* (Lexington, Mass.: Lexington, Heath, 1976), p. 3.

Different authors have identified from three to six alternative curriculum designs: subject, broad fields, experience, activity, and social process life functions.[12] These various approaches are based on some fundamental concepts about the nature of curriculum. Eisner discussed these basic concepts about curriculum under five orientations: (1) Development of Cognitive Processes, (2) Academic Rationalism, (3) Personal Relevance, (4) Social Adaptation and Social Reconstruction, and (5) Curriculum as Technology.[13] No amount of data will prove empirically what the design of curriculum should be. However, well-defined goals should help administrators and teachers make this choice.

Recognizing the burden of school leaders in keeping up with the many curriculum alternatives, the American Association of School Administrators publishes material on curriculum trends. For instance, one curriculum handbook indicated emerging concepts in curriculum, in organization of knowledge, and in concepts of instruction.[14]

The Organization of Instruction

Educational administrators face difficult decisions concerning the organization of instructional services. An obvious problem is the organization of the school district into school divisions, such as the 8-4, 6-3-3, K6-3-3, 4-4-4, or 5-3-4 centers. (These and other school center plans are discussed fully in Chapter 5.)

Although most school districts use some aspects of the graded school as a means of organizing pupils for instruction, some have developed various forms of nongraded organizations. How teachers should be organized for instructional services has also been a point of continuing concern. The self-contained classroom and departmentalized patterns have been used widely. However, other school districts have moved to other patterns, such as teaching teams. There have been recurrent waves of interest in independent study organizations since Washburne initiated what has been called the Winnetka Plan in Winnetka, Illinois.[15]

Another aspect of instructional organization is the so-called tracking procedure. Various approaches to ability grouping are used. The controversy over heterogeneous versus homogeneous grouping has

[12]Mauritz Johnson, "On the Meaning of Curriculum Design," in James R. Gress (ed.), *Curriculum: An Introduction to the Field* (Berkeley: McCutchan, 1978), pp. 278-279.

[13]Elliot W. Eisner, *The Educational Imagination* (New York: Macmillan, 1979), pp. 50-73.

[14]William J. Ellena (ed.), *Curriculum Handbook for School Executives* (Washington, D.C.: American Association of School Administrators, 1973).

[15]Carleton W. Washburne and Sidney Marland, *Winnetka: The History and Significance of an Educational Experiment* (Englewood Cliffs, N.J.: Prentice-Hall, 1963).

not been resolved. This involves how pupils should be assigned to designated grades, teams, or other groupings.

Providing Support for Instructional Programs

Decisions about content and instructional procedures are followed by the need for decisions about support services. Of primary importance is the task of providing the necessary materials and facilities. Although instructional materials alone do not make an instructional system, appropriate materials are absolutely essential in any learning system designed. The same can be said for the physical facilities and equipment.

As discussed later in this chapter, modern instructional programs must be supported by appropriate supervisory services and by well-organized in-service programs. The ultimate aim of supervisory services is to provide better instructional programs congruent with program goals. Moreover, opportunities must be provided for administrators and teachers to evaluate the effectiveness of the educational programs. The nature of this evaluation process involves basic ideas about curriculum.

Finance of Education

The subject matter of educational finance is not restricted to dollars and complicated formulas, but also involves concepts of economics, taxation, politics, and education. The curriculum and instructional program desired must be translated into the financial resources needed through budgeting. Money must be found to fund the program. After the money has been found, it must be allocated to realize the program desired and achieve equality of educational opportunity. In addition to these very complicated tasks, students of educational finance must conduct research on variations in fiscal capacity and effort, educational needs and costs, bases for achieving equality of opportunity, relationships between financing patterns and educational quality, and numerous other aspects of the economics and finance of education. Problems in educational finance involve (1) how to raise money needed to finance education, (2) how to allocate this money to optimize equal educational opportunity for students regardless of place of residence, (3) how to expend resources to optimize the attainment of organizational goals, and (4) the impact of educational expenditures on socioeconomic conditions.

The Budgeting Process

Through the budgeting process, the desired educational program is translated into fiscal terms. Within recent years educational liter-

ature has included much about PPBS (planning, programming, budgeting system) and zero-based budgeting as management techniques
for program development and budgeting. Some of the tasks in the
budgeting process are (1) identifying the purposes and priorities of
the educational program, (2) developing an educational plan to achieve
these purposes, (3) preparing a budget document to estimate the expenditures required to implement the educational plan, (4) presenting, considering, and adopting the budget, (5) administering the
budget, and (6) evaluating the budgeting process.[16]

The budget document should be well prepared and fully supported by supplementary documents. In preparing these documents
educational leaders should use simulation to anticipate any and all
possible situations and responses. There is no substitute for knowing
what one wants and thoroughly documenting that position.

Previously, emphasis was placed upon the importance of educators knowing what they want and need as a basis of improving educational opportunities for students. This involves well-established
goals, which become the personal mission of the administrators and
teachers in the system. From this point on, preparing the budget document itself is largely a means problem. Seeking support for and official adoption of the budget is, however, a very important leadership
responsibility involving value choices.

Funding of Educational Programs

Education becomes big business when one considers the financial resources spent on a state and national basis. Additional money
is not easy to obtain for many reasons, not the least of which is the
resistance of taxpayers and competition for scarce dollars among the
agencies of government. Educational administrators must be prepared for the politics of financing schools. This involves the development of expertise in such areas as taxation, preparing budget documents, and politics.

Educational leaders in public institutions must have up-to-date
information on the present use of taxes to raise funds. This involves
a well-developed data bank showing the present use of taxes and de-
lineating alternatives for raising additional monies. Also involved is
understanding of the criteria used to judge taxes and how the property tax, sales tax, personal income tax, corporate income tax, and
other taxes fit these criteria.

As is true of all major decision making in education, the funding
decisions one makes must be supported in the politics of bargaining
(if practiced), politics of the board, politics of the legislature, and pol-

---

[16]Roe L. Johns and Edgar L. Morphet, *The Economics and Financing of Education,* 2nd ed. (Englewood Cliffs, N.J.: Prentice-Hall, 1975), pp. 397–412.

itics of the Congress. The educational administrator in charge of these politics must have a strategy that will procure the resources needed.

Allocation of Funds

In public K–12 schools, the tradition of local control and financing of education has presented a difficult problem in providing equal educational opportunity for every child regardless of place or residence. The basic problem involves variation in local fiscal ability and effort among school districts and among states. The rich states and local school districts can, with much less effort, raise many times more dollars per pupil for education than can poor states or local districts making a high effort. The range in wealth per pupil within states may be 50 to 1. As a consequence, in states showing low levels of state equalization funding, the differences in program opportunities for children among districts are great.

Junior colleges and other postsecondary schools were developed initially through local funding. However, Wattenbarger and Gage predicted that there will be continued shifting of funding for community colleges from local to state and federal sources.[17] Consequently, the states must have an equitable process for allocating state funds for community colleges and other postsecondary programs, such as regional vocational programs.

Another significant problem in allocating funds for education is to account for factors that influence educational costs. The costs of special education, vocational education, compensatory education, adult education, and other programs vary from the costs of other programs of equal quality.

Allocating state funds for state-supported universities is another problem. The differences in costs of programs among and within universities (e.g., medical education versus education of social workers), whether justified or a matter of difference in political influence, are very great. Consequently, this is a process marked by sharp political conflict.

As is discussed in other parts of this text, the battle for equal educational opportunity has raged in the legislatures, the Congress, and the courts. This has stimulated much activity to develop state and federal support programs to equalize financial support for schools. Authorities involved in the National Educational Finance Project developed means through which the consequences of alternative models of state financing could be analyzed and evaluated for a prototype state.[18] Most authorities feel that complete equalization within a state

[17]James L. Wattenbarger and Bob N. Cage, *More Money for More Opportunity* (San Francisco: Jossey-Bass, 1974), pp. 73–74.

[18]Roe L. Johns and Kern Alexander, *Future Directions for School Financing* (Gainesville, Fla.: National Educational Finance Project, 1971).

requires a complete state support program. Equalization among the states would, of course, require federal funding. Either of these alternatives violates traditions of local control.

Business Management Support Services

The operation of schools and postsecondary institutions is big business. Educational administrators are confronted with providing massive support services just to keep their organizations in operation. Some of the support services provided in this task area include budget administration, purchasing and supply management, maintenance and operation of plant facilities, transportation, food services, insurance, accounting and financial management, and data processing. There is a continuing growth of tasks in the administration of support services. For example, Candoli and associates placed much emphasis upon the emerging planning function as an important aspect of business management.[19] Among the important planning activities suggested by Hentschke were enrollment forecasting and personnel and resource forecasting.[20] During the 1970s educators witnessed much growth of management information systems and of security services.

Business management tasks in the administration of higher education programs parallel those encountered in the operation of the public schools; however, some differences in the tasks and in the intensity of task performance are evident. For example, such areas as student financial aid, management of endowment funds, and investment management are major responsibilities in universities and colleges but of minor consequence in most public school systems.

Numerous management techniques have been developed within recent years, such as the planning, programming, budgeting system (PPBS) that swept the country during the 1960s. Leaders in the Association of School Business Officials developed the Educational Resources Management System (ERMS) as an application of management systems to educational organizations.[21] The Program Evaluation and Review Technique (PERT), described in Chapter 11, is another management technique. Let us now consider some of the important tasks of providing effective business management services in school systems and higher education institutions.

[19] I. Carl Candoli, et al., *School Business Administration: A Planning Approach,* 2nd ed. (Boston: Allyn, 1978), pp. 3–25.

[20] Guilbert C. Hentschke, *Management Operations in Education* (Berkeley: McCutchan, 1975), pp. 361–404.

[21] William H. Curtis, *Educational Resources Management System* (Chicago: Association of School Business Officials, 1971).

Accounting and Financial Management

There must be appropriate accounting for the funds received and expended by an educational organization. Controls over expenditures must be established to assure that the funds are spent in accordance with authorized budgetary statements. Some of the functions regularly performed by the business office are management of salary payments, purchasing, internal auditing of expenditures, preparation of financial reports, financial accounting, supervision of internal accounting of schools, provision for insurance, and accounting for property. Performance of these jobs is a major responsibility and involves many persons. Thus the volume of transactions completed and accounted for is very great each year. Although the traditional function of the accounting system was to maintain control over expenditures consistent with the budget, modern financial accounting has evolved from the traditional "bookkeeping function" to a managerial process essential to decision making and educational planning. The system provides data in an organized form to the administrative staff and governing board that are very useful in evaluating the budgeting process and in accounting to the public. The accounting function is not restricted to financial accounting. Proper means must be established to inventory equipment, to collect routine data about students, and so on. For example, statistical data concerning student enrollment and attendance are usually required for the allocation of state funds.

Operation of Plant Facilities

To keep the plant facilities in operation in a large school system or university involves a large investment in personnel. The buildings must be heated. They must be kept clean and free of health hazards to staff and students. Grounds require constant care. The facilities must be maintained. Nelson and Purdy commented:

> Citizens have placed *in trust* millions of dollars of assets for educational purposes. It is the responsibility of the school business administrator to accept responsiblity for this trust and see that this property is maintained so there will be no interruption in the educational program and maximum life and usefulness will be obtained.[22]

The thousands of persons who inhabit a large high school or university each day make the provision of custodial services necessary. These services include the selection, training, and supervision of custodians; organization of the plant staff; maintenance of buildings and equipment; operation and maintenance of utilities; maintenance of

[22] D. Lloyd Nelson and William D. Purdy, *School Business Administration* (Lexington, Mass.: Lexington, Heath, 1971), p. 185.

landscape and grounds; repairs and renovations; provision of shops; and administration of motor pools.[23]

Transportation Services

Many school systems transport thousands of pupils daily to and from schools. This was a massive operation even before the use of buses for desegregation, but it has grown demonstrably as a result of cross-busing between school centers to achieve racial balance in classrooms. For many school systems this has required the purchase and operation of many more buses than in previous years. Of course, in many city school systems the school district does not assume responsibility for transporting pupils. For the preponderance of school systems that do provide these services, however, much is involved. In most of these school systems transportation services are publicly owned rather than contracted. Other important duties in this area include the establishment of bus routes and schedules, driver training, regular safety inspections, bus maintenance, supervision of staff, and continuous evaluation of services.

Food Services

In most school systems and higher education institutions, food service programs have become a major operation in which overall coordination must be achieved. Among the numerous specific tasks in the administration of food service are staffing and supervision, menu planning, establishment of prices, maintenance of portion control, food purchasing, food preparation, accounting, reporting, and cost analysis.[24] If the choice is made to "contract out" the food service operation, as is done in many colleges and universities, the administrative responsibilities will include negotiating contracts and ensuring that the contract provisions are fulfilled.

Purchase, Storage, and Distribution of Supplies and Equipment

Instructional and other supplies must be received, stored, and efficiently distributed as needed. This involves records of goods received and distributed. To ensure economy of purchase and efficiency in having the supplies available when they are needed, warehouse facilities for storage must be provided for all but very small school systems, but even in the smallest systems there will be a need for the storage of supplies and equipment when large-scale warehousing may not be feasible.

[23]National Association of College and University Business Officers, *College and University Business Administration* (Washington, D.C.: The Association, 1974), pp. 109–116.

[24]Candoli, et al., op. cit., pp. 288–300.

Facilities, equipment, and personnel are needed to distribute the supplies as they are requisitioned. Efficient management of distribution services is especially important to ensure that classroom supplies and equipment are available when needed. Efficient recordkeeping is required; an inventory is kept of what is available for distribution.

Other Support Services

Although the services discussed are the most important supports, many others must be provided. For example, school administrators in many districts are faced with the responsibility of operating a security force for protection of persons and property. Large school systems also operate a mail service. Many persons are required for secretarial, clerical, printing, and other office services. Provisions must be made for administering personnel services for noninstructional employees.

Staff Personnel Administration

Much of what has been written about organizational effectiveness involves personnel. For example, in an earlier era, a basic theme was how personnel could be led toward optimum productivity. As a task area, however, personnel administration involves numerous management functions as well as the application of complex theories to achieve maximum attainment of organizational goals.

Before we discuss some of the tasks in personnel administration, we should point out that this is an area of great ferment and change. First, there is the redefinition of roles, norms, and administrative leadership associated with the growth of collective bargaining. Federal laws relating to affirmative action and assurance of equal opportunity employment practices have been initiated that have had an impact upon procedures for recruitment, selection, and promotion of personnel. As a result of the ferment in personnel administration created by teacher militancy, adoption of the industrial model for collective bargaining, federal and state laws, and other movements, educational administrators and teachers have been faced with radical redefinitions of roles.

During the great growth in enrollment following World War II, school systems faced critical shortages of teachers. Most staff planning in terms of organizational missions was lost in the problems of recruiting, certifying, and placing teachers and other personnel just to keep schools open. With the downturn in enrollment and availability of highly qualified personnel in many areas, educational administrators have the opportunity to regroup for short- and long-range personnel development goals.

As Castetter suggested, the success of the organization is related to sound personnel practices.

> It is generally conceded that the success of any human endeavor is closely related to the quality of the personnel who perform the tasks necessary to the achievement of purpose, as well as to the conditions that affect their physical and mental well-being. This assumption is as applicable to school systems as it is to any organized human effort.[25]

Personnel Policies

A task essential to the success of the organization includes the continuous development and improvement of personnel policies. Traditionally this developmental process was primarily a board and administrator prerogative in which the faculty might be permitted to participate; however, as will be discussed in Chapter 18, personnel policies in many school districts and colleges are presently subject to collective bargaining. Some of the important aspects of personnel policies include policy statements with reference to (1) planning, (2) recruitment, selection and placement, (3) compensation, (4) staff development, (5) evaluation, (6) collective bargaining (if applicable), and (7) other matters pertaining to the faculty and staff, such as statements referring to the quality of relationships among the staff. When adopted by the board, these policies guide the administration in the development of processes for their implementation.

Predicting Personnel Needs

The prediction of personnel needs must be based on the goals of the organization and the number of students to be educated. The goals guide the process of program development and, consequently, influence estimates of future personnel needs. The planning function must also include predictions of social trends and economic developments, which will have an impact upon the number of students who are to be educated.

Additionally, the planning of strategies for recruitment, selection, and placement should be considered. From the determination of future personnel needs will emerge implications for the development of strategies in other areas of personnel administration.

Personnel planning should facilitate the development and adoption of policies in such areas as internal promotion and external recruitment, welfare provisions (e.g., sick leave, leaves of absence, retirement, salary), tenure, evaluation of performance, and so on. Again, many of these policies are subject to negotiation through either collective bargaining or other processes.

---

[25] William B. Castetter, *The Personnel Function in Educational Administration,* 3rd ed. (New York: Macmillan, 1981), p. 4.

Recruitment of Personnel

Recruitment involves identifying and describing positions to be filled, communicating these needs, encouraging persons to apply for the positions, and giving interested persons information. As mentioned previously, educational organizations must comply with federal laws on affirmative action in recruitment, selection, promotion, transfer, and the like. The aim of all recruitment programs, however, is to locate the best-qualified persons and then to interest them in applying.

Steps in establishing the recruitment process include developing recruitment policies, allocating recruitment activities to staff, locating and encouraging qualified persons to apply for the positions, and systematizing contacts with the applicants.[26] Recruitment policies and activities vary among educational systems; however, Castetter advocates a centralized recruitment process for public school systems coordinated by the assistant superintendent for personnel in the district.[27] In higher education, at the faculty level, recruitment is usually a decentralized process. The recruitment, screening, and selection process should comply with established guidelines for equal opportunity.

Screening, Selection, and Appointment of Personnel

Processes must be established to screen the applicants for the variety of positions to be filled. What information should be collected about the applicants? How will screening be accomplished and who will be involved? How will eligibility lists be prepared and maintained? Through what formal processes will those eligible be selected and appointed? What policies should exist for promotion from within the organization?

Some of the tasks involved in the process include establishing position requirements, collecting information about candidates (e.g., application forms, placement papers, transcripts, interviews, examinations), evaluating the applicants, making employment decisions, offering positions to candidates, and placement.[28] According to Castetter,

> most selection processes include the following steps: reception, central screening interview, completion and review of application blanks, completion of tests required by the system, decentralized interview, background investigation, nomination, and appointment.[29]

[26] Ibid., pp. 133–134.
[27] Ibid., pp. 137–138.
[28] Ibid., p. 159.
[29] Ibid., p. 187.

Systematic procedures should be established to appoint personnel and process their assignments and orientation to positions. Nothing can compensate for warm, hospitable attention to persons taking positions in the organization for the first time. Moreover, personal conferences should be arranged to define expectations and provide information to optimize personal orientation.

Evaluating Performance

Procedures should be established to evaluate job performance for all instructional, noninstructional, administrative, and supervisory personnel in the organization. This is a difficult area because being evaluated is seldom, if ever, appreciated. Yet to move to where we ought to be, we must understand where we are in relation to goals.

Evaluation involves the establishment of criteria, which has a way of becoming a treacherous administrative activity. As discussed previously, personal needs and the demand dimensions of organizations frequently conflict. What persons feel that they should be evaluated on is not always consistent with what the organizational mission demands.

The process of rating performance in accordance with criteria is also sometimes emotionally demanding. Tenure, promotion, merit pay (if applicable), and other factors (including one's ego) are greatly influenced by the way one is evaluated in regard to the applicable criteria. Therefore the process must be as fair as possible and one should include provisions for appealing decisions. The process should ensure that prejudice (e.g., race, sex, age) does not enter evaluations.

Personnel Development

An evaluation system that does not have procedures to overcome limitations for optimum performance is inhuman and irresponsible. Furthermore, there are court decisions that, in effect, require the organization to provide development opportunities for employees before taking an adverse action, such as dismissal. Within recent years administrators have seen the need for comprehensive staff development programs, which assist personnel throughout the system to function productively in relation to organizational goals. However, in the past, boards have not provided much support for staff development activities. Instead, teachers and administrators had to pay for their own development. This left the preparation in specialties to the personal interests of individuals. Consequently, many who worked for master's degrees, for intance, prepared themselves not to perform better in their present positions, but to be promoted to other fields thus creating a dysfunctional system. Funding for staff development programs to meet personnel resource needs of the organization is essential.

Staff development refers to the entire personnel (administrative, instructional, and noninstructional) of a school system or university, but administrators tend to restrict professional development to the faculty. Certainly instructional improvement is the desired result of a faculty development program; however, this objective may also be achieved by improving administrative performance and noninstructional services. Therefore, any development program should include activities through which administrators learn how to become better leaders for instructional improvement. Quality custodial services are not realized by employing a person and handing him or her a broom. Proper housekeeping depends upon specific information and know-how not possessed by the average person; training is needed.

Administration of Paraprofessional and Auxiliary Teacher Programs

Within recent years the use of auxiliaries to supplement teaching and administration has gained popularity. The auxiliary has been used by hospitals and other organizations for many years.

Abbott suggested that auxiliary teacher programs (e.g., tutors, parent participants, student aides) make important contributions.[30] These programs are growing in significance, and leadership is needed to keep these programs focused upon the objectives of the educational organization.

Student Personnel Services

The term "student personnel services" is used to refer to those services provided that are not directly related to instruction. In the public K–12 schools these services include statistical accounting for pupils, school census, admission, registration, discipline, promotion, health services, counseling, special activity programs, and other direct services (e.g., voluntary financial aid to students in need). Colleges and universities also administer these services; however, they have more extensive student aid programs (e.g., scholarships and fellowships, assistantships, grants, loans, part-time employment, and deferred payment plans). Many colleges, and some nonpublic schools, have the added tasks of providing on-campus housing for students and more complete health services. A brief description of the special tasks in student personnel follows.

Admission, Census, and Enrollment Estimates

Educational authorities are required by law in many states to conduct periodic censuses of preschool children. Some authorities have

[30]Jerry L. Abbott, *The Auxiliary Teacher Program* (West Nyack, N.Y.: Parker, 1973).

recommended continuous contact and enumeration of the census. These data are important in planning for the admission of pupils to school for the first time.

In many instances the admission of children to an educational program is the first contact parents have with the school. This is also the first step of the child away from the home. Consequently, school officials should plan and execute well the processes for the admission of pupils, and provisions should be made for the orientation of pupils during the admissions procedure.

Colleges and universities must complete enrollment projections as a basis for short- and long-range planning. Some universities have had to make drastic reductions in spending, including sharp reductions of faculty, because of declining enrollments. The processes of admission and registration in large universities are complex tasks, requiring much investment in personnel and equipment. Registration procedures are a continuous source of faculty and student complaints.

Counseling Services

Providing effective counseling services is essential in elementary schools, middle or junior high schools, high schools, colleges and universities. Henderson and Henderson observed that counseling "is as much a part of college today as classes are."[31] Students need counseling concerning their study programs, vocational preferences, and many personal problems. Thus counseling services are not restricted to only those provided by professionally-educated counselors. Members of the faculty must assume much of the responsibility in the area of academic counseling and also can be helpful in personal counseling and referrals. Students have a multitude of personal problems that may become critical enough to require extended professional counseling. Vocational counseling is also a very significant task in the counseling process. Unfortunately, the professional counseling field has emphasized personal counseling and somewhat neglected this important task.

Student Discipline

For over a decade Phi Delta Kappa has sponsored an annual national poll, which is concerned with attitudes toward the public schools. Discipline has consistently been at the top of the list of what the public believes to be the most pressing problem in the public schools.[32] Although higher education administrators have tradition-

---

[31] Algo D. Henderson and Jean G. Henderson, *Higher Education in America* (San Francisco: Jossey-Bass, 1974), p. 69.

[32] For the results of the 1981 poll see George H. Gallup, "The 13th Annual Gallup Poll of the Public's Attitudes Toward the Public Schools," *Phi Delta Kappan* 63 (September 1981), 33–47.

ally had to deal with irregularities in student behavior, the campus protests of the 1960s constituted an especially serious problem of student disorder. There is some evidence, however, that the emotional involvement of the students in campus protests during the 1960s has been replaced during the late 1970s and early 1980s by student concern for professional preparation.[33]

Educational administrators must assume the task of dealing appropriately with student irregularities. Roe and Drake found that, when educators discussed discipline, two key words emerged: "order" and "respect." They wrote that the same processes that result in desirable discipline are similar to the processes required in good teaching.[34] This is no doubt a useful attitude toward the large majority of students; however, administrators frequently have to contend with some rather unusual behavior problems that require special services and programs. For example, many school systems have established so-called alternative schools with programs designed to correct very serious behavior problems. Finally, in dealing with student irregularities, their legal due process rights must be respected.

Other Student Services

Most school systems and higher education institutions provide some health services for students. Any activity to determine the health condition of students, to aid in correcting health defects, or to provide first aid may be classified as health services. Health services, especially physical examinations (e.g., identification of sight and hearing difficulties), may provide important ways in which learning may be enhanced. Schools, colleges, and universities with students in residence must provide more health services than the typical public school or community college.

School systems and most higher education institutions have individual inventory services, including a variety of individual and group testing services. The increasing interest in employment opportunities and in evaluating organizational effectiveness has brought demands for better placement and follow-up services. Individual schools must provide processes for evaluating and reporting pupil progress.

Not to be overlooked in importance is the task of servicing the many student activities traditionally referred to as extracurricular activities (i.e., entertainment, publications, clubs, interscholastic athletics, intramural athletics, band, orchestra, fraternal organizations, and so on). The administration must allocate the time of many persons to supervise and otherwise assure the success of these activities.

[33] Sandeen, op. cit., pp. 59–60.
[34] William H. Roe and Thelbert L. Drake, *The Principalship*, 2nd ed. (New York: Macmillan, 1980), pp. 311–312.

Accounting for students is also a very important administrative task. This includes systems to locate students, to account for attendance, and to record changes in membership.

Buildings and Facilities

The rapid growth of student enrollments following World War II placed heavy leadership burdens upon educational administrators to provide new plant facilities. These facilities cost the taxpayers many billions of dollars. Even though the nation may reach zero population growth, providing new school plant facilities will continue for many school districts. Population shifts are causing many school districts to grow in pupil enrollment, whereas other districts are experiencing sharply declining enrollments. Program changes, changes in population, and other conditions will cause many buildings now used to become obsolete. Consequently, educational administrators will continue to have the responsibilities associated with the planning, design, and construction of new facilities.

Administrative responsibility for satisfactory physical environment is not limited to providing new facilities. Existing buildings must be maintained. Another management task is to oversee the operation of buildings—to provide proper lighting, ventilation, temperature, and so on.

Leadership in Planning and Construction of New Plant Facilities

In the planning, construction, and renovation of plant facilities, administrators come face to face with the ancient philosophical problem of humanistic versus material values. Should buildings be designed to represent the values of ancient Greece or should they be designed to provide desirable physical environments functional for educational programs? The noted architect Walter Gropius wrote that the "sickness of our present chaotic environment, its often pitiful ugliness and disorder have resulted from our failure to put basic human needs above economical and industrial requirements."[35] Gropius further contended that our obsession with designing buildings based on values of the past and imitating existing designs were symbols of our "spiritual bankruptcy."[36]

The main objective in planning new buildings is to construct facilities that will be congruent with the educational program. The

---

[35]Walter Gropius, *Scope of Total Architecture* (New York: Harper & Row, 1955), pp. 76–77.
[36]Ibid., p. 79.

facilities should be planned to provide a functional, attractive, comfortable classroom climate, which facilitates the learning process. Planning flexibility to adjust to changing educational programs is crucial in preventing rapid obsolescence. Comprehensive studies of population growth and change, educationsl programs, and socioeconomic developments are essential in the development of building programs.

The National Association of College and University Business Officers recommended that the guidelines for new construction should be consistent with the master plan: "The physical plan, a component of the master plan, determines where a new structure will be built, and is an important part of the overall program of institutional growth."[37] These plans should include broad-based representation of the educational community.

Success in planning new plant facilities depends upon how well the leaders of an educational organization have visualized their educational mission and developed educational programs. Although buildings should provide a good physical environment for teachers and students, they should also be designed to help personnel attain the program objectives. Therefore the participation of many persons concerned with program development in planning new plant facilities is essential to success.

Projections of facility needs through adequate planning can be used to estimate the financial resources needed. Expert assistance is required to translate plant facility needs into financial needs and project a financing program. Few school districts or higher education institutions can finance building programs through a pay-as-you-go plan. Therefore, the financing program in most instances must propose long-term bonded indebtedness. For K–12 public schools, this will usually require a public referendum and will involve school officials directly in political leadership. If the referendums are not successfully passed by the electorate, the new buildings will be delayed indefinitely and the school program curtailed.

Selection of architects, preparation of educational specifications, and development of architectural plans are very important tasks. Architects should be selected who will work closely with professional educators. Architectural plans are based on the educational specifications for a building. The preliminary draft of the architectural plan should be studied and reviewed by teachers, administrators, and other personnel. Other tasks involved in the construction of new buildings are awarding construction contracts, monitoring construction, final inspection, and acceptance of the building by the board.

[37] National Association of College and University Business Officers, op. cit., p. 117.

Effective Operation of Buildings

The primary aim in operating buildings is to provide for teachers and students an optimum environment for learning. Studies have shown the importance of controlled temperature and humidity with adequate ventilation in maintaining a good thermal environment. Administrators should be wary of architectural fads that use large amounts of energy and prevent maintenance of an optimum thermal environment. One such fad in the past has been to construct buildings with great amounts of glass, making the control of heating, cooling, and lighting difficult.

Other areas of plant operation, which have already been discussed, include maintenance, custodial services, and health and safety precautions.

Scheduling Buildings

There is great demand from various faculty, student, and community groups to use the facilities of the school district and the facilities of colleges and universities. Anyone who has attempted to schedule a meeting of any kind in one of these facilities realizes the difficulties sometimes experienced. Consequently, an important administrative task is to establish a means to schedule the use of facilities.

The first step in this process is to develop and adopt policies governing the scheduling and use of buildings and grounds. For example, what are important criteria for approving the use of facilities by various community groups? What are the priorities in the use of building facilities? Should community groups pay for utilities and custodial services? These are some of the questions for which policies should be adopted. Based on these policies administrators are responsible for assigning the persons, space, equipment, and materials necessary to control the use of the plant facilities.

School-Community Relations

In enumerating the problems K–12 public school administrators face, those concerning community–school relations are among the most frequent. Educators must communicate information about the schools to citizens to promote understanding of programs, help clarify and build commitment to goals, and promote cooperation among the institutional functions of society. Effective interaction with other institutional leaders is essential in promoting interinstitutional understanding and functional congruency.

Throughout the history of public education in the United States educators have gone through cyclical periods of interactive cooperation with citizens followed by isolationist withdrawal from the public. Associated with these cyclical trends is growth in public confidence and then damaging loss in credibility of educational leaders. Within the past decade educators have been faced with lack of credibility in many, but not all, school districts. The credibility gap for college administrators has been devastating in some instances; there have been noticeable reductions in legislative appropriations and private donations. Some observers blame the era of campus unrest during the 1960s for some of the loss of credibility with the public. However, much of the cause lies with the college leaders themselves for not promoting better relations with their publics.

The Public Relations Program

Many volumes have been written concerning the development of good public relations programs. Realizing their obligation to report upon educational conditions to the public, many organizations have a director and staff for this purpose. Studies have demonstrated the need for informing the citizens about educational programs. Many citizens have only superficial and in many instances erroneous understanding of the schools, colleges, and universities. One crucial objective, then, of the public relations program is to help the public understand educational organizations and how they are operated. McCloskey emphasized this approach to administering public relations.[38]

Public relations programs that build an image that cannot be substantiated may eventually create a credibility gap, and loss of public confidence can have serious consequences. Careful planning of long-range public relations programs is important.

Of primary concern in providing information to increase public understanding of education is identification of what is worthy of communication. From the viewpoint of the educational leaders, those things that contribute most to communicating how the organization is achieving its mission should have priority. Recurring subjects of communication with the parents of elementary and secondary children include (1) marking and promotion practices, (2) homework, (3) methods of instruction, (4) materials of instruction, (5) special services available to pupils, (6) schedules, and other routine practices involving children.

Deciding how best to encode and transmit information to the public is a difficult task. How can the information be put into lan-

[38]Gordon McCloskey, *Education and Public Understanding* (New York: Harper & Row, 1967).

guage, pictures, and graphic materials readily communicated and understood? A lot of dry factual information in stilted language is almost useless.

Often overlooked in public relations programs, however, is the importance of personal interaction with other citizens. How are persons treated by teachers, administrators, and other educational personnel? How well prepared are personnel to talk intelligently about the mission of the organization and how they are attempting to accomplish this mission? In most of their interaction with parents and other citizens, do educational personnel create more friends than enemies for public education? Every attempt should be made to promote effective processes of personal interaction with the public to promote understanding, warmth of human relationships, and bases for future cooperative interaction.

Participation of Educators in Community Activities

The complete public relations program includes ways in which educators may "reach out" to participate with other citizens in community, state, and national activities. For example, educational administrators may make personal get-acquainted visits in the offices and homes of community leaders. Participation of educators in a wide variety of community organizations should be encouraged. This accomplishes several functions. The interaction provides opportunities to inform leaders in other institutional sectors about education. Through leadership in community affairs, the interests of educators in the society in general are promoted. Effective personal relationships for future cooperation of educators and other community leaders are fostered. As Kindred, Bagin, and Gallagher have observed, "constructive relationships must be developed and maintained with the community by those who are responsible for public education if the school is to meet its obligations to the cause, continuance, and preservation of democracy."[39]

The Community School

As discussed in Chapter 5, the community school has grown in significance as a result of the interest of the developmental programs in Michigan. The early development of the program was based upon the school-centered concept. Within recent years the community school movement has moved to communitywide programming; the term *community education* is more descriptive of the thrust today. In 1974 Seay and associates published a comprehensive discussion of the community education movement.

[39] Leslie W. Kindred, Don Bagin, and D. R. Gallagher, *The School and Community Relations* (Englewood Cliffs, N.J.: Prentice-Hall, 1976), p. 3.

Certainly the community school was concerned with humane values and humanitarian issues. Educators and other community leaders turned to it as the educational answer to increasingly complex problems. By the sixties, however, communities had become increasingly urbanized and their members were more expectant of educational services in great variety for everybody throughout his life cycle. And larger numbers of agencies appeared with educational programs aimed toward diverse education needs within the community.[40]

One very important aspect of the community education program is to encourage the participation of large numbers of citizens in the educational improvement of the community. Olsen and Clark identified six major components of the philosophy of community education: (1) systematic community involvement, (2) maximum use of all resources, (3) cooperation and coordination, (4) lifelong learning experiences, (5) community problem solving, and (6) life-centering curriculum.[41]

Research, Evaluation, and Accountability

Most discussions of the tasks performed by educational administrators do not include a section on research, evaluation, and accountability. Our decision to include this is based on the significant growth of tasks in these areas in all educational organizations. Maintaining responsiveness to accountability alone demands an inordinate amount of investment of administrative energy. Likewise, research tasks have grown to major proportions as have the tasks associated with evaluation.

Deciding on the Nature of Research

The first task in developing the research program is to define the kind of research that is desired. There are different definitions of research. Consequently, employing persons trained for research without reference to their definitions of research may not fulfill organizational expectations. Let us consider some alternative ways in which research programs have developed and how research is defined.

Many educational administrators view research as a process of collecting, organizing, and reporting factual information. Administrators constantly must report large amounts of factual data to state and federal agencies concerning faculty, pupils, programs, physical facilities, and many other aspects of their operation. This "research" is not

---

[40] Maurice F. Seay and associates, *Community Education: A Developing Concept* (Midland, Mich.: Pendell, 1974), p. 27.

[41] Edward G. Olsen and Phillip A. Clark, *Life-Centering Education* (Midland, Mich.: Pendell, 1977), pp. 90–100.

concerned with the development of new conceptual knowledge. It is what might appropriately be referred to as *social-bookkeeping* (fact-collecting) research. This type of research is prevalent in state education departments, where it is used for making statistical reports about education.

Another definition of research is what some have referred to as *action research* or *process improvement* research. The aim of this type of research is to develop information for solutions to problems faced by the personnel of the organization without reference to generalizing knowledge. Thus the activity starts with troublesome problems, and the aim of the research is to develop and test knowledge useful in solving these problems. External validity of the findings is not of primary concern. In this approach, however, the researchers try to produce information useful in solving problems confronting personnel in the organization, and they are concerned with the applicability of the findings in the local situation.

Another version of research is primarily concerned with the development of new knowledge that is broadly applicable. This is frequently referred to as *basic research*. A basic research program might involve testing of ideas by numerous cooperating school districts to provide sufficient replication to make the knowledge developed generalizable beyond the individual school districts. This knowledge would be assumed to be universally applicable.

What is the most appropriate research program for school systems, colleges, and universities? Before responding to this question, let us consider some concepts of evaluation and the relationship between research and evaluation.

Concepts of Evaluation in Education

Evaluation in education emerged as *measurement*. During the period of behaviorist, neorealist influence, the testmakers developed many standardized tests to measure student achievement, adjustment, personality, and the like. This was eventually expanded to include observational inventories, questionnaires, and other instruments to produce quantifiable data concerning practically every aspect of an educational operation. Large amounts of quantified facts could be manipulated statistically.

A different concept of evaluation is what Stufflebeam and associates referred to as the *congruence definition*,[42] in which evaluation is seen as the process of determining the degree of congruence between organizational goals and performance. This concept of evaluation was developed under the leadership of Ralph Tyler in the Eight-

---

[42] Daniel L. Stufflebeam et al., *Educational Evaluation and Decision Making* (Itasca, Ill.: Peacock, 1971), pp. 11–12.

Year Study sponsored by the Progressive Education Association. In this sense the main purpose of evaluation is to collect information and make judgments concerning how well the school system, college, or university is meeting stated goals. Thus the evaluation process moved away from the aimless process of collecting objective scores on anything and everything and focused upon organizational purpose.

Stufflebeam and associates have offered what they refer to as the *judgment definition of evaluation*,[43] in which evaluation is a process that links value, information, and decision-making situations in making professional judgments. This concept of evaluation would avoid the *ex post facto* effect of the congruence or measurement approaches and make evaluation influential in the decision-making process, rather than simply determining what constructive or destructive effects had already occurred. Evaluation is a key factor in making professional, enlightened decisions.

Research and Evaluation Services of School Districts

The answer to the question of which research and evaluation services should be provided depends on the purposes of the organization and the demands made on it by its clients, on the strategic location and resources available for basic research, and on decisions concerning the allocation of resources. Authorities estimate that the costs of basic research to make breakthroughs in education comparable to those made in medicine and the physical sciences will be many billions of dollars. Education is a much more complex field, and very little has been invested in basic research. The "pay-off" of basic research is very, very slow, and great patience is needed as large investments are made. Greatest progress will be made when the best scholars are organized to produce a concerted attack upon massive problems. Therefore we offer the following proposed tasks for the development of research programs in local school systems.

First, the local school district should cooperate in and vigorously support the development of state and federally funded research centers for basic research. The research specialists in school districts should cooperate with regional research agencies by submitting problems needing testing, suggesting solutions to be considered, and assisting in the development and testing of ideas. Moreover, they should help local school administrators interpret and use the results of basic research.

The costs alone, not to speak of the demands upon school systems, dictate that basic research be a cooperative effort through a regional research and development organization, such as a well-staffed university or a research corporation. In fact, the generalizability of

---

[43] Ibid., pp. 13–16.

findings would indicate the need for a national effort. Educators might well consider the agricultural model with both federal and state support and at least one critical massing of resources for basic research in each state.

Second, research directed by local school districts and state departments of education should be for process improvement. The school district research and evaluation program should emphasize designs with local applicability to assist school officials in valuing the consequences for pupils of the alternative choices considered. The research should be of high quality and offer solutions to organizational and instructional problems. This concept of research is consistent with what the Phi Delta Kappa National Study Committee on Evaluation referred to as *judgment evaluation*.[44] It is also consistent with the contingency concept of management, which, as is discussed elsewhere in this book, has some validity in educational administration.

Third, the research and evaluation programs of school districts and state education agencies must continue to conduct factual measurement, social-bookkeeping studies, and evaluations. Valuable as judgment evaluation is in improving professional decision making, legislatures and other agencies will continue to demand measurement data and factual information. The accountability demands are also in the direction of program auditing procedures in some states.

The Accountability Movement: Implications for Educational Administrators

Perusal of professional journals in education during the 1970s will reveal many articles involving the term *accountability*. The tenor of some articles is that administrators should be made accountable to a particular person or group. Some authors attempt to blunt the modern thrust of the movement by pointing out that accountability is thousands of years old, and not new, as many presume.

Many educators believe that accountability is one of the many fads that come and go in education, and it may well be. However, the high public support for such accountability-inspired legislation as minimum competency testing demonstrates continuing popularity of the concept.

Of some interest here is the study by Hedges of differences in parent attitude toward education in selected Florida schools; there was no statistically significant difference among parental attitudes between schools with high achievement and schools with low achievement on Florida's minimum competency examination.[45]

---

[44] Ibid.

[45] William D. Hedges, *Attitudes of Parents, Teachers, and Students Towards Education in Florida High and Low Achieving Schools,* National Study of School Evaluation (Gainesville, Fla.: College of Education, University of Florida, 1980).

The modern fixation on accountability is symptomatic of deeply ingrained problems in the administration of public schools, colleges, and universities. It is symptomatic of the lack of professional development, low level of research-based knowledge about how students learn, and lack of political power among educators. It is symptomatic of the loss of credibility of educational leaders and of a gulf of misunderstanding among educators, their clients, and other citizens. The demands for accountability, however, are symptomatic of much deeper social and cultural problems than these. Underneath the reasons already given for the flood of demands for educational accountability is a deep public disappointment with the basic institutions of the society. The pent-up frustrations are vented upon any institutional sector in which glaring weaknesses are obvious.

Thus the demands for accountability are based upon the belief of many citizens that education, among other institutions, has failed them. Specifically, it is a belief that educators need to be held accountable for malpractice. Let us examine two views of how educators may achieve accountability.

One view is that educators should be accountable only for the processes (or treatments) used but not the end product. In support of this view, educators point to the data, which show rather clearly that what a student learns depends on many variables within systems not controlled by the organization, such as the family and the neighborhood. Therefore holding the school accountable for producing all merit scholars would be like holding the minister accountable for not converting all souls to a religious faith or holding the physician accountable when the patient dies, even though all standard treatments were used.

Product accountability, however, focuses upon the output of the system, with less concern about the processor (e.g., the school) or the variation in inputs. Proponents of this view believe that educators should be answerable and responsible for outcomes, regardless of inputs.

The renewed demands for accountability present challenging tasks for educational administrators. They are challenging because educators have not demanded a strong basic research program to establish a basis of process accountability, as is possible in the practice of medicine. These demands are challenging because educational administrators have not been careful enough in specifying what education can and can not do and thus promised too much to too many. They are challenging because educators are not as strong politically as they should be. There are other challenging aspects not discussed here. What educational leaders must do, however, is respond to these challenges.

First, there must be cooperative participation in the development and legitimization of attainable educational goals and objectives. The people, who ultimately hold educators accountable, should be encouraged through appropriate processes to participate in the development of educational goals. The administrators, who will be held accountable, should provide leadership through the use of public relations and political techniques to legitimize cooperatively developed and officially adopted goals.

Second, professional processes and performance expectations must be developed. In response to public demands for accountability, educators must lead in developing a concept of what can reasonably be expected. This should include the compilation of careful program descriptions of specified processes for attaining the objectives. The aim should be to develop and legitimize the best processes for treating variations in learning and to specify what can be reasonably expected from these processes. In summary, educators must become much more professionally respectable than they have been in dealing with learning problems.

Third, basic research and development programs are needed. Responding to accountability requires a scientific approach to the solution of educational problems, rather than the traditional authoritative approach. There is a desperate need for the development of processes in basic research through which educators can specify that research-based practices were employed. Moreover, these research-based practices will assist educators in specifying what education can and cannot perform.

Fourth, the criteria for accountability must be specified. Leaders should see that such criteria are consistent with the accepted goals of the organization. Accountability places greater emphasis on specifying predetermined expectations and performance objectives than was traditionally found in education.

Fifth, responsibility must be fixed. Educators must decide who should be held accountable for what. Is the principal going to be held accountable for what pupils learn? If so, for what is the principal accountable? If the principal is accountable for using the correct process, control of programs need not be decentralized. If product accountability is emphasized, the principal and faculty should be given autonomy in the selection of teaching processes.

The accreditation of schools and colleges constitutes a form of accountability. To speak of a school or college as being accredited usually means that it has met the standards and has been approved by the commission of one of the six voluntary regional associations in the United States. However, many of the states also use the term accreditation with respect to the licensure of schools and colleges. Some of the tasks involved in voluntary accreditation are as follows: (1) making application for accreditation, (2) conducting a self-study,

(3) inspection by an external committee, and (4) a decision by the agency's accrediting committee.[46] The process is very time consuming for administrators.

ACTIVITIES/QUESTIONS FOR FURTHER STUDY

1. As suggested in this chapter, the tasks of educational administration change (e.g., the tasks associated with collective bargaining were almost unknown before the 1960s). Divide into small groups to discuss future changes in education and the impact of these changes upon the tasks of educational administrators. What are some important societal changes that may influence education during the next decade? How will these changes influence the tasks of educational administrators?

2. What competencies are needed to perform the many tasks associated with the administration of educational programs? Are the competencies needed by educational administrators different from the competencies of a hospital administrator, a city manager, or a president of a business corporation? Are the competencies characteristic of good school principals different from assistant superintendents, superintendents, and supervisors? Interview selected principals, assistant superintendents, and other administrators concerning what they believe to be the most important competencies. Compare what they say about competencies and also compare their views with the results of interviews with administrators in fields other than education.

SUGGESTED READINGS

CANDOLI, CARL I., WALTER G. HACK, JOHN R. RAY, and DEWEY H. STOLLAR. *School Business Administration,* 2nd ed. Boston: Allyn & Bacon, Inc., 1978.

CASTALDI, BASIL. *Educational Facilities.* Boston: Allyn & Bacon, Inc., 1977.

CASTETTER, WILLIAM B. *The Personnel Function in Educational Administration,* 3rd ed. New York: Macmillan Publishing Co., Inc., 1981.

CULBERTSON, JACK, and NICHOLAS NASH (eds.). *Linking Processes in Educational Administration.* Columbus: University Council for Educational Administration, 1977.

EISNER, ELLIOT W. *The Educational Imagination.* New York: Macmillan Publishing Co., Inc., 1979.

JOHNS, ROE L., and EDGAR L. MORPHET. *The Economics and Financing of Education,* 2nd ed. Englewood Cliffs, N.J.: Prentice-Hall, Inc., 1975.

KINDRED, LESLIE W., DON BAGIN, and D. R. GALLAGHER. *The School and Community Relations.* Englewood Cliffs, N.J.: Prentice-Hall, Inc., 1976.

LESSINGER, LEON. *Every Kid A Winner: Accountability in Education.* New York: Simon & Schuster, Inc., 1970.

MARKS, WALTER L., and RAPHAEL O. NYSTRAND (eds.). *Strategies for Educational Change: Recognizing the Gifts and Talents of All Children.* New York: Macmillan Publishing Co., Inc., 1981.

National Association of College and University Business Officers. *College and University Business Administration.* Washington, D.C.: The Association, 1974.

---

[46] Harold Orlans, *Private Accreditation and Public Eligibility* (Lexington, Mass.: Lexington, Heath, 1975), pp. 2–3.

ROE, WILLIAM H., and THELBERT L. DRAKE. *The Principalship,* 2nd ed. New York: Macmillan Publishing Co., Inc., 1980.

SEAY, MAURICE F., and Associates. *Community Education: A Developing Concept.* Midland, Mich.: Pendell Publishing Company, 1974.

WATTENBARGER, JAMES L., and BOB N. CAGE. *More Money for More Opportunity.* San Francisco: Jossey-Bass Limited, 1974.

PART TWO

Formal Organizational Arrangements for Education

BIG *organizational complexes make an impression upon all of us. Persons seeking administrative positions are in a sense committing themselves to some form of organizational existence, and their success as administrators will depend in part upon how well they are able to make use of existing organizations. This requires comprehensive understanding of governmental structure. Understanding how the schools and colleges of the nation are organized and administered requires knowledge about the formal structure of education and the various legal mechanisms at different levels of government. Chapters 3, 4 and 5 provide information about these structures and mechanisms. Described in these chapters, for example, are the influences of the federal and state judiciary, the role and function of the chief state school officer, the impact of the federal Congress and state legislatures, the status and function of regional school districts, the organization of local school centers, and the various relationships between education and general government. Additionally, numerous specific issues related to the formal structure and* *governance of education are identified and discussed. In Chapter 6 broad, basic questions concerning the governance and organization of education are detailed and alternative responses are offered. The authors believe that these questions, or some aspects of them, are important to the future of education and that debate about them will be considerable in the years ahead.*

3

The Federal Government and Education

EVEN the casual observer is aware that the United States has no national educational system comparable to the systems existing in many other nations. Yet only the most uninformed would suggest that the federal government does not have an impact on the nation's schools, colleges, and universities, both public and nonpublic. This has resulted primarily from the decisions of the U.S. Supreme Court and the lower courts in the federal system, the acts of the U.S. Congress and programs resulting from these acts, and the activities of the U.S. Department of Education and other federal agencies. Moreover, the federal government operates directly some educational institutions and programs for special purposes or in unique situations.

Influence of the Federal Courts

The federal judiciary has been quite active in regard to educational matters since World War II. During this period monumental decisions have been rendered in regard to racial desegregation, nonpublic educational institutions, religious exercises and instruction, individual rights of students and teachers, and state financial plans for schools. These decisions have resulted in fundamental changes in educational policies and practices. The decisions have been both praised and damned. Critics of the federal courts tend to feel that they have been "making" law rather than interpreting it; that is, the courts have engaged in legislative action. This charge was most frequently made during the 1950s and 1960s. Those espousing this view feel that the courts usurped the power of the Congress and state and local governments. Many believe an imbalance of power existed. Further, because federal judges are appointed officials and are immune from the election process, the people have no recourse if they are not in accord with the federal courts "legislative acts." Supporters of the federal judiciary tend to stress two points. First, most of the court decisions do nothing more than protect the rights of individuals, which are clearly guaranteed by the U.S. Constitution; that is, the federal courts are simply interpreting the Constitution. Second, because the courts must often reach decisions that are likely to conflict with values of the numerical majority, our founding fathers exhibited great wisdom by removing them from the political process. It is essential that there be a final arbitrating body for the governance structure to function. On one point the critics and supporters of the federal courts agree: no school, college, or university anywhere in the nation has been immune from the decisions of the federal courts.

Because decisions of the federal courts are based on interpretations of the U.S. Constitution, we present a brief review of the more pertinent provisions of the Constitution. The remainder of this section is devoted to a description of major decisions of the federal courts and their impact upon educational organization and administration.

Pertinent Constitutional Provisions

Education is not mentioned in the U.S. Constitution. Thus the cases involving education come to the federal courts indirectly. The Tenth Amendment; First Amendment; Fifth Amendment; Fourteenth Amendment; Article I, Section 8, clause 1; and Article 1, Section 10, clause 1, are the constitutional provisions that have been most frequently involved in cases having significance for education.

The Tenth Amendment, often referred to as the reserved-powers clause, states, "The powers not delegated to the United States by the Constitution, nor prohibited by it to the States, are reserved to the States respectively, or to the people." This amendment has been the basis upon which each of the states has assumed the primary responsibility for providing education for its citizens.

The First Amendment says, "Congress shall make no law respecting an establishment of religion, or prohibiting the free exercise thereof. . . ." This separation of church and state has been the basis for numerous legal disputes regarding religion and the schools.

The Fifth Amendment provides that persons cannot be required to be a witness against themselves nor can they be deprived of their "life, liberty, or property" without due process of law. The Fourteenth Amendment reads, in part, as follows:

> No State shall make or enforce any law which shall abridge the privileges or immunities of citizens of the United States; nor shall any State deprive any person of life, liberty, or property, without due process of law; nor deny to any person within its jurisdiction the equal protection of the law.

These provisions, one applicable to the federal government and the other to the states, have been used to safeguard the civil rights of individuals and groups in regard to schooling. Article I, Section 8, clause 1, the so-called general welfare clause, gives the Congress the power to levy and collect taxes to provide for the nation's defense and general welfare. This provision is the legal justification for federal aid to education. Article I, Section 10, clause 1, provides that no state can pass a law that impairs the obligation of contracts. This clause has served to enhance the security of nonpublic education.

Status of Nonpublic Education

Nonpublic schools, colleges, and universities have a right to exist, and parents may choose to send their children to such institutions. However, the state may exercise reasonable control over these nonpublic institutions. There are three landmark court decisions that justify these propositions. The first is the Dartmouth College case.[1] Dartmouth was established in the colony of New Hampshire under a charter granted in 1769 by the English government. In 1816, after New Hampshire became a state, the legislature passed a law that changed the power, number of members, and method of selection of the college board of trustees. Because the practical effect of the law was to give the state control of Dartmouth College, the trustees sought relief in the courts. The case eventually reached the Supreme Court. The Court ruled in favor of the trustees, noting that the charter was a contract that could not be changed by the unilateral action of the legislature.

In 1919 the Nebraska legislature passed a law prohibiting the teaching of a foreign language in any type of school below the ninth grade. A teacher in a Lutheran school taught German to a ten-year-old boy, and lengthy court action followed. The Supreme Court de-

---

[1] *Trustees of Dartmouth College* v. *Woodward,* 4 Wheat. (U.S.) 518 (1819).

cided the case by ruling in favor of the teacher. In its decision the Court noted that it desired to let the state maintain reasonable control over schools within the state, but that the law was arbitrary, without reasonable purpose, unlawfully interfered with the right of language teachers to pursue their occupation, and denied parents the right to reasonable control of their children's education.[2] This decision served to enunciate the notion of parents' rights and place a limit on the "police power" of the state over schools.

In 1922 the Oregon legislature passed a law, effective in 1926, that stated that all school-age children, with very few exceptions, would be required to attend public schools. Two nonpublic schools sought relief from the act. The Supreme Court upheld the injunction granted the nonpublic schools by the federal district court in Oregon. The Supreme Court noted that it would not interfere with the right of the state to regulate schools reasonably, but as long as nonpublic schools were developing competent citizens, the needs of the state were being met, and in such cases the state could not require pupils to attend public schools. The Court reasoned that the law would unreasonably hamper the business of the nonpublic schools and the rights of parents in rearing their children.[3]

In more recent times the rights of parents with regard to the education of their children were again affirmed in a case arising in Wisconsin. In that state an effort was made under the state's mandatory school attendance laws to require children of Amish parents to attend school beyond the eighth grade. In a 1972 decision the Supreme Court ruled in favor of the parents.[4]

The foregoing does not mean that there are no limits on parental rights. In a 1976 decision in which the Supreme Court held that private, nonsectarian schools may not deny admission to black applicants solely on the basis of race, the Court noted that parents had no constitutional right to a nonpublic school education for their children that was unfettered by reasonable government regulation.[5] In this instance, the high court reaffirmed that reasonable government controls over nonpublic institutions were acceptable.

Since the 1920s there have been no serious challenges to the right of nonpublic institutions to exist, and other than in the case of the Amish pupils, in which the question was schooling beyond grade eight, the right of parents to send their children to such schools has not been questioned. In many states a significant proportion of the school-age children attend nonpublic schools, most frequently those

[2]*Meyer* v. *Nebraska,* 262 U.S. 390, 42 Sup. Ct. 625 (1923).
[3]*Pierce* v. *Society of Sisters of the Holy Names of Jesus and Mary* (and *Pierce* v. *Hill Military Academy*), 268 U.S. 510, 45 Sup. Ct. 571 (1925).
[4]*Wisconsin* v. *Yoder,* 406 U.S. 205, 92 Sup. Ct. 1526 (1972).
[5]*Runyon* v. *McCrary,* 427 U.S. 160, 96 Sup. Ct. 2586 (1976).

operated by the Roman Catholic Church. As a general rule the states exercise minimal controls over such schools. The existing controls are designed to ensure that a reasonable level of schooling is being provided, that the children are not exploited, and that the rights of individuals are protected.

Public Support for Nonpublic Education and Students

The issue of public financial support for nonpublic educational institutions or students has generated intense debate and numerous legal actions (e.g., court cases, federal acts permitting some forms of assistance, state laws prohibiting aid, state laws permitting some forms of aid). Since most nonpublic educational institutions have been controlled to some degree by religious groups and an overwhelming majority of the nonpublic K–12 pupils have attended schools with a religious affiliation, the "church–state" relationship has been central to the legal questions involved.

Those who advocate greater public financial support, particularly at the K–12 level, tend to offer the following arguments.

1. The nonpublic schools provide a service in the interest of the nation; that is, such schools educate persons who become productive citizens.
2. Economically, public support is a wise course of action. If nonpublic schools do not receive greater public assistance, they will be forced to close, and accommodating their enrollment in the public schools would call for greater expenditures than would assisting them.
3. The presence of a viable nonpublic school system is essential to provide people with an educational choice.
4. Failure to provide assistance is a form of double taxation on the parents of nonpublic school pupils. They pay taxes to support public schools and also must pay to support their children's nonpublic schools.

The major arguments against such support include the following:

1. Public funds would be used without adequate public controls, or if public controls were imposed, the special mission of many nonpublic schools would be aborted.
2. Because the greatest benefactors would be church-related nonpublic schools, greater support would free funds to be used for religious purposes.
3. There is no tax discrimination because single persons and childless couples pay public school taxes.

4. Greater support would greatly weaken the public schools. Public schools would be schools for the "unchurched," "dullards," "have-nots," and "incorrigibles."

Central to the issue of the legality of public support to nonpublic education and its form is the establishment clause of the First Amendment. One of the early cases on the subject arose in Louisiana, where the legislature had passed a law that provided free textbooks from public funds to nonpublic school pupils of the state. The law was contested, and in 1930 the Supreme Court upheld the constitutionality of the law, ruling that the children were aided—not the parochial schools attended by most of the children who benefited from the law.[6] Thus it appeared that providing instructional materials to children was legal under the First Amendment. This aid-to-the-child concept was reaffirmed by the Supreme Court in a 1947 decision and again in a 1968 decision. The 1947 decision upheld a contested New Jersey statute that permitted a local public school district to provide free transportation, or provide reimbursement for such, to pupils attending parochial schools as well as public schools.[7] The 1968 decision upheld a New York statute that authorized the loan of textbooks, purchased with public funds, to pupils in parochial schools as well as pupils in public schools.[8] In each case the Court noted the intent of the Constitution regarding the separation between church and state, but asserted that children were being aided—not religion.

In the 1960s states began to enact statutes that provided more direct financial aid to nonpublic K–12 pupils and schools. In 1968 Pennsylvania passed a law that authorized the state to "purchase secular educational services" from nonpublic schools by reimbursing these schools for teachers' salaries, textbooks, and instructional materials. In 1969 Rhode Island enacted a statute that provided, under specified conditions, for a state-paid salary supplement to teachers of secular subjects in nonpublic schools. Both of these acts were tested in the courts and in 1971 the Supreme Court ruled both acts unconstitutional because of the religious questions involved. In rendering its Pennsylvania decision the Court set out three "tests" for determining whether a law was in violation of the establishment clause. First, it must have a secular purpose. Second, its primary effect must be such that religion is neither advanced nor inhibited. Third, it must not foster excessive entanglements between government and religion.[9]

[6]*Cochran* v. *Louisiana State Board of Education,* 281 U.S. 370, 50 Sup. Ct. 335 (1930).

[7]*Everson* v. *Board of Education,* 330 U.S. 1, 67 Sup. Ct. 504 (1947).

[8]*Board of Education of Central School District No. 1* v. *Allen,* 392 U.S. 236, 88 Sup. Ct. 1923 (1968).

[9]*Lemon* v. *Kurtzman* (and *Early* v. *DiCenso, Robinson* v. *DiCenso*), 403 U.S. 602, 91 Sup. Ct. 2105 (1971).

Using these tests and the decisions of the Court in two other cases—a 1970 decision upholding local tax exemptions for church-owned property[10] and a 1971 decision upholding federal grants to public and nonpublic colleges for the construction of facilities to be used for secular purposes only[11]—new statutes were drawn in New York and Pennsylvania. Parts of the comprehensive New York statute provided state grants for building maintenance and repair to nonpublic schools serving low-income families and tax benefits for parents who paid nonpublic school tuition for their children. The Pennsylvania law provided parents of nonpublic school pupils reimbursement for tuition expenses. In 1973 the Supreme Court declared unconstitutional the forms of aid provided for by these statutes.[12] The primary rationale of the Court seemed to be that the second test set forth in the 1971 decision was not met. More than 90 percent of the nonpublic school pupils were enrolled in schools controlled by religious groups, and the Court noted "the impermissible effect of advancing religious institutions."

In 1975 the Supreme Court ruled on two other Pennsylvania statutes. It held constitutional the loan of secular textbooks to nonpublic school pupils but held unconstitutional the loan of instructional materials and equipment to the schools and the provision of guidance and testing services to be provided by public school personnel. The potential for "entanglements" and "advancement of religion" was noted.[13] Ohio, taking into account the 1975 Pennsylvania decision, passed a law providing nonpublic school pupils with secular textbooks, standardized testing and diagnostic services (such as provided in the public schools), therapeutic and remedial services provided by public school personnel at "neutral" locations, instructional equipment and materials comparable to that provided public schools, and transportation and other services for field trips. The textbooks, testing and diagnostic services, and the therapeutic and remedial services were ruled constitutional; the instructional equipment and materials and the field trip transportation and services were not. In rejecting the latter two forms of aid, the advancement and entanglement reasons were again cited.[14]

In consideration of the judicial decisions cited, it is obvious that any public support for nonpublic K–12 pupils must be for a secular purpose, in such a form that religion is not advanced, and administered in such a way that there are no resulting "excessive entangle-

[10]*Walz* v. *Tax Commission,* 397 U.S. 604, 90 Sup. Ct. 1409 (1970).
[11]*Tilton* v. *Richardson,* 403 U.S. 672, 91 Sup. Ct. 2091 (1971).
[12]*Committee for Public Education and Religious Liberty* v. *Nyquist,* 413 U.S. 756, 93 Sup. Ct. 2993 (1973); *Sloan* v. *Lemon,* 413 U.S. 825, 93 Sup. Ct. 2955 (1973).
[13]*Meek* v. *Pittenger,* 421 U.S. 349, 95 Sup. Ct. 1753 (1975).
[14]*Wolman* v. *Walter,* 433 U.S. 229, 97 Sup. Ct. 2593 (1977).

ments" between the government and the nonpublic schools. The loan of secular texts, public transportation to and from school, testing and diagnostic services (e.g., speech, hearing, psychological), and remedial and therapeutic services performed by public school personnel and comparable to what is provided in the public schools appear to be acceptable. Furthermore, shared time arrangements whereby non-public school pupils enroll in public schools for specific courses or pro-grams, such as vocational courses, seem to meet the legal standards. The foregoing forms of aid can be provided with very minimal sur-veillance by the government to ensure that the secular purpose con-cept is upheld. However, extensive surveillance creates entangle-ments. Thus, unless there is no need for extensive surveillance, the other forms of assistance mentioned appear to be legally question-able.

At this writing, there is considerable interest in a variety of tu-ition tax credit and educational voucher plans, which are intended to allow parents to choose which school their K–12 child will attend. There are those who believe that if a nonpublic school is one of the choices provided by a given plan, it will be declared unconstitutional; others believe a plan that includes nonpublic schools can be drafted to meet the legal standards.[15] Our belief is that this will be one of the major legal questions of the 1980s in the area of public support for nonpublic education.

As suggested previously, the Supreme Court has tended to take a different view of public assistance to postsecondary education. To illustrate, in a 1976 decision, the Court held constitutional a Mary-land statute that provided public financial assistance to nonpublic higher education institutions having student bodies not enrolled pri-marily in religiously-oriented programs. The reasoning in this case, which was consistent with previous cases, was that the religious in-fluence in church-related higher education institutions is less perva-sive than in parochial K–12 schools.[16]

Religious Instruction and Exercises

Public school pupils may be released from school for instruction in religion that takes place away from school premises, and the school may provide instruction about religion. However, instruction in the tenets of a religion or religious exercises with school sponsorship and on school premises may not be provided. There are four Supreme Court decisions that support these assertions. The *McCollum* case, decided

[15] For a detailed supporting position see John E. Coons and Stephen D. Sugar-man, *Education by Choice: The Case for Family Control* (Berkeley: University of Cali-fornia Press, 1978).

[16]*Roemer* v. *Board of Public Works of Maryland,* 426 U.S. 736, 96 Sup. Ct. 2337 (1976).

in 1948, arose from a situation existing in the Champaign, Illinois, schools.[17] In these schools there was a practice of setting aside a portion of the school day and permitting representatives of various religious groups to come into the schools to instruct pupils of their faith in the tenets of that faith. This occurred during regular class hours and in school classrooms. Pupil participation was voluntary, and those who did not choose to participate pursued their regular secular studies. The Court held that this practice was unconstitutional because public school buildings were being used, and the state compulsory attendance law had the effect of aiding the religious group to secure a pupil audience. Significantly, the Court made it clear that (1) it was ruling on a particular practice and not declaring all forms of cooperation to be unconstitutional, and (2) it was not taking away the right of the school to provide instruction about religion and its values.

The second germane decision, rendered in 1952, arose from a practice in New York City whereby pupils who chose to do so were permitted to leave school during regular class hours for instruction in the principles of their religious faith that was conducted on private premises. Those who did not choose to participate attended their regular classes. The Court held this practice was constitutional because the instruction took place away from school, and there was no evidence that the school system was using coercion or in any way providing the religious groups with an audience or aid.[18]

The other pertinent cases are *Engel* v. *Vitale*[19] (1962) and the *Schempp* case[20] (1963). At issue in the first case was the legality of a New York State Board of Regents–sponsored optional program of a brief nondenominational prayer in the public schools. The Court ruled that the prayer program was unconstitutional; the decision was based primarily on the premise that the government had no business legislating on matters of religion. Again, the Court made it clear that it was not hostile to religion or to the use, in public school classrooms, of historical documents containing references to the Deity. The focus in the *Schempp* case was a Pennsylvania statute requiring the reading of ten verses of the Bible, without comment, at the opening of each day in each public school. The statute provided that any child might be excused by parental request. (In this instance there was also a similar statute in Maryland at question, but the Court, as it often does, treated them as one case and focused on the Pennsylvania statute.) The Court ruled the Bible reading to be unconstitutional and

[17]*People of the State of Illinois ex rel. McCollum* v. *Board of Education of School District No. 71, Champaign, Ill.,* 333 U.S. 203, 68 Sup. Ct. 461 (1948).

[18]*Zorach* v. *Clauson,* 343 U.S. 306, 72 Sup. Ct. 679 (1952).

[19]*Engel* v. *Vitale,* 370 U.S. 421, 82 Sup. Ct. 1261 (1962).

[20]*School District of Abington Township* v. *Schempp* (and *Murray* v. *Curlett*), 374 U.S. 203, 83 Sup. Ct. 1560 (1963).

made it clear that such religious exercises need not involve substantive expenditures of public monies or be compulsory for pupils to be unconstitutional.

Racial Desegregation

Perhaps no activity of the federal judiciary has aroused as much emotion as the decisions that have been reached relating to racial desegregation of educational institutions. The first obvious point the federal courts have made is that governmental bodies may not take actions that result in students being segregated by race.

For many years, as a result of state constitutional provisions or state legislative acts, the Southern states operated a dual public educational system. This dual system was viewed as legal as a result of several federal court decisions, including the Supreme Court decision in the *Plessy* v. *Ferguson* case of 1896.[21] In this case, which involved transportation, not education, the Court upheld the notion that "separate but equal" facilities for the races were constitutional. Following several decisions relating to segregation and education that paved the way, in May 1954 the Supreme Court ruled directly on the issue in regard to public schools where there was racial segregation as a result of governmental acts (*de jure* segregation). In that so-called *First Brown* case, the Court asked, "Does segregation of children in public schools solely on the basis of race, even though the physical facilities and other 'tangible' factors may be equal, deprive the children of the minority group of equal educational opportunities?" The Court answered, "We believe that it does."[22] A year later, in what is known as the *Second Brown* case, the Court placed the responsibility on the school authorities and the lower courts to eliminate racial segregation based on governmental acts.[23]

In the years that followed, much of the energy of school officials and the lower courts in the South was expended in desegregation matters. Further, a number of legal disputes arose relative to how far school officials must go in their efforts to eliminate the vestiges of *de jure* racial segregation. In 1971 the Court rendered a far-reaching decision on the elimination of segregation in the Charlotte–Mecklenburg County, North Carolina, schools where the segregation had a *de jure* base. In this case the Court struck down the antibusing law passed by the North Carolina legislature and identified a number of guidelines to accomplished school desegregation. Specifically, the Court suggested that (1) busing of pupils to accomplished desegregation may be done; (2) deliberate gerrymandering of school districts and atten-

---

[21]*Plessy* v. *Ferguson,* 163 U.S. 537, 16 Sup. Ct. 1138 (1896).
[22]*Brown* v. *Board of Education of Topeka,* 347 U.S. 483, 74 Sup. Ct. 686 (1954).
[23]*Brown* v. *Board of Education of Topeka,* 349 U.S. 294, 75 Sup. Ct. 753 (1955).

dance zones may be necessary as an antidote to *de jure* segregation; (3) "racial balance" of pupils within a school, though not required, may be used; and (4) when required to desegregate, one must not be "color-blind" in assigning pupils.[24]

Although much of the legal and moral pressure of the 1950s and 1960s was aimed at those sectors of the nation where there was *de jure* segregation, considerable effort was being expended to reduce the incidence of *de facto* segregation (where the segregation was the result of residential patterns), and there was no history of *de jure* segregation as usually defined. During this period the Supreme Court did not address this question; however, several conflicting decisions were rendered by lower courts in the federal system. There were decisions to the effect that affirmative action must be taken by local districts, that affirmative action may be taken, and that the local school district cannot be held responsible and required to act to overcome conditions it did not create.

In June 1973, the U.S. Supreme Court issued a detailed opinion in a case involving Denver, Colorado—the first such opinion from a school district that had no history of *de jure* segregation as usually defined. In this case the district court had found that the Denver school board had segregated seven schools (*de jure*) and that twenty-five other schools were segregated on a *de facto* basis and were educationally inferior to the district's white schools. This lower court ordered desegregation of the seven schools but left the others untouched. The appeals court concurred on the seven schools and further ordered that the other twenty-five schools be desegregated and improved. The Supreme Court, issuing its opinion on the plaintiffs' appeal, remanded the case back to the trial court with a detailed procedure for further hearings. Further, the Court noted that if the trial court found a "dual system," the school board would have a duty to desegregate the total district.[25] In a later action the trial judge ordered the elimination of the segregation. The Denver case, although not requiring the desegregation of *de facto* segregated schools, provided lower courts considerable leeway in deciding whether segregation is *de jure* or *de facto*. That is, the *de jure* concept was considerably broadened.

Two Ohio cities, Dayton and Columbus, were the settings for two other often-cited "Northern" desegregation cases. Dayton illustrates well the issues involved. The case was entered in 1972 when forty-nine of the sixty-nine schools of the district had enrollments of 90 percent or more of one race. In 1977 the Supreme Court said the lower courts had erred in ordering the Dayton Board of Education to

[24]*Swann* v. *Charlotte–Mecklenburg Board of Education*, 402 U.S. 1, 91 Sup. Ct. 1267 (1971).

[25]*Keyes* v. *School District No. 1, Denver Colorado*, 413 U.S. 198, 93 Sup. Ct. 2686 (1973).

take steps to bring each school within 15 percent of the systemwide ratio of black–white pupils, and ordered the district court to hold additional hearings. It noted there was little evidence of any constitutional violations, which had caused the segregation, and that a systemwide remedy was not appropriate.[26] As a result of the new hearings, the district court ruled the district board did not have an obligation. However, the appeals court reversed the district court on the basis that in 1954, the year of *First Brown,* the board had operated a dual system and had failed to take steps to dismantle it. Accordingly, a systemwide remedy was appropriate. In 1979, in a five-four vote, the Supreme Court upheld the decision of the appeals court noting that the schools were as segregated as they had been in 1954 and that the board of education had failed in its "affirmative" responsibility.[27]

As implied by the foregoing, as the courts began to order desegregation in "big city" school districts and/or those where there was no history of segregation by state statute, the issue of how far school officials must go became more complex. Central to the issue were questions related to the integrity of school district lines, extensiveness of busing, and the extent to which racial ratios must be maintained once desegregation had been achieved.

Regarding the integrity of school district boundaries, the Richmond, Virginia district, with a *de jure* history, composed of about 70 percent black pupils, and adjoined by the Chesterfield County and Henrico County districts, where the pupil enrollment was about 90 percent white, was the location of an intended court test. In 1972 the federal district judge ordered the merger of the three districts into a single metropolitan district. Later, the appeals court overturned the decision, noting the Tenth Amendment and saying it found no constitutional violation in the establishment and maintenance of the three school districts. In May 1973 the Supreme Court, with one justice not taking part, split four–four on the issue. Thus the decision of the appeals court stood.[28]

The legal battlefield then shifted to Detroit. The Detroit situation was "typical" of large industralized urban areas. The city school district's pupil population was about 70 percent black, and the city was surrounded by a large number of suburban districts, which were overwhelmingly white. In 1972 the district judge in the case ordered a massive busing plan, which required the consolidation of fifty-three school districts into a single attendance area. The appeals court upheld the district court on the existence and causes of the segregation

[26]*Dayton Board of Education* v. *Brinkman,* 433 U.S. 406, 97 Sup. Ct. 2766 (1977).
[27]*Dayton Board of Education* v. *Brinkman,* 443 U.S. 526, 96 Sup. Ct. 2971 (1979).
[28]*Bradley* v. *School Board of City of Richmond, Virginia,* 462 F. 2nd 1058, 1060 (1972); 416 U.S. 696, 94 Sup. Ct. 2006 (1974).

and the remedy of crossing district lines. The issue went to the Supreme Court and in July 1974, in a five–four vote, the high court struck down the cross-district busing plan. The Court accepted the findings of the lower court on Detroit's discrimination against blacks but found no evidence of suburban school district discrimination; thus, the Court reasoned, the suburban districts could not be compelled to become part of a solution to a problem they did not create.[29] As a result, a Detroit-only remedy was formulated, which included four remedial programs intended to combat the effects of the prior segregation, and in 1977 the Supreme Court upheld the district court's remedial programs including the requirement that the state pay one-half of the costs.[30]

On the matter of the extensiveness of busing to accomplish desegretation in the urban districts, as suggested before, the Supreme Court had accepted the concept in the *Charlotte–Mecklenburg* case and permitted it to be a significant part of the remedy in the Detroit-only and Dayton plans. Also, in December 1980, a federal appeals court upheld a district court ruling declaring an antibusing statute in the state of Washington unconstitutional.[31] However, in a 1977 decision involving Austin, Texas, the Court found an extensive cross-district busing plan of the appeals court exceeded what was necessary to eliminate the effects of any official acts or omissions.[32] Furthermore, the reader is reminded that the 1979 decision in Dayton was five–four.

Regarding the question of pupil racial ratios, the Supreme Court has ruled that ratios may be used as guidelines to move from segregated to unitary schools. However, school officials may not be required to make yearly adjustments within school centers to offset random population shifts in the district. That is, once desegregation is achieved, there is no requirement of a particular ratio of majority to minority pupils.[33]

From the federal court activity to date relative to racial segregation of public K–12 pupils, it is obvious that segregation by virtue of governmental acts is unconstitutional. Where there is a finding of intent to segregate, affirmative action may be required. The required action may include ratio schemes and busing plans. However, the boundaries of districts that are not a part of the intent to segregate may not be ordered violated. Furthermore, the maintenance of strict

[29]*Milliken* v. *Bradley,* 418 U.S. 717, 94 Sup. Ct. 3112 (1974).

[30]*Milliken* v. *Bradley,* 433 U.S. 267, 97 Sup. Ct. 2749 (1977).

[31]*Seattle School District No. 1* v. *The State of Washington et al.,* 633 F. 2nd 1338 (9th Cir. 1980).

[32]*Austin Independent School District* v. *United States,* 429 U.S. 990, 97 Sup. Ct. 517 (1977).

[33]*Pasadena City Board of Education* v. *Spangler,* 427 U.S. 424, 96 Sup. Ct. 2697 (1976).

racial ratios within school centers over time are not required, and the extensiveness of the busing required will be a function of the perceptions of the courts about the facts in a given situation.

In regard to pupil segregation in nonpublic schools, as previously mentioned, in the 1976 *Runyon* case the Supreme Court ruled that nonpublic, nonsectarian schools, which offer enrollment to the public at large, may not refuse admission solely on the basis of race. Relative to staff desegregation in the public schools, the ruling in the *Charlotte–Mecklenburg* case noted that it was constitutional to order teacher assignments to achieve faculty desegregation. Therefore, the racial composition of the faculty of a school has often been a part of desgregation plans. Furthermore, in 1977, the Supreme Court held that the percentage of black teachers in a school district as compared to the black teachers in the relevant labor market was an appropriate statistic to consider in determining whether a school district had engaged in employment discrimination.[34]

The erosion of the separate-but-equal doctrine in higher education preceded the landmark *First Brown* case with two 1950 cases.[35] The major question in recent years has related to how far must, *or* may, governmental officials go in higher education desegregation efforts? Specifically, operating on the general premise that the scope of the remedy must fit the violation, may the merger of institutions be ordered? In Tennessee such a merger was ordered with the historically black university being the surviving institution.[36] May so-called "reverse discrimination" be practiced? In the celebrated *Bakke* case, by a five–four margin, the Supreme Court said that student racial quotas in situations where no previous discrimination has been found are illegal. However, university admissions committees may consider race as one factor in making decisions about student admissions.[37]

Protection of Rights of Students and Staff

Obviously many of the decisions of the federal judiciary on religious exercises and instruction and racial desegregation have been for the purpose of protecting rights of individuals. However, these are but two areas in which the federal courts have acted. Basic to the decisions of the courts in cases involving the rights of individuals are the concepts of *due process* and *equal protection* contained in the Fourteenth Amendment.

[34]*Hazelwood School District* v. *United States*, 433 U.S. 299, 97 Sup. Ct. 2736 (1977).
[35]*Sweatt* v. *Painter*, 339 U.S. 629, 70 Sup. Ct. 848 (1950); *McLaurin* v. *Oklahoma State Regents for Higher Education*, 339 U.S. 637, 70 Sup. Ct. 851 (1950).
[36]*Geier* v. *Blanton*, 427 F. Supp. 644 (M.D.Tenn. 1977).
[37]*Regents of the University of California* v. *Bakke*, 438 U.S. 265, 98 Sup. Ct. 2733 (1978).

There are two aspects of due process. Procedural due process means that if an action is to be taken against a person that deprives the person of "life, liberty, or property"—expelling a pupil from school or dismissing a teacher—three basic steps are required: (1) proper notice to the individual that he or she is about to be deprived of "life, liberty, or property"; (2) an opportunity to be heard; and (3) a fairly conducted hearing. Substantive due process means that if the government is going to deprive an individual of "life, liberty, or property," there must be a valid objective, and the action to be taken must be reasonably calculated to achieve the valid objective.[38] For example, if school authorities institute a dress code for pupils, they might be required to show that the dress code is essential for orderly conduct and an adequate learning environment in the schools.

As applied to education, equal protection has had its greatest impact in prohibiting unreasonable classifications. The two tests for determining whether or not a classification is reasonable relate to *rational basis* and *fundamental interest*. The rational basis test, which is employed when a fundamental interest is not involved, requires that there must be a sound reason for the classification used and that all of those classified alike must be, insofar as possible, treated uniformly. Also, under this test, the person challenging a classification scheme has the burden of proving that the scheme has no rational basis to achieve a legitimate government objective. When a fundamental interest or *suspect classification* (e.g., race, national origin, indigence) is involved, a strict scrutiny test is used. Under this test the government has the burden of proving that it has a compelling interest that justifies the classification in question and that the scheme is necessary to further the compelling government interest. In reaching decisions regarding whether or not equal protection (or for that matter due process) has been granted, the courts appear to make an effort to examine several factors (e.g., sociological factors, the larger good of society, prevailing mores, sound educational policy) and examine the protection of individual rights in light of these.[39] This reasoning seemed apparent when the Supreme Court in 1954 reversed its 1896 separate-but-equal stance in regard to race.

Because educational administrators and teachers have historically viewed their relationship to students to be like the relationship between parent and child (where the basic right is custody, not liberty), they might question whether or not students have due process rights. The Supreme Court clearly struck down the traditional *in loco parentis* concept in a 1967 decision relating to the rights of juveniles

---

[38] Kern Alexander, *School Law*. (St. Paul, Minn.: West, 1980), p. 349.

[39] Michael W. La Morte, *School Law Cases and Concepts*. (Englewood Cliffs, N.J.: Prentice-Hall, 1982), pp. 8–9.

under an Arizona law and extended the right of due process procedures to young people.[40]

One of the leading cases on procedural due process grew out of a situation in which a group of students at Alabama State College were expelled without a hearing for allegedly having brought discord and disorder to the campus by taking part in a sit-in demonstration. The Circuit Court reversed the decision of a lower court and held that the students had not been given notice of the pending action and a chance to be heard. The Court noted that the college had the governmental power to expel the students, but this power could not be exercised arbitrarily.[41] This judicial philosophy was reaffirmed in the often-cited *Goss* v. *Lopez* case in which the Supreme Court ruled against ten-day suspensions of high school students without notice of reasons or hearings. However, the Court noted that there need be no delay in time between notice and hearing, and, if necessary, the students could be removed immediately, provided that the notice and hearing followed within a reasonable time.[42] Also, according to a 1977 ruling of the Supreme Court, notice and hearing before administering corporal punishment in accord with state law are not required. In that case the Court reasoned that the opportunity to file civil or criminal charges was sufficient to protect the student's due process rights. Incidentally, in that same case the Court held that the corporal punishment administered was not "cruel and unusual" in violation of the Eighth Amendment.[43]

In a 1969 decision, the Supreme Court applied the doctrine of the previously mentioned Arizona case to pupils and provided an illustration of the application of substantive due process. In that situation a group of pupils in the Des Moines, Iowa, schools decided to wear black armbands to school to publicize their objection to the war in Vietnam. The school officials, becoming aware of the plan, met and adopted a regulation that pupils wearing armbands to school would be asked to remove them, and if they refused to do so, would be suspended. Two Tinker children, aware of the regulation, wore armbands and were suspended; court action followed. In 1969 the Supreme Court ruled in favor of the Tinker children. The Court indicated that there was no evidence that the school authorities could have reasonably forecast disruption or interference with school activities because of the wearing of armbands, and in fact none occurred.[44]

[40]*In re Gault*, 387 U.S. 1, 87 Sup. Ct. 1428 (1967).
[41]*Dixon* v. *Alabama State Board of Education*, 294 F. 2nd 150 (5th Cir. 1961) cert. denied, 368 U.S. 930, 82 Sup. Ct. 368 (1961).
[42]*Goss* v. *Lopez*, 419 U.S. 565, 95 Sup. Ct. 729 (1975).
[43]*Ingraham* v. *Wright*, 430 U.S. 651, 97 Sup. Ct. 1401 (1977).
[44]*Tinker* v. *Des Moines Independent Community School District*, 393 U.S. 503, 89 Sup. Ct. 733 (1969).

The procedural due process concept has been applied to the employment rights of teachers. In one case, a university had hired a teacher for a fixed term of one academic year and later notified him that he would not be rehired. The Supreme Court, upholding the university, stated that reasons for the decision and a pretermination hearing were not required where there were no conditions creating an expectation of continued employment and the teacher had no constitutionally-protected "property" interest in the position.[45] In another leading case, a teacher had been employed by a college for ten years under a series of one-year contracts but had no formal tenure. In legal action following the teacher's dismissal for insubordination (he had criticized publicly the board of regents), the Supreme Court, in holding for the teacher, noted that (1) public criticism of superiors by a teacher on matters of public concern is constitutionally protected and may not be the basis for dismissal, and (2) although a "subjective" expectancy of tenure does not require reasons and a pretermination hearing, in this case, based on rules contained in the college faculty guide, there was an "objective" expectancy of reemployment, which required procedural safeguards.[46]

The due process concept has also been applied to the rights of pregnant teachers. The Supreme Court has ruled that regulations requiring teachers to take unpaid leaves of absences when they are only four or five months pregnant "sweeps too broadly." As viewed by the Court, the problem was the specific and early cutoff dates chosen by the school boards involved. The majority opinion stated that the rules set up a nonrebuttable presumption of unfitness to teach, which infringed the constitutional right to bear children. Also, the medical testimony did not justify the specific cutoff dates, nor did the boards' claims of administrative convenience and teaching continuity.[47]

In March 1973, the Supreme Court rendered what became one of the most highly publicized educational case of the 1970s. In the *Rodriguez* case, the Supreme Court, by a five–four vote, reversed a lower federal court, which had held that the Texas educational finance system violated the equal protection clause of the Fourteenth Amendment in that it created unequal treatment of poor school districts.[48] Thus the high court sustained, as far as federal constitutional questions were concerned, the existing system, which in large measure relied on the local district property tax. The Court noted that the system did not operate to the particular disadvantage of any "sus-

---

[45]*Board of Regents* v. *Roth,* 408 U.S. 564, 92 Sup. Ct. 2701 (1972).

[46]*Perry* v. *Sindermann,* 409 U.S. 593, 92 Sup. Ct. 2694 (1972).

[47]*Cleveland Board of Education* v. *Le Fleur* (and *Cohen* v. *Chesterfield County Board*), 414 U.S. 632, 94 Sup. Ct. 791 (1974).

[48]*San Antonio Independent School District et al.* v. *Demetrio Rodriguez et al.,* 411 U.S. 1, 93 Sup. Ct. 1278 (1973).

pect class," and education was not a "fundamental right" under the First Amendment (i.e., speech, press, religion, peaceable assembly, and petition for redress of grievance). Therefore the strict scrutiny test was not applied, and under the rational basis standard the Court upheld the Texas finance system because it bore a national relationship to a legitimate state purpose. It should be emphasized that this decision was in relation to federal questions only. This does not mean state financing plans might not violate state constitutional provisions (see Chapter 4).

During the 1970s great interest developed in ensuring the rights of the handicapped. Even though the federal court decisions are not extensive, the trend seems clear: Handicapped children must be identified, provided procedural safeguards, have their conditions assessed, and provided an appropriate education in the least restrictive environment. To illustrate, in a 1971 suit a federal district court-approved consent agreement was reached that provided Pennsylvania could not apply any statute that postponed, terminated, or denied mentally retarded children access to public education, including a public school program, homebound program, and tuition or tuition maintenance.[49] In 1972 a federal district court issued an order declaring the constitutional right of all children to a publicly supported education and that the policies and practices of the Washington, D.C., board of education excluded the children without provisions for an adequate and immediate alternative.[50]

A Texas school district had to pay for residential placement when the range of services offered by the public schools was deemed inadequate for a child's needs.[51] In a case where a pupil had been screened, and assigned to a special education program, expulsion of the pupil was denied when the district court reasoned that any change in a pupil's placement must be made by a planning and placement team taking into account the pupil's needs and the opportunities available.[52] A nonpublic South Carolina college was required to provide a deaf graduate student with a sign language interpreter.[53]

A 1974 Supreme Court decision involving children with a language handicap became the frequently cited basis for the federal Department of Education's controversial 1980 bilingual program plan. The decision grew out of a suit filed on behalf of about 1,800 Chinese pupils in San Francisco who charged that they needed special instruc-

[49]*Pennsylvania Association for Retarded Children* v. *Pennsylvania*, 334 F. Supp. 1257 (E.D. Pa. 1971).

[50]*Mills* v. *Board of Education of Washington, D.C.*, 348 F. Supp. 866 (D.D.C. 1972).

[51]*Howard S.* v. *Friendswood Independent School District and Texas Education Agency*, 454 F. Supp. 634 (S.D. Tex. 1978).

[52]*Stuart* v. *Nappi*, 443 F. Supp. 1235 (D. Conn. 1978).

[53]*Barnes* v. *Converse College*, 436 F. Supp. 635 (D.S.C., 1977).

tion in English, which was being provided to some 1,700 other Chinese pupils, and that failure to provide the needed instruction was a violation of the equal protection clause and the 1964 Civil Rights Act. The lower courts had upheld the school authorities on the basis that the schools had done nothing to cause the problems of the Chinese pupils and thus had no duty to correct; however, the high court held that the school authorities had a duty to rectify the situation.[54] In this instance the Court did not rely on the equal protection concept; instead, it ruled on the basis of a violation of the Civil Rights Act, which forbids discriminatiion in any program receiving federal funds (such funds were being received).

The federal courts have not limited their application of the due process and equal protection concepts to the foregoing areas of individual rights. Furthermore, in some instances the First Amendment has been applied. The high court has ruled that a school board may not condition school attendance upon overt participation in "patriotic" exercises (flag saluting) deemed offensive on religious grounds by pupils and their parents.[55] A state statute that prohibited teaching "the theory or doctrine that man ascended from a lower order of animals" has been struck down.[56] The right of the state to require a course in sex education has been upheld.[57] The Supreme Court has ruled that if a state tenure law is worded so that a contract exists between the state and the teachers affected, a later legislature cannot repeal or change the law for those affected.[58] The right of a teacher, on personal time, to criticize publicly the educational administrators has been upheld.[59] This freedom of speech has also been extended to the private communication of a teacher to his or her principal.[60] A teacher has been upheld who refused to comply with the "necktie code" of a school board.[61] The right of teachers to organize for collective bargaining has been confirmed.[62] In a case involving a power company the Supreme Court ruled that employment standards and tests that do not have a reasonable relationship to job performance violates

---

[54]*Lau* v. *Nichols,* 414 U.S. 563, 94 Sup. Ct. 786 (1974).

[55]*West Virginia State Board of Education* v. *Barnette,* 319 U.S. 624, 63 Sup. Ct. 1178 (1943).

[56]*Epperson* v. *Arkansas,* 393 U.S. 97, 89 Sup. Ct. 266 (1968).

[57]*Cornwell* v. *Maryland State Board of Education,* 428 F. 2nd 471 (4th Cir. 1970) cert. denied, 400 U.S. 942, 91 Sup. Ct. 240 (1970).

[58]*State of Indiana ex rel. Anderson* v. *Brand,* 303 U.S. 95, 58 Sup. Ct. 443 (1938).

[59]*Pickering* v. *Board of Education, District 205,* 391 U.S. 563, 88 Sup. Ct. 1731 (1968).

[60]*Givhan* v. *Western Line Consolidated School District,* 439 U.S. 410, 99 Sup. Ct. 693 (1979).

[61]*East Hartford Education Association* v. *Board of Education,* 562 F. 2nd 838 (2nd Cir. 1977).

[62]*McLaughlin* v. *Tilendis,* 398 F. 2nd 278 (7th Cir. 1968).

the 1964 Civil Rights Act.[63] However, the use of National Teacher Examination scores for teacher certification and salary purposes has been upheld.[64] The right of students to write off-campus and distribute on-campus a publication critical of the the administration has been affirmed.[65] In a case where a female student wanted to participate in some formerly all-male athletic events, such as track, skiing, and tennis—where her ability was not in question and there was no alternative competition for females—a federal circuit court ruled that banning her was arbitrary and unreasonable.[66] Lower federal courts have struck down rules excluding an unwed mother from public school[67] and excluding a married student from extracurricular activities.[68]

In sum, the decisions of the federal courts clearly indicate that where fundamental rights of students and/or teachers are involved, they will be protected. Laws, educational policies, administrative acts, and so on, must meet the conditions inherent in the definitions of due process and equal protection imposed by the courts.

Interest of the U.S. Congress

The interest of the Congress in education dates from the passage of the Ordinance of 1785. Federal legislation related to education intensified in 1958, following the 1957 Russian launching of Sputnik I, and its financial commitment increased significantly with passage of the Elementary and Secondary Education Act of 1965. To many this period marked the beginning of a new era of congressional involvement in education. Most of the congressional legislation has been designed to stimulate specific educational activities through the provision of monetary support. This categorical aid has been the subject of much criticism among educational authorities; yet many worthy purposes have been served by this approach, and it has persisted. However, for the 1982 fiscal year the Congress made a modest move toward more general aid with a "block grant" authorization. The authority to tax and expend federal funds for education is based on the previously mentioned general welfare clause of the Constitution, and this authority to tax for broad social purposes was upheld by the U.S. Supreme Court in a 1937 decision relating to the Social Security Act.[69]

[63]*Griggs* v. *Duke Power Company,* 401 U.S. 424, 91 Sup. Ct. 849 (1971).
[64]*United States of America* v. *State of South Carolina,* 434 U.S. 1026, 93 Sup. Ct. 756 (1978).
[65]*Scoville* v. *Board of Education of Joliet Township,* 435 F. 2nd 10 (7th Cir. 1970).
[66]*Brenden* v. *Independent School District 742,* 477 F. 2nd 1292 (8th Cir. 1973).
[67]*Perry* v. *Granada Municipal Separate School System,* 300 F. Supp. (D. Miss. 1969).
[68]*Davis* v. *Meek,* 344 F. Supp. 298 (D. Ohio 1972).
[69]*Helvering* v. *Davis,* 301 U.S. 619, 57 Sup. Ct. 904 (1937).

Land Grants for the General Support of Education

During the period of the settlement of the nation, Congress passed several land grant acts essentially providing that a portion of the public lands be set aside for the support of schools. The Ordinance of 1785 was the first of these acts. This act provided that the sixteenth section of each township in the state carved from the public domain was to be set aside for educational purposes. As a result of additional acts (e.g., the Ohio Enabling Act of 1802), this land grant policy continued through 1912, when Arizona and New Mexico were admitted to the Union. Other land allocations for schools were also made. These included internal improvement lands, salt lands, and swamplands. Because of a variety of circumstances, not all states participated in the original land grants (e.g., the thirteen original colonies and five states with no federally owned land). However, in the thirty-nine states that did receive some type of land grants, it has been estimated that collectively this amounted to over 154 million acres.[70]

The federal government did not exercise any control over the land grants. In some states the lands were sold at low prices; in some instances the funds derived from the lands were mismanaged; and in other cases the lands were settled by private citizens and the state lost title to them. In spite of such abuses most authorities feel that the land grants were significant in demonstrating the federal government's commitment to education and stimulating the states and local communities to establish public schools.

Encouragement of the Establishment of Public Colleges

The land grant concept was applied to higher education with the passage of the Morrill Act in 1862. This act granted to each state 30,000 acres of public land (or equivalent value in script if there was insufficient land available) for each of its congressional members to be used for the support of a college "to teach such branches of learning as are related to agriculture and the mechanic arts—in order to promote the liberal and practical education of the industrial classes in the several pursuits and professions of life." The respective state legislatures were expected to provide additional support as necessary to develop and maintain these land grant institutions. The function of these institutions was extended to agricultural research with the passage of the Hatch Act in 1887, providing for the establishment of agricultural experiment stations. A second Morrill Act, in 1890, and subsequent acts provided for direct monetary appropriations to the states to be used for these institutions. The function of the land grant

[70] Arvid J. Burke, *Financing Public Schools in the United States,* rev ed. (New York: Harper & Row, 1957), p. 241.

colleges was further extended to embrace service activities with the passage of the Smith-Lever Act in 1914, which provided for the agricultural extension service. The result was a network of extension workers, almost always associated with the land grant institution of the state, who provided instruction to rural Americans for improving farm life and agricultural production.

The significance of the legislation related to the land grant colleges is threefold. First, it established the precedent for the federal government to take action in areas deemed essential for the national welfare that were being neglected by the states. Second, it led to the creation of a network of colleges and universities that succeeded, in large measure, in providing the masses an opportunity for a college education with a different emphasis. Third, it led to the creation of a different concept in regard to the function of public institutions of higher learning (i.e., instruction, research, and service).

Youth-Oriented Legislation of the 1930s

When Franklin D. Roosevelt became president of the United States in 1933, the nation was in an economic depression. During the Roosevelt years the Congress passed a number of measures that were primarily for relief of the existing economic condition. However, several of these were of educational significance in that aid was provided for some educational activities, the attention of the nation was focused on the needs of youth, and a rough blueprint was provided for the education legislation that the Congress would enact in the 1960s.

The Civilian Conservation Corps (CCC), created by congressional action in 1933, and the National Youth Administration (NYA), created by presidential executive order in 1935, are of particular significance. The CCC, aimed primarily at relieving unemployment, enlisted more than 3 million young men between 1934 and 1941, and more than 2.7 million participated in the organized educational programs provided.[71] Even though educational opportunities were provided from the start, Congress formalized this thrust in 1937 by stating that "at least ten hours per week may be devoted to general education and vocational training," and eventually each CCC camp had an educational advisor who was appointed by the U.S. Office of Education. The mobilization effort for World War II greatly curtailed the CCC, and it was abolished in 1943. The NYA was intended to provide employment and assistance for high school and college youth. However, in time, in some states, resident centers were established

---

[71] Edgar L. Morphet, Roe L. Johns, and Theodore L. Reller, *Educational Organization and Administration,* 3rd ed. (Englewood Cliffs, N.J.: Prentice-Hall, 1974), p. 238.

and educationally related activities (e.g., guidance and testing programs) were undertaken. Approximately 2.7 million young persons were assisted by the NYA.[72] The agency was phased out in 1944.

A number of other federal relief agencies carried on educationally relevant programs during the 1933–1940 period. Among their many and varied activities, the Federal Emergency Relief Administration and the Works Progress Administration, which superseded it in 1939, provided nursery schools, hot lunches for children, public affairs education, literacy classes, vocational education, correspondence courses, and funds for school building construction and repair. The Public Works Administration made grants for school building construction up to 45 per cent of the building cost, and persons employed by the Civil Works Administration repaired and renovated many school buildings. The Surplus Commodities Corporation, created in 1935, distributed surplus agricultural commodities for public and nonpublic school lunch programs. (Federal support of the school food service program was furthered with the passage of the National School Lunch Act in 1946, special aid for the school milk program in 1954, the enactment of the Child Nutrition Act of 1966, and enactment of a 1970 law making the special school milk program permanent. The passage of amendments has extended the programs into the 1980s. However, in 1981 the Congress made significant reductions in child nutrition program funding.)

Funds for Schools in Federally Impacted Areas

In the 1930s federal funds had been diverted to school construction and repair as a result of the "depression legislation." In 1941, with the passage of the Lanham Act, the Congress focused directly upon the need in many localities for community facilities. This act provided funds for the construction, maintenance, and operation of facilities, including those for education, in communities where financial hardships had been created because of the federal activity associated with the war effort. In 1950 this concept was extended with the enactment of Public Laws 815 (funds for school construction) and 874 (funds for operating expenses). These acts, like the Lanham Act, which they superseded, provided funds to school districts affected by federal activities in the area. The funds involved were significant and only those districts that could qualify as "federally impacted" received benefits. Although these acts have been consistently renewed, they have become the focal point of considerable controversy. Some would extend the program to all school districts, whereas many oth-

---

[72] Arthur B. Moehlman, *School Administration*, 2nd ed. (Boston: Houghton Mifflin, 1951), p. 469.

ers would eliminate it. Perhaps illustrative of a trend in this controversy is the fact that in 1981 the Congress reduced significantly the
amount of impacted-areas funds.

Educational Activities for National Defense

Congress has provided major support for educational endeavors
deemed important to the defense of the nation. One major thrust has
been the establishment and support of schools to train officers for the
military services. Congressional action created the Military Academy
in 1802, the Naval Academy in 1845, the Coast Guard Academy in
1910, and the Air Force Academy in 1954. Another thrust has been
to support reserve officer training programs in schools and colleges.
The 1916 National Defense Act provided the impetus. A third thrust
has been support for the education of enlisted members of the armed
forces, ranging from literacy training to sophisticated technical programs. A fourth thrust has been support of education and training
for returning military veterans. This began with congressional action
in 1918. The concept was more fully developed by the 1944 passage
of the Serviceman's Readjustment Act. Public Law 550 provided educational benefits for Korean War veterans. In 1966 and 1967 "cold
war" and Vietnam War veterans were extended such benefits.

Although the immediate "payoff" for national defense is questionable, many authorities believe that these veterans' education and
rehabilitation acts represent one of the most significant efforts of the
federal government in relation to education. They reason that the
millions of veterans who availed themselves of the opportunities have
more than reimbursed the nation for the funds expended in their behalf through increased earning power and the subsequent payment of
more taxes and through their leadership in every walk of life, including education.

Support for Vocational, Adult, and Community Education

With the passage of the Smith-Hughes Act in 1917, the Congress reaffirmed its philosophy of stimulating the development of educational programs that equipped participants with salable skills. This
act provided funds to the states for vocational preparation below the
college level in the fields of agriculture, home economics, and trades
and industries. Also, funds were provided for teacher preparation in
these fields. The Smith-Hughes programs placed several requirements on the states. These included state legislative approval, the
creation of a state board for vocational education, the matching of
federal funds, submission of a plan for use of funds to the federal
government, and reporting how funds were actually spent. This act
marked the first effort of the Congress to stimulate specific programs
and provide support for specific educational activities below the col-

lege level. As a result of this act, vocational agriculture and home economics became an integral part of the high school curriculum. Further, in a number of cities vocational high schools were established and trade and industrial programs were added to the curriculum of many comprehensive high schools.

During the period 1918–1960, further stimuli for vocational programs were provided by other acts and amendments. For example, the Smith-Bankhead Act of 1920 provided for vocational rehabilitation and education of handicapped persons, and the George-Deen Act of 1937 provided for education in the distributive occupations.

Federal support for vocational education entered a new era, which has continued, with the passage of the Vocational Education Act of 1963. This act increased significantly federal funds for vocational and technical education and greatly broadened the concept of vocational education. It provided support for a broad range of vocational programs below the baccalaureate-degree level for persons still in high school, persons who had completed or discontinued their formal schooling, persons who needed to upgrade their skills or learn new ones, and persons with educational handicaps. One of the most visible results of this act was the creation of area vocational schools. This 1963 act is even more significant when examined in conjunction with the Area Redevelopment (1961) and Manpower Development and Training (1962) Acts and subsequent amendments that provided support for training or retraining in geographic areas where there was a high rate of unemployment or underemployment and for the training of workers whose skills had become obsolete. The 1968 Education Amendments further increased the level of federal funding for vocational education and placed greater emphasis on opportunities for the disadvantaged and the handicapped. As a part of the 1976 Education Amendments, the vocational act was revised by consolidating some categorical programs, placing greater emphasis on planning and evaluation, broadening the role of local and state advisory groups, and requiring the removal of sex bias. Through amendments in 1980 the Congress continued its basic thrust in vocational education.

Adult basic education received emphasis beginning in 1966 with the Adult Education Act, which, with subsequent amendments, has placed emphasis on basic functional skills for adults, including immigrants and refugees. Beginning in 1973 with the Comprehensive Employment and Training Act (CETA), emphasis has been placed on employment and training the underemployed and the economically disadvantaged unemployed. In 1980 this thrust was extended to support local postsecondary programs for CETA-eligible persons. However, in 1981, consistent with an overall budget reduction, major cuts were made in CETA funds and programs.

As a part of the Special Projects Act of the Educational Amendments of 1974, the Congress authorized the career education and community schools programs. The career education program, which in 1977 became the Career Education Incentive Act, was aimed at providing students with an early awareness of available career opportunities. The Community Schools Act, which was extended in 1978 as the Community Schools and Comprehensive Community Education Act, made grants available to states and local education agencies to provide, by means of community education programs, educational, recreational, and other related services in keeping with the needs, interests, and concerns of the community. Also, the act established the National Community Education Advisory Committee. In 1980 the Higher Education Act was amended to place increased emphasis on lifelong learning, which was defined to include a wide variety of activities such as adult basic education, parent education, education for older and retired people, and continuing education.

From the foregoing it seems obvious that a major concern of the Congress has been and continues to be support for programs that are seen as having immediate relevance to communities and enhancing the salable skills of the population. Furthermore, beginning in 1963 the thrust has been on programs that are relevant to an urban technically-oriented society.

National Defense Education Act of 1958 (NDEA)

In its original form the National Defense Education Act contained ten titles that authorized loans and grants to public and nonpublic institutions from the elementary level through the graduate level. This act, which explicitly recognized the importance of education to the national defense, provided financial assistance to strengthen instruction in science, mathematics, modern foreign languages, and vocational education; to improve guidance and counseling activities; to make available loans to colleges and universities to assist able and needy students to continue their education beyond high school; to foster research and experimentation with the educational uses of television and related media; to improve the statistical services of state departments of education; and to provide fellowships for teachers in service and graduate students desiring to become teachers in specified areas. Subsequent amendments broadened the original act. For example, 1964 amendments broadened the NDEA teacher institutes to include teachers of the disadvantaged, librarians, media specialists, and teachers of English, history, geography, and reading. Also, the instructional materials features were expanded to include other subjects. Furthermore, some provisions of NDEA were later incorporated into other legislation (e.g., Vocational Education Act of 1963, the El-

ementary and Secondary Education Act, and subsequent amendments
to these acts).

Elementary and Secondary Education Act of 1965 (ESEA)

The general purpose of the Elementary and Secondary Education Act of 1965 was to strengthen and improve educational opportunities and quality in elementary and secondary schools. Funds provided by the act doubled the amount of federal aid for elementary and
secondary schools, and state and local educational officials had considerable latitude in the use of these funds. It was the nearest to general
federal aid to education since the early land grant acts.

In its original form the act contained five major titles. Title I
provided funds to local school districts based on the number of children from economically deprived families. These funds were to be used
for educational activities specifically designed to benefit the children.
Title II provided funds for the acquisition of library materials, including textbooks and audiovisual materials. Title III provided support
for local school districts, working in cooperation with other educational and community agencies, to establish supplementary education
centers to provide additional services to pupils. School officials were
instructed also to make the benefits of these titles available to pupils
attending nonpublic schools. Title IV supported the creation of a series of regional educational laboratories through which innovative educational techniques and programs could be developed, tested, and
disseminated. Title V provided funds to strengthen state departments
of education.

In the 1967 amendments to this act, Titles III and V were transferred to state control, and provisions were made for bilingual programs and dropout prevention projects. In 1970, Title III was consolidated with NDEA, Title V-A (guidance and counseling). These are
but two examples of amendments to ESEA during its first decade.
The Educational Amendments of 1978 included several significant revisions to ESEA. Title I, now known as Financial Assistance to meet
Special Educational Needs of Children, was made more specific regarding the use of funds and included an emphasis on involving parents and teachers in planning and carrying out programs. Reflecting
a national concern, a new Title II focused on basic skills improvement
and incorporated the then existing Reading Improvement Act. Part of
Title IV was rewritten to focus on assistance to local educational
agencies to improve their programs and practices. Title VII, relating
to bilingual education, had several changes, including permission to
use funds to implement a *Lau* Plan (see the previously-discussed *Lau*
v. *Nichols* case).

At this writing, Title I of ESEA has become the cornerstone of federal assistance to K–12 education. As a result of the provisions of Title I, a large amount of funds has gone to geographic areas with large concentrations of the poor, for example, the rural South and inner cities. Thus to a small degree Congress has contributed to an "equalization" of funds to support education.

Assistance for Higher Education

The land grant college movement has been described. Another important form of congressional support for colleges and universities has been in the area of facilities. This began in 1950 with loans for housing (dormitories) and was broadened in 1963 with the Higher Education Facilities Act to include funds for the construction of academic facilities at a variety of postsecondary institutions. In the Education Amendments of 1978, authorization was provided for funds to be used to renovate facilities for more economical energy use, to provide easier access for handicapped persons, and to meet environmental, health, and safety mandates.

The 1965 Higher Education Act, with numerous extensions and amendments, has provided support for a variety of postsecondary programs. One long-standing thrust has been assistance to college libraries and funds for instructional equipment. Another has been student financial aid programs, including basic educational opportunity grants (BEOG), guaranteed student loans, and work–study programs. In the 1980 extensions of the Higher Education Act, concerns about increasing costs of student financial aid because of inflation created considerable controversy, and in 1981 the Congress included several cost containment measures in the legislation. Other significant higher education programs include the teacher corps, the teacher centers, and funds to improve teaching and learning.

Support of Education for the Handicapped

Another area of congressional concern is educational services for handicapped persons. This is not of recent origin as evidenced by the 1857 establishment of the Columbia School for the Deaf (which was authorized to offer degrees in 1864 and is now known as Gallaudet College), the 1879 creation of the American Printing House for the Blind in Lexington, Kentucky, and the 1920 passage of the Smith-Bankhead Act that provided vocational assistance for handicapped persons. The actions of the 1960s and 1970s suggest that such support will be a continuing aim of the federal government. In 1961 federal funds were provided to train teachers of deaf children and to make available to them services of audiologists and speech pathologists. In 1963 Congress provided matching grants for mental retardation facilities and community mental health centers. Funds to train teachers to care for retarded children also were made available. In 1966 congressional action created the Bureau for Education and Training of the Handicapped and established a National Advisory Committee on Handicapped Children. The Handicapped Children's Early Education Assistance Act of 1968 authorized model education centers for preschool-age handicapped. The Rehabilitation Act of 1973 focused on the most severely handicapped and required statewide studies of the needs of the handicapped and how these could be met, and also required that several special studies be conducted. Programs for handicapped persons have been supported under provisions of the Elementary and Secondary Education Act, and the 1974 Educational Amendments provided a significant increase in funds for such programs in order to help the states meet the requirements of court rulings regarding educational services for the handicapped.

In November 1975, Congress passed its most comprehensive and significant legislation in this area. The Education for All Handicapped Children Act (Public Law 94-142), often referred to as the handicapped persons' civil rights act, provided, in addition to financial support, the following major policy directives:

1. Each handicapped child has a right to a free and appropriate education. The impact of this is that an intensive and continuing effort must be made to locate handicapped children; a careful assessment must be made of the educational needs of each; educators in collaboration with parents or guardians and, when possible, the child, must develop an "individualized education plan" (IEP) for each child; and each child must be provided educational services consistent with the IEP.
2. Each handicapped child has the right to due process and equal protection. Tests and other evaluation instruments used in assessing a child's educational needs must be nondiscriminatory; educational placements may not be made without prior consultation with the child's parents or guardians; identifiable data about the child may not be shared inappropriately or without written consent; and the rights and guarantees of the law extend to both public and nonpublic school pupils.
3. Handicapped and nonhandicapped children will be educated together to the maximum extent possible. This "least restrictive environment" concept means that handicapped children may be placed in separate classes or schools only when they cannot, even with supplementary aids and services, be educated satisfactorily within regular classes.

The impact of PL 94-142 has been felt in every school district of the nation and the education of the handicapped enhanced greatly. IEP's, "staffings," and "mainstreaming" have become commonplace terms to educators. The most controversial part of the effort seems to be the "mainstreaming" effort resulting from the "least restrictive environment" concept.

Encouragement of Educational Research and Development

As part of the National Science Foundation Act (1950) support was provided for the promotion of basic research in the sciences. (This act also provided funds for curriculum revision and program development in the sciences, graduate fellowships, and institutes for teachers.) This encouragement of educational research became more sharply focused with the funding of the Cooperative Research Program in 1956. Under this program the government entered into contracts with institutions of higher learning and state education departments for the conduct of educational research, surveys, and demonstrations. The educational research effort received an added impetus as a result of Title IV of the Elementary and Secondary Education Act of 1965, which incorporated the Cooperative Research Program and provided funds for regional educational laboratories, research and development centers, and the training of education researchers.

In 1972 Congress created the National Institute of Education (NIE) and stated its mission as follows:

(a) help to solve or to alleviate the problems of, and promote the reform and renewal of American education;

(b) advance the practice of education, as an art, science, and profession;

(c) strengthen the scientific and technological foundations of education; and

(d) build an effective educational research and development system.

Also, the National Diffusion Network was created for the purpose of disseminating information about educational programs that have been certified as worthy of duplication.

Initially, NIE, an agency born in controversy (discussed in Chapter 16), was located in the then existing Department of Health, Education, and Welfare but independent of the then existing Office of Education. With the 1980 beginning of the Department of Education, NIE, the National Diffusion Network, and other educational improvement-oriented units were grouped under an assistant secretary for educational research and improvement within the new department. The basic mission of NIE has remained as cited above even though its priorities shift in response to the perceived research and development needs of the education community. For example, in the Educational Amendments of 1980, which extended NIE for five years, Congress instructed that particular attention be paid to the problems of the nontraditional sudent, the needs of adolescents, and international education and culture.

Even though the federal effort may appear modest when compared with research and development expenditures in other areas, when reviewed collectively these programs are of great importance. They represent an effort by the federal government to improve the knowledge base for educational practice, an area that had previously been largely neglected. Some view the 1980 consolidation of several educational research, development, and improvement programs under an assistant secretary as another significant step in overcoming the history of neglect.

Other Significant Congressional Acts

As is obvious from the foregoing, each session of Congress will result in federal legislation that has an impact on education. As suggested at the beginning of the discussion, this legislation will be in response to perceived national educational problems that need attention. In the paragraphs that follow mention is made of some other congressional acts passed in response to perceived needs that have had a significant impact on education.

The Economic Opportunity Act (1964) was reminiscent of much of the youth-oriented legislation of the 1930s. This act had as its purpose the mobilization of human and financial resources to combat poverty. Of particular importance were the youth programs that this act and later amendments generated. These included the Head Start and Follow Through programs, the Job Corps, work-training programs, and work-study programs. Some of the activities resulting from this legislation had the effect of creating competition for local public schools. For example, as Head Start programs were begun, some were under the effective control of local school district officials; yet in other situations the Head Start programs were under the supervision of local community action agencies and operated apart from the local public school structure. The Job Corps camps were in most instances operated by private corporations under a contract with the federal government. Also, the Office of Economic Opportunity, a federal government unit deriving funds from the Economic Opportunity Act, instituted pilot educational voucher programs in some communities. Essentially, the voucher plan provided parents with a voucher to cover the cost of their child's schooling, and it could be used at the school of their choice. The school, in turn, could redeem the voucher for public funds.

The 1964 Civil Rights Act contained two titles that directly affected education. Title IV gave the power to conduct surveys to determine the lack of equal educational opportunity in schools and provided funds for technical assistance in the form of materials, advice, and teacher training to communities facing problems related to desegregation. Title VI outlawed discrimination in programs aided by federal funds. Title IX of the 1972 Educational Amendments forbade sex discrimination in federally-assisted educational programs. Violations of these civil rights provisions have been the basis for efforts to withhold federal funds and deny eligibility for such funds to both public and nonpublic educational institutions. Also, Title IX has been at the base of the extensive efforts to equalize athletic opportunities for men and women in colleges and universities.

Also included in the 1972 amendments were the Indian Education Act that provided assistance in meeting the special educational needs of American Indians and the Emergency School Aid Act (ESAA). ESAA, which has been extended and amended, provided funds to local school districts that could be used in a variety of ways (e.g., new curricula, remedial programs, in-service training, community activities) as long as the use of these funds contributed to decreasing racial isolation and the alleviation of problems associated with the desegregation of schools.

In November 1974, the Family Educational Rights and Privacy Act (Buckley Amendment) became effective. This act, reflecting concern for persons' rights to information about themselves and the right to limit the access of others to such information, gave parents and the student the right to examine the educational file of the student and restricted the access of others to the file without parental and/or student consent. Also in 1974, in recognition of the needs of women and as a part of the Special Projects Act, the Women's Educational Equity program, which provides funds for demonstration, developmental, and dissemination activities, came into being.

Categorical Versus More General Federal Financial Aid to Education

As noted at the beginning of this discussion relating to the interest of the U.S. Congress in education, the basic approach to providing federal funds for education has been categorical. Both the approach and the level of funding for K–12 public schools have been the focus of much discussion. In spite of the accomplishments that can be attributed to the categorical approach of the Congress, many knowledgeable observers have advocated a more general approach. They have argued that categorical aid with its limits of flexibility has resulted in federal programs duplicating existing state–local programs. The uncertain nature of the continuation of aid in given categories has seriously hampered long-range state and local planning, and the problems of administering so many discrete allocations have resulted in a "sea of red tape." Further, it has been argued that the approach allows maximum federal control and places a premium on "grants-manship." On the other hand, general aid or at least a block-grant approach (i.e., blocks for vocational education, research and development, handicapped children, and so on) would give needed flexibility to states and local districts and make possible more simplified application and reporting procedures.

In 1981, for the budget year beginning in September 1982, the Congress authorized one block grant. Insofar as the programs having a major impact on K–12 schools, categorical funds were appropriated for ESEA Title I, handicapped education, bilingual education, impacted areas, and vocational education, and some of the requirements for these programs were eased. A number of the other smaller grant programs (e.g., teacher corps, Follow Through, emergency school aid, school library and instructional materials) were grouped together in a block with funds to be distributed through state education departments. This move by Congress marked a change in direction and could signal future steps toward more general financial aid to education in the form of large block grants.

In recent years federal funds have amounted to 7 to 9 percent of the operating expenses of K–12 public schools. Many school finance experts advocate that the proportion of federal funds should be increased to the 20 to 30 percent range. Some argue that this shift in proportion is in the interest of the national welfare, is consistent with the degree of mobility of the population, and that educational quality in one state affects all other states. The federal government is in a position to provide revenues and ensure a fair distribution of the tax burden, and only with this level of federal funding can great disparities in wealth among the states be overcome. Despite such arguments, at this writing, given the congressional educational appropriations for 1982, the outlook is that the federal share will remain at or below the 7 to 9 percent level.

Impact of the Federal Executive Branch

Schools, colleges, and universities throughout the nation are affected by the United States Department of Education. Other units of the executive branch of government administer education-related programs, and in instances the federal government directly operates educational programs. In the paragraphs that follow attention is given to these topics.

The U.S. Department of Education

The U.S. Department of Education was created by congressional act in 1867. Its original purposes were to collect and disseminate ed-

ucational information in order to describe the status of school education in the nation and to promote the cause of education. For a number of years the Office of Education, as it was then called, was a part
of the Department of Interior. In 1939 it was transferred to the Federal Security Agency. When the Department of Health, Education,
and Welfare was created in 1953, the Office of Education became a
part of this department, where it remained until 1980. In October
1979, President Carter signed the bill that created a cabinet-level Department of Education, which began in 1980.

In the law creating the Department, the Congress restated the
historic interpretation of the Tenth Amendment that the primary responsibility for public education was reserved for the states, local
school districts, and other instrumentalities of the states. However, it
was also noted that (1) there was a need for improvement in the management and coordination of the federal education programs to support more effectively the states; (2) there was no single full-time official accountable to the President for the federal education programs;
(3) the existing organization hindered presidential and public consideration of educational issues; and (4) the dispersion of federal educational activities had led to federal educational policies that were fragmented, duplicative, and often inconsistent.

The dispersion of the federal education effort has been documented frequently. For example, based on a study of the estimated
federal expenditures in fiscal year 1968, over twenty-three major federal departments and agencies as well as a number of lesser agencies
carried on some educational activities. In terms of estimated expenditures, only about 45 percent of the funds were channeled through
the Department of Health, Education, and Welfare, and of this amount
less than 75 percent was channeled through the Office of Education.[73]
This scattering of the federal educational effort was of concern to many
educators. They pointed to the frustrations and problems of states and
local school districts in dealing with a variety of agencies. Frequently
the recommendation was advanced that the federal education effort
be concentrated in a single agency. The rationale was that a single
agency with major status in the federal bureaucracy is essential to
provide the needed educational leadership for the nation, provide educators with a single point of contact with the federal government,
improve administrative efficiency, and eliminate conflicting federal
rules and regulations relating to educational grant programs.

The stated purposes of the Department of Education appeared to
be a response to these concerns of the educators. These included (1)
supplementing state–local and public–nonpublic educational efforts;

[73]Roald F. Campbell et al., *The Organization and Control of American Schools*,
2nd ed. (Columbus, Ohio: Merrill, 1970), pp. 37–38.

(2) strengthening the federal commitment; (3) encouraging increased involvement of the public in education; (4) promoting improvement of education through federally-supported research, evaluation, and sharing of information; (5) improving the coordination of the federal programs; (6) increasing accountability; and (7) improving the management and efficiency of the federal educational programs relating to both processes and organization with the intent of reducing constraints, duplication, and paperwork. Consistent with these purposes a number of programs from other federal agencies were designated for transfer to the new Department. For example, those designated included the overseas dependents' school from the Department of Defense; the vocational rehabilitation programs and four "special" institutions from the Department of Health, Education, and Welfare that were not in the Office of Education; several programs from the National Science Foundation; the Department of Agriculture's graduate school; the high school equivalency and migrant-worker education programs from the Department of Labor; and the college housing programs from the Department of Housing and Urban Development. Furthermore, to coordinate activities with other federal agencies an interagency committee was created.

In the past the federal educational agency has changed its organizational structure frequently, and such changes will probably continue. Yet in its initial organizational plan the Department of Education had units for elementary and secondary education, postsecondary education, vocational and adult education, special education and rehabilitation services, educational research and improvement, nonpublic education, civil rights, overseas dependents' schools, and bilingual and minority language affairs.

At this writing, it is not possible to judge with any validity the extent to which the new Department will fulfill the hopes of its proponents or even if it will continue to exist as a separate cabinet-level unit. Its creation represented a "victory" for President Carter and many educators. The margin in the House of Representatives was only fourteen votes and support in the education community was not unanimous. On the surface it seems to fulfill a long standing need. Yet there are numerous critics and President Reagan suggested during the 1980 campaign that it should be dismantled. The arguments of the critics center around the lack of need for a separate cabinet-level unit and/or the fear that such a unit will result in more federal control and involvement in what has historically been a state function.

Activities of Other Federal Agencies

With the creation of the Department of Education came an increase in the concentration of the educational activities of the federal government. However, there still remain many education-related activities located in other federal agencies.

The Department of Agriculture has responsibility for the school food-service programs. Furthermore, it provides support for a variety of cooperative research projects at land grant institutions and state agricultural experiment stations. Drug abuse education, Head Start, and special training programs for the aging are in the Department of Health and Human Services. The Department of Justice becomes involved in education-related legal actions and has some training programs for law enforcement and corrections personnel. The Department of Interior administers a variety of educational programs for American Indians. The apprenticeship training and Job Corps programs are in the Department of Labor. The Veterans Administration manages the educational assistance programs for veterans. There are educational exchange programs in the Department of State. Several federal agencies with international concerns assist in the promotion of education in trusteeship territories and in other nations of the world. The District of Columbia, not being a part of any state, is dependent on the federal government to develop and pass enabling legislation for a variety of public services, including schools. Obviously the Office of the President has an impact on the educational programs of Congress and the educational activities of excutive agencies.

Federally Operated Educational Institutions and Programs

As stated before, despite the historic interpretation of the Tenth Amendment there are several instances in special circumstances where the federal government runs educational institutions and programs independent of the states. These include those administered by the Department of Education as well as other federal agencies.

The largest of these directly operated programs is the overseas schools for dependents of military personnel and civilian employees. In 1980 there were more than 260 of these schools enrolling more than 136,000 students and employing almost 11,000 persons. Also there are four "special" institutions that are rather autonomous. These include Howard University, a private nonprofit institution with over 50 percent of its operating costs being federally funded, and Gallaudet, an institution for the hearing impaired that provides programs from the elementary through the graduate level. The U.S. Air Force Academy, Coast Guard Academy, Merchant Marine Academy, Military Academy, and Naval Academy are federally supported and operated. Even though existing primarily to educate military officer personnel, these institutions grant degrees in fields that are essential to the general welfare of the nation. The Department of Interior operates schools for Indian children residing on reservations. Numerous federal agencies operate schools and educational programs for personnel within the agency. For example, each branch of the armed forces operates a variety of schools for enlisted men and officers; the Department of State provides instruction for diplomatic service personnel; the Department of the Treasury operates a correspondence school for Bureau of Internal Revenue employees.

Obviously the courts and the Congress are the major sources of federal influence on education, yet the executive branch agencies also have their impact. As such, people tend to overlook the fact that in several situations the federal government directly operates educational programs.

ACTIVITIES/QUESTIONS FOR FURTHER STUDY

1. To summarize the impact of the federal courts and the Congress on educational policies and practices, prepare two charts. First, list what you consider to be the major areas of influence of the courts (e.g., religious practices) and within each area identify the two or three major court cases with a brief notation of the thrust of each decision. Second, list the several areas of congressional intervention into education and within each area note the major acts with a brief explanation of each.

2. Invite a local public school or college administrator to your class to address the topic of "The Impact of the Federal Courts on the Educational Policies and Practices on my Organization."

3. Discuss with your colleagues whether during the next decade the impact of the federal courts on education is likely to increase or decrease. The impact of the Congress. The impact of the Department of Education. Is there likely to be more or less effort to monitor and enforce federal legislation and regulations? Why?

SUGGESTED READINGS

ALEXANDER, KERN. *School Law*. St. Paul, Minn.: West Publishing Co., 1980, Chapters 1, 3, 6, 9.

American Education. A periodical of the U.S. Department of Education published ten times a year.

BENSON, CHARLES S. *The Economics of Public Education*, 3rd ed. Boston: Houghton Mifflin Company, 1978, Chapter 12.

CAMPBELL, ROALD F., et al. *The Organization and Control of American Schools*, 4th ed. Columbus, Ohio: Charles E. Merrill Publishers, 1980, Chapters 2, 7.

HOGAN, JOHN C. *The Schools, The Courts, and the Public Interest*. Lexington, Mass.: Lexington Books, D.C. Heath & Company, 1974.

HOOKER, CLIFFORD P. (ed.). *The Courts and Education*. Chicago: The National Society for the Study of Education, 1978, Chapters 1, 4, 5, 8, 9.

LA MORTE, MICHAEL W. *School Law Cases and Concepts*. Englewood Cliffs, N.J.: Prentice-Hall, Inc., 1982.

WARSHAW, THAYER S. *Religion, Education, and the Supreme Court*. Nashville, Tenn.: Abingdon Press, 1979.

ZIRKEL, PERRY A. (ed.). *A Digest of Supreme Court Decisions Affecting Education*. Bloomington, Ind.: Phi Delta Kappa, 1978.

4

State Provisions
for Education

$\mathbf{T}$HERE exists within each of the states a system of public
education. The emergence of these systems is the result of the historical interpretation of the Tenth Amendment. Even though the systems are discrete, there are many similarities. Each of the states has
constitutional provisions for education, and in each the state courts
render decisions of significance for education. The governor and state
legislature have their impact. Nearly all the states have one or more
state-level boards for the governance of some aspect of education. In
each of the states there is a chief state school officer and a state department of education, a formal structure for higher education, and
other state agencies and officials that have an impact on education.
Further, each of the states has some form of state financial support
for public education through which state influence over schools and
higher education may be exercised.

The State Constitution and Courts

State constitutional provisions and decisions of state courts, unless these are found to be in conflict with federal constitutional pro-

visions and court decisions, are two important legal bases upon which state control of schools rests. Immediately following is a brief discussion of the state constitutional provisions. Next, the impact of state courts is described.

State Constitutional Provisions

Even though in the colonial period education was frequently left to the home or church, state constitutional provisions pertaining to education are not of recent origin. Of the thirteen original states, six had some constitutional provisions relating to education at the time of the formation of the Union. (Considering both constitutional and statutory provisions, only Rhode Island of the original thirteen entered the Union with no legal provisions for education.[1]) Since that time, most states admitted to the Union have made constitutional provisions for education.

The state constitutional provisions may simply direct the state legislature to provide for the establishment and maintenance of a uniform system of free public schools that is open to all and to make provisions for higher education. However, the provisions in many states are more extensive. Some state constitutions prescribe the method of selecting the chief state school officer, set tax levy limits, define the make-up of the state board of education, indicate the method of selection of local school district superintendents, define boundaries of local school districts, and the like.

Constitutions serve the purpose of providing stability in government, and, as such, the process of changing a state constitution is generally difficult and time-consuming. For this reason most educational authorities take the position that a state constitution should include only the basic policies and provisions for education and leave the detailed provisions to the legislature and other subordinate bodies; that is, it should provide for higher education and mandate the establishment and maintenance of a free, public, uniform, nonsectarian system of schools, which is to be supported from public tax funds. To provide details, such as those mentioned earlier, may hamper the state legislature in fulfilling its mandate and make it difficult to adapt the educational system of the state to changing times. To illustrate, in one situation with which the authors are familiar, a state-level citizens' committee was appointed by the governor to make recommendations on the state organization for educational governance. This committee recommended changes related to the state board of education, the chief state officer, and local district superintendents. To implement the changes recommended by the citizens' committee would

[1] Ellwood P. Cubberley and Edward C. Elliott, *State and County School Administration* (New York: Macmillan, 1915), pp. 12–15.

have required changes in the state constitution, because in each instance specific constitutional provisions were involved.

Impact of State Courts

Even though they may serve to set a precedent, court decisions rendered in one state are not binding in another state. Further, there are instances in which a decision rendered by the court in one state appears to be in conflict with the decision of the court in another state. In spite of the areas of apparent conflict, on most major issues relating to the control of education there has been a great deal of consistency in court decisions from one state to another.

State courts have repeatedly held that public education is a function of the state, and, as such, control of the schools and school affairs is vested in the law-making power of the state. Illustrative of the consistent position of state courts is the statement of the Supreme Court of Oregon:

> Education is a function or duty not regarded as a local matter. It is a governmental obligation of the state. Few of our administrative agencies are creatures of the organic law. But, as to schools, the Constitution mandates the legislature to provide by law "for the establishment of a uniform, and general system of Common Schools. . . ." It is a sovereign power and cannot be bartered away.[2]

The state courts have also made it clear that the state controls education for the fulfillment of the public good. The Supreme Court of New Hampshire held as follows:

> The primary purpose of the maintenance of the common school system is the promotion of the general intelligence of the people constituting the body politic and thereby to increase the usefulness and efficiency of the citizens, upon which the government of society depends. Free schooling furnished by the state is not so much a right granted to pupils as a duty imposed upon them for the public good.[3]

State courts have often expressed the opinion that the legislature has the power to exercise the state's control over education, except where that power is restricted by the state or federal constitution. That is, the legislature has full or plenary power to enact laws relating to education. Recognizing the power of the legislature over education, state courts have been reluctant to substitute their judgment for that of the legislature. Part of the opinion of an often-cited Indiana case stated the following:

---

[2] *Monaghan* v. *School District No. 1*, 211 Ore. 360, 315 P. 2nd 797 (1957).
[3] *Fogg* v. *Board of Education*, 76 N.H. 296, 82 Atl. 173 (1912).

The authority over schools and school affairs is not necessarily a distributive one, to be exercised by local instrumentalities; but, on the contrary, it is a central power, residing in the legislature of the state. It is for the law-making power to determine whether the authority shall be exercised by a state board of education, or distributed to county, township, or city organizations throughout the state. With that determination the judiciary can no more rightfully interfere than can the legislature with a decree or judgment pronounced by a judicial tribunal.[4]

An Ohio court also made it clear that the legislative power extends to nonpublic schools when it stated, "the control of schools, be they public or private, providing elementary and secondary education for the youth of Ohio, reposes in the legislature. . . ."[5] The reader is reminded that this state "police power" is limited by constitutional provisions and the federal court decisions about the rights of individuals, such as those cited in Chapter 3. Thus, the power of a state legislature over nonpublic education has limitations.

The above-mentioned Indiana opinion also illustrates another concept that has often been confirmed by state courts. Local school districts are creatures of the state, which have been devised by the state for the purpose of assisting in maintaining a system of schools. This means that a local school district has no inherent powers of government and its boundaries may be changed, or the district may be abolished at the will of the legislature unless prohibited by the state constitution. In a Pennsylvania case the court said, "A school district is a creature or agency of the legislature and has only the powers that are granted by statute, specifically or by necessary implication. . . ."[6] The Minnesota high court stated, "School districts are subject to the control of the legislature, and their boundaries or territorial jurisdictions may be enlarged, diminished, or abolished in such a manner and through such instrumentalities as the legislature may prescribe, except as limited by the constitution. . . ."[7]

In a like manner, it has been consistently held that a local district board of education is a creation of the state. The import of this principle is that local boards of education have no inherent powers of government, and local board members are state officers—not local or municipal officers. In a 1927 decision the Illinois court expressed the following opinion:

A board of education is a corporation or quasi corporation created *nolens volens*, by the general law of the state to aid in the administration

[4]*State ex rel. Clark* v. *Haworth*, 122 Ind. 462, 23 N.E. 946 (1890).
[5]*Board of Education of Aberdeen–Huntington Local School District* v. *State Board of Education*, 116 Ohio App. 515, 18 N.E. 2nd 81 (1962).
[6]*Barth* v. *School District of Philadelphia*, 393 Pa. 557, 143 A. 2nd 909 (1958).
[7]*Thorland et al.* v. *School District*, 246 Minn. 96, 74 N.W. 2nd 410 (1956).

of state government, and charged, as such, with duties purely governmental in character. It owns no property, has no private corporate interests, and derives no special benefits from its corporate acts. . . .[8]

The Kentucky Court of Appeals said, "We have said that members of
a county board of education and its officers are 'state officers' although they are elected locally and function in a local capacity, because education is a state function. . . ."[9] This does not mean that
local boards are powerless. They have numerous powers granted by
legislative statutes. They have ministerial powers, which require a
local board to act. A board also has discretionary powers as are necessary to accomplish its mandated mission. The state courts will not
interfere with a local board when it exercises its powers "in good faith
for the best interests of the people." But if the board uses these powers in a "fraudulent, arbitrary, or unreasonable manner," the courts
will act.

Because local school districts and boards of education are creatures of the state, historically state courts found that they could not
be held liable for torts. In other words, under the medieval doctrine
of sovereign immunity, school districts, as state creations, could not
be sued for damages unless there was a state law that permitted such
suits. In a 1959 Illinois case arising from a suit brought on behalf of
a boy who was injured in a school bus accident, the Illinois Supreme
Court concluded that the immunity from tort liability doctrine was
unjust and ruled in favor of the boy.[10] Since 1959 some state courts
have upheld the immunity rule, in other states it has been abolished
by the courts and later restored, and in at least two cases, one in
Minnesota[11] and one in Iowa,[12] the courts upheld the rule with a clear
warning to the legislature that it must be reexamined. By 1976 at
least thirty states had some legal limits on sovereign immunity.[13]
Clearly the trend has been away from the immunity doctrine.

State courts have upheld the power of the legislatures to levy
taxes for school purposes, subject to constitutional restrictions, and
the power of the legislature to confer upon other governmental units
(i.e., municipalities and school districts) such taxing power. The precedent relative to public taxing power for schools was set with a Michigan Supreme Court decision in 1874. In this frequently cited *Kalamazoo* case, the court upheld the use of the school district's tax funds

[8]*Lincke* v. *Board of Education*, 245 Ill. App. 459 (1927).

[9]*Hogan* v. *Glasscock*, 324 S.W. 2nd 815 (1959).

[10]*Molitor et al.* v. *School District*, 18 Ill. 2nd 11, 163 N.E. 2nd 89 (1959).

[11]*Spanel* v. *School District*, 264 Minn. 279, 118 N.W. 2nd 795 (1962).

[12]*Boyer* v. *Iowa High School Athletic Association and Independent School District of Mason City*, 127 N.W. 2nd 606 (1964).

[13]Eugene T. Conners, "Governmental Immunity: Legal Basis and Implications
for Public Education" (Doctoral Dissertation, University of Florida, 1977).

for secondary schools, even though this was not required by the state constitution.[14] More recently, consider the following excerpts from an opinion of the Colorado court:

> We hold the establishment and financial maintenance of the public schools of the state is the carrying out of a state and not a local or municipal purpose. . . . Being for a state purpose, the imposition of taxes or the appropriation of monies in the treasury, the proceeds from taxes imposed, is not unconstitutional. . . . By vesting the power in districts to levy and collect taxes for the support of the school or schools in such districts, the state was but adopting a means for carrying out its purposes.[15]

Historically it was held that the state had the power to determine the method of allocating state funds for schools in order to provide each child with a minimum level of educational opportunity regardless of where the child resides in the state. This state power was upheld in an 1859 U.S. Supreme Court decision arising out of a dispute in Indiana over the distribution of income from the federal land grants.[16]

In the 1960s several cases challenged state methods of allocating and distributing public school funds. Basically the plaintiffs contended that the allocation and distribution system denied them their due process and equal protection rights because the system did not take into account differences in educational needs or the wide variations in wealth among the school districts of the state. The right of the states to determine the means of distributing funds was confirmed in both state and federal courts. For example, the South Dakota Supreme Court, in a 1964 decision, upheld the distribution system in that state,[17] and in 1968 a federal district court upheld the legality of the state aid statutes of Illinois.[18] This decision was later summarily affirmed by the U.S. Supreme Court.

In August 1971, the Supreme Court of California issued a precedent-shattering decision. In the *Serrano* v. *Priest* decision the court ruled that the state's system for financing public education violated the equal protection clause of the U.S. Constitution and of the California constitution.[19] The California case differed from previous challenges to state financing plans in that stress was placed on the differences in tax burden of raising school funds. California, like most states,

---

[14]*Stuart* v. *School District No. 1 of the Village of Kalamazoo,* 30 Mich. 69 (1874).

[15]*Wilmore* v. *Annear,* 65 P. 2nd 1437 (1937).

[16]*Springfield Township* v. *Quick,* 63 U.S. 56 (1859).

[17]*Dean* v. *Coddington,* 81 S.D. 140, 131 N.W. 2nd 700 (1964).

[18]*McInnis* v. *Shapiro,* 293 F. Supp. 327, aff'd. 394 U.S. 322, 89 Sup. Ct. 1197 (1969).

[19]*Serrano* v. *Priest,* 5 Cal. 3rd 584, 487 P. 2nd 1241 (1971).

relied heavily upon the real property tax levied within the local districts. The court noted that in the Baldwin Park district the taxpayers had to pay almost twice as much taxes per $100 of assessed property value as those in the Beverly Hills district. Yet the Baldwin Park district spent far less per pupil than the Beverly Hills district. The court summed up its position by recognizing the fundamental interest of the state in education, which could not be conditioned on wealth, stating it could find no compelling state purpose necessitating the existing method of financing education, and in keeping with the legal procedures of the state, referred the case to Los Angeles Superior Court for trial. After an extensive trial, during which the U.S. Supreme Court held in the *Rodriguez* case that, in terms of the U.S. Constitution, education was not a "fundamental interest" and not entitled to "strict" constitutional protection, a lengthy opinion was rendered. In brief, the trial court held that the financing method violated the provisions of the state constitution for equal protection of the law because of the disparity in the ability of the state's school districts to support education. This was viewed as constitutionally significant because of the state's fundamental interest in education. The trial court ordered the disparities to be corrected within a reasonable period of time. This decision did not mean equal expenditure for each child; the trial court said that there could be different expenditures if such were justified in terms of the educational needs of the children.[20]

In 1972, after the *Serrano* decision by the California high court and before the *Rodriguez* decision by the U.S. Supreme Court, the Michigan Supreme Court held that education was a fundamental interest under the Michigan constitution and that no compelling state interest was served by the disparities resulting from taxable wealth differences among the state's school districts.[21] In 1973 the high court of New Jersey ruled that the state's system of financing schools violated the state constitutional provision requiring the maintenance and support of a "thorough and efficient system of free public schools" for school-age children.[22] However, in rendering its decision, it did not pursue the equal protection argument; instead, the court ruled on the basis that the state had not taken seriously its constitutional obligation to fund education.

As it evolved, the basic requirement of the *Serrano*-type decisions was that the relative wealth, as measured by the property base of the school districts within a state, had to be equalized. In the late 1970s, in at least three states, there were lower state court rulings to

[20]Tom Shannon, "Serrano Revitalized in California—Implications for Financing America's Schools Despite Rodriguez," *The School Administrator*, (June 1974), 2, 8.
[21]*Milliken* v. *Green*, 203 N.W. 2nd 457 (1972).
[22]*Robinson* v. *Cahill*, 62 N.J. 473, 303 A. 2nd 273 (1973).

the effect that this was insufficient to ensure each child of equal educational opportunity. These rulings were related primarily to the special financial problems of the cities. Thus in the 1980s, further state court action relative to school finance issues can be expected.

In brief, the impact of *Rodriguez* was to leave to the states the responsibility for educational finance reform. State supreme court decisions, such as those in California, Michigan, and New Jersey, motivated many states to revise significantly their educational finance systems. Where the basis has been to equalize wealth, further revisions may be forthcoming. Clearly the trend of the state courts has been to require statutory and policy changes as needed to carry out state constitutional mandates regarding educational opportunities.

State courts have not limited their decisions to the areas discussed; rather, they have ruled on a wide variety of educational matters. The authority of the state to prescribe teacher qualifications has been upheld. Most state courts have ruled that state teacher tenure laws do not constitute a contract between the state and teachers. State compulsory attendance laws have been confirmed. The actions of educational authorities in promulgating rules for proper conduct and disciplining pupils are legal if the rules are reasonable in terms of the orderly operation of schools and there is no abuse of power. Generally, in recent years state courts have held that a pupil cannot be suspended or expelled merely because of marriage. Where there is statutory authority or imminent danger of an epidemic, the legality of vaccination of pupils has been confirmed. State courts have exempted schools from municipal codes and regulations in some states, but in others they have not. The point here is that the relationship between municipal government and school districts differs, depending upon state statutes (this relationship is discussed further in Chapter 5).

As is apparent, over the years state courts have rendered decisions that at one time or another have touched on almost every phase of education. However, it is important to restate the fact that state courts deal with concrete situations and generally have been loath to become "law makers" and usurp the power of the legislature and other state and local agencies. The aim of the state courts seems to be to determine the reasonableness of constitutional provisions and statutory law, not to question their wisdom.

In spite of the foregoing, many feel that state courts, like the federal courts, have become too involved in educational matters. Case law has become more dominant in educational governance than board policies and statutory law. Hazard, referring to the influence of both federal and state courts on K–12 educational policy making, put it this way:

School board decisions are rarely accepted these days as the last word; more and more, citizens regard them as the trigger for legal confrontations. . . . schooling is no longer regarded as a take-it-or-leave-it proposition but is viewed, along with the policies supporting it, as an offer negotiable in court. . . . educational policies are the product of constitutional, statutory, and case-law interpretations.[23]

The Governor and State Legislature

The creation of special state arrangements for education does not remove it from general state government. The governor, as the chief executive of a state, and the legislature, with its plenary power to enact laws, represent two most significant aspects of general government affecting education.

Influence of the Governor

Even though the powers of governors vary widely from state to state and with time in a given state, they are in a position to exercise considerable influence on a variety of educational matters. In many instances this begins with the gubernatorial campaign. Practically all the candidates will have "educational planks" in their platforms and make specific commitments to education. These may include plans for organizational reform, a promise to reduce educational spending, an intent to apply "sound business practices" to education, a proposal for restructuring the educational tax system, or a pledge to upgrade the quality of education. The successful candidate may have a strong desire to see his or her campaign promises become reality and may utilize the resources available to this end.

In accordance with political custom, the governor is the titular head of his or her political party within the state. If this party controls the legislature, to the extent that party loyalty is binding, the governor's position on educational measures before the legislature may be persuasive. Even in the absence of party control and/or loyalty, each member of the legislature is acutely aware of the many power resources available to the governor. Thus the governor's desires are not lightly ignored.

The governor's authority over state finances is usually spelled out in the law. Generally a governor is charged with making educational budget recommendations to the legislature. In many states the governor has some legal access to any accumulated balances in the state treasury. In numerous instances these have been allocated for

[23] William R. Hazard, *Education and the Law: Cases and Materials on Public Schools*, 2nd ed. (New York: The Free Press, 1978), p. 12.

educational purposes, such as to increase teachers' salaries or provide for school construction.

The power to appoint and remove personnel is another source of gubernatorial control of education. In the majority of the states the governor appoints members of the state board that exercises general supervision over the schools. Similarly, the governor generally appoints members of higher education governing or coordinating boards.

In a few states the governor has the power to appoint the chief state school officer. In some states the governor has the power to remove temporarily school officials from office for alleged misconduct and appoint their successors. These appointive powers often have restrictions (e.g., approval by the state senate of gubernatorial appointments to the state board of education); nevertheless, in many states the governor can use these personnel powers to promote desired educational goals.

In most of the states the governor has the power to veto acts of the legislature. Thus through the use of the veto a governor may "kill" educational measures that are opposed, or the threat of a veto may be used to discourage the legislature from enacting educational laws the governor does not favor.

Many educators resent what they feel to be excessive gubernatorial interference with educational governance. To be sure, there have been numerous instances in which education was used by the governor of a state as a pawn in a political power struggle. However, the governor is the chief executive of the state, and from that perspective education is another public service. As such, and we deal with the subject in greater detail in later chapters, education is not isolated from the political arena, including involvement by the governor.

The point is simple. If the governor chooses to take an aggressive position on an educational matter, this influence will be felt.

Role of the Legislature

In the discussion of state constitutional provisions, it was pointed out that in most states the legislature is charged with the primary responsibility for establishing and maintaining a system of public education. In accomplishing this mission the legislature has broad powers to enact laws pertaining to education. However, these powers are not unlimited. There are restrictions in the form of federal and state constitutional provisions and court decisions. But within these restrictions the legislature has the full power to decide basic educational policy questions within a state.

Subject to the restrictions mentioned, the legislature determines the special governmental arrangements for education. Examples of these are how the state board(s) of education will be selected, what will be the responsibilities of the state board(s), how the chief state school officer will be selected, what the duties and responsibilities of this office will be, what the functions of the state department of education will be, what the types of local and regional school districts will be, what will be the nature of the organizational and fiscal provisions for higher education, and what the composition, method of selection, and powers of local school boards will be.

Relative to education finance, the legislature usually decides the nature of the state financial plan for the equalization of educational opportunity within the state, the state tax sources to be used for education, the level of financial support for education, and the taxing power for schools to be allocated to local school districts or municipalities. Regarding educational programs, the legislature may enact laws determining what subjects may or may not be taught, how many years of education may be available to various groups of pupils, whether or not there will be a community junior college and/or vocational-technical school system, and what will be the length of the school day and year. In the area of staff and pupil personnel, standards may be set for pupil attendance, admission, promotion, and graduation; pupil–teacher ratios by types of schools and categories of pupils may be prescribed; teacher certification standards may be defined or the state board of education may be required to determine the standards; teacher tenure and retirement provisions may be enacted; and the duties of administrators and teachers may be determined. Moreover, legislatures often enact laws establishing new institutions of higher learning, authorizing specific programs in colleges and universities, setting standards for facilities construction, and providing for an array of auxiliary services, such as pupil transportation and school food services. With the advent of collective bargaining in the public sector, including education, many state legislatures passed laws relating to collective bargaining for public employees. (Chapter 18 treats this topic in detail.)

The nonpublic schools within a state are not exempt from the action of the legislature. In line with the police power of the state, the legislature enacts general laws that apply to nonpublic schools, such as those pertaining to health standards, building construction and safety, welfare of children, and the like. Legislative bodies in many states have passed laws of benefit to nonpublic school students. These have included provisions for transportation at public expense, health services, dual enrollment or shared-time plans, assistance to handicapped pupils, school lunch services, textbooks, pupil testing services, teacher salary supplements, and tuition grants to those enrolled in nonpublic colleges. (As discussed in Chapter 3, many of these laws have been found to be unconstitutional.) Laws are generally enacted regulating the details of incorporation of nonpublic institutions. Further, courts have generally held that, subject to the concept of reasonableness, the legislature has the right to pass laws providing for the supervision of such institutions. However, only a few states have comprehensive statutory or regulatory requirements in this regard. Furthermore, where these exist they are often not rigidly enforced.

Many people find "loose" state supervision of nonpublic educational institutions desirable. Extending public controls could limit many of the traditionally held freedoms of such institutions. Also, to develop and enforce comprehensive requirements would further burden frequently overloaded state educational agencies. On the other hand, state controls are essential to protect parents and students from charlatans. The late 1960s and 1970s saw an increase in "freedom schools," "street academies," "protestant fundamentalist schools," and private schools designed to appeal to parental concerns over turbulent conditions in big-city schools and the desegregation of schools. At the postsecondary level, there was an apparent increase in "diploma mills." Where such schools have continued to emerge, the question of state control of nonpublic education has become one of greater concern.

At any given session of a state legislature a plethora of educational bills will be introduced. For example, the authors made a cursory examination of the educational bills introduced at one regular legislative session in a single state. They found that 528 educational bills were introduced, fifty-five passed both houses of the legislature, and fifty-two became law. (The governor vetoed three.) The bills introduced covered almost every conceivable educational topic. To illustrate, there were bills to revise the state financial support program, grant a waiver of sovereign immunity, reorganize the state department of education, provide educational appropriations, eliminate teacher tenure, register nonpublic schools, change the school accreditation standards, set pupil assignment criteria, and remove jury duty exemptions for teachers. Fortunately, all bills introduced do not become law, and because of the committee system used by legislatures, many are never even considered by the full membership. In spite of the death of many bills, to report the education laws of a given legislative session often requires a substantial volume.

It would be an error to assume that the legislature in fulfilling its role acts in a vacuum. Members of the legislature are, as is the governor, elected public officials and must be, to some degree, responsive to the wishes of the people. Thus they are prone to support educational measures that have broad public support. Reference has been made to the committee system through which the legislature does its work. Special-interest groups, both "proeducation" and "antieducation," attempt to influence educational decisions at the committee level. Further, educational leaders frequently testify at committee hearings, provide information for legislators, and assist the governor in developing his or her educational platform and preparing educational budget recommendations.

In the opinion of many educators, legislatures often enact laws that handicap orderly development of the educational system within a state. To illustrate, in some states the legislature directs the state board to prescribe the types, classes, ranks, and requirements for teaching certificates to be issued, whereas in other states the legislature writes into law many of the details relative to teaching certificates. In a number of states there is a law requiring each teacher to keep a register of pupil attendance and the like. This task might be better performed by the data-processing installation of the local school district. The position of most educators is that the legislature should enact into law the basic framework for education within the state and the basic policies to be observed by the educational system. This means that technical requirements, minimum standards, and other details should be left to the state board of education, higher education boards, local school boards, and other education officials. At the other extreme is the position that the state constitution charges the legislature to enact laws governing education, that the legislature is far more representative of the desires of the people than the officials within the educational establishment, and that these officials cannot be counted upon to do more than required by law.

State Boards of Education

The first state-level board of education was created in New York in 1784. This board was concerned with the colleges of the state and had no responsibility for public elementary and secondary schools. The concept spread, and by 1954 there were 231 state boards concerned with some aspect or level of education.[24] Most of these were responsible for a specific educational institution, for example, a college. Even though modifications have certainly occurred, there is no reason to believe the number has changed significantly since 1954. Thus there is a multiplicity of state-level boards concerned with some facet of education. However, our focus is on those state-level boards that have general supervision over public elementary and secondary schools and, in a few states, postsecondary education—those that have the broadest powers for the state system of education. This is usually what is meant by persons who speak of "the state board of education."

[24]Fred F. Beach and Robert F. Will, *The State and Education,* U.S. Office of Education, Miscellaneous No. 23 (Washington, D.C.: U.S. Government Printing Office, 1955).

By the mid-1970s all of the states except Wisconsin had such boards.[25] About half were provided for in the state constitution and about half by legislative act.

Characteristics of State Boards of Education

Even though somewhat outdated, descriptive data from two 1972 surveys provide some insight into state boards of education. They ranged in membership size from three (Mississippi) to twenty-four (Texas), with thirty-three of the states having seven to eleven members when ex officio members were included. In total, the state boards consisted of 523 members, including forty-two ex officio members. Even though twenty-two of the forty-nine state boards had ex officio members, usually they numbered only one or two (most frequently the chief state school officer), and in only two states (Florida and Mississippi) were the state boards composed solely of ex officio members. Excluding the ex officio members, in thirty-two states the state board members were appointed by the governor and in fifteen states they were elected. In eight states the members were elected in partisan elections, in four states the elections were nonpartisan, in one state election was by the legislature (New York), in one state election was by legislative delegation (South Carolina), and in one state election was by local school boards (Washington). Terms of office for board members ranged from three years (Delaware) to nine years (Arkansas, Tennessee, and West Virginia), with terms of from four to six years being most prevalent. In terms of compensation for state board members, thirty-two states provided per diem and expenses for board members to attend meetings, and seventeen states provided for expenses only. The per diem payments were modest.[26]

Typically there are very few legal requirements for state board membership. Residency in different geographic areas of the state may be required, a few states prohibit persons employed in the schools of the state from serving, and a few states require that a percentage of the board be educators.

In spite of differences in method of selection and limited legal requirements, there are great similarities among board members. Sroufe, based on a 1970 study, described the state board of education member as follows:

[25]Roald F. Campbell and Tim L. Mazzoni, Jr., *State Governance Models for the Public Schools* (Columbus, Ohio: The Educational Governance Project, Ohio State University, 1974), p. 13.
[26]Campbell and Mazzoni, Jr., op. cit., pp. 13–15 and Sam P. Harris, *State Departments of Education, State Boards of Education, and Chief State School Officers*, DHEW Publication No. (OE) 73-07400 (Washington, D.C.: U.S. Government Printing Office, 1973), pp. 59–74.

He is a white (97 percent) male (82 percent). He is a professional (80 percent) earning a comfortable income (medium between $20,000–$25,000) and has a college degree (80 percent). The typical board member is about 53 years old and has lived most of his life in the state for which he serves. He belongs to major Protestant denominations, major political parties only and major civic or social groups only.[27]

Campbell and Mazzoni collected usable data from sixty-four voting board members (not all ex officio board members vote) in ten states. Although careful to claim no national representativeness for the sample, they noted that their data suggested the following:

> state board members are largely male, almost always white, usually over 40 years of age, half of them have annual incomes of $30,000 or more, nearly always they have graduated from college, generally they live in urban and suburban communities, they divide about evenly between Democrats and Republicans, and almost half of them have had some professional experience in education. . . . The proportion of board members who have had professional experience in education was higher than we had suspected. Much of the literature on state boards indicates that board members are made up of laymen, not educators. We now suspect that such a proposition is only half true.[28]

The domination of state boards by white, affluent, establishment males has been of great concern among many people. Such persons feel strongly that the boards should be more representative and argue for more women, members of minority groups, blue-collar workers, and so on. There is also disagreement about the presence of professional educators on state boards. As implied from the data presented, in some states specific provisions are made for professional educators to be on the board (including the chief state school officer); in other states the law prohibits educators from serving; and in other instances the law is silent on the point. The major argument for the presence of educators on the board is that they have the interest and needed expertise. On the other hand, the presence of educators violates the traditional administrative axiom of the separation of policy development and policy execution, and their presence is contrary to the American tradition of lay control of schools.

There is also controversy regarding the means by which state board of education members acquire their offices. There is considerable agreement that ex officio boards should be eliminated. The controversy focuses on elected board members versus gubernatorial appointees. The major points for popular election are (1) election provides

[27]Gerald E. Sroufe, "State School Board Members and the State Education Policy System," *Planning and Changing,* 2 (April 1971), 18.
[28]Campbell and Mazzoni, Jr., op. cit., p. 16.

the people with a more direct voice in educational governance; (2) the governor will tend to appoint persons who agree with his or her point of view; (3) an elected board will be more representative of the people; and (4) gubernatorial appointments concentrate too much power in the hand of a single official, whereas election provides for a better system of checks and balances. The major points for appointment are (1) well-qualified persons will be more inclined to accept an appointment than to be a candidate in an election; (2) appointment tends to lessen conflict between the governor and the board; (3) gubernatorial appointment is more likely to assure that the governor will have a continued interest in education; (4) if overlapping six- to eight-year terms of office are used, rarely can a single governor control a majority of the board; and (5) popular election provides a greater potential for vested-interest groups to finance and control the candidates.

As indicated by the variance in practice among the states, there is a lack of unanimity on other questions related to the characteristics of state boards of education, such as the following: What is the appropriate size? What should be the length of a term? Should geographic distribution be required? Should board members be paid or provided only expenses?

Jurisdiction and Duties of State Boards of Education

The jurisdiction of state boards of education varies among the states. Specifically, in addition to jurisdiction over elementary and secondary education, during 1972 the state board of education also served as the state board for vocational education in forty-four states. (The reader will recall from Chapter 3 that a board was a requirement of federal vocational education legislation.) Thus in only six states (Colorado, Hawaii, Indiana, Oklahoma, Washington, and Wisconsin) was there a different state board for vocational education. In twenty-seven states the state board also had jurisdiction over vocational rehabilitation, and in four states (Idaho, New York, Pennsylvania, and Rhode Island) the board had direct supervision of higher education.[29]

The major duties and responsibilities of a state board of education will vary from state to state. However, generally the state board is charged with adopting and enforcing policies, rules, and regulations necessary to implement legislative acts related to education; adopting long-range plans for development and improvement of schools; creating advisory bodies as required by law, or as it deems necessary; establishing qualifications and appointing personnel to the state department of education; setting standards for issuing and revoking teacher certificates; establishing standards for classifying and

[29] Ibid., pp. 13–15.

accrediting schools; recommending to the governor and/or legislature annual estimates of expenditure requirements for schools under its control and needed legislation for schools; managing state school funds; requiring the keeping of records and collecting data as required by law or as needed for reporting, evaluating, and planning; making annual reports on schools to the governor and legislature; approving plans for cooperation on education matters with other agencies (including the federal government); and acting as a judicial body in hearing disputes as required by law or arising from the policies or rules and regulations it has adopted. Also, in some states this board appoints the chief state school officer and sets minimum salary schedules for teachers and administrative personnel. In most states the law requires that in performing its duties the board seek and consider the recommendations of the chief state school officer.

For those facets of the state educational system under its jurisdiction, the policies, rules, regulations, and minimum standards of the state board have the force of law unless they are in conflict with constitutional provisions, court decisions, or legislative acts.

The chief question concerning the role of the state board of education relates to its jurisdiction. As previously mentioned, in some states there is a single board that supervises all aspects of education, whereas in other states there are separate boards for different aspects of education. Those who favor the single "superboard" concept argue that such a board ensures unity in direction and educational priorities; useless duplication of programs and services is avoided; competition among the several aspects of education is lessened. Those who favor several boards (e.g., different boards for K–12 schools, vocational education programs, community junior colleges, four-year colleges) argue that each aspect is important enough to warrant a board that is exclusively concerned with its problems and development; the state's educational program is so large and complex no single board can be expected to do an adequate job of supervision; the problems of duplication are not as severe as the critics suggest; unity of direction and priorities can be best achieved through voluntary cooperation among the several boards. It is of interest to note the approaches to the question of jurisdiction in the case of three states (Kansas, Illinois, Maine) that have significantly reorganized since 1968. In Kansas and Illinois the state board was given "the sovereignty of the state" for K–12 education, whereas in Maine the board was placed in an advisory role to the chief state school officer for K–12 schools. In none of the states was the board given jurisdiction over higher education. In each case the state board also became the state board for vocational education. In regard to control over cultural entities—such as museums, libraries, and agencies for the arts and humanities—Maine's board was given limited control, whereas the boards in Kansas and Illinois were confined to formal schools.[30]

The Chief State School Officer

Each of the fifty states has a chief state school officer. The title used to designate this official varies, with the most frequently used titles being superintendent of public instruction and commissioner of education. In 1972, twenty-four states used the former title and fifteen the latter.[31] In some states the position is provided for in the constitution, and in others it is authorized by legislative act. Thirty-five states had constitutional provisions for the chief state school officer.[32] The position dates from its creation in New York in 1812. During the nineteenth century the position in many states was an ex officio one and was filled by other state officials, such as the secretary of the treasury, state auditor, or secretary of state. There have been no ex officio chief state school officers since the early part of the present century.

Selection, Term of Office, and Qualifications

There are three methods used to select the chief state school officer: popular election, appointment by the state board of education, and appointment by the governor. The 1972 survey data showed that the position was filled by popular election in nineteen states (thirteen in partisan elections), appointment by the state board of education in twenty-six states, and appointment by the governor in five states. (Since 1900 the trend has been from popular election to appointment by the state board.) Twenty-one chief state school officers were serving indefinite terms (i.e., at the pleasure of the state board of education or governor in states where such appointment was the method of selection). Among those serving definite terms, the range was from one to five years, with four years being the most frequent term.[33] In about half of the states there were no educational qualifications required by law, and in those states that had such requirements, they were often not very stringent. In states where the chief state school officer was chosen by popular election, residency was a common requirement. However, as states have moved from popular election to some form of appointment, there has been an effort to appoint persons who are qualified and experienced regardless of place of residence.

[30] Ibid., pp. 28–38.
[31] Harris, op. cit., pp. 76–77.
[32] Ibid., pp. 82–83.
[33] Ibid.

The method of selection of chief state school officers has been the topic of considerable debate. One of the reasons for the persistence of popular election is the constitutional basis of the post in many states. Also, many feel election ensures greater dispersion of power (an elected official can have influence with the governor and other public officials and not be dominated by them), the selection of a person familiar with the needs and problems of the state ("outsiders" are eliminated), and a chief state school officer who is more responsive to the wishes of the majority of the people. Those who go further and advocate partisan election add the argument that the persons elected will have party support for educational reform. The objections to election include the belief that politics (particularly of the partisan variety) is potentially harmful to state educational policy; the elected person will be subject to intense pressure for patronage; and many well-qualified candidates are eliminated (e.g., those who cannot finance a campaign, persons from out of state). The proponents of state board appointment note that the chief state school officer is the executive of the state board, and they must function as a team; thus giving the state board the right to appoint their executive provides for greater cohesiveness. These persons also argue that the board is in a position to select the best-qualified candidate. There are those, however, who argue that such an appointment provides for a chief state school officer who is too far removed from the state political processes to be effective. In favor of the governor appointing the chief state school officer is the notion that as a chief executive the governor is ultimately responsible for all aspects of state government. As such, the governor should have the prerogative of appointing the officers of his or her administration. Further, such an appointment will provide for greater unity of command. Persons who espouse this view generally do not favor a strong and independent state board of education. Opponents of such appointments are also quick to note that although a chief state school officer, so appointed, may benefit from the influence of a governor who is supportive of education, such a school officer may be powerless if the governor is not supportive. In the three states having undergone reorganization in recent years, two (Kansas and Illinois) went to state board appointment and one (Maine) moved from board selection to appointment by the governor.[34]

On the matter of length of term and qualifications for chief state school officers, there is little controversy. It is generally agreed that fixed terms are essential to provide some security in the exercise of the powers of the office and sufficient time for the occupant to effectuate policies and programs and be fairly evaluated. If the chief state school officer is going to command respect both within the state and

[34]Campbell and Mazzoni, Jr., op. cit., p. 38.

at the federal level and serve as the chief educational spokesperson of the state, only persons who can provide leadership within both general governance circles and educational circles should be selected.

Relationship to State Board and Duties

According to the Harris survey, in seventeen states the chief state school officer served as an ex officio member of the state board of education, and in five of those states this person also served as chairman or president of the state board.[35] In terms of the formal relationship with the state board, Harris noted that even though such terms as *secretary, executive officer, chief administrator,* and *chairman* are used in the state laws to describe the chief state school officer's official relation with the board, the laws do not generally provide a detailed definition of the relation. Thus boards, which are usually authorized to govern their internal affairs, make their own determinations within the confines of the law.[36] Common sense suggests that in some measure the nature of the chief state school officer's selection will determine that person's relative independence or dependence of the board. Where there is board appointment for an indefinite term, greater dependence is likely; where selection is by election or gubernatorial appointment, greater independence is likely. To illustrate with the Kansas, Illinois, and Maine reorganizations: In the first two states, where board selection was chosen, the chief state school officer was made subordinate to the board, whereas in Maine, with gubernatorial appointment, the chief state school officer was placed in a superordinate position to the board.[37]

In Pennsylvania, where the chief state school officer is called the secretary of education, the relationships are unique. The secretary of education is appointed by and serves at the pleasure of the governor, is a member of the state cabinet, is the chief executive officer of the state board of education (which includes a council for higher education and a council for basic education), and is head of the state department of education.[38] Given these legal relationships, the potential for influence is great. Incidentally, in their 1974 report on state educational governance, Campbell and Mazzoni noted that four states had adopted some form of the secretary of education approach and suggested that it might represent the beginning of a broader trend.[39] However, only in Pennsylvania did the secretary serve as the chief state school officer and such a trend has not developed.

Because of the differences in method of selection, the legal rela-

[35] Harris, op. cit., pp. 76–77.
[36] Ibid., p. 95.
[37] Campbell and Mazzoni, Jr., op. cit., p. 38.
[38] Ibid., p. 57.
[39] Ibid., pp. 55–56.

tionship with the state board, the jurisdiction of the state board, and in the degree of state versus local district control of schools, the duties and powers of chief state school officers vary widely. However, the major duties associated with the office are likely to include serving as the chief administrator of the state department of education; selecting and recommending to the state board personnel for the state department of education; recommending to the state board policies, rules, and regulations deemed necessary for efficient governance of the schools; interpreting state school laws and state board of education policies, rules, and regulations; making recommendations regarding educational budgets and legislation; ensuring compliance with applicable laws, policies, rules, and regulations; arranging for studies, committees, and task forces as necessary to study educational problems and recommend plans for improvement; and reporting on the status of education within the state to the governor, legislature, state board, and public.

In actual practice, in those states where there is a considerable degree of state control of education, the chief state school officer is rather powerful. This is so because of the law, the reliance of the state board upon his or her recommendations, and the availability of the state department of education staff to assist in carrying out the assigned duties. Because of political acumen and expertise, this person, in some instances, also has considerable political power.

The State Department of Education

The state department of education (SDE) or state education agency (SEA), the major administrative agency of the state for education, generally operates under the direction of the state board of education and is administered on a day-to-day basis by the chief state school officer.

Size, Function, and Structure

State department of education staffs range from fewer than 100 in some states to more than 1,000 in others. Specifically, in 1972, nine states had total professional staffs of fewer than 100, whereas in three cases, including staff in local and regional offices and in related programs, the staff exceeded 1,000. Wyoming had the smallest headquarters staff (forty-six professionals) and New York the largest (972 professionals).[40] As a general rule, the more populous states that have a rather high degree of centralization in state school governance have the larger staffs. The staff is usually composed of professional educa-

[40] Harris, op. cit., pp. 42–43.

tors with differing areas of specialization, professionals from other fields (e.g., accountants, architects, computer specialists) as needed, and supporting secretarial and clerical personnel. In some states personnel employed in related areas—such as vocational rehabilitation, state museums, libraries, and the like—are in the state department of education. Also, some states have assigned staff to field offices in various sectors of the state in an effort to serve the state better. The number of staff members in the education departments of most states increased greatly in the late 1960s and early 1970s. To illustrate, in 1962 only ten states had departments with more than 100 professionals and twenty-one had fewer than fifty.[41] The activities of the federal government were a major cause of these increases. Specifically, the states found a need to increase staffs to administer the various titles of federal acts, such as the National Defense Education Act and the Elementary and Secondary Education Act of 1965. Title V of the latter act provided support for staff increases.

Prior to 1900, state departments of education functioned primarily as agencies to collect and disseminate statistics about the status of education. After the turn of the century, concurrent with the development of state financial support plans for schools and federal assistance for vocational programs in the high schools, an inspection or regulatory role was assumed. State departments became involved in school accreditation, teacher certification, and apportionment of funds. State department personnel were charged with ensuring that state standards relative to curriculum, attendance, facilities, transportation, financial accounting, and the like, were observed. In some states the department of education operated directly some special-purpose schools or programs (e.g., special technical schools, schools for the blind). Even though this continues today, most feel the operational function is inappropriate.

In the 1930s the emphasis within state departments was placed on providing leadership for education. The leadership emphasis has continued, even though many observers feel that even today far too much of the energies of state department personnel are devoted to the traditional dissemination, operational, and regulatory functions. In fulfilling the leadership function, state department activities include providing professional leadership for educational goal setting and policy development; long-range planning for the improvement of education throughout the state in terms of the goals, including setting priorities and devising strategies; stimulating, conducting, and supporting educational research; providing consultative assistance to local school districts; collecting and disseminating information about

[41] C. O. Fitzwater, *State School Systems Development: Patterns and Trends* (Denver, Colo.: Education Commission of the States, 1968), p. 49.

education to the general public and educators; and assisting as needed in coordinating the educational programs of federal, state, and local agencies.

The chief state school officer, within the restrictions of higher authority, determines how the state department of education will be organized. Even though the organization differs from state to state and from time to time within a state, there will frequently be divisions concerned with instruction, school finance, administrative services, and planning and research. Also, in some states there is a division concerned exclusively with higher education, such as a division of community junior colleges. Within the divisions, which are usually headed by an associate or assistant commissioner or superintendent, are various subunits (e.g., bureaus, programs). These include administration, program, and support components, such as budget, elementary education, special education, comprehensive planning, financial accounting, teacher certification, experimental programs, publications, educational statistics, and so on.

Problems and Trends

Although most writers on the subject plead eloquently for the major emphasis of state departments of education to be placed on leadership, many note that in numerous states the department has not adequately fulfilled the leadership function. Often there have not been sufficient resources and expertise to resolve major policy issues, conduct needed basic research, engage in long-range planning, attack major educational problems, stimulate major innovations, and provide high-level consultative services to complex urban districts. Many believe these shortcomings to be the result of excessive preoccupation with routine responsibilities and the failure of state departments to attract able people. Low salaries, political constraints, and lack of professional status associated with state department positions have been noted. Apparently the U.S. Congress recognized the validity of the so-called personnel problem within these state departments with the passage of Title V of the Elementary and Secondary Education Act, which provided funds to strengthen state departments.

Harris summed up the status of state departments in regard to trends and problems as follows:

> In terms of general trends, State Departments appear to be moving toward (1) long-range planning, stating goals, assessing needs, and establishing priorities; (2) closer alignment and coordination with related agencies and individuals such as higher education, state legislatures, Governors, and national education associations as well as local-Federal agencies and other State departments of education; (3) new approaches to research, development, and evaluation capabilities and exertion of accountability efforts to answer increasing demands for vis-

ible results achieved by public elementary and secondary schools; (4) shifts in general departmental orientation from regulatory and supervisory emphasis to increased leadership responsibilities and technical assistance and to improved departmental self-concept of purpose, program, goals, and priorities; and (5) significant changes in the kinds and numbers of personnel who work on State-level educational problems.

State departments are engaged in an increasing multitude of activities but continue to be hampered from playing even more vital roles in their State's educational establishments by a number of constraints, such as (1) staffing problems, including the shortage of qualified personnel; (2) low support level; (3) limitations imposed by emphasis on traditional and routine functions, antiquated personnel policies, the numerous agencies in most States having some governance over education, and resulting organizational inertia; and (4) political conflicts, which may involve rural-urban and legislative-executive representatives.[42]

Our opinion is that the 1973 forecast of trends made by Harris is fairly accurate. Since that time there does appear to have been a continued stress on planning and related activities; increased efforts at coordination with other groups, particularly the legislature; great stress on accountability measures; and, perhaps, a wider range of competencies present on state department staffs. Yet we see no real evidence of a shift away from the regulatory orientation. Relative to the problems he identified, they still appear to be present in varying degrees.

State Organization for Higher Education

In an earlier era the "typical" pattern for higher education in a state was for the legislature to authorize (if not provided for constitutionally) the formation of separate governing boards composed of lay citizens for each of the state's public institutions of higher learning. Generally such a governing board was vested with the power to hold property, approve programs, appoint administrators and faculty, approve budgets, set pupil admission standards, award degrees and diplomas, and generally oversee the operation of the institution. Said another way, historically state governance of higher education was decentralized. However, with the rapid growth of postsecondary institutions, in terms of size and type (e.g., new four-year colleges, community junior colleges, vocational-technical schools) after World War II, came the realization of the need for different state-level organizational structures.

According to Halstead, there emerged some basic consistencies in governing arrangements among most of the states that indicated

[42] Harris, op. cit., pp. 105–106.

wide acceptance of three basic principles. First, the public interest is best served if an institution or group of institutions is governed either directly or indirectly by a body of nonsalaried citizens who are not members of the operating agency. This governing body selects the chief administrative officers and assumes responsibility for needed policies, development, and planning in terms of institutional goals. Such a role gives the institutional head(s) considerable executive power. Second, a central coordinating agency is essential if there is going to be effective planning, coordination, and review of higher education throughout a state. Third, central coordination is not the same as governance; it involves coordinating among existing institutions, assessment of state needs, and developing plans to meet these needs—not responsibility for institutional operation. Halstead recognized the close relationship between governance and coordination. He suggested the challenge was, through organization and assignment of responsibilities, to achieve a proper balance between the two.[43] Abbott commented as follows on the point:

> The two functions—governance and coordination—are closely interrelated. Institutions can hardly function effectively without awareness of statewide needs and of activities going on in other places. Planning and coordination, on the other hand, must take account of current efforts in existing institutions.[44]

Even though no two states are alike, by 1980 each of the states had a statewide agency for higher education (twenty-nine had what were classified as coordinating boards and twenty-one had governing boards). However, in Delaware and Vermont, where there were governing boards, the University of Delaware and the University of Vermont had their own governing boards.[45] Callan and Jonsen, while noting that the strength and authority of those state-level boards varied, stated that such boards had three common duties: planning, budget review, and program review.[46] To illustrate the difference in this strength and authority, governing boards will often submit a consolidated budget to the legislature, whereas coordinating boards will often only recommend or review and comment on institutional budgets.

Three basic state agency models have been identified that are generally consistent with the "accepted principles" enunciated by

---

[43] D. Kent Halstead, *Statewide Planning in Higher Education,* DHEW Publication No. (OE) 73-17002 (Washington, D.C.: U.S. Government Printing Office, 1974), pp. 222-223.

[44] Frank C. Abbott, "Organization of Higher Education Coordination: The Alternatives," *Compact,* 3 (June 1969), 9.

[45] *The Chronicle of Higher Education,* XXI (September 22, 1980), 8.

[46] Patrick M. Callan and Richard W. Jonsen, "Trends in Statewide Planning and Coordination," *Educational Record,* 61 (Summer 1980), 50-51.

Halstead. One model is the single governing board for all "state-operated" higher education. (As is noted in Chapter 5, in some states, community junior colleges and/or vocational-technical schools operate under the control of local or regional districts.) In this model the single board serves both the coordinating and governing functions. Thus there is no confusion of role, centralized planning and development are possible, and needless duplications can be avoided. The limitations of this model are that lay involvement is limited, because of the single board; governance is difficult when there are several different institutions and types of institutions (i.e., the board has trouble having enough knowledge of individual institutions to respond to a presidential request for guidance); excessive standardization among institutions may occur (i.e., there may be a loss in institutional initiative and innovation); and the single board must either delegate much authority to individual institutions, which reduces the potential of centralized planning and control, or lodge much of the authority in its staff, which often results in a "superpresidency and central bureaucracy." A second model is lay governing boards for each institution, which are subject to the coordinating power of a central coordinating body. This model broadens lay participation, enhances the possibility that the governing body of a given institution is more knowledgeable of that situation and better able to provide needed guidance and review, and stresses lay rather than professional control. However, institutional competition and pressure brought on behalf of individual institutions may result in fragmented growth of higher education. There is also concern for differentiating between coordination and governance. The third model, a middle-of-the-road approach, involves a coordinating commission with governing boards for each sector of higher education. This model eases the governance problems in that only one sector is involved, provides better program control within sectors, and encourages resource sharing. On the other hand, each sector governing board will have to serve a coordinating function, which must be delineated in relation to the coordinating commission, and have a staff (as will the coordinating commission). Also, competition for students and funds among the sectors is likely.[47]

In 1980 an example of the single-governing-board model was Georgia with a board of regents consisting of fifteen persons appointed by the governor and confirmed by the state senate. The board had legal responsibility for planning and coordination, institutional budget review including recommendations for a consolidated budget, and program approval for all of Georgia's public universities, colleges, and junior colleges. (The state board for K–12 schools served as the state board for vocational education.) Indiana was an example of the

[47] Abbott, op. cit., 9–12.

second model. There the statutory state coordinating agency, consisting of twelve members appointed by the governor, was charged with planning, program review, approval of new programs, and review and recommendations relative to the budgets of the six public institutional governing boards. An example of the third model was Minnesota, which functioned with a coordinating commission made up of eleven citizens appointed by the governor with the advice and consent of the senate. The commission worked in cooperation with governing boards for the University of Minnesota, the state colleges and the junior colleges, and the state board for K–12 schools that was legally responsible for the area vocational-technical schools.[48]

Among the states there were numerous modifications of the basic models. To illustrate, Idaho's State Board of Education/Board of Regents, consisting of eight members (seven appointed by the governor and the chief state school officer), was in effect a "superboard." It was the single state board for all public education, and, in addition, it served as the "1202 commission" of the state (see below), which meant the board had some coordinating responsibilities relating to nonpublic institutions. In Iowa, the state board of regents was the governing board for all of the senior higher education institutions. The community colleges and vocational-technical schools were under the jurisdiction of the state board of education. However, the two boards had to approve the community colleges and vocational-technical schools annually in order for them to receive state aid.[49]

Another aspect of state organization for higher education is the previously mentioned "1202 commissions." In 1980 these existed in each of the states, except Wisconsin, and, as a general rule, were separate from the state's coordinating or governing board(s). These advisory commissions, which grew out of the 1972 amendments to the Higher Education Act and were established either by legislative act or gubernatorial order, are intended to enhance postsecondary education planning among the various types of institutions—public, nonpublic nonprofit, and proprietary. The commissions have no governing powers, but with the basic support received from the federal government and any other allocations provided within the state, they may conduct studies and make recommendations relative to more efficient use of the postsecondary educational resources of the state.

In our opinion, there will be a continued emphasis on state organizational arrangements for higher education. Such arrangements came into being as a result of growth pressures. However, as is discussed in more detail in Chapter 6, in a "no growth" era there is a

---

[48] Education Commission of the States, *State Postsecondary Education Profiles,* Report No. 88 (Denver, Colo.: ECS, 1980), pp. 48, 69, 112.
    [49] Ibid., pp. 56, 71.

need to avoid unnecessary program duplication and overlap, to develop cooperative arrangements among institutions, and to make difficult decisions about possible resource reallocation. Dealing with such matters requires diplomacy when there is keen competition among the universities, community colleges, and vocational-technical schools of a state for students and resources. Therefore, the scope of authority of state-level agencies for higher education can be expected to be a source of continued controversy. This is particularly true in matters related to programs and enrollments because, as a general rule, state financial aid formulas for postsecondary education take into account, to some degree, the number of full-time equivalent students enrolled in different programs (e.g., lower division, upper division, graduate).

Impact of Other State Agencies and Officials

We have discussed the impact of the state courts, the governor, and the legislature on education and the presence of special state educational governance arrangements. In addition, there are numerous other state agencies and officials who influence educational activities within a state.

The office of the state attorney general renders numerous interpretations of state laws, which are to be followed in the absence of court decisions or unless overturned by court decisions. Also, this office frequently becomes involved in litigation involving education. The state health department is often charged with conducting inspections and demanding corrections regarding sanitary conditions in educational buildings and engaging in activities aimed at the prevention of contagious diseases. In some states an agency such as the state industrial commission may approve educational building plans and exercise control over construction to ensure that specified standards are met. The state treasurer often handles the state educational funds. The finance department is generally charged with management of the overall state budget. The state auditor is usually authorized to audit educational institution accounts. Safety inspections of educational buildings may be the responsibility of the state fire marshall or insurance commissioner.

The state labor relations board or the public employees relations commission may be the agency charged with fact finding or arbitration in instances of disputes between an educational governing board and its employees. In a few states educational employees belong to a retirement system covering all state employees, and the system is administered by an agency of general state government. A state personnel board may set standards regarding conditions of employment of personnel. The state labor department will usually be charged with enforcing child labor laws and, as such, control work permits for pupils. The state corrections department usually operates various educational programs within the state correctional and caretaking institutions.

The preceding are but a few examples to illustrate the point that education is affected by many agencies of general state government. As is suggested in various other places in this book, there are many informed observers who believe the line separating educational governance from general state government is becoming more blurred with time, and the future will see even greater involvement with education by general government agencies.

State Financing of Schools

As suggested in the chapter introduction, each of the states provides some state-level financial support for public education, and this is a source of state governmental influence, particularly on the K–12 schools. Except in Hawaii, where there has been complete federal and state funding of schools, the level of K–12 support has varied widely (from less than 10 percent state support to more than 75 percent) with the national median in 1980 being around 53 percent. Also, there are differences among the states in their ability to finance schools and in their effort to finance schools in relation to fiscal ability.

The requirements placed on school districts to receive state support often include maintaining adequate records and filing required reports, providing a minimum number of days of school each year, adhering to state-required employment practices (e.g., written contracts, minimum number of days service per year, certified teachers, minimum and maximum teaching loads), meeting prescribed standards for school facilities, and providing prescribed programs and services for pupils. Thus in states that impose requirements such as these, the state finance program becomes a potent tool for state control of the activities of local districts.

Allocation Plans

Each of the states has its own method of allocating state funds for schools. There are two basic allocation plans. The flat-grant plan provides that the state funds are distributed to local districts on some uniform basis, such as a set amount per pupil in average daily attendance or per certified employee. The equalization plan provides that the state funds are distributed to local districts in varying proportions. The intent is that the less wealthy districts will receive from the state a larger percentage of the funds needed to operate their educational programs. At the turn of the century, 38 states used some type of flat-grant plan; however, since 1975 all states have some form of equalization plan.[50]

Basically there are two types of equalization plans—the foundation program and the power-equalizing plan. Historically the foundation program plan has been the common approach to equalization. However, as a result of state court decisions, such as in the *Serrano* case, there has been a trend toward some form of power equalizing.

Lindman described the essential differences between the power-equalizing plan and the foundation program plan as follows:

Power Equalizing

Purpose: To establish an equal tax base per student, thus equalizing *potential* income per student for all school districts.

State Contribution: Amount is inversely related to local taxable wealth per student and directly *proportional* to the total local school tax rate.

Required Local Tax Rate: No specific tax rate is required, but the amount of state aid is reduced if the local tax rate is reduced.

Limitation upon State's Contribution: No limit is established. If a local school district increases its local tax rate, it would be entitled to more state aid.

Source of Inequalities: Inequalities in income per student depend upon the willingness of people to tax themselves locally for public schools.

Foundation Program

Purpose: To guarantee a specific annual income per student for all school districts, irrespective of local taxable wealth per student.

State Contribution: Amount is inversely related to the local taxable wealth per student and is *independent* of the total local school tax rate.

Required Local Tax Rate: A specific local tax rate is required by law for all school districts to provide the local contribution to the foundation program.

Limitation upon State's Contribution: The state contributes toward the cost of the minimum program only. Expenditures beyond the minimum must come entirely from local taxation.

Source of Inequalities: Inequalities in income per student stem primarily from differences in taxable wealth per student for school taxes beyond the required local contribution rate.[51]

As can be seen from Lindman's description, under a power-equalizing plan, matching ratios are determined for each school district. Low-wealth districts would have high state matching ratios (e.g.,

[50] Walter I. Garms, James W. Guthrie, and Lawrence C. Pierce, *School Finance: The Economics and Politics of Public Education* (Englewood Cliffs, N.J.: Prentice-Hall, 1978), p. 188.

[51] Erick L. Lindman, "Full State Funding: Requirements and Options II. The Serrano Problem," in Kenneth H. Hansen (ed.), *The Governance of State Education Systems: Pressures, Problems, Options* (Washington, D.C.: U.S. Office of Education, 1972), p. 54.

five state dollars for each local dollar), high-wealth districts would have low state matching ratios (e.g., one state dollar for each local dollar), and in ideal form for extremely wealthy districts the ratios would be negative, resulting in a contribution to the state. Even though in its simplest form power equalizing puts no limits on local and state amounts, the matching ratio formula is designed to ensure that districts levying like tax rates for schools receive from state and local sources combined the same amount of money per pupil (i.e., the potential incomes are equalized). This feature, reflecting the value that the ability to raise money should be equalized but that the amount of money to be raised should be left to local initiative, has so much potential for disequalization that some school finance authorities would argue that in its simplest form power equalizing is not really an equalization plan. Furthermore, as noted previously, in a few states there have been court decisions that support this view.

As implied by the Lindman description, the basic value undergirding the foundation plan is that each person in the state should be provided a minimum educational program. Therefore, under the simplest form of the foundation program plan, the state, taking into account the per pupil wealth of a local school district, contributes an amount proportional to the cost of the standard state program, and expenditures beyond this come from local sources. Unless the state imposes some limitations on local expenditures, the result is an advantage to districts with high per pupil wealth. (This is the main source of the inequities cited in *Serrano*.)[52]

State Educational Finance Problems

Over the years state financing of education has been beset by numerous problems, some of which we discuss elsewhere. These include the relative balance among federal, state, and local contributions to schools; securing adequate amounts of money; identifying adequate tax sources and spreading the tax burden fairly; devising defensible measures of tax-paying ability and effort; and determining what constitutes a state minimum or standard program.[53] In the 1970s other issues and problems arose. These related primarily to fiscal neutrality and cost differentials and came in the wake of *Serrano*-type decisions.

Garms defined fiscal neutrality in terms of breaking the link between the wealth of a community and the amount that it spends for schools.[54] (Others have offered broader definitions. Benson, for ex-

---

[52] Ibid., p. 55.

[53] For a concise discussion of these and related topics see Edgar L. Morphet, Roe L. Johns, and Theodore L. Reller, *Educational Organization and Administration*, 4th ed. (Englewood Cliffs, N.J.: Prentice-Hall, 1982), pp. 401–415.

[54] Walter I. Garms, "The Financial Dimensions of Recent School Finance Reforms," *Planning and Changing*, 5 (Summer 1974), 93.

ample, said "fiscal neutrality exists when we see no warping or distortion of choice in consumption of tax-financed goods and services on irrational or social-undesirable grounds."[55]) A most obvious approach to equalizing the wealth of school districts within a state would be full state funding; that is, the state would mandate the school district expenditure levels, and these would be supported by statewide taxation. However, the full state funding concept does not eliminate adjustments among districts due to differences in pupils' educational needs or differences in the cost of providing equal educational services. The notion is that all things being equal, the state will provide equal funds to each student within the state regardless of the wealth of the community where the student resides. As previously stated, only Hawaii has full state funding supplemented, of course, by the federal educational funds received. However, several other states (e.g., Florida, Minnesota, New Mexico) have approached full state funding by using foundation-type plans with a required local district tax rate and permitting little or no local educational tax levy above the required local rate.

Full state funding, or more accurately full federal–state funding, of public K–12 schools could achieve wealth equalization. Furthermore, consistent with what many school finance experts feel is desirable, it would reduce the dependence of schools on the real property tax. Some experts believe the plan could also cause the level of support for schools to rise, for persons who reside in wealthy school districts would advocate that state government provide funds to maintain the schools to which they are accustomed. However, the plan works against the exemplary-district concept and interdistrict competition, which have served useful purposes in the past. Broadly based citizen participation, a condition seen as vital by many for the continuation of public schools, could easily be diminished. Because higher education depends largely on the state, the educational lobby would be further divided. Also, the specter of centralization, large state bureaucracies, and so on, raises questions about the political feasibility of full state funding.

A national commission, sponsored by Phi Delta Kappa, after an extensive review of different options for state K–12 educational allocations, including full state funding, recommended what they called a foundation system supplemented with equalized local initiative.[56]

---

[55]Charles S. Benson, "Accomplishing Fiscal Neutrality," in K. Forbis Jordan and Kern Alexander (eds.), *School Finance in Transition*, Proceedings of the 16th National Conference on School Finance (Gainesville, Fla.: National Education Finance Project and Institute for Educational Finance, 1973), p. 56.

[56]Phi Delta Kappa Commission on Alternative Designs for Funding Education, *Financing the Public Schools: A Search for Equality* (Bloomington, Ind.: Phi Delta Kappa, 1973), pp. 41–55.

In essence their recommendation combined the foundation and power-equalizing plans. The rationale was that the limitations of the one option could be offset with the use of the second option in conjunction with the first. What was recommended was a rather high level foundation program that was to be supplemented with an equalized local initiative plan in which the schedule would be kept short; that is, there would be a limit on the state's contribution. Regarding the advantages of their proposal, the commission noted the following:

> it (a) establishes a state defined foundation program based on educational needs of the individual child, (b) creates fiscal neutrality among all school districts, (c) provides for equalized local initiative and effort, but maintains a sufficiently high state foundation to prevent a child's education from becoming entirely a function of effort of the local school district[57]

The cost differentials question has two dimensions: (1) differences in costs among different educational programs or services and (2) differences in the cost of delivering the same program or service in different geographic areas. The first dimension really relates to individual needs, and the concern is with providing differentially for pupils with different needs. This includes providing for the handicapped (emotional, mental, physical, and socioeconomic) and for those who desire high-cost vocational programs. Even though various means have been proposed for dealing with the differing costs among programs (e.g., categorical state reimbursements for actual costs), the most common approach is some form of pupil weighting to reflect differing program costs. The commission created by Phi Delta Kappa described this approach as follows:

> Under the typical "weighted pupil" techniques a weight of 1.00 is assigned to regular pupils in the elementary (K–6) program. Other weights or indexes are expressed in relation to the cost of educating a child in a given program compared to the cost of educating the regular elementary pupil. In effect a pupil's day is prorated according to the program in which he is enrolled; and he generates a weight for state support purposes based on the amount of time he spends in various programs and the weights assigned to each program.[58]

The weighted pupil approach is based on two assumptions. First, educational needs of all children will be assessed, and programs to meet these needs will be provided. Second, cost analysis studies will be conducted on a recurring basis to validate the weights assigned to var-

[57]Ibid., p. 55.
[58]Ibid., pp. 29–30.

ious programs.[59] According to Garms and associates, the problems with the weighted pupil approach relate to these assumptions. There is

> an inability to define appropriate programs or to measure their costs accurately. Circular reasoning is involved in establishment of weightings, for these are usually based on the cost of programs that are themselves influenced by the weightings provided. Misallocation of students to programs is encouraged.[60]

Regarding the cost of delivering the same educational program or service in different school districts, at least one state (Florida) has incorporated a cost-of-living adjustment in its state allocation plan. The intent of the approach is to provide more funds for like programs in those "high cost" localities of the state. The critics of the cost-of-living adjustment approach argue that cost-of-living differences do not reflect the actual cost of delivery. Other than the cost-of-living approach and some minor special assistance for isolated small schools and the like, little has been done to deal with this dimension of the cost differentials issue.

The large cities of the nation appear to have particular problems because of the way the cost differentials are handled in state allocation formulas. Specifically, there are often inadequate allocations for the programs needed by children of minorities and the poor, and frequently there is insufficient recognition of the higher costs of delivery in urban areas. This situation is complicated by the heavy use of the property tax for other city services—municipal overburden. As suggested earlier, it is anticipated that during the 1980s there will be continued legal action intended to determine the extent to which state finance systems must take into account the special problems of big cities.

Perhaps the overriding general problem in state school finance is the political activities of special interests. (Chapter 17 contains a detailed discussion of interest groups.) The technical experts of educational finance may devise a rational means of allocating state funds so that school districts (or higher education institutions for that matter) are treated in a fairly equitable manner and may even succeed in getting these plans enacted into law. Yet, as the several special interests succeed in amending the plan to their benefit, it becomes increasingly complex and disequalizing.

[59] Ibid., p. 32.
[60] Garms, Guthrie, and Pierce, op. cit., pp. 208–209.

ACTIVITIES/QUESTIONS FOR FURTHER STUDY

1. Study the laws of your state applicable to education (i.e., the state school code) to determine the method of selection, qualifications, and duties of the state board(s) of education for K–12 schools and colleges and the chief state school officer. Also, review the laws to see if there are instances where the orderly development of education within the state has been hampered.

2. Interview one or more knowledgeable persons about the activities of your state department of education. What is the relative emphasis placed on planning and coordination, regulation, technical assistance, and so on? What appear to be the major concerns about the state department of education and its activities?

3. Examine your state educational finance system and answer the following questions: What is its basic purpose? How is local wealth measured? How is the state contribution determined? To what extent is there local leeway to tax for educational purposes? What are the major sources of inequities?

SUGGESTED READINGS

ALEXANDER, KERN. *School Law*. St. Paul, Minn.: West Publishing Co., 1980, Chapter 4.

CAMPBELL, ROALD F., and TIM L. MAZZONI, JR. *State Policy Making and Public Schools*. Berkeley: McCutchan Publishing Corp., 1976.

CAMPBELL, ROALD F., et al. *The Organization and Control of American Schools*, 4th ed. Columbus, Ohio: Charles E. Merrill Publishers, 1980, Chapters 3, 15.

FULLER, EDGAR, and JIM B. PEARSON (eds.). *Education in the States: Nationwide Developments Since 1900*. Washington, D.C.: Council of Chief State School Officers, 1969.

GARMS, WALTER I., JAMES W. GUTHRIE, and LAWRENCE C. PIERCE. *School Finance: The Economics and Politics of Public Education*. Englewood Cliffs, N.J.: Prentice-Hall, Inc., 1978, Chapters 8, 9.

HALSTEAD, D. KENT. *Statewide Planning in Higher Education*. DHEW Publication No. (OE) 73-17002, Washington, D.C.: U.S. Government Printing Office, 1974.

HANSEN, KENNETH H. (ed.). *The Governance of State Education Systems: Pressures, Problems, Options*. Washington, D.C.: U.S. Office of Education, 1972.

HARRIS, SAM P. *State Departments of Education, State Boards of Education, and Chief State School Officers*. DHEW Publication No. (OE) 73-07400, Washington, D.C.: U. S. Government Printing Office, 1973.

SORGEN, MICHAEL S., et al. *State, School and Family*, 2nd ed. San Francisco: Matthew Bender & Co., Inc., 1979, Chapter 2.

5

Local and Regional Arrangements for Public Schools

THE LOCAL SCHOOL district or local educational agency (LEA) is the basic administrative unit for public K–12 education in the United States. The development of the nationwide network of public schools—to replace the church and home as the primary institution for formal schooling—began with the local school district. Specifically, the Act of Massachusetts General Court in 1647 required towns to establish schools that would be under the control of the towns. A 1789 act granted these districts legal rights, including the right to appoint school committees, and an 1801 legislative enactment granted these districts taxing power.[1] Even though the 1647 Massachusetts act established the concept of state authority for public schools, formal state governance systems developed much later. Except for Hawaii, which has a state-financed and administered system, each of the states has local school districts that directly operate the vast majority of the public elementary and secondary schools of the state. (Even Hawaii has established "district superintendencies" on the four larger islands.)

[1] Roald F. Campbell et al., *The Organization and Control of American Schools,* 4th ed. (Columbus, Ohio: Merrill, 1980), p. 94.

153

The term *regional district* or *educational service agency* is used to describe various organizational arrangements, other than local districts, that have been created to carry out instructional, liaison, regulatory, supervisory, and/or service missions. Many writers have used the term *intermediate district* somewhat as we use the term *regional district* or *educational service agency.* The reason for the use of the term is that in many states these units originally functioned intermediately between the state and the local districts. In several states, however, the functions and status of these units have been altered in recent years; thus the regional designation seems more appropriate.

Local School Districts: Some Basic Information

The legal status of local school districts is rather special. Among the states, local school districts vary as to type, number, and size. Numerous local districts enrolling over 50,000 pupils have decentralized. In the paragraphs that follow, attention is given to these subjects.

The School District as a Quasi Corporation

In Chapter 4 the point was made that the local school district is a creature of the state that exists for the purpose of enabling the state to administer its school system. Thus local districts are generally referred to as quasi corporations or limited corporations, as distinguished from municipal corporations.

Legally, a corporation is an artificial person created so that it can act as a single person within the context of the powers granted in the charter of incorporation. Corporations are private (e.g., an automobile manufacturer), quasi public (e.g., an electric utility), or public (e.g., a city). A municipal corporation is one type of public corporation; for example, an incorporated city is granted a charter by the state primarily to regulate the local affairs of a given territory. To say a school district is a quasi corporation is to say that it operates in many ways "as if" it were a municipal corporation. However, because a school district exists to carry out a state function—not a local function—its powers are more limited. It has only those powers expressly granted by state laws, those implied by the expressed powers, and those discretionary powers essential to accomplish its specified objectives. Subject to the restrictions of the state constitution, the legislature also can modify the area of jurisdiction of a local district, change its powers, and even eliminate it.

Unless the law specifically grants or charges the municipal corporation with responsibilities for education, the municipal corporation and the quasi corporation for education are separate entities even though they may have common boundaries. However, if the state so chooses, it can make use of municipal corporations in carrying out its educational policies. For example, it may require that the local school district budget be approved by city (municipal) officials; that the city, not the local school district, levy taxes for school purposes; that school bonds be approved by city officials; or even that education be a department of municipal government. On the other hand, these powers may be granted expressly to the local school district. Edwards commented as follows on municipal corporations and schools:

> It (the state) may impose upon municipalities and their officers such powers and duties with respect to education as wise policy may seem to dictate. It may provide that school-board members be appointed by the mayor with the consent of the council, that the school budget be approved or even reduced by some city officer or agency, or that school-district bonds receive municipal approval before being issued and sold. It may even go so far as to make education a department of the city government, thus placing education under the complete control of the municipality.[2]

There are numerous specific issues regarding the relationships between the school district and municipal government, especially in those states where school districts and municipalities generally have common boundaries. For example: Should the school district be subject to municipal building codes? Should it be subject to the purchasing standards and procedures followed by other units of municipal government? Should the personnel practices and procedures for classified employees adopted by the municipal civil service board be required of the school district? To what extent should the school district and municipal government share facilities and/or equipment, such as computers? Perhaps the most debated question is, "Should the local school district be fiscally independent of the municipality or fiscally dependent?" (If the budget of the school district is subject to review and final adoption by a municipal body that holds the taxing power, such as the city council, it is said to be fiscally dependent. In practice, the vast majority of the school districts of the nation are fiscally independent; that is, they have the power to adopt a budget.)

Most educators, while agreeing that the services of the local school district should be coordinated with those of related municipal agencies (e.g., libraries, health, recreation, planning), tend to take the position that the local school district should have a large degree of autonomy. Specifically they argue for fiscal independence. Those who support a high degree of local autonomy, including fiscal inde-

---

[2] Newton Edwards. *The Courts and the Public Schools,* 3rd ed. (Chicago: University of Chicago Press, 1971), p. 94.

pendence, support their position by noting that (1) education is unique—it is a state function, and (2) a board of education is really a useless body unless it has the power to manage fully its own affairs, including fiscal control. On the other hand, there are some, including a number of political scientists, who see no reason to divorce educational and municipal affairs. These persons note that inefficiency occurs. Further, these persons contend that to grant education autonomy in fiscal matters makes unified fiscal planning for the total municipal area difficult.

Types of Local School Districts

The names applied to different types of districts may seem to be a function of the preference of the state. Yet some knowledge of these assists in understanding the diversity in local school district organization. In New England and parts of the Midwest there exist common school districts and town or township districts. Both were among the early types of districts created in the United Sates. The *common* school district is generally found in rural areas and is most often quite small in terms of pupils enrolled and territory encompassed. In fact, some of these districts may have only a single school that provides instruction on the elementary level for fewer than a dozen pupils. The *town* or *township* districts are also generally small. The name is derived from the fact that the boundaries of such districts are coterminous with those of the town or township. The term *joint district* is often used to describe a district that emerges from a joining of two township districts or a joining to provide a specific type or level of schooling. (For example, Ohio has joint high school and joint vocational school districts.) The *city* school district, the boundaries of which are usually coterminous with city boundaries, is found in a number of states. The range in size and complexity is great. There are the huge city districts of New York, Chicago, and Los Angeles. Yet there are numerous districts encompassing smaller "cities" that enroll a few hundred pupils. The large city districts offer comprehensive programs for all age groups, whereas some small city districts are limited to elementary schools. The *county* local school district, with boundaries coterminous with county lines, is found roughly in one third of the states, mostly in the Southeast. In a few states (e.g., Florida) the county districts administer all schools within the county. In other states (e.g., Alabama) there are other districts within the county (e.g., a city district). In a few states (e.g., Illinois) there are *elementary* districts and *high school* districts. Where elementary and high school districts have been merged, the resulting district is often called a *unified* district. The term *special,* or *independent district* is used in some states. This type of district usually does not have boundaries coterminous with a municipality, has its origin in a legislative act, and may offer elementary or high school education, or both. Finally some states have separate community junior college and/or vocational-technical school districts that directly administer the community junior colleges and/or vocational-technical schools within the state. On the matter of community junior colleges Thornton noted that during the early period of rapid public community junior college growth (1920–1940) these colleges were frequently "grades 13 and 14" and a part of the local high school. However, during the second period of rapid growth (1945–1965), the independent community college district emerged.[3] In the late 1960s there was a move toward more centralized systems under state governing or coordinating boards. Therefore, even though several states still maintain community college districts, as a general rule, these districts do not have as many powers as the districts that provide elementary and/or secondary schooling.

Usually more than one type of district exists within a state. For example, a state may have township, elementary, high school, and unified districts or city, county, and independent districts. A few states have basically one type of district. To illustrate, Florida, Louisiana, Nevada, and West Virginia are county district states. Regardless of type, most districts rely upon real property taxes for funds that must be provided locally to support education. Also, the vast majority of the local school districts have been granted fiscal independence to adopt a budget and to require the collection of the necessary taxes to provide the local contribution to support the budget.

Number and Size of Local School Districts

In 1931–32, the first year that adequate information was available, there were 127,531 local school districts in the United States. In 1945–46 there were 101,382; in 1959–60 the figure was 40,520; in 1975–76 there were 16,376;[4] and in 1979–80 there were 16,056 local school districts in the nation including 290 school districts that did not operate any schools.[5] Obviously, with such reductions in the total number of districts, there has been a decided trend toward increasing the size of local school districts; yet the number of districts per state and the size of districts have continued to vary widely. As has been noted, Hawaii has a state system and during the 1979–80 school year Delaware, Nevada, and Maryland each had fewer than thirty local school districts. At the other extreme, California, Illinois, Nebraska,

[3]James W. Thornton, *The Community Junior College,* 3rd ed. (New York: Wiley, 1972), pp. 89–91.

[4]W. Vance Grant and Leo J. Eiden, *Digest of Educational Statistics, 1980 Edition* (Washington, D.C.: U.S. Government Printing Office, 1980), p. 60.

[5]National Education Association, *Estimates of School Statistics, 1979–80* (Washington, D.C.: The Association, 1980), p. 26.

and Texas each had more than 1,000 districts.[6] In 1980, led by New York City with about 960,000 pupils and Los Angeles with about 545,000 pupils, sixty-seven districts within the forty-eight contiguous states enrolled 50,000 or more pupils.[7] However, in spite of the great reduction in the number of school districts, about 75 percent of the local school districts of the nation enrolled fewer than 2,500 pupils including about 25 percent that enrolled fewer than 300 pupils.[8] Taken collectively, it was estimated that in 1979–80 the local public school districts of the nation enrolled 88.5 percent of the 47.3 million persons five to seventeen years of age.[9]

What is the appropriate size for a school district? This question has persisted for several decades. There is general agreement that a school district should have a large enough pupil population to provide, at reasonable cost, comprehensive programs and services and that it should be of sufficient size to have an adequate tax base (assuming some local financing of schools). Yet it should not be so large as to become unresponsive to the people and be administratively unwieldy. In the 1930s and 1940s many expressed the view that 3,000 to 5,000 pupils was appropriate; a popular view of the 1960s was 20,000 to 30,000 pupils. Another point of view holds that the appropriate-size concept is a myth; other factors are more critical. For example: How is the district organized internally? What support services are available from a regional district, if any? What is the population density? What is the level of state support to local districts? What is the socioeconomic mix of the population? In other words, there are so many variables involved that what might be an optimum size in one situation might well be too large or too small in another situation.

Decentralized Large Districts

Since the 1950s there has been widespread interest in "decentralizing" large districts. The movement is not new; in a few places (e.g., Philadelphia, St. Louis) decentralization occurred much earlier. In a 1958 report a commission of the American Association of School Administrators described decentralization as the delegation of administrative authority and responsibility on a geographic rather than a departmental basis.[10] Usually a district adopting such an organization is divided into geographic areas, and an area or district superin-

[6] Ibid.

[7] Allan C. Ornstein, "Decentralization and Community Participation Policy of Big School Systems," *Phi Delta Kappan*, 62 (December 1980), 255.

[8] Grant and Eiden, op. cit., p. 60.

[9] National Education Association, op. cit., p. 27.

[10] Commission on School District Reorganization, *School District Organization* (Washington, D.C.: American Association of School Administrators, 1958), p. 300.

tendent is appointed to be the chief administrator of the schools in each of these areas. To illustrate, in 1980 New York City had thirty-two "community districts" with each enrolling 12,000 to 30,000 pupils. In the smaller urban communities there were usually fewer than New York's thirty-two districts. For example, in Nashville, Tennessee, the school system, with a pupil enrollment of roughly 71,500, had three geographic areas. These each enrolled 16,500 to 27,000 pupils.[11] Each area was headed by an area superintendent who reported to the director of schools (superintendent).

Some indication of the magnitude of the decentralization movement is provided by Ornstein's 1980 survey of school districts enrolling 50,000 or more pupils. He reported that forty of these local districts (excluding Hawaii and Puerto Rico) had some degree of administrative decentralization. This included four school districts with school boards operating at the decentralized level.[12] (These were in addition to the district-level school boards.)

The extent to which functions and services are decentralized varies widely. In some local districts the area offices have an area superintendent, a small staff of instructional specialists, and supporting clerical personnel. In these instances, except for serving as a contact point for citizens in the area served, acting as a liaison between the local schools and the central office, and providing instructional support to teachers, the areas remain dependent upon the central office of the district. At the other extreme, some few districts have tried to provide much greater autonomy for the geographic areas and have, to a degree, decentralized curriculum planning, personnel, budgeting, and so on. As is discussed in more detail in Chapter 6, among the major questions confronting those interested in decentralization are the extent to which such services and functions should be carried out by the several area offices and the degree of autonomy with which the area offices should be provided.

Local School District Governing Boards

The local school district governing board may be called the board of education, school board, school committee, school commissioners, school inspectors, school directors, or the like. Whatever the title, no local district exists without such a board. Furthermore, as indicated above, in a few of the decentralized districts, both a central board and boards at the decentralized level are operational.

[11]Ornstein, op. cit., p. 256.
[12]Ibid.

Some Basic Data About School Boards

Over the years there have been some reasonably broad-based surveys of school boards.[13] Based on such surveys it is possible to draw some generalizations about the size of local school boards, how they are selected, qualifications for service, characteristics of board members, meetings, and reimbursement.

Most of the local school boards have five to nine members. However, there are boards that have more than twenty members, and there is at least one small city district where the city manager serves as the school board. In about four fifths of the states some or all of the local board members are elected by popular vote from the district at large or by geographic areas within the district. Roughly 85 percent of the total number of board members are elected, most frequently on a nonpartisan basis. Those who are appointed receive their appointments from a variety of sources (e.g., legislature, governor, mayor, city council, county court, grand jury). In practically all states the law provides that local board members serve for a specified period of time. The usual practice is for board members to serve from two to six years. Most frequently members of a board serve overlapping terms with one or more new members being selected each year or every other year. The qualifications for board membership are minimal. The typical state law requires that to be a board member one must "have a practical education," "be of reputable character," be a resident of the district, and not be an employee of the district. In a few states there are requirements, such as owning property in the district or having a child in school. (If challenged in a court, it is likely that some qualifications that exist in some localities would be ruled unconstitutional.)

Local district board members, like state board members, tend to be representative of the middle and upper-middle socioeconomic classes. For example, they tend to have business or professional backgrounds (except in rural areas), to be long-time residents and home owners in the community they serve, to be white, to have higher than average incomes, to be middle-aged, to be better educated (over one-half have college backgrounds), and to be male.

In most states the law requires that the board meet at least monthly on a regularly scheduled date (e.g., the first Tuesday of each

[13] See, for example, Morrill M. Hall, *Provisions Governing Membership on Local Boards of Education*, Bull. 1957, No. 13 (Washington, D.C.: U.S. Government Printing Office, 1957); Alpheus L. White, *Local School Boards: Organization and Practices* (Washington, D.C.: U.S. Government Printing Office, 1962); National School Boards Association, *Survey of Public Education in the Member Cities of the Council of Big City Boards of Education* (Evanston, Ill.: The Association, November 1968); L. Harmon Zeigler and M. Kent Jennings, *Governing American Schools* (North Scituate, Mass.: Duxbury, 1974), p. 28.

month), that additional regular meetings may be held, and that special meetings may be held on call. In large districts, it is not uncommon to see a board have two regularly scheduled meetings per month and over the period of a year hold an additional five to ten called meetings. By law in many states board meetings are open to the public, except that most of the states that require open meetings provide for closed (executive) sessions for specified purposes (e.g., consideration of school sites, to instruct the board negotiator in regard to collective-bargaining matters). School board minutes, which are public records and open for examination by persons who have valid reasons, constitute the official record of school board meetings.

Because school board membership is by tradition a public service, most generally members have served without pay or for a nominal per meeting rate and/or reimbursement for expenses incurred. However, among the larger districts of the nation, there have been several instances in recent years where more than nominal salaries (e.g., in 1981 Washington D.C. board members were paid more than $18,000 per year) for school board service have been instituted. Furthermore, in some instances board members have been provided support personnel (in addition to the usually provided secretarial service). For example, each member of the board may be provided an administrative aide.

As in the case of the state boards, there are differences of opinion regarding how local board members should be selected, their qualifications, term of office, level of reimbursement, and whether or not meetings should be open. Most authorities have tended to advocate nonpartisan elections, residence as the only legal qualification, three- to five-year overlapping terms of office, nominal reimbursement, and open meetings except where the board is considering a sensitive personnel matter, discussing school sites, or conferring with their negotiating team. In recent years many have advocated the use of local caucuses to nominate candidates for election. The belief is that this procedure can serve to screen candidates and urge reluctant, well-qualified persons to place their names on the ballot. Also, there has been increased concern for broader representation for the underrepresented sectors of a community (e.g., minorities, women). One approach to this concern has been the school boards at the decentralized level in the big-city districts and the increased use in a wide variety of localities of school-level citizens' councils. There appears to be some rethinking among the authorities relative to nonpartisan elections, and we suspect the future will see the increased incidence of salaried school boards. Furthermore, in a few states, "government-in-the-sunshine" laws have been passed, which require almost all school board meetings to be open.

Powers and Responsibilities of School Boards

School board members, as agents of the state who are selected locally, find that they must, on the one hand, carry out the mandates of the state and, on the other hand, try to be responsive to the desires of the local people. In the event of a conflict in this dual role, legally board members must carry out the mandates of the state. Furthermore, the board is legally empowered to act only as a unit; that is, an individual board member has no legal power except as a member of the group.

The point has been made that in the legal sense a local school board has mandated and implied powers. Accordingly, as a usual practice the state law will provide that after receiving and considering the recommendations of the local superintendent, the board has the power to determine policies, adopt rules and regulations, make contracts, and prescribe minimum standards necessary for the orderly and efficient operation of the school system. In addition to this general power, in most states the law also spells out a number of specific duties for the school board: appointing personnel, adopting the school district calendar, adopting the school district budget, providing for the proper handling of school district funds, providing for curriculum development, and ensuring that required records are kept.

In fulfilling the responsibility to oversee the operation of the schools of the local district consistent with the laws of the state, the local school board will appropriately engage in policy-making, legislative, judicial, planning, interpretative, and appraisal activities. In making policy, the board describes in general terms the objectives to be achieved. Legislative activities take place by the approval in school board meetings of motions and resolutions (e.g., approval of budgets, personnel appointments, salary schedules, textbooks, curriculum changes). By such actions their policies become reality. They function in a judicial sense when as a unit they hold hearings (e.g., considering a pupil expulsion or teacher dismissal). The board engages in planning as it examines the needs of the local school district and considers alternative courses of action to meet these needs. Through their discussions with and explanations to the citizens the board interprets. In making judgments about the adequacy of the programs offered by the district, the extent to which money has been wisely spent, and the quality of performance of employees, the board is appraising.

Central and Community Boards in Local School Districts

As noted several times previously, because of a variety of economic, legal, political, and social forces, there has been, and continues to be, considerable pressure from diverse sectors of the population to broaden formal participation in educational policy making. In spite of much verbiage to the contrary, most informed observers feel that control of schools has, for the most part, been in the hands of a few persons. Those who object to the monolithic control exercised by the "establishment" and feel powerless have demanded "a piece of the action." This includes the ethnic minorities, the "have-nots," teachers, and pupils.

There are many who believe that if the local schools are to be responsive, structures must be developed to permit the underrepresented groups to have an effective voice in school affairs. The basic position is that pluralism is essential in a democracy, and two of the keys to pluralism are diversity of views and wide participation.

In a few of the large city districts of the nation, where the demand for broader involvement has been particularly intense, in addition to administrative decentralization, the response has been to create a two-tiered structure of governance. To illustrate, in 1969 New York City created thirty-one community school districts (a thirty-second district was created later) to operate elementary and junior high schools. (The senior high schools remained under control of the central board, which had final responsibility for schools in the city.) Each of the community school districts had a locally elected, nine-member board and was headed by a community school district superintendent. Even though the central board had responsibility for negotiating contracts with employee groups, the local boards had a major voice in who was employed, curriculum, and so on.

The Local School District Superintendent and Central Office Staff

Most local operating districts employ a chief executive officer. In some very small districts the school board may operate without such an executive or may "share" such an executive with an adjacent district of similar size. The chief executive is most often referred to as the *superintendent of schools*. In carrying out the responsibilities of their office, superintendents are, in most cases, assisted by a district-level staff—generally referred to as the central office staff.

Origin and Status of the Superintendent Position

As noted in Chapter 1, the position of superintendent was first established in the city districts, with Buffalo and Louisville leading the way by creating the position in 1837. By 1900 most of the city districts had superintendents who in most cases were appointed by the school board.[14] Because, outside the cities, the local school district

14Campbell et al., op. cit., p. 218.

was usually quite small, the position did not begin to develop in these districts until the twentieth century.

Campbell and associates suggested that there were four stages in the development of the position. In the first stage the position was essentially clerical; the board felt the need to hire someone to relieve them of routine details. With the expansion of the school program, the board tended to look to the superintendent for assistance in regard to educational problems. Thus in this second stage the superintendent was basically an educator. With the increased growth and complexity of school districts came the necessity to deal with budgets, school plants, tax levies, and so on. This led to the third stage when the superintendent became a business manager, often to the neglect of educational matters, or, in several localities, to a superintendent for business and a superintendent for education. The fourth stage, perhaps still evolving, is the superintendent as the chief executive of the school board for business and the chief professional advisor of the board for educational purposes and procedures.[15]

With the exception of the position of superintendent of county local districts in some of the states of the Southeast, the local district superintendent is almost always an appointee of the local school board. Furthermore, in some very small districts the person appointed as superintendent may also serve as a school principal and even as a part-time teacher.

In many states the laws do not deal in detail with the position. Often the law simply authorizes the employment of a superintendent. In those states where the position is a constitutional office, or where it is an elected position, the laws tend to be more specific. This is also true where the position is defined in a municipal charter. In one old but often-cited study it was found that in about half of the states the school code defined the relation between the school board and superintendent. In thirteen states the courts had declared the superintendent to be an officer of the board and in six states it had been ruled the superintendent was an employee.[16]

Role of the Superintendent

In view of the fact that in well over half of the states the law is not specific, the role of the superintendent is largely a function of the policies and procedures of the employing board of education. However, these policies and procedures most often reflect what authorities in the field perceive to be "best practice."

In nearly all local districts, the superintendent alone reports di-

---

[15] Ibid., pp. 219–220.
[16] Lloyd E. McCann, "Legal Status of the Superintendent of Schools as a Public Officer" (unpublished doctoral dissertation, Colorado State College of Education, 1951).

rectly to the board. All other district administrators are responsible to the superintendent. There are still a few exceptions to the single-executive practice. In a few districts the board appoints a secretary or comptroller who reports to the board directly and is charged with the management of the district's fiscal affairs.

Among the major expectancies usually associated with the chief executive role are the following:

1. To advise, counsel, and keep the school board informed regarding the achievements, needs, and problems of the school district.
2. To make recommendations to the board relative to needed policies, rules, and regulations.
3. To serve as a leader of the staff and board in long-range planning.
4. To be responsible for the day-to-day operations of the school district.
5. To ensure compliance with the directives of higher authority.
6. To prepare the school district budget for board review and adoption and administer the adopted budget.
7. To make recommendations to the board regarding the employment, assignment, transfer, development, and dismissal of personnel.
8. To ensure that needed steps are taken in planning, maintaining, and evaluating instructional programs and services.
9. To determine the internal organization of the school district.
10. To make recommendations regarding school building needs and ensure that the buildings are efficiently operated and adequately maintained.
11. To serve as a major public spokesperson for the schools.

To fulfill these expectancies, the superintendent does not work alone. This person often relies on assistance from the central office staff of the district, building-level administrators, teachers, support personnel, outside consultants, lay citizen groups, and pupil groups.

The Central Office Staff

Simply put and in the legal sense, the board, with the assistance of the superintendent, makes policy and the superintendent carries out these policies. The larger and more complex the school district, the greater the number of district-level administrative and supervisory personnel needed to assist the superintendent in implementing these policies.

As suggested in Chapter 1, in a large district the central office staff will often have five or more levels in the hierarchy, and there will be an imposing array of titles. For example, in some districts there is a deputy superintendent who accepts any responsibility delegated by the superintendent, such as directly coordinating the activities of the assistant superintendents for specific facets of the school district's operation. At the next level there may be a number of associate or assistant superintendents (e.g., for instruction, business affairs, administrative services, staff personnel, pupil personnel). Where there is no deputy superintendent, often one or more administrative assistants and the assistant superintendents report directly to the superintendent. At the next level there are numerous directors who are usually responsible to a given superintendent (e.g., directors for secondary education, vocational education, transportation, buildings and grounds, food services, guidance services). At the lower levels may be found a number of persons with such titles as assistant director, coordinator, supervisor, and consultant (e.g., assistant director for research, coordinator of testing, art supervisor, foreign language consultant). In addition, there will usually be a wide assortment of "classified" and technical personnel (e.g., secretaries, computer programmers, painters, plumbers, clerk-typists, mechanics, school bus drivers). The central office staff in large districts often includes other specialists, such as architects and attorneys. In smaller districts such specialists may be employed on a retainer basis or whenever the need arises. Obviously, with a large central office staff, personnel have more specialized assignments than central office personnel in small school districts.

The line–staff concept of organization is discussed in Chapter 8. Suffice to note at this point that many theorists have expressed reservations about the concept. Nevertheless, in many school districts the notion persists. Superintendents and school building principals are inevitably line officers. If a district has an assistant superintendent for school operations or area superintendents, the line will usually run from the superintendent to the assistant superintendent for school operations or area superintendent, to the building principal, to the teachers. With these exceptions central office administrators have staff roles. Persons such as the assistant superintendent for fiscal affairs, director of libraries, and director of planning are staff officers who perform assigned duties necessary to facilitate the operating units in the accomplishment of the primary mission of the district—instruction. Although many central office administrators often exercise effective control over line officers by virtue of their personal power and expertise and in many districts the line–staff relations are not easily defined, in the formal sense these administrators do not exercise formal general authority. In Figure 5-1, intended to assist the reader in better understanding the relationships and structure of local school

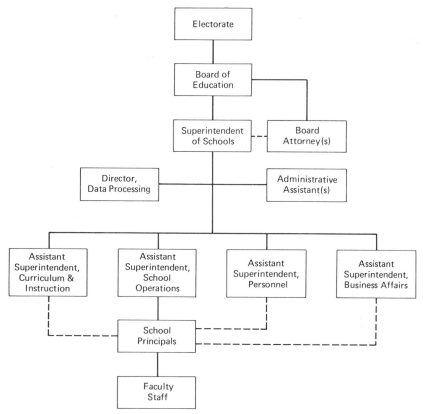

Figure 5-1. Illustrative local school district organization.

districts, the line is from the board to the superintendent, to the assistant superintendent for school operations, to the school principals, to the teachers. All other assistant superintendents are in a staff relationship to the principals. We emphasize that Figure 5-1 is just an example; probably no two school districts in the nation are exactly alike in structure and formal relationships.

School Centers

The operating units of a school district are the individual schools (i.e., attendance units, attendance centers). In 1931–1932 there were roughly 259,000 public elementary and secondary schools in the nation.[17] In 1976–77 the comparable figure was 86,501.[18] This reduction in the number of schools occurred, in spite of great increases in pupils

[17] Grant and Eiden, op. cit., p. 62.
[18] Ibid., p. 60.

enrolled, because of the consolidation of small schools. For example, by the 1976–77 school year there were only 1,111 one-teacher schools left in the nation, whereas in 1931–32 there were over 143,000.[19] In this section attention is given to school attendance areas, school organizational patterns, administrative hierarchies in schools, and organizational reform efforts in urban school centers.

School Attendance Areas

A school attendance area (i.e., zone or district) is that geographic portion of a district served by a particular school. In a small district operating a single school center, the boundaries of the district are the same as the boundaries of the school attendance area. However, in the vast majority of school districts there are many such areas. These areas are not uniform in size, and it is not unique for a single school center to have different attendance areas for different grade levels. For example, a K–12 center might have different attendance areas for grades K–8 and 9–12. Further, an attendance area for a senior high school center (grades 10–12) might include two or more junior high school (grades 7–9) attendance areas and several elementary school attendance areas. The term *neighborhood school* comes from the tendency of school districts to use geographically compact attendance areas. Historically a few districts have not used attendance areas; rather an "open-enrollment" policy has been followed—permitting a pupil to attend any school center he or she chooses within the district. Some districts have used attendance areas and open enrollment for special-purpose school centers (e.g., a vocational high school center).

Since the *First Brown* case (1954), the nature and even viability of school attendance areas has been the subject of much scrutiny among educators, the courts, and the laity. One basis for this scrutiny was that in many districts there appeared to be gerrymandering of attendance areas to perpetuate racial segregation.

In the late 1950s and early 1960s in many school districts where *de jure* segregation was practiced, as the federal courts directed the elimination of racial segregation, attendance areas gave way to open-enrollment policies. In some districts where there was a high degree of *de facto* racial segregation, open-enrollment policies were adopted voluntarily but these open-enrollment policies were unsuccessful in eliminating segregation. In the main pupils continued to attend the schools nearest their residence.

In view of the failure of open-enrollment plans, the next move was restructuring of attendance areas; larger and/or uniquely shaped areas were created. For example, in some city districts "pie" or "strip" attendance areas running from the center to the fringes of the city

---

[19] Ibid., pp. 60, 62.

were created. In the late 1960s and early 1970s terms such as *pairing* and *clustering* became commonplace in many local districts. An example of pairing would be to take one K–6 attendance area in a sector of the district that had mostly white pupils and another K–6 area in a sector that had mostly black pupils and use the school center in one area as a K–3 school and the center in the other area as a 4–6 center. Thus each school would have two noncontiguous attendance areas. The term *clustering* is used when three or more attendance areas and school centers are included in such an arrangement. Obviously almost any arrangement that has a school serving noncontiguous attendance areas results in a part of the school's pupil population being transported (i.e., "cross-bused"). As was discussed in Chapter 3, an important legal issue is how far must school districts go in reducing racial segregation. How this issue is resolved in a given school district will be a major determinant in the nature of the school zones in that district and the extent of busing for desegregation.

In light of the above, the attendance area for a given school center could well include several geographic areas in disparate sectors of the school district. Where this has occurred, there is no longer a neighborhood school in the conventional sense. This breaking up of neighborhood schools has created much controversy among educators and the laity. The advocates of the neighborhood-school concept often express the view that the demise of the neighborhood school makes it difficult for the child to adjust. The point is also made that loss of the neighborhood school means the loss of community support and involvement. Those who suggest the concept is no longer viable rebut by noting that size is not the prime factor related to the climate of a school; rather it is the organization and staff. Further, they suggest that school–community interaction is not assured by the neighborhood school and that other mechanisms are available to provide better interaction (e.g., community boards and school councils).

Organization of School Centers

In the days when a school center was most often a one-room, one-teacher affair providing instruction at the elementary level for ten to twenty-five pupils, the organizational pattern was simple—a one-teacher, nongraded arrangement. With pupil population growth, extension of public schools to provide high school education, and the consolidation of one-room schools into larger centers, graded 1–12 school centers came into being. In areas where the pupil population was sufficient, the following organizational patterns were used: 1–8 centers and 9–12 centers (8–4 plan); or 1–6, 7–12 (6–6 plan); or 1–6, 7–9, 10–12 centers (6–3–3 plan). In recent years the middle-school concept has become popular and many school districts have moved to K–4, 5–8, 9–12 centers. It is probably safe to say that a school center could be found that housed almost any grade level combination one could name.

The typical graded elementary school of the 1940s was organized around the *self-contained* classroom—one teacher charged with the instruction of a group of twenty-five to thirty pupils of a single grade. In some instances the departmentalized pattern prevalent in the secondary schools was adopted by elementary schools, but except for the seventh- and eighth-grade levels, it never gained wide acceptance. For a number of pedagogical reasons, in the late 1950s and 1960s there developed considerable interest in the *nongraded* organization, particularly at the lower levels (e.g., K–3). The modern version of the nongraded plan, far different from the one-room school of an earlier era, is an organizational arrangement in which pupils are classified and provided instruction in terms of their progress in a given area. The nongraded organization is often accompanied by some form of team-teaching arrangement. For example, a team of six persons (headed by an experienced "master teacher" and including two other professionals and three paraprofessionals or teacher aides) would be responsible for the instruction of a group of 140 to 160 pupils who, if the school were "graded," would be in grades 1–3. However, the prevailing organizational pattern within elementary school centers continues to be the graded self-contained classroom supplemented with special teachers for instruction in some areas (e.g., art, music).

At the secondary level even though there have been efforts to provide more flexibility through the use of modular-type scheduling in lieu of the traditional fifty-minute class period with the class meeting each school day, the department organization has persisted. Thus in most high school centers there are departments (e.g., English, mathematics, physical education) in which a given teacher is responsible for a single subject or a group of closely related subjects, and the pupils have different teachers for different subjects.

Administrative Hierarchy Within School Centers

As a usual practice each school center has a single chief administrative officer—a principal. In very small school centers this person may be a "teaching principal" and teach full- or part-time. Also, in a few cases a single principal will administer two small geographically separated school centers. At the other extreme, in a very large center that has different buildings housing different grade-level combinations (e.g., a K–12 center with a K–4 building, a 5–8 building, and a 9–12 building) there may be a supervising principal who is responsible for the total center and a building principal for each separate facility. In a large elementary center, in addition to the principal, the administrative hierarchy may include assistant principals (e.g., for administration, for curriculum) and grade-level chairpersons (e.g., for primary grades) or team leaders who have part-time administrative duties. In a large senior high school center (e.g., enrolling 3,000 pupils) the administrative hierarchy supporting the principal may include vice or assistant principals, deans, a registrar, a director of guidance, department chairpersons (who teach part-time), and the like.

Even though the functions vary by locality, the principal has primary responsibility for administering all aspects of the school center. This person must ensure, consistent with directives from higher authority, that instructional programs and pupil services are provided; pupils are apropriately classified and assigned; pupil conduct is such that the center can function in an orderly manner; there is adequate accounting for internal funds; the instructional personnel have needed support in terms of instructional materials and consultative assistance; the staff is appropriately assigned; required records are maintained; the building is kept clean and in good repair; and other similar duties are performed. In addition to these internal duties, the principal is also expected to serve as a major link between the center and the community served.

For many years it was common practice for school center administrators to work with some type of lay group for the improvement of all or some facet of the program of the school. This frequently took the form of parent–teacher associations, community-school committees, and the like. In most cases, such lay groups exercised little influence on school affairs. In the late 1960s there emerged a demand for greater lay voice in the affairs of a school center. This demand was most forceful in the big cities.

The lay citizen element in the hierarchy of school centers most frequently takes the form of local school councils, which advise and counsel with the school principal and staff. In this arrangement the legal authority for decision making in the school still resides with the principal, subject to the directives of the area superintendent and board (if any) and general superintendent and central board. However, there are those who advocate that school-level councils should have legal authority in such areas as personnel and curriculum. To date, this pattern (for individual schools) has not been adopted in many localities. However, in Ornstein's 1980 survey, over 60 percent of the large districts of the nation reported "extensive" community involvement at the local-school level.[20] There are also a number of states (e.g., California, Florida) that mandate some form of local citizen advisory committees. Thus there appears to be rather widespread citizen participation in school-level affairs.

The concept of increased community control through the mechanism of local school citizen councils has created considerable debate.

[20]Ornstein, op. cit., 257.

Particularly controversial are those proposals for granting legal authority to school-level boards for such matters as personnel and curriculum. However, it should be noted that there is some precedent for such control in the school trustee system that once prevailed in many rural school districts and is still provided for in the laws of some states. For example, Alabama law provides for three trustees per school within the county districts of the state, and these trustees are charged with caring for school property and reporting to the county school board on school needs and progress.

Reform Efforts in Urban School Centers

As we discuss in several different contexts, there has been much criticism of the public schools, particularly in urban areas, during the past twenty-five years. This criticism has provided the impetus for many proposals for reform—for example, community control, "free" schools, performance contracts, vouchers. At this writing, in addition to the efforts to increase citizen involvement in local school decision making, there are three organizational reform efforts that have shown some promise in the localities where they have been instituted. These are alternative schools within the public school district, schools that have been designed specifically as human or community service centers, and so-called "adopt-a-school" programs.

Because alternative schools are intended to provide persons with options, they come in a variety of forms. Smith identified eight types of alternative schools: (1) open schools—characterized by learning activities individualized and organized around interest centers within the building or classroom; (2) schools without walls—where there is extensive community and school interaction, with learning activities taking place throughout the community; (3) magnet schools, learning centers, educational parks—where there is a concentration of learning resources in one center which is open to all pupils in the community; (4) multicultural schools, bilingual schools, ethnic schools—characterized by emphasis on cultural pluralism, ethnic awareness, and racial awareness; (5) street academies, dropout centers, pregnancy-maternity centers—where the emphasis is placed on programs for a specially targeted population; (6) schools within a school—any of the foregoing organized within a traditional school; (7) integration models—any of the foregoing with a voluntary pupil population that is broadly representative of the total community; and (8) free schools—characterized by great freedom for pupils and teachers.[21]

Smith also noted that, regardless of type, alternative schools

[21] Vernon H. Smith, "Options to Public Education: The Quiet Revolution," *Phi Delta Kappan*, LIV (March 1973), 434–435.

tended to have several characteristics in common. These include (1) provision for options within public education for parents, pupils, and teachers; (2) commitment to be responsive to some felt need within the community; (3) a more comprehensive set of goals and objectives than traditional schools; (4) flexibility and responsiveness to planned change; and (5) emphasis on being humane to pupils and teachers.[22]

There are numerous illustrations of alternative schools. (In 1981 it was estimated that there were more than 10,000 alternative public schools, and about 80 percent of the school districts enrolling 25,000 or more pupils operated alternative schools.[23]) Consider the Whitney Young Magnet High School opened by the Chicago public school system in 1975. The intent was to provide high quality programs to attract middle-class and upward-mobile lower-class students from black, white, and Hispanic backgrounds. (Racial/ethnic goals for the student body were set.) The major magnet programs were in the medical arts, performing arts, and science. Also, there was a school within a school for students with hearing impairments.[24]

The community education movement has placed emphasis on the community use of school buildings after school hours and on weekends. In the extension of the concept referred to as community or human service centers, facilities are built with the notion that several people-serving groups will share available spaces. Three examples serve to illustrate this notion.

The Williams Community Center in Flint, Michigan, constructed in 1971 adjoining a 72-acre park, was designed for educational, health, recreational, and social service functions. The project included provisions for a 900-pupil prekindergarten through grade 6 school, a community recreation center, community use of the library, community meeting rooms, and a facility for community health and social services for the elderly. The John F. Kennedy Center in Atlanta, which opened in 1971, is a multistoried complex that houses community recreational facilities, day-care space, family and children services, offices of the local housing authority, performing arts facilities, and a school. The Dana P. Whitmer Center in Pontiac, Michigan, was designed to include four elementary schools, space for ten community agencies, a medical and dental clinic, a library, a field house, a community lodge, a performing arts center, and so on. Usually centers such as these are managed by a director and have a representative executive board. For example, the Whitmer Center has a coordi-

[22] Ibid.

[23] Mary Anne Raywid, "The First Decade of Public School Alternatives," *Phi Delta Kappan*, 62 (April 1981), 552.

[24] Connie Moore and Daniel U. Levine, "Whitney Young Magnet High School of Chicago and Urban Renewal," *Planning and Changing*, 4 (Winter 1977), 148–154.

nating director, a community executive board consisting of parents and teachers with advice from the social agencies, and numerous community service committees.[25]

To encourage the development of such facilities, at least one state has made funds available for this specific purpose. In New Jersey, special funds were made available for construction and/or renovation of facilities to deliver municipal, social, recreational, and/or educational services to all age groups.[26]

Based on a review of data relating to school renewal efforts from thirty large districts, Chase identified four essential conditions for success in such endeavors. Utilization of the total urban environment was one of the conditions identified.[27] The adopt-a-school programs represent one application of the use-of-the-environment concept. Adopt-a-school programs vary, however; in essence businesses, civic organizations, church groups, and/or social service agencies identify with and provide assistance to specific schools. The assistance may include in-school speakers, tutoring, providing work and field experience sites, funds for materials and supplies, and executive advisory services. An extensive adopt-a-school program has been instituted in Dallas. Some 150 Dallas schools have reported assistance from about 600 business and community organizations. Top leadership personnel of the community have served on task forces that helped to plan and organize the magnet schools of the district.[28]

Regional Educational Agencies

A regional district or service agency has been defined as an educational unit other than a local school district that has been created to carry out instructional, liaison, regulatory, supervisory, and/or service missions. Frequently such a unit will encompass two or more local school districts. To facilitate the description of the organization, control, and functions of such units, two broad categories are used: statutory regional units and voluntary regional units. By statutory units we mean there is a basis for their creation in the legislative

[25] Richard J. Passantino, "Community/School Facilities: The Schoolhouse of the Future," *Phi Delta Kappan,* LVI (January 1975), 306–309.

[26] Barry Semple, Ronald K. Butcher, and W. Frank Johnson, "State Aid Boosts Community School Construction," *Community Education Journal,* VII (January 1980), 8–9.

[27] Francis S. Chase, "The Regeneration of Public Education in Our Cities," *Phi Delta Kappan,* 60 (January 1979), 353–356.

[28] Daniel U. Levine and Nolan Estes, "Desegregation and Educational Reconstruction in the Dallas Public Schools," *Phi Delta Kappan,* 59 (November 1977), 163–167, 221.

enactments of the states where they exist. Voluntary units refer to those units created as a result of the initiative of local school districts without specific state authorizing legislation.

Statutory Regional Units

The traditional form of the statutory regional unit is the intermediate district. This was, historically, a unit of educational governance existing between the state and local districts. The intermediate district had its origin in the Midwest, and in most of the states having such units, the unit boundaries were coterminous with county boundaries. As initially conceived over 100 years ago, these units, which were created in about two-thirds of the states, were essentially an arm of the state and functioned to oversee the small, largely rural, local districts through the enforcement of state rules and regulations and the distribution of state funds to the local school districts. In addition, these units collected information from the local districts and provided some services to them. Most often these county intermediate districts were headed by an elected county superintendent, who functioned basically as a clerk.[29] In the mid-1940s, excluding New York and six New England states that had other types of intermediate units, twenty-seven states had a statewide pattern of county intermediate districts. With some few exceptions in three states, twenty of these states had an elected county superintendent, and eleven states had county intermediate school boards.[30]

As the consolidation of local districts proceeded and the means of communication and transportation improved, many authorities began to question the need for such districts to perform their historic liaison, regulatory, and supervisory functions. Since World War II some states have eliminated all or part of their intermediate units, and in many other states the functions and territory encompassed by these units have been altered. The intermediate unit has come to be seen by most authorities as an entity to provide services, including instruction that is high cost and/or very specialized, to the local districts that they can not feasibly provide for themselves. Further, in some states the county as the intermediate unit has given way to larger areas. More specifically, Benson and Barber found that since the early 1960s, about one-half of the states have promoted regional units as a means of gaining economies of scale, equalizing educational opportunities, acquiring specialized staff for special instruction

[29]Charles W. Benson and R. Jerry Barber, *Intermediate Units and Their Promise for Rural Education* (Austin, Texas: National Educational Laboratory Publishers, Inc., March 1974), p. 15 (ED 088632).

[30]Charles O. Fitzwater, "Patterns and Trends in State School System Development," *Journal on State School Systems,* 1 (Spring 1967), 26.

programs, providing services to local districts, achieving flexibility to meet demands, and providing linkages with other educational agencies.[31]

As implied above, the states proceeded differently as they took steps to create a system of regional agencies to replace or supplement the traditional intermediate units. In some of these states (e.g., Colorado) the assigned mission of the regional units was service (including instruction in special areas); in others (e.g., Illinois) the regional units also had some regulatory functions.[32] In some instances the law creating these new regional agencies was permissive and did not abolish the existing intermediate superintendency or other existing statutory cooperative arrangements, nor were local districts required to be members of the regional agency. In other cases the law totally restructured the intermediate system.

One of the first states to promote regional service units was New York. In 1948 the state legislature authorized local districts to form Boards of Cooperative Educational Services (BOCES). The existing supervisory districts were not abolished; instead, if desired, the BOCES was superimposed on them. BOCES programs and services are determined by the board, which is elected from the participating local districts. Financing is from the local districts and directly from the state. The appointed superintendent is an employee of the board and the state education agency.[33]

New York was by no means the only state to create new regional educational agencies without abolishing the existing cooperative arrangements, and where this occurred there was great potential for conflict. In Massachusetts, for example, as a result of legislative encouragement, the local school districts had created a variety of voluntary "collaboratives" to provide services that the leaders of the participating local districts thought they needed. (In 1977 it was estimated that over 100 formal/informal collaboratives existed with boundaries determined by the participants. Forty of these were active, multipurpose organizations having full-time directors.) With the reorganization of the state department of education, six regional educational centers were created with monitoring, program auditing, and regulatory/administrative responsibilities. With the regional centers, there was perceived conflict in regard to funding, authority, and role (i.e., the centers were seen as desiring a greater service role).[34]

[31] Benson and Barber, op. cit., pp. 21–22.

[32] Ibid., p. 24.

[33] Troy V. McKelvey and William B. Harris, "The Board of Cooperative Educational Services Model," in Troy V. McKelvey (ed.), *Metropolitan School Organization: Basic Problems and Patterns,* vol. 1 (Berkeley: McCutchan, 1973), pp. 112–119.

[34] Jean E. Sanders, *Education Service Centers: Some Policy Implications for Massachusetts,* part I (Chelmsford, Mass.: Merrimack Education Center, May, 1977), (ED 163-580).

Pennsylvania, Washington, and Wisconsin illustrate total state restructuring. In July 1971, the sixty-seven county units existing in Pennsylvania were replaced by twenty-nine intermediate units, each with a governing board, executive officer, and staff. One unique feature of the Pennsylvania plan is that in Philadelphia and Pittsburgh, each designated as an intermediate unit, the boards of education serve a dual role—as a "local" board and as an "intermediate" board. As a result of legislation in 1965 and 1969, Washington eliminated its thirty-nine county units and replaced them with fourteen Intermediate School Districts; later the number was reduced to twelve, and eleven were larger than a single county. These units, each governed by an elected board, have both service and regulatory functions.[35] In 1965 Wisconsin abolished its seventy-two county intermediate units and replaced them with nineteen Cooperative Educational Service Agencies. Commenting on their mission, Belton noted that the structure "is designed not as an agency for providing services but to facilitate and coordinate the development of multidistrict service programs over which it exercises little control or direction. The agency is a catalyst."[36]

At this writing, well over half the states have three levels in their K–12 educational system—the state, the statutory regional district or service agency in some form, and the local districts. These include the New England states with supervisory unions and the states having educational cooperatives with a statutory basis. The supervisory union is usually considered to be different from the traditional intermediate districts in that it serves mainly to encourage cooperation among boards of the local districts that comprise the union, and the superintendent frequently works with the several local district boards. Generally, in those states that historically have had a relatively small number of local districts (e.g., some of the southeastern states), the statutory regional district does not exist.

In most of the states with regional units, there are regional governing boards. The majority of these are elected (either by popular vote or by local district boards). In spite of a decided trend to appoint the regional unit director or superintendent, it is still an elected position in some states. These regional districts are generally financed by some combination of federal, state, and local funds. In only a few states (e.g., Michigan, Oregon) do such districts have taxing authority.

In some states the regional unit has continued to exercise, with varying degrees of effectiveness, its traditional functions. However,

[35]Robert M. Isenberg, "States Continue to Reorganize Their Intermediate Units," *Planning and Changing*, 2 (July 1971), 63–64.
[36]John R. Belton, "Wisconsin's New District Educational Service Agencies," *Journal on State School Systems*, 1 (Winter 1968), 222.

as has been noted, since the move to reorganize these units there has been a decided shift from regulation to service. As suggested above, the exact nature of the services provided by regional districts varies widely (e.g., programs for exceptional children, computer services, curriculum planning, cooperative purchasing services, media services, specialized vocational-technical programs, research services). Isenberg emphasized that the services provided should supplement those provided by the local district. He suggested such services would tend to fall into five broad categories:

1. Programs which require a large pupil population base for effective and economical operation because the incidence of need is small. . . .

2. Programs which require a large pupil population base for effective and economical operation because the kinds of equipment and/or personnel they require are highly specialized, expensive, in short supply or infrequently used. . . .

3. Programs which require a larger area in order to get an appropriate and desirable social and economic mix. . . .

4. Programs which by nature must be regional or which relate to non-school-oriented regional agencies. . . .

5. Programs of research and those which might be considered experimental, pilot or of a demonstration type. . . .[37]

In spite of efforts to revitalize the regional unit in many states, there are still those who question the need for such districts. Basic to the position that the regional district is obsolete is the reorganization and enlargement of local districts and improved means of communication and transportation.

Those who see such units as desirable point to the fact that in spite of local district reorganization, about three-fourths of the local districts still have fewer than 2,500 pupils, and because of political considerations, sparse population, and the like, small districts are likely to remain in many areas of the nation. Given this condition, the regional district is the logical unit to provide essential services that these small, largely rural local districts would not or could not provide.

In more recent years some have advocated a regional unit as a vehicle for coping with many of the educational organization problems of metropolitan areas where there historically existed a local city school district and where, as the area grew, a number of local suburban districts surrounded the city. Such advocates frequently cite the educational arrangement of metropolitan Toronto, where there was a regional unit and six local districts.[38] This kind of two-tiered

[37] Isenberg, op. cit., 66–67.
[38] For a description of the Toronto plan see E. Brock Rideout, "The Supra-System Model: The Toronto Experience," in McKelvey (ed.), op. cit., pp. 167–187.

metropolitan arrangement is seen as making it possible to share resources over the broader base while enabling the smaller component local school districts to maintain their identity.

Stephens summarized well the perceived benefits of regional service agencies for both rural and urban settings:

1. Regional units can facilitate the provision to local districts of easily accessible, definite, and self-determined supplemental and supportive services of high quality.
2. Service units can contribute to the development and/or provision of state mandated programs and services to local districts in the event the local units are unable to do so.
3. Service units can contribute to the equalization of educational opportunities for all children by minimizing accidents of geography and neutralizing artificial barriers as determinants of the educational programs available.
4. Service units can promote the better utilization of known applications and stimulation of the search for new applications of cost-benefit and cost-effectiveness principles in the delivery of educational programs and services within the state school system.
5. Service units can contribute to the healthy interface between urban, suburban, and rural interests in the search for solutions to areawide educational issues.
6. Service units can contribute to the development of a statewide research, development, evaluation, and dissemination network and promotion of best resource use to foster the network once it is in place.
7. Service units can contribute to the establishment of a statewide network of resident change agents possessing both credibility in the eyes of their principal constituencies and legal mandates, where necessary. They can more readily implement the staffing and resources necessary to effect fundamental change in the state school system on a regular and planned basis.
8. Service units can substantially promote meaningful local school district involvement in state and regional planning and decision-making processes.[39]

If the position is taken that in some localities (e.g., metropolitan areas, sparsely populated areas) the regional unit is desirable primarily for programs and service—not control—then a number of specific questions must be examined. To illustrate: Should these units be governed by a board? If so, what should be the qualifications of board members, and how should they be selected? On what basis does one determine what programs and services will be provided by the regional district and the local districts? Will local districts be required to use the regional district's programs and services, or should they be

[39] E. Robert Stephens, *Regionalism: Past, Present and Future* (Arlington, Va.: American Association of School Administrators, 1977), pp. 8–9.

made available only on demand? Should the regional units be financed by the federal government, the state, tax levies throughout the area covered, mandated contributions from local districts, contracts with local districts for programs and services, or some combination of these methods? What should be the relationship between the regional unit and the system of area vocational-technical schools and/or community junior colleges within the state, if any?

When it reorganized its regional units in 1976, Minnesota provided an example of how one state dealt with most of these questions. The educational cooperative service units are governed by a board made up of persons selected from and by the governing boards of the participating local districts; local district use of a unit's services is voluntary; the units have no taxing power, and major funding comes from participating local districts in the form of a membership charge and a per pupil fee; the programs and services offered are limited to those requested by the participating districts and regional educational planning; and out-of-area school districts and nonpublic schools can become associate members of a cooperative service unit.[40]

In an era of declining enrollments in many local districts, the question of what programs and services the regional service agencies are to provide seems particularly critical. If the regional agencies are not subordinate to the local districts by some arrangement, such as in Minnesota, the regional programs may possibly be growing while many local districts are declining in enrollments and having financial problems. On the other hand, if the regional agency is limited to providing what the local districts want and are willing to finance, it has great difficulty in becoming an independent entity that some see as important for a viable regional district. As one experienced regional agency director stated it:

> If an ESA [Educational Service Agency] is totally a "tin cup" operation, it may be difficult for that ESA to take an independent stance on an issue, when at times an independent stance might be necessary to exert leadership.[41]

Voluntary Regional Units

In numerous areas local school districts and colleges have, for many years, banded together without the benefit of specific state statutes. The general purpose in voluntarily creating some form of edu-

[40]*Southwest and South Central Educational Cooperative Service Unit, Annual Report for 1979–80* (Marshall, Minn.: Southwest and South Central ECSU, April 1980), pp. 7–8, 17, (ED 186-199).

[41]Dennis Harken, "Emerging Organizational Patterns of Educational Service Agencies," paper presented at the American Association of School Administrators Annual Meeting, February 14–17, 1979, p. 2, (ED 173-923).

cational unit or consortium that encompasses more than a single local district has been to provide one or more programs and services that the local districts felt they could not provide alone. In its earliest form these units were simply an arrangement agreed upon by the leaders of a group of local districts without any external financing. For example, the local districts might create a structure to facilitate cooperative purchasing or to administer and support a high school jointly. One of the first voluntary cooperatives of this type was formed in the late 1920s in St. Louis County, Missouri. It began as an audiovisual cooperative, and in the early 1970s it provided an audiovisual center for 300 member schools, provided educational television services, engaged in research and development activities, and maintained liaison with area legislators on educational matters.[42]

Through Title III of the Elementary and Secondary Education Act of 1965, which provided funds for supplementary services, the federal government provided encouragement for the creation of such arrangements. A "key" for small districts to receive Title III funds was to enter into a cooperative arrangement with others. As a result, "Title III Centers" involving more than a single local district came into being all across the nation. Over one-half of the first 217 proposals approved under Title III were multidistrict projects.[43]

Some of these Title III–funded units had broadly defined purposes, whereas others had very limited purposes. In the typical Title III unit, one of the member local districts was the grantee and served as the fiscal agent. The unit had a board, often educators representing each member district, that determined policies and programs. The director and staff of the unit were legally employees of the local district serving as the fiscal agent. In a few states there was a concerted effort by state department personnel to provide a network of supplementary service units encompassing almost the entire area of the state.

Perhaps because of the impetus provided by the Title III units, another form of voluntary regional unit made its appearance in the late 1960s—the *educational cooperative*. In 1967 the encouragement and development of educational cooperatives became a major thrust of the Appalachian Educational Laboratory, a regional laboratory funded by Title IV of the Elementary and Secondary Education Act. One of the first educational cooperatives that became operational included seven local districts, the largest of which enrolled about 7,500 pupils, in a three-county area of eastern Tennessee. This cooperative was governed by a nine-member board consisting of the district superintendents, a staff member from a nearby state university, and a

[42] National School Public Relations Association, *Shared Services and Cooperatives* (Washington, D.C.: The Association, 1971), p. 24.
[43] Ibid., p. 2.

representative of the state department of education. (The last two board members were selected by the other board members.) The board employed a director and the programs and services provided by the cooperative were the result of priorities established by the board. As has been implied, in a very few states (e.g., Connecticut, Rhode Island) there is permissive legislation authorizing cooperatives;[44] thus, our statutory–voluntary scheme is not as discrete as it might appear.

Based on a nationwide survey of regional educational cooperation (including both statutory and voluntary units), Achilles and associates noted that cooperatives, such as those created under the auspices of the Appalachian Laboratory, provide more than service; they provide member districts autonomy and control and encourage local district development and improvement.[45]

A third type of voluntary unit is frequently referred to as a *study council*. Study councils have been in existence in many sectors of the nation for a number of years. In the early 1970s eighty-one such councils were reported to be in operation. Some of these covered large geographic areas, including one that was open on a nationwide basis.[46] Most frequently study councils involve one or more institutions of higher learning as well as local school districts and concentrate on in-service training, educational research, program development, and dissemination activities.

Voluntary educational consortia, such as the foregoing, have come into being throughout the nation, particularly since the Title III impetus. Often such units fail, particularly where external funding has provided some "start up" assistance and the external funds are withdrawn. Thus a key question becomes, "What are the conditions that are necessary for voluntary regional units to survive?" Based on a case study of two comparable regional organizations—one that was surviving and operating on local funds and one that had collapsed when federal funding from Title III ceased—Kimbrough identified eleven conditions that appeared to characterize the surviving and effective unit. These included some history of cooperation among the participants; decision making and responsibility assignment procedures that are specified, related to organizational purposes, and involve the participants; power and political sophistication on the part of key unit administrators and board members; attainable goals and flexible ways of working with different participant districts; close communication with the participants by the unit staff; prompt and efficacious unit staff response to participant district requests; an ac-

[44]Stephens, op. cit., p. 7.

[45]C. M. Achilles, L. W. Hughes, and J. R. Leonard, "Regionalism and Cooperation in Education," *Planning and Changing,* 4 (Winter 1974), 217–218.

[46]National School Public Relations Association, op. cit., p. 21.

tion orientation with visible productivity; and a perception among the participants that the unit is effective.[47]

In concluding the discussion we emphasize that the classification used to describe the voluntary regional units is arbitrary; the differences are often not as distinct as the descriptions might suggest. The important point is that there exists throughout the nation a variety of arrangements that have been created by local district personnel to serve the needs they deem to be important. Unlike many of the statutory regional units, these units exercise no controls over the local districts, but rather, are controlled by the local districts.

ACTIVITIES/QUESTIONS FOR FURTHER STUDY

1. Select a nearby local school district and determine its fiscal powers and relationship to municipal government; method of selection, compensation, and powers of the school board; internal organization of the central office; nature of decentralization (if any); and relationship to the regional educational agency (if any).

2. Visit an alternative school or an adopt-a-school program. What are its purposes and activities? How different is it from other schools with which you are familiar? What do the pupils, teachers, and building administrators believe to be the future of the school?

3. Does your state have statutory regional educational agencies? If so, how are they governed and financed? What services do they provide and on what basis do local school districts avail themselves of the services? What are the issues, if any, about these units? If your state does not have statutory regional units, what types of voluntary units exist in your area? Is there any move to establish statutory units?

SUGGESTED READINGS

"Alternative Schools: A Question of Choice," *Phi Delta Kappan,* 62 (April 1981), 551–573.

BENSON, CHARLES W., and R. JERRY BARBER. *Intermediate Educational Units and Their Promise for Rural Education.* Austin, Texas: National Educational Laboratory Publishers, Inc., March 1974 (ED 088632).

CAMPBELL, ROALD F., et al. *The Organization and Control of American Schools,* 4th ed. Columbus, Ohio: Charles E. Merrill Publishers, 1980, Chapters 4–6, 8–10.

CHASE, FRANCIS S. "The Regeneration of Public Education in Our Cities," *Phi Delta Kappan,* 60 (January 1979), 353–356.

EDWARDS, NEWTON. *The Courts and the Public Schools,* 3rd ed. Chicago: University of Chicago Press, 1971, Chapters 4–8.

ERICKSON, DONALD A., and THEODORE L. RELLER (eds.). *The Principal in Metropolitan Schools.* Berkeley: McCutchan Publishing Corp., 1979.

[47]Ralph Kimbrough, "Lessons from the Survival and Death of Regional Educational Organizations," *Planning and Changing,* 10 (Spring 1979), 37–41.

HUDGINS, H. C., JR., and RICHARD S. VACCA. *Law and Education: Contemporary Issues and Court Decisions.* Charlottesville, Va.: The Michie Company, 1979, Chapters 3, 4, 6.

JANSSEN, K. C. COLE. *Matters of Choice.* New York: The Ford Foundation, September 1974.

MORPHET, EDGAR L., ROE L. JOHNS, and THEODORE L. RELLER. *Educational Organization and Administration,* 4th ed. Englewood Cliffs, N.J.: Prentice-Hall, Inc., 1982, Chapters 12–14.

ORNSTEIN, ALLAN C. "Decentralization and Community Participation Policy of Big School Systems," *Phi Delta Kappan,* 62 (December 1980), 255–257.

ROE, WILLIAM H., and THELBERT L. DRAKE. *The Principalship,* 2nd ed. New York: Macmillan Publishing Co., Inc., 1980, Chapters 3, 5, 9.

STEPHENS, E. ROBERT. *Regionalism: Past, Present and Future.* Arlington, Va.: American Association of School Administrators, 1977.

STOOPS, EMERY, MAX RAFFERTY, and RUSSELL E. JOHNSON. *Handbook of Educational Administration: A Guide for the Practitioner,* 2nd ed. Boston: Allyn & Bacon, Inc., 1981, Chapters 4–5.

6

Major Issues and Alternatives in the Formal Arrangements for Education

In THE PRECEDING three chapters numerous specific organizational issues related to each governmental level were identified and amplified. Many people feel that the federal courts have usurped the prerogatives of the legislative and executive branches of government at all levels. The categorical-aid approach to funding education has been seen as serving worthy purposes. Yet the critics of categorical federal aid have been legion. As discussed previously, the Congress moved slightly in 1981 toward block grants for small programs. The diffusion of the educational effort among many federal agencies has long been questioned. Yet with the considerable concentration of the federal educational effort accompanying the creation of the United States Department of Education came increased concern about federal executive branch control.

Questions have been raised regarding the method of selection and qualifications of state board members and the chief state school officer. The role and nature of service provided by the state education department has been a recurring concern. A variety of problems associated with state financial plans for education has been identified. Turning to problems and issues of regional and local school districts, we have noted questions about the selection and qualifications of school board members and chief executives. The size of school districts is a continuing issue, and the need for regional educational agencies is debated frequently. How to provide programs and services for a diverse clientele and broaden participation in local educational decision making are perplexing questions.

Such issues arise from value differences about the functions of societal institutions and how they are to be controlled and supported. For example, advocates of basic education feel that education has been used inappropriately to further broad social goals, whereas liberal-minded persons feel that education has not carried a fair share of social change. Many persons (e.g., leaders of minority groups) believe that the educational systems are no longer run by the people, but have been coopted by massive bureaucracies. During the 1960s a few leaders in the U.S. Office of Education expressed the opinion that a national system of education would enhance efficiency and effectiveness. Nearly all educational leaders believe that it is in the best interests of education to take steps to assure the separation of education from the "hurly-burly" of general government. On the other hand, some authorities of public administration believe that education is not so unique that a "fourth branch of government" is needed. Finally, the question of how to pay for education will arouse a spirited debate at almost any gathering of civic and governmental leaders.

Within this context, this chapter focuses upon four overarching and interrelated questions about formal arrangements for education: (1) How shall the state organize for educational governance? (2) How shall education at the district level be organized? (3) Who shall have the formal power in governing education? (4) How can the educational enterprise cope successfully in a demand-for-quality and no-growth era? The first three questions have persisted for a number of years. The fourth question is of more recent origin. It began to come into focus in the mid-1970s with the decline in enrollments in many public educational institutions, with the increasing cost of education, and with public skepticism about the quality of education being provided by public schools, colleges, and universities.

State Educational Organization Alternatives

What should be the relationship between the chief state school officer and the state legislature? The governor? How much coordination is needed among the different levels of schooling? Between education and other state agencies? How much control should the bureaucrats have? In the paragraphs that follow, three basic alternatives are presented for the state governance of public education. Each basic model provides a somewhat different response to questions such as these. They are not presented as ideals, nor do they represent the spectrum of options. They are conventional bureaucratic structures. These options come from the previously discussed Educational Governance Project under the direction of Campbell and Mazzoni.[1] Table 6-1 presents the essential details of the basic models.

A Strong Executive Model

The secretary of education model shown in Table 6-1 is an example of a centralized-executive approach, which maximizes the power of the governor and the chief state school officer (CSSO). As can be seen from the table, in this model the governor appoints both the CSSO (the secretary of education) and the state board of education, with the CSSO serving at the pleasure of the governor. The CSSO is the chief executive of the state board, and together they have formal authority over the total public education and cultural effort of the state. The CSSO has status as a member of the state cabinet and can provide linkage with other general governmental services as well as to the governor and legislature.

This model provides for close ties between educational and general government and maximizes opportunity for gubernatorial accountability. Coordination among different levels of education is simple in that there is a single executive and "superboard." Lay board control is minimized, and educational executive and general governmental executive control is maximized. Breadth of participation in decision making is limited. Education is treated as another major unit of state government, and as such, it is in the middle ring of state governmental politics.

The model has not been popular among educators and other political leaders. As a part of the Educational Governance Project, 465 persons who were seen as reasonably representative of the educational and political leadership of the fifty states were asked to react to eight alternatives relative to organizing for state educational governance. Two of the models were similar to the secretary of education model in that they were centralized-executive models. Only about 10 percent of these persons ranked either of these models as the one most preferred, and only about one-fourth found them to be acceptable.[2] Also, at this writing, only one state (Pennsylvania) uses such a highly centralized model. (In Tennessee the governor appoints the CSSO and the state board of education; however, all of the colleges and universities of the state are not under the jurisdiction of the state board.)

---

[1] Roald F. Campbell and Tim L. Mazzoni, Jr., *State Governance Models for the Public Schools* (Columbus, Ohio: The Educational Governance Project, Ohio State University, 1974), pp. 181–190.
[2] Ibid., p. 184.

Table 6-1. Three Different Models for State Governance of the Public Schools

	Secretary of Education Model	Elected State Board Model	Governor-Appointed Authoritative Board Model
Structural Arrangement			
	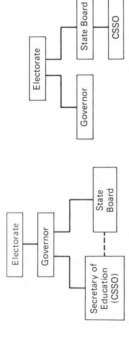		
Key authority relationships	The Secretary of Education is an appointed member of the Governor's Cabinet. The Secretary exercises the prerogatives of the CSSO and the responsibilities of this office embrace the full range of state educational and cultural programs, as well as K–12 schools. The Secretary is also chief executive authority for a Governor-appointed State Board, a body that does have, by statute, some policy-making authority.	The State Education Agency has a semiautonomous governmental status. It is governed by a State Board whose members achieve office through election. The Board appoints the CSSO to serve as its chief executive. The State Board has both constitutional and statutory authority, and has considerable policy-making authority for K–12 and vocational education, but not for higher education.	While the State Education Agency does have a special governmental status, there is direct linkage to the Governor through his appointment, subject to legislative approval, of Board members. They, in turn, select the CSSO who serves as the Board's chief executive. The State Board has both constitutional and statutory foundation, and has considerable policy-making authority for K–12 and vocational education, but not for higher education.

State board characteristics			
Selection	Appointed by the Governor	Elected from districts on either partisan or non-partisan ballot	Appointed by the Governor, subject to confirmation by the Legislature
Term of office Size Service/compensation	4 years; overlapping Medium (7–11) Part-time; compensation for expenses and small per diem allowance	4 years; overlapping Large (12–15) Part-time but more Board service (e.g., several meetings per month) than usual; expenses plus attractive per diem	4 years; overlapping Medium (7–11) Part-time; compensation for expenses and small per diem allowance
Staff information resources	Department for Research, Planning and Evaluation in the Governor's Office, as well as such units in the State Department of Education	Small staff directly responsible to Board in addition to staff resources provided by the State Department of Education	Staff resources made available by the State Department of Education
CSSO characteristics			
Authority	Statutory authority for Cabinet-level responsibilities and CSSO administrative duties; directly responsible to Governor	Statutory authority for administrative duties; directly responsible to the State Board	Statutory authority for administrative duties; directly responsible to the State Board
Selection	Appointed by the Governor	Appointed by the State Board	Appointed by the State Board
Statutory qualifications	None	None	Professional educator
Term in office Compensation	Pleasure of the Governor Comparable to those of other Cabinet positions with similar responsibilities	4-year contract; renewable Comparable to those paid local school superintendents in the largest districts	4-year contract; renewable Comparable to those paid local school superintendents in the largest districts

Table 6-1. Three Different Models for State Governance of the Public Schools (*Cont.*)

	Secretary of Education Model	Elected State Board Model	Governor-Appointed Authoritative Board Model
Scope of authority			
Higher education	Included under the authority of the Secretary and State Board	Not included under State Board jurisdiction; a separate board for higher education	Not included under State Board jurisdiction; a separate board for higher education
Vocational education	Included under the authority of the Secretary and State Board	Included under the authority of the State Board	Included under the authority of the State Board
Preparation/teacher certification	Included under the authority of the Secretary and State Board	Included under the authority of the State Board	Included under the authority of the State Board
SEA-general governance linkages			
SEA-state planning agency	To Agency through Cabinet structure, as well as informal liaison	Informal liaison only	Informal liaison only
Linkages to governor/legislature	To Governor through Cabinet structure	Through formally established Governor's Advisory Council on Education	Informal relationships and legal requirement for State Board/CSSO to report to Governor/Legislature

Source: Roald F. Campbell and Tim L. Mazzoni, Jr., *State Governance Models for Public Schools* (Columbus, Ohio: The Educational Governance Project, Ohio State University, 1974), pp. 187–188.

As do the other two models presented, the secretary of education model assumes the presence of local school districts or regional and local districts. However, the model could lend itself to a state structure in which school districts were eliminated. To illustrate, if the aim were to maximize professional control and create an integrated hierarchy of authority, the state could be divided into geographic regions containing 100,000 to 200,000 pupils each, and each region could be divided into areas of 20,000 to 25,000 pupils each. The secretary could appoint a regional superintendent for each region, and the regional superintendent, in turn, could be empowered to appoint area superintendents. The office of the regional superintendent could provide supervision and a variety of support services, including direct instruction in high-cost areas. The area units would be charged with conducting most of the instruction. Financing would be from the state and federal levels and all employment would be by the state. Obviously, if the model were extended in this manner, the formal power of the state would be greatly enhanced, and local lay participation would be nil. However, if some lay participation was desired, regional and area boards could be created and roles defined.

This model features such time-honored administration notions as efficiency in design, potential for maximum coordination, and reliance on technical competency. On the other hand, its lack of popularity in practice can probably be attributed to enhancing the power of the governor and CSSO at the expense of the state board of education, the concern that education will not be given adequate attention if it is so closely aligned with general state government, and the fear that education will become too enmeshed in gubernatorial partisan politics.

A Strong State Board Model

The strong state board of education model provides for a rather autonomous state educational organization. As shown in Table 6-1, the state board is elected by the people from geographic sectors of the state, either in a partisan or nonpartisan election. The state board has the power to appoint the chief state school officer and that person is directly answerable to the state board. The state board has jurisdiction over K–12 schools and vocational education, with higher education being under a separate board. No formal linkages are provided to ensure coordination with other state services, yet formal linkage to the governor is provided by means of a governor's advisory council on education. The role of the state board is further enhanced by provisions for a small staff answerable directly to the board and provisions for sufficient per diem and expense funds for frequent meetings.

Within the context of conventional thinking, this option represents the other end of the continuum from the secretary of education model. Lay participation is enhanced in that the voters choose the board, and the board has a power base just as do the governor and members of the legislature. The professional leadership is subordinate to the lay board. Lay participation is also enhanced in that another board, presumably composed of lay persons, is responsible for higher education. Yet this could create some problem in total educational planning. (The advisory council could alleviate some of the problems.) In terms of the balance of power between educational and general government, educational government is dominant. If a nonpartisan election were used, chances are that educational politics would be somewhat separated from general government politics. If the desire were to enhance the chances of persons representative of emerging sectors of interest to be elected to the state board, some form of party caucus arrangement could be used to encourage and nominate such persons, and the party machinery could be used to provide support.

As noted in Chapter 4, several states had elected state boards and board-appointed chief state school officers (e.g., Nebraska, New Mexico). Thus it is not too surprising that a considerable segment of the Educational Governance Project respondents favored this model. About 22 percent preferred a nonpartisan-elected board version and about 4 percent a partisan-elected board version.[3]

A modification of this model would be to elect the CSSO as well as the board. This would provide more voter control and enhance the power base of the CSSO, yet many observers would fear problems in unity of command (e.g., between the board and CSSO).

A Middle-of-the-Road Model

The governor-appointed authoritative board model shown in Table 6-1 is representative of a middle-of-the-road approach to state educational governance. As the table shows, in this model the governor appoints the state board of education, subject to confirmation by the legislature. The state board appoints the CSSO, who is directly responsible to it. The state board has jurisdiction over K–12 schools and vocational education, but not higher education, which is under the supervision of a separate board. This creates the potential for coordination problems.

There is a degree of autonomy for educational governance in that the lay board is granted policy-making authority. However, because the board is appointed by the governor, there is not the independence provided in the elected-board model. Because the board is appointed by the governor with the legislature confirming, it would seem that

[3] Ibid., p. 185.

there would be excellent linkage among the branches of general state government. However, Campbell and Mazzoni offered this comment:

> That appointment by the governor and access to that official were not related for the ten state boards we examined is an unexpected finding. Persons on the governor's staff were widely perceived by both board members and outside observers as the key influentials in recommending nominees to the chief executive for board appointment. Once the appointment had been made, however, the governor traditionally took a "hands off" policy toward the state board, a reflection undoubtedly of its lack of saliency to him or the risks involved in challenging the societal norm that the schools should be kept free of "politics." Yet just as the governor did not seek to exert much influence in state board affairs, so the members of this body had little access to his office. As one board member put it, "we go our separate ways after appointment." [4]

Nevertheless, in the Educational Governance Project this model got more support than any other reviewed. Also, this model, or some slight variation of it, was the prevailing model among the fifty states.

The model avoids the high level of centralization found in the secretary of education model. Lay participation could be further enhanced in this model if a blue-ribbon nominating committee were used to present a slate of names from which the governor made state board of education appointments.

Organizational Alternatives at the School District Level

As indicated in Chapter 5, the patterns of organizing local and regional school districts are many. However, the patterns used in nearly all the regional units and the local districts with under 25,000 to 30,000 pupils represented some variation of a centralized bureaucratic model. An illustrative local district model of this type was shown as Figure 5-1; thus it will not be repeated in this discussion of alternatives for district organization. In the paragraphs that follow, four basic options are presented. One of these includes both local and regional arrangements. Three are conventional and adaptations of them exist. One is nonconventional. All are presented to stimulate discussion about one of the more perplexing issues in the field of educational administration—school district organization. As was the case with the state options, the models are not original; they represent, with some modifications, models created by Andes, Johns, and Kim-

[4] Ibid., p. 108.

brough as a part of a developmental study of alternative models for large school districts.[5]

Two Decentralized Models

Figure 6-1 shows a fairly conventional option for local school district organization, with an elected school board and a board-appointed superintendent. It is a centralized model insofar as administrative, business, and personnel services are handled centrally and individual school principals report directly to the superintendent. Formal lay participation in major decision making is limited to the

[5]John O. Andes, Roe L. Johns, and Ralph B. Kimbrough, *Changes in Organizational Structures of Large School Systems with Special Reference to Problems of Teacher Militancy and Organizational Conflict,* Final Report, U.S. Office of Education Project No. 8-0254 (Gainesville, Fla.: University of Florida, March 1971), pp. 139–145, 157–169.

Figure 6-1.   Instructional-services-decentralization model.

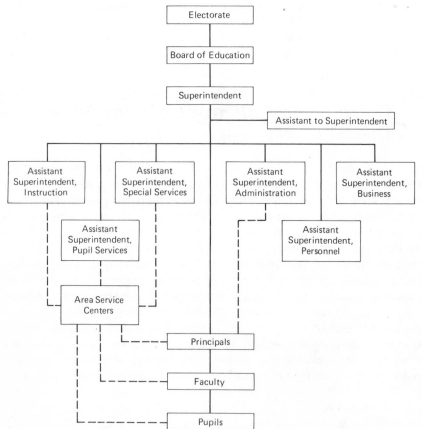

board of education. Thus a large school district employing this model would be relying heavily on its professional staff to make major decisions. No provisions are made for formal ties with the municipal governments within the territory served.

The major distinctive feature of the model is the provision for placing instructional services, special services, and pupil services in closer proximity to the operating units—the schools. Geographic areas for these services would be defined, and the majority of the coordinators and resource specialists in these service units would be housed in a facility within the geographic area served. Each regional service center would be supervised by a single director. The central office staff of the instructional, pupil service, and special service units would be minimal and their role would be to support the geographic area centers and to do needed districtwide instructional planning and development. In sum, this model is intended to make frequently used instructional and pupil services more readily available to teachers and pupils.

Perhaps the major strength of this model is that it provides the personnel in the local schools with more autonomy. In a school district that encompasses a large geographic area, this may be significant. Its major shortcomings are the high probability of role conflicts between personnel in the central office and the area service centers and perhaps the inability to make maximum use of some subject area specialists. For example, if each area is not of sufficient size to make full use of a resource person in a low-demand field, either the person is not fully utilized, the area has no such resource person, or the area shares such a person with another area.

Figure 6-2 shows a model that is similar to the instructional-services-decentralized model. The difference is the extent of decentralization. In the area-decentralized model the superintendent would maintain a minimal central staff. The central office would be expected to provide leadership in districtwide planning and development and make available high-cost, low-demand services (e.g., bulk purchasing, management information, technical programs). The majority of the supporting services and personnel would be located in geographic area offices. Each of the geographic areas would be under the direction of an area superintendent who would have administrative authority for the area and, within the guidelines established by the central board, would make decisions regarding allocation of funds, instructional programs and services, personnel, facilities, and so on. The model shown provides for four geographic areas, the number that would probably be employed in a district of 50,000 to 75,000 pupils. Assuming the use of this option in a school district of such size, each of the areas would be of sufficient size to utilize, with reasonable effectiveness, the support personnel assigned to the area offices. Where

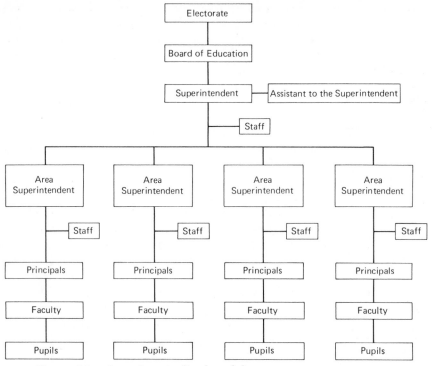

Figure 6-2. Area-decentralized model.

models of this type have been used, there have been problems in defining the role of central and area office personnel.

This model could be adapted to provide for elected area (i.e., community, local) school boards with either formal authority or advisory power. If such an adaptation were to be used, the role conflicts between the central and area levels would probably become more numerous. For example, based on her evaluation of three demonstration districts created in New York City in the 1960s, Gittell concluded that the "local" boards were determined not to be controlled by the central office on what they considered to be critical policy issues.[6] The area boards would obviously enhance lay participation. However, if they were to be advisory only, and the formal authority remained with the central board and professional staffs, the question would still remain of what happens when the advice and counsel of the area board is not sought or followed.

If the area boards are granted formal authority in areas such as program and personnel, their power is certainly enhanced. However,

[6]Marilyn Gittell et al., *Local Control: Three Demonstration School Districts in New York City* (New York: Praeger, 1972), p. 132.

this may not establish community control. With reference to such boards in Detroit and New York, LaNoue and Smith said the boards could not fully exercise their power because of budget restrictions, union contracts, and internal conflict.[7] Furthermore, there is some evidence to suggest that teachers fear the power of area boards because they may become a disruptive element in the bargaining process. Based on their study of decentralization in five major cities, LaNoue and Smith concluded that teachers tended to back decentralization in principle, while being suspicious of it in practice, and local boards, being distrustful of professional educators, have tended to be more resistant to union demands than the district-level officials.[8]

Because the two decentralized models focus on arrangements internal to a school district, the impact on the existing arrangements among local, state, and federal levels and between general and educational government is nil. Of course, if the area board adaptation were used and formal authority were granted area boards, the existing lay–professional arrangements would be affected; otherwise, the lay–professional balance really would not be disturbed.

An Urban Regional Agency–Local District Model

Shown as Figure 6-3 is a MESA (metropolitan education service agency) model that uses two levels of educational governance. It is most appropriate to an urban area as an alternative to a single school district or several totally separate districts. It represents an effort to gain the advantage of a metropolitan-area tax base for schools and centralization of high-cost educational programs and support services without the complexities of a single large district.

The operating local districts would have elected boards of education, and each operating district board would elect its representative to the MESA board. If the local districts were of roughly the same size, each would have one representative on the regional board. However, if there was considerable variation, representation could be proportional. For example, Figure 6-3 shows six operating local districts. Assume that five of these local districts had a pupil population in the 20,000 to 25,000 range and the sixth had 50,000, the latter district board could select two representatives to the seven-member MESA board. The MESA board would appoint the MESA superintendent, and each operating local district board would appoint its own superintendent.

Each local district board would depend upon MESA, and higher levels, for financing. Thus collective bargaining would be two-tiered.

[7] George R. LaNoue and Bruce L. R. Smith, *The Politics of School Decentralization* (Lexington, Mass.: Lexington, Heath, 1973), p. 227.

[8] Ibid., pp. 229–233.

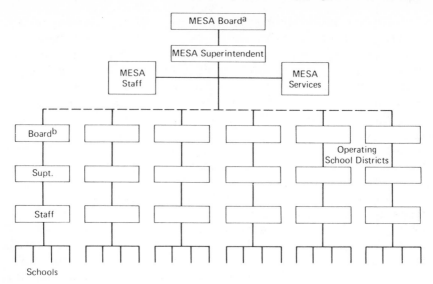

aSelected from among operating
district boards or elected by voters.

bElected by voters.

Figure 6-3. Metropolitan educational service agency model.

The basic salary and fringe-benefits package would be negotiated by MESA and other items with the individual districts. Each local district would be legally responsible for developing, maintaining, and evaluating an educational program to meet the needs of the people of the district. MESA would provide such services as educational television, personnel recruitment, computer services, and high-cost, limited-demand instructional programs. The granting of financial powers to the regional unit and not to the local units is the most unconventional aspect of this model. Yet, unless such power resides with the MESA board the advantage of the metropolitan-area tax base is lost.

If this model were to be instituted in an urban area where there was a large-city district surrounded by a number of suburban districts, it could be used in combination with a decentralized model internal to the city district. The model does not assume that each of the local districts will be similarly organized or even that each will be representative of a centralized bureaucracy.

Even though in a formal sense (except for the shifting of financing power) the MESA model may not have a direct impact on existing intergovernmental arrangements, an educational agency of this magnitude has numerous power resources. In most states there would be few such units and, given the proportion of the state's student population contained within such units, the state education agency, as well as municipal and federal education officials, would be prone to listen when representatives of the MESA unit spoke. When compared to the alternative of a single district for the area encompassed, the MESA model provides for considerably more formal lay control of schools.

A Model to Enhance Coordination Among Human Service Agencies

In recent years considerable concern has been expressed that school districts tend to operate in a manner that isolates them from the other human service agencies of the community. This concern is most often, but not exclusively, expressed in urban areas. The CCRC (coordinated community resources corporation) model, which to our knowledge is untested, is one response to that concern. The model is based on the following assumptions: (1) with the rising specialization of education, social work, and other helping professions, communication and articulation of these services are severely handicapped; (2) there is a relationship between the educational services provided by the school, educational services provided by other community agencies, and the various service functions provided by other community agencies; (3) there is a need for increased coordination and linkage among these services; (4) an organizational model that includes health, educational, and welfare services within a single structure will help provide the needed coordination and linkage.

The CCRC would be an organization composed of all health, education, and welfare agencies in the area served. These include the school system, the recreation department, the library and other media resource centers, the welfare department, the medical and dental health organizations, and rehabilitation units. The organizational chart for the central administrative structure is represented in Figure 6-4.

The board of directors of the corporation would be elected by the voters of the area served. With assistance from higher governmental levels, it would have the financial powers necessary to support the services provided and would have policy-making and related powers similar to a board of education. The board would select the chief executive of the corporation, who, in turn, would be directly responsible to the board for the total array of human services.

The chief executive would select the central staff and the directors of the six divisions and nominate members of the chief executive's advisory board. To provide a link with general government, actual appointment to this advisory board could be by a municipal body or official (e.g., the mayor). The advisory board would work directly with the chief executive and the six division directors. Within the policies, guidelines, and so on, provided, each division director would

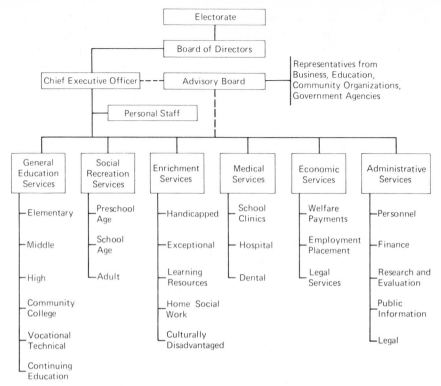

Figure 6-4. Coordinated community resources corporation, central administration.

be responsible for organizing, staffing, and operating their assigned programs. The administrative services division exists to provide support to the other divisions.

If desired, the corporation could be decentralized by use of geographic areas or regions with lay boards and administrators. The geographic areas could consist of the area served by a senior high school and its feeder schools (i.e., 6,000 to 10,000 pupils). The area administrator, who would be appointed by and directly responsible to the chief executive of the corporation, would have a support staff of specialists in the several fields of service (e.g., medical–dental, social, economic). These persons would assist in providing the several services for children and adults through the school centers, which would remain open year-round and for an extended day (e.g., sixteen hours). Lay participation in each geographic area would be provided by an elected advisory board that would work directly with the area administrator in planning programs and services of particular interest to the people of the area.

The CCRC model represents a break with most existing organizations for education and also represents an extension of the school as a human service center notion, which was discussed in Chapter 5. It creates a more complex structure than exists now in most localities. It does not have the "clean" integrated hierarchy of authority of the classical bureaucracy, as is discussed in Chapter 8.

For example, advisory boards provide an "interested party" outside of the chain of command, and if they were decentralized on an area basis, the specialists would be subject to influence from both the area administrator and the head of their respective division (e.g., economic services). Such an organization would provide a bloc for dealing with higher levels of government. With the array of human services included in one structure, it would no longer be education versus general government, but human services versus highways, utilities, public protection, and other services.

To institute such a model would require a considerable revision in the legal structure of most states. It runs counter to the existing norms in many of the agencies currently providing these services. For example, it is in conflict with the notion of education as a unique function.

Balance of Formal Power in Educational Governance

The balance-of-power question is a many-faceted issue relating to the distribution of formal power or authority over the educational enterprise. We have touched on the question in many ways previously. In this section, attention is given to four aspects of the issue: (1) among federal, state, and local levels; (2) between general government and educational government; (3) between the laity and professional educators; and (4) between the traditional sectors of influence and those emerging blocs seeking influence. The stance assumed in regard to these balances is going to affect the alternatives one is willing to consider relative to state organization for education, district organization for schools, and educational financing schemes. Thus the reader may want to review the state and local organization options presented and the financing alternatives discussed in Chapter 4 within the context of these four dimensions of the issue.

Relative Power Among Levels of Government

One key to exploring the question of the relative influence of federal, state, and local government is to examine the extent to which education should be the primary instrument for the implementation of broad economic, political, and social policies. Since World War II the federal government has made a commitment to a variety of such policies. These include elimination of racial segregation, full employment for those in the work force, conservation of our natural resources, elimination of the social and intellectual handicaps imposed by cultural and economic deprivation, protection of the environment, reduction in traffic fatalities, energy conservation, and a reduction in alcohol and drug abuse. By means of an array of programs (e.g., compensatory education, vocational training, driver training, special units on drugs, counseling services, adult education) and some organizational restructuring (e.g., use of pairing and clustering arrangements instead of neighborhood schools), education has played a major role in efforts to implement each of these policies.

It is one thing to accept the validity of these policies and another to assume that education, as a single societal institution, should be a primary instrument of implementation. If one assumes that education should serve the larger society as a basic instrument to implement broad-scale national policies, then one could argue that the federal government should assume an even more dominant role in governing education. The logic is that only through strong national governance can we achieve the unity of direction and ordering of priorities necessary to implement policies fully.

Those who advocate a greater measure of federal and state power frequently point to population mobility and the "present condition" of education, and they often note that, even though the states have the constitutional power, they have in the past delegated much of this to local school districts and semiautonomous boards for higher education institutions. Some critics blame local control for what they feel are serious limitations of education. In sum, those who feel that federal and/or state control is the appropriate option, argue, in one form or another, that education is so central to the general welfare it can no longer be left to local decision making.

At the other extreme, those who advocate a return to greater local control can be persuasive. One line of reasoning is that the whole case for a greater federal influence is based on a false premise: that the federal government can be more effective than lower levels of government. A Pennsylvania legislator expressed the antifederal premise when he noted in regard to revenue sharing:

> Anytime the federal government becomes involved in a particular situation, naturally the giant federal bureaucracy enters the picture. This can only hinder the efficiency of any program . . . when taxes are sent to collect, only about half gets sent back. The rest is swallowed up in the bureaucratic mire.[9]

[9] Max H. Homer, "Legislator's Warning: Beware of the Feds," *Compact*, 7 (February/March 1973), 19.

Local control proponents also point out that public education in our nation was built from a grass-roots base. Our many national accomplishments in the economic, political, and social realms are often noted. Advocates of local control contend that we have developed the highest standard of living (in a physical sense) in the world; our political institutions are relatively stable; and, in spite of many problems, our social accomplishments are many. Also, local control advocates contend that the closer education is to the people, the greater their participation will be. Anything so critical to the daily lives of people should be controlled by those nearest the issues.

In response to the national policy notion and mobility statistics, counterarguments are offered. First, if the policy in question is in the best interest of the nation, unity can be more effectively achieved on a voluntary basis. Second, much of our mobility occurs within a narrow geographic area (e.g., a metropolitan area).

The cause of more state power also has proponents. The Tenth Amendment and state constitutional provisions are noted. Court decisions, such as the *Serrano* and *Rodriguez* cases relating to equality of fiscal support within a state, can be offered as placing the legal responsibility for schools with the states rather than the federal government. In advancing the cause of the state rather than the local units, mention is frequently made not only of the state's legal power, but of the state's taxing power and base. A few persons believe that local school districts should be abolished in favor of a "pure" state system. They cite illustrations of state systems working in other nations and in Hawaii. Further, many point to the spread of collective bargaining and suggest that in the final analysis this should be done with the state (i.e., the legislature).

There are many options within the extremes mentioned. We suspect most persons favor some balanced federal–state–local partnership. However, there may be differences of opinion on the role of each partner. One viewpoint holds that the federal level must (1) participate significantly in the general or large block, not categorical, support of education because of the disparities in wealth and taxing power among the states; (2) promote education's role in the achievement of national policies; (3) ensure that the constitutional rights of pupils and school employees are protected; and (4) assume leadership in an educational research-and-development thrust that generates broadly applicable knowledge. The state should (1) ensure fiscal equality and a basic educational program among the schools of the state; (2) see that there is a structure and that support exists for higher education; (3) provide leadership in state educational planning and goal setting; (4) ensure that school districts of adequate size provide a broad range of educational opportunities; and (5) provide either directly or through

regional units a wide array of support services. Within this framework, local officials should be free to develop educational policies and
be charged with the day-to-day operation of educational programs.

Educational Government Versus General Government

The issue of general government powers versus educational government powers has been growing for several years. The activities of
the federal judiciary, the governor in some states, the legislature in
many states, and so on, have resulted in numerous educational leaders viewing general government as seriously encroaching upon the
prerogatives of those charged with the governance of education.

Those who feel that the historic prerogatives of educational government must be maintained and reemphasized base their position
on the uniqueness of education. The reasoning is that the scope of
education, its nearness to the daily lives of people, and its opportunity
for influence on young people demands that it be governed differently
from other governmental services and insulated from the politics of
general government.

Generally, those who espouse a strong educational government
do not question the need for the judiciary to protect the rights of individuals or for the legislative branch to fulfill its legal mandate.
Rather they would prefer an independent chief state school officer and
board of education, minimum municipal controls over schools, fiscal
independence for local school boards, and the like. They expect general government agencies to refrain from interfering in matters that
are the prerogatives of school boards and administrators. There is re-
sentment of the idea that

> [t]he policy-making role of local school boards is modified by the capac-
> ity of the courts to examine educational issues and adopt positions which
> effectively preempt the board's policies on these matters. Through fed-
> eral and state legislation, court decisions, and local opinions, the law
> clearly denies the mythology that says "educational policy making is
> the function of the local school board."[10]

Those who believe that the balance should be shifted more to
general government frequently cite the opportunity to improve accountability, economy, and efficiency in the educational system if it
is treated like any other department of government. Improved coordination with other government services is noted. Also cited are the
administrative axioms of unity of command and departmentalism that
are described in detail in Chapter 8. At the state level the ultimate
responsibility of the governor and legislature is noted. Persons opting

---

[10]William R. Hazard, *Education and the Law,* 2nd ed. (New York: The Free
Press, 1978), p. 18.

for closer ties between educational and general government are likely to argue for governor- and/or legislature-appointed chief state school officers and board members, extensive direction by the legislative branch, more control by the general executive branch, education as a department of municipal government, fiscal dependence, and so on. Also, some argue that the municipal governing bodies or officials (e.g., city council, county commission, mayor) should appoint district superintendents and/or school boards. The extreme option would be to eliminate the local school board, have the municipal governing body handle educational affairs as it does other matters of municipal government, and replace the district superintendent with a head of the department of education.

Lay Versus Professional Control

As discussed previously, the education enterprise of our nation has its origin in grass-roots lay control, and educational administration, as a field requiring specialized training and knowledge, is of recent origin. Furthermore, as is discussed in Chapter 8, traditional administrative thought held that policy development and execution were to be separated. For these reasons, among others, the concept of lay control by means of boards at various levels, citizens' committees, and legislative power is ingrained in the thinking of most people. Yet as we have noted, many fear that traditional lay control has eroded in recent decades. As was noted, expanded judicial and legislative activity are frequently mentioned as affecting the traditional power of school boards and influence of citizens' committees. However, one hears frequently that professional educators have become both the policy makers and the executors of policy. The apparent increase in the number of educators being seated in state legislatures, municipal governing bodies, state boards of education, and, in a few instances, on local boards of education is noted. The presence of large districts under a single board and state boards of education with broad jurisdiction are seen as devices for enhancing professional control. The reasoning is that no single lay body can give sufficient attention to so vast an educational operation; thus the professionals are free both to make and to carry out policy. The power of teachers and other educational employees, expressed through collective bargaining, is perceived as seriously limiting lay boards in exercising any meaningful control.

Those who feel that professional educators constitute a serious threat to lay power are likely to support a variety of mechanisms that are seen as promoting lay influence and curtailing the professionals. These may include (1) creation of smaller school districts in urban areas, (2) establishment of subdistrict-level lay boards (e.g., community boards, area boards, school councils), (3) several state-level boards of education (each with a limited scope of jurisdiction), (4) legal restrictions on the political activities of educators (e.g., laws prohibiting educators from serving on state boards of education), (5) elected local district superintendents and chief state school officers, and (6) laws severely restricting the scope of collective bargaining.

At the other extreme, one can find a few advocates for abolishing the most basic form of lay control over schools—the local school district with its lay board. Some who assume the local board and district are passé would support a state system in which a chief state school officer would be responsible for organizing the state into manageable units, appointing school executives, and the like. Or they might choose to make schools a department of municipal government.

Neither of the preceding extremes is widely advocated. Most observers feel that some form of lay–professional partnership will best provide high-quality educational opportunities. However, the exact nature of the partnership is of great concern. The issue is likely to surface in the form of questions about school district size, power of area lay boards and local school councils (if any), requests for additional support services for school board members (e.g., school board aides), elected versus appointed superintendents in some sections of the nation, power to approve instructional programs and materials, and a single state board for higher education versus a separate board for each institution.

Traditional Educational Power Blocs Versus Emerging Interests

As we suggested at the outset of this discussion, the federal–state–local question is in part a question of general government versus educational government, and these issues cannot be isolated from the lay–professional question. In like manner each of these issues is manifest in the problems of traditional versus emerging sectors of influence.

It has been charged that there has existed for several years an educational establishment that has effectively controlled the educational enterprise. This informal and frequently loosely affiliated "establishment power bloc" has been seen as consisting of educationally minded congressmen and state legislators, a few high-ranking federal and state bureaucrats, selected educator-politicians who represent long-established national and state educational organizations, some educators associated with nationally prestigious universities, long-tenured chief state school officers, veteran local school superintendents (particularly those from the big cities), long-time state board of education members, and a few local school board members (again, most frequently from the large urban districts). The "establishment" has been seen as white, male-dominated, and representative of the more affluent sectors of society.

The evidence to support the assumed presence, now or in the past, of a reasonably monolithic educational power bloc is, at best, tenuous. In fact, one author, who assumed the former existence of such a bloc, concluded that the 1970s saw its "virtual collapse."[11] Nevertheless, the presence of males, whites, and representatives of the upper socioeconomic classes in educational decision-making roles has been well documented. Seemingly to provide a counterbalance to this perceived power, there emerged in many localities opposing interests with little previous history of influence. The expressed aim of these individuals and groups has been to make schools and colleges more responsive to the needs and interests of the people. Some such groups have been dominated by representatives of racial and/or ethnic minorities, some by leaders of the lower socioeconomic classes, some by "new" special interests (e.g., special education), others by the leadership of "militant" teacher organizations, and still others by some combination of the foregoing. Further, in some localities the young have made a concerted effort to make their influence felt.

The emergence of such diverse sectors of interest in education has resulted in an increase in pluralism and mechanisms intended to provide for wider participation in educational decision making. As has been noted, efforts at decentralizing decision making in local districts have emerged in the form of community boards, local school councils, and the like. More women, members of minorities, teachers, and so on, have sought election to general and educational governing bodies. Their presence is often attributed to caucuses that make a deliberate effort to identify, encourage, and/or nominate such persons. Young people have been appointed to educational governing boards (e.g., boards of trustees for colleges and universities). Executive sessions of educational boards and other governmental policy-making bodies have been curtailed through the enactment of government-in-the-sunshine laws. In some localities more freedom is being provided at the local school level in program, financial, and personnel matters. That is, there has been a move to school-based management.

Numerous examples could be offered where efforts at broad power sharing have been resisted, where the result has been to upset the "orderly way" of doing business, or where the shift in the power balance has installed new decision makers whose actions have been socially irresponsible. Also, a few observers have expressed the view that such wide diversity of interests in educational decision making

[11] Denis P. Doyle, "Public Policy and Private Education," *Phi Delta Kappan,* 62 (September 1980), 16.

will result in instability, causing fundamental harm to the educational system. Nevertheless, various options have been and will continue to be explored in efforts to accommodate these emerging interests.

In our opinion, the various interrelated conflicts regarding who governs the educational enterprise or what is to be the relative power and role of each interest sector will continue for the foreseeable future. Decisions regarding the role of the Congress, the state legislature, the state board of education, higher education institution boards, local school boards, the minorities, the regional school districts, the teachers, the state education department, the courts, and so on, will be determined at various moments through negotiation, judicial decree, or the political process. Furthermore, prevailing opinion on the broad question of who shall govern will in large measure determine how education is to be financed, how the state organizes to carry out its responsibility for education, and how school districts are organized.

Coping Options for Education in a Demand-for-Quality and No-Growth Era

From the end of World War II until the early 1970s, educational enrollments, financial support, physical facilities, and the like, along with public expectations of education increased. Educational leaders grappled with the many problems of growth. As suggested in the chapter introduction, by the mid-1970s there was the realization that, except for a few growth states, the great growth era was at an end. Nationally, K–12 educational enrollments declined more than 10 percent during the 1970s;[12] taxpayers became increasingly resistant to higher taxes for public education, even though (because of inflation) educational costs continued to rise; hundreds of local public school centers were closed in an effort to reduce costs, and in the vast majority of these closings there was much community controversy; the age of the teaching force increased as the declining enrollments limited opportunities for new teacher education program graduates, and the less experienced teachers became casualties of reduction-in-force (RIF) plans; in many localities pupil test scores declined and the confidence of the people in public education waned rapidly. By 1980, in spite of enrollment declines, inflation-driven school costs had risen to 187 percent of the 1970 costs;[13] about thirty state legislatures had found it

[12]National Center for Educational Statistics, *The Condition of Education* (Washington, D.C.: U.S. Government Printing Office, 1980), p. 16.
[13]President's Commission for a National Agenda for the Eighties, *A National Agenda for the Eighties* (Washington, D.C.: U.S. Government Printing Office, 1980), p. 88.

necessary to alter their public school finance laws to provide a "cushion" for school districts experiencing enrollment declines;[14] in an effort to ensure a minimum quality of education, thirty-eight states had passed some kind of minimum competency testing statute;[15] and a 1981 Gallup poll revealed that only 36 percent of the population gave public schools a grade of A or B while 20 percent gave a grade of D or F (by way of comparison, in 1974 a grade of A or B was awarded by 48 percent and only 11 percent gave a D or F grade).[16] Many colleges and universities faced severe problems because of sharp enrollment declines during the 1970s.

Clearly, for the foreseeable future the growth era is over, and, based on available projections, there will be continued modest enrollment declines in many school districts. (As has been suggested, there will be exceptions; particularly in school districts located in "Sunbelt" states.) Slight increases in elementary school enrollments are projected to begin in the mid-1980s; however, these will be more than offset by projected declines at the high school level through 1988. Thus, the period ahead seems to be one of essentially no growth. Furthermore, the public school system of the nation has produced an educated population that is demanding what is perceived to be a better quality education. Said another way, "[h]aving performed the miracle of mass education we are now confronted with the results of our labors: an adult population of parents who are knowledgeable, questioning and restive."[17]

Developing governance and organizational arrangements for coping successfully with the situation is a pervasive challenge. It can not be separated from federal educational policy, educational financing schemes, state and local organizational structures, the balance-of-power issue, and each of the task areas described in Chapter 2. Accordingly, the discussion that follows is selective—not inclusive— and focuses on the basic policy options open to public educational leaders, the public–nonpublic choice, and options for making public education organizations more efficient and responsive.

The Basic Policy Options for Public Education

Simply put, public educational leaders may view their policy options as on a continuum from continued retrenchment within present programs to the minimum or of striving through careful planning to

[14]Diane Divoky, "Burden of the Seventies: The Management of Decline," *Phi Delta Kappan*, 61 (October 1979), 88.

[15]National Center for Educational Statistics, op. cit., p. 92.

[16]George H. Gallup, "Gallup Poll of the Public's Attitudes Toward the Public Schools," *Phi Delta Kappan*, 63 (September 1981), 35.

[17]Evans Clinchy and Elisabeth Allen Cody, "If Not Public Choice, Then Private Escape," *Phi Delta Kappan*, 60 (December 1978), 271.

institute selective qualitative improvements within the context of the existing economic, political, and social constraints. A case can be made for either end of the continuum; however, it seems important that educational leaders make a conscious choice with knowledge of possible consequences of the choice and not simply "drift." In our opinion, failure to deliberate and make a policy choice will result in a continuing series of "gearing down" or "holding our own" crises for public education.

If a conscious retrenchment-to-the-minimum choice is made, there will be deliberate steps taken to close underused school centers, cut programs and/or subjects that do not contribute to the acquisition of basic skills (e..g., the arts, enrichment courses), fill existing classes to capacity, cut administrative and support personnel, reduce or eliminate auxiliary services (e.g., school lunches, transportation), encourage older teachers with advanced degrees to retire and replace them with teachers who have just completed bachelor degree programs, avoid issuing bonds, cut out duplication at the postsecondary level, reduce postsecondary student financial assistance, and so on. The idea would be to "belt tighten" in order to reduce, hold-the-line, or slow the rate of increase (depending upon the rate of inflation) in public educational costs.

In defense of the deliberate continued retrenchment-to-the-minimum option, three interrelated points can be made. First, over time education as an institution has accepted too many responsibilities and usurped the functions of other basic social institutions, such as the family, church, and economic system. (Institutional roles and interaction are discussed in the next chapter.) Public educational administrators have become restaurant owners, transit system operators, health clinic professionals, sports franchise operators, and so on. Many of these activities are not educational in the sense that the primary function of education is intellectual development. Therefore, a policy of continued retrenchment will result in education "returning" to its basic function as a social institution. Second, by restricting the functions of public education, the focus will be limited to those activities educators are best equipped to do, and as a result a better job will be done. Third, the basic direction of the public educational system should be determined by the people at large, and the people want a restriction in functions, activities, and costs.

The selective improvement option requires careful planning at the several levels of educational governance and making choices about program and service priorities in terms of demographic and social changes. Such planning may result in reduction or elimination of some programs and/or services. On the other hand, demographic and social trends may support an increase of effort in some areas (e.g., compensatory programs for the disadvantaged and handicapped). The basic argument for this policy option is that in the long run a "return-to-the-basics" option is an inadequate response to the complex educational needs of a changing society. Said another way, in order to produce an educated and skilled population that is essential to the survival of the society, public educational opportunities cannot be confined to the "basics." Furthermore, such an option is one of hope as opposed to the "defeatist" stance of continued retrenchment.

The Public–Nonpublic Choice

We have discussed (1) the legal right of nonpublic educational institutions to exist and of parents to send their children to such schools and colleges, (2) the limited uses of public funds for nonpublic school students, (3) the "classic" arguments for and against public funds for nonpublic education, (4) the rise in the 1970s of the proportion of the school-age population enrolled in nonpublic schools and the projected continuance of this trend, and (5) the late 1970s efforts to provide a broader base of support for nonpublic education by means of educational vouchers that provide parents with a sum of money each year for each eligible child that can be spent at a public or nonpublic school of the parents' choice or a federal income tax credit for a part of the tuition paid for education. At this writing, some sentiment is expressed in favor of congressional action for some sort of voucher or tax credit scheme. In our opinion, a tax credit plan (particularly at the college level) is more politically feasible and legally less vulnerable; yet, any action by the Congress in this area will result in constitutional challenges in the courts.

It has been argued that the presence of a legally defensible federal income tax credit plan that allows a person to "pass on" a major part of nonpublic school or college tuition greatly enhances the possibility of persons exercising their legal right to a nonpublic education. Many see a realistic opportunity to choose between a public or nonpublic educational institution as an appropriate mechanism for dealing with many of the problems associated with the quality demands and no growth. They reason that educational competition will result, and the consumer will benefit from the efforts to improve the quality of education provided. In a similar vein, the opinion is sometimes expressed that if a realistic choice is available, there will be greater satisfaction with the public schools. The logic is that those who are not satisfied with the quality of education being provided will choose nonpublic schooling. Some supporters of a realistic choice option argue that this is one way to "hold the line" on the costs of public education. The reasoning is that public educational costs are reduced as individuals choose a nonpublic institution, and the tax loss due to the tax credits will not be so large as to offset the savings.

Those who do not see the value in such a "free market" concept tend to offer four arguments. First, there is no true competition; the public schools cannot be selective—they must serve everyone who requests it. Second, the primary beneficiaries of such schemes will be the white middle and upper classes, and the public school population will become increasingly minority poor. In the long run such segregation is not in the best interests of society in that the public education system as we know it will be destroyed. Said another way, such schemes promote private rather than public purposes. Third, the supposed savings to the taxpayers may not be realistic. Specifically, only after loss of a sufficient number of pupils in the right places can any savings occur due to reduced personnel, dropped programs, or closed facilities. Fourth, if the public educational establishment will provide more flexibility, it can meet the perceived needs of those who might be inclined to choose nonpublic schooling.

Enhancing the Efficiency and Responsiveness of Public Education

The significance of values in educational decision making is the focus of Chapter 12; suffice to say at this point that in light of our values we reject the retrenchment-to-the-minimum option (i.e., public education should be confined to "the basics") and the notion of a public–nonpublic choice underwritten by some form of governmental financial assistance. We reject the "return to basics" option in that the educational needs of many will not be met, and it will result in a stagnation that will tend to reduce the enthusiasm and motivation and increase the frustration of those associated with public education. Butts expressed well our basic concern relative to the government-assisted public–nonpublic choice when he stated that

> where there is enormous diversity of culture, of religion, of class, and of educational goals, the private schools are likely to separate and divide along homogeneous lines of one kind or another and are not likely to provide the overall sense of political community needed for a viable public life. This is especially true if the government itself and public funds are used to encourage parents and families to coalesce around other like-minded families.[18]

If one accepts our position and believes that there is need for improving the efficiency and responsiveness of public education, the selective improvement option based on careful planning is the most viable means of coping in the era ahead. This requires educational leaders to identify and consider carefully possible means to implement the option. These possibilities appear to be in three areas—a

---

[18]R. Freeman Butts, "Educational Vouchers: The Private Pursuit of the Public Purse," *Phi Delta Kappan,* 61 (September 1979), 8.

basic change in the formal structures for making educational decisions, increased use of schooling alternatives within the public system, and increased collaboration or linkage with other public and private sector organizations and individuals.

If the decision is made to move in the direction of a basic change in the structures for making educational decisions, it is obvious that a choice has been made in regard to the balance-of-power question discussed earlier. Such a basic change would substitute for the hierarchical bureaucracy, where decisions flow from the top down, a structure where important decisions about the schooling to be provided are made by parents and teachers. Decisions made at this level would

> flow up to the central administration and the board of education, whose job it will be to insure that the desired options are provided. Instead of an industrial, mass-production corporate structure, we will have developed what economist Peter Drucker describes as a model based upon "socialist competition."[19]

To ensure the power to make decisions at the parent–teacher level, some advocate "lump-sum" budgeting and school-level governing boards, such as have been discussed earlier, composed of teachers and parents. Such arrangements have great appeal and certainly provide a means for establishing educational priorities in an era when hard choices must be made. However, a major difficulty is balancing the responsiveness mechanisms with economic efficiency. Further, as is discussed in Chapter 18, the limitations imposed by collective bargaining on such a decision-making structure must be considered.

Obviously, changing the decision-making structure is conducive to increasing the schooling alternatives within the public system. If the primary decisions about educational content, delivery systems, and so on, are made at the school level (i.e., there is school-based management), then the marketplace concept can be operative—each school can reflect what the clientele wants. In order for this to work, an open enrollment plan would be necessary, educators would have to be available to offer counsel to parents, and one parental option would have to be to let the educators decide about a child's placement. The array of schooling alternatives was described in the preceding chapter and will not be repeated here; however, if an alternative was available that did not ensure competent instruction in mathematics, reading, writing, and logical thought processes, it could be argued that the public purpose was not being well served. Furthermore, there is always the possibility that, even though the choices are in the public

[19] Clinchy and Cody, op. cit., 272.

sector, there will be a decided tendency to "separate and divide along homogeneous lines."

Increased collaboration or linkage has considerable potential for enhancing operational efficiency. There are many examples of practices instituted in the late 1970s and early 1980s. The human service centers and adopt-a-school plans that have been described are obvious illustrations. As an option to closing underused schools and the concomitant controversies, some school districts have kept such schools open and rented the space not needed for educational purposes. For example, one California district was able to change a state law and rented surplus space to a variety of tenants, including "an eye clinic, an electronics firm's training program, a telephone solicitation operation, a real estate firm."[20] A few school districts have established "educational foundations" as a means of providing support for activities that the level of public funding will not permit. In a number of localities, smaller school districts "share" a variety of administrative and support personnel and services. Greater use of regional service agencies to achieve "economies of scale" was described in the preceding chapter.

There are numerous arguments, pro and con, about each of the foregoing collaborative arrangements. From our perspective, the key to judicial consideration of such arrangements is careful planning. Planning provides a basis for selective improvements and more rational choices about how to be efficient and responsive, yet responsible in regard to the public purpose of public schooling.

ACTIVITIES/QUESTIONS FOR FURTHER STUDY

1. Criticize the state and local organizational models described in terms of political feasibility, lay versus professional control, opportunity for emerging interests to have a voice, and efficiency of operation.
2. Interview a small sample of lay citizens in your community to determine the extent to which they believe schools are responsive and what they see as the major school governance issues.
3. If your community has experienced a loss in public school enrollment, determine what strategies have been used by school leaders to cope with the situation.
4. Discuss as a class the promise and problems of the "free market" concept in education.

SUGGESTED READINGS

ABRAMOWITZ, SUSAN, and STUART ROSENFIELD (eds.). *Declining Enrollment: The Challenge of the Coming Decade.* Washington, D.C.: U.S. Government Printing Office, 1978.

[20] Divoky, op. cit., 91.

BAKALIS, MICHAEL J. "American Education and the Meaning of Scarcity," *Phi Delta Kappan,* 63 (September and October 1981), 7–12, 102–105.

CAMPBELL, ROALD F., and TIM L. MAZZONI, JR. *State Policy Making for the Public Schools.* Berkeley: McCutchan Publishing Corp., 1976.

CAMPBELL, ROALD F., et al. *The Organization and Control of American Schools,* 4th ed. Columbus, Ohio: Charles E. Merrill Publisher, 1980, Chapters 17, 19.

MCKELVEY, TROY V. (ed.). *Metropolitan School Organization: Basic Problems and Patterns,* vol. 1. Berkeley: McCutchan Publishing Corp., 1973.

MCKELVEY, TROY V. (ed.). *Metropolitan School Organization: Proposals for Reform,* vol. 2. Berkeley: McCutchan Publishing Corp., 1973.

PRESIDENT'S COMMISSION FOR A NATIONAL AGENDA FOR THE EIGHTIES, PANEL ON GOVERNMENT AND THE ADVANCEMENT OF SOCIAL JUSTICE: HEALTH, WELFARE, EDUCATION, AND CIVIL RIGHTS. *Government and the Advancement of Social Justice: Health, Welfare, Education, and Civil Rights in the Eighties.* Washington, D.C.: U.S. Government Printing Office, 1980, Chapter 4.

WHETTEN, DAVID A. "Organizational Responses to Scarcity: Exploring the Obstacles to Innovative Approaches to Retrenchment in Eduation," *Educational Administration Quarterly,* XVII (Summer 1981), 80–97.

PART THREE

The Conceptual Milieu of the Educational Administrator

PROFESSIONAL identity is an important ingredient for success as an educational administrator. Moreover, one attribute of a profession is that it has a theoretical base that needs to be understood prior to the practice of that profession. To assist in the process of achieving such identity and acquaint prospective and practicing educational administrators with the rudiments of theories associated with the field, this section focuses on the "world of ideas," which has become part of the professional heritage. Schools and colleges do not operate in isolation from the other institutional sectors of society. Consequently, in Chapter 7 alternatives for relating education to other elements of the culture are explored. Some historians have contended that the influence of an idea is mightier than the sword. In Chapters 8, 9, and 10, various "theories of administration" are detailed. These theories are the heart of the ideas that have influenced the way education is organized and administered. They are the basis of administrative behavior. Consequently, to be truly educated in the profession of educational administration, one must *endeavor to learn and understand how these theories are the basis of what we know in the profession. Chapter 11 contains a discussion of the administrative functions or processes (e.g., decision making, planning, communication, controlling, conflict management) that are basic to the tasks of educational administration.*

Chapter 12 is devoted to an examination of different systems of ideas and their implications for administrative decision making and personal values. In this chapter the authors not only examine different systems but identify some of their own values, which affect much of what is written in this book. In Chapter 13 attention is given to a most important aspect of professional identity: professional ethics and moral responsibility.

7

Educational Administration and Cultural Responsiveness

CONCEPTUALIZING the culture within which educational organizations function is basic to the practice of educational administration. Several chapters of this textbook relate to this conceptual process; however, this chapter addresses directly the concept of culture and how the administrator may perceive it. The primary emphasis here is the educational leader's obligation to understand how educational organizations relate to the total culture. This is an important responsibility of leaders in all of the professions.

Professional Identity for Educational Administration in a New Era

The great social and professional upheavals since World War II have left many educational administrators with what might be appropriately termed a professional identity crisis. Examples of social changes include accelerated urbanization, rapidly changing social norms, expanded technology, and bureaucratic complexity. Reflected in these social and economic developments is an economic system wracked by recession–inflation cycles, important transformations of

219

the family, and modifications in other aspects of the culture, such as religion, politics, and education. A primary example of professional change is the growth of the industrial model for collective bargaining among school districts and colleges. Educational administrators, who traditionally thought of themselves as members of the teaching profession, have had to come to grips with a new identity.

The administrator is no longer characterized as the disciplinarian principal or the tradition-directed superintendent of yesterday. These traditional administrators met the needs of their day. Their administrative objectives were consistent with the high degree of cultural consensus of the community served. As Kimball observed, the school was largely an extension of the family, and teachers performed roles similar to those of older sisters or brothers.[1] The obvious administrative need of this era was to see that congruence of the school and community was maintained, to manage social bookkeeping operations, and to gear the standard operating procedures and programs for the transmission of the cultural heritage.

Conditions following the post-World War II period have steadily imperiled the professional future of those who follow traditional administrative practices. Massive technological advances have prevented local communities from isolating themselves from influences that are different from and challenging to community norms. Sweeping political, familial, and economic developments have, except in small segments of the population, begun to modify the congruence of education with other societal institutions. College and university student bodies have changed radically from the predominantly upper-middle- and upper-class strata of pre-World War II. Central High School may no longer transmit middle-class values to upper-middle-class white children. Hilldale High School may no longer serve the mill workers across the tracks. Instead, these schools may be caught within the tangle of culturally different families and pupils and even different economic systems. The economics of the poor (e.g., welfare, charity, low pay, unemployment, crime) cannot be compared with the economics accepted by upper-middle-class, silk-stocking neighborhoods. There is reason to believe that the extent of commonly shared values is less than it was and is getting smaller.

Except for some authoritarian countries, all societies experience some subcultural variation—groups at variance with popular conceptions of the cultural norms (e.g., "hippies" of the 1960s, the Amish). As a result of the massive immigration of non-English speaking people, the growth of egalitarianism, and the national emphasis on human rights, some writers have advocated the philosophy of cultural

---

[1] Solon T. Kimball, *Culture and the Educative Process* (New York: Teachers College Press, Columbia University, 1974), pp. 13–14.

pluralism.[2] In this view subcultural variation becomes dominant and the society becomes a kind of confederation of culturally different groups, each operating by different sets of norms. Proponents of this philosophy view the "melting pot" function of the public schools as a repressive form of imperialism. Cultural pluralism is used by some individualistically oriented groups to support legislation to supplant the public schools with private schools. Proposing a less extreme definition of cultural pluralism, Valverde wrote that the "concept requires that schools design instructional activities, organize experiences, and create curricula so that *all* pupils will explore, learn, and respect their own cultural and historical heritages as well as those of others."[3]

The important question for all Americans is whether an emphasis on cultural pluralism may move the society toward a Tower of Babel with resulting cultural disintegration and political balkanization. Haviland is among those anthropologists who warn that marked cultural pluralism would produce acute problems for the society.[4] Kimball has suggested that the culture is a variable interdependent system in which the similarities among cultural traditions are greater than the differences.[5] He took the position that the school should encourage cultural congruency; thus "the transmission of culture, inclusive of developing cognitive capacities and technical skills, should be the primary objective of an educational system."[6]

However, cultural pluralism versus cultural homogeneity may not be the central issue. Sanday wrote that the United States is more appropriately classified as a structural pluralism than as a cultural pluralism.[7] In structural pluralism culturally different groups become social class structures with widely different opportunities and rewards for members of the classes. Thus Sanday contended that an important function of the school is to assist in overcoming the bias that results in a prejudicial structural pluralism.

The conventional wisdom of educational administration has been to identify the areas of community consensus and to respond educationally to them—to find the community power structure and to work through it to improve the educational system. This is obviously an oversimplified concept of responsiveness. Consensus is difficult to find

[2]Seymour W. Itzkoff, *Cultural Pluralism and American Education* (Scranton, Pa.: International, 1969).

[3]Leonard A. Valverde, "Strategies for the Advancement of Cultural Pluralism," *Phi Delta Kappan,* 60 (October 1978), 108.

[4]William A. Haviland, *Cultural Anthropology* (New York: Holt, 1978), pp. 14–17.

[5]Kimball, op. cit., pp. 21–24.

[6]Ibid., p. 32.

[7]Peggy R. Sanday, *Anthropology and the Public Interest* (New York: Academic Press, 1976), pp. 53–72.

in many communities, and the leadership structure has changed. For example, the principal of a large consolidated high school has mobile clients from a far-flung area who may have different ideas about community living, and the principal simply cannot respond to a sense of values widely shared. Thus the first task is to work with clients and local communities to create shared values to which the school can respond. This responsiveness is somewhat complicated by the growth of state and federal influence on the administration of educational organizations. Achieving congruence of the educational organization and the culture is not restricted to the spontaneous development of local culture but includes powerful state and federal inputs.

Most school superintendents no longer have the unswerving support of teachers, as was expected in the traditional administrative view. Principals of some school systems feel that separate bargaining units for administrators are advantageous. Boards of trustees and college presidents must grapple for power in the general economic and political arenas. Attempting to quell a teacher strike may involve the school board with private-sector labor union leaders, mayors, legislators, and leaders from other areas of society. Yet administrators must regain from somewhere the influence lost through teacher defection from the traditional concept. Inevitably administrators must reach beyond the confines of the educational community for support from leaders in other sectors of society. Administrators must seek cooperation of these leaders in order to keep the educational sector compatible with other sectors of society and to provide thrust toward important educational goals and objectives.

During the 1950s and 1960s educational administrators at all levels struggled to cope with the unparalleled growth in all aspects of the society. A brave new age seemed upon us and everyone was attuned to a growth policy of bigger and better. In the 1970s, however, ecological problems, overpopulation, the threatened collapse of fossil energy resources, world inflation, and other concerns resulted in radical changes in social outlooks. Educational leaders in the 1980s are more likely to cope with problems associated with no growth instead of growth. Many school districts may have to deal with long-term losses in pupil enrollment. This is a challenge to all who have become accustomed to thinking only in terms of growth.

The authors would not be so bold as to define specifically the administrative identity with reference to cultural responsiveness. This identity is forever in the process of "becoming" because, in an open society, leadership for educational and cultural congruency is not in static equilibrium. The administrative identity will, and indeed should, vary among communities; therefore, a contingency concept for cultural responsiveness may be the most productive approach. However, formal and informal organizations on the state and local levels and the national interdependence of leaders will produce greater similarities than differences in the culture of educational organizations. Before further expanding our views, let us examine more specifically the shortcomings of traditional views and discuss in greater detail the concept of culture.

The Limitations of Traditional Approaches to Educational Administration

One of the worthy aims of traditional administrators was to maintain the system, "to run a tight ship." Potential issues were stonewalled. Erupting issues were watered down, extinguished, or the forces behind them neutralized so that they did not become lethal. Those who overemphasized this traditional view directed their efforts toward "keeping the lid on," "not rocking the boat," or "whatever is necessary to keep people still." Indeed, this intent became one of the preoccupations of theory construction about the job. How do you control the actions of teachers and optimize production?

The primary objective of much research and literature in educational administration has been to identify sets of practices ("ideas" or "theories") to maintain the system, to optimize economy and productivity, and to respond to certain professional and civic norms. The literature and many hours of professional meetings have been devoted to the identification of promising practices from experience. Action that would maintain the power equilibrium was one important criterion. Some administrators came to be known as specialists in regaining system balance in schools on the verge of anarchy. Some of these "troubleshooters" were advocates of the "Neanderthal" philosophy, controlling actors physically. Others used the cunning of the fox, manipulating the forces into balance. Some came in as lions and turned into foxes. These persons served the important function of restoring orderliness. Every student, when he or she enters the field, will find well-established professional "folkways" and "mores" about how to further the traditional aim of maintaining the organization.

Some global practices or "theories" have captured the imagination of educational administrators from time to time. One illustration of this is the "democratic administration," which, as will be discussed in Chapter 9, is an application of the human relations movement. Briefly, the idea is to find ways for teachers, parents, pupils, and other citizens to participate in establishing the objectives of education. This seems to many to be the perfect solution to the age-old problem of finding and responding administratively to consensus and, perhaps just as important, to the problem of improving productivity.

The authors begin by referring to these traditional aims as worthy. Obviously, maintaining orderliness is not only worthy but essential. Nevertheless, the traditional administrator is limited in his or her ability to be effective, for a number of reasons, not necessarily all of his or her own making.

1. The concept of system maintenance (or orderliness) and intersystem balance (or congruence) that is perceived (and desired) is a static equilibrium. Orderliness does not emphasize the concept of cultural change.

2. Too many tradition-bound administrators are predisposed to look inward to the educational organizations for solutions to problems that have their roots in the environment of the school. Attempts to improve education consists of manipulating or reorganizing the curriculum, adopting new organizational patterns, adopting new methods for teaching subjects, retraining personnel in new classroom techniques, and using a number of fads, gadgets, and so-called innovations. Great amounts of energy are consumed annually in manipulating the various aspects of educational organizations as if student learning had no relationship to the environments of schools, colleges, and universities.

3. Research and development in educational administration has been very limited and has not achieved widespread respectability. Although the value of research in medicine, agriculture, and business has been demonstrated, resources for research in education are practically nonexistent by comparison. This may be a result of the "bag-of-tricks," the "reliance-upon-experience" approach of tradition-bound administrators. In any event, lack of scientific development has left the field subject to thousands of hucksters who profess to know the answers to educational problems. All that is necessary to learn about these answers is to pay a healthy honorarium, buy an expensive new set of materials, or attend a modern "medicine show" at some costly hotel.

4. Tradition-bound administrators are not helped to assess the social and cultural conditions (basic to conceptualizing educational needs) and either adapt education to these conditions or work with persons outside of education to change the conditions. Indeed, there are "professional ethics" that discourage the participation of educators in this process. One of these is the concept that administration could be separated from policy making or that politics and education are divorced. Consequently, many tradition-bound educational leaders are expending energy to keep from doing what they need to accomplish most.

The Relationship of Education to Other Aspects of the Culture

The term culture has so many different uses that an exact definition is difficult. Some writers, intimidated by hair-splitting theoretical debates concerning its meaning, are driven to overlong discussions in their attempts to find a definition. Culture frequently is used colloquially to refer to a person as cultured "if he or she is well mannered, well read, skilled in several languages, and able to talk knowledgeably about art and music."[8] As used by anthropologist William Haviland, culture is "learned behavior, passed on from generation to generation by nonhereditary means."[9] Thus culture is whatever humankind has achieved and transmitted as a way of life—mores, taboos, norms, beliefs, behavior, ideologies—beyond mere animalistic existence.

The educational administrator needs to find a way of thinking about the culture and to discern the relationship of education to other aspects of the social order. One approach is to conceptualize the basic institutions of the society. The educational administrator may think of these institutions as a sort of taxonomy of the culture.

Basic Social Institutions

The term *institution* is imprecisely defined, even among social scientists, whose task is somewhat complicated by lay use of the term. One often hears it said that this or that person "is an institution" or that a certain university is an institution. As used by sociologists, however, a school or a university is a structure (or an organization) in education, education being one of several societal institutions. Sociologists define institutions as complexes of crystallized norms and roles of an enduring nature that are regarded as essential for the society. This could also include those practices that have wide social acceptance and more permanence than folkways and mores. The first definition emphasizes defining crystallized roles and norms independent of people, whereas the latter view includes people and their actions. In any event, humankind has certain important areas of needs and has institutionalized certain practices and activities associated with these needs. Although there are differences in conceptions of institutions, many students of the culture have identified the following: family, religion, education, economics, and politics.

One obvious area of human need involves sexual relationships,

[8] Haviland, op. cit., p. 12.
[9] Ibid.

procreation, caring for the young, intimate love, and a refuge from the struggles of daily life in the corporate society. The normative actions, or crystallized behavior patterns encompassing these functions and needs, are thought to be largely, although not entirely, institutionalized in the family. The authors accept this broader view of the family espoused by cultural anthropologists and sociologists. In the technologically oriented, corporate society, the family is an important, compassionate refuge for its members. When it fails in this function, its members may indeed be in trouble and could become dropouts from the mainstream of society.

The economic institution has emerged as extremely important to modern, industrialized, ubanized societies. People have always struggled for and worried about adequate food, clothing, and shelter. Through participation in the economic system people expect to realize physical well-being. Many persons' long and continuing struggle to avoid starvation, overcome pestilence, and live comfortably has made them overly materialistic. In his remarkable publication *The Worldly Philosophers,* Heilbroner highlighted the tremendous impact of competing economic views upon people,[10] and from the pens of these worldly philosophers (e.g., Adam Smith, Karl Marx, Thomas Malthus, John Maynard Keynes) came conceptualizations of economic systems over which wars have been fought.

People of all cultures have institutionalized religion. Participation in the religious sector helps persons adjust ideas, beliefs, and morals to what they perceive to be the supernatural. Among the many religions, denominations, and sects of the United States, one finds a variety of alternative practices. Most, however, appeal to personal needs to give expression to moral ideals. Thus religion has contributed much to people's moral conscience and ethical behavior. One example, strongly embodied in some religious structures, is the idea that all persons are equal in the sight of God and that no special intellectual activities, social standing, or political status are necessary to enjoy full societal benefits.

In the political institution one finds aspects of the society associated with governance. Through the political systems nations attempt to make decisions concerning police protection, protection from foreign invasion, provision of important services, and so on. Within recent decades the social welfare functions within the political institution have greatly expanded, to the delight of many and the dismay of others. Included in the political institution is the establishment of law and the organizational arrangements for maintaining societal order and for the adjudication of disputes.

[10]Robert L. Heilbroner, *The Worldly Philosophers* (New York: Simon & Schuster, 1953).

Education involves the function of passing on the cultural heritage, socializing persons into the basic values and practices of society, and assisting persons to adjust from the domesticated values, processes, and practices of the home to those associated with the larger society. This also includes the development of cognitive and technical capacities of persons. Education is also a resource for improving the culture and for preparing persons to accept and live in rapidly changing conditions in the future.

Other Institutions

The previously identified institutions have been traditionally advanced by sociologists and cultural anthropologists as the basic institutions of society. There may well be room for the identification of other institutional sectors, however, which are significant and yet do not fit into these traditional categories. Some authorities have included additional categories, such as recreation. Some feel that so-called normal persons survive existing institutions but that a very large (and perhaps growing) number do not. Those who do not survive become associated with the ameliorative institution—jails, prisons, hospitals. The educational administrator may indeed wish to expand upon the traditional concepts of societal institutions already discussed.

Interaction of Institutions

Any attempt to categorize the society into institutions is somewhat arbitrary because the society is complexly integrated. Although some of the agencies and organizations are engaged primarily in educational functions, other institutional agencies may also perform certain educational functions. For example, the well-functioning family contributes tremendously to the education of the young. In the economic system, large amounts of resources are invested in educational functions. Education, however, should be the primary function of schools, colleges, and other educational organizations.

In addition, the people primarily engaged in education should be constantly interacting with those primarily concerned with economics, the family, religion, and politics. Insofar as religion and the public schools are concerned, the interaction on a denominational basis is restricted because of the judicial interpretations of the First Amendment to the Constitution. Nevertheless, Judeo-Christian traditions and ethics are important in our culture. The administrator who is ignorant about religion fails to understand a very significant aspect of culture, and this could limit his or her effectiveness. Attempts to obtain more resources for education involve political activity which have consequences for the economic sector. Educators are often in interaction with families. From these interactions come developed sentiments and routinized practices for interinstitutional co-operation (or dissension). The principals and faculties of schools develop normative practices for interacting with parents and vice versa. Thus even though we can think of different institutions, we must realize that these institutions exist in interaction. The quality of this interaction is of great importance.

In the past there have been strong pressures from other institutions to compartmentalize the educational function. The Governmental Reform movement of the early part of this century led to the creation of structures to separate education from politics. For example, the model school government calls for nonpartisan election of school boards and the appointment of professionally trained school administrators.

We now realize, of course, that these and other attempts to minimize interaction of educational leaders with leaders in other institutional sectors were façades. Educational administrators now find themselves scrambling for political power. One could not foresee three decades ago that opposing a teachers' strike might throw educational administrators into open political conflict with grave diggers, sanitation workers, and other labor groups. Moreover, the principal of a prestigious city high school serving upper-middle-class children could not have foreseen having to grapple with community agitators or widespread student strikes.

Those who would attempt to compartmentalize education and isolate themselves from those in other institutional pursuits create problems for themselves and their students. In fact, such withdrawal has resulted in national demands for greater citizen participation in educational decision making. There has been a resurgence of demands to establish citizens' committees for the public schools. The problem, however, is greater than this. Looking inward or attempting to stonewall problems means that the persistent problems of education cannot be solved. In the following section, the authors amplify this point.

Persistent Educational Problems and Other Institutional Sectors

Many educators and lay citizens have ascribed to education phenomenal powers to improve the society. Education is indeed a potentially powerful regenerative force. A nation with an educational system espousing values antithetical to that nation's basic institutions has within it a force that may eventually bring about its demise. Realizing this, one of the first acts of many revolutionists is to educate the young in a manner consistent with the goals of the new regime.

This is why Hitler and Stalin placed tight controls over their educational systems. Fidel Castro also acted swiftly to revolutionize the educational system.

Powerful as education is, however, it is only one of several very important institutional sectors of the society. The educational sector can assist in solving only those problems for which it has support from the other important sectors of society, such as family, religion, economics, recreation, politics. This concept has a long history; for example, Plato feared the influence of the family upon teaching the young values conflicting with the best interests of his Republic. Education cannot function well at cross-purposes with the family, the economic system, or other institutional areas of society.

Perhaps the best current illustration of this fact is the pervasive problem of racial segregation. Following the 1954 *Brown* decision declaring *de jure* racial segregation of schools unconstitutional, much emphasis was placed upon using the public schools to desegregate the society. Although drives were undertaken to desegregate soda fountains, churches, public transportation, and so on, the public looked to school desegregation as the great hope for the racially desegregated society of the future. Proponents of the school as a force for social change almost forgot the racially segregated housing patterns.

Implementing or attempting to implement busing for racial balance in the schools brought out some important conditions contributing to the problem. In their *Busing: The Political and Judicial Process,* Bolner and Shanley demonstrated how the school busing controversy was a problem deeply ingrained in all aspects of society.[11] The movement promoted one of the great political struggles of our times. As the struggles were occurring in presidential elections, in Congress, and in state and local political arenas, the nation saw that resistance to school desegregation was a national phenomenon and not, as had been assumed, a regional issue restricted to the South. Many political and civic leaders were thought to act in what Senator Abraham Ribicoff described as "monumental hypocrisy."

The conclusion is that education alone cannot be used to solve a problem that is deeply rooted in all major institutions of the society. Racially balanced schools will not affect materially the tokenism rampant in the economic system, segregated families, segregated churches, and denial of equal opportunity in other sectors of society. Society cannot be racially integrated and equal in one institutional sector and remain racially segregated in all others. Therefore, educational organizations can effectively incorporate only those changes for which they have support from other institutional sectors of the

[11]James Bolner and Robert Shanley, *Busing: The Political and Judicial Process* (New York: Praeger, 1974).

society. However, this is not to say that education cannot lead in cultural change in cooperation with the rest of society, but educational agencies and organizations are only one aspect of all social organizations.

Institutionalized Expectations, Strengths, and Weaknesses

Basic systems (structures or organizations) exist to further institutional functions. In education, for example, there are elementary schools, middle schools, junior high schools, high schools, vocational-technical schools, colleges, community colleges, universities, multiversities, schools for the blind and deaf, adult centers, nurseries, and a host of other educational organizations. These are usually parts of other structures, such as school districts, university systems, state departments, boards of regents, or organizations by other names performing the same functions. Many elementary schools, high schools, and colleges are organized and operated under church jurisdiction; others are privately organized and financed.

Within the economic sector are many thousands of organizations. To appreciate the immensity of this sector, one only has to thumb through the classified pages of the telephone directory of any large city. These economic organizations make up what some authors refer to as the corporate society, which has always been a powerful one in the United States, because our nation was nurtured in the private enterprise philosophy.

During this century a great increase in the political sector has occurred. There has been a tremendous increase in organizations connected with social welfare services, regulatory agencies, commercial organizations, and other governmental organizations. The government has grown in influence over economic activity. Some economists separate the economic sector into the "private economy" and the "public economy."

One must not assume, however, that all institutional activities involve organizational activity. The people who live within institutionalized norms are not necessarily organizational persons. There are many highly religious persons who may not be participating church members. There are some well-educated persons who do not hold a college degree. The expectations (norms) of the corporate sector do not belong to the economic organizations; they are generalized in the population. In this generalization of institutional expectations, most persons have a generalized conception of what schooling is all about. These ideas about schooling vary, to be sure, but most citizens explaining what schooling means will describe conditions accepted by a large part of the society. When thinking about the economic sector, people think of tough competition for goods and services, the desirability of making profits, labor–management bargaining for wages, and other very important concepts and behavior associated with surviving in the world of business. As in the case of schooling, there is much agreement among many citizens concerning the normative behavior and processes in the economic sector.

Thus the "way of life" fixed within the religious, economic, educational, political, and familial sectors is said to be institutionalized. The average parent, for example, has a mental picture of what the school smells like, how pupils act, how the teachers behave, how the principal performs tasks, and so on. This parent pictures the important ceremonies associated with schooling (e.g., bells for different activities, classroom teaching, PTA meetings, sports activities, graduation exercises). This parent can also differentiate fairly well among educational roles performed by English teachers, first-grade teachers, coaches, principals, custodians, and others.

One who violates or attempts to violate these institutionalized "ways of schooling" (norms and activities) will be sanctioned or worse, and may come to be known by colleagues as "a failure." Consequently, to be an effective leader in the education sector requires a thorough feeling for and knowledge of institutionalized education. This is why experience in the educational processes is so important to the prospective administrator and why colleges offer practicums for students. Likewise, to be effective in promoting educational ideas in the economic, religious, familial, or political sectors, educators must also understand the institutional "way of life" in these areas of the culture.

Advantages of Institutionalization

Benjamin Disraeli, the noted statesman of Great Britain, once observed, "Individuals may form communities, but it is institutions alone that can create a nation." One might also add that the decay and malfunction of institutions signal the disintegration of nations. Thus the institutionalization of a way of living together is not inherently evil, as many revolutionaries have claimed.

Through the processes associated with institutionalization a nation establishes acceptable ways for responding to problems. This is necessary for any society. Think, for example, what the world would be if we had to start from scratch to create responses to the need to find food, control the sex drive, care for the young, decide how to shelter ourselves, and so on. At least we do not have to fear cannibalism as an alternative to our finding food for sustenance. Because we have inherited a culture with its institutionalized behaviors, we do not have to spend a lot of time learning how to respond to many conditions and needs. We do not have to flounder in the wilderness a thousand years to find that we need schools or to find that we should not steal, murder, or rape.

All societies must have institutionalized patterns through which responses are made to life's developmental problems and crises. Persons typical of the middle class, for example, are born and reared in a family in which responses to developmental problems produce a certain orderliness. They acquire what Kimball referred to as a psychic pattern.

> Through the formative years, each individual acquires an enormous and unpayable debt to his parents. He is in debt to them for the opportunities they have given him—for life itself. It is his duty, as a child, to utilize the benefits accorded him; as an adult, he validates the trust that has been placed in him. He does this by fulfilling his sense of their aspirations, an assignment that cannot be forgotten, even after his parents' death. It is an obligation he also transmits to his children, and hence, its perpetuation is transgenerational.[12]

In the family, economics, politics, education, and religion are fundamentally important predispositional response patterns. Regardless of their rightness or wrongness, these predispositions to act in a cultural orderliness frees us for creative activities. Full of shortcomings as the American economic system is, most Americans dress well, eat well, and have some semblance of physical well-being. Even though the education sector is severely criticized, through its institutionalized patterns, generations of Americans have acquired the education necessary to their perceptions of the "good life" and that necessary to help the economic system produce the greatest gross national product in the world. "Becoming educated" does not just happen, nor are we born in an educated state.

"Becoming educated" through those processes institutionalized for that purpose is more than cognitive development. The processes of being separated from the parents, interacting with persons from other homes, learning to cope with other adults, and so on, go into what curriculum specialists have labeled the affective domain. Many citizens fail to recognize the value of this schooling. In a very real sense, the schools are transitional institutions to help children and youth adjust in their movement from the private world of the family and neighborhood peers to the public world of the "corporate society."[13] In fact, the educational experience is so important to most of us that we look back throughout life to things that happened in school. Instead of remembering the day Mrs. Fuller taught us how to add

---

[12]Kimball, op. cit., p. 20.
[13]Solon T. Kimball and James E. McClellan, *Education and the New America* (New York: Random House, 1962), pp. 35–39.

polynomials, we recall her idiosyncrasies, which were strangely different from those of our mothers or older sisters. We also learned how men and women are supposed to behave and how organizations work, particularly the meaning of authority.

The institutionalization of life patterns is absolutely essential. The writers are not arguing that the institutions, as they are now constituted, are serving the needs of mankind in the best way possible. Indeed, we are faced once again with a two-edged sword. If one were to look not at the values of institutions but to their subversion of humanity, one could find justifiable reasons and inflammatory words for tearing down the cultural structures and starting anew. Note, however, that in the process of destroying, one must substitute some other form of institutionalization for the traditional forms. Let us discuss now the weaknesses of traditional institutions.

The Weaknesses of Institutions

Throughout history human beings have been sacrificed for institutionalized patterns. All the great martyrs of history were sacrificed to further certain institutions. Millions of people have lost their lives or have been physically mangled in wars that had economic and religious bases. Indeed, if one assumes an existentialist frame of mind, a violent internal struggle must be faced to maintain hope, not unlike the writer of the book of Ecclesiastes: "Vanity of vanities, saith the Preacher, vanity of vanities; all is vanity."

The vanities of education have been the subject of many articles, some of which are justified and many of which are unfair. Each year millions suffer through poor teaching, outmoded practices, boredom, and even discrimination in the schools, colleges, and other educational organizations. Even in the cognitive domain, the education institution is found to be weak in intellectual development, especially for children of the poor. Unfortunately, some individual schools have lost sight of the responsibility for cultural purpose.

The economic institution has also failed in some respects. In a nation that is rich in many ways, there are many poverty-stricken persons. Manufacturing processes and their products are polluting the environment. Heilbroner observed: "Thus, if we are the richest nation in the world, we are also one of the more socially neglectful—ignorant of, or acquiescent in, conditions that other, less wealthy nations no longer tolerate."[14] There is currently much concern that too much of our industrial system may fall victim to foreign competition.

The religious sector has also slipped from the mainstream to perpetuate irrelevant religious dogmas. Almost daily one reads about

[14]Robert L. Heilbroner, *The Making of Economic Society*, 4th ed. (Englewood Cliffs, N.J.: Prentice-Hall, 1972), p. 3.

churches opposing such changes as ordination of women for the ministry, population control, certain instructional materials in the schools, racial integration, and other social changes. The tragic mass suicide of members of the Peoples Temple Church in Guyana on November 18, 1978, shocked Americans and focused attention on the growth of religious cults. One frequently reads of frantic parents who charge that some religious group has enslaved their son or daughter.

There has been growing concern about the vitality of the family. Many children do not know a home characterized by genuine compassion for its members. Many families are breaking apart; many children are being reared by one parent, grandparents, aunts, and uncles. In too many cases families are "living hells" rather than places of loving refuge from the corporate world. Too many children are being sacrificed rather than being reared.

With the perils of Watergate and Abscam in our recent past, there is little need to prolong discussion about the shortcomings of the political realm.

Through all of our institutional weaknesses, we are sowing the wind and reaping the whirlwind. All societies carry within them the seeds of their own destruction. The concept of a great public school system can no longer be taken for granted. Within the society today are winds that could blow toward its destruction. Unfortunately, sacrificing the desirable aspects to destroy those that subvert human decency carries no assurance for improvement. Therefore the problem becomes one of removing the cultural decay, which produces inhumanity, and of elevating those institutional aspects that serve the best interests of humanity. This requires coordinated effort in all institutions. The situation, however, is not hopeless. Ours is neither the first nor the last generation to suffer moral decay and yet survive for a better day.

The Need for Strength and Balance

The interdependence of the institutional sectors of society has been noted. This has been demonstrated in numerous studies of the education process. The Coleman Report challenged the influence of schools independent of socioeconomic conditions in other institutional sectors (e.g., family, economics, religion).[15] As most educators have observed, "education" is not restricted to what is done in a school, college or university. The educational organization represents an attempt to mass those resources presumed to offer the student the best

[15]James S. Coleman et al., *Equality of Educational Opportunity* (Washington, D.C.: U.S. Government Printing Office, 1966).

possible opportunity to become "educated." If the child has the predisposition to learn, the school can provide for important cognitive and affective development. As a parent recently exclaimed, "I hear persons say, 'The schools do not educate the children.' Well, I didn't teach my son advanced mathematics or physics." On the other hand, weaknesses in the other institutional sectors will produce psychic patterns antithetical to cognitive development in schools, and these are difficult to overcome. Hence for better schools and colleges, we must work toward strength and balance in our culturally responsive effort in all institutional areas of society.

Confusion in Cultural Functions and the Dangers of Imbalance

The organizational systems through which the institutionalized functions are carried out are frequently in conflict. For example, there are conflicts of educational leaders with leaders in other institutional sectors for economic resources. Leaders primarily engaged in institutionalized functions, therefore, engage in "empire building" in attempts to gain power over competing leaders. These efforts, without a culturally responsible purpose, degenerate into a mindless militancy for power. From time to time one institutionalized leadership has gained ascendancy over others, and this has had harmful consequences. For example, we have known religious monarchies, economic feudalism, and political dictatorships. Plato advanced the idea of the ascendancy of the educational sector through a philosopher king. In these instances, the leadership in one institutional sector dominated all others. Where this happened, exploitation of the people resulted. The society is not well served if the leaders of any sector gain enough power to dominate. The aim always is to work toward strength, balance, and interdependence among institutions.

Another very important problem has been a confusion of institutional functions. One sees, for example, the corporate (economic) invasion of the family. Whereas the family should be based upon certain important humanistic values, one frequently reads about contractual marriage, which resembles the corporate sector. Many religious leaders have persisted in dominating education. Economic leaders have insisted that so-called business practices be used in government and in education. Callahan's *Education and the Cult of Efficiency* documented how leaders from the economic sector (businessmen) influenced administrative practices in the schools.[16] One sees how the education sector is taking on more of the economic norms of industry, including the traditional labor–management ethic.

[16]Raymond E. Callahan, *Education and the Cult of Efficiency* (Chicago: University of Chicago Press, 1962).

The problem of these confusions of functions is that people are denied important needs. Religious dogmas can adversely influence economic productivity. Schools that serve only norms of the economic sector are destroying important familial norms. Schools that serve only the purposes of a political machine are working toward the eventual demise of democratic government. Humans need strength to function. They need an economy through which they can earn a living and produce for the good of society. They need the compassionate love of a family circle devoid of scores on an intelligence test, signatures on a demanding contract, and stresses of a campaign speech. They must have a political system that provides, among many things, protection of their civil rights and beliefs conducive to the moral life. People need to learn to read and write—to have the kind of education that provides the opportunity to enjoy the economic, religious, political, and familial fruits of society.

Leadership for Educational Improvement

In approaching the institutional leadership role, the educational leader should earnestly reflect upon the cultural and educational conditions and their implications for educational development. We approach our tasks optimistically resolved to make things better. What the clients of educational organizations need are educational leaders who are genuine, compassionate, socially responsible, and thoughtful about what leadership involves.

Educational leaders should provide schooling of quality. The functions of the schools should make educational sense; schools should avoid being drowned in functions usually assumed by other institutional agencies of society. This does not mean that the schools should abandon feeding poor children or even compensating compassionately for the absence of a well-functioning family. Obviously, educational leaders should be responsive to the feelings of children, youth, and adults. Their primary function, however, should be educational and based upon sound educational objectives.

A fundamental aspect of educational leadership is to foster interinstitutional cooperation and social integration. Educational organizations eventually fail when educators turn their backs on what is "out there" and peer inward.

Schooling should facilitate the development of a democratic creed and cultural consensus, which, in turn, promote social integration. Some persons have advocated educational policies which would foster cultural feudalism. The authors see no difference in a national policy that would segregate schools on the basis of social status, ethnic origin, or philosophy of life and a national policy of racial segregation. Both would facilitate balkanization rather than unification. Our forefathers fought one civil war over this question.

Administrators should provide leadership in community affairs. Educational interests must be felt in decisions involving economics, family living, and other aspects of the society. Political leaders need to hear educators say that equality of opportunity is dependent upon equality in all institutions. Indeed, educational leaders have much to offer to strengthen other sectors of the society. Perhaps through their leadership, more parents will give more children the backgrounds essential to full participation in the fruits of schooling and even in the potential fruits of a family.

Those administering schooling processes cannot, as many seem to presume, become mothers and fathers to all the children, provide for their economic well-being, perform religious services, or run governmental social welfare services and still be primarily educational leaders. Thus one of the essential leadership tasks of the administrator is to furnish leadership energies, which help educators and other citizens agree what societal role schooling performs and how the other institutional sectors of the culture can assist in the process. Decisions on this and other matters are made in a value-laden culture.

ACTIVITIES/QUESTIONS FOR FURTHER STUDY

1. Select two school districts of a state with which you are familiar that represent the following: (a) an inner city district characterized by a marked degree of "cultural pluralism," (b) a school district characterized by a high degree of cultural congruence among institutions. Do these districts represent different challenges to one's performance as a school administrator? Would the same leadership style be successful in both communities? Should a contingency view of leadership be considered?

2. Continuing your consideration of differences in the cultures in which the schools must be administered, discuss what you know, or may discover through interview, about the functions of cultural institutions (e.g., family, religion, economics, politics, education) in different school districts. How are the schools influenced by the cultural values? What did you learn from this discussion concerning administrative leadership in promoting educational change? How can educators work with leaders in other institutional sectors to promote better educational opportunities for the people?

SUGGESTED READINGS

BEALS, RALPH L., et al. *Introduction to Anthropology,* 5th ed. New York: Macmillan Publishing Co., Inc., 1977.

COX, HARVEY. *The Secular City.* New York: Macmillan Publishing Co., Inc., 1966.

DENISOFF, R. SERGE, and RALPH WARMAN. *An Introduction to Sociology,* 2nd ed. New York: Macmillan Publishing Co., Inc., 1979.

HAVILAND, WILLIAM A. *Cultural Anthropology.* New York: Holt, Rinehart & Winston, Inc., 1978.

KIMBALL, SOLON T. *Culture and the Educative Process.* New York: Teachers College Press, Columbia University, 1974.

KIMBALL, SOLON T., and JAMES E. McCLELLAN. *Education and the New America.* New York: Random House, Inc., 1962.

OLSEN, MARVIN E. *The Process of Social Organization,* 2nd ed. New York: Holt, Rinehart & Winston, Inc., 1978.

TOFFLER, ALVIN. *Future Shock.* New York: Random House, Inc., 1970.

8

Traditional Administrative Theory and Educational Administration

THE AUTHORS NOTED in Chapter 1 that, as a field of scholarly endeavor, educational administration developed later than related fields, such as business administration and public administration. As a result, many of the concepts of relevance for educational administration practitioners and scholars have their origin in these related fields and in basic disciplines, such as political science, psychology, and sociology. A review of theory development in these related fields of administration will show that there have been eras of emphasis. The authors' choice is to focus on three eras: the traditional era, the transitional era, and the systems era. The three-era classification is somewhat arbitrary; different writers use slightly different ways of classifying the developments in administrative theory. Our intention in this chapter and the two which follow is to provide an understanding of the development of administrative thought and its impact on educational administration; consequently, the number of eras identified or labels placed on them is of secondary significance. However, before turning directly to the subject, it seems appropriate to give attention to what is meant by the term *theory*.

The Meaning and Use of Theory

To many practitioners theory is the antithesis of practice; consequently, they are skeptical of it. While recognizing that theory in educational administration is lacking in maturity and refinement and that scholars have done little to help practitioners understand and use it, our position is that one does not function without some type of theory. To illustrate: Mr. Leek, Dean of Boys at Southside High, takes every opportunity to remind the pupils that infractions of the numerous school rules governing pupil conduct will result in swift punishment. Even though he may not articulate the position, Mr. Leek is of the conviction that pupils respond to structure and negative reinforcement. Such a conviction, even though it may be naive and simplistic, constitutes a part of Mr. Leek's "theory of pupil control."

Some Definitions

Undoubtedly contributing to the skepticism of many practitioners is the lack of a commonly accepted definition of the term *theory*. The existence of such variation is not surprising when one considers the differences in philosophic orientation among scholars, the relative newness of the emphasis on theory in educational administration, and the fact that much of what has been written has its origin in pertinent basic disciplines. Following are several definitions that illustrate the variations.

One often quoted definition from Einstein follows:

> In our endeavor to understand reality we are somewhat like a man trying to understand the mechanism of a closed watch. He sees the face and the moving hands, even hears it ticking, but he has no way of opening the case. If he is ingenious he may form a picture of a mechanism which could be responsible for all the things he observes, but he may never be quite sure his picture is the only one which could explain his observations. He will never be able to compare his picture with the real mechanism and he cannot even imagine the possibility or the meaning of such a comparison. But he certainly believes that, as his knowledge increases, his picture of reality will become simpler and simpler and will explain a wider and wider range of his sensuous impressions.[1]

Central to the preceding definition is the attempt to understand reality. The definition treats theory as a continuous process that is followed in an effort to develop an increasingly simple and valid picture of reality. The definition is also very broad; any abstraction developed to understand "what is" can be called a theory.

[1] Albert Einstein and Leopold Infeld, *The Evolution of Physics* (New York: Simon & Schuster, 1938), p. 33.

Let us assume this notion of theory was accepted and one was interested in gaining knowledge of participant behavior in a faculty meeting. Based on observation of participants, one would begin to develop some assumptions, which would help explain the behavior observed. As one collected additional data in relation to these assumptions, he or she would revise the assumptions as necessary to provide an increasingly simple and "valid" explanation of participant behavior at faculty meetings. This "picture" might then be used to predict what might occur under given conditions and to explain behavior in other group settings. Note that no values of good and bad behavior are involved. The object is to gain an increasingly simple "picture" to explain what is and/or predict what will be.

Equally broad in dimension is the following definition, which is illustrative of the thinking of some educational administration scholars of the 1950s:

> A theory of educational administration is, broadly speaking, a collection of concepts or principles that define what educational administration is and that give directions to an individual attempting to be an educational administrator. It is conceivable that a theory of educational administration would include concepts relating to the nature of individual and group life, the major tenets of American democracy, the purposes of public education, the nature of the administrative process, and functions of educational administration.[2]

Even though the preceding definition is like the Einstein definition in its broad character, there is a significant difference. The Einstein definition focuses on what is—reality; whereas this definition implies that theory should encompass both what is and what ought to be. That is, the latter definition implies that theory includes values. There are those who would argue that value statements are not reducible to factual terms and as such are not productive of derivations that can be tested empirically.

A far more restrictive definition has been offered by Feigl:

> In order to provide for a terminology which will not constantly involve us in a tangle of confusion, I propose to define a "theory" as a set of assumptions from which can be derived by purely logico-mathematical procedures a larger set of empirical laws. The theory thereby furnishes an explanation of these empirical laws and unifies the originally relatively heterogenous areas of subject matter characterized by those empirical laws.[3]

[2] Southern States Cooperative Program in Educational Administration, *Better Teaching in School Administration* (Nashville, Tenn.: McQuiddy, 1955), p. 47.

[3] Herbert Feigl, "Principles and Problems of Theory Construction in Psychology," in Wayne Dennis (ed.), *Current Trends in Psychological Theory* (Pittsburgh: University of Pittsburgh Press, 1951), p. 181.

The Feigl definition, obviously reflecting a philosophical bent toward logical positivism, has gained wide acceptance among scholars of educational administration.[4] In terms of this definition, the use of the term *theory* should be restricted to a set of assumptions from which empirical laws may be derived.

A definition, which is favored by the authors, comes from psychologists Calvin S. Hall and Gardner Lindzey: "a theory consists of a set of related assumptions concerning the relevant empirical phenomena, and empirical definitions to permit the user to move from the abstract theory to empirical observation."[5] The Hall and Lindzey definition appears to be a bit less restrictive than the Feigl definition, yet it is not so all-encompassing as to lose meaning and avoids the mixing of *is* and *ought*.

To illustrate briefly the application of this definition, consider the school administrator who begins with the assumption that the morale of a group is related to the productivity of a group. Once such an assumption is made and observable measures of morale and productivity are accepted, one is in a position to collect empirical data in specific settings; that is, to observe the extent to which the assumption holds in, say, a school faculty. If observation in particular settings tends to suggest that the assumption is useful, one is in a position to extend the assumption. For example, if the school principal will engage in specified activities, faculty morale will improve and productivity will increase. However, if observation does not provide support for the assumption that morale and productivity are related, different assumptions might be made as a basis for observations in different settings. In this sense theory helps us understand what is or what may be in regard to particular relationships. However, it does not tell the administrator what should be.

Within the same vein is the definition offered by Kerlinger: *"A theory is a set of interrelated constructs (concepts), definitions, and propositions that presents a systematic view of phenomena by specifying relations among variables, with the purpose of explaining and predicting the phenomena."*[6]

In brief, there is a lack of clarity among scholars about the meaning of theory. As such, the student of educational administration will find a wide range of pronouncements that are labeled as theory.

---

[4] See, for example, Daniel E. Griffiths, *Administrative Theory* (New York: Appleton, 1959); Andrew W. Halpin, *Theory and Research in Administration* (New York: Macmillan, 1966).

[5] Calvin S. Hall and Gardner Lindzey, *Theories of Personality*, 3rd ed. (New York: Wiley, 1978), p. 15.

[6] Fred N. Kerlinger, *Foundations of Behavioral Research*, 2nd ed. (New York: Holt, 1973), p. 9.

Some Common Characteristics

In spite of differences in definition, there appears to be general agreement in regard to four essential characteristics of a theory.

1. Because a theory is the creation of the theorist, there is no prescribed procedure for developing a theory. The theorist may use direct observation, the work of other theorists, the results of other research, or some combination thereof.

2. Because the postulates that make up a theory are abstract, a theory cannot be tested directly. Because a theory cannot be tested directly, it is inappropriate to speak of a theory as being true or false. It is more appropriate to speak of theory in terms of its usefulness. On this point, Hall and Lindzey noted:

> The theory can be seen as a kind of proposition mill, grinding out related empirical statements which can then be confirmed or rejected in the light of suitably controlled empirical data. It is only the derivations or propositions or ideas derived from the theory which are open to empirical test. The theory itself is assumed and acceptance or rejection of it is determined by its *utility*, not by its truth or falsity. In this instance, utility has two components—verifiability and comprehensiveness. *Verifiability* refers to the capacity of the theory to generate predictions which are confirmed when the relevant empirical data are collected. *Comprehensiveness* refers to the scope or completeness of these derivations.[7]

3. The postulates must be internally consistent. Said another way, when viewed collectively, the elements of a theory must appear logically related and add to a consistent whole.

4. Empirical definitions are essential. Because theory leads to propositions that can be tested in the real world, there is a need to define the concepts of the theory in order that the user can have a means of moving from the abstract to the observable. Difficulties in this process are obvious; the aim should be to be as precise as the state of development permits.

Functions of Theory

Theory serves the scholar and practitioner in at least four ways. One function of theory is taxonomic, another is explanatory, a third is predictive, and a fourth is heuristic.

To say that theory has a taxonomic function is to say that theory provides a framework or classification scheme that enables the user to "fit" what is observed or known about a particular group of events. For example, some of the earlier "theories" of educational administration focused on the task areas of educational administration (e.g., curriculum, personnel, facilities, evaluation). If one were studying the

---

[7] Hall and Lindzey, op. cit., pp. 12–13.

use of time by administrators occupying different posts, some such scheme would be useful in organizing the numerous discrete observations so that meaningful conclusions could be drawn from the data. (One of the more frequent criticisms of many "theories of educational administration" is that they are merely classification schemes and are useful only as taxonomies.)

Theory also provides explanations for possible relationships among events (e.g., cause and effect, concomitant variation). For example, assume that while studying a number of different school organizations, the researcher notes that there is considerable commonality within each organization relative to the level of involvement by members of the organization. However, among the organizations the level of involvement ranges from a negative orientation to great commitment. Using Etzioni's theory of compliance relationships,[8] the differences between the organizations might be explained in terms of the dominant mode of power utilized within a given organization.

Closely related to the explanatory function of theory is the predictive function. To illustrate, let us continue with the compliance relationships. Assume that in repeated researches it has been demonstrated that in organizations where the dominant kind of power exercised is coercive, the orientation of most of its members toward the organization is negative. Such a generalization would provide a base from which to predict the kind of power exercised in an organization if the level of involvement by the members was known or vice versa.

As a theory gives rise to derivations—which enable one to describe, explain, and/or predict—the formulations may be found inadequate in any number of ways. Thus theory points the way for further problem solving (further discovery) and eventually perhaps to refined theory. This is the heuristic function, providing a conceptual framework for further discovery and refinement. Said another way, theory provides a base for further research and the extension of the state of knowledge.

Philosophy, Theory, Hypothesis, Research, and Practice

To the authors there is a logical relationship, although not necessarily a linear one, between the terms *philosophy, theory, hypothesis, research,* and *practice.* Moreover, many persons have difficulty in clarifying their thinking about these terms, and this is a factor in their confusion in understanding the meaning of theory.

As is indicated in Chapter 12, the focus of philosophy is on the

---

[8] Amitai Etzioni, *A Comparative Analysis of Complex Organizations,* rev ed. (New York: The Free Press, 1975).

overarching problems of reality, knowledge, values, and their inter-relationships. Furthermore, many ideas are not subject to empirical examination. For example: "What is the nature of reality?" "What is the source of truth?" Therefore, in a sense, one's philosophy is one's unconfirmed belief system or values.

A theory can be viewed as a set of relevant, internally consistent postulates about a particular observable phenomenon along with def-initions to enable the user to move from the abstract to the real in order to describe, explain, predict, and/or advance knowledge. Be-cause theorizing is a human endeavor, the development of a theory, or the willingness to consider the postulates of an already existing theory, is conditioned by one's belief system or philosophy. To illus-trate, if an administrator believed that people were inherently lazy and seek to avoid responsibility, he or she would have great difficulty accepting a theory of supervision that had key postulates providing that the employees would set workloads, standards of performance, and the like.

Hypothesis, a conjectural statement of the relation between two or more variables, is the link between theory and research or prac-tice. A hypothesis is an if–then statement. The logical basis for the statement of conjectural relation is theory; a hypothesis is a deriva-tion from theory.

Obviously, hypotheses give direction to research, and logically research leads to practice. However, as noted previously, the relation-ship is not always so linear. For example, if numerous hypotheses derived from a theory are not confirmed, the hypotheses and/or theory may be altered; or on other occasions, one may move directly from hypothesis to practice and the experience so gained may be used as a basis for developing a new hypothesis or altered theory.

Implication for an Overview of Administrative Theory

At this juncture the reader might appropriately ask, "What is the point?" From our perspective, there are three parts to the answer. First, recognize that historically there has not been a uniform defini-tion attached to the term *theory*. Second, theory is a creative en-deavor; there are no agreed-upon rules for theory development. Third, as a result of the lack of precision in the use of terms and personal nature of theory, the conceptual material that follows in the remain-der of this chapter and the chapters following is wide-ranging. Some of the theories are value-laden, others are not; some are global, others are specific; some have been very productive in terms of hypotheses generated, others have not; some are mere taxonomies, others repre-sent full-blown hypothetic-deductive schemes.

Scientific Management and the Bureaucratic Model

Efforts to develop a systematic conceptual base for administering complex organizations are relatively recent. In fact, most scholars reason that such efforts were closely associated with the industrial revolution and really began as the nineteenth century closed. Jenks offered the following description of the situation up to that point: "Problems of organization and the use of the labor force were solved *ad hoc,* empirically for each establishment. Knowledge about the solutions was transmitted by observation or word of mouth and had to be rediscovered by most new firms."[9]

As a systematic body of thought emerged, certain dominant themes began to take shape. These major themes characterized the preponderance of the scholarly literature in relation to organization and administration until the early 1930s.

Administration as Policy Execution

Primarily because of the efforts of municipal reform-oriented public administration theorists, one of the central doctrines of the era was the separation of policy development (politics) and policy execution (administration). In the latter part of the nineteenth century and the early part of the twentieth century, bossism, corruption, graft, and vice were commonplace in the governments of many big cities. These situations were exposed by the journalists of the day, and as a result "politics" was held in even greater contempt than had been the case previously. Woodrow Wilson, as early as 1887, stated the doctrine concisely: "administration lies outside the proper sphere of politics. Administrative questions are not political questions. Although politics sets the tasks for administration, it should not be suffered to manipulate its offices."[10]

Waldo stated the position in this way: "the process of government, analytically considered, consists of two parts only, namely, decision and execution. It is necessary to decide what should be done—the function and definition of politics—and then to carry out the decision—the role and definition of administration."[11]

In brief, the theorists of the day were careful to restrict the concerns of administrators. The common theme running through the def-

[9] Leland H. Jenks, "Early Phases of the Management Movement," *Administrative Science Quarterly,* 5 (December 1960), 424.

[10] Woodrow Wilson, "The Study of Administration," *Political Science Quarterly,* XLI (December 1941), 494. Reprinted from 1887 issue.

[11] Dwight Waldo, *The Study of Public Administration* (New York: Random House, 1955), p. 40.

initions of the traditional era was that administration was confined to those activities, powers, and techniques necessary to carry out policies established by someone else.

The practical manifestations of the notion are numerous. In the private sector the board-of-directors–president form of corporate leadership is illustrative. In the public sector the result was the city-council–city-manager form of municipal government. Ridley and Nolting, writing in 1934, stated the case as follows:

> The city manager does not let himself be driven or led into taking the leadership or responsibility in matters of policy.[12] . . . The manager may suggest ordinances to the council or methods of procedure without acquiring community leadership in a political sense—a position he carefully avoids.[13]

Historically, there have been, in many localities, legal restrictions placed on the political activities of public employees, including educators. This is a logical outgrowth of the doctrine. Finally, at the federal, state, and local levels of government the "politically neutral" career service is found (e.g., the civil service system). From the point of view of the traditional-era theorists, such a system can be supported on the basis that it protects the "bureaucrat" from the uncertainties of the policy development arena.

Scientific Principles to Maximize Worker Output

While the public administration theorists were focusing on separating administration from politics, within the industrial sector emphasis was being placed on developing a set of principles that would, if rationally applied, maximize the use of available human and material resources in achieving the goals of the enterprise. The result of this kind of emphasis is most clearly illustrated by the work of Frederick W. Taylor (1856–1915), who is frequently referred to as the father of the scientific management movement.

Taylor—trained as an engineer, experienced at all levels in industrial shops, and obviously imbued with the Protestant ethic of the day—believed in economic rationality, hard work, and defined social roles and position. His basic orientation is demonstrated by the following:

> If the writer's judgment . . . that for their own good it is as important that workmen should not be very much overpaid, as it is that they should not be underpaid. If overpaid, many will work irregularly and tend to become more or less shiftless, extravagant, and dissipated. It does not

[12]Clarence E. Ridley and Orin F. Nolting, *The City-Manager Profession* Chicago: University of Chicago Press, 1934), p. 30.
[13]Ibid., p. 31.

do for most men to get rich too fast. The writer's observation, however, would lead him to the conclusion that most men tend to become more instead of less thrifty when they receive the proper increase for an extra hard day's work. . . . They live rather better, begin to save money, become more sober, and work more steadily. And this certainly forms one of the strongest reasons for advocating this type of management.[14]

This orientation undergirds the scientific principles he advanced. Villers summarized his principles as follows:

1. *Time-study principle.* All productive effort should be measured by accurate time study and a standard time established for all work done in the shop.
2. *Piece-rate principle.* Wages should be proportional to output and their rates based on the standards determined by time study. As a corollary, a worker should be given the highest grade of work of which he is capable.
3. *Separation-of-planning-from-performance principle.* Management should take over from the workers the responsibility for planning the work and making the performance physically possible. Planning should be based on time studies and other data related to production which are scientifically determined and systematically classified; it should be facilitated by standardization of tools, implements, and methods.
4. *Scientific-methods-of-work principle.* Management should take over from the workers the responsibility for their methods of work, determine scientifically the best methods, and train the workers accordingly.
5. *Managerial-control principle.* Managers should be trained and taught to apply scientific principles of management and control (such as management by exception and comparison with valid standards).
6. *Functional-management principle.* The strict application of military principles should be reconsidered and the industrial organization should be so designed that it best serves the purpose of improving the coordination of activities among the various specialists.[15]

The essence of Taylor's position, and of others who wrote in the same vein, was that job analysis was to be used to determine each element of each job; using empirical data, "best" methods of performing each job were to be determined; standard times, rates, and equipment were to be employed; there was to be a clear division of responsibility between management and the workers. Obviously, the basis for such a point of view is that there is "one best way" to do each job in order to maximize worker output—an empirically determined, universal truth.

[14]Frederick W. Taylor, *Shop Management* (New York: Harper & Row, 1911), p. 27.
[15]Raymond Villers, *Dynamic Management in Industry* (Englewood Cliffs, N.J.: Prentice-Hall, 1960), p. 29. Quoted by permission.

The impact of such principles can be observed in almost any large organization, particularly an organization that has a production goal as opposed to a sales or service goal. For example, "job analysis" is accepted, almost without question, as the basis for the development of job descriptions. Many sales and/or production-oriented enterprises base employee pay on some unit of measured output. Also, there has been increasing use of these principles in service organizations, such as education.

Efficiency in Organizational Design

While some, such as Taylor, were focusing on the development of scientific principles that could be applied directly to the supervision of employees, other theorists focused on the structure of organizations. The aim was to develop a design to enable the objectives of the organization to be accomplished with minimum expenditure of human and fiscal resources. The resulting design came to be known as a bureaucracy. The bureaucratic model in its original form was proposed by Max Weber (1864–1920), a German sociologist.[16] Weber, who saw a bureaucratic organization as a part of a total social theory, felt it was a form of organization that could find expression in governmental, industrial, religious, and scientific organizations. He did not hold what came to be the popular view of bureaucracy, which is often described with such terms as *paper shuffling, red tape,* and *inefficiency.* Weber stated his position as follows:

> the purely bureaucratic type of administrative organization—that is, the monocratic variety of bureaucracy—is, from a purely technical point of view, capable of attaining the highest degree of efficiency and in this sense formally the most rational known means of carrying out imperative control over human beings. It is superior to any other form in precision, in stability, in the stringency of its discipline, and in its reliability.[17]

In Weber's analysis, an ideal bureaucracy encompasses many different elements. Blau suggested that these could be reduced to four basic characteristics: a hierarchy of authority, impersonality, a system of rules, and specialization.[18]

In a bureaucracy, rational or legal authority "resting on a belief in the 'legality' of patterns of normative rules and the right of those elevated to authority under such rules to issue commands" is the most relevant.[19] The hierarchy serves to assign and validate such author-

---

[16]Max Weber, *The Theory of Social and Economic Organization,* trans. A. M. Henderson and Talcott Parsons, Talcott Parsons (ed.) (New York: The Free Press, 1964).

[17]Ibid., p. 337.

[18]Peter M. Blau, *Bureaucracy in Modern Society* (New York: Random House, 1956), p. 19.

[19]Weber, op. cit., p. 328.

ity. There is a precise, impersonal system of superordination and subordination. Each office (position) is responsible to the one immediately above it and derives its authority from this superior position. Each officeholder has the right to issue orders to his or her subordinates and the subordinates have the duty to obey. This control, however, is confined to the authority assigned to the officeholder's position.

Rationality undergirds a bureaucratic organization. The organization is improved to the extent that personal, irrational, and emotional factors are eliminated from official acts. The result will be rational decision making and equitable treatment for subordinates. Weber expressed the impersonality notion as follows:

> The dominance of a spirit of formalistic impersonality, *"Sine ira et studio"*; without hatred or passion, and hence without affection or enthusiasm. The dominant norms are concepts of straightforward duty without regard to personal considerations. Everyone is subject to formal equality of treatment; that is, everyone in the same empirical situation. This is the spirit in which the ideal official conducts his office.[20]

A system of organizational rules and consistent application of them in particular instances ensures a high degree of predictable behavior and conformity with prescribed patterns of behavior. Such rules, intentionally established and recorded in writing, define responsibilities and relationships among the several offices, protect subordinates from arbitrary acts of superiors, and generally serve to enhance rationality and reduce friction within the organization.

In a bureaucracy there is a division of labor and employment in a given position. Employment is based on the individual having the technical competence to fill the special demands of the position. Abbott and Lovell offered the following description of bureaucracy on this point:

> Employment in a bureaucracy is based upon technical competence and constitutes a career. Promotions are to be determined by seniority, or achievement, or both; tenure is to be assured; and fixed compensation and retirement provisions are to be made. Since individuals with specialized skills are employed to perform specialized activities, they must be protected from arbitrary dismissal or denial of promotion on purely personal ground.[21]

The work division concept was also central to Luther Gulick's theory of organization. Gulick, who served for many years as director

---

[20] Ibid., p. 340.
[21] Max G. Abbott and John T. Lovell (eds.), *Change Perspectives in Educational Administration* (Auburn, Ala.: School of Education, Auburn University, 1965), p. 43.

of Columbia University's Institute of Public Administration, reasoned that if work division was essential in organizations, coordination was mandatory. He advanced two interdependent ways for achieving co-ordination.

1. By organization, that is, by interrelating the subdivisions of work by allotting them to men who are placed in a structure of authority, so that work may be coordinated by orders of superiors to subordinates, reaching from the top to the bottom of the entire enterprise.
2. By dominance of an idea, that is, the development of intelligent sin-gleness of purpose in the minds and wills of those who are working together as a group, so that each worker will of his own accord fit his task into the whole with skill and enthusiasm.[22]

In support of his two basic principles he advanced a number of other ideas, including span of control, unity of command, and a sys-tem of departmentalism.

Because of limits of time, energy, and knowledge, the chief ex-ecutive of an organization can personally supervise only a few subordinates. These subordinates must supervise others, who in turn supervise others, until each person in the organization is reached. The limits on the span of control (the number of employees directly supervised) are determined by the nature of the work and the capac-ity of the executive. Based on experience, Gulick cited examples in which the number supervised ranged from three to twelve.[23]

In regard to the unity-of-command idea, Gulick offered the fol-lowing:

A workman subject to orders from several sources will be confused, in-efficient, and irresponsible; a workman subject to orders from but one superior may be methodical, efficient, and responsible. Unity of com-mand thus refers to those who are commanded, not those who issue the commands. . . . The rigid adherence to the principle of unity of com-mand may have its absurdities; these are, however, unimportant in comparison with the certainty of confusion, inefficiency, and irrespon-sibility which arise from the violation of the principle.[24]

Obviously, when the notions of a hierarchy of authority, span of control, and unity of command are taken collectively, the result is a pyramidal-type organization. In this type of organization there is an integrated model of command; authority is lodged at the apex of the pyramid, and the lines of authority run directly from the top to the bottom of the organization.

[22] Luther Gulick and L. Urwick (eds.), *Papers on the Science of Administration* (New York: Institute of Public Administration, Columbia University, 1937), p. 6. Quoted by permission.
[23] Ibid., pp. 7–8.
[24] Ibid., p. 9.

Gulick's system of departmentalism is a way of "assembling" an enterprise so as to aggregate workers and enhance organizational efficiency. Specifically, he offered four bases upon which an enterprise could be organized: by major purpose, by major process, by clientele or material, and by place.

To organize by major purpose means to bring together into a single unit (department) all those persons who are working toward providing a particular service. For example, city government might have a fire department, education department, health department, police department, utilities department, and the like. Organized in such a manner, all employees concerned with schools (e.g., teachers, administrators, clerical personnel, maintenance personnel, school nurses) would be a part of the education department. The advantages of organizing by purpose are threefold: (1) a single executive has control of needed resources to accomplish the identified purpose and, as such, can give his or her energy to the job—not negotiating with others for assistance and cooperation; (2) the public, concerned with results, not methods, can more clearly recognize "who is to do what"; (3) employee understanding of objectives will be enhanced and lead to greater employee loyalty and effort.[25]

Each of the previously mentioned departments might have a number of processes in common—personnel selection, purchasing, planning, and the like. Thus units could be created for each of these processes and bring together those persons engaged in the process. Such organization enables maximum use to be made of specialized skills of workers, permits investment in labor-saving equipment that could not be afforded otherwise, and makes it possible for employees to understand the route of career service within their specific field.[26]

Organization by clientele or material, regardless of purpose or techniques, means bringing employees together on the basis of the people served or the things dealt with. An often-cited example at the federal level of government is the Veterans Administration, which deals with all problems of and services to veterans. Such an organization permits the development of increased employee skills through dealing over and over with the same situations.[27]

Organization by place refers to bringing together in some locale all those who work in a limited area, regardless of service provided or techniques used. For example, many large international business firms have geographic units (e.g., a Latin American division). At the local government level, many cities have their police departments organized by precincts, and almost all police activities in a given area

25 Ibid., pp. 21–22.
26 Ibid., pp. 23–25.
27 Ibid., pp. 25–26.

go through the precinct station. The advantages of organization by place include ease of coordination and control and adaptability of the organization to the needs of the area served.[28]

Gulick recognized disadvantages in each of the four bases of organizing and commented on the interrelationships as follows:

> If an organization is erected about any one of these four characteristics of work, it becomes immediately necessary to recognize the other characteristics in constructing the secondary and tertiary divisions of the work. . . . While the first or primary division of any enterprise is of very great significance, it must nonetheless be said that there is no one most effective pattern for determining the priority and order for the introduction of these interdependent principles. It will depend in any case upon the results which are desired at a given time and place.[29]

Another idea popularized by the traditional-era theorists which contributed to efficiency in organizational design was the line-and-staff system of organization. While recognizing that there was a lack of a precise statement of meaning and that in practice the system was a compromise, Urwick identified Mooney as having "definite and acceptable ideas" and quoted him as follows:

> A line officer exercises authority over all of the body of organization lying beneath him on the chart, whereas the influence exerted by a staff officer outside of his immediate department is, so far as it is authoritative, an authority of ideas. The staff officers are, in their functional capacities, responsible advisers to their respective line superiors, and advisers also to the corresponding staff officers in the subordinate organization strata, but any direct line instructions they may wish to see promulgated may be promulgated only back through their line of contact with their superiors and down thence to the line officers in the next subordinate stratum. . . . If the expression descriptive of a staff officer's authority—an "authority of ideas"—means anything at all, it means that the staff executives' plans and recommendations are entitled to the respect and consideration of the line executive.[30]

The concept also finds expression in terms of the employees supervised directly. The line administrator supervises directly those who perform duties related to the primary mission of the organization (e.g., production workers in a factory) or those who supervise the workers who perform such duties (e.g., the foreman of the production workers). Staff administrators, on the other hand, supervise directly support personnel only (in a factory, such personnel would include personnel specialists, maintenance workers, and the like).

[28] Ibid., pp. 25–30.
[29] Ibid., pp. 31–32.
[30] Ibid., pp. 58–59.

Administration as a Series of Elements

Henri Fayol (1841–1925)—a geologist and a mining engineer, an industrial executive, and a teacher of administration—concentrated much of his conceptual effort on top management. Perhaps his major contribution was his "elements of management." He is the father of what is called the "administrative process," and his effort is reflected in most subsequent formulations. In *Administration Industrielle et Générale,* his classic work, first published in 1916, he defined the basic process or functions of management:

> to forecast and plan, to organize, to command, to coordinate, and to control. To foresee and provide means examining the future and drawing up the plan of action. To organize means building up the dual structure, material and human, of the undertaking. To command means maintaining activity among the personnel. To coordinate means binding together, unifying and harmonizing all activity and effort. To control means seeing that everything occurs in conformity with established rule and expressed command.[31]

Gulick adapted Fayol's analysis to the organization of the work of the President of the United States. He defined the job of the chief executive with the "acronym" *POSDCORB,* consisting of initials for the following activities:

- Planning, that is working out in broad outline the things that need to be done and the methods for doing them to accomplish the purpose set for the enterprise;
- Organizing, that is the establishment of the formal structure of authority through which work subdivisions are arranged, defined and coordinated for the defined objective;
- Staffing, that is the whole personnel function of bringing in and training the staff and maintaining favorable conditions of work;
- Directing, that is the continuous task of making decisions and embodying them in specific and general orders and instructions and serving as the leader of the enterprise;
- Coordinating, that is the all-important duty of interrelating the various parts of the work;
- Reporting, that is keeping those to whom the executive is responsible informed as to what is going on, which thus includes keeping himself and his subordinates informed through records, research and inspection;
- Budgeting, with all that goes with budgeting in the form of fiscal planning, accounting and control.[32]

---

[31] Henri Fayol, *General and Industrial Management,* trans. Constance Storrs (London: Pitman, 1949), pp. 5–6.
[32] Gulick and Urwick, op. cit., p. 13.

In sum, Fayol, Gulick, and the others who followed saw a precise definition of the functions of an administrator as another important notion in the development of a "set of principles," which collectively would constitute a theory of administration.

Impact of Scientific Management and Bureaucratic Concepts on Educational Administration

In the preceding section our aim was to introduce the key notions of what we have called the traditional-era theorists. Because these ideas originated in basic disciplines or fields of administration other than education, no effort was made to show the application of the ideas to the development and practice of educational administration. We now examine the meaning of these important ideas for educational administration.

As was discussed in Chapter 1, the study of educational administration developed more slowly than some related fields. Before World War II, well-defined graduate programs to prepare educational administrators were limited. There was no effort to accredit those programs in existence, and in most states administrator certification requirements were at best undemanding and often were nonexistent. Furthermore, in the opinion of many, education has historically been viewed as unique when compared to other public services (e.g., health services, utilities). Thus one might conclude that the traditional-era theorists had limited impact on the administration and organization of the educational enterprise. However, although many of their ideas never reached full fruition and others were belatedly applied, most of the essential thoughts found at least partial expression in educational organizations.

Efforts to Separate Policy Development and Execution

Pre-World War II educational administration scholars emphasized the policy development role of the lay board both at the state and district levels and the policy execution responsibilities of the administrator. For example, one widely used 1940 text in educational administration defined the "executive activity" as "all the acts or processes essential to make policies and procedures effective."[33] The implication was that the development of such policies and procedures was to be left to someone else—the lay board. Sears, writing in 1947 relative to the problems of policy making in education, commented on the situation as follows:

[33] Arthur B. Moehlman, *School Administration* (Boston: Houghton, 1940), p. 231.

These problems exist because by tradition administering a school system has been thought of, first of all, as a task of applying authority
that has been created in laws or granted by boards of education. The
staff aspect of the job—the research, the finding out what to do and how
to do it, the development of a policy or a plan—was not treated as a
major aspect of the administrative task.[34]

As suggested by Sears, state legislative enactments made a distinction in responsibilities. Such enactments remain in vogue today.

Because the pre-World War II scholars tended to differentiate
between policy making and execution of policy, it logically follows
that they would advocate, to the extent feasible, the nonpolitical
character of educational leadership and such was the case. Texts of
the era exhorted students of educational administration to refrain,
insofar as possible, from political activity, particularly partisan politics. Consider the following from Moehlman's 1940 text:

The need for freeing the education function from partisan political domination or control cannot be emphasized too strongly. The only way in
which this aim may be achieved is through maintaining the corporate
and political independence of the local school district. The worst effects
of partisan politics upon the schools are most obvious in those urban
districts when the mayor, council, city commission, or judicial officers
are responsible for the appointment of school board members. The second worst effect is noted in urban districts when boards of education
are chosen on partisan ballot. The least political control is exercised in
cities where the board of education, even though fiscally dependent upon
municipal authorities, is still elected directly by the people at nonpartisan elections distinct and separate from regular municipal elections. The fact that the typical large urban school district is usually
coterminous with corporate boundaries may also be a contributing factor in the development of these political controls.
There is no implication in these statements that education or any other
public social activity can be completely divorced from politics in a functional sense if politics is defined as "the art of good government." . . .
It does mean that through the separation of school from other civic and
non-pertinent political issues and through concentration of the electoral
interest in the single issue of education, it is possible to maintain direct
community interest and participation and to secure a relatively high
type of instructional efficiency unhampered by the diffusion that natu-
rally results from the integration of diverse interests.[35]

As suggested by Moehlman, to try to divorce education from the
perceived evils of municipal government, a number of ideas were advocated, many of which still prevail and are encoded in state statutes.
These included appointed superintendents, district boundaries that

[34]Jesse B. Sears, *Public School Administration* (New York: Ronald Press, 1947),
pp. 210–211.
[35]Moehlman, op. cit., pp. 158–159.

were not conterminous with local municipalities (creation of a unique electorate), separate nonpartisan elections, special fiscal powers for the local school district, a directly elected governing board for the local school district that was separate from the municipal governing body, and limitations on the political activity of educators.

The tenor of the writings of many of the scholars of that era was that politics was "bad," and educational leaders who were seen as politicians were thought by many to be unprofessional.

Application of Scientific Principles

In spite of the insistence by some educators that the concepts intended to maximize the productivity of workers were more applicable in production organizations than in service organizations, such as education, some of the notions advanced by Taylor and others found expression in educational organizations, particularly in the large city districts. In fact, some of the early education scholars appeared to be avid followers of Taylorism. Consider, for example, the following statement from a 1913 paper by Bobbitt:

> In any organization, the directive and supervisory members must clearly define the ends toward which the organization strives. They must co-ordinate the labors of all so as to attain those ends. They must find the best methods of work, and they must enforce the use of these methods on the part of the workers. They must determine the qualifications necessary for the workers and see that each rises to the standard qualifications, if it is possible; and when impossible, see that he is separated from the organization. This requires direct or indirect responsibility for the preliminary training of the workers before service, and for keeping them up to standard qualifications during service. Directors and supervisors must keep the workers supplied with detailed instructions as to the work to be done, the standards to be reached, the methods to be employed, and the material and appliances to be used. They must supply the workers with the necessary materials and appliances. . . . They must place incentives before the worker in order to stimulate desirable effort.[36]

Even though other education writers of the era were not as faithful to the language of Taylor as was Bobbitt, they did emphasize the job of the educational executive as determining what is to be done to carry out policy and how it is to be done (based on scientific study), ensuring resources to do the job are provided as needed, and instructing the subordinate educators in the application of appropriate methods and materials. Clearly, the point of view was that the educational

[36]Franklin Bobbitt, "Some General Principles of Management Applied to the Problems of City School Systems," in *The Supervision of City Schools,* twelfth yearbook of the National Society for the Study of Education, part I (Chicago: University of Chicago Press, 1913), pp. 7–8.

leader was to be a possessor of superior knowledge and to exercise considerable power.

Cubberley's 1916 characterization of the superintendent is illustrative of this view. Cubberley saw the superintendent as "the organizer and director of the work of the schools in all their different phases . . . the executive officer of the school board, and also its eyes, and ears, and brains. . . . the supervisor of the instruction in the schools, and also the leader, advisor, inspirer, and friend of the teachers."[37]

In the pre-World War II era the education colleges emphasized prescriptive instruction in regard to specific and immediate educational tasks and methods. This emphasis on specific skills and mechanics was also present in the exisitng preparation programs for educational administrators. Under the primary direction of George Strayer, Teachers College, Columbia was the leader in this regard. However, the rise of the human relations and Gestalt psychology movements in the 1930s blunted the wide application of many of the specific "scientific principles" expounded. Furthermore, many school executives (particularly outside of the large city districts) of the 1920s and 1930s had little specific preparation and in general lacked knowledge of the scientific principles. Also, many of the so-called best methods were found to be less than adequate in practice. Even so, several of the notions of the traditional era, often in modified form, have been applied to education. At one point curriculum experts advocated the development of curricula on the basis of "activity analysis" (a modified version of job analysis). The development and use of pupil achievement and aptitude tests and of school surveys were products of the era. In most educational organizations with any degree of complexity, job analyses with resulting job specifications and descriptions are fully institutionalized. In-service training in methods for teachers, and most categories of support workers, receives major attention in most school districts. One could argue that many of the notions associated with the efforts at educational accountability and management by objectives of the 1970s represented updated applications of Taylorism. Taylor's piece-rate principle has seldom been applied with any degree of success in educational organizations. The obvious problem is that there is little agreement relative to the measure of output that is to be used as a basis for pay. Also, educators have frequently ignored his corollary that a worker should be given the highest grade of work he or she can perform. Even today it is not unusual to observe educational administrators and teachers performing clerical, custodial, and school building maintenance tasks.

[37] Ellwood P. Cubberley, *Public School Administration* (Boston: Houghton, 1916), p. 132.

Organizational Efficiency in Education

As enumerated previously, the traditionalists advocated a number of concepts designed to enhance the ability of an organization to accomplish its objectives with minimum expenditure of human and fiscal resources. These include an integrated hierarchy of legal-rational authority, a defined span of control, an impersonal system of superordination and subordination, a set of written rules and regulations that are uniformly applied, employment and promotion based on technical competence to fill the special demands of the job, work division, and a line–staff system. Application of these ideas to educational organizations has been widespread. However, like the application in other types of organizations, in most instances these concepts have not been operationalized in their "pure form."

The prevailing organizational form for local school districts and other educational agencies represents a kind of integrated hierarchy of authority, which appears to be rational. Also in terms of statutes, ordinances, policies, and the like, this authority structure has a legal base. Recall Figure 5-1 (shown in Chapter 5), which illustrates a basic organizational form that may be found, with variations, in many local school districts. As can be seen, the board of education is elected and subordinated to the wishes of the people, as well as being bound by statutes, court decisions, and the like. The board appoints the superintendent, who in turn controls the subordinate administrators with the teachers' line of authority flowing from the assistant superintendent for school operations to the principal. Thus in this illustration, the unity of command notion is observed.

Even though the integrated model under the control of a single executive, answerable to an elected board, is the prevailing form, it is not, and has not been, universally used. As noted in Chapter 5, in the past several districts, especially in the Midwest, employed an organizational form with dual or multiple executives—a situation where two or more administrators answered directly to the school board (e.g., a superintendent for instructional affairs and a superintendent for business affairs). Even though some state statutes still permit it, today few school districts use the multiple executive concept. Also, in many school districts in the South, both the board and superintendent are elected by the people directly. Or in some instances, either the board or the superintendent is appointed by some other governmental body (e.g., the city council). In such instances there is "split authority" at the top of the structure.

The concept of span of control is widely recognized in educational organizations. To illustrate, through the use of assistant superintendents, the superintendent's span is limited. Likewise, the building principal, by the use of assistant principals and department heads, confines the number of persons who report directly. Most educational organizations of any size operate on the basis of written policies and rules and regulations, which in theory are to be uniformly applied. Because most complex educational organizations make use of job specifications, advertise job openings, and have well-defined selection procedures, the concept of technical competence as a basis for filling a given position is institutionalized.

Since the demise of the one-room school, the work division notion has been applied in education. Where education is considered to be a unit of municipal government and is set up as a separate department, the concept of "organization by purpose" is recognized. This is also the case in a high school or college with its several departments (English, mathematics, and the like). The use of divisions of personnel and business (see Figure 5-1) represents "organization by process." (The line units have personnel to be processed and numerous business procedures in common.) The neighborhood school and, from the point of view of the state, the local school district are examples of organization by place. Nursery schools, elementary schools, middle schools, and adult centers are representations of "organization by clientele."

In educational organizations of any significant size, the line–staff system is usually present. As illustrated by Figure 5-1, the superintendent, assistant superintendent for school operations, and principals are line administrators; the other assistant superintendents and administrative assistants are staff administrators.

In sum, as schools, school districts, and colleges have grown in size and complexity, they have assumed the basic characteristics of a bureaucracy. As noted at the outset, however, many of these characteristics do not exist in the idealized form advocated by Weber, Gulick, and others. Sears identified the central point as follows:

> The authority of law is an essential element in public school administration. . . . But law is not all. To settle most questions we have also to use facts and reasoning. . . . Then there is the factor of tradition and public attitude. These cannot be set aside ruthlessly in a democracy. The power of law, of knowledge, of tradition and public opinion are not turned on and off easily, for they must flow to their tasks through a complicated system of channels and under control of many people, each person an individual, regardless of whether he may be also an officer and a part of a system of management.[38]

Administration as a Process

As suggested previously, the concept of administrative process is derived from Fayol's "elements of management."[39] The concept,

[38] Sears, op. cit., p. 107.
[39] Fayol, loc. cit.

which Campbell and associates defined as "the way by which an organization makes decisions and takes action to achieve its goals,"[40] has been given considerable attention by educational administration scholars. Sears was the first to give detailed attention to the concept, and he frankly admitted his reliance on Fayol, among others. Specifically, he noted, "The major divisions of the school administrative process were not difficult to identify, and no reason was found for departing significantly from Fayol's classification, applied earlier in the field of public administration."[41] Sears, who stressed the unity of administrative activity as opposed to separate and discrete elements, saw the process as including five different kinds of activity: planning, organizing, direction, coordination, and controlling.[42]

In 1954 the leadership of the Southern States Cooperative Program in Educational Administration suggested there were five "general administrative methods" used in the performance of the critical tasks of educational administration. These were (1) defining needs and exploring problems; (2) seeking information, determining resources, and providing consultants; (3) proposing policies, formulating possible courses of action, and offering alternative proposals; (4) initiating and implementing plans; and (5) evaluating progress.[43]

In the 1955 yearbook of the American Association of School Administrators, the "constituent functions" of school administrators were identified as planning, allocation, stimulation, coordination, and evaluation.[44] Gregg's formulation consisted of seven components: decision making, planning, organizing, communicating, influencing, coordinating, and evaluating.[45] Campbell and associates described the process in terms of decision making, programming, stimulating, coordinating, and appraising.[46]

The terms differ, yet there is great similarity in the statements. The later theorists appear to differ from the early theorists in only two significant ways. First, in the more recent formulations, decision making is seen as a critical component of the process; the earlier the-

[40] Roald F. Campbell, John E. Corbally, Jr., and John A. Ramseyer, *Introduction to Educational Administration* (Boston: Allyn & Bacon, 1958), p. 179.

[41] Jesse B. Sears, *The Nature of the Administrative Process* (New York: McGraw-Hill, 1950), p. ix.

[42] Ibid., pp. 31–37.

[43] Southern States Cooperative Program in Educational Administration, *Improving Preparation Programs in Educational Administration* (Nashville, Tenn.: George Peabody College, 1954), pp. 102–105.

[44] American Association of School Administrators, Commission on Staff Relations in School Administration, *Staff Relations in School Administration* (Washington, D.C.: The Association, 1955), p. 17.

[45] Russell T. Gregg, "The Administrative Process," in Roald F. Campbell and Russell T. Gregg (eds.), *Administrative Behavior in Education* (New York: Harper & Row, 1957), p. 274.

[46] Roald F. Campbell, Edwin M. Bridges, and Raphael O. Nystrand, *Introduction to Educational Administration*, 5th ed. (Boston: Allyn & Bacon, 1977), p. 165.

orists (e.g., Fayol, Sears) tended to ignore this component. Second, words such as *stimulating* and *influencing* were substituted for *commanding* and *directing*. In the opinion of the authors the later emphasis on decision making is a reflection of the rejection of the notion of the separation of policy development and execution, and the use of less authoritarian terms (e.g., *stimulating*) reflects the impact of the human relations movement, which is discussed in the next chapter.

In sum, the traditional theorists postulated administration as consisting of a series of elements. Educational administrator scholars have consistently viewed the concept as viable. Whatever words are used, there seems to be agreement that for an educational organization to function, decisions must be reached about what is to be done, plans must be developed in terms of the goals, fiscal and human resources must be allocated in terms of the planning, people must be motivated to act, teamwork must be ensured, and a determination must be made of the extent to which the goals were achieved in terms of the predetermined plans and standards.

A Critique of the Traditional Era

As suggested earlier, the traditional-era theorists represent a "first effort" to move to a type of administration based on an organized body of knowledge. Thus in retrospect it does not seem surprising that the critics of the traditional-era theorists were numerous and vocal. There are at least five lines of criticism, which appear to have some validity.

First, the dichotomy between policy development (politics) and policy execution (administration) came to be seen as unrealistic. That is, the notion lacked utility in that observation in real-world settings suggested that there was a large "gray area" between development and execution. Waldo, writing in 1955, probably best described what occurred:

> The rigid, even dogmatic separation of politics and administration has been almost wholly abandoned during the past fifteen or twenty years. Indeed, it has become correct to regard administration as a process diffused or permeated with politics—meaning by the term both the contest for power (whether or not it is party contest) and the making of policy.[47]

Educational administration writers were not as direct as Waldo; they tended to stress the broadened responsibilities of educational ad-

[47] Waldo, op. cit., p. 42.

ministration. Pierce and his associates, in the forefront of those rejecting the dichotomy, made the point as follows:

> Neither legal requirements nor traditional roles assigned by the community are likely to keep abreast of present demands of administration. . . . educational administration's responsibility deals with (1) the development of community policy for education, (2) the execution of educational policy, and (3) the continuous evaluation of educational policy and progress in carrying it out.[48]

Even though broader, a closely related second criticism of traditional theory is the closed-system view; that is, the theory does not really take into account the impact of forces in the environment on the organization. Again, as Pierce and associates stated it, "attitudes, understandings, and aspirations with respect to education do not exist apart from the policies and beliefs that underlie the total behavior of the community."[49] The theory is deterministic as opposed to probabilistic. Thompson, referring to traditional theory as the "rational-model approach," commented as follows:

> It seems clear that the rational-model approach uses a closed-system strategy. It also seems clear that the developers of the several schools using the rational model have been primarily students of performance or efficiency, and only incidentally students of organizations. Having focused on control of the organization as a target, each employs a closed system of logic and conceptually closes the organization to coincide with that type of logic, for this elimination of uncertainty is the way to achieve determinateness.[50]

A third criticism relates to the place afforded people. Some critics suggested that in an effort to stress economy and efficiency people were ignored by this school of thought. It has been referred to as the "man-as-a-machine" theory. Others have suggested that, in reality, the theory is based on untenable assumptions about the basic nature of human beings. McGregor, referring to traditional theory as "Theory X," suggested that the theory was based on the following assumptions:

1. The average human being has an inherent dislike of work and will avoid it if he can. . . .
2. Because of this human characteristic of dislike of work, most people must be coerced, controlled, directed, threatened with punishment to

[48] Truman M. Pierce et al., *Community Leadership for Public Education* (Englewood Cliffs, N.J.: Prentice-Hall, 1955), p. 270.

[49] Ibid., p. 225.

[50] James D. Thompson, *Organizations in Action* (New York: McGraw-Hill, 1967), p. 6.

get them to put forth adequate effort toward the achievement of organizational objectives. . . .

3. The average human being prefers to be directed, wishes to avoid responsibility, has relatively little ambition, wants security above all.[51]

Perhaps in his zeal McGregor overstated the point. Nevertheless, latter-day scholars are almost unanimous in the opinion that the theory gives inadequate attention to people or assumes that they function from purely economic motives.

The power ascribed to the executive became a fourth line of criticism. By positing such notions as a rigid hierarchy of authority, unity of command, span of control, executive control of budgets, and a line-and-staff system, the traditional theorists created a "strong-executive" theory. Some persons argued from a value base that such power in the hands of the executive is not in the best interests of the people and is inconsistent with the idea of equality. Others based their criticism of the strong executive in terms of the "generalists' power versus the specialists' knowledge." For example, Victor A. Thompson saw a basic conflict between the organizational hierarchy based upon position and the importance of technical specialization and the accompanying authority of knowledge.[52] Illustrative of Thompson's point is the situation that exists in many school districts: The school principal, as a line administrator, has organizational authority over each teacher in the school; yet, the teacher's subject matter specialist or supervisor, a central office staff administrator, presumably has the greater technical specialization.

A fifth line of criticism is logical and methodological. Specifically, critics have frequently suggested that the "principles" are too vague for utility. They are simply "proverbs," "truisms," or "common sense." The principles are also lacking in internal consistency. A frequently cited example is that the notion of specialization is often in conflict with the idea of unity of command. The situation mentioned above involving the principal, the teacher, and the central office subject matter supervisor is illustrative. The traditional theorists have also been subject to criticism about the way they derived their principles (e.g., personal experience). Furthermore, it is noted that often derivations from the principles have not been validated by application of the scientific method.

In spite of such criticisms and the many modifications made,

[51] Douglas M. McGregor, *The Human Side of Enterprise* (New York: McGraw-Hill, 1960), pp. 33–34. Quoted by permission.

[52] Victor A. Thompson, "Hierarchy, Specialization, and Organizational Conflict," *Administrative Science Quarterly,* 5 (March 1961), 485–521.

much of what the traditional-era theorists advocated can be found in large, complex organizations, including schools, colleges, and universities. For example, still much in evidence are such notions as a hierarchy of legal authority, division of labor, time-and-motion analysis, span of control, departmentalism, and the like. Furthermore, some would suggest that the 1970s emphasis on Management by Objectives (MBO) (described in Chapter 11) is representative of a traditionalist approach to controlling.

ACTIVITIES/QUESTIONS FOR FURTHER STUDY

1. Develop in your own words a working definition of the difference among the following terms: philosophy, theory, and hypothesis.
2. Review the educational laws (i.e., state school code) of your state and determine the extent to which educational policy making and execution are separated. To what extent do the laws place restrictions on the political activities of educators?
3. Using an educational organization with which you are familiar, prepare a list of examples which represent applications of scientific principles and bureaucratic characteristics in operation.

SUGGESTED READINGS

BLAU, PETER M. *Bureaucracy in Modern Society.* New York: Random House, Inc., 1956.

CAMPBELL, ROALD F., EDWIN M. BRIDGES, and RAPHAEL O. NYSTRAND. *Introduction to Educational Administration,* 5th ed. Boston: Allyn & Bacon, Inc., 1977, Chapter 6.

FAYOL, HENRI. *General and Industrial Management,* trans. Constance Storrs. London: Sir Isaac Pitman & Sons, 1949.

GULICK, LUTHER, and L. URWICK (eds.). *Papers on the Science of Administration.* New York: Institute of Public Administration, Columbia University, 1937.

HAMPTON, DAVID R. *Contemporary Management.* New York: McGraw-Hill Book Company, 1977, Chapter 1.

HANSON, E. MARK. *Educational Administration and Organizational Behavior.* Boston: Allyn & Bacon, Inc., 1979, Chapter 2.

HICKS, HERBERT G., and C. RAY GULLETT. *Organizations: Theory and Behavior.* New York: McGraw-Hill Book Company, 1975, Chapters 7–10.

HOY, WAYNE K., and CECIL G. MISKEL. *Educational Administration: Theory, Research, and Practice,* 2nd ed. New York: Random House, Inc., 1982, Chapters 5–6.

KAST, FREMONT E., and JAMES E. ROSENZWEIG. *Organization and Management: A Systems and Contingency Approach,* 3rd ed. New York: McGraw-Hill Book Company, 1979, Chapter 3.

MOEHLMAN, ARTHUR B. *School Administration.* Boston: Houghton Mifflin Company, 1940.

OWENS, ROBERT G. *Organizational Behavior in Education,* 2nd ed. Englewood Cliffs, N.J.: Prentice-Hall, Inc., 1981, Chapters 1–2.

SEARS, JESSE B. *The Nature of the Administrative Process.* New York: Mc-Graw-Hill Book Company, 1950.

TAYLOR, FREDERICK W. *Scientific Management: The Principles of Scientific Management.* New York: Harper & Row, Publishers, 1947.

WEBER, MAX. *The Theory of Social and Economic Organization,* trans. A. M. Henderson and Talcott Parsons, Talcott Parsons (ed.). New York: The Free Press, 1964.

9

Transitional Administrative Theory and Educational Administration

THE ERA OF emphasis in administrative theory, which we label *transitional,* focused primarily on people and their relationships in organizations. The movement began to gain recognition around 1930 and continued to be in vogue into the 1950s. Many of the dominant notions of the era are still most acceptable to both practitioners and scholars. In part, the "aim" was value-laden and the central thoughts related to what "ought" to be the place of persons in an organization that is a part of a democratic society. This primarily philosophic orientation was complemented, however, by the goal of understanding, explaining, and predicting human behavior and interactions based upon empirical investigations. That is, the central focus was to develop theory that dealt with human behavior and was useful in terms of giving rise to derivations, which could be subjected to application of the scientific method.

In the section immediately following, the genesis of the movement and its key ideas are described. In the next section the influence of transitional-era thought on educational administration is detailed. The chapter is concluded with a critique of the era.

Human Relations and the Behavioral Sciences

The focus on human relations, using the methods of the behavioral scientists, was a response to the perceived defects of traditional theory. Thus the scholars of the era did not develop a "complete theory," nor did they challenge some of the traditionalists' notions (e.g., the concept of the division of work was never seriously questioned). The genesis of the transitional era is found in the empirical work of Elton Mayo and his associates and the writings of Mary Parker Follett.

During the period 1923–1926, a series of experiments, in the scientific management mold, were carried out at the Hawthorne plant (near Chicago) of the Western Electric Company. The experiments were aimed at determining the relationship between the intensity of illumination and worker output. The researchers could find no clear relationship between illumination and worker productivity. For example, when illumination was decreased for the experimental group, production increased rather than decreased as predicted. This led to the notion that factors other than physical ones might have a significant impact on worker performance. That is, the basic assumptions of the traditional era—the economic motivation of the worker and the emphasis on the mechanistic elements of production—were questioned. As Roethlisberger and Dickson, two of Mayo's colleagues, were later to write:

> Although the results from these experiments on illumination fell short of the expectations of the company in the sense that they failed to answer the specific question of the relation between illumination and efficiency, nevertheless they provided a great stimulus for more research in the field of human relations.[1]

As a result of these illumination experiments, between 1927 and 1932, under the direction of Mayo, the now famous "Hawthorne studies" were conducted.[2] These studies encompassed three different inquiries: (1) the observations of six females making telephone assemblies (the relay-assembly test room experiment); (2) interviews with over 21,000 workers during a three-year period (the interview program); (3) the observation of a fourteen-member male work group (the bank wiring observation room study). In the relay-assembly experi-

---

[1] F. J. Roethlisberger and William J. Dickson, *Management and the Worker* (Cambridge: Harvard University Press, 1939), p. 19.
[2] For a detailed description see Elton Mayo, *The Human Problems of an Industrial Civilization* (New York: Macmillan, 1933).

ments, production increased regardless of the modifications made in physical working conditions. This led to the hypothesis that changed human relations had occurred concurrent with the increased production. (In designing the studies, a variety of changes had been introduced—a separate work room, personal attention, a different type of supervision, and the like.) In other words, social and psychological factors were seen as critical in worker motivation. The interviewing program, which followed, offered further substantiation for this conclusion. In the bank-wiring study the work group set its own social norms. This included norms that restricted worker output, even though the workers were paid in accord with Taylor's piece-rate principle. In sum, these empirical efforts demonstrated the inadequacy of a theory of administration that was primarily economic and mechanistic in treating human beings.

Although Mayo and his associates provided the empirical base for the era, initially the leading protagonist was Mary Parker Follett (1868-1933). Follett, who was knowledgeable in both governmental and business administration, was a contemporary of the traditional-era theorists, and her writings and speeches, which began around 1900, extended over roughly a thirty-year period. Her point of view was different from that of the traditional-era theorists. Her basic contention was that any enduring society or organization must be based upon a recognition of the motivating desires of the individual and of the group and that all organizational problems were fundamentally human relations problems. Her most frequently quoted work is *Creative Experience*,[3] which Metcalf and Urwick described as follows:

> mainly psychological in interest and content, [it] marks a definite advance both in the crystallization of thought and in style and phraseology. Its thesis is the reciprocal character—the interpenetration—of all psychological phenomena, from the simplest to the most complex. Human relationships—the warp and woof of society and of industry—are at their best when difference is solved through conference and cooperation, when the parties at interest (1) evoke each other's latent ideas based upon the facts of the situation, (2) come to see each other's viewpoints and to understand each other better, and (3) integrate those viewpoints and become united in the pursuit of their common goal.[4]

Administration as Building and Maintaining Harmonious Human Relations

If the era could be said to have a single dominant theme, it was that administration was basically concerned with "the building and

---

[3] Mary Parker Follett, *Creative Experience* (New York: Longmans, 1924).
[4] Henry C. Metcalf and L. Urwick (eds.), *Dynamic Administration: The Collected Papers of Mary Parker Follett* (New York: Harper & Row, 1940), p. 14. Quoted by permission of Pitman, London.

maintenance of dynamic, yet harmonious human relations. . . ."[5] As suggested previously, this theme was central to Follett's position. Follett saw "coordination," which she expressed in four "fundamental principles of organization," as the key to building an effective organization—one which was characterized by harmonious human relations. Her principles were stated as follows:

1. Co-ordination by direct contact of the responsible people concerned.
2. Co-ordination in the early stages.
3. Co-ordination as the reciprocal relating to all the factors in a situation.
4. Co-ordination as a continuing process.[6]

Follett defined coordination by direct contact as horizontal control between unit heads instead of the traditional notion of control up and down the hierarchy of authority. Relative to coordination in the early stages, Follett noted that if the direct contact begins while policy is being formed, not after it has been finished, successful coordination is more likely. Or as she put it, "you cannot, with the greatest degree of success for your undertaking, make policy-forming and policy-adjusting two separate processes."[7]

Relative to her third principle, coordination as the reciprocal relating of all factors in a situation, Follett commented as follows:

> You cannot envisage the process accurately by thinking of A adjusting himself to B and to C and D. A adjusts himself to B and *also* to a B influenced by C and to a B influenced by D and to a B influenced by A himself. Again he adjusts himself to C and *also* to a C influenced by D and to a C influenced by A himself—and so on and so on. One could work it out mathematically. This sort of reciprocal relating, this interpenetration of every part by every other part, and again by every other part as it has been permeated by all, should be the goal of all attempts at co-ordination, a goal, of course, never wholly reached.[8]

This principle appears to be a reflection of the influence of Gestalt psychology, which stressed that the way an entity is perceived is determined by the total context of the situation. Relationships among entities in a perceptual field rather than the fixed attributes of the individual entities determine perception.

By coordination as a continuing process, Follett meant that there had to be provided continuous machinery for working out relation-

[5] Ibid., p. 21.
[6] Ibid., p. 297.
[7] Ibid., p. 298.
[8] Ibid., p. 299.

ships. That is, people could not just meet and confer when difficulties arose and expect a great deal of success.[9]

The concern for people and their relations was also central to the thought of Mayo and his associates. Mayo pointed out that for the workers involved in his studies a different social milieu was created, one "in which their own self-determination and their social well-being ranked first and the work was incidental."[10]

Roethlisberger and Dickson noted the following:

> Adequate personnel administration in any particular industrial plant should fulfill two conditions: (1) Management should introduce in its organization an explicit skill of diagnosing human relations. (2) By means of this skill management should commit itself to the *continuous* process of studying human situations—both individual and group—and should run its human affairs in terms of what it is continually learning about its own organization.[11]

An integral part of the human relations theme was the interest in group dynamics and interpersonal relations in small groups. Two pioneer theorists in this area were Kurt Lewin and George C. Homans. Lewin advanced propositions to the effect that behavior is a function of the interaction of the individual, group, and cultural norms. Change in individual behavior is most likely when it is supported by the group and the cultural norms.[12] Lewin's theory became the basis for the sensitivity training movement, which emerged in the 1950s. Homans, in his often-cited 1950 book *The Human Group,* offered a comprehensive view of the functioning of small groups. Among his major ideas was the notion that there is a reciprocal relation between activities and interactions, and that, as activities and interactions are increased, more sentiments come to be shared, including sentiments that are germane to topics beyond the group itself.[13]

The harmonious human relations theme continued to be prominent in the writings of the scholars throughout the dominant era of the movement. Also, more contemporary writers, such as Argyris[14] and McGregor,[15] have stressed the importance of internal relations being in harmony and human collaboration. The focus on human beings and their relation to organization is reflected in the three other "big ideas" of the transitional era.

[9] Ibid., pp. 303–305.

[10] Mayo, op. cit., p. 73.

[11] Roethlisberger and Dickson, op. cit., p. 604.

[12] Kurt Lewin, *Field Theory in Social Science* (New York: Harper & Row, 1951).

[13] George C. Homans, *The Human Group* (New York: Harcourt, 1950).

[14] See, for example, Chris Argyris, *Integrating the Individual and the Organization* (New York: Wiley, 1964).

[15] See, for example, Douglas M. McGregor, *The Human Side of Enterprise* (New York: McGraw-Hill, 1960).

Emphasis on Meeting the Psychosocial Needs of Employees

The emphasis put on the psychological and social needs of persons as motivating forces was a major departure from the strict economic motivation concept. As suggested before, almost paralleling the emphasis among administrative theorists on the nonphysical needs of persons was the rise of Gestalt psychology. From the point of view of many such psychologists, a person's behavior is determined by his or her "field" (including his or her own "needs"), characteristics of his or her reference group, and cultural norms. That is, behavior is a function of a person's personality in interaction with his or her environment.[16] Thus thought in the field of psychology offered support for this and other doctrines espoused by the transitionalists.

Other than Follett and Mayo and his associates, one of the first administration writers of note to stress the importance of the psychosocial factors in organizations was Chester I. Barnard (1886–1961). Barnard, a practitioner, was experienced as the chief executive of New Jersey Bell Telephone and later the Rockefeller Foundation. Based on a series of lectures he had delivered the previous year, Barnard's classic book *The Functions of the Executive*[17] was published in 1938. Germane at this point are his ideas on why people choose to enter into a cooperative system (an organization), the conditions necessary for the persistence of the cooperative system, and incentives in organizations. In regard to why persons choose to enter into a cooperative system, Barnard suggested this is a function of their purposes, desires, impulses of the moment, and alternatives they see as being available[18]—quite a contrast from rational, economic motivation. The persistence of the cooperative system is dependent upon what Barnard called "effectiveness" and "efficiency." The degree of effectiveness is a function of the extent to which the cooperative purposes (organizational purposes) are achieved. Effectiveness is essentially nonpersonal. Efficiency is personal. It refers to the extent to which the motives of individuals are satisfied. If an individual derives sufficient satisfaction from involvement in the cooperative effort, he or she will continue it; if not, he or she will not continue it. On this point Barnard commented as follows:

> For the continued existence of an organization, either *effectiveness* or *efficiency* is necessary; and the longer the life, the more necessary both are. The vitality of organizations lies in the willingness of individuals

[16]See, for example, Kurt Lewin, *A Dynamic Theory of Personality* (New York: McGraw-Hill, 1935).

[17]Chester I. Barnard, *The Functions of the Executive* (Cambridge: Harvard University Press, 1938).

[18]Ibid., p. 17.

to contribute forces to the cooperative system. This willingness requires the belief that the purpose can be carried out, a faith that diminishes to the vanishing point as it appears that it is not in fact in process of being attained. Hence, when effectiveness ceases, willingness to contribute disappears. The continuance of willingness also depends upon the satisfactions that are secured by individual contributors in the process of carrying out the purpose. If the satisfactions do not exceed the sacrifices required, willingness disappears, and the condition is one of organization inefficiency. If the satisfactions exceed the sacrifices, willingness persists, and the condition is one of efficiency of organization.[19]

Incentives cause individuals to contribute their effort to the organization. Barnard divided incentives into two classes: specific inducements and general inducements. Specific inducements include material offerings, personal opportunities, and desirable working conditions. Among the general incentives are "associational attractiveness" (social compatibility), opportunity for enlarged participation, and the possibility of "communion" with fellow contributors (social integration). There is difficulty in distributing incentives in that different individuals are motivated, at different times, by different incentives or combinations of incentives. Beyond the level of bare physiological necessities, material incentives alone are very weak motivators. Incentives of a personal nonmaterial nature (e.g., opportunity for distinction, prestige, and personal power) are more powerful than monetary rewards in the development of an organization, unless the money is an indirect means of satisfying nonmaterial needs (e.g., as a symbol of worth).[20]

Within the same vein is the fusion notion, advanced by Bakke[21] and Argyris.[22] As Argyris stated, the objective is optimum self-actualization:

> effective leadership behavior is "fusing" the individual and the organization in such a way that both simultaneously obtain *optimum* self-actualization. The process of the individual using the organization to fulfill his needs and simultaneously the organization "using" the individuals to achieve its demands has been called by Bakke the *fusion process.*[23]

During the latter years of the transitional era, much of the writing relative to psychosocial needs reflected Maslow's hierarchy-of-needs theory. Maslow postulated that a person's needs were hierarchical and that "higher-order" needs become motivators to the extent that "lower-

[19] Ibid., p. 92.

[20] Ibid., pp. 142–149.

[21] E. W. Bakke, *The Fusion Process* (New Haven: Labor and Management Center, Yale University, 1955).

[22] Chris Argyris, *Personality and Organization* (New York: Harper & Row, 1957).

[23] Ibid., p. 13.

order" needs become satisfied. One's lower-order needs relate to physiological and safety needs (e.g., need for food, water, sleep, sex; need
for protection from danger). One's higher-order needs are psychosocial
(e.g., need for love, affection, status, self-fulfillment). Lower-order
needs are never permanently satisfied. They manifest themselves pe-
riodically if one is deprived; thus when they recur, they are motivators. Nevertheless, a satisfied need is not a motivator. Higher needs
are rarely satisfied. Further, they are not active motivators if one is
struggling to satisfy lower needs.[24] Maslow did not believe that the
needs hierarchy was absolutely rigid. Therefore, some persons may
be motivated by the need for status even though their safety needs
have not been met fully.

The influence of Maslow's hierarchy of needs seems apparent in
the work of McGregor, who advanced Theory Y as an alternative to
Theory X. McGregor noted that a satisfied need is not a motivator of
behavior, a fact ignored by Theory X. He further suggested that the
typical industrial enterprise provided reasonably well for the fulfillment of physiological and safety needs, but offered few opportunities
for lower-level employees to satisfy their "egoistic needs." Because a
satisfied need is not a motivator and organizations have done relatively well in regard to physiological and safety needs, management
must shift its focus to social and egoistic needs. Failure to do so will
result in underutilization of human potential.[25]

Maslow's concept can also be related to the job satisfaction theory advanced by Herzberg and his associates.[26] On the basis of several studies, Herzberg postulated that in the work situation there are
two rather different sets of factors—those that relate to extent of job
dissatisfaction (e.g., pay, fringe benefits, nature of supervision) and
those that relate to job satisfaction (e.g., job content, achievement,
recognition). The dissatisfiers ("hygiene factors") can be seen as
roughly paralleling Maslow's lower-order needs, and the satisfiers
("motivators") can be related to the higher-order needs. If the job environment does not provide reasonably well for a person's physiological and security needs, the person will likely become disenchanted
and not perform adequately; yet, enhancing these "hygiene" conditions is not likely to improve performance greatly (a satisfied need is
not a motivator). On the other hand, employee growth (satisfaction)
may be seen as a function of psychosocial needs being met through
work that is inherently interesting, achievement of work goals, and
recognition for that achievement.

[24] A. H. Maslow, "A Theory of Human Motivation," *Psychological Review,* 50 (July
1943), 370–396.
[25] McGregor, op. cit., pp. 35–43.
[26] Frederick Herzberg, Bernard Mausner, and Barbara Snyderman, *The Motivation to Work* (New York: Wiley, 1959).

As implied previously, the transitional-era theorists were of the conviction that the needs of employees could not be met fully within the context of the formal structure of the organization. Thus, it is not surprising that they placed emphasis on informal relationships among people in an organization.

The Informal Organization as a Major Consideration

Formal organization refers to the planned structure of an enterprise—a deliberate effort to prescribe relationships, ways decisions are to be made, activities to be accomplished, and the like. Within a formal organization many interactions occur that are not planned; communication networks are built; ways of behaving are defined; cliques emerge and disappear. The informal organization is portrayed in those human aspects of an enterprise that are not described in organization charts and official documents.

Roethlisberger and Dickson, members of the Mayo team, probably best stated the importance of the informal organization. In commenting on the findings of the Hawthorne studies, they made the following observation:

> It became clear to the investigators that the limits of human collaboration are determined far more by the informal than the formal organization of the plant. Collaboration is not wholly a matter of logical organization. It presupposes social codes, conventions, traditions, and routine or customary ways of responding to a situation. Without such basic codes or conventions, effective work relations are not possible.[27]

Barnard also stressed the importance of informal as well as formal organization. He defined formal organization as the activities of conscious, deliberate, and purposeful cooperation and informal organization as people who come in contact and interact without specific conscious joint purpose.[28] Formal and informal organizations were related. As he stated, "the attitudes, institutions, customs, of informal society affect and are partly expressed through formal organization. They are interdependent aspects of the same phenomena—a society is structured by formal organizations, formal organizations are vitalized and conditioned by informal organization."[29]

Whereas Barnard saw the formal and informal organization as intertwined, other writers, both before and after him, tended to treat them as separate entities. However, the intermeshing of the two became the prevailing viewpoint. Writing almost twenty-five years after Barnard, Blau and Scott stated it well:

[27] Roethlisberger and Dickson, op. cit., p. 568.
[28] Barnard, op. cit., p. 114.
[29] Ibid., p. 120.

It is impossible to understand the nature of a formal organization without investigating the networks of informal relations and the unofficial
norms as well as the formal hierarchy of authority and the official body
of rules, since the formally instituted and the informally emerging patterns are inextricably intertwined. The distinction between the formal
and the informal aspects of organizational life is only an analytical one
and should not be reified; there is only one actual organization.[30]

From Barnard's perspective, informal organizations are essential because the informal society facilitates communication, promotes
cohesion, and protects an individual's feeling of choice, integrity, and
self-respect. Also, the informal organization serves to establish attitudes, customs, habits, and understandings. Since Barnard, numerous
scholars of the human relations-behavioral sciences persuasion have
focused on the significance of the informal organization, which has
been thought important for various reasons. Specifically, it serves to
ratify or legitimize authority of superiors, provides a source of com-
panionship and sense of belonging, helps protect the membership from
external pressures, is a major source of assistance for individuals in
job-related problem solving, and sets guides of acceptable behavior,
including quality and quantity of output.

Organizational Authority Based on Knowledge, Participation, and Reason

Throughout the transitional era, and continuing even today,
there was considerable focus on the nature and place of authority in
an organization. In reality, this was a response to the strong executive concept advocated by the traditionalists, at the heart of which
was Weber's legal-rational, impersonal hierarchy of authority. The
alternative ideas relating to authority took several forms, and Mary
Parker Follett, early in the era, advanced important ideas on the topic.
For example, her principles of coordination suggest the importance of
involving people in the decision-making process, the need for horizontal control, and the necessity for meeting and conferring. She also
advocated the following: (1) authority and responsibility should go
with function and not depend upon "hierarchy of rank"; (2) legitimate
authority is the interweaving of all the experience concerned; it comes
from coordination, not the reverse; (3) the leader is to create group
power, not to express personal power; and (4) leadership in a given
situation should be exercised by the person possessing the needed
knowledge.[31]
While Follett provided the genesis for many of the ideas relative

---

[30] Peter M. Blau and W. Richard Scott, *Formal Organizations* (San Francisco:
Chandler, 1962), p. 6.
[31] Metcalf and Urwick, op. cit., pp. 173, 204, 248, 277.

to authority and leadership behavior, the 1938 study by Lewin, Lippitt, and White provided the empirical impetus. The research involved eleven-year-old children who were organized into three groups of five children each for the purpose of engaging in hobby activities. The leadership behavior of the adult leaders was deliberately varied, and three "styles" were followed—autocratic, democratic, and laissez-faire. They found the following: under autocratic leadership there was discontent, submissiveness, dependence, and aggression; under the laissez-faire leadership there was lack of purpose, less work done, and frustration; under democratic leadership there was stronger work motivation, greater originality, more sharing, and more group-mindedness. The great majority of the participants expressed a preference for the democratic leadership.[32] Reseach of this type led to the often-cited postulate that if people participate in the planning and decision-making process, they will be more likely to be committed and "follow through" on the decisions made.

From Barnard's perspective, organizational authority is dependent upon its acceptance by individuals. An individual will accept authority if he or she understands the order, sees it as being consistent with organizational goals, views it as compatible with his or her own personal interests, and is mentally and physically able to comply.[33] Simon and associates, influenced by Barnard, suggested that acceptance of authority by an individual is conditioned by legitimation, technical skills, social approval, and sanctions and rewards.[34]

As mentioned previously, Thompson, among others, suggested that in the traditional model there was a conflict between the concept of authority based on rank and the technical knowledge of the specialist.[35] Thus another approach, consistent with Follett's notions of authority based on function and leadership based on knowledge, was to advocate "functional authority." Etzioni went so far as to suggest that in professional organizations (e.g., hospitals, research laboratories, universities) the traditional line–staff authority should be reversed; that is, "to the extent there is a line–staff relationship, at all, professionals should hold the major authority and administrators the secondary staff authority."[36]

McGregor argued that, in contrast to Theory X (see Chapter 8),

[32] Kurt Lewin, Ronald Lippitt, and Ralph K. White, "Patterns of Aggressive Behavior in Experimentally Created 'Social Climates'," Journal of Social Psychology, X (May 1939), 271–299.

[33] Barnard, op. cit., p. 165.

[34] H. A. Simon, D. W. Smithburg, and V. A. Thompson, Public Administration (New York: Knopf, 1950), pp. 189–201.

[35] Victor A. Thompson, "Hierarchy, Specialization, and Organizational Conflict," Administrative Science Quarterly, 5 (March 1961), 485–521.

[36] Amitai Etzioni, Modern Organizations (Englewood Cliffs, N.J.: Prentice-Hall, 1964), p. 81.

controls should be more consistent with the view that a person does not inherently dislike work, will exercise self-control under certain circumstances, has the capacity for creativity, and under certain conditions seeks responsibility (Theory Y). In commenting on Theory Y, McGregor stated it this way:

> Theory Y points to the possibility of lessening the emphasis on external forms of control to the degree that commitment to organizational objectives can be achieved. Its underlying assumptions emphasize the capacity of human beings for self-control, and the consequent possibility of greater managerial reliance on other means of influence. Nevertheless, it is clear that authority is an appropriate means of control under certain circumstances—particularly where genuine commitment to objectives cannot be achieved. The assumptions of Theory Y do not deny the appropriateness of authority, but they do deny that it is appropriate for all purposes and under all circumstances. . . . Theory Y is an invitation to innovation.[37]

Also contributing to the concept of lessened external control and enhanced self-control was the client-centered therapy movement in counseling. The movement's principal advocate, Carl R. Rogers, in contrast to the then prevailing view of counseling, advocated a permissive, nondirective role for the counselor. The client, not the counselor, determined his or her goals and direction of change.[38]

Likert, among others, addressed himself to the notions of horizontal control and group-centered leadership. As a device for achieving greater integration, he suggested that there should be persons within each organizational unit who are designated to serve as "linking pins" between their units and those on the same level as well as those above and below. Such a concept has the effect of creating a multiple, overlapping organizational structure. He summed up as follows:

> To perform the intended coordination well a fundamental requirement must be met. The entire organization must consist of a multiple, overlapping group structure with every work group using group decision-making processes skillfully. This requirement applies to the functional, product, and service departments. An organization meeting this requirement will have an effective interaction-influence system through which the relevant communications flow readily, the required influence is exerted laterally, upward, and downward, and the motivational forces needed for coordination are created.[39]

[37]McGregor, op. cit., pp. 56–57.
[38]Carl R. Rogers, *Counseling and Psychotherapy* (Boston: Houghton, 1942).
[39]Rensis Likert, *The Human Organization* (New York: McGraw-Hill, 1967), p. 167.

In sum, whether the term used is *functional authority, group decision making, democratic leadership, participative management, situational leadership, authority based on acceptance,* or *collegiality,* the aim was to offer an alternative to the traditionalist notion of authority from the top to the bottom. That alternative was some form of power equalization. Leavitt offered a concise description of the concept:

> Besides the belief that one changes people first, these power-equalization approaches also place major emphasis on other aspects of the human phenomena of organizations. They are, for example, centrally concerned with affect; with morale, sensitivity, psychological security. Secondly, they value evolutionary, internally generated change in individuals, groups and organizations over externally planned or implemented change. Thirdly, they place much value on human growth and fulfillment as well as upon task accomplishment; and they often have stretched the degree of causal connection between the two. Finally, of course, the power-equalization approaches, in their early stages at least, shared a normative belief that power in organizations should be more equally distributed than in most existent "authoritarian" hierarchies.[40]

Influence of the Human Relations-Behavioral Sciences Movement on Educational Administration

The transitional-era movement, which began with an emphasis on treating employees in a humane manner and evolved into a series of key ideas derived from the behavioral sciences (the latter phase of the movement has been referred to by some writers as the "human resources" emphasis[41]), affected educational administration on two fronts. First, there were efforts to democratize the practice of educational administration. Second, there was a growing emphasis on the utilization of concepts from anthropology, psychology, sociology, and the behavioral elements of economics and political science (when considered collective, the term *social sciences* was frequently used) for the study and practice of educational administration.

From the 1930s until the mid-1950s one could hardly attend a meeting, scan a journal, or read a text in the field without being admonished to observe the "principles of democratic administration" (a

[40] Harold J. Leavitt, "Applied Organizational Change in Industry: Structural, Technological and Humanistic Approaches," in James G. March (ed.), *Handbook of Organizations* (Chicago: Rand McNally, 1965), p. 1154.

[41] Raymond E. Miles, *Theories of Management: Implications for Organizational Behavior and Development* (New York: McGraw-Hill, 1975), pp. 41–43.

frequently used phrase intended to cover a wide range of humanitarian considerations) and to give attention to the leadership role (as opposed to the managerial role). Spears, in 1953, offered the following description:

> No subject has challenged the pen and vocal chords of the educator during the past twenty years as has the subject of democratic school operation. He has filled the educational journals and the shelves of his professional library as he has pleaded with the school to promote to the fullest the democratic ideal. . . .[42]

Spain and associates noted the following regarding the social sciences and leadership:

> situations differ and it is difficult, therefore, to generalize concerning effective leadership. . . . answers once thought to be satisfactory regarding administrative leadership are not harmonious with what has been learned through basic researches in industry, sociology, psychology, psychiatry, and group dynamics.[43]

Though the behavior is not always consistent with the words, it seems fair to say that both educational administration practitioners and scholars have enthusiastically embraced the tenor of this aspect of the movement, if not all of the substantive ideas.

Beginning in the early 1950s and blending into the social system emphasis, the scholars of educational administration have made a concerted effort to apply concepts derived from the behavioral sciences to the development of a science of educational administration. These efforts were enhanced by the creation of a "national network" consisting of professors of educational administration, behavioral science scholars interested in the application of their concepts to educational administration, and leading practitioners. This network was in large measure a result of the creation and activities of the previously described National Conference of Professors of Educational Administration (NCPEA), Cooperative Program in Educational Administration (CPEA), University Council for Educational Administration (UCEA), and Committee for the Advancement of School Administration (CASA).

In sum, the impact of the transitional-era ideas began in the 1930s with education writers urging democracy in educational administration. The 1950s saw the creation of a national social system, made up of key professors and leading school practitioners, which focused much

---

[42] Harold Spears, *Improving the Supervision of Instruction* (Englewood Cliffs, N.J.: Prentice-Hall, 1953), p. 97.

[43] Charles R. Spain, Harold D. Drummond, and John I. Goodlad, *Educational Leadership and the Elementary School Principal* (New York: Holt, 1956), p. 2.

of its effort on the application of concepts from behavioral sciences to educational administration. Following is a detailing of nine overlapping ideas of the era. The first five reflect the democracy movement, and the remaining four are representative of the behavioral sciences emphasis.

The Administrator as a Promoter of Staff Harmony and Morale

During the era it was commonplace for speakers and writers to advance the notion that educational administrators were responsible for the promotion of relations between organizational members that were mutually satisfying. This was often accompanied by a listing of techniques that could be used to promote the desired state of relations. Frequently harmony and high staff morale were considered essential for improved teaching and learning (e.g., the relations affected morale and morale affected the teaching-learning situation), or they were considered desirable because they were philosophically consistent with the tenets of a democratic society.

Kimball Wiles was one of the leading proponents of the importance of staff harmony and morale. In the 1950 version of his widely used text, he detailed twenty-six suggestions that could be used by the educational leader to promote staff harmony. These included being polite and courteous, being accessible, taking prompt action on a request, letting people know when they did a good job, being willing to listen, offering assistance in settling group disagreements, giving credit where due, and being cheerful.[44] Wiles saw morale as an individual phenomenon (i.e., a person's emotional and mental reaction to work) that influenced the amount of work done. Citing his own research as well as that of others, he posited that teachers want security and a comfortable living, pleasant working conditions, a sense of belonging, fair treatment, a sense of achievement, a feeling of importance, a part in policy formulation, and a situation in which they can maintain their self-respect. He argued that an effective school leader must give attention to these wants and constantly demonstrate that the morale of teachers is one of his or her major concerns. To this end he offered twenty-nine suggestions for the leader.[45]

Some of the earlier scholars struggled with the problem of how an educational leader could engage in behavior seen as appropriate to the promotion of harmony and morale and maintain a position of authority in the organization. This was a reflection of being "caught" between the views of the traditionalists and transitionalists. One au-

[44] Kimball Wiles, *Supervision for Better Schools* (Englewood Cliffs, N.J.: Prentice-Hall, 1950), pp. 109–129.
[45] Ibid., pp. 39–60.

thor dealt with the dilemma by suggesting that the school principal had a parental role in the school, and in this role was a "parent-person" to teachers. To maintain desirable relations and high morale among teachers, the principal was advised to give attention to the economic and social aspects of the teacher's life, moderate criticism, make judicious use of praise, be mindful of the personalities and problems of teachers, and give advice conducive to the development of the full potential for growth.[46]

Administration as a Service

Educational administration came to be seen as an activity contributing to the instructional program, as a means, not an end in itself. The object was to engage in activities that made it possible for teachers and pupils to work together under conditions deemed conducive to learning. This was Moehlman's central thesis, and he stated it as follows:

> Administration is essentially a service activity, a tool or agency through which the fundamental objectives of the educational process may be more fully and efficiently realized. In the development of this point of view the teacher emerges as the most important agent, with administration in the position of ministering to his needs and thus increasing the efficiency of the teaching process . . . advocates of this school of thought proceed to examine, appraise, and orient objectively all structure and organizational practices in terms of instructional purposes.[47]

Reeder, as well as many others, echoed the Moehlman point of view:

> School administration does not exist for itself, it is only a means, not an end . . . school administration, therefore, exists only for the pupil, and its efficacy must be measured by the extent to which it contributes to teaching and learning; to teaching and learning it must always be a servant.[48]

Participation in Decision Making

There emerged in the 1930s almost universal support among educational administration scholars for cooperative decision making. There was recognition of the problems associated with this approach to decision making, yet the belief was that decisions made in such a manner were more valid and more likely to be implemented at various levels within the educational organization.

[46]Norman Fenton, *Mental Hygiene in School Practice* (Stanford, Calif.: Stanford University Press, 1943), pp. 335–344.
[47]Arthur B. Moehlman, *School Administration* (Boston: Houghton, 1940), p. v.
[48]Ward G. Reeder, *The Fundamentals of Public School Administration* (New York: Macmillan, 1941), pp. 6–7.

The notion was seen as central to the concept of democratic administration. Consider, for example, the five principles to govern democratic action of educational administrators advanced by Koopman and associates:

1. To facilitate the continuous growth of individual and social personalities by providing all persons with opportunities to participate actively in all enterprises that concern them.
2. To recognize that leadership is a function of every individual, and to encourage the exercise of leadership by each person in accordance with his interests, needs, and abilities.
3. To provide means by which persons can plan together, share their experiences, and cooperatively evaluate their achievements.
4. To place the responsibility for making decisions that affect the total enterprise with the group rather than with one or a few individuals.
5. To achieve flexibility of organization to the end that necessary adjustments can readily be made.[49]

To implement the cooperative decision-making notion, open discussions, standing and ad hoc committees, task forces, and the like, came into use in educational organizations at all levels. The impact of these entities on the decisions made varied widely, yet they remain an integral part of educational organizations.

Group-Granted Administrative Authority

In general, the advocates of democratic educational administration stressed the exercise of group authority within the legal framework governing educational organizations.

That is, the only meaningful authority that could be exercised was that granted by the people affected. Illustrative of this point of view, which prevails even today, is the following paragraph from a widely used 1938 text on educational supervision:

Democratic authority rests not upon force or power but on demonstrated ability and upon delegation by the group. Democratic authority will be exercised, not for the selfish ends of those possessing it but for the common good, for the furtherance of those policies predetermined by the group in free discussion. Inevitably there will be authority in democracy, the issuance of orders, obedience to leaders. This authority, however, will be as indicated, derived from "the consent of the governed," will continue so long as efficiently exercised in the interests of the group. Democratic authority is subject to recall.[50]

[49] Robert G. Koopman, Alice Miel, and Paul J. Misner, *Democracy in School Administration* (New York: Appleton, 1943), pp. 3–4.
[50] A. S. Barr, William H. Burton, and Leo J. Brueckner, *Supervision* (New York: Appleton, 1938), p. 49.

Commenting directly on the implications of group-given authority for educational administrative practice and the relation to legal authority, Hagman noted the following:

> this means that the superintendent of a school system must provide leadership which is pleasing to the group led or suffer defeat of his plans when the group he is endeavoring to lead no longer grants him recognition as their spokesman and withdraws the support which had been his. As long as he is in office as superintendent, his legal authority will be undisputed but the authority to act as leader of the group, while much more subtly granted and withdrawn, must be his, or he will stand impotent as a titular leader.[51]

Obviously, emphasis on the service function of educational administration, wide participation in decision making, and group-granted authority struck at the heart of the "strong-executive" concept advanced by the theorists of the earlier era. Therefore there were some efforts aimed at changing the formal structure of educational organizations to make it more compatible with these notions (e.g., as suggested previously, the use of dual and multiple executives); yet these efforts have not been widespread. This is not to say that the previously mentioned notions have had little or no impact on practice in educational organizations. The impact has been in the manner with which school executives exercise their legal authority. In large measure, unless required by law, they are loathe to issue edicts or move in directions that do not have the support of at least a significant segment of the organization.

Administrators Enhance the Satisfaction of Individuals

As suggested in the discussion dealing with the promotion of staff harmony and morale, another theme of the advocates of democratic administration was that the executive should take steps to satisfy the psychosocial as well as the economic needs of teachers and other organizational employees. Simply put, the rationale was that the relative happiness of the teacher (and any other employee who came in contact with pupils) would be transmitted directly to the pupils. Thus, viewing the charge of the school as the development of the "whole child," it logically followed that unless the teachers' psychosocial needs were attended to, the teachers would be in a poor position to make a contribution to the psychosocial needs of their pupils.

To the end that individual needs would be met and the welfare of individuals would be enhanced, the educational executive was exhorted to create opportunities for each individual to participate in

[51] Harlan L. Hagman, *The Administration of American Public Schools* (New York: McGraw-Hill, 1951), pp. 39–40.

decision making, treat each person in a manner that is perceived as fair, create conditions where individuals can have a sense of achievement, give attention to individual interests in assignments, provide recognition for deserving individuals, provide aesthetically pleasing work surroundings, be sensitive to the nonjob-related problems of employees, provide opportunities for individuals to accept responsibility, and make an effort to develop a sense of belonging and psychological security in each subordinate.[52] In sum, the belief was, in the words of Shane and Yauch, "Teachers will, beyond question, work best under conditions which they recognize as fostering their maximum growth and satisfaction."[53]

Emphasis on the Use of Social Sciences Methodologies

As suggested previously, there was frequent criticism of the notions of the traditional-era scholars and the early transitional-era scholars because of the methodologies employed in the validation of their ideas. In the 1950s this same basic criticism of the prevailing ideas in educational administration began to be heard. Specifically, many of the "theories" focused on what "ought to be" and as such were not productive of hypotheses that could be empirically tested (i.e., many of the ideas had little explanatory and predictive value); too little of the research conducted focused on significant questions (i.e., the same survey-type studies were done over and over again); and often the conditions under which the research was conducted were such that the results were not generalizable (i.e., the prevailing mode was raw empiricism in particular settings). Halpin summarized well the then prevailing criticisms of educational administration research. He declared that there was a failure to recognize the importance of theory (frequently the term was used naively) and too much reliance on raw empiricism; a disproportionate amount of effort was devoted to ad hoc problems and peripheral studies rather than to studies that would produce broad generalizations; the research outlook was parochial (i.e., too much emphasis was put on the uniqueness of educational administration and too little use was made of important related disciplines); and there was a lack of precision in defining concepts ("is" terms and "ought" terms were used indiscriminately).[54]

[52] For illustrative books devoted to this and the staff harmony theme see American Association of School Administrators, Commission on Staff Relations in School Administration, *Staff Relations in School Administration,* (Washington, D.C.: The Association, 1955); Wiles, loc. cit.; Wilber A. Yauch, *Improving Human Relations in School Administration* (New York: Harper & Row, 1949).

[53] Harold G. Shane and Wilbur A. Yauch, *Creative School Administration* (New York: Holt, 1954), p. 104.

[54] Andrew W. Halpin, "A Paradigm for Research on Administrative Behavior," in Roald F. Campbell and Russell T. Gregg (eds.), *Administrative Behavior in Education* (New York: Harper & Row, 1957), pp. 197–198.

A valid conceptual scheme was lacking and, because of methodological considerations, it was not possible to describe the conditions under which administrative principles were applicable. From the perspective of many of the educational administration scholars, the remedy lay in the application of the methodologies of the social sciences. Goldhammer offered a concise statement of the meaning of the idea.[55]

While stressing the necessity of theory to guide scientific research, Goldhammer used "six key words" to characterize the social sciences: *empirical, patterns, classification, systematic, predict,* and *human.* The *empirical* characteristic refers to the replicability of the observation. *Pattern* refers to the notion that social scientists endeavor to find regularities in the relationships among people and in the processes by which groups function. *Classification* has reference to the interest in the classification of data and the creation of a standardized language. Relative to *systematic,* Goldhammer noted that there is an emphasis on systematic techniques to minimize, or at least recognize, erratic, impressionistic, value-laden, and/or uncontrolled observations. *Predict* refers to the aim of the social sciences, which is being able to predict the consequences of human behavior. *Human* means that the social sciences are focused on the study of a person as an individual, as a group member, and in interaction with the environment.[56]

In sum, to improve the knowledge base of educational administration, the adoption of the methodologies of the social sciences was widely urged. This was consistent with the point of view that had been espoused a few years earlier by Barnard and others.

Individual and Organizational Dimensions of Leader Behavior

Throughout the era, the scholars of educational administration showed a concern for leaders and leadership acts. Numerous studies of leaders and leadership were conducted. In the earlier days of the era most studies assumed that administrators (e.g., superintendents) were leaders. Further, many of the studies focused on either the psychological or the sociological aspects of leadership. The focus of the psychological approach was on the determination of the personal characteristics of leaders. Initially, the effort was to identify leadership traits (e.g., forceful, creative), but this gave way to an emphasis on the identification of the personality syndrome that characterized leaders. However, neither emphasis led to the discovery of a universal "leadership personality." As Pierce and Merrill noted in 1957, "one of

[55] Keith Goldhammer, *The Social Sciences and the Preparation of Educational Administrators* (Columbus, Ohio: University of Alberta and the University Council for Educational Administration, 1963).
[56] Ibid., pp. 10–11.

the chief results of the research is the conclusion drawn that the study of personal characteristics, *per se,* is only one aspect of the study of leadership"[57] With the recognition of the inadequacies of the psychological approach, the focus shifted to the group—the sociological approach. Such an approach was characterized by a comparative study of groups to identify their major dimensions (e.g., norms, expectancies). Again, this approach alone was not too productive (i.e., in many group-oriented studies leadership was treated only incidentally).

The recognition that the "heredity-environment" argument was futile led to an emphasis on what was called the "leader-behavior" approach. Halpin described the approach as follows:

> it focuses upon observed behavior rather than upon posited capacity from this behavior. No presuppositions are made about a one-to-one relationship between leader behavior and an underlying capacity or potentiality presumably determinative of this behavior. By the same token, no *a priori* assumptions are made that the leader behavior which a leader exhibits in one group situation will be manifested in other group situations. . . . Nor does the term "leader behavior" suggest that this behavior is determined either innately or situationally. Either determinant is possible, as is any combination of the two, but the concept of leader behavior does not itself predispose us to accept one in opposition to the other.[58]

Recognizing the limitations of focusing on either the leader or the group, the educational administration scholars in the later years of the transitional era concentrated on an analysis of how leaders behave.[59] This emphasis led to the social system model of the social behavior of administrators, which is described in the next chapter.

Impact of Political-Social Environment

The transitionalists, particularly in the later years of the era, stressed the proposition that education is affected by and affects the environment of which it is a part. Accordingly, educational leaders were advised to look beyond the formal organization into the "real world" in an effort to understand how decisions were really made and how various economic, political, and social forces combined to influence educational organization and administrative behavior. Further, some scholars suggested that educators should go beyond understand-

[57]Truman M. Pierce and E. C. Merrill, Jr., "The Individual and Administrator Behavior," in Campbell and Gregg, op. cit., p. 332.

[58]Andrew W. Halpin, *The Leadership Behavior of School Superintendents* (Columbus, Ohio: College of Education, Ohio State University, 1956), p. 11.

[59]For a concise summary of the emphasis see James M. Lipham, "Leadership and Administration," in Daniel E. Griffiths (ed.), *Behavioral Science and Educational Administration,* sixty-third yearbook of the National Society for the Study of Education, part II (Chicago: University of Chicago Press, 1964), pp. 119–141.

ing and trying to cope, positing that education should make a concerted effort to shape the nature of society. For example, Counts, as early as 1932, suggested that schools promote a social order that would eliminate scarcity, unemployment, and other social ills.[60] By the 1950s many scholars were advocating that educational leaders become active in the process of developing public policy for the benefit of education and society in a reconsideration of the previously advocated role of political neutrality.[61]

Numerous interacting external factors were seen as potentially conditioning the administration and organization of the educational enterprise. These included community beliefs, demographic structure, nature and interaction of formal and informal groups in the community, bases of the economy, socioeconomic class structure, power structure, state of technology, role played by higher levels of government, and degree of urbanization.

In consort with interested social scientists and using their methodologies, studies were conducted of the environmental factors and their impact. Many of these were conducted under the auspices of the several CPEA centers, particularly those located in the Midwest, Northwest, Southeast, and Southwest.[62]

Interdisciplinary Preparation for Administrative Leadership

The pioneering programs for preparing educational administrators emphasized "scientific principles of school management." Prospective educational administrators were taught the "best" methods and techniques for dealing with the issues, problems, and tasks associated with the operation and management of educational organizations.

In the early days of the transitional era, when there was a strong emphasis on democratic leadership, preparation programs emerged that gave less attention to the scientific principles. In many instances they stressed what administrators ought to do as educational leaders in a democratic social order. Concurrently, there was a recognition that if administrators were going to deal adequately with the psychosocial needs of people, greater knowledge of human behavior must be provided. Thus anthropological, psychological, and sociological content began to appear in the curricula. With the 1950s emphasis on

[60] George S. Counts, *Dare the Schools Build a New Social Order?* Pamphlet No. 11 (New York: Day, 1932).

[61] See, for example, Truman M. Pierce et al., *Community Leadership for Public Education* (Englewood Cliffs, N.J.: Prentice-Hall, 1955).

[62] For a summary of such studies see Roald F. Campbell, "Situational Factors in Educational Administration," in Campbell and Gregg, op. cit., pp. 228–268.

social science methodology, organizational influences on administrative behavior, and situational factors associated with educational administration, the scene was complete for an interdisciplinary approach, both in method and content, to the preparing of educational administrators. Minors or collateral study in the social sciences, courses in theory, seminars in social sciences research methods, case studies, field experiences, and the like, became commonplace.[63] For example, one leading program of the 1950s was described as having a core of increasingly complex experiences including each of these elements.[64]

A Critique of the Transitional Era

The efforts of the transitional-era theorists did not result in the demise of the numerous applications of traditional theory. What did result was a humanizing of management, a sense of flexibility in bureaucratic enterprise, a lessening of the emphasis on "one best way." The human relations-behavioral science emphasis, narrowly defined, has passed its zenith. However, among educational administrators in particular, most of the doctrines are still in vogue in one form or another and provide an important base for the "systems era." For example, even though the term most frequently used is "participative management," the power equalization idea is still considered useful. As would be expected, the critics of this point of view are not as numerous or vocal as are the critics of traditional theory.

First, some of the theorists of the era, particularly those who were basically "human relationists" and were prominent in the 1930s and 1940s, gave more attention to "ought" than to 'is." Consequently, some of the postulates advanced did not give rise to derivations that were subject to empirical testing. Second, there was a lack of comprehensiveness in the notions advanced. Simply put, the primary focus was on people and their interrelations, and there was little emphasis placed on organizational tasks and processes. Stated differently, the psychosocial aspects were emphasized at the expense of the structural-technical aspects. Furthermore, in reference to the "human relationists" of the early part of the era, some writers have stated that not only was the emphasis restricted, it was also a simplified and incomplete statement of human behavior in the work situation, and its in-

---

[63] For more detail see Donald E. Tope (ed.), *A Forward Look—The Preparation of School Administrators 1970* (Eugene, Ore.: Bureau of Educational Research, University of Oregon, 1960).

[64] *A Doctorate Program in Administration,* Graduate Brochure (Cambridge: Harvard Graduate School of Education, 1954).

tent was manipulative—to secure worker compliance with the directives of management.[65] Third, there was a lack of evidence to confirm some of the derivations from the postulates advanced. Further, the research methodology of some of the empirical studies, which formed a major basis for many of the formulations, as applied to educational administration, was questionable. To illustrate: The evidence is less than conclusive in regard to the often assumed relationship between increased employee satisfaction and increased productivity. On the other hand, such an assumption was not made by the "human resources" oriented theorists of the latter part of the era; rather, it was "generally assumed that good and meaningful performance leads to job satisfaction and not the reverse. . . ."[66] Fourth, dilemmas were posed but no solutions formed. For example, several of the theorists stressed the importance of satisfying both individual needs and organizational goals, but in the event of unresolved conflict between the two, what should be the direction?

As has been implied repeatedly, the formative years of educational administration as a field of inquiry coincided with the development of the human relations-behavioral sciences emphasis. Therefore, it is not surprising that, in spite of the criticisms enumerated, the basic viewpoint of the era is still widely accepted by educational administrators.

ACTIVITIES/QUESTIONS FOR FURTHER STUDY

1. Considerable speculation has been expressed concerning the effect of collective bargaining and administrator accountability upon the sharing of decision making. Some persons express the view that cooperative decision making by school principals is no longer practical. Other persons disagree and insist that participative decision making is the only practical way to proceed. As a class, discuss the relative merits of each point of view.

2. Study the faculty of a school or a college division and determine the informal cliques and identify the leaders and members of the cliques. See if you can observe examples of the cliques setting norms of behavior, satisfying or thwarting the authority of supervisors, and/or providing individuals with a sense of belonging.

3. Discuss as a class the extent to which an educational administrator of the 1980s should serve teachers. Is he or she personally responsible for promoting good human relations within the teacher group? In assisting individual subordinates in economic and social matters?

[65] Richard M. Steers and Lyman W. Porter, *Motivation and Work Behavior* (New York: McGraw-Hill, 1975), p. 19.

[66] Ibid.

SUGGESTED READINGS

ARGYRIS, CHRIS. *Integrating the Individual and the Organization.* New York: John Wiley & Sons, Inc., 1964.

CAMPBELL, ROALD F., and RUSSELL T. GREGG (eds.). *Administrative Behavior in Education.* New York: Harper & Row, Publishers, 1957.

Center for the Advanced Study of Educational Administration. *Perspectives on Educational Administration and the Behavioral Sciences.* Eugene, Ore.: University of Oregon Press, 1965.

GRIFFITHS, DANIEL E. (ed.). *Behavioral Science and Educational Administration,* sixty-third yearbook of the National Society for the Study of Education, part II. Chicago: University of Chicago Press, 1964.

HALPIN, ANDREW W. *Theory and Research in Administration.* New York: Macmillan Publishing Co., Inc., 1966.

HICKS, HERBERT G., and C. RAY GULLETT. *Organizations: Theory and Behavior.* New York: McGraw Hill Book Company, 1975, Chapter 11.

KAST, FREMONT E., and JAMES E. ROSENZWEIG. *Organization and Management: A Systems and Contingency Approach,* 3rd ed. New York: McGraw-Hill Book Company, 1979, Chapter 4.

KOOPMAN, ROBERT G., ALICE MIEL, and PAUL J. MISNER. *Democracy in School Administration.* New York: Appleton-Century-Crofts, Inc., 1943.

MAYO, ELTON. *Human Problems of an Industrial Civilization.* New York: Macmillan Publishing Co., Inc., 1933.

McGREGOR, DOUGLAS M. *The Human Side of Enterprise.* New York: McGraw-Hill Book Company, 1960.

METCALF, HENRY C., and L. URWICK (eds.). *Dynamic Administration: The Collected Papers of Mary Parker Follett.* New York: Harper & Row, Publishers, 1940.

PORTER, LYMAN W., EDWARD E. LAWLER, III, and J. RICHARD HACKMAN. *Behavior in Organizations.* New York: McGraw-Hill Book Company, 1975, Chapter 2.

WILES, KIMBALL, and JOHN T. LOVELL. *Supervision for Better Schools,* 4th ed. Englewood Cliffs, N.J.: Prentice-Hall, Inc., 1975.

10

Systems Theory and Educational Administration

IN THE LATE 1950s scholars concerned with the administration of complex organizations began to think of an organization as a system; the "systems era" in administrative thought had begun. The basic idea is that to understand a phenomenon we must recognize that the whole is greater than the sum of the parts. Any analysis of the parts without consideration of how they interact is inadequate. Said another way, the systems approach challenges the reductionist approach where the individual part is the level of analysis and emphasizes that "it is the whole, the combination and interrelationships of parts that will provide the greatest insights."[1] There is a focus on unifying principles that serve to integrate knowledge and understanding from many diverse fields. The movement's foundation is in the efforts of scholars from many fields, including the behavioral and social scientists, who made important contributions to the transitional era. It represents a logical refinement of some of the key ideas of the human relations-behavioral sciences era. In fact, some have suggested that as applied to theories of administration and organiza-

[1] Terence R. Mitchell, *People in Organizations: Understanding Their Behavior* (New York: McGraw-Hill, 1978), p. 25.

292

tion, the systems era combines the better ideas from the traditional and transitional eras.

The basic format of the two preceding chapters is followed here. In the first part of the chapter "systems theory" is explained, next its relevance to educational administration is discussed, and a critique of the movement completes the chapter.

Systems Thought: Definitions and Rationale

In spite of some differences in words used, there is considerable agreement about the definition of a system. Consider the following illustrative definitions from scholars representing a wide spectrum in terms of academic background.

- From Flagle and associates: "a system is an integrated assembly of interacting elements designed to carry out cooperatively a predetermined function."[2]
- According to Chorofas, "A system is a group of interdependent elements acting together to accomplish a predetermined purpose."[3]
- Blendinger said, "A system is an organized 'something' that has direction to it and some degree of internal unity. The structure or organization of an orderly whole which clearly shows the interrelationships of the parts to each other and to the whole itself."[4]
- Kast and Rosenzweig saw a system as "an organized, unitary whole composed of two or more interdependent parts, components, or subsystems and delineated by identifiable boundaries from its environmental suprasystem."[5]
- To Hall and Fagen, "A system is a set of objects together with relationships between the objects and between their attributes."[6]
- In very similar fashion, Immegart and Pilecki viewed a system as "an entity composed of (1) a number of parts, (2) the relationships of these parts, and (3) the attributes of both the parts and the relationships."[7]
- And finally, a pioneer systems theorist, Rapoport, said a "system is: (1) something consisting of a set of (finite or infinite) entities; (2) among which a set of relations is specified, so that (3) deductions are possible

[2] Charles D. Flagle, William H. Huggins, and Robert H. Roy, *Operations Research in Systems Engineering* (Baltimore: Johns Hopkins University Press, 1960), p. 58.

[3] Dimitris Chorofas, *Systems and Simulation* (New York: Academic, 1965), p. 2.

[4] Jack Blendinger, "ABC's of the Systems Approach," *Education,* 90 (September–October 1969), 56.

[5] Fremont E. Kast and James E. Rosenzweig, *Organization and Management: A Systems and Contingency Approach,* 3rd ed. (New York: McGraw-Hill, 1979), p. 98.

[6] A. D. Hall and R. E. Fagen, "Definition of System," in Walter Buckley (ed.), *Modern Systems Research for the Behavioral Scientist* (Chicago: Aldine, 1968), p. 81.

[7] Glenn L. Immegart and Francis J. Pilecki, *An Introduction to Systems for the Educational Administrator* (Reading, Mass.: Addison-Wesley, 1973), p. 30.

from some relations to others or from the relations among the entities
to the behavior or history of the system."[8]

There are common threads running through these definitions.
Note the reference to "elements," "parts," or "objects." This refers to
the components of a system and can take any number of forms (e.g.,
atoms, genes, persons, processes, stars). Hall and Fagen spoke of "attributes," and the other scholars made a similar point; all objects of a
system have describable properties (e.g., an atom can be described by
atomic weight, electron configuration, energy state), which are essential to a system. Use is made of the terms *interdependent, interrelated,*
and *relationships,* which means that the parts and their properties
are "tied together" in time and space. Such a concept is broadly applicable, having utility in the life sciences, physical sciences, and social sciences as well as in applied fields, such as engineering and administration. Miller perhaps said it best: "General systems theory is
a set of related definitions, assumptions, and propositions which deal
with reality as an integrated hierarchy of organizations of matter and
energy."[9]

To further assist in understanding the concept, several authors
have offered a classification of systems (i.e., a system of systems).
Boulding offered a scheme based on a hierarchy of levels. His first
level he called "frameworks," referring to a static structure (e.g.,
anatomy of the universe). The second level was "clockworks," meaning a "simple dynamic system with predetermined, necessary motions" (e.g., a steam engine). The next level was the "thermostat" or
control system. His fourth level was the "cell," which is the level that
begins to "differentiate itself from not life" and is an open or self-
maintaining system. The fifth level was the "plant" characterized by
division of labor among cells and mutually dependent parts. Next was
the "animal" level, in which there is "increased mobility, teleological
behavior, and self-awareness." Boulding's seventh level was the "human" level, in which there is self-awareness coupled with the ability
to use language and symbols. The next level is that of "social organization" or "social system," in which the unit is not the person but
the "role" and the system is a set of roles tied together with channels
of communication. His "transcendental systems" complete the hierarchy. These are "the ultimates and absolutes and the inescapable
unknowables, and they also exhibit systematic structure and relationship."[10]

[8] Anatol Rapoport, "General Systems Theory," in David L. Sills (ed.), *International Encyclopaedia of the Social Sciences,* vol. 15 (New York: Macmillan & The Free
Press, 1968), p. 453.
[9] James G. Miller, *Living Systems* (New York: McGraw-Hill, 1978), p. 9.
[10] Kenneth E. Boulding, "General Systems Theory: The Skeleton of Science,"
Management Science, 2 (April 1956), 197–208.

Miller wrote of "conceptual," "concrete," and "abstracted" systems. The units of conceptual systems are terms that are related (e.g., words, numbers). A concrete system is a "nonrandom accumulation of matter-energy, in a region in physical space–time, which is nonrandomly organized into coacting, interrelated subsystems or components."[11] These systems can be either closed (having impermeable boundaries) or open (having at least partially permeable boundaries). They can be living or nonliving, with all living systems being open systems. Abstracted systems, selected by the observer, are composed of relationships based on interest or viewpoint. In an abstracted system "some relationships may be empirically determinable by some operation carried out by the observer, but others are not, being only his concepts."[12]

Not all systems are isomorphic (i.e., where either may serve as a model for the other). However, the closer two systems are in level of complexity the greater the degree of isomorphism. Thus such classification schemes are important in that one can focus on the type of system(s) of interest. To persons whose interest is human beings in social organizations, Boulding's "social" system, which is a type of concrete, open, living system in Miller's scheme, is of primary concern.

The goal of general systems theory is to provide a vehicle for understanding and integrating knowledge from diverse, highly specialized fields. This goal is based on the conviction that there are certain principles that are common throughout the various fields of study and can serve as unifying principles. Ludwig von Bertalanffy is generally credited with being the first advocate of this parallelism notion and is generally acclaimed as the "father" of general systems theory. (He claimed he first advanced his ideas in 1937, but because of the "bad reputation" of the theory did not begin to publish in this regard until after World War II.[13]) In 1952 he commented as follows on the idea of parallelism:

If we survey the various fields of modern science, we notice a dramatic and amazing evolution. Similar conceptions and principles have arisen in quite different realms; although this parallelism of ideas is the result of independent developments, and the workers in the individual fields are hardly aware of the common trend. Thus, the principles of wholeness, of organization, and of the dynamic conception of reality become apparent in all fields of science.[14]

[11] Miller, op. cit., p. 17.
[12] Ibid., p. 19.
[13] Ludwig von Bertalanffy, "General Systems—A Critical Review," in Buckley, op. cit., p. 13.
[14] Ludwig von Bertalanffy, *Problems of Life* (New York: Wiley, 1952), p. 176.

Hearn made the point as follows:

> General systems theorists believe that it is possible to represent all forms of animate and inanimate matter as systems; that is all forms from atomic particles through atoms, molecules, crystals, viruses, cells, organs, individuals, groups, societies, planets, solar systems, even the galaxies, may be regarded as systems. They are impressed by the number of times the same principles have been independently discovered by scientists working in different fields.[15]

The parallelism concept is consistent with the functionalism notion in the behavioral and social sciences. In essence, the term means a focus on networks of relationships of entities and the integration of the entities and subsystems into a whole. Martindale described functionalism in the social sciences as follows:

> This point of view has had both theoretical and methodological dimensions. Theoretically, it consists in the analysis of social and cultural life from the standpoint of the primacy of wholes or systems. Epistemologically, it involves analysis of social events by methods thought peculiarly adapted to the integration of social events into systems.
>
> The functionalistic point of view has been manifest in all of the social sciences from psychology through sociology, political science, economics, and anthropology to geography, jurisprudence, and linguistics.[16]

The parallelism–functionalism movement suggests two essential points. First, systems theory is, in part, an approach, a frame of reference for analysis. The term applied is *systems analysis*. On this point, Blendinger said, "Systems analysis is the process of breaking down or taking apart an existing whole into its constituent parts or elements for the purpose of depicting the relationships of the parts to the whole and to each other."[17] Granger stated it as follows: "the generic term system analysis is employed to describe a general planning or macroanalytic process which involves looking at a problem or system organismically as well as analytically."[18]

Second, the general system–social system movement is a logical extension of the work of many scholars of the transitional era, not a radical departure from their efforts. Said another way, even though it has been suggested that the "systems era" began in the 1950s, it

---

[15]Gordon Hearn, *Theory Building in Social Work* (Toronto: University of Toronto Press, 1958), p. 38.

[16]Don Martindale, *Functionalism in the Social Sciences,* Monograph 5 (Philadelphia: American Academy of Political and Social Science, February 1965), pp. viii–ix.

[17]Blendinger, loc. cit.

[18]Robert L. Granger, *Educational Leadership: An Interdisciplinary Perspective* (Scranton, Pa.: Intext, 1971), pp. 94–95.

has its roots, as related to individuals and groups, in the work of many of the behavioral and social scientists who were identified as making a major contribution to the "transitional era." To illustrate, Barnard decried the lack of a systematic conceptual scheme grounded in the social sciences, for he saw such a scheme as necessary for communication and for the understanding of organizations.[19] Also consider the following comments: "the most useful concept for the analysis of experience of cooperative systems is embodied in the definition of a formal organization as a *system of consciously coordinated activities or forces of two or more persons.*"[20]

> If organizations are systems, it follows that the general characteristics of systems are also those of organizations. For our purposes, we may say that a system is something which must be treated as a whole because each part is related to every other part included in it in a significant way.[21]

In 1945 Simon further advanced Barnard's point about the lack of a conceptual scheme when he suggested that what was needed in administrative theory was an approach that focused on the conditions under which administrative principles were applicable.[22] In the field of psychology, the Gestaltists, with their emphasis on the whole being greater than the sum of its parts and on the influence of one's "field" on behavior, provide another basis for the systems movement.[23] In his study of small groups Homans viewed them from the perspective of a social system. He defined a social system as consisting of "activities, interaction, and sentiments of the group members, together with the mutual relations of these elements with one another during the time the group is active. . . ."[24] Argyris conceived of an organization as an open system that acted on and reacted to its external environment. He projected three essential core activities for an organization: achievement of objectives, internal maintenance, and adaptation to the external environment. Organizational growth was seen as a function of the extent to which these activities were carried out.[25]

[19] Chester I. Barnard, *The Functions of the Executive* (Cambridge: Harvard University Press, 1938), p. 289.

[20] Ibid., p. 73.

[21] Ibid., p. 77.

[22] Herbert A. Simon, *Administrative Behavior* (New York: Macmillan, 1945), p. 240.

[23] See, for example, Kurt Lewin, *A Dynamic Theory of Personality* (New York: McGraw-Hill, 1935).

[24] George C. Homans, *The Human Group* (New York: Harcourt, 1950), p. 87.

[25] Chris Argyris, "The Integration of the Individual and the Organization," in George B. Strothers (ed.), *Social Science Approaches to Business Behavior* (Homewood, Ill.: Irwin & Dorsey, 1962), p. 61.

Talcott Parsons developed a detailed treatise of social systems. From Parson's perspective, a social system

> consists in a plurality of individual actors interacting with each other in a situation which has at least a physical or environmental aspect, actors who are motivated in terms of a tendency to the "optimization of gratification" and whose relation to their situations, including each other, is defined and mediated in terms of a system of culturally structured and shared symbols.[26]

Basic Systems Concepts of Relevance to Organizations

Systems theorists have offered several concepts relative to the nature and functioning of systems. In the paragraphs that follow there is an elaboration of those that are basic to understanding organizational systems—social systems that are concrete, open, and living.

Boundaries of Organizations: Adaptable and Permeable

As suggested previously, systems may be viewed as being either open or closed. A closed system is one with rigid, impermeable boundaries; as such, there are neither inputs nor outputs—no exchange of matter and energy with the environment. Many scholars, including Miller, note that no concrete system is completely closed; thus it is more accurate to speak of concrete systems as being relatively closed or open.[27] Open systems have relatively permeable boundaries. As such, they receive inputs and provide outputs; energy and matter exchange occurs between the system and the environment. Note the term *relatively permeable.* Some social systems have considerable exchange, and there is a relatively free flow of information across the boundaries. Other social systems are characterized by boundaries that serve as significant barriers to information flow. Thus some scholars speak of the degree of openness of a social system. Some open systems have easily identifiable, "fixed" boundaries (e.g., biological systems), whereas the boundaries of social systems are not so easily identifiable; that is, they are subject to change over time or subject to definition on the part of the observer.

The significance of the concept for organizational systems is obvious. First, the boundaries of an organization are "vague," subject to definition. Second, organizational boundaries must be transcended for units within the organization to interact with units in the environment. Third, because the boundaries can be transcended, events in

---

[26]Talcott Parsons, *The Social System* (New York: The Free Press, 1951), pp. 5–6.
[27]Miller, op. cit., p. 18.

the environment can affect the internal structure and activities of the system. The latter point is well illustrated by Homans in one of his postulates relating to small groups. He posited that a decrease in the frequency of interaction between group members and "outsiders," accompanied by an increase in group members' negative feelings toward "outsiders," would increase the frequency of interaction and the strength of positive sentiments among group members and vice versa.[28] Also, while it is conceded that most mainstream organizational theorists recognize the effect of the environment on internal organizational behavior, some of the critics of mainstream organizational theories have contended that there is inadequate attention given to this most powerful influence on organizations.[29] Fourth, the boundaries of a given organization will be in contact with the boundaries of numerous other organizations. For example, a school as an organization will be in contact with other schools, the central office of the district, various civic groups, municipal agencies, and so on. Because these boundaries are relatively permeable, many authors have suggested that one major function of organizational management is to serve as an agent to ensure integration and cooperation.[30]

Organizations as Hierarchical, Integrated Systems

Systems theorists posit that all concrete systems with any degree of complexity are hierarchical. That is, conceptually, all systems, except the very smallest, are composed of subsystems; and all systems, except the very largest, are part of a suprasystem. In applying the hierarchical concept to living systems, Miller identified the applicable levels as cell, organ, organism, group, organization, society, and supranational system.[31] Illustrative applications of the hierarchy in organizations abound. For example, if an individual school in a decentralized school district is defined as the system, its subsystems at successively lower levels may include departments and classes. At successively higher levels its suprasystems may include the subdistrict and the district.

Kast and Rosenzweig have provided a concise application of the hierarchical and integrated notions to an organization. They defined an organization as an open, sociotechnical system. Because the system is both social and technical, the technologies affect the types of inputs, nature of the internal transformations, and output; and the

[28] Homans, op. cit., p. 113.

[29] See, for example, Charles Perrow, *Complex Organizations: A Critical Essay* (Glenview, Ill.: Scott, Foresman, 1979) and Jeffrey Pfeffer and Gerald R. Salancik, *The External Control of Organizations: A Resource Dependence Perspective* (New York: Harper & Row, 1978).

[30] Kast and Rosenzweig, op. cit., p. 114.

[31] Miller, op. cit., p. 4.

social system determines how well the technologies are used. Internally, an organization is composed of five interacting subsystems: goals and values, technical, psychosocial, structural, and managerial.[32]

As was discussed in Chapter 7, many organizational values come from the environment; further, an organization as a societal subsystem (institution) exists to accomplish certain goals that are "assigned" by the society. To sustain itself (continue to receive needed inputs) the organization must give attention to the values and goals of the society. The technical subsystem includes the knowledge and techniques needed to transform the inputs into outputs. The form of the technical subsystem is determined by the special knowledge and skills, types of equipment, and layout of facilities required by the tasks of the organization. The form will vary from organization to organization, depending upon the tasks (e.g., the technical subsystem of a school will be quite different from that of a coal mine). The psychosocial subsystem refers to groups and individuals in interaction. As Kast and Rosenzweig put it, the psychosocial subsystem "consists of individual behavior and motivation, status and role relationships, group dynamics, and influence systems. It is also affected by sentiments, values, attitudes, expectations, and aspirations of the people in the organization."[33] The structural subsystem, in the formal sense, defines the relationship between the technical and psychosocial subsystems. The focus is on the configuration of authority, communication, and work flow. It is characterized by policy, rules and regulations, organizational charts, job descriptions, and the like. The managerial subsystem, spanning the total organization, is concerned with environmental linkages, goal setting, planning, designing structure, and setting up control processes.

In sum, the systems theorists view organizations, as well as other systems, as composed of interacting subsystems, each of which makes a contribution to the system of which it is a part. This prevailing view, as typified by the conceptualization of Kast and Rosenzweig, stresses integration and holism. It represents a departure from the discrete and narrow emphasis of the traditional era and the transitional era.

Organizations as Systems Capable of Combating Entropy

According to Miller, the second law of thermodynamics can be stated as follows:

> one cannot convert an amount of heat into its equivalent amount of work, without other changes taking place in the system. These changes, expressed statistically, constitute a passing of the system from ordered

[32] Kast and Rosenzweig, op. cit., pp. 108–111.
[33] Ibid., p. 110.

arrangement into more chaotic or random distribution. This disorder, disorganization, lack of patterning, or randomness of organization in a system is known as *entropy*.[34]

Thus all systems will, over time, tend toward an increase in entropy. However, this tendency toward a decrease in order and an increase in disorder may be minimized in open systems. The reason is that open systems exchange matter, energy, and information with their environment, and these inputs can serve virtually to arrest the tendency toward entropy and on occasion can even serve to establish greater order. Bertalanffy put it this way:

> the general course of physical events (in closed systems) is toward increasing entropy, leveling down of differences and states of maximum disorder. In open systems, however, with transfer of matter import of "negative entropy" is possible. Hence, such systems can maintain themselves at a high level, and even evolve toward an increase of order and complexity—as is indeed one of the most important characteristics of life processes.[35]

When an open system—by continually using the inputs of matter, energy, and information; by transforming these; and by providing outputs to the environment—achieves a state of balance internally and with its environment, it is said to be in steady state or *dynamic equilibrium*. It is in a state of adapting in response to changes in the environment. Changes in the environment will throw the system into a state of imbalance, and an open system will make an effort to accommodate these changes and return to a steady state that is as much as possible like its previous state. If the environmental changes are too great for the system to accommodate internally and a "new" steady state cannot be achieved, death will occur.

Organizations, as open, living systems, operate in accord with these concepts; yet organizations are contrived systems (as opposed to natural systems). This means that even though entropic changes occur, by the continued appropriate use of inputs they appear capable of indefinitely "arresting" the entropy process. Through shifting its objectives, reallocating resources, restructuring, and the like, in response to changes that occur in society, an organization may survive far longer than any known biological organism. In striving to survive and maintain some balance, social systems make use of both adaptive and maintenance devices. The maintenance devices ensure that the system does not respond so rapidly that the several subsystems get out of balance. The adaptive devices ensure that some response is provided to changes that are occurring both internally and exter-

---

[34] Miller, op. cit., p. 13.
[35] Bertalanffy, "General Systems Theory—A Critical Review," op. cit., p. 18.

nally. Without the maintenance devices, changes could occur so rapidly that the system could not accommodate them. Without the adaptive devices, there can be no dynamic equilibrium. As applied to social organization, Katz and Kahn stated the point as follows:

> If the system is to survive, *maintenance substructures* must be elaborated to hold the walls of the social maze in place. Even these would not suffice to insure organizational survival, however. The organization exists in a changing and demanding environment, and it must adapt constantly to the changing environmental demands. *Adaptive structures* develop in organizations to generate appropriate responses to external conditions.[36]

In sum, organizations, as contrived subsystems of the larger society, which are in the process of change, must maintain balance both internally and externally if they are to "arrest" the process of entropy.

Feedback as a Means of Organizational Control

Feedback, as used in a mechanical sense by Wiener, means "control of a machine on the basis of its *actual* performance rather than its *expected* performance. . . ."[37] Wiener saw feedback as the central ingredient of *cybernetics,* a term he coined, meaning literally "steersman" or "governor." This definition of *feedback* is most often associated with nonliving systems, and the feedback received leads to "automatic" adjustments in the system. The often-cited example is the home heating system that is controlled by a thermostat. When the temperature drops to the previously set level, the thermostat receives the "input" and "activates" the system. This concept of "self-regulation," based on input about actual performance rather than intended performance, can be applied to the human organism. For example, within limits, the human body can maintain a constant body temperature even though there are variations in the temperature of the environment. This is so because the change of temperature in the environment affects the temperature of the blood, which, in turn, activates brain centers that control body heating and cooling mechanisms.

In the broader sense, feedback is a concept that refers to response to output, which enables a system to modify its subsequent functioning. Granger offered the following definition: "a return communication or reaction to information processing behavior; a control process transmitting a portion of the output behavior of a producing system back to the control or decision center or property in the same

---

[36] Daniel Katz and Robert L. Kahn, *The Social Psychology of Organizations,* 2nd ed. (New York: Wiley, 1978), p. 51.

[37] Norbert Wiener, "Cybernetics in History," in Buckley, op. cit., p. 35.

system."[38] Feedback may be either positive or negative. Positive feedback serves to reinforce the system's action and can result in the system not adapting to change. Negative feedback is in opposition to a system's action and stimulates the system to corrective activity in order to adapt to change—that is, to maintain a steady state. Furthermore, feedback may have both internal and external sources; for example, the temperature control mechanism in the human body uses internal feedback, whereas in social systems much of the feedback comes from sources external to the system.

The application of the concept to organizational control is straightforward. First, since organizations vary in openness, the nature of the feedback, the amount of feedback, and the adequacy of processing of the feedback will vary. Only positive feedback, too little feedback, or inadequate processing can be damaging to an organization in that it will lack appropriate information upon which to decide whether its outputs need modification. Too much negative feedback can be depressing to organizational members. Because the transmission and use of feedback brings about a dissipation of energy, too much feedback results in "system overload" and enhances the movement toward entropy. Therefore an organization needs a balance of positive, or reinforcing, and negative, or critical, feedback in amounts that can be processed if it is to maintain a steady state. Second, the feedback must be from both internal and external sources. The feedback from internal sources will serve primarily to keep the several organizational subsystems in balance, whereas the information from external sources will serve primarily to tell the organization how its outputs are being received by the environment.

Equifinality of Organizations

In closed systems there is a direct cause-and-effect relationship between inputs and outputs. On the other hand, open systems display equifinality. According to Granger, equifinality refers to "a property of a system which permits different results from similar inputs and similar results from alternate inputs."[39] Bertalanffy stated the point succinctly as follows:

> The steady state of open systems is characterized by the principle of equifinality; that is, in contrast to equilibrium states in closed systems which are determined by initial conditions, the open system may attain a time-independent state independent of initial conditions and determined only by the system parameters.[40]

[38] Granger, op. cit., p. 30.
[39] Ibid.
[40] Bertalanffy, "General Systems Theory—A Critical Review," op. cit., p. 18.

Application of the concept to organizations suggests at least three ideas. First, the initial inputs to an organization do not determine the extent to which a goal will be realized. That is, organizations may have differing levels of inputs of human and fiscal resources and have similar goal achievement. Second, organizational outputs may vary widely even though the inputs are "equal." Third, there is no "best way" to achieve a given organizational goal; rather there may be a number of acceptable alternative ways. This mode of thinking gives rise to what is generally referred to as *contingency theory,* which is in effect an indictment of the notion of a universal theory of organizations. The essence of contingency theory is that "it depends." To illustrate, in some situations, such as military combat, a directive leadership style may be most effective, yet, in other situations, such as a research and development team, it may not. Where the goal is production, the technology is stable and routine, and the personnel are unskilled, a highly-structured, mechanistic organizational design may be most appropriate; on the other hand, given other conditions (e.g., a service goal, skilled personnel), a low-structured, nonbureaucratic design may be better. (The two leadership theories to be described in Chapter 11 reflect the contingency approach.) Contingency theory has a basic soundness, yet, as Miles noted, there are two potential limitations:

> First, contingency models, unless carefully constructed, tend not to have major impact on behavior. Practitioners tend to greedily accept the notion that every situation is different as justification for current practices. Second, to be operational, contingency models require certain core concepts and prescriptions which are thus amenable to modification according to situational demands. In the absence of these, a separate model must be constructed for each different set of conditions (a limitless task).[41]

Immegart and Pilecki offered a concise summary of the application of the concept of equifinality.

> *The greatest implication of this property of the open system is that it opens the horizons regarding alternatives, and it underscores the need for goals and the rational progression from an initial state using appropriate procedures to the goal.* Initial states or procedures, in and of themselves, do not condition or determine goal realization. More precisely, goal realization results from appropriate, planned system activity directed toward real and feasible goals.[42]

[41]Raymond E. Miles, *Theories of Management: Implications for Organizational Behavior and Development* (New York: McGraw-Hill, 1975), p. 237.

[42]Immegart and Pilecki, op. cit., p. 42.

Application of Systems Theory to Educational Administration

There are numerous ways of applying systems thinking and concepts to the study and practice of educational administration. In the paragraphs that follow four applications are offered: (1) educational administration is described as a social process within a social system, (2) schools and school districts are viewed as social systems, (3) the use of systems propositions to guide research in educational administration is demonstrated, and (4) how systems theory can be used by the practitioner in his or her day-to-day activities is shown.

Educational Administration as a Social Process

Among the earlier theorists to apply systems concepts to educational administration were Getzels and Guba.[43] Admittedly influenced by Parsons,[44] they set out to develop "a model that was at once heuristic, operational, and that had the elegance and power of parsimony.[45] Administration is conceived of structurally as a hierarchy of superordinate–subordinate relationships within a conceptualized social system. Functionally, this hierarchy constitutes the locus for the allocation and integration of roles and facilities to achieve the goals of the system. In these relationships statuses are assigned, facilities are provided, procedures are organized, activities are regulated, and performances are evaluated. These functions are the responsibility of the superordinate, but each is effective only as it "takes" with subordinates. Thus administration operates in an interpersonal or social relationship—the crucial factor in the administrative process.[46]

For the purpose of analyzing the administrative process, the social system is conceived as consisting of two classes of phenomena. These are viewed as conceptually independent but practically interactive. One of these classes of phenomena constitutes the nomothetic or normative dimension (the sociological level of analysis), and its elements are institution, role, and expectation. The other class of phenomena makes up the idiographic or personal dimension (the psychological level of analysis), and its components are individual, person-

---

[43] See Jacob W. Getzels and Egon G. Guba, "Social Behavior and the Administrative Process," *School Review*, LXV (Winter 1957), 423–441; Jacob W. Getzels, "Administration as a Social Process," in Andrew W. Halpin (ed.), *Administrative Theory in Education* (New York: Macmillan, 1958), pp. 150–165.

[44] Parsons, op. cit.

[45] Getzels, "Administration as a Social Process," op. cit., p. 151.

[46] Ibid., pp. 151–152.

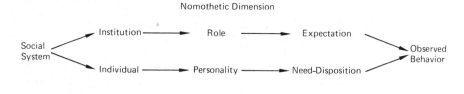

Figure 10-1.   General model showing the nomothetic and idiographic
dimensions of social behavior. [Source: Jacob W. Getzels,
"Administration as a Social Process," in Andrew W. Halpin (ed.), *Administrative Theory in Education* (New York:
Macmillan Publishing Co., 1958), p. 156. Reprinted by
permission.]

ality, and need-disposition. Observed behavior within the social system
is a function of these two dimensions. The model may be diagrammed
as shown in Figure 10-1.

Noting that social systems have certain essential functions that
come to be carried out in routinized ways (e.g., governing, educating,
policing), institution is defined as an agency created to carry out these
institutionalized functions (e.g., schools are devoted to educating). The
analytic subunit of institution is role. Roles refer to the "dynamic
aspects" of the positions, offices, and statuses of an institution and
define behavior for role incumbents.[47] The analytic subunit of role is
expectation. Role expectations are the normative obligations and responsibilities of a given role. They define for the role incumbent what
he or she should and should not do. Roles are complementary and
interdependent. A given role cannot be adequately defined or implemented except in relation to other roles. For example, the role of
teacher cannot be defined or implemented apart from the role of principal, pupil, and so on. It is the interactive character of roles that
enables an institution to be viewed as having a characteristic structure.[48]

Relative to the idiographic dimension, the subunit of individual
is personality, meaning "the dynamic organization within the individual of those need-dispositions that govern his unique reactions to
the environment."[49] Using Parsons and Shils terminology, need-dispositions are defined as "individual tendencies to orient and act with
respect to objects in certain manners and to expect certain consequences from these actions."[50]

[47]Linton's terminology, see Ralph Linton, *The Study of Man* (New York: Appleton, 1936), p. 14.
[48]Getzels, "Administration as a Social Process," op. cit., pp. 152–153.
[49]Ibid., p. 154.
[50]Ibid.

Because a given act is the result of interaction between role factors and personality factors, the general equation derived is $B = f(R \times P)$, where B is observed behavior, R is the role defined by its expectations, and P is personality of the role incumbent defined in terms of need-dispositions. The relative impact of the role and personality factors on behavior will vary with the act, the personality, and the role.[51] To illustrate, the behavior of an inmate in a maximum-security prison will in most instances conform to role expectancies and will be determined to a very limited extent by the personality of the inmate. At the other extreme, the behavior of a free-lance artist or writer will be determined largely by personality factors because the externally determined role expectancies are few.

Realizing the basic model provided an oversimplification of the determinants of social behavior and in recognition of a frequently voiced criticism that the model was inadequate to handle out-of-organization relationships, Getzels and associates expanded the basic model with the inclusion of biological and cultural dimensions. The biological dimension means that since a person is a biological organism, there are certain constitutional potentialities and abilities within which the personality develops. It is considered relevant only to the extent that it affects one's personality.[52]

The cultural dimension is considered the more directly relevant. It represents the context within which the social system functions. Said another way, role expectations in a social system are derived not only from the institutional requirements but from the culture within which the social system operates. To illustrate, in some encapsulated communities that are steeped in traditional values, persons filling the role of teacher are expected to display a standard of personal behavior not demanded of all other persons in the community. These same standards of personal behavior do not apply to teachers in other settings. The analytical units of the cultural dimension are ethos and values. Ethos refers to the distinguishing pattern of values of a particular culture. In regard to values (i.e., moral standards) the language of Parsons and Shils is accepted and values "set the limits of the permissible costs of an expressive gratification or an instrumental achievement. . . ."[53]

Theory is useful to the extent that it serves as a mechanism for understanding events, is productive of hypotheses, and leads to the identification of new issues and problems. As noted, early applications of the model led to the conclusion that refinements were neces-

[51] Ibid., pp. 157–158.
[52] Jacob W. Getzels, James M. Lipham, and Roald F. Campbell, *Educational Administration as a Social Process* (New York: Harper & Row, 1968), pp. 90–92.
[53] Talcott Parsons and Edward A. Shils, *Toward a General Theory of Action* (Cambridge: Harvard University Press, 1951), p. 166.

sary to deal with the out-of-organization relationship. This illustrates that the heuristic function of theory is to a degree served. Furthermore, the model has been most productive of hypotheses for research and as an aid to understanding reality.

One general derivation, which logically follows from the model, is that when the role incumbents in an interaction within the social system have overlapping perceptions of expectations, they will feel more satisfied with what was accomplished, no matter what the actual accomplishment, than they will if the perceptions of expectations do not overlap. Results from the studies conducted relative to the interactions of educational consultants and administrators and principal-teacher expectancies of leadership behavior offered some confirmation of this general hypothesis. More specifically, in situations where consultants and administrators agreed on the consultant role, both tended to rate the actual consultation more favorably than in situations where they did not agree; and in situations where teachers and principals had high agreement on expectations of leadership, the attitudes toward the work situation were more positive than in situations where there was low agreement, regardless of the actual situation.[54] As a guide for practice, the foregoing suggests that an administrator who desires to enhance the chances of mutual satisfaction in an administrative interaction should strive in the initial steps to clarify expectancies. Also, where dissatisfaction is observed, lack of congruence of expectancies might be explored as a possible cause of the dissatisfaction.

The model suggests three sources of conflict: intrarole conflict, intrapersonality conflict, and role-personality conflict. Role conflict refers to a situation where a role incumbent must at the same time respond to exclusive, contradictory, or inconsistent expectancies. This may be the result of disagreement about expectancies among the primary reference groups (e.g., role of the teacher as seen by the principal, by parents, and by pupils), disagreement about expectancies within a given reference group (e.g., some teachers expect a principal to provide close supervision, whereas other teachers expect to be left alone and treated as a professional), or attempts to fill two different roles at the same time (e.g., the superintendent as a leader of teachers and as a board negotiator). Personality conflicts arise as a result of opposing needs within the personality of a role incumbent. For example, a graduate professor may feel the need to maintain "distance" with students; nevertheless, he or she may also feel the need for extensive interaction on a peer basis with students. Such a conflict in needs would make it difficult to maintain a stable relationship. Role-personality conflict occurs when there is a lack of congruence between

[54]Getzels, "Administration as a Social Process," op. cit., pp. 160–161.

expectancies of a role and the need-dispositions of the role incumbent. For example, assuming the role of school superintendent requires high visibility and extensive community contact, a person with a high need for anonymity and privacy would have a conflict in personality and role if placed in the role of superintendent. Empirical research in various settings tends to confirm the validity of the notion of the primary types of conflict in an administrative setting.[55] At a practice level, the concept is useful to the administrator as he or she defines jobs in the organization (e.g., making sure there are no built-in conflicts in role expectations) and selects role incumbents (e.g., making a conscious effort to explore needs of people in relation to demands of jobs to be filled).

Three leadership–followership styles may be derived from the model: normative (nomothetic) style, personal (idiographic) style, and transactional style. The normative style stresses fulfilling institutional requirements rather than individual needs. Emphasis is placed on role definition, authority vested in roles, and organizational goal accomplishment. The personal style is characterized by minimum role definition, diffused authority, and effort to make it possible for each member to contribute meaningfully to the organization. The transactional style seeks to balance the institutional requirements and individual needs which must be met; the leader moves toward the normative style when circumstances demand and toward the personal style in other circumstances.[56] This framework can be used as a basis for classifying observed behavior of administrators and/or as a basis for research relative to the effectiveness of the various styles of leadership.

Schools and School Districts as Social Systems

Schools include pupils, teachers, support personnel, administrators, school board members, school advisory councils, buildings, instructional materials, equipment, and so on. Furthermore, schools operate within given localities with particular beliefs, economic resources, decision-making structures, and so on. The notions of environment, suprasystems, systems, and subsystems in interaction can be used to conceptualize these various components in whole or in part.

To illustrate, assume Zach Elementary School to be a social system. Within the confines of this school, a number of subsystems can be found: classrooms, faculty cliques, informal leadership structure, decision-making structures, interaction patterns, pupil friendship groups, group norms, allocation patterns, tasks to be performed, and so on. These several subsystems in interaction define what Zach is

[55] Ibid., pp. 161–165.
[56] Getzels, Lipham, and Campbell, op. cit., pp. 145–150.

and conditions what it will be in the future. The central office regime may be seen as the suprasystem of the school. This suprasystem includes various groupings of people, interaction patterns, control patterns, processes for accomplishing tasks, and so on. The suprasystem and its various elements, which could likewise be conceptualized as systems and subsystems, also affect Zach Elementary School. The environment of the school includes socioeconomic forces of the community; the power structure; various governmental structures at the local, state, and federal levels; and so on. Obviously, what is in the environment and within the system will be a function of how the boundaries of the system are defined for purposes of conceptualization, and different elements of the environment will differ in the impact they will have on Zach Elementary School. Furthermore, the system may be aware of certain parts of the environment and not be aware of other parts. (Immegart and Pilecki defined the environment of which the system is aware as proximal and that of which the system is unaware as distal.[57])

Another application of the notion of schools as integrated systems, subsystems, and the like, can be found in the work of Parsons. He suggested that education, like other complex organizations, could be conceptualized in terms of technical, managerial, and institutional systems. The technical system is involved in actual task performance within the organization (e.g., teaching), and in education the technical system consists largely of teachers and their support personnel. The managerial system functions to coordinate task performance and to ensure the presence of needed resources to the technical system. Educational administrators at various levels largely make up the managerial system. The institutional system serves to relate the organization to its environment. In education this includes, but is not restricted to, the various boards of control, such as the district school board.[58]

All schools are open in that they all have certain exchanges with their environment (e.g., receiving and processing pupils, fiscal resources). However, schools differ in the nature and quantity of outputs and in external feedback (e.g., nature, amount, processing). Thus schools can be viewed on a continuum from a high to a low degree of openness. Too much openness can create chaos within the school, whereas a low degree of openness can have a negative effect on the efforts of the school to maintain internal balance and adapt to its environment.

To illustrate, it has been frequently charged that in the 1960s and 1970s many schools in the big cities were not responsive. The

[57]Immegart and Pilecki, op. cit., p. 36.
[58]Talcott Parsons, "Some Ingredients of a General Theory of Formal Organizations," in Andrew W. Halpin (ed.), op. cit., pp. 40–72.

demography of the city changed, and some schools made no real effort
to alter their objectives, activities, and processes in response to these
changes. The people viewed these schools as archaic and uncaring;
school personnel were seen as more concerned with protecting what
they had than with providing meaningful opportunities for pupils.
School personnel came to view the environment as hostile and threat-
ening. Such schools exhibited a low degree of openness; environmental exchanges were difficult and limited. Seemingly, much more of the
energy of these schools was devoted to maintenance than to adaptation. On the other hand, there were other schools that made a concerted effort to adapt to the environmental changes: staffs were restructured, objectives were changed, curricula were altered, activities
were broadened, and citizen participation in school affairs was greatly
increased. In some instances schools attempted to respond to so many
diverse demands from the conflicting interests in the environment that
the internal balance was upset.

The point was made that open systems receive a variety of inputs, process these, and provide outputs. Because the processing subsystems vary from social system to social system, there is no direct
cause-and-effect relationship between input and output (i.e., social
systems possess the property of equifinality). Furthermore, the outputs result in internal and external feedback, both positive and negative, which, in turn, affects future input. A given school organization
includes a wide variety of input–output subsystems. For example, there
are decision-making subsystems, supervisory subsystems, teaching
subsystems, personnel subsystems, recordkeeping subsystems, and so
on.[59]

To illustrate the concept, Zach Elementary School may be conceptualized as an input–output system with the following illustrative
inputs, processing subsystems, and outputs:

Illustrative Inputs	Illustrative Processing Subsystems	Illustrative Outputs
pupils	curriculum organization	pupil attitudes
teachers	teaching methods	pupil knowledge
support personnel	data collection	decisions
community norms	data analysis	staff attitudes
community demography	communication	problem solutions
problems and alternatives	decision making	
financial resources	financial allocation	
	facilities	

[59] For a concise summary of the input–output model applied to schools see Immegart and Pilecki, op. cit., pp. 77–97.

Simply put, Zach Elementary, a social system, takes pupils, teachers, and resources within a given environment and by means of several internal processes transforms these inputs into outputs related to both pupils and staff. These outputs, in turn, provide feedback and condition future inputs.

Social Systems Concepts as a Guide to the Study of Educational Administration

As has been repeatedly emphasized, a primary measure of the adequacy of a theory is the extent to which testable hypotheses may be generated from it. In addition to the model proposed by Getzels and associates, several other "middle-range" formulations have been created that can serve as a fertile source of systems hypotheses to guide the study of educational administration. These include Homans's exchange theory for explaining social behavior,[60] Stogdill's formulation of an organized group as an input–output system,[61] and Halpin's paradigm for research on administrator behavior.[62]

One of the more comprehensive frameworks for the study of organizations was advanced by Miller.[63] Miller generated 173 systems propositions, which can be used to construct an infinite number of more specific hypotheses to direct research in educational administration. Miller focused on hypotheses (a term used interchangeably with *proposition*) that apply to two or more levels of living systems; these are called *cross-level hypotheses*.[64]

Miller did not argue that his framework, in the form of logically interrelated propositions, was original. He noted that many of the hypotheses had been proposed by others. Further, he suggested that although some of the hypotheses had been partially confirmed, some were probably erroneous, in whole or in part, and research data would provide a basis for needed refinement or modification.

The authors believe that many of Miller's propositions are useful in educational administration. Therefore some illustrative ones are cited below, along with more specific author-generated hypotheses related to educational administration.

> In general, the more structurally different types of members or components a system has, the more segregation of functions there is.[65]

[60] George C. Homans, *Social Behavior: Its Elementary Forms* (New York: Harcourt, 1961).

[61] Ralph M. Stogdill, *Individual Behavior and Group Achievement* (New York: Oxford University Press, 1959).

[62] Andrew W. Halpin, *Theory and Research in Administration* (New York: Macmillan, 1966).

[63] Miller, op. cit., pp. 89–119.

[64] Ibid., p. 90.

[65] Ibid., p. 92.

The functional segregation of components means that each one receives some information which others do not. The greater this segregation of information, the more do the components differ in decoding and deciding.[66]

These two related general hypotheses can give rise to an infinite number of more specific hypotheses related to educational organizations. For example, when compared to a comprehensive high school, the departments of a college preparatory school will be more functionally integrated, the members of the various departments will have greater commonality in perception of the needs of pupils, and the several departmental staffs will experience less difficulty in reaching agreement relative to programs and activities to meet pupil needs. Applying Miller's propositions to the school district level, one might suppose that as a school district expands programs and services (e.g., early childhood services, adult vocational programs) (1) functional segregation among the several central office units will increase and (2) difficulty in defining priorities relative to needed programs and services will increase. Obviously, either of these hypotheses could be broken into more specific ones, and before testing in a particular setting, empirical definitions of key terms would be needed.

Associations established early in the life of a system are more permanent than those established later.[67]

This proposition refers to customs, expected behavior, procedures, and so on, which are adopted by systems. Those adopted early in the life of a system tend to persist and have a significant impact on later experiences of the system. Two possible hypotheses of relevance to educational administration are the following: (1) During the first year of operation of a newly organized school, the informal staff groups will be more fluid than they will be in later years. (2) If a school board has become accustomed to a particular style of superintendent behavior (e.g., a strong executive posture) because of long experience with an incumbent, the board will view a new superintendent as ineffective if his or her behavior deviates sharply from that of his or her predecessor.

The longer the time during which a system has made decisions of a certain sort, the less time each decision takes, up to a limit.[68]

Miller saw this hypothesis as closely related to other hypotheses about communication (e.g., the less decoding and encoding required,

66 Ibid., p. 97.
67 Ibid., p. 99.
68 Ibid., p. 100.

the more a channel is used).[69] However, as applied to decision making in education, one could hypothesize that if the participant group remains reasonably stable, the length of time required by administrators and teachers to reach accord on a collective bargaining agreement will tend to decrease over the first five years following the institution of the collective bargaining process. The rapidity with which a board of education will reach a decision on an issue will be a function of the extent to which the issue is like issues that have been previously decided.

> The more two or more systems interact, the more they become alike in storing and processing common information.[70]

This proposition suggests several testable hypotheses regarding relationships between educational social systems and other social systems that have an interest in educational affairs. For example, the requests for information and the willingness to share information between school district planners and municipal planners will be greater in those localities where the two groups share a common facility (e.g., city hall) than in those localities where there is a geographic separation. If school district personnel and university personnel have been closely associated for a considerable time, then they will demonstrate more openness toward each other, even when there is a conflict in interests.

> A minimum rate of information input to a system must be maintained for it to function normally.[71]
> If the rate of information input into a system falls below a specific lower limit, normal growth of the system is impossible.[72]

These two related propositions about system inputs and functioning are pertinent to educational organizations and their environment. To illustrate, one could hypothesize that if a school district becomes isolated from its environment so that there is very limited information flow into the district, then the school district will gradually cease to function effectively.

> Segregation increases conflict among subsystems or components of a system, and a higher proportion of adjustment processes must be therefore devoted to resolving such conflicts, which means they cannot be devoted to advancing goals of the system as a whole.[73]

[69] Ibid., p. 97.
[70] Ibid., p. 103.
[71] Ibid., p. 105.
[72] Ibid., p. 109.
[73] Ibid., p. 107.

This hypothesis suggests that if an enterprise is so designed that the various units have a high degree of autonomy, in that much authority has been delegated to the several units, there will be a greater possibility for conflict, and it will be necessary for a greater proportion of the energy of the system to be expended to resolve conflicts. Applying the notion directly to educational administration, one could hypothesize that if a district superintendent provides little overt direction and tacitly encourages the assistant superintendents to define goals, programs, and activities for their respective divisions, then the conflict level among the assistants will be high, and each will devote a large portion of his or her available resources to resolving the conflicts on terms he or she deems favorable.

> The greater the resources available to a system, the less likely is conflict among its subsystems or components.[74]

The application of this proposition to schools seems self-evident. For example, if a school district's initial budget request is filled, during the budget year there will be (1) fewer grievances filed, (2) less hostility among the several departments of the schools, and (3) greater trust between administrators and teachers than if the operating budget is only 80 percent of the initial budget request.

> As a system's components become more numerous, they become more specialized, with resulting increased interdependence for critical processes among them.[75]

The thrust of this hypothesis is that as organizations increase in complexity the more numerous will be the subunits and the more narrow will be the range of activities of each. As a result, each becomes more dependent on others to carry out processes that are no longer carried out "in-house." One could apply this to schools by hypothesizing that as a school district grows in size and complexity, there will be increased demands and use by an increasing number of units (schools, central office divisions) of the personnel and finance departments for such processes as personnel selection, orientation of personnel, evaluation of personnel, financial accounting, financial allocation, and so on.

The foregoing are but a few illustrations of Miller's framework and how it might be used to generate hypotheses to guide research in educational administration. As noted at the outset, other systems schemes could have been used to demonstrate the essential point: systems theory is useful as a research framework.

[74] Ibid., p. 108.
[75] Ibid., p. 109.

The Practitioner and Social Systems Concepts

The authors contend that the ideas generated by the systems-era theorists are of practical, day-to-day value to the educational administrator. Previously presented material suggests that systems concepts are of use to the practitioner in two basic ways, as a way of thinking and as a source of substantive ideas.

Thinking in a systems mode is an intelligent approach to dealing with the many issues and problems that confront the practicing educational administrator. The practicing administrator who approaches his or her job from a systems viewpoint will think in conceptual as opposed to concrete terms, focus on both wholes and parts, recognize the dynamic interrelationships among various aspects of a situation, and be goal-oriented.

In many cases administrators seemingly approach events and problems in a concrete, isolated, and specific manner. They deal with the immediate realities of the situation, with little thought given to anything other than solving the crisis of the moment. Their behavior from one situation to another seems to indicate that they lack a set of abstractions that they use to deal with the specific concrete situation. The systems-oriented administrator, although recognizing the necessity for dealing with the immediate realities, approaches events with the conviction that there are general principles that can usually be applied to the specific. For example, assume that after several hours of serious and sometimes heated discussion, the superintendent and the school board chairperson agree on a critical policy issue facing the district but that within twenty-four hours the chairperson begins to waiver and behave as if the extended discussions had never occurred. If the superintendent thinks only in concrete terms, there will be an attempt to deal with the behavior as a specific isolated instance; if the superintendent is conceptually oriented, he or she will think in such terms as, "behavior is caused," "the parts of a system are related," "specifics must be examined within their context," "negative feedback stimulates a system to change its output," and so on. In approaching the changed behavior of the chairperson by first examining it at the abstract level and in terms of certain principles that are broadly applicable, the superintendent is far more likely to identify intelligent steps to be taken.

Focusing on broadly applicable concepts that may be applied to specific problems does not mean that an administrator has a "stock" solution to given types of problems or that there are no values involved. Conceptual thinking in this sense means the examination of general propositions to determine their relevance for the specific problem.

Systems thought is both analytic and holistic. The administrator who accepts this will approach a problem by first trying to conceive of it in its totality and then by breaking it down into relevant parts. Such an administrator begins by defining some meaningful unit as the "system" with which he or she is concerned (e.g., a single school) and identifying the suprasystem and environment of the system. This provides the framework within which the problem may be examined. The administrator, having developed a concept of the "whole," can then proceed to deal with the parts of the problem.

Systems theorists stress the relationships among the parts of a system and in open systems the relationships between a system and its environment. The administrator who is thinking from a systems framework will realize that the parts of a situation and their properties are in some manner related, so that a change in one part will be reflected in changes in another. For example, for the purpose of allocating instructional materials within a given school, the school may be conceived as the system, with the several programs being the parts. Assume that the staff of a particular program demands an increase in its allocation. The granting of this demand would have to be considered in relation to what impact this would have on the allocations for the other programs.

If an administrator approaches situations conceptually, tries to examine the parts in relation to the whole and in relation to each other, he or she will also look at the impact of a given action in terms of both its short-term and long-term effects. That is, if there is concern for linkages in time and space, there will also be concern for the future—the realization that systems exist to carry out some purpose. Long-term goals will be recognized and short-term goals will be accepted that are consistent with them. Then as a problem is analyzed and alternatives proposed, they will be evaluated in terms of the goals to be achieved.

Consistent with the systems point of view, a number of substantive ideas about organizations, leadership in organizations, and organizational behavior have been developed and at least partially confirmed. Several of these ideas have been described previously. Our contention is that ideas such as these can be used by practicing administrators as a way of explaining what they observe, making predictions about what will occur in given circumstances, and guiding action. In the paragraphs that follow, other examples of using systems ideas to explain, predict, and serve as guides for action are offered.

Most experienced administrators have seen cases where two schools seemingly had similar inputs. That is, the schools were "alike" in regard to pupil population, physical facilities, size, teaching staff, support services, financial support, administrative staff, curriculum, and so on. Yet in terms of output, as measured by pupil achievement and perceptions of the school, one school was highly productive and the other was not. A person conversant with systems concepts does not have to explain the plight of the low-productive school in terms of the "wrath of the gods." Rather, such a person recognizes that schools are examples of open systems and that open systems display the property of equinfinality.

In a similar vein, acquaintance with such concepts as dynamic equilibrium, entropy, and internal elaboration can be useful in explaining differences among educational organizations. These notions are also useful as a basis for prediction. For example, using the concept of entropy, one might predict that if a school staff engaged in actions that greatly limited interaction with the several sectors of the environment, the result would be that the school would quickly be viewed as "out of touch," "dying," and "not relevant."

Parsons's formulation of a complex organization as consisting of technical, managerial, and institutional systems can be useful as a framework for viewing a school district or university in its totality. Also, the formulation provides a basis for explaining differences in activities among different classes of employees (e.g., teachers and assistant superintendents) and assigning priorities within given classes of employees.

The model developed by Getzels and associates is of use to the practitioner. For example, the model "forces" an administrator to be cognizant of both organizational demands and the needs and concerns of individual employees when confronted with a decision. It can be used as a frame of references to explain various kinds of conflict that may be observed within an educational organization. Study of the model can also suggest courses of action that might be fruitful. To illustrate, it suggests that in making assignments care should be taken to ensure that the various expectancies of a job are, at least on the surface, compatible. Also, it can be used to build a logical case for a complete orientation program. If roles are defined by expectancies and are in part a function of the culture within which an organization functions, it can be argued that if a person is carefully oriented to the demands of a job, both formal and informal (e.g., band director at Old Tradition High), and accepts the job with this awareness, there is a greater likelihood that the individual will meet the demands of the job.

Many of Miller's cross-level hypotheses have sufficient confirmation that practitioners can feel comfortable using them to explain, predict, and guide action. For example, the proposition to the effect that decision time decreases with experience in making decisions of a similar nature seems sufficiently supported to be followed as a general rule. That is, plan for and expect more time to be used when a "unique" decision is needed.

A Critique of the Systems Movement

There appears to be considerable consensus that the systems approach represents a viable response to the administrative theory needs enunciated by scholars of an earlier day. The systems approach appears to provide a systematic conceptual scheme for the understanding of organizations. The focus on wholes, parts, and the relationships among the parts provides an opportunity for logical linkage among many conceptualizations of a nonglobal nature. For example, "theories" of planning, evaluation, decision making, organizational compliance, and conflict management may be logically related within the systems framework. Also, because the systems concept provides a set of unifying postulates and a means of communication among several fields of study, greater opportunities are provided for cooperative effort among scholars.

Systems theory also provides a framework for research related to organizations and their administration. As illustrated by Miller's propositions and the model by Getzels and associates, several of the substantive notions that have been developed consistent with the systems movement have been most productive in terms of generating hypotheses for research. Because the systems movement has emphasized mathematical and quantitive procedures, research methodology has been advanced.

As a way of thinking, the systems movement is of great value to the practicing administrator. An administrator given to this approach will be goal-oriented; will examine the context of problems faced (e.g., consider the totality of the situation); will be aware of the dynamic interrelations among groups, events, and ideas; will seek feedback; will examine various alternatives, and will be cognizant of possible long-range impact.

Those who stand apart from this mainstream approach tend to be proponents of the "garbage can" model or embrace the loose-coupling notion. The garbage can model assumes that organizations are organized anarchies. As such, the goals are hazy, varied and/or inconsistent; the techniques and processes to be used are not clear or understood by organization members; and the organizational members and decision makers change frequently. Within this context, the relationships among problems, decisions alternatives, decision makers, and solutions are not clear (e.g., solutions may seek problems, problems and solutions may be independent). The garbage can is a simulation model taking into account problems, decision structures, solutions, and potential energy of the organization.[76]

[76]Michael D. Cohen, James G. March, and Johan P. Olsen, "A Garbage Can Model of Organizational Choice," *Administrative Science Quarterly*, 17 (March 1972), 1–25.

According to loose coupling, numerous parts of some organizations (i.e., an educational institution) are weakly or infrequently related and their interdependence is minimal. For example, at times there will be an excess of resources relative to demand, and often any one of several means will produce the same end. When there is a breakdown in one part, the effect on other parts is minimal, and there is low coordination and high decentralization.[77] Thus, the garbage can/loose coupling advocates are very skeptical of rational organizational models.

If one expects the systems movement to produce a theory in the sense defined by Feigl,[78] he or she is likely to be disappointed. Systems theory is not a set of assumptions from which empirical laws can be derived by logico-mathematical procedures; it does not constitute a universal, all-inclusive, substantive body of thought. In fact, some scholars have suggested it is not even a "theory," but a methodology, and one that is empirical and interdisciplinary. Perhaps Rapoport said it appropriately when he noted that general systems is described best "as a program or a direction in the contemporary philosophy of science" aimed at "the integration of diverse content areas by means of a unified methodology of conceptualization or of research."[79]

ACTIVITIES/QUESTIONS FOR FURTHER STUDY

1. Review to ensure that you understand the meaning of the following and can illustrate their application to organizations: entropy, negative entropy, maintenance substructure, adaptive substructure, dynamic equilibrium, feedback, equifinality.
2. Attend a meeting of a school board, the administrative staff of a school district or college, or some other group that gives attention to organizational policies and problems. Observe and evaluate the extent to which the organizational leaders think conceptually, holistically and analytically, and in terms of long- and short-range goals.
3. Give consideration as a class to each of the following assertions: (1) The ideology of educational administration can be logically integrated within a systems framework. (2) Schools and colleges can accurately be described as having vague and often inconsistent goals, lacking adequate knowledge about teaching and learning, and controlled by decision makers who change frequently.

[77] Karl E. Weick, "Educational Organizations as Loosely Coupled Systems" *Administrative Science Quarterly,* 21 (March 1976), 1–19.

[78] Herbert Feigl, "Principles and Problems of Theory Construction in Psychology," in Wayne Dennis (ed.), *Current Trends in Psychological Theory* (Pittsburgh: University of Pittsburgh Press, 1951), p. 181.

[79] Rapoport, op. cit., p. 452.

SUGGESTED READINGS

BECKETT, JOHN A. *Management Dynamics: The New Synthesis*. New York: McGraw-Hill Book Company, 1971.

BUCKLEY, WALTER (ed.). *Modern Systems Research for the Behavioral Scientist*. Chicago: Aldine Publishing Company, 1968.

GETZELS, JACOB W., JAMES M. LIPHAM, and ROALD F. CAMPBELL. *Educational Administration as a Social Process*. New York: Harper & Row, Publishers, 1968, Chapters 1–3.

HANSON, E. MARK. *Educational Administration and Organizational Behavior*. Boston: Allyn & Bacon, Inc., 1979, Chapter 5.

HERBERT, THEODORE T. *Dimensions of Organizational Behavior*, 2nd ed. New York: Macmillan Publishing Co., Inc., 1981, Chapter 3.

HICKS, HERBERT G., and C. RAY GULLETT. *Organizations: Theory and Behavior*. New York: McGraw-Hill Book Company, 1975, Chapter 12.

IMMEGART, GLENN L., and FRANCIS J. PILECKI. *An Introduction to Systems for the Educational Administrator*. Reading, Mass.: Addison-Wesley Publishing Co., Inc., 1973.

KAST, FREMONT E., and JAMES E. ROSENZWEIG. *Organization and Management: A Systems and Contingency Approach*, 3rd ed. New York: McGraw-Hill Book Company, 1979, Chapter 5.

KATZ, DANIEL, and ROBERT L. KAHN. *The Social Psychology of Organizations*, 2nd ed. New York: John Wiley & Sons, 1978, Chapters 2–3.

MARCH, JAMES G. (ed.). *Handbook of Organizations*. Chicago: Rand McNally & Co., 1965.

MILES, RAYMOND E. *Theories of Management: Implications for Organizational Behavior and Development*. New York: McGraw-Hill Book Company, 1975, Chapter 1.

MILLER, JAMES G. *Living Systems*. New York: McGraw-Hill Book Company, 1978, Chapters 2, 4, 10.

PARSONS, TALCOTT. "Social Systems," in David L. Sills (ed.). *International Encyclopaedia of the Social Sciences*, vol. 4. New York: Macmillan Publishing Co., Inc. and The Free Press, 1968, pp. 458–472.

WEICK, KARL E., "Educational Organizations as Loosely Coupled Systems," *Administrative Science Quarterly*, 21 (March 1976), 1–19.

11

Key Administrative Functions

$\mathbf{A}$S IMPLIED in Chapter 8, an analysis of the many treatises regarding administrative/managerial functions or processes within the past 50 years will reveal much similarity. The terms and relative emphases may differ but there is general agreement about the functions that are central to the role. These include making decisions about purposes and procedures, providing leadership, securing compliance from subordinates, dealing with conflict, managing change, relating to the environment of the organization, planning, organizing, communicating, and controlling. Given such agreement, one is not surprised that the literature is replete with conceptual material about these topics. In the first edition of this book we used the term "nonglobal theories" to describe these ideas; others have used the term "middle-range theories." Which term is used is of little note; what does matter is to understand that constructs have been developed to assist the administrator in carrying out these key functions. Furthermore, some of the ideas advanced do not meet all of the criteria for theory as defined in Chapter 8.

To assist the student in understanding this part of the conceptual heritage of educational administration, with two exceptions, attention is given in the following sections to each of the above-mentioned functions. Organizing, which refers to developing and maintaining a formal structure of authority and groupings between people and the tasks to be accomplished within the confines of the purposes to be achieved and the resources available, was examined in some detail in parts of the preceding three chapters. The organizational environment is the focus of Part IV.

Making Decisions in Organizations

As we have noted, many theorists accept the idea that administration and decision making are almost the same, or at least that decision making is the most critical aspect of administration. Simon is representative of this posture.

> If any "theory" is involved, it is that decision-making is the heart of administration, and that the vocabulary of administration theory must be derived from the logic and psychology of human choice.[1] . . . The task of "deciding" pervades the entire administrative organization quite as much as the task of doing—indeed, it is integrally tied up with the latter. A general theory of administration must include principles of organization that will insure correct decision-making, just as it must include principles that will insure effective action.[2]

Given the prevalence of the notion that decision making is "the heart of administration," it is not surprising that the literature is abundant with discourses on the topic. Most frequently the writers have given attention to a definition of *decision making,* classes or types of decisions, occasions for decisions, the role of administrators in decision making, and the steps in the process. To provide an overview to the concepts, two theories proposed by scholars concerned directly with education, are reviewed briefly. (The place of values in decision making is discussed in the next chapter and is not considered here except as is related to the formulations reviewed.) The section is concluded with a brief review of quantitative techniques appropriate for decision making.

Decision Making Central to Administration

Griffiths, influenced by Barnard and Simon, in his often-cited 1959 book *Administrative Theory,* took the position that decision making was central to administration in that it was more important than other functions and that other administrative functions can be

---

[1] Herbert A. Simon, *Administrative Behavior* (New York: Macmillan, 1950), p. xiv.

[2] Ibid., p. 1.

best interpreted in terms of the process of decision making.[3] Basic to Griffith's theory (he accepted Feigl's definition of the term) were four assumptions about administration:

> 1. Administration is a generalized type of behavior to be found in all human organizations. . . . 2. Administration is the process of directing and controlling life in a social organization. . . . 3. The specific function of administration is to develop and regulate the decision-making process in the most effective manner possible. . . . 4. The administrator works with groups or with individuals with a group referrent, not with individuals as such.[4]

Relative to the third assumption, Griffiths emphasized that there was a difference in controlling the process and the executive making the decisions alone. Said another way, the executive makes a decision only when the organization fails to do so. In a brief 1969 restatement of the theory the fourth assumption was dropped.[5]

The position was taken that in order to use these assumptions a set of clearly defined, relevant concepts was needed. The key concepts identified by Griffiths are *decision making, organization, perception, communication, power,* and *authority.* The decision-making process was defined as including a decision—a judgment made relative to a state of affairs that influences the course of action that follows—and the acts necessary to put the decision into effect. Within organizations most decisions are based on one or more previous decisions; that is, they are sequential. Two types of organizations were viewed as affecting decisions: the formal and the informal. The form of the formal organization is seen as a function of the decision-making process. If decisions are made on a centralized basis, then the formal organization will be "tall"; if decisions are made on a decentralized basis, then a "flat" organization is built. Informal organizations (dynamic structures representing special interests and subject to continual revision) serve to alter the decision-making process of the formal organization. Perception can be examined only in relation to specific persons dealing with specific situations—a transaction. Perception enters the transaction in that each person involved enters from his or her own unique position. Thus in each situation, different individuals will see it differently and each will perceive what is seen to be real. Perception defines the limits of communication, which is the process by which cooperation and coordination in organizations occur. Cooperation and

---

[3] Daniel E. Griffiths, *Administrative Theory* (New York: Appleton, 1959), pp. 74–75.

[4] Ibid., pp. 71–74.

[5] Daniel E. Griffiths, "A Taxonomy Based on Decision-Making," in Daniel E. Griffiths (ed.), *Developing Taxonomies of Organizational Behavior in Education Administration* (Chicago: Rand McNally, 1969), pp. 63–65.

coordination are necessary if decisions are to be made and effected. Power is defined in terms of decisions made. Thus the power of an individual in an organization is a function of control over the decision-making process. Authority refers to the willingness of some members of the organization to accept the legitimacy of others in making decisions and controlling the process.[6]

Within the context of the foregoing, three major propositions relating to decision making were offered:

> The structure of an organization is determined by the nature of its decision-making process. The issues of organizational structure such as "span of control" can be resolved if viewed as the outgrowth of a particular type of decision-making process.[7]
>
> If the administrator confines his behavior to making decisions on the decision-making process rather than making terminal decisions for the organization, his behavior will be more acceptable to his subordinates.[8]
>
> If the administrator perceives himself as the controller of the decision-making process, rather than the maker of the organization's decisions, the decisions will be more effective.[9]

Griffiths conceived the decision-making process as consisting of six steps. First, the problem must be recognized, defined, and limited. This, to a degree, sets the boundaries within which the problem will be handled. Second, the problem is analyzed and evaluated. Critical at this point is a decision about whether or not an attempt should be made to solve the problem. Borrowing from Barnard, Griffiths identified three occasions when an administrator makes a decision: when given an authoritative communication from a superior, when a case has been referred from a subordinate, and at the personal initiative of the administrator. The third step is to establish criteria of judgment—set standards so a decision can be evaluated in terms of its success. The fourth step in the process is to collect relevant (free from bias or bias indicated) and repeatable (the same when viewed by others) data. The fifth step is to select a solution. This involves the formulation of several alternatives, weighing the consequences of each, and selecting the alternative seen as more likely to succeed. The sixth step is to put the solution into effect. This includes using or creating a structure to do what is demanded by the decision, assuring that the performance in implementing is consistent with the plan, and evaluating the results and process.[10]

[6] Griffiths, *Administrative Theory,* op. cit., pp. 74–88.
[7] Ibid., p. 89.
[8] Ibid., p. 90.
[9] Ibid., p. 91.
[10] Ibid., pp. 92–113.

Decision Making and Evaluation

Functioning as the Phi Delta Kappa National Study Committee on Evaluation, Stufflebeam and six associates advanced a theory of decision making that was linked directly to educational evaluation.[11] The position taken was that decision making is a four-stage process, occurs in four different settings, may be effected by three alternative models, and involves four different types of questions. Furthermore, it was recognized that in most instances more than one decision maker contributes to a decision, and decisions generally stand in a contingent relationship to other decisions.

The four stages in making a decision are (1) becoming aware that there is need for a decision, (2) designing the situation, (3) selecting an alternative, and (4) taking action in terms of the selected alternative. (Information collection is not identified as an explicit stage because it is needed at each stage.) There are three major sources for becoming aware of the need for a decision. One source is decision situations that have been identified and decision-making responsibilities fixed well in advance. These are programmed situations that can be anticipated by the logical nature of the organization. A second source is unmet needs or unsolved problems. An evaluation system for monitoring is important in this instance. The third source is opportunities, representing the difference between the present state of affairs and what desirable better state could be achieved if a change was made. The decision design stage includes six steps: stating the decision situation in question form, fixing authority and responsibility for the decision, formulating decision alternatives, determining criteria for assessing alternatives, defining the rules to be used in choosing an alternative, and determining when an alternative must be chosen. The third stage is the choice stage. This involves collecting information in light of selected criteria, applying the accepted decision rules, reflecting on the logic of the indicated alternative, and confirming the indicated alternative or recycling. The final stage is taking action. This includes fixing responsibility for implementing the selected alternative, operationalizing the alternative (specifying procedures, resources, and so on), reflecting on the efficacy of the choice, and executing the action plan or deciding to recycle.[12]

Decision setting refers to the total set of environmental circumstances governing analysis and choice. The critical dimensions are the degree of change resulting from a choice and the amount of information grasp that exists to support the change. Using these two dimensions, four different decision settings are identified. A metamor-

[11] Daniel L. Stufflebeam et al., *Educational Evaluation and Decision Making* (Itasca, Ill.: Peacock, 1971).
[12] Ibid., pp. 50–61.

phic decision setting (utopian and extremely rare) exists when a complete change will result and there is an understanding of all relevant information. This setting assumes adequate theory and information systems. A homeostatic setting, the most prevalent in education, involves a low degree of change and requires a high degree of information grasp. The information needed is provided by existing technical standards and a quality-control data-collection system, including achievement test data, attendance data, grades, and so on. In comparison to a homeostatic setting, incremental settings are those that result in a shift to a new balance by the process of a series of small changes as opposed to merely correcting to maintain a balance. In incremental settings there is great reliance on expert judgment, special studies, committees, and the like, rather than on routinely collected information. In neomobilistic decision settings, there is considerable change (new solutions for significant problems) but little theory or information. Obviously, such settings afford great opportunity but also represent high risk.[13]

Excluding metamorphic decision settings (which were seen as having only theoretical relevance), a decision model was identified that corresponds to each of the settings. The synoptic ideal model was thought to be appropriate for homeostatic settings. This model requires the collection and analysis of "all" relevant information. It does not deal with value conflicts. Though not generally useful, it does have value in homeostatic settings where the resulting change is small and restorative and the amount of information about the limited alternatives is high. The disjointed incremental model was seen as relevant for incremental settings. This model is based on the assumption that the change desired is small and only incrementally different from what is, and there is little available information. The focus is primarily on present time needs and problems, and the problem-solving approach is employed. The range of possible alternatives is confined. Improving what currently exists is a major criterion for considering alternatives. The planned change model was identified as appropriate for neomobilistic decision settings. This model is complex and time-consuming. The planned change model proposed involves four major phases, each of which includes a series of steps. The major phases are research, development, diffusion, and adoption.[14]

Four different types of decisions were conceptualized. Two postulates were basic to the typology proposed. First, decisions should be classified as to ends or means. Second, decisions should be classified as relating to intentions or to actualities. Looking at the two postulates in relation to each other, decisions in education may be classi-

[13] Ibid., pp. 61–69.
[14] Ibid., pp. 69–70.

fied as relating to goals (intended ends), procedural designs (intended means), attainments (actual ends), or procedures in use (actual means). Within this context there are four types of educational decisions: (1) planning decisions to determine goals; (2) structuring decisions, which specify means to achieve goals; (3) implementing decisions, which refer to carrying through on plans (i.e., actual means); (4) recycling decisions, which focus on actual attainments in relation to intended ends at a given point in time.[15]

For the administrator engaged in the decision-making process, the model suggests four basic concepts. First, after becoming aware of the need for a decision, make a determination of the amount of information available and the degree of change that may result. Second, within the context of the information available and degree of change, select a decision model (e.g., with low information and large change use a planned change approach). Third, recognize that decisions will relate goals, means to achieve goals, implementation of means, and actual accomplishments in relation to goals. Fourth, the process does not end with the selection of an alternative; rather, the process includes putting the selected alternative into effect and evaluating the results.

Quantitative Tools and Decision Making

Since World War II several sophisticated, mathematically oriented techniques have been developed that are relevant to the decision-making process. These techniques are most appropriate for programmed decisions and are most useful at the analysis-of-alternatives stage of the process. Given such tools, which generally require use of computer facilities, it becomes possible to analyze far more variables than can be done otherwise; as a result, the consequences of a wide array of alternatives can be explored hypothetically with little risk and at relatively low cost. However, these tools cannot serve to answer the what-ought-to-be question.

Banghart identified linear programming, gaming, queueing, inventory control, and simulation as the more well-established quantitative techniques available to the decison maker.[16] Linear programming is useful where the intent is to optimize some objective with scarce resources and at minimum cost. That is, there are given amounts of A to be distributed among B's, and there is not enough A to fill the total requirements of the B's. Linear programming is useful in resource allocations, pupil scheduling, personnel assignment, and

[15] Ibid., pp. 80–84.
[16] Frank W. Banghart, *Educational Systems Analysis* (New York: Macmillan, 1969), p. 68.

the like. Game theory is most appropriate in conflict situations involving a limited number of opponents. As Banghart put it,

> game theory is concerned with the basic conflict situation where certain strategies are available to each opponent and clear-cut rules of the game are stipulated. The objective for each opponent is to maximize his gains and minimize his losses under the circumstances.[17]

Queueing theory is focused on waiting time situations. The aim is to minimize the waiting time to use given facilities while having no more of these facilities available than is required for efficient operations. The aim of inventory control is to keep costs to a minimum while having adequate supplies available to meet current needs. The two primary cost considerations involved are the administrative costs, associated with ordering and handling, and the cost of maintaining the supplies in inventory. In the quantitative sense, simulation involves the application of mathematical models to complex decision situations. By the use of such models an infinite number of conditions and possibilities can be simulated. Thus the possible consequences of given decisions can be determined without damage to the actual functioning of the organization.

Given the emphasis beginning in the late 1970s on management information systems (MIS) within educational organizations as a necessity in decision making and the need some have for quantification, we emphasize that these techniques, which essentially provide objective methods of analyzing alternatives, have significant limitations. As Robbins noted, the techniques are only as good as the assumptions that underlie them, and "they can never replace decision makers and their judgments."[18]

Providing Leadership

In Chapter 9 we noted that even though extensive attention had been given to leadership, often there was no distinction made between administration and leadership. Thus leadership research has been hampered by the problem of definition. Furthermore, it was pointed out that there has been extensive interest in leadership "styles" and that the focus of leadership research has gone through three phases: (1) the personal traits and characteristics (psychological aspects) focus, (2) the situational factors (sociological aspects) focus,

---

[17]Ibid., p. 69.
[18]Stephen P. Robbins, *The Administrative Process: Integrating Theory and Practice* (Englewood Cliffs, N.J.: Prentice-Hall, 1976), p. 165.

and (3) the interactional focus, which includes both the psychological and sociological aspects. Halpin described this as the "observed behavior approach"[19] and more recently the phrase used is "contingency approach."

In spite of the problems of definition and methodology, the literature provides several valuable ideas to the student of educational administration. In the paragraphs that follow, the contributions of the personal and situational emphases are discussed, and two prevailing formulations from the contingency point of view, which is consistent with open systems thought, are reviewed. Before turning to these topics, three assumptions, which appear basic to much of the literature, should be identified. First, administration is broader than leadership (i.e., administration encompasses other activities, such as maintenance tasks). Second, leadership in organizations and groups is not restricted to those who hold status positions. Third, leadership refers to a person behaving in such a way as to influence others to seek willingly and enthusiastically the achievement of group objectives.

Contributions of the Personal and Situational Emphases

The usual approach to studying the psychological aspects of leadership has been to identify a group of "leaders" (often persons holding status positions), use some measure(s) of effective performance, and determine the extent to which the level of effectiveness correlated with selected traits and/or behavioral characteristics. Several scholars have prepared summaries of the research relative to the psychological aspects of leadership.[20] There is considerable similarity among these summaries; as such, it appears that the following generalizations are reasonably valid:

1. Leaders tend to be slightly higher in intelligence than the average of the group led.
2. Leaders tend to be emotionally mature, to exhibit self-confidence, to be goal oriented, to initiate action, to be dependable in exercising responsibilities, to have insight into problems faced by the group, and to have a strong continuing drive to succeed.
3. Leaders realize that people are essential for goal achievement. Therefore they attempt to communicate with others,

---

[19] Andrew W. Halpin, *The Leadership Behavior of School Superintendents* (Columbus, Ohio: College of Education, Ohio State University, 1956), p. 11.

[20] See, for example, Ralph M. Stogdill, *Handbook of Leadership* (New York: Free Press, 1974), pp. 35–127; Robert B. Myers, "The Development and Implications of a Conception for Leadership Education" (Unpublished Doctoral Dissertation, University of Florida, 1954).

tend to be sociable, show consideration for people, and seek cooperation of others.

4. The presence of such traits and characteristics does not guarantee effective performance as a leader, nor does their absence preclude effective performance; rather, the presence of these traits and characteristics enhances the probability of effective performance as a leader.

Given the absence of "universal" personal traits and/or characteristics, attention has also been given to the dimensions of the situation as factors in the determination of leadership. Gibb, as a result of an extensive review of leadership literature, suggested that the group factors related to leadership included the expectations of the followers, the nature of the tasks of the group and the conditions under which the tasks were undertaken, and the institutionalization of the group (i.e., whether formal or informal).[21] Similarly, based on a synthesis of the work of other theorists, Filley, House, and Kerr suggested that the situational variables included the task requirements of the leader and the subordinates; attitudes, needs, and expectations of subordinates; and the organizational and physical environment.[22]

As noted above and described briefly in relation to the Getzels-Guba model presented in Chapter 10, many scholars have focused on leadership or managerial styles. This includes the democratic, authoritarian, and laissez-faire styles identified by Lewin, Lippitt, and White[23]; McGregor's X and Y styles[24]; the "initiating structure" and "consideration" dimensions of leader behavior resulting from a series of studies conducted in large part at Ohio State and used by Halpin as a basis for his paradigm[25]; and Likert's "four systems of management."[26] Some critics have suggested that the leadership styles thrust was essentially personal in that inadequate attention was given to the situation in which given styles were appropriate. Such criticism appears to be a bit harsh, particularly in relation to the Halpin and Likert formulations, because these efforts represented the logical next step in leadership theory development—to offer a set of constructs

[21] Cecil A. Gibb, "Leadership," in Gardner Lindzey and Elliot Aronson (eds.), *The Handbook of Social Psychology*, vol. 4, 2nd ed. (Reading, Mass.: Addison-Wesley, 1969), p. 272.

[22] Alan C. Filley, Robert J. House, and Steven Kerr, *Managerial Process and Organizational Behavior*, 2nd ed. (Glenview, Ill.: Scott, Foresman, 1976), p. 241.

[23] Kurt Lewin, Ronald Lippitt, and Ralph K. White, "Patterns of Aggressive Behavior in Experimentally Created 'Social Climates'," *Journal of Social Psychology*, X (May 1939), 271–299.

[24] Douglas M. McGregor, *The Human Side of Enterprise* (New York: McGraw-Hill, 1960).

[25] Andrew W. Halpin, *Theory and Research in Administration* (New York: Macmillan, 1966).

[26] Rensis Likert, *The Human Organization* (New York: McGraw-Hill, 1967).

that combine leadership behavior with the requirements of the situation to predict group response. The two formulations that follow are often-cited examples of this contingency thrust.

Fiedler's Contingency Theory of Leadership

Based on the assumption that "good" and "poor" leaders cannot be defined in the abstract and that the task is to specify conditions under which a leader will perform well or poorly, Fiedler offered a model of leadership effectiveness.[27]

Fiedler developed his model on the basis of extensive research over an extended time period. During his earlier research Fiedler used two measures to define two leadership styles: Assumed Similarity Between Opposites (ASO) and Least-Preferred Coworker (LPC). The human relations style leader is one who perceives very little difference between the least-preferred and most-preferred coworkers (ASO) or who perceives the least-preferred coworker relatively favorably (LPC). The task-oriented style leader is one who perceives a great difference between the least-preferred and most-preferred coworker (ASO) or who perceives the least-preferred coworker very unfavorably.[28] Extensive efforts were undertaken in various settings to relate leadership style and group performance. However, no simple relationships were found. As a result, Fiedler posited that leadership style in combination with the situation determined group performance (the measure of leader effectiveness). He suggested that there were three situational dimensions of major importance: the leader–members interpersonal relationships, the structure of the task, and the leader's position power. The most critical dimension, interpersonal relationships, is affected by both the task structure and leader's position power as well as by the personalities of the leader and other members of the group. The second most critical dimension is task structure; in some situations the operations are routine and highly structured, whereas in other situations the task is ambiguous and relatively unstructured. The third dimension, position power, refers to the formal authority associated with a leader's position in the organization. It may or may not be commensurate with personal power. Fiedler saw the situation as most favorable if the leader was well liked and accepted (high interpersonal relations); the task was highly structured (high task structure); and the leader had a high degree of organizational authority (high position power). It was most unfavorable if all three dimensions were low.[29]

Within the two factors—leadership style and degree of favor-

[27]Fred E. Fiedler, *A Theory of Leadership Effectiveness* (New York: McGraw-Hill, 1967).
    [28]Ibid., pp. 36–37.
    [29]Ibid., pp. 22–32, 142–144.

ableness of the situation—two basic propositions were advanced. First, under very favorable conditions and very unfavorable conditions, the task-directed leader will tend to be most effective (i.e., engage in influence efforts that result in group behavior toward organizational goals). Second, in situations where the conditions are in the intermediate range of favorableness (i.e., high on some dimensions and low on others or in the middle range on each), the human relations style of leader will tend to be most effective. The task-directed leader's relative effectiveness under extreme conditions probably requires amplification. Where conditions are very favorable, the group expects to be told what to do. At the other extreme, very unfavorable conditions, the task-directed leader who makes decisions is probably better off than a leader who hesitates to engage in extensive task-directed behavior.[30]

In sum, Fiedler contended that the performance of a group is affected by a combination of leadership style and situational dimensions, which are related in specified ways. If one assumes that many educational situations are staffed by persons who view themselves as "professional equals," the task is broad and loosely structured, and the leader's formal power is limited by statutes and collective bargaining agreements; then it could be hypothesized from Fiedler's model that over an extended period the human relations style of leader will tend to be most effective.

The Path–Goal Theory of Leadership

The path–goal theory, another contingency formulation, has received much attention in recent literature. The theory, which is a derivation of expectancy theory of motivation,[31] represents an effort to link leadership styles with two types of situational variables—environmental factors and subordinate personality characteristics.[32]

As House stated it, central to expectancy theories is the notion that

the force on an individual to engage in a specific behavior is a function of (1) his expectations that the behavior will result in a specific outcome; and (2) the sum of the valences, that is, personal utilities or satisfactions, that he derives from the outcome. . . an individual chooses the behaviors he engages in on the basis of (1) the valences he perceives to be associated with the outcomes of the behavior under consideration; and (2) his subjective estimate of the probability that his behavior will indeed result in the outcomes.[33]

[30] Ibid., p. 147.
[31] See Victor H. Vroom, *Work and Motivation* (New York: Wiley, 1964).
[32] Terence R. Mitchell, *People in Organizations: Understanding Their Behavior* (New York: McGraw-Hill, 1978), p. 320.
[33] Robert J. House, "A Path Goal Theory of Leader Effectiveness," *Administrative Science Quarterly*, 16 (September 1971), 322.

Given the foregoing,

> the strategic functions of the leader consist of: (1) recognizing and/or
> arousing subordinates' needs for outcomes over which the leader has
> some control, (2) increasing personal payoffs to subordinates for work–
> goal attainments, (3) making the path to those payoffs easier to travel
> by coaching and direction, (4) helping subordinates clarify expectancies,
> (5) reducing frustration barriers, and (6) increasing the opportunities
> for personal satisfaction contingent on effective performance.[34]

In fulfilling these functions the leader must adjust his or her leadership style to the situation faced. Four styles of leadership are identified: (1) directive (where structure is provided in the work situation
through specific expectations and standards for subordinates); (2) supportive (where concern for subordinates is shown and open, friendly
relationships are maintained); (3) achievement-oriented (where excellence is emphasized, challenging goals are set, and high levels of productivity are expected); and (4) participative (where there is consultation with subordinates and serious consideration of their opinions
before making a decision). The situational/environmental factors,
which are significant in performance but beyond the control of the
subordinate, include the degree of structure and complexity of the
task, the extent to which the formal authority system helps or hin-
ders subordinate work behavior, and the extent to which the relationships in the primary work group are supportive. The subordinate personality characteristics relate to the extent to which the subordinate
perceives that he or she is able to complete the task assigned, the
subordinate's need for directive or nondirective leadership (degree of
authoritarianism), and the extent to which the subordinate believes
what happens to him or her is a function of his or her behavior or is
a result of chance or luck (internal or external locus of control).[35]

In the seminal article relative to the theory, House projected
eight hypotheses about leadership style and the situational variables
and stated that there was research support for seven of the eight.[36]
Subsequently, Mitchell and associates reported that a set of studies
had been made to support the notion that subordinates with an internal locus of control are more satisfied with a participative management style than are external-type subordinates; however, externals
are more satisfied with a directive management style.[37] House and

[34]Robert J. House and Terence R. Mitchell, "Path–Goal Theory of Leadership,"
Journal of Contemporary Business, 3 (Autumn 1974), 84.

[35]Mitchell, loc. cit.

[36]House, op. cit., 321–338.

[37]Terence R. Mitchell, Charles M. Smyser, and Stan E. Weed, "Locus of Control:
Supervision and Work Satisfaction," *Academy of Management Journal,* 18 (September
1975), 623–630.

Dessler later offered support for the idea that a directive style is more effective when the task is relatively unstructured and, when the task is relatively structured, the supportive style is more effective.[38]

In sum, the central thesis of the path–goal theory is straightforward: the basic function of a leader is to influence subordinate behavior, and "the way to motivate subordinates is to link hard work frequently and consistently to goals that are highly valued by the subordinate."[39]

Securing Subordinate Compliance

Barnard suggested that an essential executive function is "eliciting of the services" of organization members.[40] Other scholars have used different phrases, but there is general agreement that administrators must ensure that subordinates do *what* is needed *when* it is needed. Etzioni used the term *compliance,* which he defined as a "relationship consisting of the power employed by superiors to control subordinates and the orientation of the subordinates to this power."[41] Compliance was seen as related to other organizational variables.

Organizations which differ in their compliance structure tend also to differ in the goals they pursue; in the kind, location, power, and interaction of their elites; in the level and kinds of consensus attained and in the communications and socialization employed to attain it; in recruitment, scope, and pervasiveness; and in the distribution and control of charismatic participants. Moreover, organizations which differ in their compliance structure tend also to differ in the way they allocate tasks and power over time.[42]

Power, Involvement, and Compliance Relations

Etzioni identified three types of power that could be used to induce organization members to comply: coercive, remunerative, and normative. Coercive power relies on the use or threatened use of physical sanctions (pain, deformity, death), restriction of movement, or forced control of efforts to satisfy basic needs (comfort, food, sex). Remunerative power rests on control of material rewards and re-

---

[38]Robert J. House and Gary A. Dessler, "Path–Goal Theory of Leadership: Some Post Hoc and A Priori Tests" in James G. Hunt and Lars L. Larson (eds.), *Contingency Approaches to Leadership* (Carbondale, Ill.: Southern Illinois United Press, 1974), pp. 29–59.

[39]Mitchell, loc. cit.

[40]Chester I. Barnard, *The Functions of the Executive* (Cambridge: Harvard University Press, 1938), p. 216.

[41]Amitai Etzioni, *A Comparative Analysis of Complex Organizations,* rev ed. (New York: The Free Press, 1975), p. xv.

[42]Ibid.

sources (salaries, fringe benefits, commodities). Normative power depends upon regulation of symbolic rewards and deprivations; these include esteem, prestige, ritualistic symbols, social acceptance, and "positive response." To be effective an organization must use the type of power that ensures appropriate involvement of lower participants. Thus organizations, although they may utilize to some degree all three types of power, will tend to emphasize one type of power.[43]

Involvement, defined as "the cathectic-evaluative orientation of an actor to an object,"[44] was seen as ranging from high to low in intensity and from positive to negative in direction. Three basic types of involvement of organizational participants were identified: (1) alienative (intense negative orientation, such as that found among prisoners), (2) calculative (low-intensity negative or low-intensity positive orientation, such as that shown by production workers in a factory), and (3) moral (intense positive orientation, such as that of devoted party workers to their political party). It was suggested that moral involvement could take the form of internalization of organizational norms and identification with authority or social commitment based on peer pressure.[45]

Using the factors of power and involvement, nine possible compliance relations were identified:

1. Coercive power–alienative involvement.
2. Coercive power–calculative involvement.
3. Coercive power–moral involvement.
4. Remunerative power–alienative involvement.
5. Remunerative power–calculative involvement.
6. Remunerative power–moral involvement.
7. Normative power–alienative involvement.
8. Normative power–calculative involvement.
9. Normative power–moral involvement.

Even though all nine relationships are possible, three are found more frequently than others because they are congruent. The congruent patterns are items 1, coercive power–alienative involvement (coercive compliance); 5, remunerative power–calculative involvement (utilitarian compliance); and 9, normative power–moral involvement (normative compliance). Congruent relationships are said to be most effective; thus an organization striving for effectiveness will resist moving from a congruent relationship and when possible will move from an incongruent to congruent relationship.[46]

---

[43] Ibid., pp. 4–7.
[44] Ibid., p. 9.
[45] Ibid., pp. 10–11.
[46] Ibid., pp. 12–14.

In terms of the dominant compliance mode, Etzioni categorized organizations as coercive, utilitarian, or normative. In coercive organizations, force is used to control lower participants, whose degree of alienation is affected by the amount of force used. In utilitarian organizations remuneration is likely to be more effective with blue-collar workers than with white-collar workers as a means of control. In normative organizations, where there is reliance on normative power and high commitment, some secondary controls may be used, if properly segregated. For example, schools may employ coercion as a secondary means. Etzioni suggested that if segregated in time and distance, "dual" compliance patterns might exist. For example, a military combat unit might have both normative and coercive relationships in dynamic balance.[47]

Etzioni posited that the compliance structure among organizational elites varies less from one type of organization to another than the structure for lower participants. Further, coercive power is rarely applied to elites, and the use of remunerative power is fairly infrequent; most typically, normative power is used, particularly with high-ranking elites.[48]

Compliance Structures and Other Organizational Variables

Several relationships between compliance structure and other variables were proposed. However, it was not argued that the compliance structure is the causal factor or vice versa. Specifically, relationships were suggested in regard to organizational goals, organizational elites, consensus, cohesion, communication, socialization, recruitment, and charisma.

Etzioni theorized that organizations with similar compliance structures will tend to have similar goals and vice versa. To illustrate: where the goals relate to order, the compliance structure is likely to be coercive; where the goals are economic, the structure is likely to be utilitarian; and where the goals are cultural, the structure is likely to be normative. Even though any combination is possible, those illustrated are seen as congruent, and congruence between goals and structure is seen as a condition of effectiveness.[49]

Three types of organizational elites were identified. Those whose power (generally utilitarian) comes primarily from their position in the organizational hierarchy are officers; those whose power (generally utilitarian and normative) is derived from both organizational position and personal characteristics are formal leaders; and those

[47]Ibid., pp. 27–59.
[48]Ibid., pp. 303–304.
[49]Ibid., pp. 103–107.

whose power (generally normative) is derived from personal characteristics but have no position in the formal hierarchy are informal leaders. Furthermore, two types of organizational activities are suggested—expressive (those dealing with social and normative integration) and instrumental (those dealing with input and allocation). Because expressive activities require moral involvement, it can be hypothesized that they are most likely to be controlled by informal leaders, can be controlled by formal leaders, and are not likely to be controlled by officers. Because instrumental activities tend to rely on calculative involvement, it can be hypothesized that they are most likely to be controlled by officers, can be controlled by formal leaders, and are not likely to be controlled by informal leaders. However, these relationships may vary with different types of organizations. For example, in coercive organizations expressive activities are controlled in large measure by the informal leaders and only the most instrumental by officers. However, in normative organizations the relationships are more highly integrated; officers and formal leaders tend to lead lower participants; informal leaders cooperate with other elites or are absorbed into formal leadership positions; and, as a result, the distinction between who can best control different types of activities is less clear.[50]

The degree to which lower participants accept the organizational position as theirs is descriptive of level of consensus. If an organization is highly integrated, a high degree of consensus would be expected. Organizations differ not only in the degree of general consensus they require, but also in the degree of consensus they require in various spheres. It was suggested that normative organizations require high consensus on all spheres directly related to expressive activities, and less consensus in spheres related to instrumental activities. Utilitarian organizations are characterized by high consensus (when operating effectively) in spheres related to the instrumental activities. Coercive organizations can function with both the degree and range of consensus being limited; however, some degree of consensus may, to a limited extent, increase organizational effectiveness.[51]

Two classes of cohesion were identified: peer (among persons of like rank) and hierarchical (among persons of different rank). Peer cohesion was seen as affecting the orientation of nonconforming persons within a rank by enforcing whatever norms are adhered to by the majority of the group or its more powerful members. If higher-ranking persons are committed to the organization's norms, hierar-

50 Ibid., pp. 153–176.
51 Ibid., pp. 232–241.

chical cohesion may be directly related to lower participants' positive involvement in the organization.[52]

Two organizational communication networks were suggested: instrumental (focusing on information and knowledge) and expressive (serving to change or reinforce attitudes, norms, and values). Further, the possibility of horizontal and vertical flow was noted. It was suggested that in coercive organizations instrumental communication will predominate, vertical expressive communication will be rare, and horizontal expressive communication will flourish. In normative organizations instrumental communication will be limited and expressive communication (especially downward) will predominate. Utilitarian organizations will stress instrumental communication both up and down as a condition of effective production.[53]

It was posited that socialization in coercive organizations will be ineffective. In utilitarian organizations there will be a tendency to rely on external agencies (e.g., the school, home) to provide "socialized" participants. In normative organizations there will be greater efforts at socialization, and it will be mainly expressive.[54]

In regard to recruitment it was suggested that coercive organizations recruit by force, utilitarian organizations tend to use compensation, and normative organizations tend to depend upon expressive communication and outside socialization. Further, if the recruitment is selective and results in new members who accept organizational goals and norms, then fewer resources will have to be devoted to socialization.[55]

Etzioni defined *charisma,* as related to organizational elites, in terms of ability "to exercise diffuse and intense influence over the normative orientations"[56] of another person. It may be personal (achieved) or associated with one's office (ascribed). Charisma distributed in an organization may aid in increasing the commitment of lower participants and thus organizational effectiveness if the person having charisma is representative of the organizational norms as well. Chrisma may also be a positive factor in the socialization of new members and in the maintenance of already existing compliance structures. Normative organizations, which tend to rely on moral involvement, will have a greater need for charisma than will coercive or utilitarian organizations.[57]

In brief, Etzioni offered a framework for securing subordinate

[52] Ibid., pp. 279–300.
[53] Ibid., pp. 241–245.
[54] Ibid., pp. 245–249.
[55] Ibid., pp. 255–264.
[56] Ibid., p. 305.
[57] Ibid., pp. 305–306, 310–316.

compliance that suggests that the administrator has three possible types of power, and there are predictable relationships between the type exercised and the subordinate reaction and other organizational variables. In some instances the empirical data to support hypotheses derived from the theory are considerable.

Dealing With Conflict

The term *conflict* has been defined in a number of ways. However, for a person viewing conflict from an administrative post, the definition offered by March and Simon is appropriate. They noted that, most generally, "the term is applied to a breakdown in the standard mechanisms of decision-making so that an individual or group experiences difficulty in selecting an action alternative."[58]

To most theorists, conflict is thought to be inevitable where alternatives are present and there are decisions to be made. Further, it is seen as both functional and dysfunctional. Coser stated it this way:

> no group can be entirely harmonious, for it would be devoid of process and structure . . . both "positive" and "negative" factors build group relations. Conflict as well as cooperation has social functions. Far from being necessarily dysfunctional, a certain degree of conflict is an essential element in group formation and the persistence of group life.[59]

It is within the functional–dysfunctional dimension that conflict management is often defined. Specifically, conflict management refers to understanding and dealing with conflict in such a manner that it serves a functional rather than a dysfunctional purpose.

Theorists have frequently focused their attention on the types of conflict, sources of conflict, and strategies for responding to conflict. However, a few have offered formulations of conflict as a process in order to stress the dynamic nature of conflict. For example, Pondy identified five stages in a conflict episode: latent conflict (ever present in organizations); perceived conflict (when threats to value systems are recognized); felt conflict (when focused anxieties are created); manifest conflict (when conflictual behavior is exhibited); and conflict aftermath (the conditions existing after the conflict is resolved or suppressed).[60]

[58] James G. March and Herbert A. Simon, *Organizations* (New York: Wiley, 1958).
[59] Lewis A. Coser, *The Functions of Social Conflict* (New York: The Free Press, 1956), p. 31.
[60] Lewis R. Pondy, "Organizational Conflict: Concepts and Models," *Administrative Science Quarterly*, 12 (September 1967), 300–306.

Types and Bases of Conflict

March and Simon identified three major classes of conflict: individual conflict (in individual decision making), organizational conflict (involving individuals or groups within the organization), and interorganizational conflict (between organizations or groups)[61] Even though other terms are often used, the March and Simon typology is sufficient to examine the bases of conflict. From an administrative viewpoint, there may be a tendency to ignore individual conflict, but some scholars argue that this is improper because organizational conflicts may arise from individual decision problems.

According to March and Simon, individual conflict can result from "incomparability of alternatives," "unacceptability of alternatives," or "uncertainty about the consequences of alternatives."[62] They assumed that when conflict is perceived an individual is motivated to reduce it, and the reaction will depend on the perceived source. Where the source is incomparability, decision time will be brief and the choice will be a function of attention and the order in which alternatives are presented. Where the source is unacceptability, the reaction will be a search for new alternatives, and if there is repeated failure to find acceptable alternatives, there will likely be a redefinition of what is acceptable. In cases of uncertainty about consequences, the first reaction will be to seek clarification of consequences of the existing alternatives; failure to achieve the desired clarification will usually lead to a search for new alternatives.[63]

A different typology of individual conflict was offered by Argyris. He posited that conflict will tend to exist when an individual (1) wants to do two things that are liked equally well but can do only one, (2) has a choice of doing two things that are equally disliked, (3) has the choice of doing something that is liked but runs the risk of loss or punishment, or (4) has several alternatives of doing something, each of which is liked but has an equal risk of some loss or punishment.[64]

Luthans examined conflict from the perspective of an individual as an organizational member and from the point of view of organizations. Relative to the individual aspects, he theorized that conflict rose from frustration, goal conflict, and role conflict. Frustration is the source when the drive toward a desired goal is blocked. In such situations even though the reaction is most frequently negative (e.g.,

[61] March and Simon, op. cit., p. 112.
[62] Ibid., p. 135.
[63] Ibid., pp. 115–116.
[64] Chris Argyris, *Personality and Organization* (New York: Harper & Row, 1957), p. 39.

aggression, rationalization, fixation, withdrawal), it is not always so. For example, a teacher with a high need to succeed with underachieving pupils might react to frustration by trying harder and employing different techniques in teaching the underachievers. Goal conflicts for an individual occur when a goal has positive and negative aspects or two or more goals compete for attention. A threefold typology of goal conflict is identified: (1) approach–approach conflict (when a person wants to approach two or more positive but mutually exclusive goals), (2) approach–avoidance conflict (when a person sees both positive and negative features in the same goal, and as a result, he or she is motivated to approach it and avoid it), and (3) avoidance–avoidance conflict (where a person wants to avoid two or more negative but mutually exclusive goals). Relative to individual behavior in an organization, the most relevant is approach–avoidance conflict. Role conflict results from conflicting expectancies associated with a job. Often where there are conflicting expectancies, the role incumbent and those with whom he or she works do not know or agree about the expectations that should be followed.[65]

Relative to conflict within an organization, March and Simon suggested the conditions included a felt need for joint decision making and either a difference in goals, a difference in perceptions of reality, or both. Two factors were identified as critical in creating the felt need for joint decision making—resource allocation and scheduling. It was hypothesized that (1) the greater the mutual dependence on a resource that is limited, the greater the felt need for joint decision making relative to the resource and (2) the greater the interdependence of timing of activities, the greater the felt need for joint decision making relative to scheduling the activities. Goal conflict is more likely in organizations in which (1) individuals are recruited who have widely differing specializations and backgrounds, (2) the purpose is research or service, as opposed to production, and (3) the number of employees is large. Furthermore, goal conflicts are more likely at the higher levels of the hierarchy than at the lower levels. Perceptual differences are related to differences in goals (e.g., the greater the differences in goals, the greater the differences in perceptions). Also, perceptions are related to the information system of the organization (e.g., the greater the number of different information sources, the greater the differences in perceptions).[66]

Viewing conflict as arising out of a process in which one organizational unit seeks to advance its own interests over those of other units, Schmidt and Kochan posited that the potential for conflict is a

---

[65] Fred Luthans, *Organizational Behavior*, 2nd ed. (New York: McGraw-Hill, 1977), pp. 385–394.

[66] March and Simon, op. cit., pp. 121–127.

function of the degree to which resources are shared; there is inter-dependence of activities, and there is perceived incompatibility of goals.[67] Thus in situations where organizational units hold highly incompatible goals, are highly dependent on limited and shared resources, and have a high interdependence of activities, the potential for conflict is great. Scott and Mitchell suggested that conflict arising in closely knit organizations and in organizations where there was no agreement on basic values tended to be destructive, but in flexible organizations and where there was no questioning of basic values, conflict could be useful.[68]

Some theorists have examined the bases for organizational conflict from a structural perspective. Luthans suggested that in complex organizations there are four structural areas where conflict is most evident. These are (1) hierarchial conflict (e.g., the school principal in conflict with the superintendent and immediate staff), (2) functional conflict (e.g., the division of instruction in conflict with the division of operations), (3) line–staff conflict (e.g., conflict between the principals and subject matter supervisors), and (4) formal–informal conflict (e.g., conflict between the norms of teacher cliques regarding participation in in-service activities and the demands of the board of education).[69]

Many writers see the features of interorganizational conflict as almost indistinguishable from intergroup conflict within an organization. Also, this type of conflict is more frequently seen as being functional. Conflict with an "outside entity" may serve to create greater unity within the organization, bring about a reaffirmation of organizational goals and values, and contain organizational "ambitions" (i.e., the organization will tend to stay within "territorial" limits because of the power of the external force). It is not argued that the results of interorganizational conflict are all positive. Coser warned that if there is a lack of basic consensus within the organization, an external threat may lead to apathy instead of increased cohesion, and then the organization is threatened with disintegration.[70] Scott and Mitchell theorized that where a group was in continual conflict with the outside the internal conflict would be reduced, flexible organizations could adapt more readily than rigid ones to outside conflict, and general external conflict would tend to vitalize organizational values.[71]

Katz and Kahn proposed six categories of variables as predictors

[67] Stuart M. Schmidt and Thomas A. Kochan, "Conflict: Toward Conceptual Clarity," *Administrative Science Quarterly,* 17 (September 1972), 363–365.

[68] William G. Scott and Terence Mitchell, *Organizational Theory: A Structural and Behavioral Analysis,* 3rd ed. (Homewood, Ill.: Richard D. Irwin, 1976), p. 248.

[69] Luthans, op. cit., p. 398.

[70] Coser, op. cit., p. 93.

[71] Scott and Mitchell, loc. cit.

of organizational or interorganizational conflict. Their variables, which appear to incorporate much of the foregoing, were: (1) organizational properties (size, structure, resource needs, ideology), (2) incompatible needs or preferences, (3) role expectations, (4) behavioral predispositions of individuals, (5) rules and procedures, and (6) previous conflict.[72]

Managing Conflict

A number of writers have suggested approaches to reducing or resolving conflict within and among groups, and there is considerable similarity in their formulations. Further, they have emphasized that the approaches are not mutually exclusive, and when considered over time, more than one approach may be employed for a given conflict episode.

Follett offered three ways of dealing with conflict—domination, compromise as a way to achieve a lasting solution to a conflict because the parties gave up something, and at some point the conflict sense, but in the long run is not usually successful. Compromise involves each party giving up something so that the organizational activity that was interrupted can be continued. Follett did not think of compromise as a way to achieve a lasting solution to a conflict because the parties gave up something, and at some point the conflict would rise in another form. Integration, to Follett the only truly effective method of dealing with conflict, is a process by which the involved parties seek a new solution rather than staying within the confines of existing, mutually exclusive alternatives. In integration all parties to a conflict "win." The steps in integration include bringing the difference out in the open for examination and evaluation, taking the demands of the parties and breaking them into their constituent parts or identifying the whole objective, and anticipating and preparing for response (i.e., trying to behave in a different manner so as to integrate the different interests). Even thought Follett's position was that integration was the most fruitful approach to handling conflict, she recognized that it was difficult to achieve, and in some conflicts it was not possible.[73]

March and Simon suggested four basic processes by which an organization may react to conflict: problem solving, persuasion, bargaining, and "politics." In problem solving, shared objectives are assumed, collection of information is stressed, and emphasis is placed on identifying alternatives that meet the shared objectives. In persuasion it is assumed that at some level there are shared goals and that

[72] Daniel Katz and Robert L. Kahn, *The Social Psychology of Organizations,* 2nd ed. (New York: Wiley, 1978), pp. 618–637.

[73] Henry C. Metcalf and L. Urwick (eds.), *Dynamic Administration: The Collected Papers of Mary Parker Follett* (New York: Harper & Row, 1940), pp. 31–44.

the disagreements are over subgoals. The emphasis is on testing such goals for consistency. In bargaining, disagreement over goals is assumed to be fixed and agreement without persuasion is sought. On some occasions the approach is through shared values (e.g., fairness) and on other occasions bargaining involves gamesmanship. The principal difference in bargaining and "politics" is that in "politics" the basic arena is not seen as fixed. Coalitions are formed and the solution reflects the relative strength of the various parties.[74]

Citing Litterer, Luthans identified three strategies for conflict management. First, a buffer can be created between the parties to a conflict. Second, the structure of the organization can be altered. Third, the conflicting parties can be helped to understand themselves better and how they affect others.[75]

In a rather comprehensive statement, Robbins offered nine approaches to organizational conflict resolution and suggested the first two were the more widely acceptable. Specifically, he said administrators could use face-to-face confrontation between the parties, rely on highly valued goals that subordinate the conflict, avoid it, play down differences (smoothing), expand resources, compromise, use authoritative commands, alter the behavior of those involved, or change the organizational structure.[76]

In sum, the scholars suggest there are a limited number of strategies for handling organizational conflict. Conceptually, there seems to be agreement that the preferred approaches are those that enable the various parties involved to gain better insights into themselves and to the critical elements of the conflict to the end that "win–win" solutions are created. Within this context, a means often proposed is organizational development. Its advocates also see it as an effective way to facilitate organizational change; thus, it is described in the section following.

Managing Change

Given the changes occurring in the larger society, from the systems point of view, organizational change is essential for dynamic equilibrium. Yet there is need for the organization to maintain enough stability and continuity to function. If it is assumed that (1) societal change is inevitable, (2) change is essential to organizational survival, (3) change may take any one of a variety of forms, and (4) a degree of stability and continuity is essential in organizational life,

[74] March and Simon, op. cit., pp. 129–130.

[75] Luthans, op. cit., pp. 399–400.

[76] Stephen P. Robbins, *Managing Organizational Conflict: A Nontraditional Approach* (Englewood Cliffs, N.J.: Prentice-Hall, 1974), pp. 67–77.

the need for an organization is to balance the adaptive and maintenance mechanisms in order to achieve a state of dynamic equilibrium. Kast and Rosenzweig posited four ingredients for such equilibrium: enough stability for achievement of existing goals, enough continuity for orderly change in ends or means, enough adaptability to react appropriately to changing internal conditions and external demands and opportunities, and enough innovativeness to initiate changes when conditions warrant.[77]

Organizational change is usually defined as an alteration in the status quo of the system that affects the goals, personnel, technology, and/or structure of the system. It may be planned or unplanned, anticipated or unanticipated, brought about by forces external and/or internal to the system, evolutionary or revolutionary, and desirable or undesirable, and it may proceed from the top down or the bottom up. Within the context of deliberateness, goal setting, and power distribution, Bennis offered an exhaustive typology of change. According to Bennis, planned change required mutual goal setting, equal power ratios, and deliberateness on both sides.[78] Much of the conceptual material focuses on what Bennis called "planned change," yet not all writers have emphasized the mutual goal setting and equality of power as the only way to planned change.

Forces For and Against Change

Conceptually, from a systems point of view, organizational change will occur when there is an imbalance between the total of the forces for change and the total of the forces against change. The forces may be internal to the organization or in the environment of the organization. The imbalance "unfreezes" existing patterns, and changes will occur until a new state of equilibrium is achieved.

Internal to the system there are numerous forces acting for and against change. To facilitate recognition, Watson grouped the internal forces of resistance into two categories: those that operate within the individual personality and those that operate within the social system. Among the resisting forces within an individual are these: given relative stability in the situation, the tendency of an organism to respond in familiar ways (habit); the tendency of an organism to respond to a situation in the manner that was initially successful (primacy); once an attitude has been established, the tendency of an individual to respond to new input within the context of the established attitude (selective perception and retention); the tendency of an individual to enforce standards and expectancies learned early in

[77]Freemont E. Kast and James E. Rosenzweig, *Organization and Management: A Systems and Contingency Approach*, 3rd ed. (New York: McGraw-Hill, 1979), p. 565.
[78]Warren G. Bennis, *Changing Organizations* (New York: McGraw-Hill, 1966), pp. 83–84.

life from authority figures (superego); personality forces that repress impulses that are different from the established (self-distrust); and the tendency of persons to seek security in the past (insecurity and regression). Among the forces within the social system that resist change are customary and accepted ways of behaving (conformity to norms); given the interdependence and interaction of system parts, the difficulty of making a change in one part without affecting the others (systemic and cultural coherence); threats to economic interests or status of groups and individuals (vested interests); the presence of activities and ideas that are held as sacred (the sacrosanct); and given the impetus for change from outside forces, suspicion and hostility toward strange outsiders (rejection of "outsiders").[79] A few of Watson's forces may also serve to promote change. For example, if an individual or group saw a proposed change in the organization as enhancing their prestige or economic position, it would probably be a force for change. Or if the organization norms placed high value on innovativeness (e.g., a school district where there is a long tradition of "being on the cutting edge"), this would be a driving force. Other driving forces within the organization include new or altered goals, the presence of new technical capacity, new structural forms, and a change in leadership. Obviously, many of these forces represent change in themselves, which might have occurred because of "inside" and/or "outside" forces. Thus it might be hypothesized that changes in one part of a system will tend to induce further changes in various parts of a system.

The organization environment contains an infinite number of forces that seem to inhibit or promote change. These include advances in technology, demographic factors, legal decisions, economic factors, prevailing norms, political factors, and activities of competing systems. To illustrate the point, consider the number of changes brought about in schools because of the court decisions relative to racial desegregation, due process for pupils and employees, and religion in the schools. Or consider two hypotheses relative to the nature of community political power structures and educational change advanced by Kimbrough: (1) competitive elite and pluralistic power structures tend to be associated with system openness to educational changes and (2) monopolistic and multigroup noncompetitive power structures tend to be associated with system closedness to educational change.[80]

From the framework of a systems model, Griffiths advanced a

[79] Goodwin Watson, "Resistance to Change" in Warren G. Bennis, Kenneth D. Benne, and Robert Chin (eds.), *The Planning of Change*, 2nd ed. (New York: Holt, 1969), pp. 489–496.

[80] Ralph B. Kimbrough, "Power Structures and Educational Change," in Edgar L. Morphet and Charles O. Ryan (eds.), *Planning and Effecting Needed Changes in Education* (New York: Citation, 1967), p. 122.

series of propositions about "conditions" that aid or inhibit organizational change. Among his propositions were the following:

> The major impetus for change in organizations is from the outside. . . .
> When change in an organization does occur, it will tend to occur from
> the top down, not from the bottom up. . . . The number of innovations
> expected is inversely proportional to the tenure of the chief administra-
> tor. . . . The more hierarchial the structure of an organization, the less
> the possibility of change. . . . The more functional the dynamic inter-
> play of subsystems, the less the change in an organization[81]

Change Processes and Strategies

Most proposals relative to organizational change assume that the organizational membership will remain relatively stable. Thus, the change must be accomplished with the continued presence of these persons. Further, most of the proposals advanced appear to be consistent with Lewin's three-step change model: unfreezing an old pattern, changing to a new pattern, and refreezing in the new pattern.[82] Or they may be consistent with the Lippitt, Watson, and Westley model, which represents an expansion of Lewin within a specific context (i.e., involving a client system–change agent relationship).[83] However, the specific approaches to the unfreezing, moving, and freezing differ.

Numerous typologies of change strategies have been proposed. For example, shown as Table 11-1 is one proposed by Porter and associates. In their typology, approaches have been linked to intervention techniques, intended immediate outcomes, and assumptions about major causes of organizational behavior.

In a retrospective examination of administrative efforts to bring about change in an organization, Margulies and Raia argued that change efforts have tended to focus on one, or perhaps two, of the following organizational subsystems: technological, managerial, or human. From a systems point of view such a limited focus is inadequate. If an organization is an open, sociotechnical system, the focus must be on the culture of the organization. The culture includes the informal organization and status hierarchies; values about what should and should not be; what is and is not important; and norms,

---

[81] Daniel E. Griffiths, "The Nature and Meaning of Theory," in Daniel E. Griffiths (ed.), *Behavioral Science and Educational Administration,* sixty-third yearbook of the National Society for the Study of Education, part II (Chicago: University of Chicago Press, 1964), pp. 117–118.

[82] Kurt Lewin, *Field Theory in Social Science* (New York: Harper & Row, 1951) p. 41.

[83] Ronald Lippitt, Jeanne Watson, and Bruce Westley, *The Dynamics of Planned Change* (New York: Harcourt, 1958), pp. 129–131.

Table 11-1. Comparison of Three General Approaches for Initiating Organizational Changes

Approaches for Initiating Change	Typical Intervention Techniques	Intended Immediate Outcomes	Assumptions About the Major Causes of Behavior in Organizations
Individuals	Education, training, socialization, attitude change	Improvement in skill levels, attitudes, and motivation of people	Behavior in organizations is largely determined by the characteristics of the people who compose the organization
Organizational structure and systems	Modification of actual organizational practices, procedures, and policies which affect what people do at work	Creation of conditions to elicit and reward member behaviors which facilitate organizational goal achievement	Behavior in organizations is largely determined by the characteristics of the organizational situation in which people work
Organizational climate and interpersonal style	Experiential techniques aimed at increasing members awareness of the social determinants of their behavior and helping them learn new ways of reacting to and relating to each other within the organizational context	Creation of a system-wide climate which is characterized by high interpersonal trust and openness; reduction of dysfunctional consequences of excessive social conflict and competitiveness	Behavior in organizations is largely determined by the emotional and social processes which characterize the relations among organizational members

Source: Lyman W. Porter, Edward E. Lawler, III, and J. Richard Hackman, *Behavior in Organizations* (New York: McGraw-Hill, 1975), p. 440. Reprinted by permission.

usually supported by rewards and punishments, about what is appropriate behavior.[84]

An often-cited typology, offered by Chin and Benne, suggested that the various strategies could be placed into three main groups: empirical-rational strategies (those based on the assumption that people are rational and will follow their self-interests), normative-reeducative strategies (those that assume the need for changes in sociocultural norms and commitments of individuals but that do not deny the need for the rationality and intelligence), and the power-coercive strategies (based on the application of power, such as economic, moral, political, or social power).[85]

The power-coercive strategies include the use of existing political institutions (e.g., the court system), the "nonviolence" tactics refined by Mahatma Gandhi, and redistribution of socioeconomic power or manipulation of the power holders. The notion of change as an orderly process from research to development to use is central to the empirical-rational family of strategies. Illustrative of this approach is the Clark-Guba model, which includes the following steps: basic research, development (including design and invention), diffusion (including dissemination and demonstration), and adoption (including trial, installation, and institutionalization).[86] Difficulties related to application of this process are seen to lie with the persons involved. Thus, this group of strategies also places emphasis on proper personnel selection using "scientific testing" and, if necessary, personnel replacement.[87]

Most contemporary change theorists favor what Chin and Benne labeled normative-reeducative strategies (which appear to be similar to Margulies and Raia's focus on organizational culture and Porter and associates' "organizational climate and interpersonal style approach"). The techniques appropriate to apply this approach are usually referred to under the rubric of *organizational development* (OD), which was mentioned previously as a means of resolving conflict.

The essence of organizational development is contained in the following definition:

> a long-range effort to improve an organization's problem-solving and renewal processes, particularly through a more effective and collabora-

[84] Newton Margulies and Anthony P. Raia, *Conceptual Foundations of Organizational Development* (New York: McGraw-Hill, 1979), pp. 9–20.

[85] Robert Chin and Kenneth D. Benne, "General Strategies for Effecting Changes in Human Systems," in Warren G. Bennis et al. (eds.), *The Planning of Change*, 3rd ed. (New York: Holt, 1976), pp. 22–45.

[86] David Clark and Egon Guba, "An Examination of Potential Change Roles in Education," in *Rational Planning in Curriculum and Instruction* (Washington, D.C.: Center for the Study of Instruction, National Education Association, 1967), pp. 117–122.

[87] Chin and Benne, op. cit., pp. 25–26.

tive management of organization culture—with special emphasis on the culture of formal work teams—with the assistance of a change agent, or catalyst, and the use of the theory and technology of applied behavioral science, including action research.[88]

From the perspective of the outside specialist, the stages of the OD process include gaining entry into the system in such a manner as to enable the organization to obtain its improvement objectives; sensing the problems in relation to the objectives; collecting and analyzing data for problem diagnosis and prioritizing of issues; identifying and evaluating alternative courses of action (determining where and how to intervene); implementing the action plan; assessing actual improvements against anticipated improvements; and withdrawing from the system in such a way that it will maintain its own resources for continued improvement.

Interpersonal interventions (e.g., T-group or laboratory method[89]) and team building activities (e.g., the survey–feedback–discussion–action process, process consultation[90]) are often used as a part of the OD effort. An often advocated OD program is *grid training*. In grid training a variety of intervention techniques are used in a planned sequence of activities, which may extend over a three- to five-year period. The conceptual framework for grid training is the managerial grid developed by Blake and Mouton.[91] The formulation is two-dimensional. One dimension is concern for people in the organization, and the other is concern for production. The aim of grid training is to move toward what Blake and Mouton called a 9.9 management style (high concern for people and high production). This ideal style describes an organization in which "work accomplishment is from committed people; interdependence through a 'common stake' in organization purpose leads to relationships of trust and respect."[92] A 1.9 style represents high concern for people and low concern for production, a 9.1 style represents low concern for people and high concern for production, and a 1.1 style represents low concern for both. The middle-of-the-road style, 5.5, is represented in the following statement: "Adequate organization performance is possible through balancing the necessity to get out work with maintaining morale of people at a satisfactory level."[93]

[88]Wendell L. French and Cecil H. Bell, Jr., *Organization Development* (Englewood Cliffs, N.J.: Prentice-Hall, 1973), p. 15.

[89]See Kenneth Benne, Leland Bradford, and Ronald Lippitt, "The Laboratory Method," in Leland Bradford, Jack R. Gibb, and Kenneth Benne (eds.), *T-Group Theory and Laboratory Method* (New York: Wiley, 1964).

[90]See Lyman W. Porter, Edward E. Lawler, III, and J. Richard Hackman, *Behavior in Organizations* (New York: McGraw-Hill, 1975), pp. 458–466.

[91]Robert R. Blake and Jane S. Mouton, *The Managerial Grid* (Houston, Texas: Gulf, 1964).

[92]Ibid., p. 10.

[93]Ibid.

Grid training is conceived as having six phases. In phase 1, participants, beginning with top-level administrators, are acquainted with the concepts of grid training, including the array of management styles. In comparison to T-groups, the group sessions have more structure and there is more emphasis on leadership styles than on understanding of self and others. In phase 2, which is really an extension of phase 1, the emphasis is on team building. Small groups, often representing a "diagonal slice" of the organization, focus on applying what was learned in stage 1 to the organization (e.g., "How are we going to achieve a 9.9 grid position?"). At this stage there is extensive use of simulation, problem solving, evaluation of team performance, and so on. Beginning with phase 3, the attitudes and skills developed are extended throughout the organization. In phase 3, the focus is on intergroup development. Intergroup conflict situations are identified and analyzed; interventions are made where coordination among groups can be improved. Organizational goal setting occurs in phase 4. Using participants' input and data from other sources, organizational "ideals" are developed and agreed upon. In phase 5 organizational teams are formed to begin to put into operation the agreements reached. In phase 6 there is an evaluation of the improvements that have been made, support is marshaled to stabilize the improvements, and future goals are established.[94]

The appropriateness of OD as an approach to change in schools has been a topic of much debate. The most defensible position appears to be that OD is useful in school settings if its limitations are recognized.[95]

As is obvious from the foregoing, most approaches to deliberate change involve the use of change agents. Agents who are internal to the target organization can provide needed intimate knowledge of the organization, often the status necessary for legitimation, and more acceptance and credibility than an external agent. The skilled external agent can provide detachment and a different perspective. Thus, an argument can be made that an internal–external team provides for a set of complementary skills, statuses, and roles.[96]

The subject of change-agent roles is one that has been frequently addressed. Havelock identified four basic roles, which are not mutually exclusive, that a change agent may play: a catalyst (serves to

[94]Robert R. Blake, Jane S. Mouton, Louis P. Barnes, and Larry E. Greiner, "Breakthrough in Organization Development," *Harvard Business Review*, 42 (November-December 1964), 137–138.

[95]For a detailed review see Michael Fullan, Matthew B. Miles, and Gib Taylor, "Organizational Development in Schools: The State of the Art," *Review of Educational Research*, 50 (Spring 1980), 121–183.

[96]Lippitt, Watson, and Westley, op. cit., p. 138.

upset the status quo, reduce system complacency, and energize the problem-solving process); a solution giver (provides an appropriately timed solution in an acceptable form); a process helper (serves as an expert on the "how to" of change by providing assistance in the various states of problem solving); and a resource linker (involves assisting the client to identify and use resources both within and outside the system). He stressed the process-helper role.[97]

The foregoing is representative of the concepts that have been developed to aid the administrator in managing the change process. Many scholars have advanced the notion that in spite of extensive attention to the subject there still does not exist an adequate theory.[98] Therefore, even though a bit outdated, Giacquinta's postulates (based on an extensive literature review) about the state of knowledge concerning organizational change process still appear to be appropriate:

> (1) . . . organizational change when successfully completed proceeds in three distinct stages: initiation, implementation, and incorporation. Successful completion of one stage, however, does not guarantee successful completion of the next. (2) . . . these stages are influenced by attributes of the innovations that are introduced, the manner of their introduction, characteristics of the school personnel who must make the changes, and the structural properties of the school setting. (3) . . . these factors do not influence initiation completely in the same way they influence implementation or incorporation.[99]

Planning

As implied in the discussions about decision making, change, and so on, the administrator is responsible for the planning of almost every major activity he or she undertakes (e.g., goal setting, accomplishing the tasks described in Chapter 2). As Robbins stated it:

> Planning gives directions, improves continuity of actions, and reduces overlapping and wasteful activities. Through the formulation of objectives, policies, procedures, rules, and other types of guides, direction is provided for organizational members.[100]

Planning is a consideration of the future. Ziegler suggested that planners could approach the future from a preventive, adaptive, or

---

[97] Ronald G. Havelock, *The Change Agent's Guide to Innovation in Education* (Englewood Cliffs, N.J.: Educational Technology, 1973), pp. 7–15.

[98] See, for example, Margulies and Raia, op. cit., pp. 41–46.

[99] Joseph B. Giacquinta, "The Process of Organizational Change in Schools," in Fred N. Kerlinger (ed.), *Review of Research in Education,* vol. 1 (Itasca, Ill.: Peacock, 1973), p. 200.

[100] Robbins, op. cit., p. 178.

inventive perspective.[101] The preventive and adaptive perspectives are essentially deterministic, and the future is considered a projection of the past. The inventive perspective rejects the deterministic notion, and the assumption is made that through appropriate planning one may bring about "desirable" futures. This difference in perspective reflects a basic difference in two approaches to planning—"conventional" and "futures." Shane identified five ways in which futures planning differs from conventional planning. First, it is value-directed and action-oriented, stressing alternatives as opposed to linear projections. Second, futures planning seeks to identify and explore possibilities often overlooked in conventional planning. Third, the assumption is rejected that a desirable future is the present without its problems in favor of the notion that "different tomorrows" need to be anticipated. Fourth, in comparison with conventional planning, there is less stress in statistical analysis and projection and more on rational study of anticipated developments. Fifth, creating a probabilistic environment of alternative possibilities and consequences is emphasized, not reform of the past.[102]

We are of the conviction that both the "conventional" and "futures" approaches are important to the educational administrator. He or she will need to plan for the short term, most often with reference means and continuing tasks; however, long-range planning, most often relative to ends (e.g., goals, policies) is also necessary if the organization is to maintain a dynamic equilibrium. Inbar has provided a "conceptual frame of reference," which appears useful in relating different planning aims, knowledge, strategies, and so on,[103] and in the following paragraphs, his formulation is synthesized. Next, a model of the planning process is provided. The discussion of planning closes with a description of some planning tools and techniques.

A Conceptual Frame of Reference for Educational Planning

Based on an analysis of planning literature and theoretical assumptions about the educational process, Inbar suggested that five categories were necessary for a planning frame of reference:

1. Type of knowledge—explicit, tacit
2. Goal orientation—allocative, behavioral

---

[101] Warren L. Ziegler, "The Potential of Educational Futures," in Michael Marien and Warren L. Ziegler (eds.), *The Potential of Educational Futures* (Worthington, Ohio: Jones, 1972), pp. 5–6.

[102] Harold G. Shane, "U.S. Futures Research in Education: The Status of the Field in 1972," in Marien and Ziegler, op. cit., p. 9.

[103] Dan E. Inbar, "Educational Planning: A Review and a Plea," *Review of Educational Research*, 50 (Fall 1980), 377–392.

3. Planning strategies—rational, mixed scanning, incremental, linkage
4. Patterns of implementation—institutionalized discipline, manipulative persuasion, reeducational, explorative
5. Planning objects—system and subsystem parameters, role and personality, group and individual, environment and organization.[104]

Even though stressing that the categories are not mutually exclusive, no planning activities will be exclusively in one set of categories, and various interrelationships are possible (especially with reference to the planning objects), Inbar posited four basic sets or quadrants of relationships. The first quadrant of planning activities is based on explicit knowledge (well-formulated and transmittable in operational terms) and allocative goals (those related to distributing needed resources, such as people, money, materials). With such knowledge and goals, a rational planning strategy (emphasis on analysis and maximization of alternatives) and implementation by means of institutional discipline (activating people to act on the basis of formal contractual relationships backed by formal sanctions) are logical. Examples of quadrant one planning could include that relating to teacher supply and demand, pupil population forecasting, and financial allocations.

Second quadrant planning is based on explicit knowledge and behavioral goals (where the planning is focused directly on specific educational behaviors). Given this knowledge and goals, a mixed-scanning strategy (the basic planning objects are "givens," but within this context the implementation is incremental) and manipulative persuasion (a deliberate increase in awareness of selective values and sanctions so that those being influenced are not aware of it while it is occurring) are appropriate. Planning related to teacher or administrator preparation for clearly defined roles and curriculum planning within the context of well-defined objectives are examples of quadrant two planning.

Third quadrant planning also has behavioral goals (they are frequently vague and qualitative) but the available knowledge is tacit (implied, improvement can occur without knowing specifically how it was done). In this case the logical planning strategy is incremental (based on trial and error, intuition, insight, inspiration) and the implementation pattern is reeducational (using participation and involvement to bring about attitude and value changes). Planning for program change or preparation of staff where the value of the transfer of explicit knowledge is limited and the desire is to develop sen-

---

[104]Ibid., 380.

sitivity and insight represents the planning that fits into quadrant three.

Fourth quadrant planning is focused "on the relationships and impact of environment and organizations on the educational process."[105] The knowledge is tacit and the objective is allocative in the sense that education is allocative in providing consumers for the economic system, voters for the political system, and so on; as such, it needs to build support systems in the environment. In such situations the planning strategy would logically be linkage (planning and developing "islands of excellence" to act as catalysts) and the implementation explorative (a contingency approach where implementation is a part of a continuing process of seeking interaction). Planning that focuses on preparing educators for a future urban environment fits into this quadrant.

In a comparative sense, movement from quadrant one to quadrant four represents a movement from the quantative to qualitative, from "hard" data to "soft," from a logical step-by-step process to a more vague one, and from a focus on the system to the individual to the environment. Yet the basic assumption is that planning in education must be somewhat all-inclusive.

With full recognition of Inbar's cautions about other possible relationships and that the four sets he proposed are only the basic ones, the framework seems to be useful as a basis for projecting hypotheses relative to planning research and/or practice. For example, from the framework one could hypothesize that if educational administrators plan in a rational and step-by-step manner, use "expert" knowledge, and try to implement by means of formal authority, the implementation will be successful when the aim of the planning does not require a change in individual or group behavior that violates or disregards group norms or individual values; if it does, the implementation will not be successful.

Planning as a Seven-Phase Process

Planners, particularly those whose orientation is to conventional planning, tend to view planning as a logical, sequential process. The model of planning as a cyclic, seven-phase process offered by Banghart and Trull is illustrative.[106] The phases they proposed are as follows:

1. *Defining the educational planning problem.* The focus and boundaries of the problem are delineated, an analysis is made of historical forces, a determination is made of "what is" and

---

[105] Ibid., 386.

[106] Frank W. Banghart and Albert Trull, Jr., *Educational Planning* (New York: Macmillan, 1973).

"what should be" (a reflection of prevailing values), potential individual and institutional resources and constraints are identified, and planning priorities are established.

2. *Analyzing planning problem areas.* Using the systems approach, the problem is studied in detail, a data base is established, data are synthesized, and forecasts are made.

3. *Conceptualizing and designing plans.* Within the context of the planning problem defined (Phase 1) and specified (Phase 2), prevailing trends (social, economic, political) are identified, goals and objectives are prepared, and plans for their achievement are designed.

4. *Evaluating plans.* Using simulation models and other approaches, the plans designed (Phase 3) are evaluated in light of the problem and the optimum plan selected.

5. *Specifying the plan.* This phase "is essentially one of communicating to those interested in the selected plan."[107]

6. *Implementing the plan.* Implementing includes preparing a program of action, securing appropriate approval from authorities, and organizing the needed operational units.

7. *Plan feedback.* Obtaining feedback includes monitoring activities, evaluating what is happening, and adjusting, altering, and redesigning as necessary. (This final phase is really the beginning of a new planning cycle.)

Tools and Techniques

The tools and techniques available to administrators engaged in planning are numerous. The choice of techniques can be viewed as a function of the planning quadrant most characteristic of the activities (from the perspective of Inbar's framework) and the phase in the planning process. To illustrate, if the goal is basically allocative and the knowledge explicit (quadrant one), such techniques as linear programming (recall the discussion of quantitative decision-making tools) at the "evaluating plans" phase of the process would be useful. On the other hand, if the goal is to change behavior and if the knowledge is tacit, implementing the plan could require a reeducational strategy, such as OD (recall the discussion of change processes and strategies). The illustrations serve to make another basic point: Such tools and techniques may be of use in relation to different administrative functions and activities. Also, some tools are useful at more than one phase of the planning process. PERT (Program Evaluation and Review Technique) is an example. It can be of value in "planning for planning" and in relation to monitoring (a part of Banghart and Trull's

---

[107] Ibid., p. 341.

phase 7). PERT is essentially a scheduling and control tool that uses a graphic display (network) to show the relationships among the several tasks necessary to accomplish a specified objective.

The basic steps in a PERT implementation are (1) definition of the objective, (2) development of a work-breakdown structure, (3) network design, and (4) computation of time estimates. Because the objective is the final event and all that precedes it is done in terms of this objective, it must be defined in specific terms and communicated. After definition of the objective, the project must be analyzed and subdivided into its several components. Then each task must be identified and subdivided until the desired level of detail is reached. A work-breakdown structure will usually take the form of a pyramid, with the apex being the total project, the first level being the major components, the second level being the tasks within each major component, and so on. The network shows the plan to reach the objective, interrelationships and interdependencies of the tasks, and the priorities involved. The network consists of two basic elements, events and activities. Events (usually shown as circles, rectangles, squares, or triangles) represent the start or completion of an activity. Events do not use personnel or consume resources or time. Events are connected by arrows, which represent activities. Real activities use personnel, resources, and/or time. (Dummy activities, represented usually by dotted arrows, are used as needed to depict the dependency of one event on another but involve no personnel, resources, or time.) Another concept in network development is constraint; a constraint exists when an activity cannot take place until all preceding events and activities have been completed. Thus a network consists of a number of events connected by activities. It begins with a single event (e.g., "project start"), expands into a number of paths connecting events, and terminates with a single event (e.g., "project completion," objective achieved). In practice, the level of detail in networks is usually a function of the nature of the critical activities, the relative difficulty of controlling these activities, time allowed in relation to time needed, level of delegated responsibility, and availability of information.

Once the logic and detail of the network have been set up, the next step is to make time estimates. Because PERT is most often applied to "unique" projects where exact activity times are unknown, three time estimates are made—optimistic, most likely, and pessimistic. Given completion of the network and time estimates, the "critical path" can be identified. The critical path is the longest or most time-consuming path through the network. This path places the greatest time constraint on the completion of the end event. Time slippages in activity completion along this path can result in project time overrun. Thus the critical path, which will change as the project moves along and the tasks are completed ahead or behind schedule, is a major focus for successful management.[108]

There has been a tendency to group planning tools and techniques according to whether they are deterministic or goal setting in orientation. Martino offered an often used twofold classification—exploratory and normative. Exploratory methods start with the present and forecast the future changes in terms of assumptions about the continuation of past or present trends. Normative methods are goal-setting methods. That is, based on some projected future, an effort is made to determine the activities or technological capabilities that would be required to reach the objective.[109] The authors believe that at the forecasting step in the planning process, educators tend to rely on exploratory methods, such as trend extrapolation, scenario writing, and Delphi probes. Trend extrapolation appears to be more appropriate for Inbar's quadrant one activities and the other two for quadrant four. Also, depending on the questions posed, the Delphi technique could be considered a normative method.

Trend extrapolation, based on the notion of continuity, involves projecting some characteristic—one that can be quantified—beyond the limit of present knowledge or technology. The extrapolation is frequently just a linear projection of the historical trend exhibited by the characteristic; however, it could be several trends treated under a single curve based on expected changes from presently unavailable resources or projecting a continued historical relationship between two or more trends. Joseph suggested that trend extrapolation includes the following:

- persistence forecasting; assumes the future will be the same as the past;
- trajectory forecasting; assumes a constant rate of change and at the same rate as in the past (includes change acceleration);
- cyclic forecasting; assumes that the past cyclic pattern of change will continue;
- associative forecasting; assumes that a given event or force always (or usually) follows or is associated with another specific event or force; the causality approach; and
- analog forecasting; assumes that analogous trends can be used as "models" for other trends.[110]

[108] For more detail about PERT see, for example, Desmond L. Cook, *Educational Project Management* (Columbus, Ohio: Merrill, 1971); Banghart and Trull, Jr., op. cit., pp. 387–402.

[109] Joseph E. Martino, *Technological Forecasting for Decisionmaking* (New York: American Elsevier, 1972), p. 287.

[110] Earl C. Joseph, "An Introduction to Studying the Future," in Stephen P. Hencley and James R. Yates (ed.), *Futurism in Education* (Berkeley: McCutchan, 1974), pp. 15–16.

Lonsdale stated that scenarios "indicate the step-by-step developments from the present to an hypothetical future situation. They lay out alternatives available at each step for preventing, changing, or enhancing the process. There may be more than one scenario leading to an alternative future. . . ."[111] He also noted that "system breaks" (representing sharp changes in an evolutionary system) might be inserted in scenarios to focus on the possibilities of disruptive uncertainties.[112] Martino described scenarios as combining a set of forecasts into a composite picture, depicting the combined efforts of individual forecasts, permitting the checking for internal consistency by examining contradictions among individual forecasts, and providing a description of the path from the present to the time described.[113]

Weaver offered a concise description of the Delphi technique as usually applied:

> the procedure includes a questionnaire, mailed to respondents who remain anonymous to one another. Respondents first generate several rather concise statements of events, and in the second round give estimates as to the probability of each event occurring at a given date in the future. Once the respondents have given their answers, the responses are collated and returned to each respondent, who is then invited to revise his estimates. The third-round responses are made with the knowledge of how others felt regarding occurrence of each event. Again, the responses are assembled and reported back to the participants. If a respondent's estimate does not fall within the interquartile range of all conjectures, he is asked to justify his position, whether or not he wishes to change it.[114]

In brief, the planning effort may be short or long term, the perspective may or may not be deterministic, the focus may be allocation or behavior, and the data base "soft" or "hard." Regardless, the planner has available a variety of tools, techniques, and strategies (some of which may be useful for other functions or activities) from which to choose.

Communicating

Barnard identified communication as an essential executive function and noted that in a comprehensive theory of organization

---

[111] Richard C. Lonsdale, "Futurism: Its Development, Content and Methodology," in The 1985 Committee, The National Conference of Professors of Educational Administration, *Educational Futurism 1985* (Berkeley: McCutchan, 1971), p. 10.

[112] Ibid., pp. 10–11.

[113] Martino, op. cit., p. 270.

[114] W. Timothy Weaver, "The Delphi Forecasting Method: Some Theoretical Considerations," in Marien and Ziegler, op. cit., pp. 29–30.

"communication would occupy a central place, because the structure, extensiveness, and scope of organizations are almost entirely determined by communication techniques."[115] In other words, it is basic to other functions, activities, and tasks. As Lesikar said,

> communication is the ingredient which makes organization possible. It is the vehicle through which the basic management functions are carried out. Managers direct through communication; they coordinate through communication; and they staff, plan, and control through communication. Hardly an action is taken in any organization without communication leading to it.[116]

As noted previously, Etzioni suggested that communication could be instrumental (relating to information and knowledge) or expressive (relating to norms and values).[117] From an administrative point of view, communication may be regulative (task-related directions and feedback between superiors and subordinates), informative (related to knowledge and instructions to subordinates), innovative (dealing with the means and ends of bringing about change), or integrative (value-laden and attitude-oriented, which can serve to reinforce and build consensus). Further, it may be immediately one-way or two-way; formal or informal; vertical, horizontal, or diagonal.

In recent years, scholars from many fields—linguistics, mathematics, psychology, sociology—have contributed to our understanding of communication. Thus it is not surprising that the approaches and definitions have been varied. For our purposes, communication can be defined as that dynamic process by which a person "consciously or unconsciously affects the cognitions of another through materials or agencies used in symbolic ways."[118] This definition includes several basic characteristics of communication. It is "dynamic" in that it is continuing and requires linked energy and action. From "one person to another" limits it to human beings. The "consciously or unconsciously" suggests that it is not always deliberate. The "affects the cognitions" excludes communication attempts; there is no communication unless there is an impact upon the receiver, even though the impact may not be what was intended. The "materials or agencies used in symbolic ways" suggest that communication generally involves the use of abstractions through which the sender attempts to convey a specific meaning to the receiver (e.g., "we must increase our *commitment*") and that a variety of channels or mediums (e.g., memo,

---

[115]Barnard, op. cit., p. 91.

[116]Raymond V. Lesikar, *Business Communication Theory and Application,* 3rd ed. (Homewood, Ill.: Richard D. Irwin, 1976), p. 4.

[117]Etzioni, op. cit., p. 242.

[118]Kenneth E. Andersen, *Introduction to Communication Theory and Practice* (Menlo Park, Cal.: Cummings, 1972), p. 5.

voice, gesture, physical object) may be used.[119] The definition also is broad enough to include the types and directions of communication described in the preceding paragraph.

The Communication Process

Figure 11-1 shows a communication episode as consisting of six elements, occurring within a specific environment, affected by "noise," and resulting in feedback.

The episode begins with someone having orders, facts, instructions, or ideas intended for an individual or group. The sender organizes this by the use of symbols and abstractions into a message (encoding) and transmits the message by means of some channel, for example, letter, voice, gesture. The receiver is the recipient of the transmitted message and this may or may not be the intended receiver; that is, others may intercept the message. The receiver attaches some meaning to the symbols and abstractions that result in an understanding, which may or may not be what the sender intended (decoding). On the basis of the understanding, the receiver responds—does nothing, carries out the order, stores the information. The feedback loop in the figure is intended to convey that the sender will in turn receive a message about the impact of the original message even though it may not be expected, direct, or immediate. That is, the communication process tends to be cyclic, not linear. As Dance, who represented the process as a three-dimensional helical spiral,

[119]Theodore T. Herbert, *Dimensions of Organizational Behavior,* 2nd ed. (New York: Macmillan, 1981), pp. 95–96.

Figure 11-1.   A Model of the Communication Process

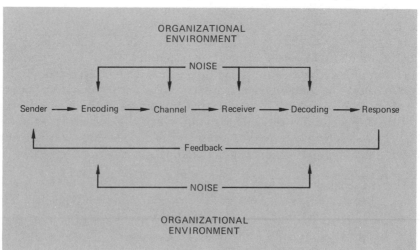

stated, "communication while moving forward is at the same moment coming back upon itself and being affected by its past behavior, for the coming curve of the helix is fundamentally affected by the curve from which it emerges."[120] Noise, which refers to any stimuli that serve to distort, filter, or interfere with the reception of the intended message, can occur at any one or several points in the process (e.g., with the sender encoding, along the channel(s), with the receiver decoding). Finally, the process does not occur in a vacuum; it occurs in an organizational system or subsystem, which is part of a suprasystem.

When the process involves more than two persons, communication networks emerge. Based on small group studies,[121] scholars suggest that such networks tend to be centralized and in the form of a wheel, chain, or Y with a central figure (e.g., "hub" of the wheel), or they tend to be decentralized in the form of a circle where communication is with adjacent members, or the network may be a "free" circle where all members communicate with all other members of the group.

Some Propositions About Communication in Organizations

Numerous scholars have offered propositions about organizational communication. Based on a review of such literature, seven propositions are presented in the following paragraphs, which we believe to have some merit; that is, they have some degree of supporting evidence and are relevant to educational administrators. Furthermore, some of Miller's cross-level hypotheses presented in Chapter 10 are germane.

The context within which a message is transmitted may have a greater influence on the meaning attached by the receiver(s) than the words used. Oral or written words are the most frequently used channels within an organization. A wide variety of variables external to the words will influence the message received. If the words are oral and face-to-face, the nonverbal cues, such as voice inflection and body language, must be considered. For example, a superior may tell a subordinate that he or she wants to hear about the subordinate's problem and then proceed to open the mail while the subordinate is relating his or her story. The message transmitted by the nonverbal behavior is that the superior really does not want to hear about the problem. The receiver's perception of the sender's credibility is often significant as is the degree of congruence between sender and receiver(s) in re-

---

[120]Frank E. X. Dance, "Toward a Theory of Human Communication," in Frank E. X. Dance (ed.), *Human Communication Theory* (New York: Holt, 1967), p. 296.

[121]See, for example, Alex Bavelas and Dermot Barrett, "An Experimental Approach to Organizational Communication," *Personnel,* 27 (March 1951), 366–371.

gard to attitudes, experience, expectations, and motivations. If the receiver is suffering from "information overload" (i.e., receiving more messages than can be handled), the words may be filtered or simply ignored. Events beyond the sender–receiver(s) will influence the meaning attached to words. For example, assume in a large high school with a rapidly declining enrollment, over a period of several days different probationary teachers have been called by the principal's secretary and asked to "come by the office at the close of school today." Once there, the principal tells them their contracts will not be renewed. During that time period, if that message is received by a probationary teacher with whom the principal wants to discuss some unrelated matter, the teacher will probably attach a "non-renewal of contract" meaning to the secretary's words. Davis made the point succinctly when he noted: "Individual words have so many meanings that they become meaningless until they are put in context."[122]

In downward communication, distortion and filtering increase as the size of the communication loop and/or the number of levels in the hierarchy increase. An organizational communication loop may be as large as the organization itself (e.g., school districtwide) or confined to a single subsystem (e.g., a single department within a school). Also, organizations vary widely in terms of hierarchical levels. Repeated experiments have shown that those more distant from the source are less likely to receive the message intended. The implication is that in downward communications, top administrators are likely to overestimate the number of persons reached by their intended messages, and those at the higher levels of the organization are likely to be better informed than those at lower levels. To put it another way, unless the necessary energy is expended to "shape" the intended message for each of the organizational subsystems, messages from near the top of a "tall" organization will be so general and remote from those near the bottom that it is unlikely that they will convey their intended meaning. Katz and Kahn suggested that such messages "need to be translated at critical levels as they move down the line, that is, translated into the specific meanings they have for given sectors of the structure."[123]

As a message moves up the levels in the hierarchy, it will be distorted and filtered to make it more optimistic, consistent with existing policies, and/or compatible with the predispositions of the intended receiver(s). Experienced practitioners and scholars alike have noted frequently that the upward communication process, particularly if the message is negative, is often the most inadequate in an organization.

[122]Keith Davis, *Human Behavior at Work,* 5th ed. (New York: McGraw-Hill, 1977), p. 381.
[123]Katz and Kahn, op. cit., p. 443.

There appears to be a number of reasons for such distortion and filtering. Miller hypothesized that a system will tend to distort in a direction to elicit rewards rather than punishment.[124] Wofford and associates noted that subordinates strive to put their "best foot forward" and refrain from transmitting to superiors information that casts them in an "unfavorable light."[125] Insecurity of subordinates, lack of trust in superiors, and the desire of subordinates to be upward mobile have also been advanced as contributing factors. Whatever the reasons, it is important to recognize that in upward communication, "editing," over and beyond that associated with the size of the loop and number of organizational levels, will likely occur. Thus, a major problem for administrators, particularly at higher levels, is "finding out what is out there."

As blockage in vertical communication increases, horizontal and diagonal communication will increase. A synthesis of organizational communication studies suggests that for managers about two-thirds of their communication time is spent on vertical communication.[126] In such downward and upward communication the needs of the superior(s) and subordinate(s) are not always congruent (e.g., what a superior wants to find out may not be what a subordinate wants to reveal). Therefore, to the extent the vertical receptability is limited, there is likely to be a tendency to turn to peers or those at a different level but in other organizational units. It is not argued that increased communication with peers and superiors or subordinates in other units has a negative impact; in fact, it can serve to provide an outlet for frustration or accomplish organizational business. Rather, the intent is to alert administrators to a likely result of the inability of persons to communicate vertically.

When the problem/task is simple a centralized communication network is more effective; with a complex problem/task a decentralized network is more effective. As noted previously, in a centralized structure one person processes a large amount of information. In simple situations, such a person can process the required information; as a result, communication is more rapid and accurate than with decentralized structures. However, in complex situations with a centralized network, the central person becomes overloaded and some persons become isolated; thus the decentralized network is more rapid and accurate. Herbert summarized the point as follows:

[124]James G. Miller, *Living Systems* (New York: McGraw-Hill, 1978), p. 96.

[125]Jerry C. Wofford, Edwin A. Gerloff, and Robert C. Cummins, *Organizational Communication: The Keystone to Managerial Effectiveness* (New York: McGraw-Hill, 1977), p. 376.

[126]Lyman W. Porter and Karlene H. Roberts, "Communication in Organizations," in Marvin D. Dunnette (ed.), *Handbook of Industrial and Organizational Psychology* (Chicago: Rand McNally, 1976), pp. 1573–1574.

When centralized and decentralized networks are compared with each other on simple problems, decentralized networks are *slower* in solving the problem and *less accurate,* yet *morale* is reported as being higher and *more* messages are transmitted among members than in centralized networks. For *complex* problem situations, however, the centralized networks are inferior; *centralized* networks are slower in problem solving as well as less accurate, with lower morale and fewer messages than in decentralized networks.[127]

Organizational communication is enhanced when the choice of the channel(s) to be used takes into account the purpose of the communication. Studies have been done comparing oral, written, oral/written, and written/oral communication. From such research it seems reasonable to suggest that oral communication is appropriate in conflict resolution efforts, when confidentiality is desired, when precision is not essential, or in some organizational integration efforts. Written communication is sufficient for general information, when impersonality is desired, when a record is required, or for required action at some future date. Oral/written or written/oral is preferred when immediate action is required, work progress is being reviewed, a specific policy change or directive is being communicated, or an employee accomplishment is being recognized. In general, for most purposes, and in most settings, some combination of oral and written communication is likely to be most effective.

The "grapevine" is ever present and may be more informative and rapid than the formal channels of the organization. The presence of informal communication channels (the "grapevine") and their use by organizational members have been repeatedly verified. Such informal channels originate spontaneously outside of the formal channels and cannot be eliminated; suppression of one informal channel merely causes organization members to move to another. Grapevine sources may exist within and outside the receiver's chain of command. A major reason for the wide reach of grapevines is the existence of social groupings that are across levels and units of an organization and even outside the organization (e.g., spouses of organization members). With such interpenetration, persons will often receive messages through the grapevine that are never received through formal channels, or they are received before and/or in greater detail than by means of the formal channels. Davis offered the following summary comment about grapevines:

They move upward, downward, and diagonally, within and without chains of command, between workers and managers, and even within or without a company. The grapevine is a normal part of a total com-

---

[127]Herbert, op. cit., p. 303.

munication system; so managers who do not wish to be bypassed by the grapevine need to learn about it, relate to it. . . .[128]

Controlling

Planning and decision making relative to ends and/or means result in organizational activities. Controlling is the process of monitoring these activities to determine the extent to which what is expected is actually occurring and where discrepancies exist to take corrective action. Thus, planning, decision making, and controlling are closely linked processes with each influencing the others. Controlling is essential to assist the total organization in meeting expectations; however, to do this it is necessary to monitor and take corrective action as needed at the individual and unit level. The process, regardless of the level at which it is applied, involves four basic elements: *standards relative to objectives, measurements of the standards, comparisons of expected and actual performance,* and *means to correct deviant performance.* A number of questions must be answered about each of these elements. For example, who sets the standards? What devices are used to bring behavior in line with the standards? The manner in which these questions are answered will determine the nature of an organization's control system and the organization members' likely reaction to it. Etzioni's compliance theory, which has been described, is one framework for examining this relationship. For example, if the standards are set externally and force is used to bring the behavior of the members in line, then they are likely to be alienated (i.e., the compliance structure is coercive).

Following is a discussion of the four elements of the control process. Then an often-advocated system—Management by Objectives (MBO)—for planning and controlling is described.

Key Elements of the Control Process

Based on an extensive review of the organizational control systems literature, Lawler identified the critical questions relative to each element of the system and offered some generalizations about the impact of alternative answers to these questions.[129] Lawler's review provides the basis for the discussion that follows.

There are three key questions that must be answered about

[128]Keith Davis, "Grapevine Communication Among Lower and Middle Managers," in Keith Davis (ed.), *Organizational Behavior: A Book of Readings,* 5th ed. (New York: McGraw-Hill, 1977), p. 353.
[129]Edward E. Lawler, III, "Control Systems in Organizations," in Dunnette, op. cit., pp. 1249–1291.

standards: At what level of difficulty will they be set? Who will set them? How precise will they be? If standards are too low, employees are likely to ignore them and not be affected by them. If they are too high, employees are likely to engage in such behavior as falsifying reports, neglecting unmeasured activities, and resisting the standards. Similar types of responses are likely to occur if the standards are set by persons who are not seen by those affected as being legitimate and expert. If the standards are too exact, they may be seen as not providing enough leeway. On the other hand, if they are too ambiguous, they are easier to distort by employees who want to "look good."

There are two important questions relative to measurements: How inclusive will the measures be? How objective will the measures be? If the measures do not include those facets of performance related to standards that employees feel should be included, they will tend to lack confidence in the measures and overemphasize those facets of the performance that are measured. On the other hand, if the measures include an area that has not been stressed before, resistance and other dysfunctional behavior will likely result. When the measures are viewed as subjective, distortion of the data is likely, particularly if the measures make a difference in what happens to a person.

Who will do the comparisons between expected and actual performance? This is the key question relative to this element. If employees are excluded from the process and the comparisons are made by those having reward power, rigid adherence to the system is likely, and, if possible, distorted data about actual performance may be reported.

Regarding the means used to correct deviant performance, the critical questions relate to the extent to which those affected are permitted to make their own corrections and the extent to which the measures taken are used to administer rewards and penalties. If there is no opportunity to receive feedback about the measures and no opportunity provided for self-corrective action, resistance and other dysfunctional behaviors are likely. If the measures are used principally for administering rewards and penalties, employees may resist, but they will tend to "meet the letter of the law." On the other hand, if the data are used primarily for planning purposes, the employees are likely to be more accepting of the control system.

Thus far the focus has been on the dysfunctional effects of certain responses to the key questions. However, the discussion may be summarized positively by means of the alternative posits that follow:

1. Standards set by a process that includes those who are affected by them, that are viewed as moderately challenging and objective but not rigid are much more likely to be ac-

cepted by employees. Such standards are also thought to motivate employees to perform better.

2. Measures that include the kinds of behavior that must be performed if the organization is to function effectively, and which require objective data, create more employee trust in the system, enhance the probability of more valid data being provided, and reduce resistance.

3. If employees are involved in making comparisons about whether they have met expectations, they will be more motivated to maintain high performance levels.

4. Corrections by means that provide feedback to those affected, give opportunity for self-correction, and use measurements for both planning and rewards or penalties, are more likely to serve the long-run interests of the organization, and are more likely to be within the tolerance limits of employees.

One caution should be offered: Individual differences cannot be ignored when giving consideration to a control system. Lawler made the point as follows:

Self control seems to be most likely to be present in people who desire intrinsic rewards. Participation seems likely to be helpful in producing self-control only among individuals who desire and are comfortable with power equalization in decision making.[130]

MBO as a Control System

As indicated previously, MBO is often advocated for planning and controlling. (Similarly, PERT, which was described as a planning tool, is useful as a control tool where scheduling is involved.) Drucker is credited with having introduced the term; he saw it as a philosophy of management and a system of controlling.

[MBO] substitutes for control from outside the structure, more exacting and more effective control from the inside. It motivates the manager to action not because somebody tells him to do something or talks him into doing it, but because the objective needs of his task demand it. . . . It rests on a concept of human action, human behavior and human motivation. Finally, it applies to every manager, whatever his level and function, and to any business enterprise whether large or small. It insures performance by converting objective needs into personal goals.[131]

Odiorne offered this frequently cited definition:

The system of management by objectives can be described as a process whereby the superior and subordinate managers of an organization

---

[130] Ibid., p. 1283.

[131] Peter F. Drucker, *The Practice of Management* (New York: Harper & Row, 1954), p. 136.

jointly identify its common goals, define each individual's major areas of responsibility in terms of results expected of him, and use these measures as guides for operating the unit and assessing the contribution of each of its members.[132]

The MBO concept, like many of the other concepts presented, has its origin with theorists who were primarily concerned with corporate management. However, the tenor of the movement has been accepted by many concerned with education. For example, the American Association of School Administrators (AASA), coining the acronym *MBO/R* ("management by objectives and results"), offered the following definition: "a system of operation that enables the organization and its personnel to identify, move toward, and lock into objectives as well as to manage more effectively for desired results."[133]

A review of the literature suggests that there are four assumptions that are basic to MBO. First there is the assumption of the desirability of McGregor's Theory Y (e.g., given objectives to which they are committed, people will exercise self-direction and self-control; given appropriate conditions, people will accept and seek responsibility; people generally are capable of applying a high degree of imagination, ingenuity, and creativity to the solution of organizational problems).[134] Second, it is assumed that persons are motivated by a variety of factors beyond economic rewards, such as achievement, challenging assignments, recognition, responsibility, organizational policy, and the work itself (i.e., the validity of a multifactor theory of job motivation, such as that advanced by Herzberg and associates, is accepted).[135] Third, integration of functions, decentralization, and a results orientation are assumed to characterize management. Fourth, wide participation in determining goals/objectives, setting standards, and making comparisons between expected and actual outcomes is assumed. These assumptions are logically consistent with the posits advanced relative to the basic elements of a control system and suggest that in its idealized form MBO may be a viable control system.

In a definitive statement of the MBO process, AASA offered the model shown as Figure 11-2. As can be seen from the figure, the process begins with organizational goals. Indicators and standards are selected to determine the extent of goal achievment. Objectives consistent with organizational goals are set for each major subunit of the organization and acceptable standards and indicators are specified.

---

[132] George S. Odiorne, *Management by Objectives* (New York: Pitman, 1965), pp. 55–56.

[133] American Association of School Administrators, *Management by Objectives and Results* (Arlington, Va.: The Association, 1973), p. 5.

[134] Douglas McGregor, loc. cit.

[135] Frederick Herzberg, Bernard Mausner, and Barbara Snyderman, *The Motivation to Work* (New York: Wiley, 1959).

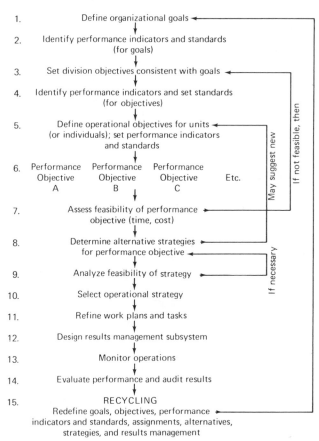

Figure 11-2. General systems MBO/R model. [Source: American Association of School Administrators, *Management by Objectives and Results* (Arlington, Va.: The Association, 1973), p. 27. Reprinted by permission.]

Steps 5 and 6 involve the assignment of specific objectives and performance standards to lower-level subunits (or administrators). Next, these "performance objectives" are examined to determine if they are feasible, given the existing situation. If they are not, recycling to generate new and more realistic objectives, consistent with higher-order objectives, must occur. Given feasible objectives, the next steps are to define alternative strategies for achievement and analyze their feasibility. Again, there may be recycling if the assessment process suggests it is necessary. At steps 10 and 11 a strategy is selected and translated into a work plan. This must be detailed and must include sequence and schedule of events, time lines, resource requirements, group and individual assignments, training needs, and so on. The next step is to ensure that a system is designed to manage for the results expected, including a system for allocation of resources, type and frequency of reports required, and so on. Monitoring is the process of determining if activities are leading to achievement of desired results and of making adjustments if they are needed. At the end of a stated time period, there is a complete appraisal of performance in terms of previously agreed-upon objectives, standards, and strategies. At step 15 the recycling process is begun. In sum, the AASA model involves a rational approach to management with built-in corrective mechanisms to ensure that organizational effort remains "locked in" to objectives. Although not highlighted in the model, staff involvement is assumed in the process of assigning objectives, setting standards, selecting strategies, making comparisons between what is expected and what actually occurs, and so on.[136]

The research data regarding the effectiveness of MBO are mixed. Some evidence exists of enhanced needs satisfaction, improved communication, more positive attitude toward evaluation, improved planning, and innovativeness. Yet there is some evidence of increased paper work, lack of participation, distortion of management philosophy, lack of incentives, and an overemphasis on production.

The key to whether or not an MBO system will produce the desired results is objectives. The approach is predictated on the presence of agreed-upon, concrete objectives and defensible measures of the extent to which these are achieved. Given the lack of unity about educational objectives, the relatively intangible nature of many educational outputs, and the shortage of acceptable measuring devices, the major problem for educational organizations is defining meaningful objectives, standards, and indicators.

ACTIVITIES/QUESTIONS FOR FURTHER STUDY

1. Techniques and tools—such as linear programming, management information systems, organizational development, PERT, normative planning methods, and MBO—were identified as being useful to administrators in carrying out one or more key functions and other such techniques (e.g., program, planning, budgeting systems or PPBS, zero based budgeting or ZBB) could have been so described. Invite to your class a panel consisting of an educational administrator, a municipal government administrator, and a business administrator to discuss the extent to which and how their organizations use techniques such as these.

2. Organize the class into small groups and have each group identify three practical suggestions for an educational administrator to follow in regard to each of the key functions discussed in the chapter.

3. A review of the chapter will show that many of the concepts related to decision making, leadership, conflict, change, planning, and controlling place an emphasis on the wide involvement of people and cooperative ef-

---

[136]American Association of School Administrators, op. cit., pp. 26–29.

fort among the several levels of the hierarchy of an organization. Drawing upon the experience of the class members, discuss the means that educational organizations use to involve people and secure cooperation relative to these functions. How successful are these endeavors?

SUGGESTED READINGS

BANGHART, FRANK W., and ALBERT TRULL, JR. *Educational Planning.* New York: Macmillan Publishing Co., Inc., 1973.

BASS, BERNARD M. *Stogdill's Handbook of Leadership.* New York: The Free Press, 1981.

BENNIS, WARREN G., et al. (eds.). *The Planning of Change,* 3rd ed. New York: Holt, Rinehart & Winston, Inc., 1976.

DAVIS, KEITH. *Human Behavior at Work: Organizational Behavior,* 5th ed. New York: McGraw-Hill Book Company, 1977, Chapters 7, 10, 11, 21.

ETZIONI, AMITAI. *A Comparative Analysis of Complex Organizations,* rev ed. New York: The Free Press, 1975.

FIEDLER, FRED E., and MARTIN M. CHEMENS. *Leadership and Effective Management.* Glenview, Ill.: Scott, Foresman and Co., 1974.

HENCLEY, STEPHEN P., and JAMES R. YATES (eds.). *Futurism in Education.* Berkeley: McCutchan Publishing Corp., 1974.

HERBERT, THEODORE T. *Dimensions of Organizational Behavior,* 2nd ed. New York: Macmillan Publishing Co., Inc., 1981, Chapters 9, 15, 17, 20.

KATZ, DANIEL, and ROBERT L. KAHN. *The Social Psychology of Organizations,* 2nd ed. New York: John Wiley & Sons, Inc., 1978, Chapters 14–16, 18, 19.

LAWLER, EDWARD E., III. "Control Systems in Organizations," in Marvin E. Dunnette (ed.). *Handbook of Industrial and Organizational Psychology.* Chicago: Rand McNally & Co., 1976, pp. 1249–1291.

MITCHELL, TERENCE R. *People in Organizations: Understanding Their Behavior.* New York: McGraw-Hill Book Company, 1978, Chapters 9, 11, 13, 16.

OWENS , ROBERT G. *Organizational Behavior in Education,* 2nd ed. Englewood Cliffs, N.J.: Prentice-Hall, Inc., 1981.

ROBBINS, STEPHEN P. *The Administrative Process: Integrating Theory and Practice,* 2nd ed. Englewood Cliffs, N.J.: Prentice-Hall, Inc., 1980.

STUFFLEBEAM, DANIEL L., et al. *Educational Evaluation and Decision Making.* Itasca, Ill.: F. E. Peacock Publishers, Inc., 1971.

WOFFORD, JERRY C., EDWIN A. GERLOFF, and ROBERT C. CUMMINS. *Organizational Communication: The Keystone to Managerial Effectiveness.* New York: McGraw-Hill Book Company, 1977.

12

Valuing and Educational Decision Making

$\mathbf{T}$HE THEORIES THAT were discussed in previous chapters are not value free. As Willower has demonstrated, theories tend to harmonize with some values and conflict with others, and "theories may reflect the dominant values of a culture or a time, not to mention those of individual theorists or groups of theorists."[1] Greenfield's and Griffiths' discussions concerning the "naturalistic" versus "phenomenological" positions and the commentaries on the issue by other writers have highlighted philosophical ideas that have been debated for many years in the field.[2] Thus a discussion of values is appropriate as a basis for a further grasp of theories and also because values are inevitably an essential element of the administrative decision-making process. As was discussed in Chapter 11, Griffiths is among those authors who have emphasized effective regulation of the decision-

[1] Donald J. Willower, "Ideology and Science in Organizational Theory," *Educational Administration Quarterly*, XV (Fall 1979), 21.

[2] See Daniel E. Griffiths, "Some Thoughts About Theory in Educational Administration—1975," *UCEA Review*, XVII (October 1975), 12–18; T. Barr Greenfield, "Theory About What?" *UCEA Review* XVII (February 1976), 4–9. Also see May 1976, October 1977, and Summer 1979 issues of *UCEA Review* for further comments on the issue by A. R. Crave and W. G. Waller, Jean Hills, Richard Kendell and David R. Byrne, and Frank W. Lutz.

making process as an essential function of administrators.[3] If the administrator is not thoughtful about the matter of purpose and the function of education in the society, he or she may not provide effective leadership in the decision-making process. Moreover, as discussed in this chapter, educational administrators must understand the values of ideologically oriented interest groups.

As suggested above, practically all administrative decisions are made in a "better-or-worse" context. Graff and associates presented this as an if–then process.[4]

> A person concerned with values proceeds in similar fashion. First, there is a determination of what seems to be good and desirable from a world of competing values. Next is the if–then process: If these things are good and worth striving for, then we ought to proceed in this fashion in order to assure their enhancement.[5]

This explanation by Graff and associates does not approach the actual, complex process. Educational administrators can seldom clarify the "if" part of the valuing process. The variables in a sociopolitical situation are incompletely defined and seldom completely understood. Theory to help us understand the relationships among the things we observe and to help predict what will happen under given conditions is not well developed. The alternative value choices are fuzzy and their implementation seldom produces the results desired. Finally, valuing involves intensive efforts to anticipate and measure scientifically the consequences of the various alternatives.

If these foregoing propositions about valuing are relevant to administrative behavior in decision making, there are some important implications for those preparing to be educational administrators. One rather obvious implication is that administrative valuing in decision making should not be an armchair exercise. The aspects of "what is" and "what ought to be" are interrelated. The decisions made are as good as the objective data one has about "what is" and the clarity in which those deciding understand alternative values and their massive interaction with "what is." If the prospective educational administrators are relatively ignorant of cultural values, of their own value system, and of the nature of values held by others, they could become Dr. Strangeloves at the control of educational systems. Being an intelligent, responsible educational administrator involves much personal study of one's own value system and of the nature of valuing in decision making. Valuing in decision making involves important con-

[3] Daniel E. Griffiths, *Administrative Theory* (New York: Appleton, 1959), p. 73.
[4] Orin B. Graff et al., *Philosophic Theory and Practice in Educational Administration* (Belmont, Calif.: Wadsworth, 1966).
[5] Ibid., p. 64.

siderations about the nature of truth, the nature of reality, and other philosophical questions. And for the educational administrator the manifestations of the basic philosophic considerations in political ideologies must be considered.

The Nature of Reality

Most of us have a way of viewing things about us or a way of perceiving the nature of things. A sophisticated philosopher of a university has no corner on this aspect of life. The most illiterate person in the world can discuss the meaning of existence, although he or she may not put his or her expressed assumptions about the nature of reality in sophisticated language. Nevertheless, concepts about the nature of reality influence one's mental processes. These, in turn, help structure the personal beliefs and the cultural mind-sets, which are our predispositions to act in certain ways when facing crises. Therefore, regardless of the aversion that practical-minded educators have to the study of philosophical precepts, we must use the contributions of philosophers to illustrate the point that our personal philosophies affect our behavior.

Our concepts of what we accept as knowledge are colored by what we believe about the nature of reality, traditionally referred to as metaphysics. Although some schools of philosophy, such as logical positivism, refrain from speculating about the nature of reality, a concept of how things are may be implied in their criterion (or criteria) for true knowledge.

True Reality is Nonmaterial

A school of thought referred to as idealism accepts a dual concept of reality consisting of (1) the perfect world of ideas and (2) the imperfect world of everyday existence. True reality is in the perfect world of ideas, which can be grasped only by the mind. Material existence is an imperfect manifestation of the real world of ideas. Therefore, true reality is a deductive process of mind and is a nonmaterial idea. This dualism is deeply ingrained in our culture, and all of us are influenced by its thought processes.

Immanuel Kant, who some have called the child of the eighteenth-century Enlightenment, provided the intellectual spring for modern idealism. Kant did not accept the "other worlds" of ancient idealism. In the place of the other worlds, he escalated mind and the exercise of pure reason. True reality is what comes from pure reason.[6]

[6] Immanuel Kant, *Critique of Pure Reason*, trans. J. M. D. Meiklejohn (New York: P. F. Collier, 1900).

Writing concerning what Kant meant by pure reason, Durant stated, "For 'pure' reason is to mean knowledge that does not come through our senses, but is independent of all sense experience; knowledge belonging to us by the inherent nature and structure of the mind."[7]

Butler expressed the view that philosophies are based upon attitudes that are widely accepted by many persons in the society.

> Just how much the unconscious influence of our classical and Christian traditions is responsible would be hard to determine; but most men of the street, the farm, the market place, or where you will, have the idea that they have a soul which is different from their bodies and somehow more enduring and permanent. Although it may not be this particular phrasing of it for all idealists, it is this motif common in human life which is refined and brought into full bloom intellectually by idealism.[8]

Many practical-minded educational administrators would scoff at this discussion as philosophical mumbo jumbo. On the other hand, let us examine how relevant it is today. As one example, administrators are forever reorganizing. A fairly typical way to reorganize is to engage consultants to assist key administrators in generating alternative structures for the operation of the school system. In many instances this is an ivory tower exercise, although, in all fairness, the participants may have years of experience as a foundation for making decisions. What those involved finally come to is to select the organization that at the time and in that particular group seems to be the most *rational* way to organize.

This preferred rational model is consciously or unconsciously assumed to be the "perfect" model for the verbally described situation. Yet there is no experimental evidence that would indicate this perfection. The next step, of course, is to adopt the rational alternative. When problems arise in the functioning of the model, the idealist-oriented educational administrator assumes the two-world stance. The problems are not with the rationally designed model but with the irrationality of teachers, principals, parents, and others who did not accept it as a basis of organizational behavior. Thus the two-part (ideal and imperfect, unreal) worlds are expressed as rational-irrational perspectives. This was a good organization, but the people would not accept it. Why was it good? Because a group of our best minds got together and decided that it was the best—the exercise of pure reason.

The authors are not suggesting that all persons who idealize about alternative solutions to problems are idealists. All of us engage

[7] Will Durant, *The Story of Philosophy* (New York: Washington Square Press, 1961).

[8] J. Donald Butler, *Four Philosophies and Their Practice in Education and Religion* (New York: Harper & Row, 1957), p. 173.

in such activity. Even the most empirically oriented sciences have their theoreticians. The important question is how these ideal convictions are interpreted and used. Based upon their metaphysics, idealists assume that these reasoned ideals represent true reality, which is not subject to further testing other than to the rigors of the logical processes. As the subsequent discussion will demonstrate, the results of such reasoning processes would not be interpreted as true reality in other schools of thought.

The Material Real World

The growth of scientific inquiry eventually precipitated what White referred to as warfare of theology in the Western world with science.[9] As indicated previously, the truths or pure reason cannot be tested in an imperfect, unreal world. Galileo, sometimes referred to as the founder of modern experimental science, was subjected to inquisition, publicly humiliated, and imprisoned by church authorities for extolling the Copernican theory. Nevertheless, the triumph of science and its methods for determining true reality eventually ended in a rout of pure reason. The naturalistic philosophies, such as realism, became popular. A 1912 publication entitled *The New Realism* was the manifesto of scholars bent upon founding a new and distinctive philosophy of realism.[10]

Realism had a straightforward concept of reality. The everyday physical world is reality and exists independently of pure reason. Reality exists "out there" in the material world with which we deal every day of our existence. Electricity, fire, and the concept of a school existed in nature independently of the knowing mind. This true reality can be discovered in this real, rationalistic world through the use of scientific method. "Knowing the law is knowing the reason. A rational world and one that operates according to law are identical. In this sense, the approved scientific sense, the world is found to be more rational today than it was known to be yesterday, and who will censure the scientist if he is encouraged on these grounds to adopt the hypothesis that this trend may continue indefinitely."[11] Wild stated the basic tenets of realist philosophy as follows:

> These basic beliefs of mankind are also the three basic doctrines of realistic philosophy? (1) There is a world of real existence which men have not made or constructed; (2) this real existence can be known by

[9] Andrew D. White, *A History of the Warfare of Science with Theology in Christendom* (New York: Appleton, 1896).

[10] Edwin B. Holt et al., *The New Realism* (New York: Macmillan, 1912).

[11] Frederick S. Breed, *Education and the New Realism* (New York: Macmillan, 1939), p. 44.

the human mind; and (3) such knowledge is the only reliable guide to human conduct, individual and social."[12]

Even though the philosophies of realism and idealism have contradictory metaphysics, both encourage educators to believe in universal truths. The realist discovers the immutable laws of nature through scientific research and is thus incurably materialistic. This emanates from the metaphysical assumption that the real world is a final and fixed, rational world independent of the knowing human being. Put another way, the realist is of the view that the physical world in which we live is the basic reality and that its component elements all move and behave according to fixed natural laws. We do not know all these laws, but we discover them year by year through the instrumentality of science.[13]

Let us revisit the illustration of school reorganization given previously and demonstrate how realism influences practice. Let us assume, for example, that we substitute consultants and administrators with a realist metaphysics instead of an idealist persuasion to develop a new organization for the school system. In this case the consultants will be persons with a national reputation in research about how organizations function. Through this research, they have discovered a lot of universally applicable answers about the real nature of organizations. Their answers are assumed to be relevant for any school district regardless of the conditions given.

Out of the expertise of the organizational efficiency experts, tempered by the experiential discoveries of the practitioners, a rational model for organizing the school system will be constructed. However, in this instance this rational model is based more upon what has been learned from research about organizations than from what logically would be good for the school district. To use the slang expression, "It is based on the best that research tells us." Note that this model does not need to be subjected to experimentation. Those irrational people who did not understand or accept this reality must bear the consequences for not following empirical laws.

The Logical Positivist's View of Reality

Every pervasive intellectual force seems to run a course to its inevitable extreme. The materialistic metaphysics of realism may well have reached one of its extremes in logical positivism. This philosophy was given impetus by the Vienna Circle, a group of scholars at

[12]John Wild, *Introduction to Realistic Philosophy* (New York: Harper & Row, 1948), p. 6.
[13]Van Cleve Morris and Young Pai, *Philosophy and the American School* 2nd ed. (Boston: Houghton, 1976), pp. 53–54.

the University of Vienna during the 1920s. Insofar as metaphysics is concerned, this is a know-nothing philosophy and has been labeled by some writers as an epistemology. The logical positivist does not speculate about a real, rationalistic world.

> Let me illustrate what I mean by a pseudoexplanation. The desire to understand the physical world has at all times led to the question of how the world began. The mythologies of all peoples include primitive versions of the origin of the universe. The best known story of creation, a product of the Hebrew imaginative spirit, is given in the Bible and dates about the ninth century B.C. It explains the world as a creation of God. Its explanation is of a naive type that satisfies a primitive mind, or a childlike mind, proceeding by anthropomorphic analogies: as humans make homes and tools and gardens, God made the world.[14]

Although the positivist accepts the world as real, speculation about it or attaching unverified meanings to it are considered meaningless. Schlick commented that either to deny or to affirm a metaphysical speculation about the nature of reality is meaningless because it cannot be verified empirically.[15] All that we know is what is verified empirically, and even this is not necessarily universal. The implied reality in some statements of positivism is a world of chance.

> Gone is the ideal of a universe whose course follows strict rules, a predetermined cosmos that unwinds itself like an unwinding clock. Gone is the ideal of the scientist who knows absolute truth. The happenings of nature are like rolling dice rather than like revolving stars; they are controlled by probability laws, not by causality, and the scientist resembles a gambler more than a prophet. He can tell you only his best posits—he never knows beforehand whether they will come true. He is a better gambler, though, than the man at the green table, because his statistical methods are superior.[16]

How would commitment to the views of logical positivists influence the problem or reorganization alluded to earlier? As we have seen, they do not choose to speculate about reality. Persons committed to these views are unwilling to speculate about whether one alternative organizational scheme is better than another. As will be seen, this involves a value question impossible to verify. Thus speculation is meaningless. Some positivists are prone to ask a lot of questions for which they presume no answers exist. This may sometimes go on and on to the point of much frustration among the members of the group. As one colleague expressed his frustration from such an

[14] Hans Reichenbach, *The Rise of Scientific Philosophy* (Berkeley: University of California Press, 1951), pp. 8–9.

[15] Moritz Schlick, "Positivism and Realism," in Alfred J. Ayer (ed.), *Logical Positivism* (New York: The Free Press, 1959), p. 107.

[16] Reichenbach, op. cit., pp. 248—249.

experience, "These fellows spent all of their time sharpening the axe but no time cutting wood." However, when decisions have to be made among alternatives, positivists explain these choices as preferences. That is, the decision about how to reorganize the school system is simply a predispositional preference devoid of values.

The Precariousness of Reality

Experimentalists, or pragmatists, also reject the fixed and final world of realists and the dualism of idealists. They are equally uncomfortable with the empirical probabilities of positivists. To the experimentalist the world is precarious, changing, incomplete, and indeterminate. The world of things is real; however, there is constant evolution.

Experimentalists think of people as purposeful and in interaction with the environment. In an oversimplified explanation, the experimentalist is somewhere between the neorealist and the idealist. Instead of a passive, inductive discovery of the reality that is "out there" (as in realism), experimentalists view thinking persons as constructing reality through interaction with a real but somewhat precarious universe.

Reality is what emerges from the interaction of a person with the environment. However, because both the person and the environment have no fixed, inherent nature and the precarious environment is constantly evolving, today's reality may not be that of tomorrow. This has always been an anathema to both the idealists, with their perfect world of reason, and the realists, who see, through all the confounding variables of the world, eternal verities.

Among those associated with the development of experimentalist concepts of reality (including William James and Charles Sanders Peirce), John Dewey is best known to most educators. In his *Democracy and Education,* Dewey focused upon the implications of experimentalism for education and the improvement of the society. He was greatly influenced by Darwin's interpretation of evolution and the changeable aspect of nature.

Experimentalism has been interpreted by many persons as promoting a form of sophisticated opportunism. If there are not bases for eternal verities, what is to prevent mankind from cannibalism or some other equally repugnant behavior? The opponents of experimentalism say that the lack of affirmation of ultimate goodness unleashes people to follow any scheme to satisfy their self-interest. They must be protected from themselves by God-given Commandments, the tenets of philosopher kings, or the natural laws of a rational world.

The point is, however, that in the metaphysics of experimentalism there are known realities. There are indeed laws to govern human activities. Persons are creative and constantly reflect upon experiences in such a way as to find a precept from the consequences. Through many years of experience people reflected upon the consequences of murder, theft, and falsehoods, for example. Ethical values are created from reflections upon the consequences of such acts. Thus the experimentalist escapes arbitrary opportunism through faith in the realities born in reflective thinking processes.

We have discussed previously how the views about the nature of reality influence the acceptance of assumptions concerning school reorganization. The experimentalist would approach the problem of reorganization through purpose in relation to existing conditions and projections of future changes. A fixed and final world of ideas or laws of nature from "out there" are unacceptable, just as universal principles of educational organization are unrealistic. There are changes and evolution in nature. The ideal organization today would be obsolete tomorrow. Thus the experimentalist would have the predisposition to view any organizational plan proposed as subject to change and variation in relation to the changing nature of the society and of education. Much emphasis would be given to what will work best in terms of the objectives of the school system.

Other Naturalistic Concepts of Reality

The realist or positivist concepts extolled by such persons as Herbert Spencer, Francis Bacon, Auguste Comte, and Charles Darwin spawned numerous concepts about the nature of reality, which seriously challenged traditional epistemology and the nature of values. For example, Friedrich Nietzsche's extensions of naturalistic metaphysics challenged traditional Christian ethics. Life was seen as a battle for existence. For this battle we need strength, not goodness; pride, not humility; the exercise of intelligence, not altruism; rule by aristocracy, not democracy by the masses; arbitration by power, not ethically based justice; and the production of supermen instead of preoccupation with the masses and their mediocrity.[17] The Nazi leaders of Germany took intellectual refuge in some of these views; however, some scholars insist that the Nazi "philosophy" was a perversion of Nietzsche's views.

Naturalistic concepts of reality have greatly influenced economics. Moreover, the pens of what Heilbroner called the "worldly philosophers" have had, and continue to have, tremendous impact upon American society and education.[18] The popular classical economic theories promulgated by Adam Smith and extolled by many economists, businessmen, and citizens are based on naturalistic concepts of

[17] Durant, op. cit., p. 402.
[18] Robert L. Heilbroner, *The Worldly Philosophers* (New York: Simon & Schuster, 1953).

reality. The real world was the Darwinian world of natural selection. Selfish, competing persons need only to be left alone to compete for the scarce resources, which Reverend T. R. Malthus predicted would, through unchained population growth, become ever more reduced. The real world was one wherein persons might pursue their self-interests, limited only by protection of property rights and the "invisible hand" of the free market. The naturalistic realities of the corporate world have become institutionalized values in the culture.

Educators are pressured to accept the realities of the marketplace. Callahan has documented how the values of the corporate society become values in the administration of education.[19] Within recent years educators have been hard pressed to adopt management concepts and practices used in certain sectors of the corporate society. These proposed changes range from the adoption of a simple practice in the management of personnel to the rather ambitious voucher schemes to realize freedom of choice objectives.

The Inner Person as True Reality

The Danish writer Søren Kierkegaard devoted his life to understanding the real qualities of human existence. In the process he championed the realities of the inner person and became the father of modern existentialism. Some writers have described existentialism as a convulsive rejection of naturalistic philosophies, the dehumanizing influences of war and automation, and the inhuman consequences of materialistic or technological developments. "Man cannot hope for guidance from universal laws and principles, the lessons of history, government, other human beings, God, or even the logical empiricism of modern science."[20] Only the person is reality and what one chooses free of external control. Although trees, animals, mountains, rivers, and other natural things exist, only a person is conscious of and consequently responsible for human development and existence.[21]

> What reality is without man's existence in it can only be surmised, it cannot be known. Man is the definer, nothing has meaning except as man gives it meaning. Reality is precisely what man, as a result of his existence in it, says it is. Except as man exists, reality is nothing. Further, man must exist as a completely free, self-choosing human being with nothing to impinge upon his absolute freedom of choice if he is to know true reality. To the extent that man relies on factors outside him-

---

[19] Raymond E. Callahan, *Education and the Cult of Efficiency* (Chicago: University of Chicago Press, 1962).

[20] Graff, op. cit., p. 193.

[21] Rollo May, "Contributions of Existential Psychotherapy," in Rollo May, Ernest Angel, and Henri F. Ellenberger (eds.), *Existence: A New Dimension in Psychiatry and Psychology* (New York: Basic Books, 1958), pp. 37–91.

self, science, God, government, or social conformity, as determinants of his choices, precisely to that extent, does he fail to know true reality.[22]

If human beings are the only reality, what do we know about their nature? Dupuis indicated that a person's nature is what one affirms it to be: "The notion that man has no predetermined nature is the central reason for the existentialist doctrine that 'existence is prior essence.' It affirms that man exists *first;* then, because he is free, he creates his own essence."[23]

Because existentialism was given impetus by the dehumanizing influences of war, rampant materialism, economic determinism, automation, and despotism, the written concerns of many existentialists focus upon the realities of human despair, dread, loneliness, anguish, and the meaninglessness of life enslaved by materialistic axioms. Thus existentialist reality in some respects is expressed as a gloomy reality. When the existentialist turns from the melancholy aspects of reality to the reality of the humanistic future, the terms *freedom, decision,* and *responsibility* emerge as important realities. Reality is human freedom to make choices on the basis of humanistic ethics. Humans will make decisions in the interest of humans rather than in the interest of gross national product, computer printouts, or other nonpersonal realities. Finally, there is the requirement to be responsible for the decisions made. There are no "cheap cop-outs." One must stand up and be counted even if an act in the interest of humanity results in imprisonment, possible injury, or even death.

Existentialists insist that formal education activities be organized so that the student may experience complete and absolute freedom to make choices and pursue his or her reality without the hindrance of administrative or teacher imposed structures. For example, such managerial structures as those discussed in previous chapters are unacceptable impositions that interfere with the freedom of students to choose. Even the imposition of democracy, promoted by the experimentalist, is unacceptable, not to speak of the autocracy of certain idealists or the competitive jungle of realists. The best illustrations of the administrative and organizational priorities of existentialists were seen in many of the "free" or "alternative" schools organized during the 1960s.

The Nature of Knowledge or Truth

The discussion of the nature of reality provides a basis for a discussion of the nature of knowledge or truth (epistemology). Keep

---

[22] Graff, op. cit., p. 199.

[23] Adrian M. Dupuis, *Philosophy of Education in Historical Perspective* (Chicago: Rand McNally, 1966), p. 228.

in mind that valuing in administration involves understanding of knowledge of "what is" in complex interaction with "what ought to be." All of us have predispositions to think and act in certain ways based upon the interplay of our personal "truths" of where we are with "where we ought to be." We are well aware that, by defining valuing this way, logical positivists can no longer "stay aboard" because they cannot entertain normative questions. However, their views are exceedingly important to educational administration.

Educational administrators facing crises or difficult problem situations are frequently heard to say, "If only I had enough facts to go on!" Having the data necessary to conceptualize given conditions is one of the greatest needs of practitioners. The uneasiness of making decisions is as much a result of no empirical understanding as it is unsureness of where we ought to be going. When we are forced to combine lack of evidence and unsureness of purposes in making decisions, which, unfortunately, is so often true, the prospect of having to decide is frightening. Within recent years the prospects of storage and retrieval of knowledge through management information systems have given hope for relief. However, few enthusiasts of this view have considered the nature of knowledge that should be collected, stored, and retrieved. This is the question at hand.

Knowledge by the Exercise of Pure Reason

As implied in the discussion of the idealist position about reality, the truth is determined by the process of deduction. True and lasting knowledge is a product of pure reasoning by "great minds."

Idealism is the basis of some research and literature used in educational administration. Griffiths pointed to the large amount of so-called research in educational administration, which was based upon what the "great minds" or "authorities" said.

> There is an alarming amount of respect for the authority of persons or principles in the field of educational administration. One need only to point to the widespread use of the "jury" technique in research to use as validating criteria the "opinions of experts in the field." As another example, one should look to the conventions and conferences of school administrators. The report of a genuine research study on administration at such a meeting is a rarity and even when presented is greeted with skepticism. One such occasion dealt with a review of the research on pupil promotion. After listening to a recounting of the research, one principal excitedly asked, "Say, do you believe this, or is it just research?"[24]

Another illustration of acting upon ideas from the processes of secluded mediation is many so-called innovations foisted upon the

[24] Griffiths, *Administrative Theory*, op. cit., p. 9.

schools during the 1960s. The National Defense Education Act (NDEA) and other federal acts (e.g., Title III, Elementary and Secondary Education Act) provided funds for innovation. Many of the instructional gadgets and innovative programs were not tested before they were marketed. They were untested ideas. Because there were no stated experimental conditions and results, the user had no idea what would occur when the innovation was introduced.

Unlike the fields of agriculture, medicine, and industry, those promoting educational change failed to provide effective research and development as a basis for experimenting with these products of reason. Educators were descended upon by hucksters, fanatics, and marketers, who were not challenged to demonstrate the potency and side effects of their medicines. On the other hand, quackery could not thrive without willing clients. Many administrators and teachers have never demanded much more than the authority of the great minds for the validation of professional principles and practices. In fact, this has been an issue in Congress, which has considered legislation requiring that federal funds not be used for educational programs and equipment not supported by research data.

Universal Truths Discovered

Most early scientific thought followed realist assumptions that knowledge was scientifically discovered and unchanging; that is, the true realities of the real world exist independent of mind but may be known through the inductive process of scientific inquiry. The ultimate truths discovered are the immutable laws of nature: for example, the Newtonian laws of motion. Through the inductive processes of science, the scholars of administration can discover the natural laws of how to organize school systems and other educational organizations.

To the realist, the scientific truths of administering good educational programs are unchangeable; only the circumstances in which they are administered change. The naturalistic epistemology of realism spawned the behaviorism of John Watson. Principles of learning were developed from the "objective" study of persons. The test makers had a "field day" in education. Tests were developed that everyone really believed measured intelligence. There were personality tests to tell pupils what they should be in life, tests to determine college admission, and so on. School curricula were developed from the discovery of material in the real world. Bobbitt, a leader in what some critics referred to as the "wastepaper basket" curriculum movement, stated:

> The central theory is simple. Human life, however varied, consists in the performance of specific activities. Education that prepares for life is

one that prepares definitely and adequately for these specific activities. However numerous and diverse they may be for any social class, they can be discovered. This requires only that one go out into the world of affairs and discover the particulars of which these affairs consist. These will show the abilities, attitudes, habits, appreciations, and forms of knowledge that men need.[25]

Subject matter for the field of educational administration was heavily influenced by neorealist epistemology. Through normative survey techniques, reflection upon experience, and observation, definitive answers to questions of how to administer schools were discovered.

The Empirical Verification of Truth

Empiricist or positivist concepts of truths or knowledge grew with the acceptance and growth of science. Logical positivist epistemology is much more demanding than that of the realists. Although not expressly stated by positivists, knowledge somehow exists in the complex rubric of the universe independent of values. Through a rigid application of scientific method one can empirically verify that which is to be exalted as knowledge. Knowledge is the end state of scientific inquiry independent of the nonconfirmed intellectual activities of persons.

As discussed previously, the realist epistemology was challenged by other naturalistic views: namely, logical positivism and experimentalism. The logical positivists reject the fixed realities and universal truths of realism. Knowledge exists only through empirical verification. Some positivists altered this demanding basis for truth by allowing in-principle verification of knowledge. In-principle verification means that a statement may not have to be completely confirmed empirically. The primary purpose of philosophizing is to clarify and express in exact language the verifications of science. Consequently, the educational administrator or theorist of a positivist persuasion is preoccupied with language rather than being preoccupied with metaphysical speculation about the results of scientific inquiry. By refining what has been verified through scientific inquiry and expressing it in precise language free of speculative metaphysics and value-laden assertions, a respectable subject matter for educational administration can be developed as the end state of scientific method. Griffiths decried the lack of scientific processes in educational administration.

The second criterion of scientific knowledge is concerned with the degree to which a bit of knowledge can be verified by confirmation from

[25] Franklin Bobbitt, *The Curriculum* (Boston: Houghton, 1918), p. 42.

others working on the same problem. Probably the surest way to distinguish between *opinion* and *knowledge* (a well-substantiated belief) is in terms of the degree to which the same conclusion is arrived at by numerous investigators using the same data in the same manner. In educational administration we have generally not subjected our findings to the test of reliability. As a consequence we have published endless lists of *principles* which are actually little more than lists of unverified *opinion.*[26]

Knowledge from the Interaction of Human Intelligence with Nature

Like realism, experimentalism is a naturalistic philosophy. Although the experimentalist embraces the methods of science, knowledge so gained is less certain than that of the positivist and not universal as in the idealist's or realist's view. The experimentalist is much occupied with values and treats them as verifiable in human experience, whereas the positivist does not even consider normative questions.

The experimentalist-oriented educational administrator has no problem including statements of values as part of knowledge. Knowledge of "what is" or scientific evidence about the workings of an educational organization is likewise acceptable. Through the interplay of creative intelligence with scientific observation of and experience with the natural environment, knowledge of how to achieve desired goals is created. This knowledge is not the result of pure reason or of discovery of real knowledge independent of intellectual activity. Educational administrators are stimulated by problems of the real world to think. As they think reflectively and apply methods of science, alternatives are created. Knowledge results when the best alternatives are found through experimentation.

The criterion for judging the worth of knowledge about how to organize and operate schools and colleges is how well the use of such knowledge helps administrators and teachers attain objectives. Experimentalists insist that many facts about how reading is taught are meaningless unless translated through creative thought into superior methods for teaching children to read well. The real meaning of a proposition can only be determined by putting it into action and observing the consequences.

Because experimentalists placed much emphasis upon the cooperative use of intelligence, they became strong advocates of democratic administration, and their precepts would be consistent with the presently advocated participative management.

If the leaders of a school or college desired to create a better organization, the cooperative application of the reflective thinking

---

[26] Griffiths, *Administrative Theory,* op. cit., p. 22.

process would be used to isolate alternatives. From these alternatives one would be tried and the consequences observed. Verified knowledge consists of what has been thoughtfully tried, evaluated, and determined to be the best solution to achieve objectives.

The experimentalist insists upon the orderly application of scientific method as a basis of thinking, of searching for alternatives, and of experimentation. Persons truly representative of experimentalist thought are willing to speculate about meanings and values. However, until these speculations, or hypotheses, are tested empirically and in the light of purposes, they are not reliable knowledge for the educational administrator.

The Introspective Knowledge of Existentialism

The epistemological assumptions of existentialism stand in stark contradiction to positivism or neorealism. Positivist knowledge is the end state of scientific inquiry, regardless of what an educational administrator or group may think, whereas existentialist knowledge begins and ends with what the free, responsible administrator declares independent of naturalistic realities. The source of truth or knowledge for the administrator in existentialist terms is the self, acting responsibly and decisively free of external constraint. Consequently, what the "group," "crowds," "computers," or other external sources may confirm should not deter the administrator from making the right decision and standing responsible for the consequences.

The existentialist administrator would tend to accept knowledge attuned to freedom and individuality rather than to conform to societal demands and group norms.

> To the extent that education contributes to the submersion of the individual in the group, the existentialists believe it is failing in its task. They point to the fact that in most educational programs a premium is placed on orthodoxy and conformity. The student who wants to go off on his own, who wants to assume some direction for his own education and free himself from the patterns and procedures of the classroom, and who wants to pioneer is frequently penalized for his departure from the group norms. Yet, the existentialists remind us that these are precisely the personal characteristics from which much of human progress springs. They see the emphasis on socialization and group progress as a deadening pall, suppressing creativity, originality, and the free development of the human personality.[27]

As discussed previously, the high value that existentialists place on the right of the person to make decisions, free of external restraint, is a strong antidote to many highly organized schools and colleges. This value has resulted in much emphasis upon what advo-

[27] Graff, op. cit., pp. 206–207.

cates term humanistic education and upon strong opposition to the perceived dehumanizing influence of technological society. Those persons administering the Summerhill school (described by A. S. Neill), the British primary schools, and the "free" schools in the United States might be seen as prototype administrators by many existentialists.

On the other hand, trying to generalize about decisions that existentialists may make is hazardous, because their truths need stand no external test. All that is necessary is that decisions be made of one's own free will and that one assume full responsibility for them. Of course, willingness to be responsible tests how deeply one is personally committed to a decision because unpopular actions are not without dire consequences for a person taking them. The point, however, is that existentialist epistemology leads different persons to different knowledge about education.

The Nature of Values

Most persons speculate freely about the nature of things about them. As mentioned previously, what we value is related to our perceptions of reality and our perceptions about the nature of knowledge. If reality is perceived as survival of the fittest, competition is valued highly. Although often difficult to discern, there is a close relationship between what we value, how we perceive truths or knowledge, and our realities of everyday existence.

Among the animals of earth, human beings have the greatest flexibility in placing values upon the objects and ideas of everyday living. We are influenced in our value choices by brothers, sisters, parents, aunts, uncles, and neighbors. We accept many of the values of those most important to us, usually our parents or those who act for them. We also engage in fixing our own values upon material and nonmaterial aspects of experience. Each of us develops from experience complex systems of values for getting along in the environment, making decisions, and ordering things and ideas.

We use these values to attach "prices" to everything and every idea in our existence. Some are "priced" higher than others. The concept of differences in or priorities among values is important. One may, for example, value such objects as automobiles, houses, clothes, money, and food. Yet one may value some more than others. Our values motivate us even in the little decisions we make.

Some place different values upon nonmaterial ideas. For instance, reading the Declaration of Independence may be a valuable experience for one who greatly appreciates certain democratic ideals. Nothing stirs the emotions of persons as valued ideas that have no material reality. An illustration of such ideas is the "other world" of many religions, which still moves persons to important decisions. Thus we can and do value ideas that cannot be seen or touched.

Most of us assign priority to values when we budget for education. Because we cannot fund everything we value, we must decide which of the elements of the educational program we value most and least. In these value decisions all the facts we can attain and run through the computer will not tell us what should be funded and what should be left out. We are left to struggle with the decision on the basis of our values.

How can we be sure that our values are superior to alternative values? How do we prove that to love is more acceptable than to hate? What is the verification for the belief that freedom is to be valued and slavery deplored? The problem of how we decide normative questions has been the object of much controversy. As discussed previously, the logical positivists contend that normative statements are impossible to verify empirically and are therefore meaningless. On the other hand, to the idealist ideas constitute true values, and materialism is abhorred.

Scholars of educational administration have had many time-consuming debates concerning whether a science of administration includes values. Some assert that true science cannot include values. One counterargument to this view is that the acceptance of scientific method is a value decision.

Merton has written that the basic values of those who place faith in scientific truth are the values of universalism, communism, disinterestedness, and organized skepticism.[28] Merton suggested that these values exercise control over those in the scientific community and are used as a basis for sanctioning behavior. *Universalism* refers to statements that are true on the basis of observation and entirely impersonal criteria, not on the basis of ethnic, racial, religious, or nationalistic traditions. *Communism* implies that anything discovered belongs to the entire scientific world, and no one has property claims or patent rights on scientific truths. *Disinterestedness* denotes valuing empirical validity for truth more than personal preference. One is accountable for assertions of scientific truths, and what is observed must be subjected to the scrutiny of peers. A person in Communist China should be able to replicate the experiments to test reported truths of a citizen of the democratic United States and obtain similar results.

If Merton is correct, acceptance of logical positivism does not free one from normative problems. How does one verify empirically the superiority of scientific method over all other sources of truth?

[28]Robert K. Merton, *Social Theory and Social Structure* (New York: The Free Press. 1957).

How will acceptance of positivist concepts of scientific method lead one to better sources of truth than experimentalist concepts of scientific method? Only a change in values will cause one to question the universality of the end product of scientific method. This raises the all-important point of how we question values.

Values Verified by Pure Reason

Values from the other worlds of idealism are not subject to empirical tests. According to this view, one must have faith in the exercise of pure reason. Through the process of logical deduction, well-educated persons of superior intellectual powers can discern universally applicable, unchanging values.

> True propositions like "my mother loves me," "this rose is beautiful" do not rest on the method of experimental inquiry and the proven hypothesis. The awareness of religious and other values is of the same kind. In fact, one may say in all matters involving the appreciation of persons and beauty, the further the scientific method of knowing goes, the less it tells us about reality.[29]

Validation of values is through accepting the assertions of those authorities thought to have superior ability to exercise reason. This has not appealed to many American educators. The American spirit is too tied to the pioneer pragmatism—that whatever works is what is valued—to accept the results of pure reason as valid.

Natural Laws as Moral Laws

In realism we find the ultimate materialistic basis of valuing: Scientific method is the valued technique or process through which the natural laws can be discovered. The natural laws, which govern the materialistic universe, become the moral laws, which should govern people.

> It follows that the forces of circumstances, which is and always has been the law, is inevitably always forcing the individual into conformity with the general trend of all evolution, sometimes with misery to himself and disaster to society, sometimes—always in the long run— with happiness to himself and hence to society. It is as ridiculous to suppose that we can invent education or society as it would be to suppose that we could invent a new and better body, or a better body of natural law.[30]

[29] Herman H. Horne, *This New Education* (New York: Abingdon Press, 1931), p. 111.

[30] Henry C. Morrison, *Basic Principles of Education* (Boston: Houghton, 1934), p. 365.

Could Lincoln ever have discovered from observing nature that free men are to be valued more than enslaved men? How can we inductively discover from the trees, oceans, rivers, grass, mountains, and so on, that the young should be educated? In fact, from studying the instinctive behavior of animals, we might never value education.

Indeed, we have discovered so many conflicting laws in our material universe that one is hard put to say how any one value can be validated empirically over another. Through empirical observation one finds lifeguards and murderers, beneficial bacteria and harmful bacteria, deserts and fertile valleys, and many other conflicting discoveries. Finally, both realistic and idealistic axiologies fail to account for evolutionary change. Can we assume that the valued truths, which might have been discovered a million years ago, are what we would discover in our modern, technologically oriented world?

Values Verified by Consequences

Experimentalists, or pragmatists, also claim the use of scientific method to confirm values. However, experimentalists will have none of the realist's belief that values exist "out there" in nature independent of the person, nor do they accept the "other worlds" of idealism. Speaking of the relation of moral values and science, Dewey stated:

> For Moralists usually draw a sharp line between the field of natural sciences and the conduct that is regarded as moral. But a moral that frames its judgments of value on the basis of consequences must depend in a most intimate manner upon the conclusions of science. For the knowledge of the relations between changes which enable us to connect things as antecedents and consequences *is* science.[31]

If persuaded by the weight of opposition to the experimentalist's position that values can be verified scientifically, one concludes that values cannot be confirmed through the application of scientific method. Romanell is among those who have expressed opposition to the experimentalist position on the scientific verification of values.

> There are several reasons why ethics, no matter how scientific in intent, cannot have its problems settled by the experimental method as we have come to understand that method. The first and most obvious reason is that the experimental method is only good for questions of fact, that is, for determining what-is-so, and hence not good for ethics proper, which deals with questions of norms or what-ought-to-be-so. Descriptive ethics is not normative ethics.[32]

[31] John Dewey, *The Quest for Certainty* (New York: Putnam, 1929), p. 266.
[32] Patrick Romanell, *Toward a Critical Naturalism* (New York: Macmillan, 1958), p. 43.

Numerous other writers have expressed the opinion that through scientific method we can determine what is but cannot confirm empirically what ought to be. Yet Hook insisted, "Since human values acquire their quality of value by being related to human desire, only the use of scientific intelligence can help us discover the difference between reliable and unreliable values."[33] Even though criticized severely for their "scientific" confirmation of values, the experimentalists offer a methodological objectivity in the realm of valuing, which the educational administrator may find useful.

To the experimentalist, scientific method is an inductive–deductive process of solving the decision problems facing us. Indeed, the person does have the natural ability to think creatively. Just as theoretical physicists struggle with the manipulation of complex ideas and create new concepts worthy of experimentation, all persons exercise intelligence in daily living independently of any materialistic determinism or appeals to supernatural worlds.

Where do we get the higher order of purpose? Through the intelligent reconstruction of experience, we visualize the consequences of decisions and actions. With years of experience, an intellectually active, resourceful educator can discern the consequences of not teaching youth to be good citizens. The consequences of not educating thousands to be able to hold good jobs are obvious. As we reflect upon our own experiences and use vicariously the experiences of others in other societies and from history, we can begin to visualize what our purposes ought to be.

As indicated, we do not have to experience everything to be intelligent about higher-order purposes or values. We have the vicarious, reconstructable experiences of history. One does not have to go to other worlds to learn that rampant murder, theft, and so on, are detrimental to society. One cannot learn from simple factual information about hawks, sharks, and other predators how people ought to behave toward each other. What are the consequences of human predation in the schools, in the city, and in the nation? Will the logical empiricist application of scientific method tell us what schools should teach us about desirable ecology? We do not think so.

Affirmation of Values by the Individual

The philosophy of existentialism offers a different source of values. As we have already discussed, the existentialist's value decisions are based upon the affirmations of the individual. No basis for validation is needed, except that the person is acting responsibly, decisively, and free of external restraint. Ozmon and Craver wrote:

[33] Sidney Hook, "On the Battlefield of Philosophy," *Partisan Review,* XVI (March 1949), 262.

The existentialists view individual man as a being who first exists and then defines his essence, for it is from individual man that all ideas, values, and institutions come. This is radically different from Platonic idealism where all ideas or essences are in a realm pre-existing independent from man.[34]

Although pointing to the fact that "existentialists have little to offer in the way of a method of knowing, a systematic epistemology," Morris and Pai suggested:

Existentialists, however, do not spend all their time in such carping dialectic. What they are interested in is simply reminding us that there is an element of *personal appropriation* in all knowing. When all the data are in, each individual must make a personal choice to believe something. Indeed, we must each make our own personal appropriation of an epistemology.[35]

As a key element of the "counterculture" of the 1960s, existentialism produced a reexamination of the society concerning the dehumanizing bureaucratization of large educational organizations, societal materialism, the dehumanization of workers, and other onslaughts on the personal well-being of individuals. However, should educational administrators be persuaded that the materialism of modern society, stimulated by technology and the poisoning of the environment, is reason to escape into the intuitive, subjective processes of existentialism? One may seriously question whether the complex problems facing educators can be solved through the individualistic pursuits of values. A process that is based on purposeful, cooperative action and experimental inquiry may be a more feasible pursuit of values as bases for administrative behavior. Existentialist valuing does have an appealing aspect: The person must stand responsible—must be willing to stand up and be counted.

Some Questionable Bases of Valuing

What are some alternatives to responsible administration in decision making? One would be to avoid a purposive stand and be blown by the winds. Another would be to establish a value supermarket in which those values that suit one's opportunistic whims of the moment are selected. At the opposite pole of value randomness is the zealot who fastens onto a value position and refuses to question or think about consequences. This is the attitude embodied by the statement, "Don't bother me with the facts, my mind is made up." Some claim to take refuge in the law as a basis of values in decision making. Of

[34] Howard Ozmon and Sam Craver, *Philosophical Foundations of Education* (Columbus: Merrill, 1976), p. 168.
[35] Morris and Pai, op. cit., p. 155.

primary consideration in some organizations is personal loyalty to top executives. In his widely read *The Lonely Crowd*, Riesman bemoaned the extent to which other-directed tendencies had pervaded the larger society.[36] In *Management and Machiavelli*, Jay reminded us that the pursuit and use of power over others may be the value held highest by many persons.[37] Teyve, the milkman in *Fiddler on the Roof*, epitomized those who adhere strongly to tradition and custom as a source of truth. All of these are considered by most authorities as unacceptable bases for personal values in decision making.

Opportunism inevitably leads to the use of other persons for one's own ends. Although some writers may support a form of sophisticated selfishness, the authors do not believe any should support it in a human operation, especially where the education of the young is concerned. Randomness of behavior, especially in the top levels of administration, tends to produce organizational ineffectiveness and inability to respond to demands. If the law is the guide, how can one condemn the Nazis who faithfully followed the law as they understood it? Numerous authorities have pointed to the fallacies of assuming that legality is morality. Riesman is essentially correct in extolling the value of inner-directed responses over other-directed and tradition-directed behaviors. However, one of the most serious problems arises from following custom and tradition in school systems.

Those who adhere strictly to custom and tradition as sources of truths in educational decision making tend to lose sight of socially responsible purpose. Ask a teacher why a certain practice is followed in a school; if she answers something like, "Oh! I never thought about it; we have done it this way since I joined the faculty," the practice is probably based upon custom and tradition as a basis of truth. Some educational administrators become so tradition-bound that their practices grow irrelevant to changing conditions.

When educational faculties follow customs and traditions and lose sight of purpose, a form of mindless activity prevails. Moreover, if our only value is to follow custom and tradition, we have no basis for claiming superiority of one culture over another or of one school over another.

Political Ideologies: The Influence of Values on Education

Some of the discussion to this point has illustrated how values influence the practice of educational administration, particularly their

---

[36] David Riesman, *The Lonely Crowd* (New Haven: Yale University Press, 1953).
[37] Antony Jay, *Management and Machiavelli* (New York: Holt, 1967).

influence on administrative behavior in decision making. The influence of values on the nature of administration becomes very visible when one focuses attention on the process of educational policy making. This involves analysis of political ideologies, and these are supported by the philosophies discussed previously.

Viability of Ideologies as an Influence

There is some controversy concerning the viability of ideology in modern politics. Bell is among those writers who have noted that traditional ideologies—liberalism, socialism, conservatism, communism—have lost their hold on people as "secular religions."[38] Many traditional positivists treat ideologies as meaningless myths and explain political motivations as expressions of interests or as based on certain behaviorally explained predispositions or preferences. Other observers believe that present day society is so complex that a person is seldom consistent; consequently, a person may be a liberal on economic issues, a conservative on such issues as abortion, and assume a moderate stance on foreign affairs. In this latter view, most Americans are philosophically eclectic in political decisions.

Numerous studies have demonstrated that ideologies are indeed viable and are influencing the way people and groups think about educational issues. Lane's study of the common men of a seaboard city and Ladd's analysis of three cities in Connecticut demonstrated the viability of ideology as an important aspect of political behavior, including educational decisions.[39] Agger, Goldrich, and Swanson discovered eight competing ideologies in their study of four communities.[40] Several studies have indicated that political ideologies influence the structure of education in the United States.[41] However, the ideologies do not always follow the logically constructed views of academicians. Litwak and associates argued forcefully that "many people

[38] Daniel Bell, *The End of Ideology* (New York: The Free Press, 1962), pp. 399–400.

[39] Robert E. Lane, *Political Ideology: Why the American Common Man Believes What He Does* (New York: The Free Press, 1962), pp. 15–16; Everett C. Ladd, Jr., *Ideology in America* (Ithaca: Cornell University Press, 1969), p. 343.

[40] Robert E. Agger, Daniel Goldrich, and Bert E. Swanson, *The Rulers and the Ruled* (New York: Wiley, 1964), p. 16.

[41] For illustrations of other studies see Robert D. Lee, "Educational Ideology and Decision-Making in the San Francisco Public Schools, 1956–66" (doctoral dissertation, Syracuse University, 1967); Keith Goldhammer and Frank Farner, *The Jackson County Story* (Eugene, Ore.: Center for the Advanced Study of Educational Administration, 1964); George J. Crawford, "Conflict in the Board Member-Board Member, Board Member-Superintendent Relationship: A Case Study" (doctoral dissertation, Ohio State University, 1973); Ralph B. Kimbrough, *Informal County Leadership Structure and Controls Affecting Educational Policy Decision-Making*, Final Report, Cooperative Research Project No. 1324 (Washington, D.C.: Department of Health, Education, and Welfare, Office of Education, 1964), pp. 105–112; Laurence Iannaccone and Frank W. Lutz, *Politics, Power and Policy* (Columbus: Merill, 1970).

have 'consistent positions' but express them in forms that differ from those expected by researchers."[42]

Contrary to popularly expressed opinion, McClosky and associates demonstrated that analysis "of the opinions of Democratic and Republican [party] leaders shows them to be distinct communities of co-believers who diverge sharply on many important issues."[43] They reported, "Democratic leaders typically display the stronger urge to elevate the lowborn, the uneducated, the deprived minorities, and the poor in general; they are also more disposed to employ the nation's collective power to advance humanitarian and social welfare goals," whereas Republican leaders subscribed "in greater measure to the symbols and practices of individualism, *laissez-faire,* and national independence" and believed that the human misfortunes of society could best be overcome through reliance on personal effort, private incentives, hard work, and personal responsibility.[44] Ideological visibility varies among elections. For instance, people expressed stronger ideological commitments in the 1964 presidential election between Goldwater and Johnson than they did in the 1960 election between Kennedy and Nixon.[45]

How Ideologies Influence Education

The new liberal ideology is based on ideas clearly consistent with the philosophy of experimentalism. Very briefly, new liberals disavow the existence of natural law and believe in the superiority of intelligence as a basis for solving political, social, and economic problems. They believe strongly in the concept that freedom is the power of effective choice. The person achieves equality and becomes fully human through participation in a society that provides a floor of support for his or her fundamental and derived needs. In general, new liberals have urged government-sponsored social welfare and education programs to elevate the poor, to broaden educational opportunity for the disadvantaged, to further civil rights for minorities, and to advance humanitarian and social welfare goals. The New Deal programs sponsored by President Franklin Roosevelt were strongly supported by new liberals. New liberal influence was evident in the progressive educa-

---

[42] Eugene Litwak et al., "Ideological Complexity and Middle-American Rationality," *Public Opinion Quarterly,* XXXVII (Fall 1973), 331. See also Norman R. Luttbeg, "The Structure of Beliefs Among Leaders and the Public," *Public Opinion Quarterly,* 32 (Fall 1968), 400–409.

[43] Herbert McClosky, Paul Hoffman, and Rosemary O'Hara, "Issues Conflict and Consensus Among Party Leaders and Followers," *American Political Science Review,* LIV (June 1960), 426.

[44] Ibid.

[45] John O. Field and Ronald E. Anderson, "Ideology in the Public's Conception of the 1964 Election," *Public Opinion Quarterly,* 33 (Fall 1969), 380–389.

tion movement, which was described by Cremin.[46] The ideology of President Johnson figured prominently in the passage of the Elementary and Secondary Education Act of 1965 and the extensive social welfare legislation of the Great Society. According to Bass and DeVries, President Johnson had very strong populist, or new liberal, beliefs.[47] He was a New Deal ideologue who, as a young congressman, was said to "worship" President Franklin Roosevelt. Both Meranto and Thomas credit President Johnson's powerful support for passage of this 1965 act.[48]

The new left, which emerged on college campuses as an ideological movement in the 1960s, had a profound influence on the American political system. Ericson is among various writers who saw the philosophy of existentialism as an important underpinning of the new left ideology.[49] Freedom for each person to make decisions and seek self-fulfillment with emphasis on democratic socialism was an important tenet. Violence or "disorderly processes" were thought to be necessary to confront and change the establishment. According to Sargent, education was a particular target of the new left in promoting participatory democracy, in emphasizing greater need for program relevance, and in emphasizing human needs.[50] As discussed earlier, leaders of the new left pressed for the development of alternative or "free" schools in which the freedom of students to decide is maximized. They demanded the relaxation of bureaucratic ("repressive") control of schools. Administrators were faced with new concepts for observing student and faculty rights. The renewed emphasis on humanistic education during the 1960s and 1970s had overtones of new left ideology. The leaders of the new left had particularly strong influence in changing the traditional administration of colleges and universities. The result was greater self-determination for students and lesser control by college administrators.

Various groups with a right-of-center orientation also have had great influence on the structure of education. Certain radical right groups, whose ideology is consistent with the philosophy of idealism, particularly religious idealism, have been thorns in the sides of many

[46]Lawrence A. Cremin, *The Transformation of the School* (New York: Knopf, 1961).

[47]Jack Bass and Walter DeVries, *The Transformation of Southern Politics* (New York: Basic Books, 1976), pp. 8–9.

[48]Philip Meranto, *The Politics of Federal Aid to Education in 1965* (Syracuse: Syracuse University Press, 1967); Norman C. Thomas, *Education in National Politics* (New York: David McKay, 1975), pp. 3–12.

[49]Edward E. Ericson, Jr., *Radicals in the University* (Stanford: Hoover Institution Press, Stanford University, 1975), pp. 1–58.

[50]Lyman T. Sargent, *Contemporary Political Ideologies: A Comparative Analysis* (Homewood, Ill.: The Dorsey Press, 1969).

boards of education and school administrators. According to Auerbach, Burkean ideology, a conservative view, figured prominently in Southern politics before the Civil War.[51] This conservative ideology is still held by certain radical right groups throughout the United States. Some of these groups press for a return to the basics in education with an emphasis on the classics (e.g., the Great Books), particularly at the college and university level. Religious idealism has been a philosophical support for ultraconservative groups involved in controversies relative to the expulsion of certain library books, prohibition of sex education, restoration of prayer in the schools, and other such issues. In 1980, one of these groups established a national power group under the banner of the "Moral Majority."

One must look at classical liberal ideology, however, to find the most powerful influence on the education of right-of-center groups. The political system of the United States was born of classical liberal ideology with its emphasis on the ideology and free enterprise precepts of John Locke, Adam Smith, and others. Classical liberalism is clearly consistent with the philosophy of realism and the belief in the natural law as the basis of society.

Liberty is defined as the absence of restraint, particularly of governmental restraint. Equality is the absence of social or legal barriers toward the pursuit of one's self-interest. The consistency of this view with the tenets of certain naturalistic ideals of realism discussed previously is self-evident.

Illustrations of the interests of classical liberals (frequently called "conservatives") in education abound in the literature. Some of these groups champion tuition tax credits and freedom of choice proposals, emphasis on nonpublic education, and other changes consistent with their beliefs. Other reconstructed classical liberals strongly support public education; however, they emphasize a "no-frills" program with grounding in the fundamentals and vocational programs geared to the needs of the economic system. They do not favor heavy program emphasis on social development. Gubser described how very conservative groups had successfully gained much control of the Arizona schools. Through their influence in the legislature, the state board of education, the state curriculum commission, and the state department of education, these conservative forces promoted impressive changes in and control over the curricular offerings, textbooks, and instructional processes in Arizona. For example, high school graduates were required to complete a course in "the essentials and benefits of the free enterprise system."[52]

[51] M. Morton Auerbach, *The Conservative Illusion* (New York: Columbia University Press, 1959), p. 69.
[52] M. M. Gubser, "Accountability as a Smoke Screen for Political Indoctrination in Arizona," *Phi Delta Kappan,* LV (September 1973), 64–65.

Space does not permit full discussion of political ideologies in the United States; nevertheless, the authors chose a few of those frequently named to illustrate the influence of various ideologies. We emphasize the limited nature of the discussion. For example, at this writing, several far right groups are claiming greater newsworthiness: the so-called New Right holds a point of view very close to traditional classical liberalism; the Libertarian party seeks to advance concepts close to laissez-faire or unreconstructed classical liberalism. Groups with ideologies to the left of new liberalism field national candidates for president. Educators should be aware that the ideological groups with the greatest national influence (e.g., classical liberalism, new liberalism) are collections of subgroups with competing beliefs. Thus we speak of the right or left or moderate wings of the national political parties. The most important point is that basic philosophical values consistent with the philosophies, which were discussed previously, undergird and support these ideologies.

Personal Beliefs for Policy Leadership in Education

The primary implication of the discussion in this chapter is that educational administrators should act thoughtfully. To prepare for thoughtful administration is to read and think deeply about the nature and source of knowledge or truth, the relationship of truth to the nature of reality, one's personal values, and the consequences of one's values and beliefs for action.

Hodgkinson contended that, since the administrative process is value-laden with significant impact upon organizational quality, the administrator should have knowledge of value superior to that possessed by ordinary persons.[53] Ostrander and Dethy also emphasized knowledge of one's value system.[54] To act thoughtfully, then, is to monitor continuously what we are doing and how we are doing it, where we are and why we are there; and we must consider the consequence of our decisions and actions.

> To have a mind to do a thing is to foresee a future possibility; it is to have a plan for its accomplishment; it is to note the means which make the plan capable of execution and the obstructions in the way—or, if it is really a *mind* to do the thing and not a vague aspiration—it is to have a plan which takes account of resources and difficulties. Mind is

[53] Christopher Hodgkinson, *Towards a Philosophy of Administration* (New York: St. Martin's Press, 1978), p. 103.

[54] Raymond H. Ostrander and Ray C. Dethy, *A Values Approach to Educational Administration* (New York: American Book, 1968), p. 46.

capacity to refer present conditions to future results, and future consequences to present conditions.[55]

Scientific Basis for Knowledge

The authors are not persuaded that intuitive processes of pure reason are the final source of knowledge. One must be able to expect knowledge to be relevant to the real world of administering educational organizations. Consequently, the thoughtful educational administrator has faith in the knowledge achieved through scientific inquiry.

The superiority of scientific inquiry over desperate attempts to reach other worlds of knowledge through pure reason is seen in agriculture, medicine, and science. Indeed, there is little basis for arguing that educators continue to use "educational magic" as a basis for behavior. Moreoever, we should not choose a materialistic interpretation of scientific method in which we are distracted by a mass of facts that have no relation to objectives.

Thoughtful educational administration demands the application of reflective thinking and experimental inquiry to the problems of achieving schools of quality. The practicing educational administrator must demand that those who claim to have answers to these problems make public the scientific basis for their findings.

Finally, the educational administrator and the students for whom responsibility is assumed have the right to demand thorough testing and development of an educational innovation before it is employed generally. What will the innovation do under controlled circumstances? What are the side effects after prolonged usage? Unless the practitioners of our schools and colleges demand a scientific basis for knowledge, education will be characterized by indecisiveness, irresponsibility, and goal conflicts.

Administrators' Concern with Personal Beliefs

Preoccupation with "what is" to the exclusion of the values used as a basis for goals is nonsense. To survive and help educational organizations thrive demands personal attention to what one believes. Indeed, there is some evidence that belief consistency, as a basis of behavioral consistency, may be an important element in attaining leadership in groups. Thus all of us should search our belief systems for internal consistency. Again, we do not recommend a pure exercise of reason for this process. Dewey wrote that mind is "the power to understand things in terms of the use made of them."[56]

Setting up dual concepts of personal values and administrative

---

[55] John Dewey, *Democracy and Education* (New York: Macmillan, 1916), p. 120.
[56] Dewey, op. cit., p. 39.

knowledge has caused many educational problems. This inevitably makes one's values completely subjective and empirically irrelevant. For example, through scientific processes we know that smoking tobacco is related to cancer. The dualist in valuing would accept this as truth but attach no value to it. Value to some persons is a personal feeling of the worth of a thing or idea regardless of empirical consequences. Thus one may both accept the truth that smoking is harmful to health and also value smoking.

This dualistic thinking may result in nonsensical administrative practices in education. True values of the individual are seen in personal action. If one values knowledge as a basis for solving problems and achieving personal aims and objectives, knowledge and value are continuous with each other. Personal values run much deeper than how we feel about educational procedures and purposes.

> The moral factor in any choice-situation is proportional to the consequences which follow from the alternative courses of action. To discriminate and anticipate such consequences is an intellectual act of the highest quality. Decisions that are thus related to all aspects of our complex social experience cannot be safely taken merely on the basis of what "feels right" in the situation as immediately experienced.[57]

As the authors have indicated, tremendous gaps in empirical research exist in our field. Much of what we call knowledge is borrowed from other disciplines, and not enough has been done in developing these concepts to observe the consequences of their uses in educational organizations. Thus there is quite a way to go in achieving a high degree of expertise in valuing. Nevertheless, achieving this high degree of professional excellence should be a goal of supreme importance to all who enter the field.

ACTIVITIES/QUESTIONS FOR FURTHER STUDY

1. Through a perusal of documents (e.g., school board minutes, newspapers, newsletters) of a college or school system, identify some important educational decisions. Think through what your personal position would have been on each of these decisions. What were the bases of your decisions? Were personal values involved? If so, was your valuing process consistent or eclectic?

2. As you listen to presentations, try to identify the assumptions made by the speakers. Consider whether the speakers' views correspond to any of the systems of philosophical thought discussed in this chapter.

3. Ask several of the most powerful political leaders in a community to state why they took a position on several recent important issues. Keep careful

[57] John L. Childs, *Education and the Philosophy of Experimentalism* (New York: Appleton, 1931), p. 109.

notes on why they favored their position in the issues. Try to describe some important elements of each leader's ideology. How would each leader's ideology tend to influence his or her actions in educational decisions?

SUGGESTED READINGS

DEWEY, JOHN. *Democracy and Education.* New York: Macmillan Publishing Co., Inc., 1916.

DUPUIS, ADRIAN M. *Philosophy of Education in Historical Perspective.* Chicago: Rand McNally & Co., 1966.

DURANT, WILL. *The Story of Philosophy.* New York: Washington Square Press, Inc., 1961.

GRAFF, ORIN B., et al. *Philosophic Theory and Practice in Educational Administration.* Belmont, Calif.: Wadsworth Publishing Co., Inc., 1966.

HEILBRONER, ROBERT L. *The Worldly Philosophers.* New York: Simon & Schuster, Inc., 1953.

HODGKINSON, CHRISTOPHER. *Towards A Philosophy of Administration.* New York; St. Martin's Press, 1978.

LADD, EVERETT C., JR. *Ideology in America.* Ithaca: Cornell University Press, 1969.

MORRIS, VAN CLEVE, and YOUNG PAI. *Philosophy and the American School.* Boston: Houghton Mifflin Co., 1976.

OSTRANDER, RAYMOND H., and RAY C. DETHY. *A Values Approach to Educational Administration.* New York: American Book Company, 1968.

OZMON, HOWARD, AND SAM CRAVER. *Philosophical Foundations of Education.* Columbus: Charles E. Merrill Publishers, 1976.

REICHENBACH, HANS. *The Rise of Scientific Philosophy.* Berkeley: University of California Press, 1951.

13

Ethics and the Educational Administrator

$\mathbf{A}$S WE DISCUSSED in Chapter 12, educational administrators act on a hierarchy of values in which some have greater significance than others. For example, one may overlook the school principal who habitually commits minor breaches of etiquette; however, toleration of acts of dishonesty, embezzlement, unjust treatment of students, or other failures in moral character is very unlikely. This is not to say that failure to observe accepted practices of etiquette may not reflect badly on one's promotion to high posts in educational administration. These failures may result in several forms of social sanctions against the offender; however, failure to observe the more basic moral expectations could result in loss of license, imprisonment, and the ruin of one's professional career not to speak of the blight visited on the profession itself. Ethics or moral philosophy concerns the values about one's moral character; as Morris and Pai have written, "At the base of all ethical considerations lies the question of morals."[1]

Immegart and Burroughs observed that the educational admin-

[1]Van Cleve Morris and Young Pai, *Philosophy and the American School,* 2nd ed., (Boston: Houghton, 1976), p. 209.

istrator has certain duties and obligations to societal ethics as well as to professional ethics. Concerning obligations to social ethics, they wrote:

> These *societal ethics* apply whether one is a professional or not and tend to be controlling in all aspects of societal life. Thus the ethical standard of honesty, fairness, and compassion apply to the doctor, the merchant, the housewife, or the paperboy as well as the unemployed.[2]

And they further noted, "the professional also has certain duties or obligations re his profession."[3]

Importance of Ethics

Because they hold visible positions of leadership, administrators will face more situations that test their moral character than many other persons. The higher up in the organization one goes, the more critically important high moral character becomes. An organization can survive immorality at the lower levels of leadership. However, when the top decision makers are corrupt, they may very soon corrupt the entire organization. This happens in several ways. First, young intentionally ethical administrators in the organization will go along out of loyalty to the organization and respect for status. Those very capable administrators who do not go along may become ambivalent or leave the organization. Second, there will be a tendency for the unethical to select persons like themselves to fill the positions vacated. In time this selection of morally questionable cronies will lead to a morally corrupt organization.

Living by a defensible and widely acceptable code of ethics is essential for the well-being of the profession. Educational administrators are assumed by many parents and other citizens to represent their profession; thus how they conduct themselves affects how people view the moral status of the entire profession. About this point, Knezevich made the following observation:

> The school administrator works in a goldfish bowl of public attention. This is more so today than ever before in history. To many he represents the school system. He is the symbol of its successes or failures. Few would logically exempt the chief executive from the fortunes or misfortunes of the organization he directs.[4]

---

[2] Glenn L. Immegart and John M. Burroughs (eds.), *Ethics and the School Administrator* (Danville, Ill.: Interstate, 1970), p. 93.
[3] Ibid.
[4] Stephen J. Knezevich, "The Ethical Concerns of Professional School Administrators," in Immegart and Burroughs, op. cit., p. 15.

Think of the great harm that unprofessional conduct may visit upon students. We become privy to some of the most intimate information about the private lives of students. In the absence of high ethical standards, this information could harm the students and their families. When some faltering administrator engages in the shamefully low level of gutter politics for self-aggrandizement, the consequences may include a loss of educational quality for thousands of students. Immense damage to a generation of students results when they are discriminated against because of their social class, ethnic background, or skin color. Physicians have had great debates concerning euthanasia; however, educators face even more serious ethical questions of "euthanasia of the mind." Suffering experienced in a terminally ill cancer patient is usually for a short period, but the suffering of children deprived of an education is life-long and torturous. The effects of administrative acts perceived to be clearly biased or unfair may be devastating to organizations. Of course, when the more blatant acts of immorality on the part of top administrators become front page news, an unbelievable pall is cast over an entire educational system and the professional leaders in it. Moreover, members of a profession who do not possess the knowledge, concepts, and skills necessary to perform their leadership tasks well contribute to program failure and denial of educational opportunity.

Some Dimensions of Ethics

Educational administrators are faced with a bewildering array of problems involving ethics. For example, there is the ethics of obligation involving laws, policies, regulations, rules, and "oughts." Educational administrators are obligated to act in consistency with state statutes, state board of education regulations, and school board policies. There is the further obligation to observe in action certain "oughts" as may be stated in a code of ethics or as thought by citizens to be the expected behavior of administrators.

Another dimension is the ethics of responsiveness involving, among other aspects, what Mayeroff called caring or helping others to grow.[5] Thus an administrator may exhibit questionable ethics through any behavior that thwarts the growth and development of the faculty, other administrators, or students. A person bent on self-aggrandizement at the expense of others exhibits questionable ethics. The administrator with a "don't-give-a-hang" attitude may commit breaches of ethics of responsiveness or caring that are beyond discussion here. The community, faculty, and students may reasonably ex-

[5] Milton Mayeroff, *On Caring* (New York: Perrennial Library, 1971).

pect the school administrator to have prepared himself or herself adequately for the position held and to have kept current in the research
and literature. There is the obligation to have a high degree of expertise in one's area of emphasis.

Ethics also involves actions to establish goals, objectives, and
priorities. As an illustration, priorities may be so manipulated as to
reflect more favorably on one's career, or the goals established may
discriminate against certain classes of pupils in a school system.

Administrators should exercise obligations to students; for example, there are moral obligations to recognize and respect the basic
human rights of students. Serious ethical questions are involved in
the misuse of personal information about students. What are students' rights of privacy? Students have a right to know the rules as
opposed to the questionable practice of making-up-the-rules to fit the
administrative situation. In many school systems and colleges procedures exist for students to have redress of grades received. At present
educators are faced with very serious ethical issues concerning the
use of standardized tests in education. Finally, administrators have
the obligation to protect the physical well-being of students and to
protect them from unfair punishment. Administrators are obligated
to provide for the appropriate education of the handicapped, to provide adequate counseling services, to protect privacy, and to ensure
adequate supervision.

The point of this discussion is that ethics is not restricted to such
gross failures of character as indicated by the headlines announcing
that the school superintendent is convicted of stealing thousands of
the taxpayers' dollars or for receiving kickbacks for the purchase of
school supplies. The student of educational administration who just
wants to learn enough to "get by" and, because of lack of expertise,
fails in his or her obligations to the faculty and students may contribute to the failure of some students to realize their educational
aspirations. Who commits the greater crime—the one that destroys
the physical well-being of a person or the one who causes the mental
stagnation and life-long suffering of the person and of the society?
Space does not permit the exploration of this and many other aspects
of the ethical administrator. The discussion now turns to the professional code of ethics as a source of ethical behavior.

A Professional Code of Ethics

As discussed in Chapter 1, the American Association of School
Administrators adopted a code of ethics in 1966. This statement contained a preamble alluding to basic concepts of the democratic society, professional ethics and responsibilities, the importance of profes-

sional dignity, and references to the purposes of the code. This was followed by nine policy statements and an overview statement including in each case illustrative examples of behaviors consistent with the policies. Among the policies were obligatory assertions to uphold the honor and dignity of the profession; to obey local, state, and national laws; to show loyalty to country; to master specialized knowledge, concepts, and skills; to honor contractual commitments; to carry out board policies; to place the public trust above economic or social rewards; to avoid conditions involving conflict of interest; and to adhere to the public's right to be informed. Each policy statement was followed by several specific statements of behavior that might illustrate applications of this policy.

The 1966 policy statement was revised in 1976 into the *AASA Statement of Ethics for School Administrators and Procedural Guidelines.*[6] This 1976 statement has been adopted as a standard of professional ethics by most national school administrators' associations, including the National Association of Elementary School Principals and the National Association of Secondary School Principals. The statement contains ten standards and detailed information about the procedural guidelines for administering them. These standards, which are clear as to their meaning and implications for administrative behavior, are as follows:

The educational administrator:

1. Makes the well-being of students the fundamental value of all decision making and actions.
2. Fulfills professional responsibilities with honesty and integrity.
3. Supports the principle of due process and protects the civil and human rights of all individuals.
4. Obeys local, state, and national laws and does not knowingly join or support organizations that advocate, directly or indirectly, the overthrow of the government.
5. Implements the governing board of education's policies and administrative rules and regulations.
6. Pursues appropriate measures to correct those laws, policies, and regulations that are not consistent with sound educational goals.
7. Avoids using positions for personal gain through political, social, religious, economic, or other influence.
8. Accepts academic degrees or professional certification only from duly accredited institutions.
9. Maintains the standards and seeks to improve the effectiveness of the profession through research and continuing professional development.

[6] American Association of School Administrators, *AASA Statement of Ethics for School Administrators and Procedural Guidelines* (Arlington, Va.: The Association, 1976).

10. Honors all contracts until fulfillment, release or dissolution mutually agreed upon by all parties to contract.[7]

The results of the study by Dexheimer indicated that a discrepancy may exist between what members of the American Association of School Administrators (AASA) proclaim publicly as a Code of Ethics and their standards of conduct. Dexheimer reached the following conclusion:

> The findings just outlined point to at least one inescapable conclusion: there is a significant discrepancy between acceptance of a professional code of ethics and adherence to that code in actual practice by chief school administrators. Closely allied to this major finding are two corollaries: ethical behavior as measured by the AASA *Code of Ethics* is more likely to occur among chief school administrators in larger school districts; and ethical behavior is also more likely to be found among the more highly paid members of the AASA who are chief school administrators.[8]

Dexheimer's finding that the obligations to follow a professional code are taken more seriously by persons in the higher-salaried and larger superintendencies offers some reassurance. Perhaps these persons offer a leadership core upon which to build greater professional status. On the other hand, his study also showed that people do not become ethical in practice because a code of ethics exists to which lip-service is given. Following a professional code of ethics or the law does not make one moral.

This latter point has many implications, not the least of which is that there is a need for greater attention to admitting those who have high morals and to educating those in preparation programs about their obligations to make personal commitments to ethical conduct. The authors suggest that greater attention must be given by all of us (students, professors, and practitioners) to what we believe and the basis of our moral convictions. This process may include personal reading and thinking based upon the formal study of ethics. Educational administrators may at first feel that the books on moral philosophy are too complicated. In time, however, they will begin to appreciate the importance of understanding the bases of their personal systems of morals and better fathom what they really believe about right and wrong.

---

[7] Ibid., pp. 12–13.
[8] Roy Dexheimer, "Administrative Ethics: A Study in Accommodation," in Immegart and Burroughs, op. cit., p. 35.

Alternative Bases of Ethics

During the decades of the 1960s and 1970s educational administrators faced many new problems involving ethical behavior. College presidents were confronted with a wave of militant activity, which was seen often by the American people on the national news programs. Elementary and secondary school administrators also grappled with riotous acts, long hair, rowdy manners, slovenly dress, and repulsive language. Administrative behavior, consistent with long-held norms, did not fit these new situations and frequently became the object of court cases. This period was characterized by greater intensity of challenge to conventional ethics than previous decades; however, educational administration has always been a profession confronted with challenging situations involving ethics. There is no possible way to program ethical behavior for all situations through written codes of ethics or books no matter how voluminous they may be. Consequently, the educational administrator must, to some extent, be his or her own moral philosopher. In the following paragraphs, an introductory discussion is provided about alternative bases for discerning what is ethical.

Intuitionism as the Standard of Ethics

There have been many expressions of intuitionism—the concept that within the realm of the human being is the capacity to discern right from wrong without appeals to supernatural authority or other worlds of ideas. People are frequently heard to express the view that there is a real conscience in each person.

We are indebted to Immanuel Kant for giving intuitionism scholarly respectability. The views, which Kant amplified and clarified, have for many years been popular underpinnings for the traditional humanist approach to ethics. Throughout his discourses, Kant exhibited a profound faith in reason itself. We need not attempt to follow the laws discovered in nature (naturalism), appeal to the higher authorities of religions, or reason from other worlds of reality. Through mediation and the exercise of pure reason, we can know what is right or wrong. "The moral life, as distinct from mere sentient existence, depends upon the employment of reason or rational will in the projection of its own purposes and upon the exercise of freedom in obedience to these purposes."[9] Titus made the following comment about Kant's views:

[9] William A. Banner, *Ethics: An Introduction to Moral Philosophy* (New York: Scribner, 1968), p. 99.

The moral law appears within man as a sense of *ought* or what is popularly called conscience. It is this sense of duty which originates through
man's creative intelligence. According to Kant, it is clear that all moral
conceptions have their basis and source in reason as a regulative principle in human affairs. They are recognized by the ordinary reason of
men as well as by reason in its more speculative activity. The true
object of reason is to produce a will that is good in itself. The pure idea
of duty or the moral law influences man, in so far as he is moral, much
more strongly through his reason than do the motives that have their
origin in the fleeting experiences of life.[10]

Stroh's review of leading American idealists revealed that, although the external world was accepted as objective, the "only morality worth having is one that is achieved by careful, coherent
thought."[11] The idealist believes that only the mind can know moral
values and establish order, harmony, and unity; empirical processes
cannot reveal moral truths.

If educational administrators are to be moral from the intui-
tional perspective, they must trust pure reason and disregard what
Kant referred to as inclination (the motives to act on the basis of
pleasure, human desires, happiness, and so on). Through rigorous exercise of reason, independent of such inclinations, the school administrator can discern either hypothetical or categorical imperatives.
Hypothetical imperatives do not involve the moral law but are guides
to action based upon given circumstances in the empirical existence.
"The hypothetical imperative is one in which a purposive end demands a means to attain that end."[12] The hypothetical imperatives
are conditional and the administrator is not duty bound to follow them.
The categorical imperatives, however, are expressions of the moral
law.

The categorical imperative is the voice of duty, the sense of "ought,"
the dictate of conscience, or the positive command which arises within
the morally sensitive person. It is *a priori* or derived from the reason
itself, and it is applicable to experience everywhere. This voice of duty
has reference not to what *is* but to what *ought* to be.[13]

What Kantian ethics demands is a very rigorously rational educational administrator who is obligated to act in conformity with the
moral law.

Revelation and Christian Ethics

Morality based upon divine revelation as a source of truth serves
as the standard of ethics for many persons. The principles of morality

[10] Harold H. Titus, *Ethics for Today* (New York: American Book Co., 1954), p. 140.
[11] Guy W. Stroh, *American Ethical Thought* (Chicago: Nelson-Hall, 1979), p. 114.
[12] Stephen C. Pepper, *Ethics* (New York: Appleton, 1960), p. 251.
[13] Titus, op. cit., p. 142.

may be received directly by chosen ones, as Moses received the Ten Commandments. The Book of Mormon was translated from divinely inspired golden plates, which Joseph Smith was led by the spirit to discover. The angel Gabriel revealed the Koran to Mohammed. Revelation for the Christian is in the life of Jesus as recorded by divinely inspired writings in the New Testament. Many scholars view Christianity as having considerable influence upon the moral philosophy of Western civilization.

Affirmed through Christian ethics is the great worth of human beings. Jesus proclaimed the idea of the supreme worth of every person to God.[14] Persons are of greater value than the most cherished traditions. "And he said unto them, the sabbath was made for man, and not man for the sabbath." As W. J. Henderson expressed it, "Jesus asserted the immense value of the individual."[15]

In the Sermon on the Mount, as recorded in Matthew, Jesus gave the essence of Christian ethics as direct imperatives to his disciples. The sermon begins with the beatitudes concerning the blessedness of humility, kindness, mercifulness, and purity of heart. Special mention is made of the blessedness of those who are persecuted because they are good, those who long to be good, and those who strive for peace. The Sermon on the Mount is a moving proclamation of Christian teachings about love, the commitments of marriage, prayer, the emptiness of materialism, the person's proper relationship to God, purity of thought, and other aspects of Christian ethics.

Love is one of the primary elements of Christian ethics. Knudson observed, "Love is clearly the chief of New Testament duties and virtues."[16] Beach and Niebuhr stated, "Here in the Sermon on the Mount, the enemy is counted among those to whom men have an obligation under the rule of God."[17] Niebuhr stated, "The ethic of Jesus is the perfect fruit of prophetic religion. Its ideal of love has the same relation to the facts and necessities of human experience as the God of prophetic faith has to the world. It is drawn from, and relevant to, every moral experience."[18]

The ethics of Christianity provides for the growth of human personality. According to this view, there is something in persons that will respond to patience, benevolence, purity, humility, and under-

[14]Georgia Harkness, *Christian Ethics* (Nashville, Tenn.: Abingdon Press, 1952), p. 57.

[15]W. J. Henderson, "Ethics," in James Hastings (ed.), *Dictionary of the Bible* (New York: Scribner, 1937), p. 242.

[16]Albert C. Knudson, *The Principles of Christian Ethics* (Nashville, Tenn.: Abingdon Press, 1929), p. 118.

[17]Waldo Beach and H. Richard Niebuhr (eds.), *Christian Ethics* (New York: Ronald, 1955).

[18]Reinhold Niebuhr, *An Interpretation of Christian Ethics* (New York: Meridian, 1956), p. 43.

standing compassion. Often overlooked in the discussion of Christian ethics is Jesus's great compassion for the downtrodden. He treated women as emancipated human beings (e.g., Woman at the Well, John 4:7–38) and was concerned with the suffering of people.

The educational administrator following Christian ethics must be obedient to a standard that, admittedly, is interpreted differently by different scholars. That standard is what we can know about the life and teachings of Jesus as compiled in the Bible. Many Christian moralists place love of others as the all-encompassing theme.

Utilitarianism and Ethics

The theory of utilitarianism is often referred to by moral philosophers as a revival of hedonistic thought. Early advocates of the utilitarian ethic were Jeremy Bentham and John Stuart Mill.[19] Bentham maintained that the basis of moral action is the balance of pleasure over pain. The end of moral action is the happiness of the community—the greatest happiness to the greatest number of people. Mill posited that the maximum enjoyment or pleasure with the minimum of pain is the standard of all morality. The primary basis of moral judgment is whether there is positive increase in pleasure and enjoyment over negative pain or misery. The aim of all leaders should be to increase happiness and diminish misery. Commenting upon Bentham's views, Banner wrote, "An individual acts properly and wisely, according to Bentham, only when he acts in a way that is productive of pleasure and free of pain, and he is prompted to act in this way only through the fact or expectation of pleasure or pain."[20]

The question arises immediately concerning the great variation in pleasures appreciated by people. Pleasure for some of us may inflict pain and misery upon others. Moreover, there is the widely accepted belief that persons are so flexible and pliable that some rather strange practices can be interpreted as pleasures. Therefore some criteria for interpreting pleasure are needed. Bentham produced the "hedonistic calculus" to describe the dimensions of pleasure or pain.[21] The discussion of these by Titus is as follows:

> Pleasures vary in: (1) *intensity*, whether they are strong or weak; (2) *duration*, whether they are lengthy or short in temporal existence; (3) *certainty*, or the degree of probability that they will occur; (4) *propinquity*, or nearness in time; (5) *fecundity*, or the chance that they will be

[19] See, for illustration of their works, Jeremy Bentham, *A Fragment on Government*, edited by F. C. Montague (London: Oxford University Press, 1931). First published in 1776. John Stuart Mill, *Utilitarianism* (New York: Dutton, 1951). First published in 1863.

[20] Banner, op. cit., p. 117.

[21] Titus, op. cit., p. 156.

followed by more of the same kind of sensations; (6) *purity,* or the likelihood that they will not be mixed with or followed by sensations of the
opposite kind (pain); (7) *extent,* or the number of persons who will be
affected.[22]

The administrator who follows the utilitarian school of ethics
should be primarily concerned with making decisions that will bring
the greatest pleasure to the greatest number of people. In determining this, however, the administrator must put it to the tests of intensity, duration, certainty, propinquity, fecundity, purity, and extent.
Some decisions that might seem to promote pleasure may be questionable from the calculus of *purity* because they could bring on unforeseen pains. Therefore what brings pleasures of the moment for
some may be of short *duration* and not meet the *purity* principle in
producing continued enjoyment of life without pain.

Thus, contrary to some subversion of the idea in modern society, utilitarian-oriented educational administrators would not appear
as shallow-thinking persons driven by momentary desires. In fact, they
would probably be rigidly opposed to many of the currently popular
"pleasures" of modern society.

Naturalism as the Ethical Standard

As discussed previously, individual interpretations of ethical
standards are unique and different. Therefore, even though many
writers may be referred to as naturalistic, there are unique differences among them. In view of the impact that the writings of American naturalists (e.g., John Dewey, William James) have had on
American education, they are discussed separately. Immediately following is a discussion of the naturalism generally associated with the
realist view of the superiority of the laws of nature. In commenting
upon the philosophical views of naturalism. Mann and Kreyche wrote:

> As to his teaching on man, the naturalist grants that man is unique
> among animals in ability and accomplishment but denies that he has a
> special place in nature. Between man and his animal ancestors there is
> only a difference of degree, not of kind. Consciousness, like any other
> phenomenon, can be described empirically, at least in its effects, and
> accounted for in terms of matter and organization of matter. Presup-
> posed by the naturalist is a theory of biological evolution that declares
> that nature in its evolutionary process regularly gives rise to operations
> and functions on newer and higher levels. Consciousness and thought
> are regarded as two such higher levels of operations. They have their
> sole cause in the organism in which they appear. Admittedly, thought
> and consciousness are distinct from any previous products of an evolv-
> ing nature, but the factors from which they arise are no different, ex-

[22]Ibid., p. 157.

cept for their particular organization, from the factors from which physical, chemical, and biological processes arise.[23]

Naturalists differ, however, in their identification with nature. Some of the early naturalists were heavily influenced by the Darwinian concepts of evolution and of the need to see human beings from the materialistic perspective. To view consciousness and thinking as more than the imprints of nature upon the mind might again open the Pandora's box of religious idealism from which the early realists were trying to escape.

The immutable laws of nature are the standards of morality for the naturalist. That which is good is in harmony with nature. In the struggle for existence, that which survives is good and that which fails or expires in the struggle is bad. Thus strength is the ultimate virtue.[24] Titus wrote the following about the views of Herbert Spencer concerning morality:

> Spencer exhibits an unshakable conviction that the natural laws of the evolutionary process itself lead in the direction of the good. As the individual improves physically, he is also passing from crude gregariousness to conscious sympathy and intelligent co-operation. The laws of nature are gradually bringing a harmony, so that acts which are good for the individual are also good for the group and for the race.[25]

Many naturalists are preoccupied with Darwinian precepts concerning the precariousness of nature, the survival of the fittest, and the struggle for existence. This includes the American naturalists such as Dewey, who are discussed later. However, individual naturalists approach the precariousness of nature somewhat uniquely and evolve very different standards of ethics. Nietzsche, who Durant described as the "child of Darwin and the brother of Bismarck," represents one of the unique interpreters of the moral laws of nature.[26]

Nietzsche's views reject Christian ethics. Rather than the humility, benevolence, and altruism emphasized by theological ethics, Nietzsche held that all human behavior could be reduced to the will to power. All living creatures, he said, are motivated in the struggle for existence by the will to power, which is the ultimate good. Out of the struggle for existence will come "supermen," who represent the highest morality. These "supermen" will set the standard of morality for those who have not reached the top. Nietzsche viewed democracy as being at cross-purposes with the natural morality.

[23] Jesse A. Mann and Gerald F. Kreyche (eds.), *Approaches to Morality* (New York: Harcourt, 1966), p. 289.

[24] Will Durant, *The Story of Philosophy* (New York: Washington Square Press, 1961), p. 401.

[25] Titus, op. cit., p. 171.

[26] Durant, loc. cit.

The naturalist-oriented educational administrator would subscribe to the view that if a natural struggle for existence is characteristic of the faculty and the students, good will triumph over evil. Competition among underlings in the organization, therefore, is to be encouraged. Morphet, Johns, and Reller described traditional, monocratic bureaucracy as based on such principles as "Maximum production is attained in a climate of competition" and "The image of the executive is that of a superman."[27] Shepard has also labeled administrators who operate from an extreme position of this ethic as following the "Primary Mentality."[28] Those who follow the Primary Mentality view life as mutual competition for everyone in the organization.

The Ethics of the American Experimentalists

In the works of William James, Charles Sanders Peirce, John Dewey, and other American experimentalists, or pragmatists, there is what many writers have referred to as a distinctly American moral philosophy. Peirce taught that values for living can be determined by the practical results observed from their use. James further developed the concept that the goodness or badness of an idea depended upon how satisfactorily it worked in practice.

Dewey was by far the most influential of the American naturalists. He embraced a scientific process for the verification of morality. Ethical values, he said, grow out of a person's interaction with the environment, in which value judgments are made. Thus they have no "other-world" or intuitive quality. The values develop from the process of reflective thinking or the experimentalist's interpretation of the "scientific method" in arriving at solutions to problems. For most experimentalists the ultimate determination of the moral existence is in the consequences of acts. Thus the principle of the morality of consequences becomes a very important guide to conduct.

Dewey is probably most renowned for his writings on the democratic ethic. Indeed, one can pick up few books about political systems or the educational process in which Dewey is not mentioned.

The naturalist views of Dewey and others have had broad application in American education. There has been a strong emphasis on the development of the democratic ethic. Bode, a leader in the experimentalist school, wrote the following:

> The question cannot be avoided by saying that the purpose of the schools is to develop individual capacity or talent, since this applies in some

---

[27] Edgar L. Morphet, Roe L. Johns, and Theodore L. Reller, *Educational Organization and Administration,* 4th ed. (Englewood Cliffs, N.J.: Prentice-Hall, 1982), p. 78.

[28] Herbert A. Shepard, *"Changing Relationships in Organizations,"* in James G. March (ed.), *Handbook of Organizations* (Chicago: Rand McNally, 1965), pp. 1115–1143.

sense or other to all schools of whatever kind. The task of the democratic school is to develop individual capacity with a specific reference. This reference is to the issue of democracy as a whole way of life. This reference to democracy is of a twofold kind. A democratic school may be expected both to give actual experience in democratic living and to foster intellectual insight, or understanding of the principle on which democracy is based and which gives it a distinctive character.[29]

If one could summarize the ethics of experimentalism for educational administrators, the obligation to democratically derived values would have high priority. The administrator would exhibit faith in the morality gained through the application of intelligence in the reconstruction of experience. The primary criterion for the moral life is the morality of consequence. The highest good is the cooperative, democratic application of intelligence in the reconstruction of experience. Thus the principles of ethics are derived from the rigorous application of reflective thinking concerning the consequences of actions.

Existentialism as the Basis of Ethics

As was discussed in Chapter 12, the philosophy of existentialism has influenced thought in many fields. There are, for example, existentialist theologians, existentialist educators, and existentialist social scientists. The writings of Søren Kierkegaard (the father of existentialism), Albert Camus, and Jean-Paul Sartre have been influential. Banner summarized the basic tenets of existentialist ethics as follows.

> Existentialism, simply expressed, is the ethics of self-affirmation. This affirmation is expressed as subjective inwardness (Kierkegaard) or freedom (Sartre) or lucidity (Camus). Consciousness is not a glass which simply mirrors endlessly what is given in awareness. Consciousness has its own being and its own concerns; it has its own way of asserting itself against the anonymity and vacuity of the world of objects and events. Existentialism is thus the ethical (and religious) dimension of phenomenology, presenting consciousness under the aspect of the intentionality of interest or passion. In this respect, existentialism opposes all forms of rationalism and objectivism which appear to reduce the life of reflection to a neutral account of experience and which do not account for individual life itself.[30]

The highly individualistic expressions of the conscience of existentialist philosophy militate against a systematic view of ethics. Mann and Kreyche stated the following:

> Our examination of ethics in existential philosophy has revealed that none of the philosophers considered had a systematic moral philoso-

---

[29] Boyd Henry Bode, *How We Learn* (Boston: Heath, 1940), p. 272.
[30] Banner, op. cit., p. 150.

phy; yet all were strangely obsessed by ethical problems. Notwithstanding their unwillingness to present things in an orderly fashion, they nevertheless have left a mark upon ethical thought as a whole. This obsession with ethics is actually linked with their principal concern, which is man himself.[31]

Existentialist writings often emphasize that the free expression of the self is good. Perhaps the highest of moral acts is when the person who makes a decision of conscience assumes responsibility for it. Moral strength is measured by the willingness of the person to stand by these freely expressed moral convictions regardless of the odds.

The existentialist administrators, therefore, must make their personal decisions, based upon their own conscience, concerning what is best for people instead of what might be best for business, education, religion, or other institutional areas of the society. If, after in-depth "soul searching," the administrator believes that certain practices in educational organizations are in error, a personal decision must be made. Having supporting data or the overwhelming support of parents does not matter where a practice is obviously wrong and needs to be corrected.

Emotivism: The Metaethics of Logical Positivism

The positivist's conclusion that value statements are impossible of empirical verification and, consequently, meaningless was discussed in Chapter 12. Where does this proposition leave one concerning personal and professional ethics? Ayer's *Language, Truth, and Logic* and Stevenson's *Facts and Values* are the two frequently cited sources in answer to this question.[32] Since ethical assertions can be said to be neither empirically verified as true or false, they are nothing more than expressions of the speaker's feelings, attitudes, or emotional preferences. Such terms as "good" and "bad" are merely the expressions of one's feelings.[33] The primary objective of what is known among analytic philosophers as metaethics is to clarify the language used in moral expressions.

For Ayer, however, it is not the business of philosophy to make moral judgments or formulate normative principles. Philosophy has no special competence to make moral judgments since its sole purpose is to seek clarification of conceptual issues by logical analysis. Once the philoso-

[31] Mann and Kreyche, op. cit., p. 578.

[32] A. J. Ayer, *Language, Truth and Logic* (New York: Oxford University Press, 1936); Charles L. Stevenson, *Facts and Values* (New Haven: Yale University Press, 1963).

[33] Mary Warnack, *Ethics Since 1900* (New York: Oxford University Press, 1978), pp. 53–61.

pher has discovered that moral judgments have only emotional meaning and that they cannot be proved or disproved, his work in ethics is,
for all practical purposes, finished.[34]

Emotivism simply reduces judgments made about professional
ethics to personel preferences. Values are viewed as pseudoconcepts
expressing individual feelings. The educational administrator does not
have, as guidelines to ethical behavior, an established set of verified
moral values. Any statements to this effect, such as "serving the
counseling needs to students is good" or "embezzlement is bad," are
cognitively meaningless, cannot be verified empirically, and are simply the subjective expressions of one's attitude or feelings. Hodgkinson characterized positivism or metaethics as a means of retreat from
the consideration of values.[35]

Other Expressions of Ethics

The authors have not discussed all the views of ethics found in
the literature on the subject. The object has been to describe briefly
some of the bases of ethics found frequently in the literature. However, we do want to mention some of the other views on the subject.

Much has been written about the possibility of a science of morals. From our view of what has been written, there appears to be no
clearly identified support for the proposition that there can be a science of morals. Most writers seem to agree that normative, or "ought,"
propositions cannot be verified empirically.

Most educators are, no doubt, familiar with *The Republic of Plato*
and other Greek contributions. Plato's two-world views constitute a
different form of intuition. Instead of deriving our ethical views from
pure reason (Kantian idealism), the ideal ethics are found in another
world. Through proper concentration of the philosopher kings, these
ideas can become known.

There are other variations of ethics. For example, there is much
discussion of situation ethics. This view was extolled in *Situation
Ethics* by Fletcher.[36] All moral principles are relative with the exception of love. Love is described as the ruling norm in situation ethics.
Another frequently heard view is that if one follows the law, one will
need no other ethics. Some persons claim to follow tradition as a standard. Others simply "follow the crowds," with whom they become in-
timately associated.

A very basic question, which administrators must answer indi-

[34]Stroh, op. cit., p. 213.

[35]Christopher Hodgkinson, *Towards a Philosophy of Administration* (New York:
St. Martin's Press, 1978), p. 122.

[36]Joseph F. Fletcher, *Situation Ethics: The New Morality* (Philadelphia: West-
minister, 1966).

vidually, is whether they will be (in Riesman's terms) "tradition-directed," "other-directed," or "inner-directed."[37] As is seen in the discussion that follows, the authors encourage the administrator to strive toward inner-directed ethics. In addition to this individual decision, there are some important professional concerns.

The Uses of Ethical Systems

The problem of achieving the moral life is too complicated to be directed by a computer programmed with all the answers for what is right and what is wrong in every aspect of human behavior. Administrators must continually make personal decisions on the basis of the rightness and wrongness of actions. Therefore they need to be very intelligent about the basis for these decisions. If one is to be judged intelligent about how personal moral judgments are rendered, a personal philosophy of morals is necessary. The formal study of ethics provides a basis for thinking through the alternatives available for the most intelligent act of all, the decision concerning one's personal basis for moral standards.

Some persons suggest an eclectic approach to assuring personal morality. Perhaps some thinking along this line may not be harmful. However, attempting the eclectic approach is almost sure to create personal conflict and a Dr. Jekyll and Mr. Hyde existence. How, for instance, could one possibly be personally committed to both the naturalism of Nietzsche and Christian ethics? These are very different moral philosophies and the standards that result from following them are different.

The moral standards of Kantian intuitionism and revelation have universally applicable features. The morality of the early naturalists was of the same quality because they were consistent with the unchangeable moral laws of nature. However, in such moral philosophies as experimentalism, utilitarianism, and existentialism persons are not assumed to be inevitably adaptive to a fixed moral law. In these systems the moral practices and principles are changeable and flexible.

The processes for achieving the moral answers are vastly different among the moral philosophies discussed. In intuitionism the confrontation of a moral problem is solved through secluded meditation or the exercise of pure reason. The Christian would approach the same problem through prayer and would attempt to apply revelations from God. The utilitarian would apply the hedonistic calculus and be heavily influenced concerning what actions would result in the greatest

[37] David Riesman, *The Lonely Crowd* (New York: Doubleday Anchor, 1953), p. 23.

pleasure to the largest number of people. The naturalist of the realist school would find the answer in the scientifically derived knowledge of the moral law of nature. Naturalists of the experimentalist school would be guided by an ordered reflective reconstruction of experience and by the morality of consequence and the values of the democratic society. An existentialist would appeal to the conscience and be guided by what is in the humanistic interests of persons exclusive of all other considerations. Positivists would disavow moral values as a basis of behavior.

In summary, these moral philosophies are different in the processes, and there are differences in principles of morality among them. However, for the most part, the advocates of these moral philosophies are similarly motivated to find and explain the moral action and the good life. The enthusiasm of a John Stuart Mill, a John Dewey, and an Immanuel Kant for their views is a quality that we may all learn to have for our own views. We need to decide for ourselves what the basis of our moral standard will be after prolonged examination of what we believe. When we reach this point, we will also have enthusiasm for morality in our personal and professional lives. We will have become more inner-directed than tradition-directed, or other-directed. Even if each of us were at this point, we would still need a professional code of ethics.

Personal Morality in the Practice of Educational Administration

When school administrators discuss their concepts of ethical behavior, the discussion frequently involves such terms as *trustworthiness, responsibility, loyalty, honesty, legality, personal productivity,* and *persistence.* Working hard at one's assigned tasks is more valued than laziness. Bravery in the face of strong pressures to stray from acceptable educational procedures is more valued than cowardice. Loyalty is more valued than treachery. Yet all of these valued concepts, which most educational administrators espouse, may present some very difficult moral problems. One such concept is loyalty.

Administrative Loyalty

The Nuremberg Trials brought out the moral problems associated with personal loyalty to superiors, to official orders, to the law, and to political parties. Problems associated with loyalty to persons were illustrated in the Watergate affair. In fact, loyalty to superiors has produced some very difficult problems of organizational morality in local school systems. As Appleby noted, by the nature of their positions, administrators frequently experience personal conflict between loyalty to persons and loyalty to organizations.[38]

Some unscrupulous administrators may attempt to use the concept of personal loyalty to force subordinates to make unlawful or unethical decisions. These subordinates may have family obligations that would place them in a weak position to disobey orders. Other autocratic-minded administrators use loyalty as a basis for disciplining persons for failure to follow top-level decisions.

On the other hand, as Appleby indicated, loyalty is essential for developing school organizations of quality. No organization could survive and be effective unless those in it held relatively strong feelings of loyalty to its common purpose and to other persons in the organization. The key appears to be whether the loyalties are to ideas, which can be defended as morally acceptable, and whether the loyalties are freely elicited. Thus the individual administrator is back to basic ethics or to the sources of moral standards, which were illustrated earlier. One may well defend loyalty to morally acceptable ideas that are widely shared in the educational organization and within the society.

Executive Responsibility

The authors stated previously that being a top leader in an educational organization heightens the need to assume responsibility for moral behavior and judgment. If allowed to go unchecked, immorality at the top of the bureaucracy soon corrupts the entire organization. Appleby used the office of the President as an illustration of the need to be morally responsible.

> For all the executive government—and indeed for the political government as a whole—the obligation to support integrity is greatest on the President and on his staff, who partake of his influence. The obligation is greatest at that point because any deviation there multiplies itself in levels below. Lower levels are more vulnerable, and on them there is a moral obligation in behalf of responsible government to bend to presidential guidance.[39]

School superintendents, college presidents, and their top executive assistants must assume moral responsibility. Otherwise, the undesirable effects of corruption present at the top will be multiplied many times within the lower reaches of the organization. To be responsible is to assume personal commitment to act in accordance with high moral standards.

On the other hand, responsibility is not limited to being of good

---

[38] Paul H. Appleby, *Morality and Administration in Democratic Government* (Westport, Conn.: Greenwood, 1952), p. 178.
[39] Ibid., p. 130.

character. Educational administrators are responsible for developing programs of quality for students. Through the board of education the people have placed responsibility on educators to carry out the educational function. To assume this responsibility is to be accountable. Those administrators who fail to assume their obligations of leadership are guilty of unethical conduct. Those who do not assume their obligations toward the education of students should experience the weight of conscience as heavily as they would for other more widely recognized crimes against the society.

This responsibility permeates all professional behavior in the educational system. It obligates us to protect the dignity and worth of people. Therefore, students should not be "written off" as educationally incorrigible. Students should not be willfully and purposefully discriminated against for whatever situation that may exist. Education should be defended against irresponsible public attacks. Teachers, students, and parents have every right to expect more than a "gutless wonder" at the head of the organization.

Yet responsibility for education is not wholly that of the educational administrators. The people share some of the responsibility, as do the students themselves; they cannot expect miracles. If the community, the state, and the nation do not uphold their responsibilities for the support of education, educational administrators may be unfairly held accountable. Therefore, administrators must constantly remind themselves, the board, and the clients of the limits of responsibilities that the school or college can assume. However, administrators must assume professional responsibility. In our modern, complex society, people look more and more to professional educators to exert leadership. Thus a very important responsibility is to lead the people into assuming their own obligations for education.

Educational leaders are responsible for leadership in forming policies conducive to quality, whether these policies are made by the local board, state board of education, legislature, or Congress. Moreover, educational administrators have the responsibility of seeing that educational government is consistent with democratic ideals.

Other Aspects of Personal Ethics

Several important dimensions of ethics were discussed previously. What the authors can include in this discussion of personal ethics is only illustrative of the much broader aspect of personal and professional ethics. A full discussion of all behavior seen as unethical by educators would be quite lengthy. However, before concluding, we mention a few other facets of moral conduct of school administrators.

Nepotism has always been a source of conflicting values. This involves any practices that would favor relatives in the job situation.

For example, the school superintendent or members of the board might award a contract to teach to a relative when other qualified persons had applied. Closely associated with this is the conflict of interest in which the officeholder benefits personally from his or her official actions. Such breaches of ethics must be guarded against. Because of the positions they hold, educational administrators will be shown many personal favors. Personal involvements may sometimes lead to the inability to discriminate clearly between the welfare of students and the welfare of those who would use the educational organization. Appleby observed in this regard that public officials should guard their social lives.[40]

Financial management is an area filled with the possibilities of criticism and the tarnishment of one's character. Many educational administrators have been dismissed because of criticism about the manner and method of receiving, accounting for, and spending money. Embezzlement is frequently referred to as the most "honest" crime people commit. Improper financial management can only lead to widespread loss of public confidence, which causes shortfalls of support for education.

Maintaining high moral character involves such attributes as truthfulness or intellectual honesty, living within the critical ethical norms of the society, and the general demeanor of the person. Within the culture are many customs, values, mores, and normative expectations of leaders. There is no way in a free society in which we can force people to accept us as leaders. We must win this leadership. George Homans wrote that the leader is the person who comes nearest to fulfilling the norms of the group.[41] Therefore when we accept a position as an educational administrator, our responsibilities for the way we act, dress, and talk go beyond friendship and family groups. We may violate the norms of the community, but if we do, we will not be accepted as a leader. Becoming an educational administrator without eventually gaining support in the community to lead is irresponsible.

Democracy as A Basis of Conduct

Appleby stated that democracy provides a sound basis of values for administrators.[42] That is, of course, consistent with the experimentalism of John Dewey, which was reviewed previously. If Appleby's premise is accepted, one must define democracy very succinctly. The reader will recall that experimentalism demands very rigorous application of the reflective thinking process by a group. This is not

[40] Ibid., p. 221.
[41] George C. Homans, *The Human Group* (New York: Harcourt, 1950).
[42] Appleby, op. cit., pp. 29–36.

characteristic of many pseudodemocratic decision-making groups. Appleby expressed his position as follows:

> For the purposes of this discussion, the administrative pattern of responsibility must be described as within existing social, political, and Constitutional structures and procedures. We begin by accepting democracy itself as the basic means by which values will be identified, pursued, and kept in moving balance. We accept for the present the conditioning social and political mores and structures and look within all these for the somewhat specialized pattern of administrative responsibility. This pattern in turn we relate to four central concerns. However these concerns arise, however they are compounded and proliferated in differentiated problems, they seem rather clearly to be essentially these: concern for the maintenance and development under modern conditions of a capacity for popular controllability; concern for method, manner, and equities humane and considerate of persons; concern for utilizing and nurturing an advancing, pluralistic civilization; and concern for provision and exercise of responsible and unifying leadership.[43]

Persons of different persuasions (e.g., intuitionism, existentialism, Christianity) would not accept the cooperative use of intelligence as a defensible basis of morality. In defense of his position, however, Appleby contended that pluralistic democracy is a process in which persons holding the different bases for morality can participate in the process of producing the public morality, which he saw as being of a higher order than private morality.[44]

Personal Development of Professional Ethics

What are some immediate steps open to educational administrators interested in developing their personal concepts in the field of ethics? Of importance is the need to study carefully the AASA code of ethics. This code is the result of the compilation of many years of experience and has had wide acceptance in the field. Consequently, it provides ready access to some basic normative expectations within the field of practice. Since knowledge of the law is an important resource for ethical behavior, beginning administrators should invest considerable effort in learning the laws governing educational programs. This should include knowledge of state and local regulations and policies, which in practice have the effect of law.

As has been emphasized previously, the code of ethics and the law are not substitutes for a personal moral philosophy. Helpful as they are in assisting one to understand the expected behavior of a profession, the statutes and codes of ethics will never substitute for a personal commitment to a moral philosophy. Life is too complex to live by a set of rules. Thus the student of educational administration

[43] Ibid., p. 219.
[44] Ibid., pp. 29–36.

will have to invest in diligent study for the development of his or her own philosophy of morals. This must include much reading and personal introspection in the formal study of ethics.

Perhaps of greatest importance is that one make a strong commitment to a high standard of ethics. Making such a personal commitment lays a very important cornerstone for ethical behavior.

ACTIVITIES/QUESTIONS FOR FURTHER STUDY

1. Make a list of situations describing what you and other experienced educators believe involve important questions of ethics. Would a thorough knowledge of the AASA code of ethics provide a guide for ethical behavior in each of the situations?
2. Ask well-experienced educators to lead a group discussion concerning acceptable ethical behavior. What did you learn from the discussion concerning the alternative bases of ethics (e.g., intuitionism, revelation, utilitarianism, existentialism, and so on) used by the participants concerning acceptable standards of ethics?
3. Review your college library for published cases available for use in instructional programs for educational administrators and select from among these those that have high relevance for administrative ethics. Conduct small group and class discussions of several of these selected cases and attempt to reach consensus regarding ethical administrative behavior in each case.

SUGGESTED READINGS

APPLEBY, PAUL H. *Morality and Administration in Democratic Government.* Westport, Conn.: Greenwood Press, Inc., 1952.

BANNER, WILLIAM A. *Ethics: An Introduction to Moral Philosophy.* New York: Charles Scribner's Sons, 1968.

FINDLAY, JOHN N. *Values and Intentions: A Study in Values Theory and Philosophy of Mind.* New York: Macmillan Publishing Co., Inc., 1961.

FULMER, ROBERT M. *The New Management,* 3rd ed. New York; Macmillan Publishing Co., Inc., 1982, Chapter 20.

GIROVETZ, HARRY K. *Beyond Right and Wrong.* New York: The Free Press, 1973.

IMMEGART, GLENN L., and JOHN M. BURROUGHS (eds.). *Ethics and the School Administrator.* Danville, Ill.: Interstate Printers and Publishers, 1970.

MANN, JESSE A., and GERALD F. KREYCHE (eds.). *Approaches to Morality.* New York: Harcourt Brace Jovanovich, Inc., 1966.

STROH, GUY W. *American Ethical Thought.* Chicago: Nelson-Hall Publishers, 1979.

WARNACK, MARY. *Ethics Since 1900.* New York: Oxford University Press, 1978.

PART FOUR

Socioeconomic and Political Influences Upon Educational Administration

T*HROUGHOUT THIS BOOK it has been emphasized that educational administrators should avoid concentrating upon internal organizational concerns to the disregard of the powerful forces in the environment. Educational administrators must wrestle with bewildering educational changes wrought by rapidly changing socioeconomic, technological, political, and professional conditions. In this part of the book the discussion focuses on the importance of understanding some of these conditions and of providing political leadership.*

Much of this part is devoted to the political arenas through which the pressures generated by societal trends inevitably find expression in educational policy. Finally, the discussion is focused on the exchanges of professional power as a result of the collective-bargaining movement in education. In Chapter 14 we discuss some of the important socioeconomic and technological developments that are influencing the practice of educational administration. Chapters 15, 16, and 17 are devoted to local, state, and federal political forces and the functions of interest groups. The collective-bargaining movement is discussed in Chapter 18, the concluding chapter of the book.

14

The Impact of
Societal Trends
on Education

THE ADMINISTRATION of education is not isolated from the influence of other forces of the society. Any strong force operating in the society will inevitably have an influence upon the educational process. In this chapter we examine some of these forces to illustrate their connection with education.

Far more important than knowledge of the developments discussed here, however, are those socioeconomic forces that are still in the future and unknown to us now. Educators must constantly "read" the forces influencing the society and predict how they may affect education. What are the forces at work in the nation, the continent, and the world that will change the society and eventually influence what we do in education?

At this writing, for example, the entire world has experienced an energy crisis. We have come to realize that all of what we have accomplished goes back to a fixed amount of energy. Without a substitute for fossil energy, many of our children are faced with starvation. The implications of the energy problem for education are far more fundamental than the struggle to raise additional funds to pay utility bills or procedures instituted to conserve electricity. Without

431

a large and continuing source of energy, the entire technological revolution will diminish and collapse.

Or consider the possibility that an endless source of cheap energy is discovered. How we use this new knowledge could be as ominous for humanity as the way technology was used to destroy humanity in wars, to pollute the environment, and to sentence large segments of the society to an urban slum. Thus a cure for the energy problem could be as important for educators as the prospects of again resorting to muscle power.

Urbanization and Education

In 1790 about 5 percent of the people of the United States lived in the cities. If past trends continue, the reverse may be true in the future. What is interesting about the growth of cities is the rate of urbanization of the population after 1870. From 1790 to 1890 the percentage of urban population rose from about 5 percent to about 35 percent. Between 1890 and 1980 this percentage more than doubled.

Many conditions were associated with the tremendous growth of cities. One obvious factor was the industrial revolution. The growth of commerce and industry made jobs available in the cities. The mechanization of farming produced a steady decline in employment on farms. There were, however, other magnets, which pulled people by the thousands into cities. To the young they offered "bright lights" and things to do. They were viewed as centers of cultural activities and learning. In reality, the institutions of the cities, including education, during the 1920s and 1930s were somewhat like Mumford's description of nineteenth-century cities, "They were responsible for most of what was good and almost all that was bad."[1]

The rapid growth of urbanization led to concentrations of industry, commerce, and people in some areas of the nation. However, Geruson and McGrath observed that the dispersal of the population to regions outside the central city boundaries, largely stimulated by the use of the automobile and other technological developments after 1915, was one of the most significant developments during the past generation.[2] This urban sprawl accelerated after World War II, producing great problems for educators in the central cities and resulting in the development of the *megalopolis,* which Goldfield and Brownell described as follows:

[1] Lewis Mumford, *The Culture of Cities* (New York: Harcourt, 1938), p. 144.
[2] Richard T. Geruson and Dennis McGrath, *Cities and Urbanization* (New York: Praeger, 1977), pp. 171–173.

The *Megalopolis* or *conurbation* composed of two or more metropolitan areas might cover hundreds and even thousands of square miles and cut across the boundaries of several states and scores of counties and other civil divisions. Perhaps the best single example is the highly urbanized region extending from Boston in the North to Washington, D. C., and Richmond, Virginia, in the South, and passing through New York City, Philadelphia, Wilmington, and Baltimore.[3]

The results of the 1980 census demonstrated the continued dispersal of the big city population to the surrounding areas. Small towns and suburbs in areas 25 to 100 miles from large cities had substantial increases in population during the 1970s—some grew at astronomical rates. Many large cities, however, showed an appreciable loss of population. Even where some cities increased in population the urban area surrounding them experienced a higher rate of growth during the 1970s. Consequently, the administrators and boards of some city districts are struggling with problems associated with the management of decline, whereas some suburban educational leaders are faced with the management of expansion. The enrollment decline for some of the larger city districts, such as Boston, Cleveland, Milwaukee, St. Louis, and San Francisco, surpassed 25 percent between the late 1960s and the late 1970s. Between 1967 and 1978, for example, St. Louis experienced a 37.4 percent enrollment decline.

Urbanization, Population Shifts, and Segregation

In his 1938 landmark publication, Mumford explained the culture of the cities as the continuation of events begun in European cities.[4] He led the reader back in time through the monstrous struggles of the industrial revolution and the medieval towns and described the influences of economic, religious, political, and other institutional leaders upon city life. Vivid portrayals of the nineteenth-century cities (e.g., unimaginable pollution, economic domination, urban slums, urban blight) are reminiscent of what one reads about the cities today.

In *The Urban Wilderness*, Warner confined his historical analysis of the forces, conditions, and consequences of urbanization to the American scene.[5] He traced at length the struggle between the protection of property rights of individuals and the human rights of people for a decent, healthful life. The development of zoning ordinances to protect the value of downtown commercial property was later used as the primary means to segregate the city by social status and race.

---

[3] David R. Goldfield and Blaine A. Brownell, *Urban America: From Downtown to No Town* (Boston: Houghton, 1979), p. 298.

[4] Mumford, loc. cit.

[5] Sam Bass Warner, Jr., *The Urban Wilderness* (New York: Harper & Row, 1972).

Technological developments brought new answers along with the creation of new problems.

The development of cheap steel and engineering advances brought the skyscraper as the symbol of progress along with a crush of people. Highspeed transit, bridges, viaducts, electricity, and other technological developments allowed the cities to expand. These developments when used as old answers, however, helped people to do the wrong things better. The automobile made urban development and so-called urban sprawl possible. It also placed new unmerciful demands upon land for streets, highways, superhighways, belts, and parking lots. Used to help people do what they wanted to do and could afford to do, the automobile and other technological developments further segregated the cities into poor and rich, not-so-poor and not-so-rich, black and white, and other segregated groups. Its use congested streets, took huge amounts of land, and polluted the air.

One theory of the ecological growth of American cities is that it followed variations of the *concentric-zone* concept. According to this view, cities grew and expanded radially from the central core, which was the familiar downtown business district. Encircling the central core was a transitional wholesaling and light-manufacturing area. The third circle was a low-class residential area. The next area consisted of heavy industry and workers' homes. Encircling this industrial area were single-family dwellings, commercial establishments (including shopping centers), and some high-rent apartments. Beyond the city boundaries lay the suburbs and urban sprawl. Another growth pattern is the *sector* concept in which each residential section (e.g., low-class, high-class residential) grows out like a slice of pie from the commercial core. These tend to grow along and are divided by railroads or major highways. A third theory of urban development is known as the *multiple-nuclei* model, which posits that the city grew outward from a number of distinct nuclei instead of from one central core. As Goldfield and Brownell suggested, even though these theories are different, there are important similarities in that "all assume the outward growth and development of the city; and all are based on the division of the city into areas of different land use."[6]

The concentric-zone theory was used by Lightfoot to explain the development of six different types of urban schools: inner-city schools, transitory schools, common-man schools, main-line schools, high-status schools, and private schools.[7] Except for the private schools, these schools serve different social classes, have different curriculum orientations, have different dropout rates, among other differences. For

[6]Goldfield and Brownell, op. cit., p. 13.
    [7]Alfred Lightfoot, *Urban Education in Social Perspective* (Chicago: Rand McNally, 1978), pp. 40–47.

example, the central city schools (approximately 50 percent of the total) serve lower-lower and lower-middle class families and experience a 50 percent dropout rate, whereas the high-status schools (3 percent of the total) serve the upper-middle and middle-middle class and have a dropout rate of less than 5 percent.[8] Like the concentric-zone theory of the ecological growth of a city, Lightfoot found that, starting with the inner-city schools and moving outward, the different types of public schools were located in concentric zones in the order in which they are named above.

As has been suggested the complex forces of urbanization produced cities that are segregated by social status, race, ethnic group, and other social and cultural qualities. Sirjamaki noted:

> According to the ecologists, such segregation is both voluntary and involuntary. Some groups choose to reside in certain neighborhoods because of social, economic, religious, prestige, or other reasons; others must live in neighborhoods because they are forced to by customs, laws, or their own poverty.[9]

Within recent years much of the literature about city life has concentrated upon involuntary segregation. The forces accompanying urbanization trapped the poor in low-grade residential areas. By studying the complexity of forces involved, one begins to appreciate the systematic relationships of elements in city life. Segregation in the cities is not explained by one simple cause. Indeed, forces in all the social institutions (religion, economics, education, family, politics) contributed to the process of segregation and the concentration of the poor in the inner city. Economics is a very important factor because many of the poor have no effective choice. Politicians made planning and zoning decisions, which were used either by them or by others to segregate further, drive up land prices, and rob a large segment of the city of a voluntary choice. Organized religion aided social segregation.[10] Of much concern to scholars is the possibility that the family itself contributes to a kind of culture-of-poverty that is passed from one generation to another. As the authors emphasized in Chapter 7, organized educational offerings without the active support of other institutions will not produce the system break necessary for change.

Numerous studies have shown that the schools have become segregated by race as whites move to the suburbs. Levine and Havighurst found that "central-city school districts have experienced a decline in middle-class and white enrollment that appears to be

[8] Ibid., p. 46.
[9] John Sirjamaki, *The Sociology of Cities* (New York: Random House, 1964), p. 202.
[10] Goldfield and Brownell, op. cit., pp. 161–164.

associated with actual or imminent desegregation."[11] Thus the older segregation of education by ethnic group, social class, religion, and race is being rearranged by the forces of urbanization. The result is segregation by race and economic status.

Influence of Urbanization on Education

The neighborhood-school tradition effectively segregates the school population according to the segregation in the city. For the past three decades this segregation of education by poor-white, black, middle-class, and upper-class neighborhoods has been expedited by the massive shifts of middle- and upper-class families to the suburbs and the migration of the poor to the city. This is not to say that the schools of the towns and countryside of rural America were not segregated by social class, race, and economic background. Even the smaller municipalities had their "milltowns" and "snobhills," and in the South there was *de jure* racial segregation before 1954. Moreover, as Hollingshead wrote about the fictitious Elmtown, segregation will be practiced within socially mixed schools.[12] Nevertheless, one of the problems of urbanization with which educators are confronted is how to educate children of segregated families. Nowhere is this more challenging than among the poor of the central city.

Education of the Poor or Desperately Disadvantaged. Teachers of the towns and countryside know the challenges of helping the few disadvantaged in their classes to achieve up to the standard of children from middle-class homes. Yet never in past history have educators faced the challenge of very large central-city schools full of the very poor, many of whom come from broken homes or homes where conditions do not motivate one to learn. There is substantial agreement that the severe climate of the inner-city families promotes educational disadvantages for many of the children. For example, the authors of a research report about selected inner-city families in England well expressed the sources of this educational deprivation.

> Early severance of mother-child contact and delegation of mothering to siblings affect the training of the young child in the achievement of age-appropriate behavioural standards. It does not stimulate language development. Children learn to adapt to situations of play in which only aggressiveness or withdrawal guarantee survival. The scarcity or total absence of toys and equipment suitable for play, and the absence of privacy allowing intensive play prevent the development of creative activities, powers of concentration, manipulative skills, and the re-enactment of experiences in imaginative role play. The absence of personal

[11]Daniel U. Levine and Robert J. Havighurst, *The Future of Big-City Schools* (Berkeley: McCutchan, 1977), p. 269.
[12]August B. Hollingshead, *Elmtown's Youth* (New York: Wiley, 1949).

possessions deprives children of a culturally essential experience, the care of valued objects. Limited patterns of parental hobbies and interests and family activities deprive children of many enriching experiences, and thus many behavioural competences useful in school and in society at large cannot be developed.[13]

Consistently reported in the literature is the view that an unusually high level of the students from inner-city families come to school educationally disadvantaged. This disadvantage consists of such characteristics as language inadequacies, visual or perceptual deficiencies, limited imagination, preoccupation with immediate gratification, low self-image, low motivation, restricted attention span, feeling of little control over events, antischool attitudes, readiness to resort to physical force, limited initiative, and a resulting achievement score below national norms.[14] Various special programs (e.g., adopt-a-school programs, alternative schools, Head Start, Follow Through, child–parent centers) have been employed to overcome the educational overburden of inner-city schools; however, too much may have been expected of the schools. Despite much expression about the failure of urban schools, there is reason for optimism. Based on a review of 1,200 studies, Clark and associates identified the characteristics and resources that have much promise of success in urban elementary schools.[15] For example, the things associated with success were leadership of the designated leader, staff development activities, clearly stated curricular goals, availability of special project funds, structured learning environments, high levels of parental contact with school, and so on.

Unreasonable Demands on the Schools.   The writers who have been most critical of what they claim is the failure of the public schools of the city make unreasonable demands. The concentration of poverty, extreme deprivation of the children, smoldering hostility, brutality, and hopelessness of the slums places very harsh tests upon all social institutions. Politics have failed to quell rampant crime and to protect the health and safety of citizens. Religion has not transformed the moral values of the urban jungle. The economic system has not provided work opportunities and the wealth needed by the people to escape their entrapment in the slums. Why, then, do we expect miracles of the schools?

Kimball suggested that these strong critics of the schools are,

[13] Harriett Wilson and G. W. Herbert, *Parents and Children in the Inner City* (London: Routledge & Kegan Paul, 1978), p. 185.

[14] Lightfoot, op. cit., pp. 205–206.

[15] David L. Clark, Linda S. Latto, and Martha M. McCarthy, "Factors Associated with Success in Urban Elementary Schools," *Phi Delta Kappan* 61 (March 1980), 467–470.

either through irresponsibility or improper knowledge of the process of education, making false assumptions about how to improve educational opportunity. He insisted that the schools cannot be studied or evaluated in isolation from the social institutions in interaction with them. He observed that "no anthropologist could accept the implicit assumption that the educative process is divorced from its social environment."[16] He further stated:

> If we took seriously all that the critics have said about education in recent years, we might give over to despair. The effectiveness with which our schools fulfill their mission has been questioned at many levels and from many sources. Some critics have hacked at bits and pieces of the education edifice, exposing deficiencies and nonsense; others have leveled charges that are broad, sensational, and frequently ill-informed, if not irresponsible; others have struggled to evolve constructive reforms. All, however, appear unconscious either of the social issues that are currently agitating our society or of the relation between these issues and the process of cultural transformation that has generated them. They seem not to understand the interdependence between school organization and educational process, nor even, perhaps, the unique solitary responsibility of the schools as the means of transition between the nuclear family and corporate organization.[17]

Problems Created for Urban Higher Education.   Urban colleges and universities are beset by inner-city problems similar to those described for schools. For example, the commuter college or university serving the central city has a clientele that is increasingly poor, many of its prospective students are more than one grade below national norms in reading, and the college or university faces a dwindling source of financial support. Many of the enrollees are part-time students who hold full-time jobs. Urban universities faced severe crises during the 1960s when students and community challenged them for lack of relevance, for being economic barriers to the urban poor, and for their support of the status quo in government. As Berube observed, "The urban university was viewed by students and community activists as being part of the national urban problem rather than a part of the solution."[18] Some colleges and universities—for example, City University of New York—faced rather tumultuous crises concerning the establishment of an open admissions policy, minority studies, and other demands. In 1970, City College of New York adopted an open admissions policy, including free tuition; however, this short-

---

[16] Solon T. Kimball, *Culture and the Educative Process* (New York: Teachers College Press, Columbia University, 1974), p. 102.

[17] Ibid., pp. 101–102.

[18] Maurice R. Berube, *The Urban University in America* (Westport, Conn.: Greenwood, 1978), p. 4.

lived policy was abandoned in 1975–76 when the city faced a severe financial crisis. In addition to the open admissions development, urban universities led in the development of urban studies programs, black studies programs, and the like. Feldman and Hursh noted that an additional problem of urban commuter colleges is the development of a sense of community among the faculty, students, and others affiliated with the college.[19] Finding solutions to the educational problems of urban universities is important to the nation because a large majority of college students attend urban colleges and universities, most of which are public.

Declining Enrollments and Financial Crises. As discussed previously, many large central-city school systems are experiencing declining enrollments. They are also facing opposition to property taxes. In November 1979, the school system in Chicago faced a financial catastrophe, and for several weeks the teachers did not know whether their checks would arrive on payday.[20] Duke and Meckel discussed the effects of depleted resources or, as they termed it, "the slow death" of San Jose High School.[21] City colleges and universities in inner cities are also experiencing severe financial problems. The effects of city conditions do not always emerge as a crisis—they also appear over a long period of deprivation and undernourishment.

Interaction and Cooperative Involvement of Education with Other Social Institutions. The great social problems resulting from urbanization cannot be solved if the basic institutions of the society have conflicting goals. Coordinated action toward common goals is essential. In a free society this coordination must be accomplished through the cooperative involvement of leaders from the various institutional sectors of the society.

> If we are to avoid a cultural Tower of Babel, we must somehow restore the oneness of our collective experience. We must deal with the pluralism and fragmentation of our collective experience *first*. Only then can we deal with the resulting pluralism and fragmentation of our collective value system—the core culture. Only then can we restore our sense of community.[22]

[19]Reynold Feldman and Barbara A. Hursh, "Establishing an Urban Commuter University: The Need for Community," in W. Franklin Spikes (ed.), *The University and the Inner City* (Lexington, Mass.: Lexington, Heath, 1980), pp. 1–20.

[20]Casey Banas, "The Chicago School Finance Catastrophe," *Phi Delta Kappan* 61 (April 1980), 519–523.

[21]Daniel L. Duke and Adrienne M. Meckel, "The Slow Death of a Public High School," *Phi Delta Kappan* 61 (June 1980), 674–677.

[22]H. G. Vonk, "Education and the 27-Year Countdown," *Phi Delta Kappan,* LIV (April 1973), 516.

Solving our problems will require the coordinated effort of leaders in all institutional sectors. These leaders and their followers must be committed to commonly held goals. Moreover, the success of the effort will depend upon the strength and vitality of the institutions. If they are weak, they must be strengthened. Jane Jacobs contended that schools alone will not be the salvation of the cities:

> It is even the same with schools. Important as good schools are, they prove totally undependable at rescuing bad neighborhoods and at creating good neighborhoods. Nor does a good school building guarantee a good education. Schools, like parks, are apt to be volatile creatures of their neighborhoods (as well as being creatures of larger policy). In bad neighborhoods, schools are brought to ruination, physically and socially; while successful neighborhoods improve their schools by fighting for them.[23]

The Rising Rate of Crime in Many Cities of the United States.   Again, the schools are somewhat reflective of the social problems of society in that the rise of criminal acts in schools and colleges is alarming. Marolla, Williams, and McGrath found that disorder and violence have increased dramatically in the schools and that the "incidence of violence, especially vandalism, increases with the size of school and urban density."[24] They stated that educators must attack this acute problem by reestablishing closer identification with students and their parents or guardians. Using data from the Bayh subcommittee survey of 750 school districts for a three-year period (1970–73), they pointed to the following trends:

(a) homicides increased by 18.5 percent;
(b) rapes and attempted rapes increased by 40.1 percent;
(c) robberies increased by 36.7 percent;
(d) assaults on students increased by 85.3 percent;
(e) assaults on teachers increased by 77.4 percent;
(f) burglaries of school buildings increased by 11.8 percent; and
(g) drug and alcohol offenses on school property increased by 37.5 percent.[25]

Much has been published about ways to stem and reduce this wave of violence. There is certainly much that educators can do: increase surveillance against vandalism, train teachers to cope with acts

[23] Jane Jacobs, *The Death and Life of Great American Cities* (New York: Vintage, 1961), p. 113.
[24] Joseph A. Marolla, J. S. Williams, and J. H. McGrath, "Schools: Antiquated Systems of Social Control," *The Educational Forum* XLV (November 1980), 77–92.
[25] Ibid., 77–78.

of violence, increase patrol of the facilities, and so on. However, as has been suggested repeatedly, education is only one of the institutions through which a solution can be found. A really workable solution to the crime problem depends on a cooperative institutional approach and particularly an economic system that offers full employment. This does not absolve educational administrators of responsibility for acting to reduce acts of violence in schools before the more encompassing social solutions are activated.

The New Technology and Beyond

Sometime before the dawn of written history, humans are presumed to have done everything by hand. In time these human forms began to invent tools to assist in their sustenance. These crude tools represented a great advance in technological thinking—the use of tools and machinery to supply the material needs of humanity. Yet we know today that the machine-intensive industrial revolution made the previous tool-age technology small in comparison.

Western civilization was plunged into the industrial revolution without much thought about its consequences for human life. Nevertheless, as we were thrust headlong into the machine-intensive world of the industrial revolution, many warned of the influence of technology on human values. Charles Dickens, for example, poured out his heartfelt concerns for the slum-dwelling poor of the cities, for the abuses of child labor, and for the inhuman qualities of schools. We have seen in the preceding section how technology was a primary force in urbanization. In retrospect we can see that even though machines supplied people's material needs, the industrial revolution addicted them to machines and made them, to some extent, slaves of technology. The machines that provided for human wants exacted a price.

As we rethink machine-intensive technology, however, we are impressed that it provided a largely physical challenge. Near Talcott, West Virginia, stands an imposing statue of the legendary John Henry, the steel driving man, symbolizing the adversary relationship between machine power and muscle power during the 1870s. The primary fear of laborers for many years has been that machines would rob them of a means of livelihood. What a change of events from the days of human development when tools helped meet human needs rather than threaten human deprivation. Yet the great challenges of the machine technology have been superseded by the new technology. We turn now from the machine-intensive society of the industrial revolution to the human struggle for control over what is being created.

Problems and Promises of the New Technology

By the new technology we mean the very rapid developments in automation and computer technology and their application to many aspects of human existence. As Susskind observed,

> Whereas the first Industrial Revolution saw machines put in place of animal and human muscles, the Second Industrial Revolution began the use of machinery for some of the functions performed by the senses and the human mind.[26]

Many scholars have been busy attempting to conceptualize in the brain-intensive technology and what the prospects are for the future.

Many fear that the new technology is moving society ever closer to Huxley's *Brave New World*.[27] Ellul advanced the opinion that we have already lost the opportunity to control science for the advancement of humanity and that, indeed, we may already be at the mercy of the monster.[28]

In *The Children of Frankenstein* Muller wrote that people still may exercise effective choice; however, he cautioned that people must critically assess their value systems.[29] Like most other aspects of life, technology is not inherently good or bad. The question is whether people, who are capable of following alternative values, choose to live by those that will allow technology to elevate or to destroy humanism.

Although the so-called student revolution of the 1960s was based on numerous conditions, one important target of the protest was the presumed dehumanizing influence of technology. Probably in the minds of many were thoughts of the destructive force of the hydrogen bomb. Would the computer eventually take charge and signal the final dehumanizing act? Eventually some came to see that the environment was being made uninhabitable by unrestrained technological developments, such as the automobile, and by the great unrestrained dumping of chemical and human wastes. Finally, as Burke suggested, there were ominous changes in human values.[30]

Educational Implications of the New Technology

One of the functions of schooling is to help the young child make the transition from the very familiar world of family and friends to

[26]Charles Susskind, *Understanding Technology* (Baltimore: Johns Hopkins University Press, 1973), pp. 33–34.

[27]Aldous Huxley, *Brave New World* (New York: Harper & Row, 1932).

[28]Jacques Ellul, *The Technological Society* (New York: Knopf, 1964).

[29]Herbert J. Muller, *The Children of Frankenstein* (Bloomington: Indiana University Press, 1970).

[30]John Burke (ed.), *The New Technology and Human Values* (Belmont, Calif.: Wadsworth, 1972).

the big, changing, technologically oriented corporate society. The realities of this task are becoming ever more complex because of the changes wrought by the new technology.

> Thus, automated machines can mine coal, pick cotton, cast and finish engine blocks, sort bank checks, roll aluminum, grade oranges, and weave cloth. Computers are devices which rapidly perform traditional human tasks involving experience, memory, analysis, logic, and decision making. Such devices now can diagnose symptoms for the physician, research a case for the lawyer, read envelopes for the postman, design a plant for the architect, prepare war and defense plans for the military, screen volunteers for the Peace Corps, and keep inventory for the merchant. These machines are being "taught" to translate languages, compose music, play chess, transcribe speech, and "see" objects; already they correct their mistakes and identify trouble spots in their mechanisms.[31]

Venn pointed to some figures showing displacements in the work force. For example, automatic elevators displaced 40,000 elevator operators in New York City. Machine displacement reduced jobs in coal mines tremendously, from 415,000 in 1950 to 136,000 in 1962. Computers do the work of millions of clerical personnel in banks, transportation, government, and other organizations and agencies. Venn further observed, "The full impact of the new technology has been slow to register on the American consciousness. To date, the instances of 'technological unemployment' are like the tip of an iceberg: the difficulty of appreciating what is below lures many into believing we can sail blithely ahead without changing course."[32]

The ever-changing world of work demands that persons be able to undergo retraining for new positions and responsibilities as the old are displaced. Some authorities feel that this places greater emphasis upon general education for personal flexibility. Moreover, this need for retraining has resulted in demands for continuing education and a commensurate extension of educational opportunities throughout life.

The so-called knowledge explosion, and its forecasted continued expansion, has very important implications for educators. One obvious implication is the need for continuous curriculum adaptation and change. Another is the need for better understanding of how instructional programs can be structured.

There has been strong advocacy from numerous quarters for the application of technology to the teaching process itself. In *The Technology of Teaching,* B. F. Skinner claimed that mechanical and elec-

---

[31] Grant Venn, *Man, Education, and Manpower* (Washington, D.C.: American Association of School Administrators, 1970), p. 27.

[32] Ibid., p. 28.

trical devices could provide better reinforcement for learning than a person.[33] There have been strong demands for large scale computer-assisted instruction, with the prediction by some that someday the teacher would become obsolete. Most advocates for strong emphasis upon technology of instruction are of the behaviorist or operant conditioning school of educational psychology. Educational psychologists of other persuasions feel that the new technology may be as unwisely used in education as it has been in some other sectors of society, except that in education, the consequences for society would be even more severe.

Another very important concern is the direction of the new thrust for knowledge. According to some writers, too much knowledge has been developed in areas that might further dehumanize society, and there has not been enough emphasis on knowledge about people. Thus within recent years many have worked to increase interest in and emphasis upon humanistic education.

Those who held to the view that we were experiencing a process of dehumanization gained many followers during the 1960s. This reaction against technology was spearheaded by the student revolutions. The students called attention to the progressive pollution of the air we breathe and the water we drink. Their strong campus protests called to the attention of the nation how much was invested in research on college campuses to produce new, inhumane devices for war and destruction.

The ecology movement became a powerful political influence. In nearly every town and city of the United States the politicians have listened to leaders of ecology-minded people, who have become a force to be reckoned with in making policy. In time the feelings about the dehumanizing influences of technology found expression in education.

One modern expression of humanism, which may be viewed as a very strong reaction against the dehumanizing influences of technology, is existentialism. Existentialists led in the popular emphasis during the 1970s upon humanizing the process of education. This is not to say that all educators and others who gave expression to this movement are existentialists. Many others—experimentalists, idealists—have been an important part of this emphasis upon humanism.

Patterson specifically warned about the possible dehumanizing consequences of a technology of education. "But the danger of technology in education is a real one, and its real danger lies in the fact that while it may produce technically skilled individuals it cannot produce free, reasoning, responsible individuals."[34]

---

[33] B. F. Skinner, *The Technology of Teaching* (New York: Appleton, 1968).
[34] C. H. Patterson, *Humanistic Education* (Englewood Cliffs, N.J.: Prentice-Hall, 1973), p. 16.

As a result of a four-year study of education in which he visited over 100 schools, Silberman advocated renewed emphasis upon humanizing education. He observed, "More important, education should prepare people not just to earn a living but to live a life—a creative, humane, and sensitive life. This means that schools must provide a liberal, humanizing education."[35]

If there is a lesson to be learned by educational administrators from the humanist thrust, it is that the humanizing purposes of education are of critical importance. The critical norms of schools and colleges should facilitate and continuously elevate above all else individual dignity. In all aspects of policy development and decision making the person is to be valued as a human being. Human dignity and worth is a precious value as is reaffirmed in our most basic documents.

One encounters numerous conflicting views concerning the eventual impact of the new educational technology. Previously discussed was the view that humanistic values would suffer. These fears are frequently stimulated by extreme predictions that teachers are obsolete and that machines will assume the entire process of educating. Shostak wrote, "synergistic linkage of communications and computer capabilities makes possible bookless libraries, paperless news (teletext), teleconferencing, portable language translators, and campusless and professorless universities—among myriad other mind bogglers."[36] Obviously there is the possibility that educational technology may be used to deschool and dehumanize the educational process. The authors, however, believe that the new wave of educational technology will assist and facilitate the teaching process and that schools and colleges will not go out of style as places for important socialization functions.

All too often the fear is voiced that with the rise of technology the schools will become barren, humorless places with children pushing buttons all day. A more inviting prospect is that the technological assistance will assume its proper role of freeing human beings to do the things to which they are particularly well suited—like loving, laughing, caring, and listening—while the onerous, deadening tasks are taken over by mechanical equipment. . . . The real task in the next wave of educational technology will be to find those aspects of teaching and learning which are uniquely suited to being handled by machines and to help teachers identify the skills they have which can only be performed by real, live human beings.[37]

[35]Charles E. Silberman, *Crisis in the Classroom* (New York: Vintage, 1971), p. 114.

[36]Arthur B. Shostak, "The Coming Systems Break: Technology and Schools of the Future," *Phi Delta Kappan* 62 (January 1981), 357.

[37]Dwight W. Allen and Lawrence N. McCullough, "Education and Technology: The Changing Basics," *Educational Technology* 20 (January 1980), 49.

Technology Based on the Biological Revolution

The new technology may well pale in significance in comparison with the potential developments in the biological sciences based on the discovery of the structure of the DNA molecule, the double helix. Anxieties are already high concerning the cultural impact of the creation of new life, cloning, and so on.

Coulson pointed to the close relationship between scientific discovery and the technological development that resulted in the great industrial progress after 1900.[38] Science, according to Coulson, furnishes the fundamental knowledge upon which modern technological developments are realized. He defined technology as "the concentrated, relentless study of the ways in which things may be made, or changed: or [how] the new knowledge of science may be pressed into human service."[39] The biological revolution in genetic research is thought by many observers to be connected principally to medical technology, agricultural technology, and other fields closely associated with the biological sciences. However, one may rest assured that this technology will not be restricted to miracle cures and the breeding of super cows. The power of parents to control the color of their children's eyes and the shape of their bodies foretells significant cultural changes and the possibility of direct influence upon the field of education. The educational impact of this is, of course, a development about which one may only speculate now.

The Shifting Moral Climate of Politics

The United States has gone through several periods of political scandal followed by reforms. As referred to elsewhere in this book, the pens of the muckrakers at the turn of the century initiated a governmental reform movement that greatly influenced politics. This movement had a strong influence upon the governance of education. These journalists exposed unscrupulous politicians, bankers, industrialists, and others who acted for their own interests at the expense of the public interest. Ida M. Tarbell's "History of the Standard Oil Company," Upton Sinclair's *The Jungle,* David Phillips' "The Treason of the Senate," and Lincoln Steffens' "The Shame of the Cities" are examples of these exposés.

Most historians credit the work of the muckrakers with adding much thrust to governmental reform and stimulating the passage of social legislation preventing child labor, shortening working hours,

[38]C. A. Coulson, *Science, Technology and the Christian* (Westport, Conn.: Greenwood, 1978).
[39]Ibid., p. 17.

and improving working conditions. There was a strong movement to democratize government. Laws soon were passed to place greater control upon commerce and industry.

The movement toward governmental reform, with its emphasis on the unscrupulous aspects of business and politics, had some aspects detrimental to education. Many citizens became predisposed to judging politicians as unprincipled and self-aggrandizing; this predisposition may indeed have created a long-lasting and almost inherent credibility problem for public officials, who, of course, also operate the public schools and colleges.

Because any serious governmental scandal is likely to influence public opinion about all public officials, educational administrators may well be concerned about effects of the Watergate affair and the Abscam revelations. The question is not whether these scandals will affect the administration of colleges and schools but rather how they will affect them. How can educational administrators provide leadership in the reaction to public scandals to optimize conditions for better education and minimize overreactions that would be harmful to students?

Speculation about political backlash to scandals is hazardous, to say the least. Some believe that the presidency has been weakened and that the Congress has become stronger than it has been for many years. If this shift in power occurs, there will be a long period of readjustment of national power, and possible consideration of the parliamentary system. Also related is the move for congressional reform and further democratization of the Congress. Any shift in the traditional power relationship is, of course, of much importance to educational administrators interested in federal funding of education.

There will be continuing and persistent demands for policies of openness. The demand for openness could result in more stringent "government-in-the-sunshine" laws. These laws have already been passed in several states, and there will be strong pressure for national legislation. The Congress has established sanctions against educational organizations unwilling to open student files for the inspection of parents. As a result many schools and colleges have had to revise their practices.

Of much interest to educators, however, was the ascendancy of ideology on the political right and the election of Ronald Reagan as President. The political right supporting Reagan consisted of power groups with somewhat conflicting interests: for example, neoconservatives, old right, new right, GOP establishment, and religious right.[40] The priorities of most of these groups have involved economic policies, reduction of governmental interference, and the support of free enter-

---

[40]"The Right: A House Divided," *Newsweek*, XCVII (February 2, 1981), 59–63.

prise principles. However, the religious right "has focused largely on social and moral issues including abortion, homosexuality, busing, school prayer and a defense of traditional family values."[41] If this new political surge on the ideological right succeeds in its efforts to change public policies, it will have great influence on how schools and colleges are managed.

The Civil Rights Movement

In 1948 President Truman proposed the enactment of civil rights legislation. However, Congress did not pass a major civil rights act until 1957, which was three years after the 1954 decision of the Supreme Court. The Civil Rights Act of 1957 prohibited action to prevent citizens from voting in national elections. It also created a Civil Rights Commission and established a Civil Rights Division in the Department of Justice. Major civil rights acts were passed in 1960, 1964, 1965, and 1968, and covered many areas of discrimination, such as public accommodations, employment practices, public school attendance, housing, and loans.

What started as a movement to prevent acts of discrimination and bring down racial barriers in the South became a generalized movement throughout the nation. One aspect of the movement involved discrimination because of sex. Leaders in the "women's liberation" or feminists' movement have used the legal machinery established by civil rights legislation to seek equality for women. Another aspect of the civil rights movement involved Hispanic groups. Americans are also aware of the American Association of Retired Persons, the Gray Panthers, and other politically active groups interested in the rights of senior citizens. Strong sentiment for the rights of students was generated by the movement during the 1970s.

The problems associated with the civil rights movement have greatly increased the involvement of educational boards and administrators in legal action. As discussed in Chapters 3 and 4, the courts have rendered decisions about a wide range of educational procedures. There is much action concerning the legal rights of students, teachers, parents, and others.

The history of the rights of women is illustrative of the difficulties of promoting cultural change in the society. Although Americans are very conscious today of the pressure for equal opportunities for women, a perusal of library shelves will reveal that this had been an issue waiting for political action for many years. Even though the slaves were given full rights of suffrage after the Civil War, women

[41] Ibid., 63.

did not win this right nationally until 1920. The nation has been in the midst of the so-called new feminist movement. Strong political movements seem inevitably to encounter opposition, and the women's liberation movement is not an exception to this observation. Strong opposition has emerged to such policies as the adoption of a proposed equal rights amendment (ERA) and the right to abortion. This opposition seems to be a generalized movement that may oppose many other aspects of civil rights demanded by some women's groups.

The civil rights movement has profoundly influenced the way educational organizations are administered. Educational administrators have had to establish affirmative action programs to assure that people are not discriminated against in employment practices. They encounter problems of equality of men and women in such areas as sports activities. Parents now are bringing suits in behalf of pupils, and due process in the disposition of pupil behavior problems has taken on new meaning.

One obvious influence of the civil rights movement is in curriculum and instruction. Instructional materials have been revised and rewritten to eliminate discriminatory portrayals concerning race, ethnic minorities, or sex. Minorities have demanded a variety of special programs, such as black studies programs. Schools, colleges, and universities have experienced strong pressures to eliminate sex bias in all aspects of their programs and administrative procedures. Barnett and Baruch probably expressed the general sentiment of leaders for women's rights when they wrote, "the schools are viewed by many not only as potential agents of social justice but also as in part responsible for the present difficulties women face." [42]

Influence of the Economic System

Economics has traditionally had a pervasive influence on American society. We have described how the industrial economy and new technology contributed to great population shifts, urbanization, and other consequences. And we have discussed how these changes in the society have directly influenced the administration of educational organizations. The economic sector also has had a direct influence upon the operation of schools and colleges. The discussion here will touch upon only a few of the many aspects that could be analyzed.

The Dow-Jones averages, wholesale price index, and the Federal Reserve discount rates may seem by many educators to be far removed from teaching first grade children to read or teaching college

[42] Rosalind C. Barnett and Grace K. Baruch, *The Competent Woman* (New York: Irvington, 1978), p. 108.

students freshman English. On the other hand, these and other economic barometers indicate business conditions that vitally influence what goes on in the first grade and in the beginning freshman English course. Educational funding has been reduced by the growing inflation of the 1970s, not to speak of the effect that the unemployment–inflation dilemma has had on the well-being of families. The economic system has an incalculable influence on the educational process and in ways difficult to predict. As a specific illustration, Cox discussed how, during the 1960s and 1970s, large numbers of college graduates could not find employment and decided to continue in college for advanced degrees.[43] The result was a glut of highly educated men and women in the labor market.

One problem that has a vital influence upon the opportunity for children and youth to obtain an education is the great inequality in income, resulting in poverty or near poverty for many families. As was discussed previously, educating the children of the inner city where there is a concentration of poverty is a very difficult task in comparison to educating those in affluent communities. Conditions in the economic system are obviously important constraints upon educational organizations. Another aspect of economic activity involves the direct influence of business organizations upon societal values. Concerning this point, Kaysen wrote:

> The mass media, newspapers, magazines, television, radio, are the great teachers in our society, far more pervasive in their reach and far more persistent in their influence than school and church. A major part of their content, verbal and pictorial, is explicitly "sales talk"; the whole of it is shaped by the sales purpose that is their essential aim. The words, slogans, pictures, symbols, jingles have one major message: consumption is happiness.[44]

As discussed in Chapter 12, the corporate society has represented different views of free enterprise, such as classical liberalism and new liberalism; but classical liberalism has been the mainstay ideology of business. That these views should become infused in the practice of education is of little surprise. Some of the current pressure for freedom of choice emanate from classical liberal thinking. One of the chief advocates for the freedom of choice in education is Friedman who, among others, has advocated a voucher system for funding edu-

[43] William A. Cox, "The U. S. Economy in the Eighties," in Nake M. Kamrany and Richard H. Day (eds.), *Economic Issues of the Eighties* (Baltimore: Johns Hopkins University Press, 1979), pp. 73–74.

[44] Carl Kaysen, "The Business Corporation as a Creator of Values," in Sidney Hook (ed.), *Human Values and Economic Policy* (New York: New York University Press, 1967), p. 213.

cation.[45] Spring is among several educational historians who has expressed the opinion that schools are primarily structured by corporate interests to serve corporate interests.[46] Private foundations established by corporate interests have sponsored many programs in colleges and schools that became permanently funded by local, state, and national governments.

Corporations have for many years sponsored programs aimed at solving societal problems in which educational programs at all levels have been prominently represented. Koch has suggested a renewed effort by corporations to make an impact on the social problems of the society, and he has contended that educational organizations, especially primary and secondary schools, should be given high priority.[47]

In a study reported in 1927 Counts found a high representation of businessmen on boards of education in the United States,[48] and, as indicated in Chapter 5, more recent studies have shown that this pattern persists. Some object to the assumption that high representation of businessmen on school boards means that schools are necessarily influenced to accept normative practices from the economic sector. On the other hand, Callahan's documentation of the adoption of business practices in educational administration indicates that the assumption made by Counts has some validity. In his study Callahan found that the adoption of many of these practices was not voluntary.

> So I was not really surprised to find business ideas and practices being used in education. What was unexpected was the extent, not only of the power of the business-industrial groups, but of the strength of the business ideology in the American culture on the one hand and the extreme weakness and vulnerability of schoolmen, especially school administrators, on the other. I had expected more professional autonomy and I was completely unprepared for the extent and degree of capitulation by administrators to whatever demands were made upon them.[49]

Political and business leaders provided the principal thrust for the accountability movement in education. It certainly was not fueled by teachers and educational administrators. Accountability emerged during a period in which there were strong emphases in industry to maximize economy and production. Accountability, simply put, was thought to show the cost effectiveness of education just as on the assembly line.

[45] Milton Friedman, *Free to Choose: A Personal Statement* (New York: Harcourt, 1980).

[46] Joel Spring, *The Sorting Machine* (New York: David McKay, 1976).

[47] Frank Koch, *The New Corporate Philanthrophy* (New York: Plenum, 1979).

[48] George S. Counts, *The Social Composition of Boards of Education* (Chicago: University of Chicago Press, 1927).

[49] Raymond E. Callahan, *Education and the Cult of Efficiency* (Chicago: University of Chicago Press, 1962), preface.

The Politics of Population and Demographic Changes

For many years nations have engaged in a heated controversy concerning the ethics of population control. Faced with the growing realization of the Malthusian specter of populating ourselves into starvation, advocacy for population control grew significantly during the 1950s and 1960s. Statistics on world population growth were alarming, to say the least, particularly with many persons already starving. This raised the very important question of how well the nations could cope with the food problem, not to speak of housing, schools, and other necessities. Discussing the problem of population growth, Morse stated:

> It is hard to understate pressures that governments—especially in the developing world—will have to confront as a result of the magnitudes involved in population increases. The world's population, which was about 3 billion in 1960, reached 4 billion by the mid-1970's and will exceed 5 billion by 1990, regardless of how effective fertility control policies may be. Depending upon how rapidly fertility rates fall and when a targeted net reproduction rate of 1.0 is achieved, the world's population will likely be stabilized somewhere between 8 and 14 billion by the end of the next century. The difference between these two estimates—6 billion persons—is enormous, representing twice the total population of the world two decades ago.[50]

Hauser described the acceleration in the rate of the world population increase as follows:

> It took most of the time humankind (or close relatives of humankind) has been on the earth, perhaps up to 4 million years, to reach 1 billion people. This is the estimated number of total world population in about 1800. It required another 130 years to add a second billion persons, the estimated world population in about 1930. It took only another thirty years for world population to add a third billion—it was 3 billion in 1960; and it took only an additional fifteen years to add a fourth billion, for world population reached 4 billion in about 1975.[51]

The controversy over population control has become a value conflict. Many religious leaders have leveled strong attacks upon the establishment of national policies favoring population control. For sev-

[50] Edward L. Morse, "Population and World Politics," in Georges Tapinos and Phyllis T. Piotrow (eds.), *Six Billion People* (New York: McGraw-Hill, 1978), pp. 7–8.
[51] Philip M. Hauser, "Introduction and Overview," in Philip M. Hauser (ed.), *World Population and Development* (Syracuse: Syracuse University Press, 1979), p. 3.

eral years the controversy has raged over the use of contraceptives as public policy. As in the case of all great cultural debates, people participating in the issue have had to deal with cherished values. This was particularly true of the battle to legalize abortion as a means of controlling the population and preventing unwanted births. Entering the fray were leaders in the women's liberation movement who asserted that a woman's body was her own and that she should have freedom of choice; otherwise, women would continue to be slaves of the state, a man, or others. Against this expressed human right was what many churchmen asserted was the dignity of human life itself. This, of course, involved the deep philosophical, medical, and legal question of when human life begins.

As a result of the population control movement, the United States has for several years experienced a declining birthrate and, consequently, declining school enrollments. To predict what influence declining enrollments will have upon education is hazardous. First of all, one must consider demographic trends other than birthrates. As has been noted, some states of the nation have continued to grow, whereas other states have experienced continuing population declines.

In school districts experiencing a declining school enrollment, administrators have had to make appropriate adjustments. For example, personnel policies had to be changed in terms of a surplus of teachers coupled with a loss of financial resources. Thus some difficult decisions had to be made about who stays and who goes.

School district administrators must also be responsive to changes in the demography of the district. In the section on urbanization, massive population shifts were discussed. When areas of a city are "invaded" by persons different from the existing population or when people move out of areas, these movements change the community served by the schools and involve commensurate changes in political leadership, economy, and social norms.

Changing age statistics are another important demographic trend. Statistics show that the population has grown proportionately older since 1900. In 1900 the statistics indicated a preponderance of youth and few aged. Increases in life expectancies have radically changed this picture. Moreover, the age of the population varies greatly among the school districts of the nation. For example, certain popular retirement areas may have large numbers of aged persons. In the past educators have not been as responsive as they should have been in providing adult education programs of interest to older persons.

Demographers have demonstrated that one may, as expressed by Zito, "connect population change with social change and with the emergence of new definitions of social problems."[52] For example, street crimes tend to be committed more frequently by males under twenty-five years of age; consequently, crime rates may be affected by changes in the preponderance of males under twenty-five. Differences in densities of population affect social problems.

The divorce rate has increased in the United States throughout this century. As educators know, divorce can be a traumatic experience for the children involved and influence their pursuit of an education. As we have already discussed, population shifts have completely changed the clientele of schools and colleges of large cities. The influx of millions of Hispanic and Asian refugees and illegal aliens into the United States since the early 1950s placed severe burdens on school systems in some states. For example, the 1980 "boatlift" from Cuba resulted in the immediate enrollment of thousands of Spanish-speaking children in the Dade County, Florida, school system. The high birthrate and poverty conditions in the developing nations foreshadow a continued "entrant" or immigration problem for the United States and additional demands on the educational systems signaling new ethnic problems for educators and additional financial burdens for the school districts affected.

New Problems of Ethnicity

Americans often forget that they are part of everyone in the world. We came voluntarily from many nations, races, and cultures. We came as refugees from religious, political, and economic repression. Some of us came as slaves and indentured servants. Many of us came because we were hungry, had committed criminal acts, or wanted to escape from some situation. We came by the millions, bringing our institutions with us and establishing ghettolike communities to preserve them. About 3 million of us immigrated in the decade from 1845 to 1855, which was three times what the immigration had been before national independence. A huge number of immigrants had arrived by 1860. Most of those who came were desperately poor. The world had never seen anything like it.

Of considerable importance is that the immigrants came for mixed reasons. The process of assimilation was very different for people who were motivated differently. Whether through discrimination upon arrival, by their own choice, because of need for security, or all of these, the influx of "new" people formed very large racial and ethnic groups. Through or because of these groups people could segregate

[52] George V. Zito, *Population and Its Problems* (Syracuse: Syracuse University Press, 1979), p. 115.

and maintain culturally different values and institutions. This was particularly true in the large cities. Royko used rather expressive language to describe Chicago.

> But Chicago, until as late as the 1950's, was a place where people stayed put for a while, creating tightly knit neighborhoods, as small-townish as any village in the wheat fields.
> The neighborhood-towns were part of larger ethnic states. To the north of the Loop was Germany. To the northwest Poland. To the west were Italy and Israel. To the southwest were Bohemia and Lithuania. And to the south was Ireland.
> It wasn't perfectly defined because the borders shifted as newcomers moved in on the old settlers, sending them fleeing in terror and disgust. Here and there were outlying colonies, with Poles also on the South Side, and Irish up north.
> But you could always tell, even with your eyes closed, which state you were in by the odors of the food stores and the open kitchen windows, the sound of the foreign or familiar language, and by whether a stranger hit you in the head with a rock.[53]

Again, speaking in his expressive style, Royko described some problems among these ethnic groups.

> The ethnic states got along just about as pleasantly as did the nations of Europe. With their tote bags, the immigrants brought along all their old prejudices, and immediately picked up some new ones. An Irishman who came here hating only the Englishmen and Irish Protestants soon hated Poles, Italians, and blacks. A Pole who was free arrived hating only Jews and Russians, but soon learned to hate the Irish, the Italians, and the blacks.[54]

The European ethnic groupings, described by Royko, have subsided in significance because of the movement of these families to the suburbs and the process of assimilation. However, the school systems are now in the midst of new ethnic crises brought on by the large immigration of Asian and Hispanic groups to the United States. In his discussion of ethnicity and education, Glazer discussed three alternative policies for educators: positive hostility, official disinterest, and positive reinforcement.[55] Positive hostility involves demanding the use of English in schools with punishhment for noncompliance and other rather strict demands for compliance with American ways. Official disinterest is a policy of taking no official action with the assumption that the ethnic-oriented newspapers, schools, and

[53] Mike Royko, *Boss: Richard J. Daley of Chicago* (New York: Signet, 1971), pp. 30–31.
[54] Ibid., p. 31.
[55] Nathan Glazer, "Ethnicity and Education: Some Hard Questions," *Phi Delta Kappan* 62 (January 1981), 386–389.

churches will disappear. Positive reinforcement involves bicultural and bilingual programs that are financed by the government and advocated by those aspiring to a policy of cultural pluralism. There is considerable resistance to programs of positive reinforcement. As Glazer commented, "the fear that the new responsiveness to ethnicity is undermining what has been on the whole a success will not go away."[56] Consequently, the positive reinforcement approach will likely continue to be an issue in the 1980s.

ACTIVITIES/QUESTIONS FOR FURTHER STUDY

1. Select a locale (e.g., school district or region of the state) for analysis of the kinds of societal trends and events discussed in this chapter. What are some significant socioeconomic and population trends in this locale that are influencing educational programs? Are there noticeable influences from ethnic and economic sectors? How will these influence educational programs in the future?

2. Make a special study of how students, parents, teachers, and other citizens of a selected area feel about equal opportunity for employment, promotion, and compensation. Are there valid evidences of bias in these areas? If so, what solutions do you suggest for promoting equal opportunity?

SUGGESTED READINGS

BERUBE, MAURICE R. *The Urban University in America.* Westport, Conn.: Greenwood Press, Inc., 1978.

BURKE, JOHN (ed.). *The New Technology and Human Values.* Belmont, Calif.: Wadsworth Publishing Co., Inc., 1972.

GEHLEN, ARNOLD. *Man in the Age of Technology,* Trans. Patricia Lipscomb. New York: Columbia University Press, 1980.

KAMRANY, NAKE M., and RICHARD H. DAY (eds.). *Economic Issues of the Eighties.* Baltimore: Johns Hopkins University Press, 1979.

KOCH, FRANK. *The New Corporate Philanthropy.* New York: Plenum Press, 1979.

LEVINE, DANIEL U., and ROBERT J. HAVIGHURST. *The Future of Big-City Schools.* Berkeley: McCutchan Publishing Corp., 1977.

LIGHTFOOT, ALFRED. *Urban Education in Social Perspective.* Chicago: Rand McNally & Co., 1978.

McBRIDE, ANGELA BARRON. *A Married Feminist.* New York: Harper & Row, Publishers, 1976.

PATTERSON, C. H. *Humanistic Education.* Englewood Cliffs, N.J.: Prentice-Hall, Inc., 1973.

SPIKES, W. FRANKLIN (ed.). *The University and the Inner City.* Lexington, Mass.: Lexington Books, D. C. Heath & Company, 1980.

WARNER, SAM BASS, JR. *The Urban Wilderness.* New York: Harper & Row, Publishers, 1972.

ZITO, GEORGE V. *Population and its Problems.* Syracuse: Syracuse University Press, 1979.

[56] Ibid., 389.

15

Local Politics
of Education

THE LEGAL and structural aspects of local educational
government were discussed in Chapter 5. In the present chapter the
focus is upon the political dynamics of local educational government.
Although the concepts developed in this chapter are applicable to college administrators as they work with local communities, the focus is
primarily on the politics of establishing educational policy at the level
of the school district. What are the sources and uses of political power
in the decision-making process?

The theory of democratic pluralism undergirds the traditional
concept of an elected lay board of education accountable directly to
the people. For the most part, the American people have never favored using the schools to further partisan interests. Thus the elective school board and its employees do not represent a bureaucrat in
the mayor's office or the leaders of a national political party. Theoret-
ically the local board's responsibility is to establish policies for the
operation of schools—policies that have the broadest support among
the people. Different interests can be expressed directly to the members of the board. The board functions to resolve value conflicts,
adopting educational policies as widely accepted as possible by people
in the school district.

This is in great contrast to the governance of education in many countries. For example, in China, Russia, and Cuba the schools have been basically instruments of the party ruling elite, whose leaders insist that the schools further the interests of the party. This has been an unthinkable alternative to most Americans. This is not to say that the schools have not, because of external pressure, responded to partisan interests. However, to legitimize such a process has never been condoned in the United States.

Educational Politics: Definition, Importance of, and Dimensions

In its broadest sense educational politics is the process of governing schools and colleges. More specifically, it involves the formulating and legitimizing of educational policies. It involves all aspects of deciding what kind of schools we want. Central to these processes is the control and exercise of power and influence. Therefore to understand local educational politics is to understand how political power is distributed in the school district and how this power is used or may in the future be used to establish the policies by which schools are operated. As Lutz observed, "Everyone involved in politics, from ward heelers to statesmen, from the naive beginner in the study of politics to the most eminent political theoretician, needs some kind of conceptual framework in order to understand or to affect political power."[1]

Importance of Educational Politics

During the 1960s and 1970s the traditionally accepted system for the governance of schools came under criticism by some interest groups. Some of this criticism was directed at what was presumed to be the centralized bureaucratic control of the public schools. These critics often advocated proposals to effect a decentralization of school governance. As discussed in Chapter 6 and elsewhere in this text, during the 1970s and early 1980s some of the critics of public education were advocating a freedom of choice policy, which was primarily aimed at giving parents more control and providing financial assistance to private schools and colleges through various proposals for tax credits and vouchers.

Decentralizing the control of education, however, does not eliminate the need for some process for decision making. Neither would a private school operate as a utopian system, free of parental conflict

[1] Frank W. Lutz, "Methods and Conceptualizations of Political Power in Education," in Jay D. Scribner (ed.), *The Politics of Education*, seventy-sixth yearbook of the National Society for the Study of Education (Chicago: University Chicago Press, 1977), p. 30.

and without some organizational machinery to make decisions and resolve differences. Even in the smallest groups, the members have differences in opinions about the educational process. Not even the closest-knit families realize unanimity of opinion on everything. Consequently, a process must exist by which these differences are resolved and decisions are made, or the group will fail.

Agger and Goldstein wrote that the public schools are political systems that are influenced by and, in turn, influence other political systems.[2] Thus the quality of schools is influenced by educational politics and the political leadership of educators. As Hough has written, the influence of politics on curriculum is a reality, and curriculum workers must be effective in the political arena.[3]

Finally, we must consider the power of education to influence the culture. As the profession of education develops better educational processes, this power may grow so vast as to influence the society greatly. Such power in the hands of an elitist group of whatever persuasion could be ominous to American democracy. Therefore this power should be kept directly accountable to the people.

Good and Bad Educational Politics

Whether we view the politics of education as good or bad is a value decision. The one lesson that everyone must learn and relearn is that many things under the control of humans may be used for either good or evil purposes. Politics is no exception to this rule. Politics can indeed be dehumanizing and evil. Politics can also further the most cherished human values in the culture.

As we discussed previously, the people in school districts will not all hold the same values about schooling. There must be a way to resolve these differences and establish policies. Politics is the process through which this is accomplished. If the political process is exemplary of democratic values and is aimed at providing quality educational opportunity for all, it can be described as good politics. Politics based on graft, disregard for the educational needs of students, or autocratic domination of decisions is bad politics.

The Dimensions of Educational Politics in School Districts

One of our principal purposes is to assist the educational administrator in understanding the political process in the school district. First the basic dimensions of the political system must be understood. The political system of the local school district should be conceptual-

[2] Robert E. Agger and Marshall N. Goldstein, *Who Will Rule the Schools: A Cultural Class Crisis* (Belmont, Calif.: Wadsworth, 1971), p. 3.
[3] Wendell M. Hough, "Power and Influence in the Change Process," *Educational Leadership*, 36 (October 1978), 55–59.

ized as a complex system in interaction with other political systems. The leaders and followers, both groups and individuals, in the local systems are interested in many kinds of political decisions involving all institutional areas of the society. Moreover, the schools will be influenced by policy decisions concerning planning and zoning, population control, health services, the environment, economics, and energy.

Educational politics involves knowledge and practice within several dimensions. First, when viewed from the local school district level, there is the politics of the community. Second, because the school district (community) is in interaction with suprasystems, there are the politics of the state and of the federal government. Third, there is the politics of the profession, which has been very active with the spread in influence of the collective-bargaining movement. Fourth, there is the politics of the local board of education. Fifth, the educational administrator encounters a politics of the bureaucracy. All these dimensions of politics are important and are discussed in this book. In this chapter we are principally concerned with (1) the politics of the community, (2) the politics of the board of education, and (3) the politics of the bureaucracy.

Some educators may disagree with the idea that the relationship between the superintendent and the school board is political. This would obviously be objectionable to those who believe that the board should take care of political questions, whereas the superintendent should administer policies made by the board. Objections may also be raised to the description of organizational leadership (politics of the bureaucracy) as a political process. However, empirical research supports the view that there is a politics that encompasses the community, the board of education, and the bureaucracy.

There is also logical support for these dimensions of politics, as we can see by returning to the definition of politics. Politics has been defined as the process of exercising power and influence in formulating and legitimizing policies. If administrators consciously attempt to exert influence upon the formulation and adoption into practice of any educational policies, they are to that extent exercising political leadership. If a power relationship exists between the school board and the superintendent or other administrators, there is a politics of the board. Collective bargaining is a political process because it involves the use of power in decision making. If one does not have political power, one does not bargain effectively. Wiles and associates have described how politics pervades many aspects of administering schools.[4]

---

[4]David K. Wiles, Jon Wiles, and Joseph Bondi, *Practical Politics for School Administrators* (Boston: Allyn & Bacon, 1981).

On the other hand, all school board–superintendent relationships are not political. Neither could one describe all staff leadership in organizations as politics. One could hardly say that supplying the many support services for classroom instruction involves great policy questions. To describe the attempts of teachers to teach children how to read as politically motivated would be ludicrous. For the most part educational politics involves actions to formulate and legitimize basic questions of educational policy.

The Politics of the Community

As discussed previously, educational administrators should have an accurate understanding of community politics to participate effectively in influencing community values. Although the schools are technically under the board of education, they are also a subsystem of the larger political system and are influenced by the exercise of political power in the larger system. Because political decision making involves the use of power, the educational administrator should endeavor to understand the community power structure. Who are the persons exercising the most power in decisions? How do they provide leadership in the process? What, if any, are the linkages between educational governance and the total community power structure?

Power Structure and Decision Making

In any local political system, such as the special school district, county, or city, public decisions must be made. Unless anarchy exists, there will be a complex structure through which these decisions are initiated, made, and implemented, and political power is exercised through this structure. Not all persons and groups in the system are equal in exercising power in decision making. The dynamic system through which political power is exercised in making decisions is what many writers refer to as the power structure.

Power structures are a part of the lives of all of us. For example, the family may be viewed as a social system with a power structure. Not all members of the family are equal or play similar roles in the decisions made. Families will differ in the processes through which decisions are made. The individual schools in which administrators practice will have a power structure. Some of the teachers on the faculty will have much more influence on the way the school is run than others. The custodian may have greater influence on some kinds of decisions in some schools than teachers. This school power structure will also be a mix of formal and informal arrangements. For example, there may be a formal arrangement for equal participation in decision making through faculty meetings. Yet an informal system, traditionally referred to as cliques, will be present in the faculty.

In the school district the power structure becomes much more complex and difficult to comprehend than the leadership structure of a school. There are many more participants in the power structure of the school district. These participants represent a variety of normative perceptions about community living and personal interests. Moreover, there are vast differences in political power among those active in the structure. Through a complex process, within the state and national constraints given, citizens attempt to influence decisions concerning the kind of community they want.

Sources of Political Power

People have influence in a power structure by virtue of their control over and effective use of certain resources. Some important resources used in community, state, and national power establishments are wealth, charisma, knowledge, official position, control over jobs, family ties, control of credit, leadership ability, access to the mass media, high social status, leadership in informal groups, expertise, control over votes, friendship ties, and knowledge of the political system. Listing all the resources that people use to gain power is an endless task. The principle to remember is that anything people value, tangible or intangible, may be used to gain power. The Arabs gave the world a lesson in the use of oil to gain political advantage. Such valued intangibles as life after death may also be used to influence people.

Power accrues to those who use these resources effectively. For example, a wealthy man may not have much political power if he is not politically active. He may also misuse his wealth in the political process and create hostility toward himself, which will result in loss of power. Thus, in addition to controlling power resources, those who would have power must use the resources according to the principles of leadership (norms) acceptable to the group or groups in which power is used.

The football coach of a senior high school may accumulate considerable political power in the community. He controls a resource (football) highly valued by many pupils and patrons of the school. He can influence the school sports boosters or persons who follow sports. Also, he has access to the media much more frequently than the teacher of English. This gives him visibility in the community. He can capitalize upon these resource advantages by demonstrating expertise (e.g., a winning season), establishing friendship ties with community influentials, shrewd leadership, and so on.

An English teacher in a high school studied by the authors also has influence over faculty opinion within a school system. She is widely recognized for her ability to teach her subject (expertise), and parents want their children to be in her classes. She has taught in the school for over twenty years, and her colleagues value her opinion highly on a wide range of professional matters. Her positions as president of the local teachers' association and member of the board of the state professional association are sources of power in the community and state.

A mathematics teacher on the aforementioned faculty also has much influence. She comes from a family highly recognized in the community and is the daughter of a wealthy trial lawyer. Her husband is president of the First National Bank, and several brothers are successful businesmen and lawyers. She is recognized for her expertise in teaching and has held important leadership positions in professional organizations in past years.

In the community served by the high school, there is an influential banker who has several power resources. He pyramids these resources to obtain more esteem and power. He controls credit, which gives him power. His importance in this respect helps him acquire positions of power in civic organizations, government, and the economic system. He is widely acclaimed as a progressive civic leader and as a leader in cultural activities. Thus he interacts with other influential people and creates important friendship and business ties. Liberal contributions to the campaigns of state and local office seekers provide him a source of personal influence in government. Renowned expertise in finance gives him a position as counsel concerning matters of public finance.

Astute politicians learn how to pyramid a variety of resources (e.g., friendship ties, mass media, patronage, family ties, expertise) to be elected to public office. From their public position they gain additional power. On the other hand, many politicians have personal commitments to those powerful persons who used their resources to get them elected and who assist them after election. Therefore the political friends may at the same time be political masters.

We could offer many other illustrations of how people control and use resources to gain political power in the community. One need not have ownership to exercise control. The school superintendent, for example, is in a position to allocate the resources available in the school system. The teachers' union may use the threat of a strike to disrupt educational services. In neither of these cases is there personal ownership; however, there is an element of control exercised over things, services, or ideas—all of which people value.

To reiterate, mere control of resources does not give one power in decision making. The person exercising control must use the resources effectively. The arbitrary use of power will result in failure to influence decisions in a free society. Even the most powerful leaders in the political system use their influence within the critical norms of the structure. Of considerable importance to school administrators is the fact that many people do not use the resources they control. Thus in all political systems there is latent power. Locating centers of latent power can be very important in the development of educational strategies to influence the system.

Interacting Local, State, and National Structures

Traditionally, educators have had a "local" concept of power and control over education, and much local control has been exercised over the operation of schools. Thus there has been considerable interest in community power structure. Educators, however, must not concentrate their entire attention upon community power structure.

Extending upward from sources of community power are leaders of power and influence who concentrate upon state and national decisions. These leaders are not restricted to members of legislatures and Congress, although the more influential ones are obviously keys to educational decision making. Informal aspects of power also operate in the state and national power structures so that very powerful groups of leaders who may not hold elective positions may influence the opinions of the governor, legislators, the Congress, and the executive branch of the national government. Consequently, a discussion of state and national politics is included in Chapter 16.

Early Studies of Community Power Structure

Studies describing the political power structures of local communities were fully developed during the 1950s and 1960s. The earlier research of Warner and the Lynds provided considerable evidence about political power in various communities.[5] However, for the most part these studies did not focus on the political power structure. During the 1950s numerous authorities became involved in studies of community power structures. Some important techniques were developed to uncover the "Mr. Big's" who really ran the community. These studies provided fascinating descriptions of how the public schools and other public agencies were influenced by community leaders.

The setting of most studies was usually a city or town. This research was heavily influenced by the idea, once popular in the social sciences, that the power structure of one large, "typical" city was very

[5] See, for example, William L. Warner et al., *Democracy in Jonesville* (New York: Harper, 1949); Robert S. and Helen M. Lynd, *Middletown in Transition* (New York: Harcourt, 1937).

likely similar to the power structures of most large cities in the nation. The books by Dahl[6] and Hunter[7] exemplify this case study approach. Dahl used the decision analysis technique, whereas Hunter used the reputational approach. (These techniques are discussed later in this chapter.)

The assumption that results could be generalized from one "typical" city to most other cities proved to be erroneous and resulted in much controversy among authorities. For example, the findings of Hunter were inconsistent with those of Dahl. Hunter found a monopolistic power structure wherein a few powerful leaders made all significant policy decisions in Regional City. On the other hand, Dahl found a pluralistic power structure in New Haven characterized by competition between numerous groups, strong citizen participation, and participation in decision making by many leaders. These discrepancies were thought at first to be a result of the bias of the techniques used in the research.

When viewed in retrospect, it appears that the descriptions of power structures by different researchers, even though conflicting, may have been accurate for the cases cited. Since these earlier studies were reported, analyses have shown that the power structures among communities are different. Some school districts are controlled by a monopolistic elite, whereas others have a pluralistic democracy. Each power structure has unique characteristics, and one cannot generalize from one district to another, although similar patterns may be found among districts of similar types of control.

Comparative designs were also used in studies of community-power structures in two or more cities or school districts, which helped to dampen the tendency toward overgeneralizing about power structure from one case study. The studies reported by Agger, Presthus, and Kimbrough had comparative designs.[8] In these studies the same technique was applied in two or more local governments, and the results compared and analyzed. When the same procedures were used for two different school districts in the study by Kimbrough, the findings concerning the community power structures were vastly different.[9]

[6] Robert A. Dahl, *Who Governs?* (New Haven: Yale University Press, 1961).

[7] Floyd Hunter, *Community Power Structure* (Chapel Hill: University of North Carolina Press, 1953).

[8] Robert E. Agger, Daniel Goldrich, and Bert E. Swanson, *The Rulers and the Ruled* (New York: Wiley, 1964); Robert Presthus, *Men at the Top: A Study in Community Power* (New York: Oxford University Press, 1964); Ralph B. Kimbrough, *Informal County Leadership Structure and Controls Affecting Educational Policy Decision Making*, Final Report, Office of Education, Cooperative Research Project No. 1324 (Gainesville, Fla.: University of Florida, March 1964).

[9] Kimbrough, loc. cit.

Types of Community Power Structures

This section is devoted to a general description of what has been learned about community power structure and decision making. The key point to remember is that the power structures of local school districts are very different. This generalization is supported by numerous investigations. Discussing the different types of politics found in large cities, Burns, Peltason, and Cronin observed that one experiences difficulty in generalizing about city structures.[10] Similarly, suburban school districts vary in the structure and processes of decision making, as was shown in the study of the Chicago suburban districts by Minar.[11] Agger, Goldrich, and Swanson presented four types of community power structure based upon two variables: (1) whether the political ideology of the influential leaders in the structure converges or diverges and (2) whether the distribution of power in the structure is broad or narrow.[12] Using data collected from twenty-four school districts in four states, Johns and Kimbrough developed a typology of power structures based on the following variables: (1) structure of the power groups or factions, (2) leadership overlap on different kinds of issues, (3) degree of competition on decisions, (4) membership among groups, (5) communication structure, (6) participation of citizens by voting and in interest groups, and (7) the kinds of issues existing in the school district. The results of this research and the research of others indicate that at least four types of power structures may be found in school districts.[13]

Monopolistic Structures

In a monopolistic power structure, decision making and community policies are dominated by a single group of leaders or coalition of groups. This domination is great enough to stifle viable conflicts concerning community living. Most decisions are formulated and controlled by the most powerful leaders in the system. Viable citizen participation is not realized, which results in much latent power in

[10]James M. Burns, J. W. Peltason, and T. E. Cronin, *State and Local Politics: Government by the People*, 2nd ed. (Englewood Cliffs, N.J.: Prentice-Hall, 1978), pp. 211–213.

[11]David W. Minar, *Educational Decision-Making in Suburban Communities*, Final Report, Office of Education, Cooperative Research Project No. 2440 (Evanston, Ill.: Northwestern University Press, 1966).

[12]Agger, Goldrich, and Swanson, op. cit., pp. 72–78.

[13]Roe L. Johns and Ralph B. Kimbrough, *The Relationship of Socioeconomic Factors, Educational Leadership Patterns and Elements of Community Power Structure to Local Fiscal Policy*, Final Report, Cooperative Research Project No. 2842 (Washington, D.C.: Department of Health, Education, and Welfare, Office of Education, Bureau of Research, 1968).

the structure. Most of the citizens in the system either are satisfied with the way things are run or loathe the consequences of getting involved more than the consequences of going along.

There are many expressions of monopolistic structures. One form of monopolistic power structure is the political machine. Americans have experienced and read for many years about the control of communities by political machines. One of the noted machines, for example, was the Tammany Hall machine in New York City.[14] Key and Miller discussed the famous E. H. Crump machine in Memphis.[15] Other writers have provided historical accounts of machines elsewhere, such as the Pendergast machine in Kansas City and the Byrd machine in Virginia. In more recent times, Royko, a news columnist, provided a very readable and interesting description of the Daley machine in Chicago.[16] Gabriel observed that machine politics was very much alive in Rhode Island.[17] Based on his extensive study of school politics in Chicago, Peterson wrote, "Renowned for its power, internal organizational efficiency, and the shrewdness of its political leadership, Chicago's machine structured the pattern of school politics as it did all other political relationships in the city."[18]

The economic elite is another form of monopolistic structure. Decision making in some school districts is overshadowed by the great power and resources of the several industrial and commercial enterprises that constitute the economic support of the community. Leaders associated with these industrial and commercial establishments can generate enough political power in the community to dominate most significant decisions.

Another form of monopolistic power structure is the one-industry town. Although nineteenth-century one-industry towns do not exist today in quantity, the politics of many cities and towns are still overshadowed by a major industry. When the economic elite is primarily from one industry, it may effectively control those community policies in which it is interested. Such power may even be statewide, as described in Phelan and Pozen's report on the state of Delaware.[19]

Many political scientists have taken exception to the idea that monopolistic structures exist. Some writers have suggested that such

[14]Gustavus Myers, *The History of Tammany Hall* (New York: Dover, 1971).

[15]See V. O. Key, *Southern Politics in State and Nation* (New York: Knopf, 1949), pp. 58–81; and William D. Miller, *Mr. Crump of Memphis* (Baton Rouge: Louisiana University Press, 1964).

[16]Mike Royko, *Boss: Richard J. Daley of Chicago* (New York: Signet, 1971).

[17]Richard A. Gabriel, *The Political Machine in Rhode Island* (Kingston: Bureau of Government Research, University of Rhode Island, 1970).

[18]Paul E. Peterson, *School Politics Chicago Style* (Chicago: University of Chicago Press, 1976), p. 8.

[19]James Phelan and Robert Pozen, *The Company State* (New York: Grossman, 1973).

structures are restricted to a few rural school districts in the Southeast. Yet the evidence continues to indicate that strong economic control may sometimes appear anywhere. Hayes' analysis of Oakland, California, for instance, indicated the "city's large and medium businesses qualify as the major political force in the city's politics."[20] As most readers know, Hunter reported in 1953 that Atlanta was dominated by an economic elite.[21] His research was roundly criticized by those persuaded toward a pluralist concept; however, until the recent publication of his second study of Atlanta, Hunter avoided answering his critics. In his second study Hunter reported structural changes in the Atlanta power structure; yet, he contended that the preponderance of power in the city remained with the economic interests.[22] Moreover, he reiterated his earlier belief in elitism at all governmental levels.

Multigroup Noncompetitive Structures

The multigroup noncompetitive structure is typical of some provincial school districts that are highly closed to innovation and change. In this structure several important power groups participate in decision making. Unlike the competitive elite structure, however, the leaders of these groups are in basic agreement concerning the policy directions of the district. That is, they have little difference of opinion concerning what the community should be or concerning the nature of the schooling desired. Thus there are really few issues concerning economic, governmental, educational, religious, or social policies. Considerable disagreement may exist concerning who gets what within the system, which results in family fights for the awarding of fees, positions, contracts, changes in zoning, and other matters. Locating the site for a new consolidated school may embroil such systems in conflict. However, these conflicts do not involve questions of policy concerning what social views should be taught, what kind of person a teacher ought to be, or what constitutes a desirable national welfare program. This strong tendency toward ideological consensus on what the community and schools should be like produces much closedness to change.

Competitive Elite Systems

The monopolistic and multigroup noncompetitive power structures are both noncompetitive concerning community policies, whereas the competitive elite structure is embroiled in regime conflicts. The

[20]Edward C. Hayes, *Power Structure and Urban Policy: Who Rules in Oakland?* (New York: McGraw-Hill, 1972), p. 197.

[21]Hunter, loc. cit.

[22]Floyd Hunter, *Community Power Succession: Atlanta's Policy-Makers Revisited* (Chapel Hill: University of North Carolina Press, 1980).

community is in the midst of a power struggle concerning the kind of a community it should be. Should the economic base be tourism, industry, or trade, or should the district be residential? Should the schools teach the fundamentals and the values of rugged individualism, or should they exemplify the values of an interdependent society? Should the government have a strong planning and zoning function or restrict its functions to protecting the property rights of individuals? The conflicts between leaders frequently involve ideological differences (e.g., new liberal versus classical liberal, new left versus neoconservative, and so on).

Although it is open to debate upon policies, the competitive elite structure is not pluralistic. The groups involved in the struggle are elite groups. Participation of the general public in the decision-making process is weak. The structure is more what old-line politicians refer to as palace struggles to determine which group of leaders and which ideal of community living will prevail. To use the term popularized by Dye and Zeigler, the competitive elite system is a pluralism of elites.[23]

As with other power structure typologies, there are many kinds of competitive elite systems. For example, some competitive elite systems may be restricted to a struggle between two powerful elite-run groups. In other communities the struggle may be among three or more groups or coalitions of groups. The structures also vary in the normative processes for decision making and in the extent of formality or informality of the groups involved.

Democratic Pluralisms

Pluralism has traditionally been held high in the literature as the ideal power structure of democracy. As Connolly has written, the pluralistic theory is in the legacy of Tocqueville.[24] There is viable, widespread participation of the citizens of the school district in decision making. They participate effectively in selecting elected public officials who are responsive to the will of the people. The citizens further form voluntary associations through which their will can be expressed effectively to public officials. Decision making is an open process that is governed by a commonly held democratic creed.

Dahl described a pluralism in his study of New Haven.[25] Unlike monopolistic structures, pluralism provides open access to decision making by persons and groups. Moreover, as expressed previously, a high percentage of the people in the community participate and make

[23]Thomas R. Dye and L. Harmon Zeigler, *The Irony of Democracy* (Belmont, Calif.: Wadsworth, 1972).

[24]William E. Connolly (ed.), *The Bias of Pluralism* (New York: Atherton, 1969), pp. 4–8.

[25]Dahl, loc. cit.

their views felt in decisions. Thus there is little latent power in the system. Elections are effective processes for deciding who the community leaders are and for making choices on public policies. Competing organized interest groups provide means for expressing the will of the citizens.

Pluralisms have emerged in many school districts through the pressure tactics of various underrepresented groups, such as women, blacks, and ethnic groups. Organized interest groups are important elements of pluralistic structures. These groups are discussed in Chapter 17.

Pluralism is the ideal democratic power structure so often praised in much of the literature. This system for decision making is open to the emergence of new leaders. Citizen participation is effective, and those who govern are responsive to the will of the people.

Types of Power Structures Among Selected School Districts

The power structure studies of the 1950s and 1960s showed that a variety of different power structures may be found among the school districts of the nation. The studies indicate that the differences in expressions of power structures are endless. As an illustration of how the application of the same technique will produce findings supporting different types of power structure, let us examine the four-state study by Johns and Kimbrough.[26] This research provided an analysis of twenty-four school districts in four states by the same research team using the same research technique. Included in the study were six school districts in each of these states: Illinois, Kentucky, Georgia, and Florida. Three of the highest financial effort and three of the lowest financial effort school districts above 20,000 population (including large, medium, and small) in each of these states were selected for the power studies.

Using the typology of power structure discussed previously, Table 15-1 shows the frequency in which each type appeared among the twenty-four school districts. All types of power structures are represented. Different types of power structures were found in the districts of each of the states, the multigroup noncompetitive structure occurring most frequently.

Obviously one cannot generalize from this sample. However, these data, coupled with the large amount of research conducted in all sections of the United States since the 1950s, support the generalization that educational administrators cannot hold only one textbook generalization of how political decisions are made in all school districts. Community power structures are molded by many variables,

[26]Johns and Kimbrough, loc. cit.

Table 15-1.   Distribution of Power System Typologies Among Selected Districts

	Pluralism	Competitive Elite	Multigroup Noncompetitive	Monopolistic
High financial effort	2	5	2	3
Low financial effort	1	1	7	3
TOTAL	3	6	9	6
Percent all districts (four categories)	12.5	25.0	37.5	25.0

such as (1) influential leaders, (2) participation of citizens, (3) norms of leaders and citizens, (4) civic beliefs of leaders and citizens, (5) formal and informal groups, (6) patterns of communication, (7) creeds concerning the decision-making processes, and (8) local traditions. The only generalization that the educational administrator can rely on about the school district in the absence of empirical data is that any one of the several different types of power structures may exist in a variety of forms. However, some speculate that monopolistic power structures may not be as numerous in the future, and competitive elite and pluralistic structures could increase.

Change of Power Structures

As with all social systems, community power structures are constantly undergoing change. There are internal changes—new leaders emerge, old leaders become inactive, and latent power interests are activated. The structure must also respond to powerful inputs from its environment. Such dynamics produce changes in the qualities of the elements so that no power structure is today exactly like it was yesterday. Sometimes communities undergo abrupt power exchanges because of massive inputs. One example of this is large increases in the population, particularly where the new population is different from the indigenous population. Power structures often change from one type to another. For example, massive inputs into a monopolistic power structure may result in the development of a competitive elite structure. Kammerer and associates reported that the power structures of cities in their study had changed from one type to another over time.[27] In some cases the change was from competitive to monopolistic and in others from monopolistic to competitive.

The implications of change of power structures are that the educator-politician must not only study the structure for what it is

[27] Gladys M. Kammerer et al., *City Managers in Politics* (Gainesville: University of Florida Press, 1962), pp. 27–53.

today but also continuously update information. Conceptualizing the dynamics of the power structure in educational policy is a continuous process.

Occupations of Leaders in Community Politics

As suggested previously, the makeup of the leadership classes of a community power structure is an important variable producing significant differences in politics among school districts. Thus, again, the educational administrator is cautioned not to make generalizations about who is influential in a community in the absence of empirical data. Indeed, one of the first tasks for the administrator is to make personal analyses through empirical observation to discover who is influential and who may hold latent power in the structure.

The large number of power structure studies reported confirm the variation in who is influential in different communities by wealth, social class, occupation, public office, and other aspects. In many studies, such as Hunter's seminal publication and the more recent study reported by Hayes, leaders from the economic institutional sector had the strongest representation.[28] Other studies, of which Dahl's analysis of New Haven was illustrative, point to the viability of elected public officials in community politics.[29] Gabriel's study of Providence was among those showing viable ethnic community politics.[30] Johns demonstrated that one Kentucky school superintendent dominated all politics in the community.[31] To summarize, leaders of a great variety of characteristics and occupations have been found to have influence in community power structures.

The study by Johns and Kimbrough provided a comprehensive view of who held power in the selected districts of four states.[32] The economic and political leaders were heavily represented in the top ranks of power in many of these school districts. This is consistent with the findings of numerous consumer interest studies (e.g., Ralph Nader's group) that the laws seem heavily favorable to business. Political leaders were the next most prevalent group with the other occupational groups a close third. One must not generalize from these data for any particular system; that is, educators may inaccurately assume in the absence of empirical observation that economic leaders are more prevalent in their school district than other types. Actually, in many districts the economic category may be very weak in the

[28] Hunter, loc. cit.; Hayes, loc. cit.
[29] Dahl, loc. cit.
[30] Richard A. Gabriel, *Ethnic Voting in Primary Elections* (Kingston: Bureau of Government Research, University of Rhode Island, 1969).
[31] Thomas L. Johns, "Analyses of Power Systems of Three Selected Low Effort School Districts in Kentucky (unpublished doctoral dissertation, University of Florida, 1967).
[32] Johns and Kimbrough, loc. cit.

structure. Labor leaders dominate the decision-making structures of some school districts.

What is the relative power of educators and school board members in community political decision making? Educators have greatly increased active interest in politics since the middle of 1960s. The growth of collective bargaining in education attests to the increased militancy of teachers in the political arena. Unquestionably, in many school districts teachers have improved their position of power in the political process; nevertheless, they have encountered some formidable opposition to their demands. For example, several states have already passed various forms of initiatives, following the trend set by the Proposition 13 initiative in California. Lieberman is one among numerous writers who warn that powerful opposition to educational leaders may radically change public support for education.[33] Moreover, teachers are handicapped to some extent by the fierce competition among rival unions vying for political control of the profession. Examination of the results of political studies indicates that the relative power of school superintendents varies greatly from the highest extent-of-influence to very low power ranking. This is also true of the power ranking of school board members. In the twenty-four school district study by Johns and Kimbrough, twenty-one of the school superintendents had enough influence to be ranked among the top leaders of their political structures.[34] However, there is rather conclusive evidence that the power of teachers, educational administrators, and board members varies greatly among the school districts of the nation. One should not make sweeping generalizations in the absence of data concerning the relative power of educators in local politics.

The Process of Decision Making in Community Politics

How do the political systems of communities make decisions? What are the normative processes for exercising leadership in the system? What is the relationship among the community influentials in the decision-making process? In what ways do the decisions made in the political system influence the school program?

Decision making may be open and formal or informal and behind the scenes. The norms governing the process may vary from graft and corruption to altruism and democratic ethics. In any event educational administrators must understand the dynamics of political power in the community if they are to exert influence.

[33]Myron Lieberman, "Against the Grain," *Phi Delta Kappan* 61 (May 1980), 635–637.

[34]Johns and Kimbrough, loc. cit.

The conceptualization of the political decision-making process has been the focus of much literature. For example, Peterson explored the applicability of four models for educational politics: pluralist bargaining, ideological bargaining, the organizational hierarchy, and rational decision making.[35] Pluralist bargaining describes a situation in which the participants in bargaining are primarily interested in enhancing their personal or organizational political advantages with little reference to ideological concerns. In ideological bargaining the participants are motivated by and committed to ideological concerns. The organizational hierarchy model was derived from the theory of bureaucracy as an explanation of educational decision making. In the rational model the participants are assumed to be rational, goal oriented, and value directed in making political decisions. Wiles and associates did not accept the rational concept of educational politics. They advocated an arena model, characteristic of loose-coupling thought, that was discussed as follows:

> Finally, the arena model is a candid admission that real decision making is messy, confusing, and often contradictory. Players and rules for deciding may be constantly changing. The actual trading associated with a particular decision may be a blur of long- and short-range objectives and symbolic and concrete options. It is not necessary that deciders agree or be like-minded. In fact, a person can influence a particular choice without even being aware of the arena for deciding.[36]

In some contrast to the models discussed above is the technological model of decision making proposed by Zeigler and associates. They contended that, in the present technological age, school board members are faced with issues that are too complex for them to comprehend; consequently, they must rely on the school superintendent for knowledge as a basis for policy decisions. Thus the technical expertise of the superintendent propels him or her into a dominating role in the establishing of educational policies.[37]

Agger, Goldrich, and Swanson presented four regimes, or rules of the game, for decision making.[38] These were oligarchy, underdeveloped democracy, guided democracy, and developed democracy. They established two variables to describe these regimes for decision making as follows: (1) the sense of electoral potency, and (2) the probability of illegitimate sanctions being used to block efforts to change the scope of government. Illegitimate sanctions include loss of employ-

---

[35] Peterson, op. cit., pp. 1–128.

[36] Wiles et al., op. cit., p. 12.

[37] L. Harmon Zeigler, Harvey J. Tucker, L. A. Wilson, "Communication and Decision Making in American Public Education: A Longitudinal and Comparative Study," in Jay D. Scribner (ed.), op. cit., pp. 218–254.

[38] Agger, Goldrich, and Swanson, op. cit., pp. 82–90.

ment opportunities, extreme social ostracism by other means, or other very harsh treatment. The sense of electoral potency refers to the extent to which the people believe that authorities will respond to their preferences through elections. In an oligarchy the sense of electoral potency is low and the probability that illegitimate sanctions will be used upon those attempting to disturb the status quo is high. The underdeveloped democracy is characterized by a low sense of electoral potency and low probability that illegitimate sanctions will be used. Guided democracies, on the other hand, have a high sense of electoral potency and a high probability that illegitimate sanctions will be used. Developed democracies are characterized by a high sense of electoral potency and a low probability that illegitimate sanctions will be used.

Regardless of whether the regimes are accepted as described and whether they are accepted on the basis of the variables provided, they do provide a helpful way to think about local school districts. Persons who have had opportunity to work in many of the districts (e.g., state department of education personnel) can attest to the great differences in the governance of school districts. Some really can be described as oligarchies ruled by a few elites who do not hesitate to use illegitimate sanctions against political upstarts. At the other extreme are those with highly developed democratic processes for citizen participation in decision making.

In their analysis of the politics of education, Iannaccone and Lutz classified school districts according to "sacred" and "secular" types.[39] The sacred community resists change, whereas the secular community places high positive value upon change. Sacred community politics emphasize intimacy, friendship, loyalty, patriotism, and strong emotional attachment to the place of one's birth. Secular communities, on the other hand, display emotional neutrality to these values and are characterized by emotional recklessness, openness, and fanaticism toward change and thrill.

Iannaccone and Lutz found that educational politics in sacred communities is low-key. Educational administrators function in the structure to keep potential issues defused and to maintain equilibrium. They also found that the control of schools in the sacred community was in most instances monolithic.

Lutz and Iannaccone also offered a dissatisfaction theory of democracy to explain school district governance.[40] In this view school boards inevitably drift toward elitism, stability, and closeness to citizen demands, whereas the larger community is influenced by inevitable change in the society. In time this produces a widening gap

[39]Laurence Iannaccone and Frank W. Lutz, *Politics, Power and Policy: The Governing of School Districts* (Columbus, Ohio: Merrill, 1970).

[40]Frank W. Lutz and Laurence Iannaccone (eds.), *Public Participation in Local School Districts* (Lexington, Mass.: Lexington, Heath, 1978), p. 130.

between the board and the community, resulting in community politics to bring the board into line with the larger community demands.

Various authors have emphasized that educational politics of many school districts may be somewhat insulated from the general partisan politics of the community. Iannaccone and Lutz felt that this may be a tendency in those school districts that are not coterminous with the boundaries of other local governments.[41] Zeigler and Jennings wrote that the emphasis upon the reform concept of politics has made educational politics somewhat unique.[42]

In their four-state study discussed earlier, Johns and Kimbrough found that there was considerable variation in the amount of direct participation of community influentials in educational decision making among the school districts studied. Moreover, considerable variation existed in the extent of school superintendent participation in community issues not directly related to schools.

The research evidence suggests, however, that one cannot make generalizations about direct community involvement in educational decisions because the pattern of participation will be influenced by the type of decision being made. A group of businessmen is not likely to become motivated to enter a decision concerning a promotion policy in the schools. Yet a proposal to increase greatly the school millage to fund additional programs may not escape their attention.

Another factor often overlooked concerning the processes of community influence upon educational programs is that for community leaders to do nothing is often effective. Many school elections to fund new programs are lost because top leaders in the power structure did nothing, and a power vacuum was created spelling defeat for the measure. In their analysis of referenda to approve water fluoridation in over 700 cities, Crain and associates concluded that many failed because community influentials did not actively support the proposals.[43] Also, as Iannaccone and Lutz have expressed, many school superintendents put a lot of effort into keeping issues from arising, to preserve the school system in a state of static equilibrium.[44] This not only provides job security for the administrators but aids familial control of the school system as well. However, administrators frequently are unable to keep educational decisions from becoming generalized issues in the larger power structure of the community. When this happens, the administrator's ability to discern and influence the gov-

[41] Iannaccone and Lutz, op. cit., p. 29.

[42] L. Harmon Zeigler and M. Kent Jennings, *Governing American Schools* (North Scituate, Mass.: Duxbury, 1974).

[43] Robert L. Crain et al., *The Politics of Community Conflict: The Flouridation Decision* (Indianapolis: Bobbs-Merrill, 1969).

[44] Iannaccone and Lutz, loc. cit.

erning process is critical. In the following discussion an illustrative case is provided of some of the power processes involved in a millage election.

The Millage Election in a Selected School District

The power structure of the school district was competitive elite. Seven very powerful groups were known to be active in the system along with numerous local community interests. To levy more than a 10-mill property tax, the school board had to submit its proposal to a referendum of the people. After considerable study, the board decided to ask for approval of an additional 5 mills. The board stated publicly that it would not use the entire levy of 5 mills unless it was needed in the school program.

The superintendent of schools was largely instrumental in organizing the campaign for the additional millage. He developed his proposal carefully and influenced the board to set an October date for the election, which his colleagues had suggested as the best date. A public relations firm was contacted to furnish consultative advice in organizing and conducting the campaign. Important educational leaders were alerted to speak publicly for the levy. Plans were made to use the mass media to support the board decision. A list of organizations was made before which people could appear to speak for the board proposal. Finally, the superintendent decided against a hard-sell highly organized campaign.

Soon after the school board announced its decision, Mark Simpson, a newspaper publisher and key leader in the power structure, raised questions about the proposal. The school superintendent met several times with Mr. Simpson in an attempt to win his support for the board proposal. He also made the rounds of offices of other leaders in the community and sought their assistance in convincing the newsman that the board proposal was needed. With the exception of the president of the parent–teacher association, he was unsuccessful in obtaining commitments from these leaders to help. The attitude of one of the most powerful leaders is shown in the following statement: "Bob Ingram tried to talk to me. They did not need 5 mills. Taxes are too high now. Bob Ingram was just reaching for too much power. I'm in favor of good schools but that school board is getting out of hand."

The newspaper editor produced editorials explaining that the school board demands only required 2 mills. Information about the school proposal was obviously slanted in the newspaper accounts.

With the exception of the parent–teacher association and the classroom teachers' association, organizations did not take a public position in the decision. They did serve as centers for propaganda for and against the school board proposal; that is, speakers for and against the proposal made speeches at formal meetings of numerous community organizations. The activity of leaders in well-known informal power groups in town was another matter.

The Old Guard, a group of conservative business, professional, and political leaders, quietly discussed how the school board proposal should be defeated. In fact, the newspaper publisher who emerged as the public spokesman against the proposal was an important leader in this group.

Coercion was used. Nat Singletary, the Chairman of the Board, First National Bank, let key leaders know of his strong opposition. A school board member stated, "I saw almost immediate change among many businessmen, particularly loan and financial establishments, when old man Singletary cracked down."

Telephones were busy among the leaders in the power structure as the campaign neared October. Mrs. Ed Whitcomb, wife of one of the teachers and secretary to the president of a federal savings and loan association reported, "Mr. Slamon (president of the association) was on that phone day and night lining up opposition to Mr. Ingram."

As opposition to the 5-mill plan mushroomed, Ingram stepped up his grass-roots campaign. Failing to get support among most of the community leaders, he went directly to the people with his message. He distributed attractive literature to community groups focused upon the consequences for children should the 5-mill proposal fail.

The West End Crowd, a powerful influence, was busy passing the word to its constituency that a vote for the proposal would be unsound. The leaders in this group were community developers and retired persons. One of the largest developers in the state let it be known that, in his opinion, "Ingram's idea had unsound features, and I did not want to support it."

Groups referred to by their opposition as the McCall Democrats and the Farmdale Clan were solidly opposed to the proposal. They influenced a prominent rancher, who was highly respected, to run full-page ads in the newspaper and spots on television in opposition to the 5-mill levy and in favor of a 2-mill write-in.

A liberal group of business and professional leaders known as the New Democrats did not exert leadership in the issue, nor did two other prominent political groups.

Much of the leadership opposition was through the informal political cliques. As indicated earlier, Mark Simpson, the newspaper publisher, was the chief public spokesman for a swift, broad-flowing underground stream of political power against the board of education.

Leaders for the opposition groups made a counterproposal for a write-in vote of 2 mills. Apparently their logic was not entirely inaccurate because the superintendent informed associates privately that, assuming assessments were set at reasonable levels, the schools could obtain enough money to operate at the expected desirable levels with a 2-mill rate. His argument was that a "cushion" should be set for the board in case assessments did not rise to certain levels.

In the campaign one could easily see that the board was opposed by most leaders in the power structure. Many others sat out the election. Leaders important in parent organizations and teachers were the main source of support for 5 mills. The result was a defeat for the school board proposal and a winning write-in vote for a 2-mill levy.

Concepts Derived from the Millage Referendum

Some important concepts about the process of decision making may be seen in this briefly described referendum. The public schools are obviously involved in politics because they are public. School personnel face great difficulty in improving schools unless the proposed methods for improvement have the support of most of those who hold power and influence in the power structure.

Another important concept is that power is exercised formally and informally. The educator cannot restrict attention to the formal groups and elected public officials as the only users of power. Much of the activity by leaders involved in the referendum was through informal groups as well as formal organizations.

There were unmistakable signs in the school millage issue that Superintendent Ingram had violated group norms of the political system. Certain of the leaders viewed his actions as a "grab for power" rather than as an unselfish attempt to improve education. If Ingram continued to present this image, regardless of his personal intentions, he would surely lose most of his influence in that system. Existing in all political systems are normative concepts concerning how leaders ought to, and indeed are expected to, use influence in making decisions. One cannot violate these critical norms of the power structure continuously and maintain a position of influence in that system.

Public elections provide opportunities for large-scale citizen participation in decision making. In the case just described, the school board had to seek citizen approval for a millage levy for schools through referendum. Unfortunately, elections often fail to demonstrate the viable mass participation hoped for by students of government. In the election discussed, only 35 percent of the registered voters actually cast a ballot in the millage election. When one realizes that in this school district less than 85 percent of those eligible to register had registered and only 35 percent of those eligible actually voted, one can see that the possibility for elitism exists. Educators should not overlook the significance of the elective process in educational improvement. They should endeavor to improve their expertise in influencing elections. Leaders in the community power structure are vitally concerned with election outcomes. Riding on these outcomes is control over numerous boards, commissions, and executives.

The preceding illustration of decision making was for one issue in one school district. The process for another decision in education or other interest sectors (e.g., health, religion, general government) will very likely be different.

Decision making in a pluralistic power structure would seldom, if ever, be similar to that characteristic of a monopolistic power structure. In the first place many more people participate in decision making in a democratic pluralism. Competitive groups usually characterize the process in a pluralism, whereas dominance by a few is central to monopolistic structures. The student is encouraged to observe the formal and informal processes in decision making in his or her own community. In doing so, the student should attempt to look under the surface of the formal actions of school board and city commission (or council) meetings. The formal meetings of these bodies may well be what Dahl referred to as democratic ceremonials.[45] The dynamic process that preceded the culmination of official decision by the board is crucial to understanding the process.

Finally, educational politics in the community is not restricted to elections. In fact, elections may be the least important aspect. All educational programs must eventually be legitimized (made acceptable) within the community power structure. This process of legitimization, by whatever strategies used, is fundamental to schools of quality.

The Politics of the Board of Education

Before the revival of interest in the politics of education on community, state, and national levels, much of the literature in educational administration dealt with the political relationship of the board of education to professional school personnel. As has been discussed previously, much of this literature took the view of reform model government ethics that politics (a function of the board) should be separate from administration (the function of professionally educated persons). In the present discussion, we consider the politics of the board from three perspectives: (1) the politics of the selection of the board, (2) the politics of the board as representatives of the community, and (3) the politics of school board–superintendent relations.

[45] Dahl, loc. cit.

The Selection of Board Members

In his comprehensive analysis of school governance in Massachusetts, Gross obtained data from school board members and superintendents concerning the selection of board members.[46] Some of the data related to why people sought election to the school board. The most frequently mentioned motivations expressed for seeking office were that the candidate (1) felt a civic duty to run, (2) felt that a certain group should be represented on the board, (3) was interested in some experience in politics, (4) felt general disapproval with the way schools were run, and (5) felt that schools should be improved (e.g., increase expenditures for education).[47]

Considerable speculation exists that citizens seek school board positions as a steppingstone to higher political positions. Based on the data from his national sample, Zeigler found that very few school board members expressed these upward-bound aspirations.[48]

Gross was much concerned with what he termed the "bad" motivations of many school board members. "Some school board members felt their jobs were political-patronage posts and many of them sought election to the board to represent special segments of the community."[49] Gross felt so strongly about this matter that he recommended the enactment of state laws forbidding board members from engaging in personal and business patronage.

What are the political pathways for selection to the board of education? Zeigler and Jennings found great variation in the steps board members reported prior to successful candidacy for office. The most prominently mentioned preentry steps to school board membership were (1) activity and leadership in civic and business organizations (more than 40 percent), (2) apprentice leadership in political-government activities (29 percent), and (3) leadership in educational activities (28 percent). The majority of the school board members had come up through "apprentice leadership" in appointive governmental positions, civic associations, and educational organizations (e.g., PTA). However, a small number (13 percent) reported no previous steps involved before selection to the board.

Numerous authors have expressed disapproval of what they interpret as lack of participation and competition in school board elections. For example, about one third of the school board members in the Zeigler and Jennings study were either elected without opposition or appointed. On the other hand, until we have more comparative data, education should not be singled out as unique. Many govern-

[46] Neal Gross, *Who Runs Our Schools?* (New York: Wiley, 1958).
[47] Ibid., p. 78.
[48] Zeigler and Jennings, op. cit., pp. 39–42.
[49] Gross, op. cit., p. 136.

ment officials are elected either without opposition or with token opposition. Therefore education may not be greatly different from other areas of governance. Moreover, as noted later in this section, in many districts there is viable competition for office.

To be elected to the board of education, one usually must have had considerable visibility of leadership in the community.

> In this stage a great deal of self-selection takes place. People become involved differentially in endeavors which convince them and others that they are among the pool of eligibles. Sometimes this is done through sheer dint of occupational visibility. The head of the largest bank, the most successful farmer, the prominent educator, and the leading physician are examples of immediate eligibles. More often, however, there must be something else accompanying this visibility or acting in place of it.[50]

Cistone also found that nearly all school board members "had been active in some civic, educational, or occupational organization prior to standing for election."[51]

Zeigler and Jennings found that most members of boards of education were encouraged to run for office or to consider appointment to office. Significantly, however, almost one fourth of the respondents in their study indicated that no one had encouraged them to run—attesting to the ease of their election to office. Of those encouraged to run, 29 percent were encouraged by other board members, 21 percent by members of formal organizations, 21 percent by friends or neighbors, 14 percent by professional school personnel, and 13 percent by politicians.[52]

Iannaccone and Lutz examined the social system constraints that accompany the election of school board members to office. Their data led them to propose that sacred community ethics, which they felt tend to predominate in educational politics, accompanied monopolistic closedness of school governance. School board membership tended to be predicated upon conformity to the social norms of the ruling elite group.[53]

Other authors have indicated that school board elections more frequently resemble popularity contests than they do competition about what kind of school policies should be established. Iannaccone and Lutz pointed to the possibility that even in some communities with open systems (e.g., competitive elite or pluralistic power struc-

---

[50] Zeigler and Jennings, op. cit., p. 29.

[51] Peter J. Cistone, "The Recruitment and Socialization of School Board Members," in Peter J. Cistone (ed.), *Understanding School Boards* (Lexington, Mass.: Lexington, Heath, 1975), p. 54.

[52] Zeigler and Jennings, op. cit., pp. 33–34.

[53] Iannaccone and Lutz, op. cit., pp. 86–87.

tures) the schools may be run by an elite group. They hypothesized that in this situation the school system would become increasingly segregated from and incongruent with changing community norms, producing opposing candidates for school board office.[54]

One should not assume, however, that all school board elections are principally popularity contests. Much evidence, such as that presented by Goldhammer and Farner, indicates that many school board elections involve deep-seated ideological differences between the contestants.[55] School board elections frequently involve contests for control of the board for the advantage of interest groups. For example, throughout the period of teacher militancy following the 1950s, teachers' unions have actively supported candidates for the board and have been successful in many instances. Thus school board elections may or may not involve basic ideological differences about educating.

Board and Community Politics

What kinds of relationships exist among board members and the citizens of the community? After election to office for the first time, most school board members face identity problems. They must decide whether they are to be responsive to their constituents, other leaders on the board, professional leaders, national demands, or state policies. Finding a political identity produces widely different patterns of responsiveness. If, as Iannaccone and Lutz suggested, sacred community politics predominates, board members may be drawn into responsiveness to the ruling elite.[56] On the other hand, persons elected for the express purpose of changing the control of education may take their cues from their constituents unless won over by the ruling elite. Community conflict will produce additional problems of identity for board members.

The study by Zeigler and Jennings indicated that about three fifths of the board members reported pressure to support certain group positions.[57] When asked to reveal sources of information useful to them, the members indicated many different persons and groups. However, there were no clearly evident patterns of responsiveness generalizable for the total group. This again attests to the variant ways in which school board members achieve identity in different communities with variations in complexity and power structure.

Like all other groups and individuals in the district, board members will be responsive to sources of political power. Consequently,

[54] Ibid., pp. 85–94.
[55] Keith Goldhammer and Frank Farner, *The Jackson County Story* (Eugene, Ore.: Center for the Advanced Study of Educational Administration, University of Oregon, 1964).
[56] Iannaccone and Lutz, loc. cit.
[57] Zeigler and Jennings, op. cit., p. 78.

the power configuration in community decision making will influence the behavior of board members. For example, the responsiveness of board members to elite leaders in monopolistic power structures has been documented in a variety of studies.[58] Moreover, these studies have shown how patterns of power group representation may occur in communities with competitive elite structures.

The preceding discussion suggests that the educational administrator cannot make textbook assumptions about patterns of responsiveness of school board members for different school districts. Each school district must be treated as a special case for analysis. This analysis may indicate that the board members and certain key professionals have formed a reference group that dominates most educational decisions, insofar as no major policy questions arise that are of concern to politicians outside this group. On the other hand, an analysis may reveal a community and school board in the midst of a power struggle for the control of education (e.g., competitive elite). In those communities severely splintered by ideological differences concerning the kind of town the citizens want, the school board is almost always characterized by crises and conflicts.

However, not all community conflicts are ideological. In the multigroup noncompetitive power structure, for example, conflicts may arise over which firms get the contracts for school services, supplies, and equipment. For instance, the insurance agencies are eager to write the school insurance. Banks become jealous about where the school monies are deposited. Firms compete to supply the school lunchrooms. Even where the participants in the competition for these services have no ideological differences about schooling, there may be many split votes on the board unless policies are established to contain these contractual conflicts.

Political confrontations between school boards and teachers are commonplace; yet, many board members and superintendents have not developed the mental attitude necessary to cope with dignity. Since the industrial model of collective bargaining creates an adversary relationship between administrators and teachers, there is an inevitable scramble for community support by the leaders of the two groups. Krajewski described the rough-and-tumble "dirty tricks" that were employed in a teachers' strike and suggested that board planning for political action is essential.[59] He recommended that the board keep in very close communication with leaders in the community power structure during these confrontations.

There is reason to believe that ideological conflicts, which typi-

[58] Ralph B. Kimbrough, *Political Power and Educational Decision Making* (Chicago: Rand McNally, 1964).
[59] Robert Krajewski, "Planning is the Best Strike Strategy," *The American School Board Journal*, 167 (July 1980), 26–28.

cally occur in communities with competitive elite structures, run much deeper and are more difficult to deal with than "palace" conflicts over contracts. One reason for this is that all school districts, regardless of the type of power structure they have, must deal with contractual conflicts. However, in the competitive elite and many pluralistic districts, the ideological regime conflicts must be faced in addition to the economic conflicts.

Moreover, school superintendents and boards have developed some fairly sophisticated procedures to defuse crises that could arise over contractual relations. For example, fairly administered competitive bidding procedures are effective in many instances. Fair and reasonable policies can be established to remove many of these economic conflicts as governmental problems and place them in the category of major nuisances.

Although we may not like to admit it, not all school board members have the highest motivation. There is the board member with the so-called axe to grind. As discussed previously, Gross expressed great concern about the evidence from the study that indicated "bad" motivations of board members. An illustration of a "bad" motivation is the board member who uses the position for political patronage or favoritism. There is always the niece who needs a job or a friend who desires a contract. The prospective school administrator must be forewarned that, as stated earlier, politics can be either good or bad. Even where we describe politics as good, there are pressures to be unethical. The schoolteacher gets less of this than the principal, and the principal much less than the superintendent. The person holding the highest office is more likely to be the target of those following the animal instinct in politics. These must be counteracted by responsible and logically defensible political ethics.

Board–Superintendent Politics

In school board and superintendent relations the politics of the bureaucracy and of the board intermingle. Based upon his study of the Chicago Board of Education, Pois wrote the following:

> The board–general superintendent relationship is inherently one that cannot be defined precisely and that injects an element of uncertainty into the organization and its operations. The fact that any sharp dichotomy between policy formulation and administration is unreal makes it all the more difficult to implement the notion that the board should function in a purely policy-making or quasi-legislative capacity and keep itself aloof from the administrative processes that give full meaning to programs, policies, and standards.[60]

[60] Joseph Pois, "The Board and the General Superintendent," in Alan Rosenthal (ed.), *Governing Education* (Garden City, N.Y.: Anchor, 1969), p. 427.

The presently accepted concept about the roles of the school board and the superintendent of schools is the result of many years of conflict. Callahan traced the history of this conflict, which became an open conflict during the 1890s.[61] A feasible settlement was not reached until well into the 1900s. However, the question of school board–superintendent relationships represents a continuing struggle and frequently is the basis of open controversy.

The primary responsibility of the board is to make policy and the primary role of the superintendent is to administer it, but in reality the two functions intermingle. The superintendent and the board start their political relationship by discussing their expectations of each other, leading to contractual arrangements. However, as the school superintendent and board interact in decision-making situations and personal interactions, a complex interpersonal relationship results. The quality of this relationship may influence the quality of the decision-making process.

Part of this relationship involves the politics of running the schools. In one type of superintendent–board relationship, the superintendent assumes a strong political position in school policy and succeeds in coopting the board. Critics of this political relationship contend that the school board becomes a rubber stamp of the professional bureaucracy. Very different from this is the weak superintendency in which the board all but operates the schools, in total disregard of the superintendent. Between these two extremes are a variety of other political relationships for which one could develop a typology.

As a result of many circumstances, the internal dynamics of the board of education are often marked by severe conflict. Clark described school board politics as a game of numbers—for example 4–3, 5–2 votes.[62] School boards often become fragmented into political factions during the process of appointing a school superintendent. Parker described how errors during the process further fragmented an already divided board membership in Memphis.[63] To avoid the possibility of the creation of membership divisiveness, many boards contract for the services of consultants in the recruitment and selection of a superintendent.

How important is the politics of school board–superintendent relations? Authors have, for many years, pointed to the supreme importance of establishing a productive working relationship between the superintendent, other professional staff, and the board. When these

---

[61] Raymond E. Callahan, "The American Board of Education, 1789–1960," in Peter J. Cistone (ed.), op. cit., pp. 19–46.

[62] Evelyn Clark, "Board Power: A Game of Numbers," *The American School Board Journal*, 168 (January 1981), 27–28.

[63] Barbara Parker, "When a Board is Divided, Almost Anything Can Go Wrong—and Does." *The American School Board Journal*, 166 (February 1979), 21–25.

relationships deteriorate, much disruption is experienced in school organizations. In some instances the politics of the board and the superintendent degenerate to the point that decisions cannot be made. These situations are frequently the basis of community crises and create personal animosities.

Politics of the Bureaucracy

The politics of the bureaucracy refers to the exercise of power in decision making within, by, and through the central staff organization of the school district. Staff organizations vary in complexity, depending on the size of the enrollment in a district—the larger the enrollment, the more complex the bureaucracy becomes. Disagreements concerning goals and empire building among administrators and teachers may lead to factional competition among leaders in the bureaucracy, giving rise to an internal political process. Bacharach and Lawler hypothesized that interest group politics, coalition politics, and bargaining formed the main themes of the internal politics of organizations and that "most organizational politics involve the efforts of actors to mobilize interest groups and coalitions for the sake of influencing the decisions of those in authority."[64] There are few, if any, school district organizations in which administrators do not become active in influencing different aspects of the political process of the community. Thus organizational politics includes internal power struggles as well as external political strategies to influence environmental conditions.

Those in authority in the educational organization are delegated the power to allocate resources, to promulgate rules, and to regulate and control the actions of those in the lower echelons of the hierarchy. Also, they have judicial-like powers to settle disputes. The school superintendent often has a powerful community constituency that will lend support to his or her recommendations.

During the 1960s much literature appeared that was critical of educational bureaucracy, particularly the complex organizations of large city school districts. Most of these critics viewed the bureaucrats as dominating the school system, as slow in responding to needed changes, and somewhat self-serving. Gittell was among those who believed that breaking central organizational control and stimulating citizen participation through local control would result in educational improvement in city school systems.[65]

[64]Samuel B. Bacharach and Edward J. Lawler, *Power and Politics in Organizations* (San Francisco: Jossey-Bass, 1980), p. 213.

[65]Marilyn Gittell, *Participants and Participation: A Study of School Policy in New York City* (New York: Center for Urban Education, 1967).

The Bureaucracy as a Political System

As a reaction to the spoils system, beginning in 1883 many governmental employees were placed under the merit system of career service in which, presumably, they were accountable to no political party. The concept of civil service was established earlier in England with reforms dating from 1855. The governmental reform concept of the separation of politics and administration was very popular until the late 1940s. Consequently, much that has been written about governmental bureaucracy is based upon the predisposition to view bureaucrats as political eunuchs preoccupied with maintenance of rules and regulations, development of guidelines, and inflexible administration of policies. The literature about bureaucracy in big business and government has tended to emphasize what the bureaucracy does to people rather than how people use bureaucracy to realize personal and group goals.

Literature abounds with critical, damning statements about bureaucrats who have job anxiety and are masters of red tape and seven copies of everything. In our lighter moments we can enjoy the satire of *Parkinson's Law, The Peter Principle* or *When in Doubt, Mumble*.[66] Yet we are impressed with the political vitality of big organizations. Instead of seeing the personalities of all the people warped by their concern with job security and status, we see persons motivated to obtain power for personally valued social positions in addition to ego and status motivations.

In *Management and Machiavelli* Jay examined private corporations as political structures. Concerning the view that management personnel are mainly concerned with accommodations to organizations for personal satisfactions of status, Jay stated,

> I suppose there are people in management who seek power for the sheer pleasure of exercising it, but I have never encountered them. Most people who aspire to power within organizations will tell you that they want it so as to achieve objects they believe in, but even that does not go to the heart of the matter. The real pleasure of power is the pleasure of freedom, and it goes right back to one of man's most primitive needs, the need to control his environment.[67]

In his critical analysis of the bureaucratic control of education in New York City, Rogers stated that the major divisions formed strongly loyal "baronies." According to Rogers, these baronies competed for larger shares of the scarce resources available in the system.[68]

---

[66] See C. N. Parkinson, *Parkinson's Law* (Boston: Houghton, 1957); L. J. Peter, *The Peter Principle* (New York: Morrow, 1969); James H. Boren, *When In Doubt, Mumble* (New York: Van Nostrand, 1972).

[67] Antony Jay, *Management and Machiavelli* (New York: Holt, 1967), p. 38.

[68] David Rogers, *110 Livingston Street* (New York: Random House, 1968).

Regardless of the motivation, we have observed many persons in educational organizations striving for power. Sometimes, for example, a power struggle develops, as was described by Jay, as a struggle between the king (the superintendent) and the barons (the area superintendents). Area superintendents often build a strong power base among their immediate constituency as a countervailing power to the superintendent. Some school principals become politically powerful barons. Jay further illustrated the modern line and staff as barons and courtiers. Anyone familiar with school organizations has seen the situation in which the king (the school superintendent) was influenced more by the courtier (a staff officer) than by the assistant superintendents (the barons).

The prospective educational administrator should assume that, in addition to its other aspects, the large educational bureaucracy is an active political system in interaction with other political systems. There is in Appleby's term an "intermingling" of the politics of the board of education, the politics of the community, and the politics of the bureaucracy.[69] Mainzer also contended that most political observers today see the policy-making and administrative processes as interwoven.[70] In this regard Mainzer wrote, "The bureau and its chief are key characters in shaping policy. It is not parties as a whole nor Congress as a whole nor the administration as a whole that copes with most problems; it is interest groups, committees, and bureaus."[71]

Some authorities attempt to fit all bureaucratic organizations everywhere into the same descriptive mold, but educational organizations are very different, even though they may be more bureaucratic than collegial. There are some monocratic bureaucracies led by an elite that makes arbitrary demands on those in the lower hierarchies. On the other hand, there are bureaucracies in which leadership is more pluralistic. The point is that, just as community political systems fit different types, bureaucracies have different structures and processes for decision making.

Differences Between the Politics of the Bureaucracy and the Politics of the Community

In his examination of the role of bureaucracy in the political process, Rourke argued persuasively that the politics of the bureaucracy is different from the politics of the legislative sector.[72] These

[69] Paul Appleby, *Policy and Administration* (Tuscaloosa: University of Alabama Press, 1949), p. 6–10.

[70] Lewis C. Mainzer, *Political Bureaucracy* (Glenview, Ill.: Scott, Foresman, 1973), p. 70.

[71] Ibid., p. 72.

[72] Francis E. Rourke, *Bureaucracy, Politics, and Public Policy* (Boston: Little, Brown, 1969), pp. 103–115.

differences exist for the following reasons: (1) authority and power in the bureaucratic organization are hierarchically structured; (2) the professional expert has strong influence in the decision-making process of bureaucracy, whereas the legislative body is primarily affected by political considerations; and (3) the politics of the bureaucracy is less public than the politics of the legislative branch.

The politics of the board or other legislative bodies, particularly in a pluralistic power structure, is legally a politics of equals, although legal equality never assures equality in practice. In the bureaucracy persons are legally unequal, and as a consequence, the ruling elite of a bureaucratic system may exercise much greater control over subordinates and make more frequent use of arbitrary power than a board of education may exercise over its constituents or the elites of a monopolistic power structure may exercise on followers.

The politics of bureaucracy may be more heavily influenced by professional expert opinion than the politics of the legislative bodies or the public politics of the community. Many decisions in the organization hinge upon technical advice, whereas political considerations weigh heavily upon politics of the public. Rourke noted that professionals may participate in organizational decision making without facing the political reprisal inherent in public politics.[73] This last point may be questionable, particularly in some organizations. Finally, Rourke pointed to the obvious difference in visibility between the politics of the bureaucracy and public politics or the politics of the board of education. The opinion has persisted that decision making should have an invisible aspect. For example, school officials have insisted that discussions concerning the specific location of schools should not be public because of the high interest in land speculation and development. Rourke felt that many proposals benefited from private discussion because people would be more candid and compromise would be facilitated.[74]

However, as mentioned previously, within recent years educators have experienced increased pressure concerning secrecy. Legislatures have passed laws prohibiting secret meetings of boards of education and other public bodies. These "government-in-the-sunshine" laws place heavy penalties upon those participating in invisible government. Moreover, the mass media have greatly increased coverage of what goes on within the bureaucracy of school systems. The likelihood exists that the politics of the bureaucracy will continue to be more open to the public than it has been in the past.

[73] Ibid.
[74] Ibid.

The Political Culture of the Community

In Chapter 12, we discussed briefly the ideologies that influence politics in America. Carried within these concepts of life in the community are shared norms, beliefs, and attitudes that make up the political culture of the community. Nimmo defined political culture as "a widely shared pattern of tendencies of beliefs, values, and expectations."[75] This involves shared ideas about the proper functions of government (what government should do), participation and decision making (how government ought to be conducted), concepts about governmental interaction with the economic system, and so on. Thus political culture refers to the shared normative system that gives meaning to the political process.

Educational administrators from colleges and universities to elementary schools are influenced by political culture. In every state, for example, there are districts with the reputation of being "conservative" (beliefs shared that are right of center) and other districts that are spoken of as "liberal" (or left of center). Referring again to our discussion of ideologies in Chapter 12, we note the many school districts of the nation in which new liberal ideology underlies the political culture, in others classical liberalism may be the prevailing view, and so on.

The most likely prospect, however, for the educational administrator is that he or she will be faced with conflicting political cultures; that is, there will be a conflict of political cultures among competing political groups. Thus the political groups on the right press for the restriction of education to the basics, and groups on the left demand a broadened program of schooling to offer special opportunities to the unfortunate. These conflicts also involve emotional differences about library holdings, sex education, teaching materials in social studies, and the like.

Methods of Studying Community Power Structure

Prior to the community power structure studies of the 1950s and 1960s, the position method was primarily used to locate persons of power. The underlying assumption in this method is that the persons who hold the highest official positions in formal organizations are the

[75]Dan Nimmo, *Political Communication and Public Opinion in America* (Santa Monica, Calif.: Goodyear, 1978), p. 254.

most powerful leaders in the community. For example, the most powerful person in a civic organization is assumed to be the president.

The position method has lost favor as a means to locate power because it gave inaccurate results. Empirical analyses of power structures showed that many office holders were not influential in policy decision making. The results obtained by the position method left much to be desired in describing the dynamics of the power structure. Moreover, because of the emphasis on formal processes, the influence of informal groups was neglected.

Hunter is credited with developing the reputational technique and used it as a basis for collecting data for his *Community Power Structure*.[76] The reputational technique involves several steps. First, persons at the center of community activities who are knowledgeable about civic affairs are asked to provide lists of persons of prominence in important interest areas of the community (e.g., business, government, civic groups, social sectors). Second, the lists are submitted to a panel of persons knowledgeable about community affairs. This panel is asked to select the most prominent of the prominent persons nominated. Third, in-depth interviews are conducted with all persons whom the panel of judges unanimously found to be the most prominent. In these interviews the researcher probes for answers concerning the dynamics of the power structure in the decision-making process. What important decisions have been made recently or are pending now about community policy? Who are the persons who participated (or are participating) and what was (or is) the extent of their influence? How (through what processes) did the leaders in the power structure reach a decision? These are but a few general questions of the many the researcher tries to answer from the interviews. The data so collected are then analyzed to provide a view of the power structure.

In the decision-analysis technique, as developed by Dahl and used in his New Haven study, the first step is to select several decision areas (e.g., education, urban renewal, partisan politics) for study and interview persons affiliated with programs in these areas to identify the most important decisions made.[77] Pools of names of persons are developed from interviews and documents. Who were involved in these decisions? In-depth interviews are conducted with the persons known to have exerted leadership. Documentary evidence (e.g., newspapers, board minutes) is also used to reconstruct as much as possible who did what and how much. From the evidence collected and analyzed the researcher develops a description of the power structure.

In recent years the strengths of the reputational and decision

[76] Hunter, loc. cit.
[77] Dahl, loc. cit.

analysis techniques have been merged into one combined technique to study community power structure. In reality, neither of these techniques can be employed by the practitioner. They are primarily useful to those engaged in basic research. The practitioner needs to learn how to make in-service analyses that are accurate and usable. Nunnery and Kimbrough described how practitioners may make "live-in" studies of the political systems in which they practice.[78] They recommended five steps as follows: (1) study background material about power structures as described in studies of communities to increase knowledge about politics; (2) make a special effort to obtain information about local problems, issues, and decisions; (3) piece together information obtained from conversations and documents; (4) record information as it is obtained; and (5) observe leader behavior in community decisions and participate in community activities.

ACTIVITIES/QUESTIONS FOR FURTHER STUDY

1. Plan and conduct a mini-study of the power structure of a local community, town, school system, or any other organized group or locale in which you are interested. Make approximately 10 to 12 well-placed interviews with knowledgeable persons and try to obtain answers to the following questions: Who are the persons most influential in making significant decisions? How (through what process) are decisions made? What ideologies motivate the participants in the process?

2. Conduct a small group discussion about strategies that educators should use to influence different kinds of political systems with different power structures (e.g., monopolistic, multigroup noncompetitive, competitive elite, pluralistic). What strategy would be best for the communities discussed? What specific techniques should be employed? Discuss the entire process recommended from initiation of the strategy through completion of the change process.

3. Teachers' organizations in many school districts have been actively supporting candidates for boards of education who might be more supportive of teachers' interests. What are the implications for educational administrators of such attempts to control the board of education? Should the administrative establishment take any action to support or oppose the control of the board by any interest group?

SUGGESTED READINGS

AGGER, ROBERT E., and MARSHALL N. GOLDSTEIN. *Who Will Rule the Schools: A Cultural Class Crisis.* Belmont, Calif.: Wadsworth Publishing Co., Inc., 1971.

IANNACCONE, LAURENCE, and FRANK W. LUTZ. *Politics, Power and Policy: The Governing of School Districts.* Columbus, Ohio: Charles E. Merrill Publishers, 1970.

[78]Michael Y. Nunnery and Ralph B. Kimbrough, *Politics, Power, Polls, and School Elections* (Berkeley: McCutchan, 1971), pp. 27–30.

KIMBROUGH, RALPH B. *Political Power and Educational Decision-Making.* Chicago: Rand McNally & Co., 1964.

NUNNERY, MICHAEL Y., and RALPH B. KIMBROUGH. *Politics, Power, Polls, and School Elections.* Berkeley: McCutchan Publishing Corp., 1971.

PETERS, B. GUY. *The Politics of Bureaucracy.* New York: Longman Inc., 1978.

PETERSON, PAUL E. *School Politics Chicago Style.* Chicago: University of Chicago Press, 1976.

ROYKO, MIKE. *Boss: Richard J. Daley of Chicago.* New York: Signet Books, 1971.

SCRIBNER, JAY D. (ed.). *The Politics of Education,* seventy-sixth yearbook of the National Society for the Study of Education. Chicago: University of Chicago Press, 1977.

WILES, DAVID K., JON WILES, and JOSEPH BONDI. *Practical Politics for School Administrators.* Boston: Allyn & Bacon, Inc., 1981.

ZEIGLER, L. HARMON, and M. KENT JENNINGS. *Governing American Schools.* North Scituate, Mass.: Duxbury Press, 1974.

16

State and Federal Educational Politics

FOR many years educators have attempted to influence state and federal legislation concerning education. Because public colleges and universities are principally state funded, they traditionally have been concerned with the state politics of education. Those educators in the public school programs have, through the past three decades, also turned to the state politics of education in seeking solutions to many of their problems. The increased interest of the federal and state governments in funding educational programs during the 1960s further kindled educators' interest in the nature of political power and decision making at these levels.

Politics Among the States

With the growth of federal influence in many aspects of living some observers have asked whether the states have lost their sovereignty and are becoming an administrative arm of the federal government. Moynihan is among those who have viewed with alarm the increased power of the federal government to dominate colleges and universities.

496   Socioeconomic and Political Influences on Administration

The federal government has acquired the power to shut down any university it chooses. The more important the university, the greater the power. And the greater the concentration of federal power in one place, the greater the danger.[1]

The question of how independent the states should be from the federal government has been debated for several decades and was an underlying issue in the 1980 presidential election. Press and VerBurg saw considerable increase in federal influence in certain areas (e.g., welfare, civil rights, housing) following legislation passed in the mid-1960s; however, they viewed state and local governments as exercising much independence in other areas, such as police and fire protection, and education.[2] Sharkansky championed the viability of state politics and governance and believed that the states are maligned by journalists, social scientists, and politicians for their inability to solve extremely difficult problems, which by force of circumstances are beyond immediate solution.[3] If the state governments exercise powerful influence in the development of educational politics, the important question is what distinctive differences in politics exist among the states and whether these differences result in differences in the organization and administration of education?

Differences in State Political Cultures

Press and VerBurg discussed the distinctive differences among the states, including differences in political cultures.[4] The states vary in the structure and exercise of politics, economics, extent of ethnic influence, political participation, urbanization, industrialization, wealth, and so on. These conditions presumably have some influence on the political process. For example, the influence of unions is likely to be greater in highly industrialized states than in states with little industrial strength, and, as discussed in Chapter 14, the extent of urbanization also may change the nature of politics.

The concept of political culture is useful in considering the way in which cultural differences among the states influence the structure of state governance and the structure of education. As discussed in Chapter 15, the term political culture refers to the system of beliefs, attitudes, norms, and sentiments that provide order and meaning to the political process. Elazar completed some pioneer work in this area and suggested the possible domination of any one of three political

---

[1] Daniel Patrick Moynihan, "State vs. Academe," *Harper's*, 261 (December 1980), 31–40.

[2] Charles Press and Kenneth VerBurg, *State and Community Governments in the Federal System* (New York: Wiley, 1979), pp. 18–19.

[3] Ira Sharkansky, *The Maligned States: Policy Accomplishments, Problems, and Opportunities*, 2nd ed. (New York: McGraw-Hill, 1968), pp. 1–7.

[4] Press and VerBurg, op. cit., pp. 42–63.

cultures among the states.[5] The *moralist* political culture emphasizes government for the common good, the maximization of citizen participation, and high ethical principles. Emphasized in the *individualist* culture are the concepts that the least governed are the best governed, that minimum emphasis should be placed on social welfare services, that whatever rules are necessary to the marketplace should be adopted, and that one should participate in self-interests as he or she desires. The *traditionalist* culture emphasizes elite rule by "best" families, chivalrous conduct toward women, a code of honor, and a paternalistic view of society by rulers.

Sharkansky examined the utility of this concept by analyzing the relationship of these cultures to political participation, bureaucracy, and governmental service levels.[6] Using a scale to measure the political cultures developed by Elazar, Sharkansky found statistically significant relationships between political culture and several characteristics of state politics and public service. For example, the states marked by high traditionalism had the lowest levels of participation and the most restrictive suffrage laws, whereas moralist states were characterized by high participation in governance and open suffrage laws.

In another analysis, Ritt reviewed the research on state cultures and examined the relationship of political culture to political reform. In his study he found that states with moralistic political cultures fostered reform, whereas states with individualistic or traditionalistic political cultures did not engage in reform.[7]

Wirt considered the relationship of Elazar's categories of state culture to the centralization of state authority over educational policy.[8] Using six categories of the extent of centralization, from "absence of state authority" to "total state assumption" of authority, Wirt conducted a content analysis of the laws in the fifty states. A range of the extent of centralization resulted with Wyoming having the least centralization and Hawaii the greatest. Although Wirt found a relationship between Elazar's political cultures and state centralization of authority, he was surprised to find that the states with traditionalistic cultures were more highly centralized than the states believed to have moralistic cultures. The opposite would have been expected.

[5] Daniel J. Elazar, *American Federalism: A View from the States,* 2nd ed. (New York: Crowell, 1972).

[6] Ira Sharkansky, The Utility of Elazar's Political Culture," *Polity,* II (Fall 1969), 66–83.

[7] Leonard G. Ritt, "Political Cultures and Political Reform: A Research Note," *Publius,* 4 (Winter 1974), 127–133.

[8] Frederick M. Wirt, "School Policy Culture and State Decentralization," in Jay D. Scribner (ed.) *The Politics of Education,* seventy-sixth yearbook of the National Society for the Study of Education (Chicago: University of Chicago Press, 1977), pp. 164–187.

Consequently, more research needs to be completed in order to reach any meaningful conclusions in this area.

The research concerning the relationship between political cultures and the structure of education is limited in both the amount and the lack of empirically derived data. Moreover, the cultures described by Elazar are impressionistic. Thus generalization in this area is not possible. On the other hand, the data available do suggest that the political structure for education varies among the states. One may logically expect that differences in structures, ideologies, and cultures produce some distinctive qualities in the organization and administration of education among the states.

Variations in State Power Structures

As found in studies of communities, state power structures exist for decision making in education. In their study of educational decision making in Missouri, Illinois, and Michigan, Masters and associates concluded that educational decisions were made within clearly identifiable power structures.[9] Based upon his review of studies available from eleven states, Iannaccone postulated four types of state power structure.[10]

Iannaccone saw one type of state structure that was a loose confederation of very independent educational leaders of local school districts in interaction with legislators of their districts. In this *locally based disparate* structure, the leaders of the school districts were able to coalesce their forces to deal with extremely pressing educational decisions. Yet as these emergencies were dealt with, the statewide coalescence moved back into a weak confederacy of independent school districts.

In the *statewide monolithic* structure, state education policy was dominated by a single-minded elite. Iannaccone indicated that this elite could be a coalition from several professional education groups or dominated by one group.[11]

Some states have strong competition among groups (e.g., teachers' unions, professional associations, administrator associations, school board associations). This competition is among elite-run groups; hence the state power structure is a pluralism of elites. This type of structure is referred to as the *statewide fragmented* type by Iannaccone.[12]

Iannaccone described as *statewide syndical* the structure where

[9]Nicholas A. Masters, Robert Salisbury, and Thomas Eliot, *State Politics and the Public Schools* (New York: Knopf, 1964).

[10]Laurence Iannaccone, *Politics in Education* (New York: Center for Applied Research in Education, 1967), pp. 37–63.

[11]Ibid., p. 48.

[12]Ibid., pp. 48–49.

an organization or commission was officially designated by the legislature to be a brokerage agent for educational interests and recommend legislative policies.[13] The School Problems Commission used then in Illinois was cited as exemplary of this structure.

As we indicated in Chapter 4, one of the more recent state-level studies was the Educational Governance Project.[14] In commenting upon the fit of the Educational Governance Project (EGP) findings in relation to Iannaccone's typology, Nystrand stated:

> The general impact of the EGP data upon the Iannaccone typology is to suggest a more complex system of state educational policy making. To be sure, the relationship between interest groups and the legislature is important and the developmental aspects of the typology have led to important understandings. However, an adequate portrayal of state policy systems at the present time must take into account the fact that there are multiple authoritative policy arenas.[15]

Nystrand felt that Iannaccone gave too much attention to educational interest groups and legislatures and did not focus enough upon the influence of state boards of education, governors, and chief state school officers. Moreover, he felt that the models proposed oversimplified reality. According to Nystrand, the EGP data indicated that mixtures of processes may erase discrete lines differentiating the types. For example, one may point to instances of states with statewide monolithic or statewide fragmented politics, where legislatures respond to local constituents in making major policy changes. Thus what should be a process characteristic of locally based disparate politics appears in what is thought to be a predominantly monolithic structure. Summarizing the data, Nystrand noted,

> In summary, the most important finding of the EGP with regard to policy-making systems for education is that these systems are considerably more open than previous researchers have suggested. While educational interest groups and/or chief state school officers continue to hold a preponderance of power regarding some issues in some states, the more general finding was that parties interested in affecting educational policy making usually had multiple opportunities to do so.[16]

Phelan and Pozen, members of Ralph Nader's Center for Study of Responsive Law, provided a comprehensive picture of domination

[13] Ibid., pp. 49–50.

[14] Roald F. Campbell and Tim L. Mazzoni, Jr. (eds.), *State Policy Making for the Public Schools: A Comparative Analysis* (Columbus, Ohio: Educational Governance Project, Ohio State University, 1974).

[15] Raphael O. Nystrand, "State Education Policy Systems," in Campbell and Mazzoni, op. cit., p. 384.

[16] Ibid., p. 385.

by economic and family interests in Delaware.[17] The political powers of the Du Pont family, its financial institutions, its industries, and its other business activities in state and local policy making were traced. There was evidence of Du Pont power in many sectors—for example, commerce, finance, government, politics, education, health, media, recreation, taxation.

The Du Pont family owned the two large daily newspapers in Delaware. These newspapers had a statewide circulation of 140,000. The next largest newspaper in the state had a circulation of about 20,000. The Du Pont industrial, commercial, and other business interests represented many jobs and contributed much to the state economy. A substantial amount of money was donated for various charitable purposes through numerous foundations controlled by the Du Ponts. Control of large banks and financial organizations gave the Du Pont family tremendous resources for moving people in decision making. The laws of Delaware were favorable to business. The trust fund laws, for example, encouraged passage of large fortunes through generations of heirs without payment of inheritance taxes.[18]

Some of the information contained in the report dealt with control of elective and appointive officers. The congressman for Delaware was a Du Pont. The governor was a Du Pont executive before being elected to office. One fourth of the legislators were employees, former employees, or wives or husbands of employees. The official positions of leadership of education boards and commissions showed similar patterns. The board of trustees of the University of Delaware was depicted as dominated by Du Pont family connections. The programs of the university evidenced the strong influence of the Du Pont interests.[19]

Dimensions of State Education Politics

In considering the dimensions of state politics, one is immediately confronted with the great differences in traditions among the states. The legally prescribed powers of the governors vary, although the executives in state governments are generally perceived to be much weaker than the executive in the federal government. Thus we are confronted, as we were in considering the politics of local communities, with the possibility of serious error in attempting to generalize about the political power and decision-making process among the states.

What then can we say about the decision-making aspects of the state politics of education? The following dimensions are discussed in

[17]James Phelan and Robert Pozen, *The Company State* (New York: Grossman, 1973).
   [18]Ibid.
   [19]Ibid.

the literature: (1) state legislative politics, (2) politics of the governor or state executive branch, (3) politics of the state board of education, (4) politics of the chief state school officer, including the state department of education, and (5) interest groups. Because Chapter 17 is devoted to the politics of interest groups, we will not discuss this dimension here.

A word of caution to the educational leader is in order. Authorities of state government have the predisposition to view state politics as separated from the politics of local governments. Yet in observing the way people get statewide power, one must conclude that to have state power is also to have a power base in local communities. This works both ways, of course. That is, persons who move up in the legislative establishment also enhance their power and prestige in local governments, and vice versa. Also not to be overlooked is the interrelationship of state politics with national politics. Holding a very strong statewide base of power will enhance one's prestige in national politics, and vice versa.

The Politics of the Executive (Governor)

The most influential politician in the executive office, the governor, obtains and holds political power by virtue of his or her position in formal and informal associations. As described previously, the governor has legally prescribed, or formal, controls over the decision-making process. The governor may exercise the veto, influence budget proposals, exercise some control over expenditures, appoint officials, and influence the awarding of contracts. In addition to these legally ascribed powers, the governor exercises much influence through the informal aspects of the power structure. The governor is usually a very popular leader with a strong state following. Thus he or she can bring powerful forces to bear upon the consciences, if not the pocketbooks, of legislators.

To win the office of governor usually requires ties and commitments with powerful leaders and local power groups all over the state. Furthermore, decisions on patronage and various legal problems of local government require that the governor have persons in each local governmental unit who can be trusted. For example, an elective public official may die in office or need to be removed for malfeasance. Being much removed from the local situation, the governor must seek advice from some one or a few people who are familiar with the community. This, and the supporters in the political organization, gives the governor a broad base of power, which can be called upon in the legislative process. These people, in turn, have "IOU's," which they can "cash in" with the governor and other high officials.

There has been much interest in the power of the governor relative to the power exercised by the legislature. Rosenthal reviewed research in this area and concluded that considerable variation exists.[20] There were states (e.g., Alabama, Illinois, Louisiana, New Jersey, New York) in which the power exercised by the executive branch was great. However, in some states (e.g., Arizona, Florida, South Carolina) the legislature dominated the executive. Milstein and Jennings found that in New York State the governor was very influential in the establishment of educational policy.[21] There is considerable agreement among authorities of state government that the power of the governor and of the legislature in making state policies varies from state to state and from time to time.

As practiced by the legislatures of many states, governors are increasing the size and expertise of their staffs in education. This is making the governor less reliant on the members of state departments of education and educational lobbyists for information.

How much actual influence do the governor and members of the executive branch have upon educational policy? Answering this question, of course, depends upon empirical descriptions of the unique political power structure of the state. Generalization is hazardous. The political power of governors varies as well as their interest in educational policy. However, in the ultimate determination of educational policy, the financial decisions, there is evidence that support by the governor and his lieutenants is a critical element in educational policy. Campbell and his colleagues found that even though governors varied in interest and activity in education, they were heavily involved in decisions on state financing programs in all twelve states studied.[22] Thus the support of the governor's office appears to be a crucial political factor in the most important policy question—the financial decision. Some of them were not very interested in other aspects of education even though they were concerned with finance.

Politics of the Legislature and Educational Interests

The legislature is a complex structure with well-established norms of leadership behavior. If persons are to have power in the legislature, they must have influence within the legislative establishment, the formal and informal leadership structure through which important leadership roles and committee assignments are arranged. The formal leadership in the legislature is important (e.g., speaker of the house, speaker of senate, committee chairperson). Productivity of the legislature in meeting the needs of education is heavily dependent upon the choice of the leaders. Decisions on legislative leaders

[20] Alan Rosenthal, *Legislative Performance in the States: Explorations of Committee Behavior.* (New York: The Free Press, 1974), pp. 59–61.

[21] Mike M. Milstein and Robert E. Jennings, *Educational Policy-Making and the State Legislature: The New York Experience* (New York: Praeger, 1973), p. 126.

[22] Campbell and Mazzoni, loc. cit.

are usually made much in advance of the legislative sessions, and in some states informal party decisions are made several years in advance.

Much power is used to influence the legislators on important decisions. This power tends to be concentrated in those with high leadership status in the establishment and those who hold important official leadership positions. The power of well-organized interest groups is very noticeable in state legislatures. The point is that the legislature does not operate in a vacuum. Its operations occur within a definable state power structure not unlike those structures described for local governments. This structure responds to the demands of formally organized interest groups as well as powerful informal groups.

McMillan's description of the interaction of state leaders in reversing the position of legislators of South Carolina on a school desegregation decision provided an excellent illustration of the mix of formal and informal activities in state decision making.[23] His description had much similarity to Hunter's earlier discussion of decision making in South Carolina.[24] In McMillan's account, powerful business and educational leaders worked together for months to change the opinions of legislators concerning state racial policies.

In their studies of the legislative process in Louisiana, concerning a bill mandating a course on the free enterprise system, Duet and Newfield found that special interest groups were actively lobbying the legislature during its deliberation on the bill. Somewhat disturbing, however, was the lack of educational leadership in the lobbying process.[25]

Increased dependence on larger, well-educated, politically experienced, specialized legislative staffs since the early 1960s has been an important factor in the increased power of legislatures. This has also made legislatures more independent of lobbies. Balutis wrote the following concerning the staff role:

> For example, a number of legislators interviewed felt that increased leadership staffs had helped to solidify the position of the leaders. The staff publicized leadership positions and activities, giving them increased coverage in the press. They also served, as was noted earlier, as buffers to absorb pressures which the leadership wanted to avoid or divert. This was variously labeled in interviews as "taking the heat,"

[23] George McMillan, "Integration with Dignity," *The Saturday Evening Post*, CXXVI (March 16, 1963), 15–21.

[24] Floyd Hunter, *Top Leadership, USA* (Chapel Hill: University of North Carolina Press, 1959).

[25] Claude Duet and John Newfield, "The Free Enterprise System: A Case Study of Legislative Influence on the Curriculum," *Peabody Journal of Education*, 56 (October 1978), 1–8.

"acting as fall guy," "getting him off the hook," and so on. Thus, increased leadership staffs were seen as tools to increase the leaders' influence over the legislature. Further research on this matter certainly is warranted.[26]

Similarly, Fuhrman found that both the legislature and the governor are placing greater reliance upon staffs.

> Professionalization and modernization have intruded on out-dated part-time legislatures, turning them into streamlined, more efficient arenas for policy formulation, deliberation, and monitoring. The staffed, committed legislature is more likely to initiate its own policies, question the proposals of schoolmen, and insure appropriate implementation of its policies by departments. Reapportionment has lessened the rural bias of state legislatures, giving urban interests at least a reasonable chance, and has, in some cases, made for greater legislative turnover and a more youthful membership. The governor's office, too, has changed. Governors have more of their own staffs and are less reliant on state departments.[27]

The staffing practices of legislators have in effect created another barrier between educational interest groups and members of the legislature. The members of these staffs frequently possess expertise equal to members of state departments of education and educational lobbyists. Leaders of the educational staffs may in some instances have greater influence on legislative policies than any other group around the legislature. Thus educators are frequently forced to lobby the staff for education as well as the members of the legislature.

State Board of Education Politics

The prevalent opinion among most observers is that the state board of education in most states is politically weak. This observation was confirmed by the analysis of ten states by Campbell and Mazzoni. They observed, "Still, we think that our data, on balance, point unmistakably to the weakness, rather than the strength, of state boards of education as policy making participants."[28] Elaborating further on the matter, Campbell and Mazzoni stated the following:

> Their policy-making role in the legislative arena was marginal. And these boards were so overshadowed by the CSSO (Chief State School Officer) in the agency arena as to raise doubt about what policy-making

[26] Alan P. Balutis, "Legislative Staffing: A View From the States," in J. L. Heaphey and A. P. Balutis (eds.), *Legislative Staffing* (New York: Halsted, 1975), pp. 133–134.

[27] Susan Fuhrman, "The Politics and Process of School Finance Reform," *Journal of Educational Finance,* 4 (Fall 1978), 175–176.

[28] Campbell and Mazzoni, op. cit., p. 98.

functions, if any, they performed beyond the one (i.e., formal enactment) that was legally required.[29]

Thus the evidence suggests that in many states the state board is politically weak in the establishment of educational policy.

Writing from his experience as Chancellor of the New York State Board of Regents, Black found that the regents had to rely on the power of persuasion.[30] He saw the board of regents as actively participating in the state political arena in support of educational legislation.

The Politics of the State Bureaucracy: Chief State School Officer and State Department

A discussion of the politics of the bureaucracy in relation to local school district politics was presented in Chapter 15. How powerful is the counterpart of the local school bureaucracy in state politics? In our discussion we are including in the state bureaucracy the chief state school officer and the state department of education, which he or she heads.

The chief state school officer is the most important power wielder within the state education bureaucracy. Based upon the limited studies available, this domination is almost without exception. These same studies show that the chief state school officer may also have influence upon the legislature. However, in the legislative arena the power of the chief state school officers varies greatly among the states.[31]

A part of the variance may be accounted for by varying legal power; however, this is only one aspect of the source of power and influence. As described previously, power is not only ascribed legally but also earned within the dynamic climate of the total political arena. Somewhat interesting is Campbell and Mazzoni's finding that in certain states the chief state school officer may be strong within the legislature but weak in the state education agency, and vice versa.[32]

Usdan found that leaders in the state bureaucracy were viably involved in most educational legislation.[33] Unfortunately, too little in-depth research is available concerning the political role played by the chief and his or her lieutenants. Obviously, the role of the bureaucracy varies greatly among the states. In some states a well-developed bureaucracy does not exist, whereas in others it looks like a small federal bureau.

[29] Ibid.

[30] Theodore M. Black, "The Political Role of Educators," *Educational Leadership*, 34 (November 1976), 122–25.

[31] Campbell and Mazzoni, op. cit., p. 161.

[32] Ibid., p. 162.

[33] Michael D. Usdan, *The Political Power of Education in New York State* (New York: Teachers College, Columbia University, 1963), p. 69.

In those states in which a well-organized bureaucracy exists and state financing of education is moderately high, the power of the state bureaucracy is very likely to be felt in educational legislation. The processes through which the will of the leaders in the state bureaucracy is joined in legislative proposals will vary. In one state the chief and the "barons" may take a low-key, responding approach. Even with all their reference services and aides and information, key legislators feel that they must listen to top leaders of the bureaucracy who are seen as trustworthy, honest, and capable.

Persons who have influence with key leaders of the legislature are very skillful. They have learned how to work with the "in-house" professionals of the legislature and legislative aides to influence the wording of bills to be sure that a "bad" bill has a minimum disruptive effect upon educational policy. They know how to use the influence of the bureaucracy to see that "good" bills are initiated and promoted.

Again, as we have cautioned throughout, the politics of education in different communities, regions, and states is different in structure and dynamics. The educators of each state must objectively analyze the dynamics of the state power structure as a basis for developing strategies to influence educational policy.

Federal Politics and Educational Policy

Although educational interest groups had attempted to exercise political power in the development of national policies in education, a new era of educational politics may have had its inception with the passage of the Elementary and Secondary Education Act of 1965. In fact, the 1960s ushered in greater interest among educators in federal politics than they had displayed previously. The extensive efforts of school superintendents throughout the nation to lobby in behalf of PL 815 and 874 during this period are illustrative of this interest. Educational groups, including the enthusiastic support of the National Education Association, were especially active in the decision to create the Department of Education. In the sections that follow we explore briefly the area of the federal politics of education.

Who Runs the United States?

Some fascinating literature has been written in answering the intriguing question. "Who runs the United States?" The muckraking journalist may tend to see a conspiracy behind big policy-making events. Watergate and related events provided a field day for such journalists. Even less serious students of history cannot escape the "jugular vein" thrusts at the throats of business and financial moguls by Ida M. Tarbell, Upton Sinclair, and other muckraking journalists at the turn of this century.

In their anguish, dread, and despair some existentialist observers may see governments drifting inevitably into policies in a nation out of control. People have lost effective choice and are being drowned by monsters of which many are of their own creation. "I beheld the wretch—the miserable monster whom I had created."[34]

The presidency has traditionally had an aura of royalty for many Americans. Many historians, particularly those leaning toward the great-man theory, helped us to see the presidency as a secular papacy of the democracy. This thinking carries in it the blessings of national unification—the common belief in the defense of the free spirit. Unfortunately, in it also are the shadows of Nietzsche's superman and the dark clouds of dictatorship.

The scholarly student of Tocqueville sees in the politics of the national government a viable democratic pluralism characterized by (1) competition among many interest groups primarily representing openness and the interests of everyone, (2) a process of decision making representative of the commonly shared democratic creed, and (3) viable participation of the citizenry in policy formulation based upon direct involvement through various channels, including the vote.

Perhaps national politics has represented some aspects of all of these views. Perhaps, as some philosophers feel, we have either consciously or through the inescapable conditions of nature had only one policy we could follow. There seems little doubt that at times the nation was dominated by elite economic moguls, as the muckrakers contended. Their case was believable enough to stir national reform. Perhaps historically interspersed in the process is a discernible pluralism. The basic question, however, is how we can conceptualize the process now. On what basis of national power structure must strategies for educational improvement be constructed?

The Structure of National Politics: Two Views

As indicated in Chapter 3, the federal government has played an increasingly important role in the control and administration of education. Financial support for education from the federal government increased greatly during the 1960s. Therefore the views of citizens and educators need to be felt by those involved in formulating federal policies in the field of education. An important step in assuring that these views have influence is to understand how political power in decision making is exercised at the national level.

Students of government fall within two views concerning the national power structure. Traditionally, the most popularly read writers

[34]Mary W. Shelley, *Frankenstein* (London: Dent, 1921), p. 52.

in political science described the federal power structure as a democratic pluralism. The idea that the federal government could be controlled by a group of elites was unthinkable. On the other hand, supporting evidence indicates that the power structure for decision making in the federal government may not be as pluralistic as many students have been taught. As a consequence of this change in perspective, an elitist concept of democracy has been amplified within recent years.

Discussion of Democratic Pluralism.   As indicated earlier, beliefs in the efficacy of democratic pluralism are widely held among political scientists in the United States. The concepts are traceable to the persuasive works of Alexis de Tocqueville. David Truman's *The Governmental Process* represents an exemplary view of the pluralistic power structure from the perspective of interest-group theory.[35]

In discussing the nature of the pluralistic power structure, Truman centered attention upon the functions of interest groups and what he termed unorganized or potential interests. The following basic themes of pluralism were emphasized: (1) participation of the people in governance is through membership in interest groups; (2) there is competition among these interest groups in decision making; (3) a widely shared ideological consensus or "rules of the game" governs the activity of politicized interest groups.

Organized interest groups are the lifeblood of governmental policy. Truman described the controversy and conflict among these groups as the "essence of politics."[36] These interest groups function to exercise power (1) to control their members, (2) to control other groups, and (3) to make claims upon the government. Governments were described as "centers of interest-based power."[37] "Both the forms and functions of government in turn are a reflection of the activities and claims of such groups."[38] Truman described governmental decisions as follows: "The product of effective access, of the claims of organized and unorganized interests that achieve access with varying degrees of effectiveness, is a governmental decision."[39]

A problem with which most pluralists labor concerns who or what acts as the governor or control over the selfish appetites of these powerful interest groups. What is to keep several of the most powerful interest groups from dominating the federal power structure? According to Truman, two factors serve to keep balance in the system: (1) the multiple memberships in interest groups that produce divided

[35] David B. Truman, *The Governmental Process*, 2nd ed. (New York: Knopf, 1971).
[36] Ibid., p. 503.
[37] Ibid., p. 506.
[38] Ibid., p. 505.
[39] Ibid., p. 507.

loyalties to group goals; (2) the widely held but unorganized interests (ideological consensus) concerning the "rules of the game" or the democratic creed.

Multiple memberships provide the basis for competing ideas within interest groups. For example, members of teachers' unions are also members of a variety of other groups with different objectives. Some of the members may also be members of taxpayers' associations and business organizations. As a result of these overlapping memberships, Truman saw the interest groups themselves as having to accommodate different interests. Thus these interests groups never become solidified or monolithic.

Through the family, education, and other institutional areas, people develop what Truman referred to as the "rules of the game." These are very pervasive norms concerning how persons ought to behave and how political decisions should be made. These widely held unorganized interests or core of widely shared democratic values, coupled with the moderating influences of multiple-group membership, serve as the governor or, as Truman expressed it, "balance wheel" of the power structure.

There are, of course, numerous variations in expressions of the pluralistic power structure. However, nearly all of them profess allegiance to the following assumptions, which were stated by Presthus.

1. That competing centers and bases of power and influence exist within a political community. . . .
2. The opportunity for individual and organizational access into the political system. . . .
3. That individuals actively participate in and make their will felt through organizations of many kinds. . . .
4. That elections are viable instruments of mass participation in political decisions, including those on specific issues. . . .
5. That a consensus exists on what may be called the "democratic creed."[40]

The Elitist View of Democracy. Within the past thirty years various elitist views of democratic power structure in national government have been proposed. In 1956 Mills wrote about the control of the federal government by political, corporate, and military elites.[41] There is much evidence to support his documentation of the power wielded by the corporate and military leaders. The term *military–industrial complex* has become a household word to describe the interdependence of industry upon the production of military goods and

---

[40]Robert Presthus, *Men at the Top* (New York: Oxford University Press, 1964), pp. 22–24.
[41]C. Wright Mills, *The Power Elite* (New York: Oxford University Press, 1956).

services financed by the federal government. On the other hand, the interrelationship of the federal government with powerful groups in the economic system is not restricted to the military. Galbraith used knowledge about the inextricable ties of government and business to suggest that federal decisions are made by corporate and political elites.[42] Kolko concluded that despite what Americans want to believe, there are very powerful concentrations of economic power in a very small elite.[43] Domhoff also reached the decision that elites control political decision making in the United States.[44] Other writers, such as Lundberg[45] and Berle,[46] have provided information about the concentrations of persons with economic power.

In their popularly read *The Irony of Democracy,* Dye and Zeigler attempted to refine an elitist concept of national power structure and democratic governance.[47] In broad terms they described the general outline of what they termed a pluralism of elites, otherwise discussed in other literature as competitive elite structures. Instead of openness to the decision-making process, the individual is powerless to deal with huge concentrations of resources and power—mostly economic. Instead of taking comfort in the existence of a widely shared democratic creed, Dye and Zeigler warned of the ominous indications that only a small minority of Americans are committed to democratic principles. Concerning the viability of elections (one of the pillars of democratic pluralism), the authors noted, "The ballot is widely considered a panacea for social ills, but there is little evidence that voters can directly affect public policy through the exercise of their franchise.[48]

Writing in a more recent publication, Dye proposed the elite oriented "oligarchic model" to describe the structure for national policy making. According to him, corporate and personal wealth is channeled into "foundations, universities, and policy-planning institutions, where corporate representatives and top wealth-holders exercise ultimate power on the governing boards."[49] These agencies and institutions produce the results of studies, investigations, and analyses that are fed to the leaders of elite groups (e.g., leaders of mass media, financial institutions, universities). This process results in a

---

[42]John Kenneth Galbraith, *The New Industrial State* (New York: Houghton, 1967).

[43]Gabriel Kolko, *Wealth and Power in America* (New York: Praeger, 1962).

[44]William G. Domhoff, *Who Rules America?* (Englewood Cliffs, N.J.: Prentice-Hall, 1967).

[45]Ferdinand Lundberg, *The Rich and the Super-Rich* (New York: Lyle Stuart, 1968).

[46]A. A. Berle, Jr., *Economic Power and the Free Society* (New York: Fund for the Republic, 1958).

[47]Thomas R. Dye and L. Harmon Zeigler, *The Irony of Democracy* (Belmont, Calif.: Wadsworth, 1972).

[48]Ibid., p. 167.

[49]Thomas R. Dye, *Who's Running America: The Carter Years,* 2nd ed. (Englewood Cliffs, N.J.: Prentice-Hall, 1979), p. 244.

kind of consensus building among the elites and develops general support for specific policies.

> Eventually, the federal executive agencies, in conjunction with the intellectuals, foundation executives, and policy-planning-group representatives, prepare specific legislative proposals, which then begin to circulate among "the proximate policy makers," notably White House and congressional committee staffs.[50]

Finally, according to Dye, the decision-making process involves the competition, bargaining, and compromise characteristic of the pluralist concept of politics; however, this "occurs *after* the agenda for policy making has been established and the major directions of policy changes have already been determined."[51]

The Dimensions of Federal Politics

The Congress, the president, the federal bureaucracy, and single interest groups have been the subject of much that has been written about politics in the federal government. The federal courts are another important dimension. In the critically important political issues, such as racial integration and civil rights, the decisions of the United States Supreme Court are frequently split along "liberal versus conservative" lines.

The United States Supreme Court. The Supreme Court has traditionally been the point of political activity with appointments made specifically to represent the ideological perspective of the president then in office. Thus there are ideological and political differences among the members of the Court. However, until Woodward and Armstrong published the results of their report, little had been published about the internal politics of the Court.[52] Woodward and Armstrong presented a picture of the justices as engaging in petty dealing, participating in acts of intrigue, and cultivating friends to get their way. The total picture is a Court enmeshed in power struggles that unfortunately included petulant personality differences one might expect to find in any small-town courthouse. What is not known is how this process may influence decisions about education.

The Executive Office of the President. Students of government have discussed the growth of the power and influence of the President since the beginning of the nation. Writing about the relative power of the President, Califano referred to the Congress as the "separate

[50] Ibid., p. 245.
[51] Ibid.
[52] Bob Woodward and Scott Armstrong, *The Brethren: Inside the Supreme Court* (New York: Simon & Schuster, 1980).

but unequal branch."[53] The Watergate tragedy resulted in the general awareness of just how powerful the President had become, and there were voices raised demanding that the Congress regain some of the initiative "surrendered" over the decades to the executive branch. Despite these feelings, the power of the executive in making policy remains. In the modern presidency the tendency for the White House staff to dominate the executive branch is a point of growing concern. Thus, even though they sit as the heads of a great bureaucracy, cabinet officers may not exercise real power in making public policy. Among other writers, former Vice-President Mondale pointed out that this domination of the White House staff has been most clearly evident in foreign affairs.[54] There is clear evidence that the activities of the White House staff have influenced educational policy. For example, the idea for the creation of the National Institute of Education was developed and promoted by the White House staff with Daniel Patrick Moynihan, then on President Nixon's staff, as the prime mover.[55] Consequently, if educators are to influence presidential actions in the field of education, they must have access to and influence with the White House staff.

The Congressional Establishment.   Fritschler and Ross pointed to the fact that the number of persons involved effectively in congressional decisions is small. Although the proposed bills must be sent to the floor for action, "it is the chairperson of the subcommittees, two or three other subcommittee members, and a handful of staff who are important."[56] As is true of state legislatures, the congressional staff has grown in number, professionalism, and influence. The formal operation of the Congress in decision making (actions on the floor, committees, investigations, and the like) is well known by educators. What is not as widely understood is the complex power arrangement through which the deliberative process of the Congress results in the passage or defeat of bills. Dye saw the primary role of the Congress as a deliberative one in considering the program proposals presented by the President.[57] Congressional power is more important in the development of domestic policies—foreign policies being more in the control of the executive. Most authorities perceive a hierarchical structure of

[53]Joseph A. Califano, Jr., *A Presidential Nation* (New York: Norton, 1975), pp. 53–79.

[54]Walter F. Mondale, *The Accountability of Power* (New York: David McKay, 1975), pp. 83–84.

[55]Lee Sproull, Stephen Weiner, and David Wolf, *Organizing an Anarchy: Belief, Bureaucracy, and Politics in the National Institute of Education* (Chicago: University of Chicago Press, 1978), p. 33.

[56]A. Lee Fritschler and Bernard H. Ross, *Executive's Guide to Government: How Washington Works* (Cambridge: Winthrop, 1980), p. 80.

[57]Dye, op. cit., pp. 82–88.

power in both houses of the Congress.[58] The President of the Senate, Speaker of the House, minority leaders, majority leaders, and committee chairmen are among the important leaders in these hierarchies. Powerful political cliques operate within the congressional establishment. The leaders of these groups have important ties to leaders in the bureaucracy, of corporations, and of powerful interest groups. This will become evident in the discussion that follows on congressional action with reference to the establishment and funding of the National Institute of Education.

The Politics of the Federal Bureaucracy. We discussed in Chapter 15 some of the basic characteristics of the politics of bureaucracy. This arena of politics is most highly developed and effective in the federal government. A growing number of volumes is being written about bureaucratic politics. The typical concept of most Americans is that bureaucrats are activists playing political games to realize their own goals.

Pemberton is among the writers who believe the opposite of this concept is true.[59] Based on his study of attempts of presidents through the years to reorganize the bureaucracy, he saw bureaucrats as primarily "captive" of and acting in the interest of entrenched special interests. These groups (e.g., veterans, bankers, farmers, truckers) use the influence of bureaucrats to create and maintain public policies conducive to their interests. Chapman wrote that before deregulation the Interstate Commerce Commission had "compiled an almost spotless record of guarding and promoting the interests of the dominant companies and unions in its jurisdiction."[60] When presidents have tried to reorganize federal agencies to make them more responsible to the people, they have faced overpowering opposition from executive agencies, congressmen, and pressure groups. On the other hand, as discussed in Chapter 15, bureaus frequently become goal-oriented in establishing specific policies and programs. Educational administrators experience the constant pressure contained in the specific guidelines developed by federal agencies.

The leaders in bureaucracies control important power resources. As discussed by Peters, bureaucrats have information and expertise, the power to make rules, and powerful political supporters.[61] Fritschler and Ross pointed to these as important resources and added

[58] Ibid., pp. 82–83.

[59] William E. Pemberton, *Bureaucratic Politics: Executive Reorganization During the Truman Administration* (University of Missouri Press, 1979).

[60] Stephen Chapman, "The ICC and the Truckers," in Charles Peters and Michael Nelson (eds.), *The Culture of Bureaucracy* (New York: Holt, 1979), p. 158.

[61] B. Guy Peters, *The Politics of Bureaucracy: A Comparative Perspective* (New York: Longman, 1978), pp. 169–173.

such resources as the ability to concentrate attention on specific areas and access to historical data about past decisions.[62] Perhaps the most powerful resource is the control of federal funds. Rohr noted that the power of bureaucrats to control money under the Economic Opportunity Act of 1964 reached directly into local communities. The bureaucrats had considerable discretion in the community action programs.[63]

The Process of Decision Making in National Politics

Through what processes or steps is educational policy established at the national level? One approach to understanding this process is to analyze the activities and actors engaged in a significant decision involving educational policy. One such decision would have to be the Elementary and Secondary Education Act of 1965.

Meranto's analysis of the passage of this act was based upon viewing the decision-making process as a system of interrelated forces and conditions. Meranto identified the following conditions as favorable for the passage of the Elementary and Secondary Education Act of 1965: (1) the overwhelming victory of the Democrats in 1964, (2) very strong support of the President, (3) skill of the executive branch in writing a bill favorable to interest groups, (4) interest-group alignment for the bill, (5) ingenuity of the drafters of the proposal, such as linking its provisions to poverty, and (6) strong support in the Congress.[64]

Turning to the question of whether any single important factor explained passage of the 1965 act, Meranto found that there was no single political input or special turning point that was the deciding factor.

> The most fundamental finding that emerges from this endeavor is that the final passage of the school-aid bill cannot be explained by a single major change at the exclusion of others. The long-waited proponent victory must be viewed in the context of several inextricably interrelated factors.[65]

The establishment of the National Institute of Education (NIE) represented another departure from previous federal policy in education. As discussed previously, many educational reforms are shaped by key leaders on the White House staff. The idea for NIE resulted from the work of a "Working Group" on President Nixon's White

[62] Fritschler and Ross, op. cit., pp. 93–95.
[63] John A. Rohr, *Ethics for Bureaucrats* (New York: Marcel Dekker, 1978), p. 32.
[64] Philip Meranto, *The Politics of Federal Aid to Education in 1965* (Syracuse: Syracuse University Press, 1967).
[65] Ibid., p. 131.

House staff, which was heavily influenced by the views of Daniel Patrick Moynihan who at the time headed the Domestic Council.[66] President Nixon proposed the establishment of NIE in his message on educational reform on March 3, 1970. Needless to say, his proposal unleashed the political maneuvering one would expect in Washington.

In the June, 1971, issue of the *Phi Delta Kappan,* the U.S. Commissioner of Education, Sidney P. Marland, Jr., wrote about the proposed establishment of the NIE.[67] The general tone of this article was to explain and make acceptable the idea that NIE needed to be separated from the Office of Education, or what he termed the "vagaries of bureaucratic life."[68] As one can imagine, much behind-the-scenes political activity and bureaucratic struggle always accompany such changes in policies. Moreover, there is need for the visible leaders of the educational establishment to legitimize (make acceptable) new policies. The February following Marland's persuasive arguments for the establishment of NIE, another article by Finn (Moynihan's deputy on the White House staff) defended the need for NIE.[69] Both of these articles were full of optimism concerning the need for and opportunities of such a new agency, which could employ outstanding persons to conduct needed research.

In the October 1972, issue of the *Educational Researcher,* Welsh described the fluid situation surrounding the organization of NIE.[70] He called attention to "a tug-o'-war" with Congress over the confirmation of Sidney Marland as Assistant Secretary of HEW and the extent of power he would have over NIE. Obviously, there were political interventions for and against the independency of NIE from the assistant secretary. Of considerable significance was Welsh's account about the possible strong objections the teacher organizations and other interests might have to the first director appointed for NIE.

Sproull, Weiner, and Wolf saw the problems of NIE as the result of using rational organizational theory as the basis of organizing an agency with a "loosely connected set of ambiguous goals, unclear technologies, and fluid participants."[71] However, they also pointed to some weaknesses in the political expertise of the first director.

In 1973 Stivers wrote an article entitled "NIE: Learning About

[66]Sproull, Weiner, and Wolf, op. cit., p. 33.

[67]Sidney P. Marland, Jr., "A New Order of Educational Research and Development," *Phi Delta Kappan,* LII (June 1971), 576–579.

[68]Ibid., 576.

[69]Chester E. Finn, Jr., "What the NIE Can Be," *Phi Delta Kappan,* LIII (February 1972), 347–351.

[70]James Welsh, "NIE: Lining Up the Leaders," *Educational Researcher,* 1 (October 1972), 17–18.

[71]Sproull, Weiner, and Wolf, op. cit., p. 6.

Congress the Hard Way."[72] In the article she pointed to the lack of political effectiveness of NIE officials with key leaders in the Congress. Stivers attributed this ineffectiveness to the following conditions: (1) a serious communication gap between the NIE leaders and congressmen, (2) congressional dissatisfaction with NIE procedures, (3) lack of support for the program by educational groups, and (4) criticism of the agency by college officials and other educators. In any event, the NIE, which had been launched with so much optimism and executive support, was in serious political trouble. There was evidence that either the NIE had never had a constituency among the educational politicians or, if it had, it had alienated them.

In an article printed the following March (1974), Congressman John Brademas discussed the problems of NIE.[73] First, according to Brademas, most members of the Congress had little appreciation of the nature of educational research. Second, there was either apathy or opposition to NIE from influential professional groups of teachers, chief state school officers, and other educational interests. Third, the executive branch failed to move effectively to carry out the will of Congress.

From all accounts the NIE either could not or did not build a constituency to support its programs. As mentioned previously, there was opposition to the NIE program from such groups as the chief state school officers. With lack of support in the Congress, executive branch, and interested educational groups, the NIE faced even more serious obstacles in the 1974 Congress. At one point the Senate Appropriations Committee recommended zero dollars to support NIE during the 1975 fiscal year. Stivers reported that one senator had confided to a lobbyist that this was to "shake a few teeth."[74] Stivers reviewed again the great dissatisfaction with the agency in Congress. However, there were written statements of support for funding the agency from fifteen educational associations. There was mention in Congress that the wise thing to do might be to return the NIE function to the Office of Education.[75]

What has been reported concerning NIE treats the surface of what went on behind the scenes; therefore to draw conclusions about national politics from this case is difficult. Nevertheless, the politics of NIE seemed to involve the following political dimensions: (1) the

[72] Patricia E. Stivers, "NIE: Learning About Congress the Hard Way," *Educational Researcher*, 2 (November 1973), 8–9.

[73] John Brademas, "A Congressional View of Education R and D and NIE," *Educational Researcher*, 3 (March 1974), 12–15.

[74] Patricia E. Stivers, "NIE: Another Appropriations Crisis," *Educational Researcher*, 3 (November 1974), 9–15.

[75] Ibid.

committees of Congress, (2) the office of the President, and (3) educational interest groups.

The Political Arenas in National Politics

We have seen from the foregoing discussion that there are several dimensions in national politics. There is the Congress and, more specifically, certain key committees of the Congress. The office of the President looms very great in national politics. Strong professional support of educational interest groups is a critical dimension. Although not supported by the observations written, the support of the educational bureaucracy may be a very important dimension in national politics.

The message to educators desirous of influencing national politics begins to emerge. Washington politics is in a sense a matter of building power from the state and local arenas into support for education sufficiently strong to provide countervailing power against the interests of financial, commercial, military, and other groups. However, successful politics is more than applying great pressure. There must be well-developed objectives and programs supported by meaningful logic and experimental inquiry, because any force educators can build will probably be more than matched in the total arena of politics. The support of the Congress is essential, as well as the support of the office of the President. Finally, nothing can compensate for a bureaucracy as a professionally responsive countervailing power to other bureaucracies and as a source of wily political support for educational programs.

As we noted in Chapter 3, under the leadership of the Carter administration, with the powerful support of educational groups, the Department of Education was created. However, the future of the Department is much in question. Desirous of reducing federal influence upon education, President Reagan, supported by some members of Congress, announced in 1980 his intention to abolish the Department of Education. This is likely to be an issue of considerable significance for educators. If more federal participation and influence in education is desired, a strong federal bureaucracy at the cabinet level would be a political asset. If one desires greater state control, the cabinet level bureaucracy might be seen as a political liability.

Finally, in considering the dimensions of federal politics, one would miss the mark by far if the power of leaders in local and state governments was not included as an important dimension. All power exercised in federal politics is not downward to the states and local governments. State political leaders can move some people in Washington. U.S. congressmen often feel that they need key power wielders in local governments more than they need the support of colleagues in the Congress. Big-city mayors, for example, have influenced the administration of federal educational programs.

ACTIVITIES/QUESTIONS FOR FURTHER STUDY

1. Studies of state governance indicate rather clearly that the politics of education varies among the states. Through documentary evidence and discussions with educators experienced in state politics, prepare a general description of the legislative decision-making process in your state. Does this description fit any of the structures discussed in this chapter? Compare the relative power of the legislature, the governor, the state board of education, the department of education, and educational interest groups. How influential is the legislative staff for education in state legislation? Is there a strong probability of a transformation of power in your state?
2. Select from among current national proposals for education one that you and your group want to promote or oppose. Discuss at length how you would mount a political campaign to influence the Congress and the executive branch. Who are some people who might influence those holding influence in the executive branch? Describe how you would attempt to influence the Congress.

SUGGESTED READINGS

BOLNER, JAMES, and ROBERT SHANLEY. *Busing: The Political and Judicial Process.* New York: Praeger Publishers, Inc., 1974.

CAMPBELL, ROALD F., and TIM L. MAZZONI, JR. (eds.). *State Policy Making for the Public Schools.* Berkeley: McCutchan Publishing Corp., 1976.

DYE, THOMAS R. *Who's Running America: The Carter Years.* 2nd ed. Englewood Cliffs, N.J.: Prentice-Hall, Inc., 1979.

FRITSCHLER, A. LEE, and BERNARD H. ROSS. *Executive's Guide to Government: How Washington Works.* Cambridge: Winthrop Publishers, Inc., 1980.

MASTERS, NICHOLAS A., ROBERT SALISBURY, and THOMAS ELIOT. *State Politics and the Public Schools.* New York: Alfred A. Knopf, Inc., 1964.

MERANTO, PHILIP. *The Politics of Federal Aid to Education in 1965.* Syracuse: Syracuse University Press, 1967.

PETERS, B. GUY. *The Politics of Bureaucracy: A Comparative Perspective.* New York: Longman, Inc., 1978.

PHELAN, JAMES, and ROBERT POZEN. *The Company State.* New York: Grossman Publishers, 1973.

PRESS, CHARLES, and KENNETH VERBURG. *State and Community Governments in the Federal System.* New York: John Wiley & Sons, Inc., 1979.

SPROULL, LEE, STEPHEN WEINER, and DAVID WOLF. *Organizing an Anarchy: Belief, Bureaucracy, and Politics in the National Institute of Education.* Chicago: University of Chicago Press, 1978.

17

Influence of Organized Interest Groups

I N THIS CHAPTER we discuss an important dimension of educational politics that was only mentioned in passing in Chapters 15 and 16: namely, interest groups. In his often-cited *Democracy in America*, Alexis de Tocqueville described the Americans of the 1830s as "a nation of joiners." A directory of organizations for a city certainly demonstrates that there is a plethora of formal groups. Many of these have an active interest in, and actively attempt to influence, educational policy. Thus the college or university president, the school superintendent, and other educational leaders should have knowledge about the nature of such groups and how they influence the objectives, structure, and processes of education.

Participation of Interest Groups in the Political Process

The more highly active politicized groups do not enjoy a good reputation among Americans. We frequently picture these groups as somewhat sinister and selfish in lobbying the legislature or the Congress to "feather their own nests." Thus they are often referred to as pressure groups, special interests, or lobbies. A more recent term for lobby is the "single-interest group," which, according to much of the press, is the scourge of what could be an enlightened government in Washington.

A 1978 issue of *Newsweek* discussed single-issue politics as increasing alarmingly and seriously fragmenting the American political system.[1] The writer pointed to the fact that the number of lobbyists in Washington had grown from 2,000 to 15,000 in the thirty-year period before 1978. These groups use sophisticated new techniques, such as computerized mailing lists, and spend large sums of money to influence national political decisions. According to the *Newsweek* article, the Congress, and indeed the entire nation, "is caught up in a rugged new game of single-issue politics."[2]

Is the use of such negative terms as special interest groups and pressure groups justified? Truman provided a somewhat more balanced discussion of these groups and the governmental processes and referred to them simply as interest groups.[3] He presented these groups as going about the regular process of making claims on each other and upon the government, and referred to the institutions of government as "centers of interest group power." Thus what may be called pressure groups, single interest groups, or special interest groups are nothing more than the primary means by which people in a representative democracy influence what goes on in city hall, the state capitol, or in Washington.[4]

Politically active lobby groups attempting to influence national policy are on the increase. Over a three-year-period in the food industry alone, Guither found hundreds of groups that had registered lobbyists in the Congress.[5] From many accounts the Washington educational lobby has grown steadily in numbers, in diversification of interests, and in influence during the past three decades.[6] Group theorists, such as Salisbury, predicted some time ago that "over time there will appear more and more different, diverse, specialized groups in the political arena as the processes of social fission continue."[7] In other words, as social differentiation and technical specialization occur, there will be greater proliferation of different kinds of groups.

---

[1]"Single Issue Politics," *Newsweek*, XCII (November 6, 1978), 47–50.
[2]Ibid., 48.
[3]David B. Truman, *The Governmental Process*, 2nd ed. (New York: Knopf, 1971).
[4]Ibid., pp. 503–516.
[5]Harold D. Guither, *The Food Lobbyists* (Lexington, Mass.: Lexington, Heath, 1980), pp. 181–311.
[6]Stephen K. Bailey, *Education Interest Groups in the Nation's Capital* (Washington, D.C.: American Council on Education, 1975), p. 6.
[7]Robert H. Salisbury, "An Exchange Theory of Interest Groups," in Robert H. Salisbury (ed.), *Interest Group Politics in America* (New York: Harper & Row, 1970), p. 35.

Thus we have seen considerable proliferation of special interest groups in the field of education during this century, and this process will probably continue.

The Nature of Formal Groups

An informal organization, such as a faculty clique, has some of the following characteristics. Members of the clique do not keep a membership list. The group does not elect or appoint officials—whoever heard of anyone claiming to be president or secretary of a clique? No constitution or bylaws exist for the group. Decision making is not formalized by any prescribed rules, although the process may be fairly well structured. Official minutes of meetings and records are not kept. On the other hand, formal organizations have constitutions or by-laws, elected or appointed officers, membership lists, and official records.

Because there are so many and varied kinds of formal groups at the community, state, and national levels, some scheme for classification is greatly needed. However, among the various schemes used to classify these organizations, none seems to be completely satisfactory. Blau and Scott provided a discussion of the various attempts to classify formal organizations.[8] For example, distinctions between private and public ownership have been offered. Size, criteria for membership, functions performed (e.g., economic, religious, educational), and other schemes based upon observed differences have been used. One frequently hears persons talk about service as opposed to product-producing organizations. The term *civic,* or *service, club* is frequently used to include voluntary, nonprofit, and service-to-people community organizations.

Blau and Scott proposed an encompassing classification based upon the prime beneficiary of the organization. This produced four types of formal groups: mutual-benefit associations, business concerns, service organizations, and commonweal organizations.[9] The prime beneficiary of mutual-benefit associations is the membership. Unions, professional associations, and fraternal organizations were cited by Blau and Scott as examples. Teacher associations and unions would fall into this category. They exist for the benefit of the members. The owners are the prime beneficiaries of business concerns. This does not mean that businesses do not provide important services, but the prime reason for their existence is to make a profit for the owners.

---

[8] Peter M. Blau and W. Richard Scott, *Formal Organizations: A Comparative Approach* (San Francisco: Chandler, 1962), pp. 40–42.
[9] Ibid., pp. 45–48.

According to Blau and Scott, the client is the prime beneficiary of service organizations that provide professional services. Examples include social-work agencies, hospitals, schools, and legal-aid agencies. The prime beneficiary of commonweal organizations is the public at large. Examples cited by Blau and Scott were governmental agencies, such as the military services, police, and fire departments.

The suggested classifications by Blau and Scott are useful for many organizations. As in the case of all approaches for classifying organizations, one encounters much difficulty placing many groups into any one of the four categories offered by Blau and Scott. One example is the mutual company. Are the shareholders really operating for a profit or is the association for the mutual benefit of its members? Is the public school organization, with extensive adult, preschool, and community junior college functions, a service or a commonweal organization?

Because our primary concern is with the relationship of formal organizations to the organization and administration of education, the discussion in the two following sections focuses on (1) those interest groups directly related to educational agencies, particularly the public schools, and (2) other noneducational interests that have a significant impact upon education.

Educationally Related Groups

In reviewing the large number of educational interest groups represented in national politics, Bailey reported that he was unable to offer a "tidy" taxonomic categorization for the diverse groups. He did, however, suggest the following categories: (1) umbrella organizations (e.g., American Council on Education); (2) institutional associations (e.g., Association of Independent Colleges and Schools); (3) teachers' unions (e.g., American Federation of Teachers, National Education Association); (4) professions, fields, and disciplines (e.g., Music Educators National Conference); (5) librarians, suppliers, and technologists (e.g., American Library Association); (6) religion, race, sex (e.g., National Catholic Education Association); (7) "lib-lab" (liberal-labor) lobbies (e.g., AFL/CIO); (8) institutions and institutional systems (e.g., Pennsylvania State University); (9) administrators and boards (e.g., American Association of School Administrators, National School Boards Association); (10) miscellaneous (e.g., Council for Basic Education, United States Student Association).[10]

The one or two illustrative examples given under each category are part of a very large number of national, state, and local affiliated

[10] Bailey, op. cit., p. 9.

organizations interested in local, state, and national policies. For example, at the time Bailey made his study (1973), there were over thirty nationally organized interest groups in the "professions, fields, and disciplines" category.[11] This number has no doubt multiplied. The educational interest groups represent every conceivable aspect of public schools, private schools, public colleges and universities, and private colleges and universities. In his discussion of increased political activity in higher education, King documented the great increase of lobbying efforts by colleges and universities since World War II, reaching a high point in the 1960s and 1970s.[12]

Parent–Teacher Associations

Parent–teacher associations have been important in the development of education in the United States. The most influential and largest of these organizations is the National Congress of Parents and Teachers. There are branches of this organization in each of the fifty states and the District of Columbia as well as in U.S. possessions and schools overseas. The entire organization includes many thousands of local groups.

The National Congress of Parents and Teachers is not the only parent–school-related group. In many schools parent–teacher associations are not affiliated with the National Congress of Parents and Teachers. However, because the National Congress of Parents and Teachers (PTA) is much larger than most of the other parent–school associations, primary attention is given to it.

The activities of many local PTA's are rooted in well-defined goals. On the other hand, many PTA groups are either inactive or become absorbed in activities not entirely defensible. Some local PTA's fall prey to inept leadership on the part of parents, educational leaders, or both. Insecure educational administrators may consciously or unconsciously lead PTA memberships into roles counterproductive to the national goals of the PTA.

Strong PTA's cannot be developed unless administrators and teachers, in cooperation with parents, provide effective leadership. All successful organizational activity is a result of the exercise of creative leadership toward some mutually accepted, attainable objectives. If the organization fails to keep worthy objectives as a basis of activities, it is likely to degenerate into aimless meetings.

How much influence does the PTA have in the operation of schools? Opinions differ somewhat in answering this question. Campbell and associates expressed the opinion that the PTA has much in-

[11] Ibid., p. 17.
[12] Lauriston R. King, *The Washington Lobbyists for Higher Education* (Lexington, Mass.: Lexington, Heath, 1975), p. 110.

fluence locally, effective influence upon state legislation, but little influence at the national level.[13] A majority of school administrators
interviewed by Gross in Massachusetts felt that PTA leaders were
very influential in school affairs.[14] The point was made earlier that
the PTA has been a valiant force in opposing extremist attempts to
run the schools. Throughout the period of radicalism following World
War II, the PTA protected the schools from witch hunts, book burn-
ings, malicious firings of teachers, and other radical activities.

Moreover, the PTA has, in many instances, provided strong support for state legislation to improve financial support for the public
schools. PTA organizations provide much influence locally in many
districts. One thing seems clear: the power of PTA's over local government varies tremendously. Consequently, the question of how much
power the PTA exercises in controlling schools can be answered only
for each district and each state. In some districts the PTA is the most
powerful organization exercising influence over the schools; in others
the PTA (or another parent–teacher group) is without influence.

Teachers' Interest Groups

Many teachers' organizations are important in the operation of
schools. The National Education Association (NEA), with its state and
local affiliates, is one of the most influential teachers' organizations
at the national level. The NEA has exerted political influence upon
the Congress and the executive branch. Moroever, through its former
departments (e.g., Department of Classroom Teachers, Association for
Supervision and Curriculum Development, American Association of
School Administrators, and various subject matter departments), the
NEA has provided much influence within the teaching profession itself; however, many of these departments have severed relationship
with the parent organization. The NEA has, in past years, produced
a vast amount of research and literature. It also established important commissions that made influential reports. For example, the report of the Commission on the Reorganization of Secondary Education
in 1918 resulted in widespread adoption of the Seven Cardinal Principles of Education.

Since World War II the American Federation of Teachers (AFT)
has grown in power and influence to rival the NEA for the control of
teachers. The AFT used tough-minded, aggressive bargaining to
achieve important gains for teachers in some of the largest cities of
the nation. The strike was used to advantage to increase financial
support and other welfare measures.

[13] Roald F. Campbell et al., *The Organization and Control of American Schools,*
4th ed. (Columbus, Ohio: Merrill, 1980), p. 300.
[14] Neal Gross, *Who Runs Our Schools?* (New York: Wiley, 1958).

The competition from the AFT produced agonizing changes in the NEA, which was transformed from an umbrella organization with many diverse departments and interests into a union representing classroom teachers and college professors. At first reluctant to employ union tactics, the NEA is now a strong advocate of collective bargaining, the strike, and other processes normative to industrial worker unions.

The AFT and NEA have expended much energy and financial resources fighting each other for the right to represent teachers. Such states as New York and Florida have been the sites of intense struggles between the two national interest groups. The prospects of a merger of the two organizations have been discussed for some time; however, little progress has been made in this regard.

The scope of the political activities of teachers' interest groups is very difficult to conceptualize because there is such great variation among the states. Almost every conceivable state organizational arrangement exists, from the traditional teacher-administrator interest group without collective bargaining to the highly developed labor union norm with agency shops and collective bargaining. Data concerning the activities of local organizations in local school politics are very limited; however, teachers have been very active in all aspects of politics in school districts. In discussing the situation, Browne reported that most political activity of teachers has been aimed at (1) fostering legislation for collective bargaining, (2) increasing federal and state funding, (3) influencing local decision making, and (4) "power brokering" within the Democratic party.[15]

Many observers have pointed to the rivalry between the AFT and NEA as counterproductive to the acquisition of political power. In the meantime, the two organizations have exerted strong influence in local, state, and national politics. The NEA was apparently a very powerful influence upon the Carter administration and, as has been noted, was one of the important factors resulting in the creation of the cabinet-level Department of Education. The election of President Reagan brought considerable loss of influence to the NEA. Nevertheless, the militant approach by the national teachers unions has provided classroom teachers with access to the decision-making process at all levels of education.

Organizations for Educational Administrators

There are a number of organizations representing educational administrators in colleges, universities, and elementary and sec-

[15] James Browne, "Power Politics for Teachers, Modern Style," *Phi Delta Kappan*, 58 (October 1976), 158.

ondary schools. Bailey provided the following examples of higher education-related administrative groups.

> Council of Graduate Schools in the United States, the National Univer-
> sity Extension Association, the National Association for Women Deans,
> Administrators, and Counselors, American College Health Association,
> Council for Advancement and Support of Education, National Associa-
> tion of College and University Attorneys, American Association of Col-
> legiate Registrars and Admissions Officers, College and University Per-
> sonnel Association, National Association of College and University
> Business Officers.[16]

Following are some important interest groups for administrators, supervisors, and board members of elementary and secondary
schools: American Association of School Administrators, Council of
Chief State School Officers, National Association of Secondary School
Principals, National Association of Elementary School Principals,
National School Boards Association, National Public Relations Association, School Business Officials of the United States and Canada,
and Association for Supervision and Curriculum Development.

Several of these organizations (e.g., AASA, NASSP, NAESP, and
ASCD) have developed close ties in lobbying. In a number of states
umbrella-type affiliations of these administrator interest groups have
been formed in recognition of common interests and the need to make
administrator views felt on legislation.

The Education Commission of the States

As discussed in earlier chapters, many Americans have dis-
trusted federal control of education. Feeling among state leaders concerning reassertion of state initiative in the control of education provided motivation for the formation of a state Compact for Education
during 1965 and 1966. The compact created the Education Commission of the States, which has central offices located in Denver, Colorado. The idea was suggested by James B. Conant in his report *Shaping Educational Policy* published in 1964.[17] Conant recommended that
governors, legislators, and educational leaders form a commission to
seek solutions to educational problems.

The Education Commission of the States has grown in membership until most of the states belong. Each state is represented on the
commission by a delegation, including the governor, two members of
the legislature, and four members chosen by the governor. The compact is supported by membership fees based upon population and per
capita income

The Education Commission of the States holds annual meetings

---

[16]Bailey, op. cit., p. 25.
[17]James B. Conant, *Shaping Educational Policy* (New York: McGraw-Hill, 1964).

from which positions on educational issues are forthcoming. The commission publishes *Compact,* a bimonthly magazine devoted to discussions of current problems in the administration of education, and assists states in making special studies. However, much of the work of the commission is devoted to the discussion of educational policies for the states.

Accrediting Associations

Voluntary (nongovernmental) accrediting agencies have influenced education in the United States. These accrediting associations are voluntary agencies and should not be confused with the accrediting process by state departments of education. There are six regional accrediting associations in the United States: Middle States Association of Colleges and Schools, New England Association of Schools and Colleges, North Central Association of Colleges and Schools, Northwest Association of Schools and Colleges, Southern Association of Colleges and Schools, and Western Association of Schools and Colleges. The primary aim of these voluntary associations is to accredit colleges and schools.

The college or school must seek admission by meeting the standards established by the association. These standards are established through the decision-making machinery of each association, which is representative of the member schools and colleges. Membership is granted after the petitioning school or college has met the standards and has satisfied study committees of program quality in keeping with association expectations. In the case of secondary schools the association may employ the *Evaluative Criteria* as a basis of self-study by the school faculty and administration followed by the report of an external visiting committee.[18] The school may be admitted or denied admission to the association on the basis of the data and recommendations coming before the annual meeting of the association. Once a school (or college) is admitted it must have periodic reevaluations, and if found deficient it is dropped from membership in the association.

The National Council for Accreditation of Teacher Education (NCATE) is another important agency for the accreditation of educational programs. NCATE accredits the teacher education programs of most of the colleges and universities in the United States.

Private Foundations

Not to be overlooked in the control of education is the influence of private philanthropic foundations. These foundations have flour-

[18] For an understanding of criteria that may be used by secondary schools see National Study of Secondary School Evaluation, *Evaluative Criteria,* 5th Ed. (Arlington, Va.: National Study of School Evaluation, 1978).

ished in the United States and represent immense fortunes. Many of the foundations have educational development programs. The Ford Foundation has invested many millions of dollars into educational projects, as have the Carnegie Foundation, W. K. Kellogg Foundation, and others.

Many examples of foundation influence could be cited. Development of the use of educational television in the schools received much support from foundations. The W. K. Kellogg Foundation has had much interest in the development of programs for health-related services, the development of community colleges, and other educational endeavors. The Charles S. Mott Foundation provided funding for the development of community education. The Carnegie Foundation sponsored a national assessment program. Much foundation money has gone for the support of innovative instructional programs in the schools.

For many years, the foundations have been exceedingly generous in the financial support of colleges and universities. The foundations have also provided much financial support for the development of national interests in higher education (e.g., American Council on Education, National Center for Higher Education).[19] Colleges and universities have been particularly sensitive to the ideas promulgated through foundations.

In summary, foundations have been instrumental in financing educational practices that were not, at the time, possible through public taxation. As foundation executives express their function, they are in positions to advance "risk capital"; that is, they frequently back what many would believe to be high-risk operations. If the practices are successful, the public will demand continuation of the practices through public funds. Thus through the resources of foundations many practices have been introduced to education. Many of these practices eventually become permanent tax-supported functions of schools and colleges.

The National School Boards Association

State associations for school boards began to appear around the turn of this century. By 1940 the National Council of State School Boards Association was formed. During its formative stages, the national association was closely associated with the annual meetings of the American Association of School Administrators. The National School Boards Association is organized as a federation of the state school boards associations. It serves as a clearinghouse of information on problems confronting state associations and local boards of educa-

---

[19]King, op. cit., p. 20.

tion. State associations lobby for legislation that is thought to be important.

The National School Boards Association has been beset with numerous organizational and ideological crises from its beginning. For example, the membership had much difficulty with the question of federal aid to education. These ideological problems combined with its federation type of organization have, in the past, made the association more powerful at the state level than at the national level.

Organizations Critical of the Schools

The public schools are frequently subjected to severe criticism by persons organized to change the direction of education toward specific goals. These organizations foster positions that their members feel are very different from current practices in education. The formation and development of these organizations are accompanied by literature of the "Why Johnny can't add" type, which is very critical of the schools. Frequently these organizations make sweeping generalizations about the public schools, which, upon examination, may not be borne out in fact.

The Council for Basic Education is an example of this type of organization. During the 1950s its spokesmen deplored what they thought to be the neglect of teaching organized subject matter in the public schools. The council opposed the "progressive education" movement, supporting a return to the traditional subject curriculum. Unfortunately, in supporting this position the literature for basic education often gives a distorted idea of what goes on in most schools. For example, the public schools may be pictured as recreation centers opposed to teaching children subject matter, which has little support in fact. Yet in the view of many other citizens, the schools have been too subject-oriented. Some titles of books that reflect concern with maintaining the subject orientation were written by Bestor, Keats, and Rickover.[20]

Other groups, however, are interested in much more radical revision of the public schools. Of considerable interest is the great amount of literature of those advocating free choice.[21] The Center for Independent Education in San Francisco publishes *Inform*, which advocates freedom of choice as an alternative to public schools.

[20] Arthur E. Bestor, *Educational Wastelands: The Retreat from Learning in our Public Schools* (Champaign: University of Illinois Press, 1953); John Keats, *Schools Without Scholars* (Boston: Houghton, 1957); H. G. Rickover, *American Education: A National Failure* (New York: Dutton, 1963).

[21] John E. Coons and Stephen D. Sugarman, *Education by Choice: The Case for Family Control* (Berkeley: University of California Press, 1978); Ivan D. Illich, *Deschooling Society* (New York: Harper & Row, 1971); Joel Spring, *The Sorting Machine* (New York: David McKay, 1976).

Special Commissions and Study Groups

Special study committees, commissions, advisory groups, and other specially created groups should not be overlooked in considering the control of education. These organizations are usually short-lived, are created to accomplish a specific task, and are usually disbanded once this task is accomplished and the report is presented. They appear at the local, state, and national levels. For example, the local board of education may appoint an advisory committee to study the need for additional school plant facilities. The governor of a state may appoint a commission to produce a master plan for education. Special commissions and study groups are frequently employed in the federal government.

Few areas of government have been subjected to more study by groups than education. In fact, when demagogic governors or legislative leaders want to maintain the status quo in educational financing, they frequently escape taking action by ordering a comprehensive study of education. The shelves of state capitols contain the dusty educational reports of many commissions, committees, and task forces, which were motivated by nothing more than the desire to take demands for educational financing off politicians' backs.

Yet these do-nothing commissions, committees, and task forces do play a part in the control of education. They serve as tools of power interests to preserve the status quo. Control of education can be measured as much by what is done to prevent making changes as by actions to produce innovation. If the governor or legislature can spend $200,000 to study education, they may avoid raising millions to create better educational opportunities.

This is not to say that the work of special commissions and other study groups has been in vain. Some are used to legitimize ideas predetermined by powerful leaders in the local, state, and national structures. Reports of such groups are frequently followed by board policy changes or new legislation. For instance, the governor, top legislative leaders, and other leaders may desire to bring about reorganization of education. Their task may be greatly assisted by appointing a blue-ribbon commission to make a study of education. The report of this commission may contain little that is different from what the governor desired in the first place. Yet the citizen report may help legitimize the practice and facilitate legislative enactment. Many study groups are formed in honest attempts to solve difficult educational problems. The recommendations of these groups have also changed the opinions of policy-making bodies.

Examples of influence upon subject matter is seen in such groups as the Physical Science Study Committee (PSSC), which produced materials for teaching high school physics. Other groups for mathematics, chemistry, foreign languages, and the like, have had much influence upon the high school curriculum. Many of these national studies were financed by federal and foundation grants.

Special Voluntary Associations for Education

Organizations are frequently formed on the local and state level for the support of or opposition to public school programs. These are what many educators call pressure groups, especially if they happen to be opposed to certain programs in the schools.

The opposition groups often form around some emotionally charged issue, such as sex education. However, the special organization may be formed for more broadly based interests than the emotionally laden question. For example, the group may represent an organized attempt to make basic changes in the organization and operation of the schools.

An example of such a group was what we shall call the Ocean Beach School Improvement Association. This association was formed by citizens interested in improving the quality of education in the school district. Most of the leaders were newcomers who would suggest in private conversation that they were dismayed by the lack of quality in their schools. Basically, this organization represented a political power group that was determined to bring about changes in local governance and education.

These special associations may be known by various names, such as Concerned Citizens for the Public Schools, Citizens for the Advancement of Education, Committee for School Development, and so on. They may be either fervent supporters of the school organization or its bitter enemy, regardless of name.

Other Education Interest Groups

The groups discussed above are but a small number of the organizations that have interests in educational policies. For every subject of special interest in education, there is an interest group. Several of the groups most directly connected with the study of educational administration are discussed elsewhere in this textbook.

Student interest groups became more politicized following the mid-1960s. In 1978 the United States Student Association was created through a merger of the National Student Association and the National Student Lobby. Aaron wrote that college professors had significant influence in the development of the Great Society programs during the Johnson Administration.[22]

[22] Henry J. Aaron, *Politics and the Professors: The Great Society in Perspective* (Washington, D.C.: Brookings Institution, 1978).

Civil, Business, Political, and other Interest Groups

Up to this point the focus has been upon those interest groups that have education as their main reference of activity. However, these are but a few of many interest groups that attempt to influence schools and colleges, even though their main activity is not concentrated in the field of education. For example, local (and national) chambers of commerce frequently become involved in the development of education. Extremist left- or right-oriented organizations frequently attack educators. In this section some of the many groups that have become involved in the decision-making process for education are discussed.

Social Organizations and Service Clubs

In each school district one will find various community clubs that perform a variety of functions in the community power structure. In the first place many of these groups provide an opportunity for informal communication among community leaders. Newly formed groups may represent people with a point of view that has been latent. Community groups provide excellent opportunities for young persons to be trained in leadership. The membership of these groups is frequently propagandized by speakers and other organized programs.

The educational administrator will find in cities many knife-and-fork social-service clubs. These clubs usually meet for lunch or dinner once each week and are chartered by national or international organizations. Examples are Rotary, Lions, Civitan, Kiwanis, and Jaycees Internationals. Many of them sponsor high school organizations.

Although these clubs do provide important services, their main activities are social and political. One or the other of the clubs tends to have a preponderance of the important power wielders of the community as members. This, then, becomes the club that many would like to join. In one city, for example, the Kiwanis was seen as the important club in town. Many of the influentials in the power structure were members. In another city the Rotary was the preferred club, and in still another the Civitan was most important, and so on.

In addition to these knife-and-fork clubs are social, community service, fraternal, hobby, and other types of clubs. The local chamber of commerce usually keeps a list of many of these clubs and other types of organizations. In looking over such a list, one is impressed that there is an organization for everyone. Few of these clubs may have any direct activity in political decision making. They exist for a great variety of social, economic, and recreational functions other than politics. Moreover, incorporating as a nonprofit organization restricts their participation in certain political activities.

Nevertheless, these organizations must not be overlooked in the political process. As mentioned previously, they afford ready communication among their membership, provide means for propagandizing for reinforcement of community norms, and are a resource for training the future leadership of the power structure. A young professional person desiring to be recognized as a leader will attempt to gain recognition by serving as a leader in these organizations.

Business Organizations Related to Educational Organizations

An examination of the educational budget of a large city reveals that education is big business. Indeed, if one considers all the money spent for all forms of education in the United States, education is a multibillion dollar business. Many business establishments have, for many years, produced the equipment and supplies especially needed in school and college operation.

Numerous writers have pointed to textbook publishers as having much control over what is taught. Because teachers have traditionally followed the organization of subject material as given in adopted textbooks, there is some truth to the purported influence of publishers. On the other hand, because publishers are concerned with profits, they are going to adhere as strictly as possible to the normative perception of teachers and parents concerning what should be printed.

If the reader attends the exhibits of the annual meeting of the American Association of School Administrators, he or she will be impressed with the large number of manufacturers engaged in producing equipment, building supplies, and services for schools. As the population increased following World War II, the nation became heavily involved in purchasing such services, equipment, and materials. In order to construct a new building, the services of architects, construction engineers, contractors, equipment manufacturers, and other interests are necessary. The multiplicity of persons, business firms, agencies, and manufacturers involved represents a great input to education. Architects may, for example, assist in designing school plant facilities, which vitally influence the educational program. Manufacturers are constantly engaged in technological developments to control the physical environment in which the teacher practices.

Many other businesses are engaged in supplying schools and colleges. For example, local businesses are particularly interested in contractual arrangements for fuel, food, and other supplies. In many instances these business interests may be important in the election of school board members, in the placement of custodians, or in the unpopularity of school superintendents. Administrators may feel that they should not be concerned with this minor aspect of politics. However, these business interests do influence the administration of schools and colleges.

Economically Related Organizations

Studies show that the economic sector usually has strong representation in community power structures. This strong position is reason enough for administrators to understand organizations related directly to the institution of economics. In what organizations of the community, state, and nation are there the largest concentrations of wealth? How active are these organizations in the political arena? What influence does their activity have upon the improvement of education?

Corporate interests form national lobbying organizations, such as the National Association of Manufacturers, American Farm Bureau, Chamber of Commerce, and other associations. These national associations, although not directly associated with educational organizations, use their power to influence national policies, including educational policies. Many powerful corporations are particularly interested in developing educational technology. Such corporations as General Electric, International Business Machines, Bell and Howell, and American Telephone and Telegraph have realized that educational budgets may provide a rich source for business expansion.

Not to be overlooked in studying economic organizations are banking and commercial interests. Banks represent centers of wealth in the community. Various banking organizations represent economic leaders with different political interests. Forming a bank gives these different interests a means to pool their financial resources for community, state, and national development consistent with their policy interests. Their policy interests will, in the long run, influence the development of education.

Real estate companies and community developers become greatly involved in political activity to locate schools in areas that will stimulate land development. These companies are, of course, tied to big money interests in the school district and state. Much money has been made through the location of schools so that property near the school will readily sell. Developers can exercise considerable influence in school bond elections through their ties with financial interests.

Taxpayers Associations

Taxpayer associations are seen by many persons as resisting any and all additional taxes regardless of their purpose. As a consequence, educators frequently find themselves in opposition to the demands of these taxpayer associations. However, many taxpayer associations have actually helped schools obtain better bases of support.

In general, taxpayer groups have been interested in reducing inefficiency in government and minimizing the tax burden.

Political Parties

Although political parties are not mentioned in the Constitution, they have had much influence upon national policies. Party
leaders develop policy statements designed to help elect their candidates to office. The party organization may be used as a vehicle to
pool resources and elect persons to office. Leaders of the minority party
in Congress frequently serve in the "loyal opposition" role.

Americans have traditionally believed in the two-party system.
Although "third" parties have appeared from time to time, and some
acquire a rather large following, the Democratic and Republican
parties remain the major political party organizations in state and
national elections.

The party organization includes procedures to formulate policies, nominate candidates for office, raise money for election campaigns, distribute patronage, and perform many other political functions. The convention and the primary election may be employed in
different states and localities to nominate candidates for office. The
national organizations have various committees to develop positions,
make studies, and recommend the adoption of positions. State and
local committees are maintained. The national committee is made up
of representatives of states and territories. This committee fixes the
time and place for the national convention, decides upon the delegates, and, in the event of victory, may have much to say about appointments. Traditionally, the presidential candidate has selected the
national committee chairperson.

The platforms of the two parties usually have different positions
concerning educational policies. This was particularly the case in the
1980 national election. Thus the differences in ideologies of leaders
in the two parties do influence the administration of education.

The New Right

Of particular interest to educators is what is often expressed as
the conservative political turn in the United States. If indeed the political system continues toward the right of center, this trend will
signal significant shifts in educational policies. Park has written a
review of some of the New Right interest groups that are prominent
in the perpetuation of ideologies to the right of center.[23] These include such organizations as the Conservative Caucus, Committee for

[23]J. Charles Park, "Preachers, Politics, and Public Education: A Review of Right-
Wing Pressures Against Public Schooling in America," Phi Delta Kappan, 61 (May 1980),
608–612.

the Survival of a Free Congress, National Conservative Political Action Committee, Moral Majority, and Christian Voice. These organizations are bolstered by many conservative groups of long standing (e.g., John Birch Society, Heritage Foundation). Among the direct educational goals of these groups are prayer in the schools, removing humanistic ideas from school practice, returning to stern discipline, removing obscene and vulgar textbooks, returning to the basics, and teaching the creationist theory of the beginning. Many leaders in the New Right movement support tuition tax credits and a system of vouchers.

Labor Organizations

Interest groups for organized labor have for many years had an interest in educational policy. Some of the labor unions are enormous organizations. An example of one of the largest unions is the American Federation of Labor/Congress of Industrial Organizations (AFL–CIO). To illustrate the complexity of large labor interest groups, the AFL–CIO is an umbrella organization "consisting of 106 separate affiliate unions from teachers and plumbers to meat cutters and government employees."[24]

Civil Rights Associations

Associations connected directly to the civil rights movement have had considerable interest in education. Some of the national organizations have persons who serve as educational advisers. The National Association for the Advancement of Colored People (NAACP) and the Urban League have had many years of activity in negotiating changes and in litigation. Other active organizations have included the Congress of Racial Equality (CORE), Student Nonviolent Coordinating Committee, Southern Christian Leadership Conference, and their local and/or state affiliates.

Several national organizations for women have been active in the political arena (e.g., National Organization for Women, National Women's Political Caucus). Women's groups are active in attempting to influence educational programs, and activities associated with women's rights have influenced employment policies of colleges and school districts. Groups supporting the interests of Spanish-speaking Americans and American Indians have also been active.

These associations have constantly negotiated with national, state, and local officials in bringing about equal educational opportunity, acting as powerful forces in promoting racial desegregation of schools and equal rights for women. These groups have provided legal

[24]Norman J. Ornstein and Shirley Elder, *Interest Groups, Lobbying and Policymaking* (Washington, D.C.: Congressional Quarterly Press, 1978), p. 24.

assistance in seeking change through the courts. Some groups provided leadership for school boycotts and other activities to force changes in schools. Federal legislation has forced schools to observe affirmative-action programs.

Other Organized Interests

To discuss all the organized interest groups that, from time to time, exert influence upon the schools would fill many volumes. The purpose of the discussion at this point is to show that there are many different organizations. The same organizations will not appear in different local school districts or different states. For example, we would not expect to find organizations for citrus fruit growers in Alaska. A yacht club is not as probable in the Nevada desert as in San Diego. Furthermore, a Rotary Club in Bay City may not be as influential as one in Syracuse. Thus educational leaders must consider each school district as unique and as probably having different organizational characteristics from other districts.

We have not discussed patriotic groups, such as the American Legion. Members of this organization have had a strong interest in educational policies. The League of Women Voters has achieved considerable respect in politics, and has made positive contributions to the reorganization of educational governance. The American Association of University Women has also maintained an interest in education.

Functions of Interest Groups in the Control of Education

Organized interest groups are one among numerous important elements of the complex system of power in which the schools are controlled. In this chapter some of the organized interest groups in the system have been discussed. Writers about American democracy have traditionally assumed that organized interest groups were the primary means for citizen participation in governance. Within recent years, however, this generalization has been shown to be a much oversimplified concept insofar as community decision making is concerned. Organized interest groups may be run by a small group of leaders (elites) rather than serving as avenues for mass participation in governance. Presthus's finding that the activity of organized interest groups in decision making was relatively weak is fairly typical of many community power studies.[25]

[25]Robert Presthus, *Men at the Top: A Study in Community Power* (New York: Oxford University Press, 1964).

As implied above, interest groups must be viewed as only one of several important elements in the political system. The total system of power is a complex of influential power wielders, officials, informal groups, organized groups, leg men, neighborhood leaders, and other persons interwoven by group norms, beliefs about community living, concepts about education, patterns of communication, friendships, and other system variables. When seen in this setting, one can define the roles organizations play in the control of education. A discussion of these roles follows.

Solidary organizations actively exercise group power directly in the political system. For example, the leaders of an association of teachers speak forcefully for proposals to improve the welfare of teachers. These leaders are fulfilling role expectations. On the other hand, the association may experience considerable difficulty in agreeing to pursue a political position concerning city planning and zoning, partisan elections, or other areas outside their special interest. Truman's views on this matter were discussed in Chapter 16.[26] Because people hold multiple memberships in groups, few groups are able to achieve solidarity concerning objectives. This lack of solidarity on decisions outside the welfare of teachers limits the influence of the association.

We have discussed previously how the interests of business concerns lead to influence upon schools. Collectively, the economic sector of the power structure may be interested in educational quality as an aspect of community development. For example, the chamber of commerce in a city may desire growth in manufacturing. The quality of schooling available to the families of workers may be an important factor in the location of new industries in the city. Persons influential in the economic sector tend, through friendship, business, and other ties with other leaders, to form important informal groups. At this point their power is more an expression of their personal influence within the informal group. In this way the power clique becomes a complex system with objectives somewhat independent of the business concerns that give rise to personal power.

In some instances a solidary interest group is observed to exercise political influence in different areas of the political system. This requires membership consensus and solidarity not found in most interest groups. Most of the politicized groups discussed in this chapter are somewhat restricted to a single interest and would experience difficulty holding their memberships outside that interest (e.g., teacher welfare, tax breaks for business). A typical church probably has in its membership persons who are opponents in political life. Except for certain moral issues, this church would be destroyed in an attempt to

[26]Truman, loc. cit.

back openly one or another candidate in a city school board election. Yet these groups play other very important roles in the control of education.

One very important role of organizations is the training and development of leaders. Those who hold the official leadership positions in community organizations may or may not be the most influential leaders in the community. Many are young or middle-aged persons who aspire to positions of power. They view holding official positions as a means of access to the power structure. Being the chairman of fund drives, a PTA president, or a leader in other acceptable situations gives visibility that may be useful in achieving public positions.

Through the creation of an organization, persons can pool their power resources. For example, teachers' associations and unions can collect dues from members that amount to millions of dollars on a statewide basis. Moreover, the organization also has available to it the combined intellectual resources of the membership. The organization can use these resources to acquire information useful in decision making.

The advantages of organized interest groups over many disparate persons working alone are obvious. Consequently, persons finding themselves unrepresented by organizations soon form one. As one example of this, several years ago teachers of many cities began to exclude school administrators from their ranks in negotiation procedures. Principals and other administrative and supervisory personnel soon formed their own association to seek negotiated agreements with the board of education.

Organizations tend to stimulate political participation. Milbrath noted that numerous studies indicate a relationship between organizational membership and participation in political activity; that is, persons active in organized interest groups are more likely to exercise their influence in politics.[27] The point is made, however, that this may vary with groups. Membership in an apathetic group may have no influence in the direction of greater participation. Organizational mobilization has been especially important in advancing the active participation of minority groups in voting.

Many organized interest groups are sensitive to the resources provided by certain leaders, and these groups may be used to represent the views of such persons or informal groups of the power structure. For instance, many civic groups are especially sensitive to the will of persons providing large sums of money for activities.

Organizations provide convenient means for communication among the leaders and followers of power structures. First of all, they

[27] Lester W. Milbrath, *Political Participation: How and Why Do People Get Involved in Politics* (Chicago: Rand McNally, 1965), pp. 16–22.

are convenient means for propagandizing. Speakers are frequently selected because they represent the interests of leaders. Persons promoting new projects use the meetings to provide information about
the proposals. The meetings of organizations provide formal and informal communication among the members. This serves to reinforce
group norms and promote discussions of projects.

ACTIVITIES/QUESTIONS FOR FURTHER STUDY

1. Continuing your discussion of state politics suggested in Chapter 16, identify the interest groups primarily concerned with education in your state.
   Do all of these groups have full-time lobbyists? What is the relative power
   of these various groups with the legislature and governor? What educational legislation are the various interest groups promoting in your state?
   How influential are groups representing educational administrators?
2. In many of the states there has been a growing fragmentation of professional interest groups for educators. How does this fragmentation, as it
   exists in many of the states, affect the power of educators in state decision
   making? Should leaders of these groups attempt to form coalitions as is
   frequently done by national groups? If so, what are some steps that should
   be taken by educational leaders to form political coalitions?

SUGGESTED READINGS

BAILEY, STEPHEN K. *Education Interest Groups in the Nation's Capital*. Wash-
inton, D.C.: American Council on Education, 1975.
BLAU, PETER M., and R. A. SCHONHERR. *The Structure of Organizations*. New
York: Basic Books, Inc., 1971.
GUITHER, HAROLD D. *The Food Lobbyists*. Lexington, Mass.: Lexington Books,
D. C. Heath & Company, 1980.
KING, LAURISTON R. *The Washington Lobbyists for Higher Education*. Lexing-
ton, Mass.: Lexington Books, D. C. Heath & Company, 1975.
ORNSTEIN, NORMAN J., and SHIRLEY ELDER. *Interest Groups, Lobbying and
Policymaking*. Washington, D.C.: Congressional Quarterly Press, 1978.
SALISBURY, ROBERT H. (ed.). *Interest Group Politics in America*. New York:
Harper & Row, Publishers, 1970.
TRUMAN, DAVID B. *The Governmental Process*, 2nd ed. New York: Alfred A.
Knopf, Inc., 1971.

18

The
Collective-Bargaining
Movement
and Education

PRIOR to the 1960s, educators paid little attention to the collective-bargaining movement, which had drastically changed labor–management relations in the private industrialized sector of the nation. By the 1980s, collective bargaining had become an integral part of the educational scene and the subject of debate involving board members, parents, governmental officials at all levels, civic leaders, teachers, students, educational support personnel, and educational administrators—almost everyone with an interest in the schools, colleges, and universities of the nation. More importantly, in many localities the pattern of educational governance and employee–administrator relations had changed as a result of collectively-bargained agreements.

Collective bargaining as a process of resolving issues in educational organizations has been praised and damned; we do not propose to do either. Because collective bargaining is a part of the milieu within which educational institutions function, no person contemplating an educational leadership role can afford to be uninformed about the process and its impact. Accordingly, our primary intent in this chapter is to provide an understanding of how collective bargaining influences educational practices. However, to provide the reader with a context for understanding the significance of the collective-bargaining movement, we focus first on its meaning and growth. The chapter is concluded with an examination of some of the major problems and questions associated with collective bargaining in education.

The Meaning of Collective Bargaining

Collective bargaining is the process whereby representatives of the employees and the employer meet at reasonable times and negotiate in good faith in regard to the terms and conditions of the employment relation to the end that mutually acceptable agreements are reached. The product of the process is a written contract regarding the agreed-on terms and conditions of employment. Unless required by law, neither party is compelled to agree with a proposal or to make a concession.

Distinctive Features of the Process

A basic feature of the process is that fundamental conflicts of interests between employer and employees are assumed and that these can only be resolved through the process of negotiation and compromise. This is not to say that mutual interest and interdependence are not recognized; if there were no mutual interests and interdependence, the conflicts would be of no significance. The point is that under collective bargaining an adversary relationship on conflicts is assumed, but this adversary posture does not extend to the totality of the relationship. Seemingly, this concept has been difficult for teachers, school board members, and administrators to understand and/or accept. In many situations the institution of collective bargaining has been marked by hostility in the entire scope of relations—even in areas where there were no conflicts of interest.

The collective-bargaining process assumes that the parties come to the tables as equals, and each must bargain in good faith and refrain from engaging in other unfair labor practices. The idea of equality at the table means that agreements will be reached bilaterally—not unilaterally. The confrontation is between peers, not between superordinate and subordinate. It does not mean that both sides are always equal in their ability to persuade the other side to accept their proposals. This power shifts from side to side, depending upon a multitude of factors within both the social system and the environment. The notion of bargaining in good faith means that both parties accept the obligation to try and reach an agreement. To this end they act honestly and forthrightly with the intent of trying to ascertain the facts and reach accord. To come to the table and state a position, a first and final offer, while refusing to consider other information or alternatives is an example of not bargaining in good faith.

Refusing to bargain in good faith is an unfair labor practice. Other unfair labor practices on the part of the employer include coercing employees either in an effort to encourage them to join or to refrain from joining an employee organization; refusing to employ, terminating, or providing differential working conditions to an employee in an effort to encourage or discourage employee organization membership or activity; and dominating, assisting, or interfering with the affairs of an employee organization. Illustrations of unfair labor practices on the part of an employee organization, its members, or representatives include interfering with administrative (supervisory, managerial) employees in the conduct of their duties or causing or attempting to cause the employer to discriminate against an employee because of activities in relation to an employee organization. As applied to teachers, instigating or advocating support of pupils for the employee organization in a dispute and instigating, supporting, or participating in a strike—unless provided for by law—are usually considered unfair labor practices. Also, interfering with or coercing in regard to membership in an employee organization is unfair labor practice.

Collective bargaining does not necessarily mean that all employees must belong to the "union." Under collective bargaining there are three types of shops: *union security,* a *closed shop,* where membership in the union is required within a specified period of time, as a condition of employment; *union agency* or *agency fee shop,* where membership is not required but support of the union, for its efforts on behalf of the employee is required; and an *open shop,* where union affiliation or financial support is not required as a condition of employment. In education, collective bargaining is conducted either under "open shop" or "agency fee" conditions with about sixteen states having laws that permit agency fee agreements.[1] (In 1977, the U.S. Supreme Court upheld the legality of an agency fee agreement in the Detroit School District.)[2]

A fourth characteristic of the process is that the employer officially recognizes the employee representative (bargaining agent) as speaking on behalf of the membership of the group (bargaining unit). In the absence of specific laws, in some localities the procedure of determining who is to be recognized as bargaining for whom is negotiated. In other cases the state law specifies the process by which an employee organization is recognized for bargaining purposes, criteria

[1] Thomas J. Flygare, *Collective Bargaining in the Public Schools* (Bloomington, Ind.: Phi Delta Kappa Educational Foundation, 1977), p. 13.
[2] *Abood* v. *Detroit Board of Education,* 431 U.S. 209, 97 Sup. Ct. 1782 (1977).

are set forth on what is a bargaining unit, and the state agency administering the process (e.g., public employee relations commission, state labor relations board) has a role in the determination of the nature of the bargaining unit and who is recognized. As a general practice, there is one bargaining agent for each class of employees (exclusive representation). However, where the employer bargains with different employee groups (e.g., teachers, clerical workers), each may be considered a "class" and have its own bargaining agent.

The presence of a collective-bargaining arrangement does not eliminate meeting, conferring, or soliciting opinions from various groups or individuals; however, neither the employer or employee organization can act unilaterally on matters covered by the contract. The point is that collective bargaining does not usually cover all aspects of the employer–employee relation, and beyond the contract the parties are free to develop other arrangements as they see fit. What is to be the subject of bargaining may be determined by mutual agreement, or it may be set forth in the law as interpreted by the courts and the state administrative agency. To illustrate, a board of education may agree, as required by law, to bargain with a teachers' group regarding salary and fringe benefits, and this may result in a contract. Thus both sides are bound in regard to salaries. However, even though the board is not required by law and refuses to bargain about a teacher's evaluation procedure, it may choose unilaterally to set up a representative committee to offer recommendations and teachers may choose to participate.

A sixth distinctive feature of the process is the use of an impartial third party in dispute settlement when the parties cannot reach an accord. A deadlock may occur when trying to resolve a grievance under an existing contract or when trying to agree on a new contract. Three types of third-party intervention are mediation, fact finding, and arbitration. If a grievance brought under a contract cannot be settled informally or by means of the in-organization mechanisms, the grievance procedure defined in a contract often provides that the next step is mediation; that is, a third party (in the form of a team or single individual) is brought in to interpret, counsel, and offer suggestions to help the parties to the dispute reach an agreement. In education, if mediation fails, often the next step in the grievance process is fact finding, and the final step is arbitration. In some instances, fact finding may be the final step; in other situations the grievance procedure may provide for arbitration following mediation. Fact finding and arbitration are alike in that a mutually agreed-upon third party conducts hearings, takes testimony, and renders a decision on the issue. In both fact finding and arbitration the third party is guided first by the contract language. The essential difference is the power of the third party. In fact finding the decision is a recommendation. (Some persons use fact finding and advisory arbitration as synonymous terms.) In arbitration the third-party decision is binding and must be followed. Arbitrators' decisions, unless there was some "flaw" involved, are enforceable in a court of law. Where two parties cannot agree on a new contract (i.e., have an interest or contract dispute), the impasse procedures are essentially the same except that fewer states have statutes that permit arbitration of contract disputes. (As the 1980s opened, of the thirty-two states having collective-bargaining laws affecting public education at some level, nineteen permitted some form of arbitration in contract disputes.)[3]

The Steps in the Process

The movement from having no collective bargaining in an educational organization to operating under one or more collective-bargaining contracts may be described as encompassing five basic stages. First, the rules of procedure must be determined. This may be as simple as determining what the procedures are under the state law and under rules promulgated by the state agency charged with administering the process. Or in the absence of state law, the rules of procedure may be adopted by the governing board based upon the advice and counsel of interested employee groups. Whatever the origin, answers must be provided to questions such as, "What are the areas that are subject to bargaining?" "What are the rights of employers and employees?" "What will constitute a bargaining unit and how is this to be determined?" "What is the process by which an employee group obtains recognition for purposes of bargaining?"

The second stage is recognition. In this stage various employee groups, consistent with the rules of procedure, seek to be recognized for purposes of bargaining with the board on behalf of some class of employees (e.g., bus drivers). This may involve a petition requesting an election for the purposes of selecting an agent, an election, certification by the state administrative agency, and so on.

After there has been a determination of who is going to bargain for whom, the next stage is preparing to negotiate. In this stage both the employer and employee groups will (1) select negotiating teams (or negotiators) and clarify the teams' authority and responsibility; (2) determine the objectives they have in the bargaining (i.e., determine goals, order these, decide where concessions might be considered); (3) decide on table tactics and strategies; and (4) collect and analyze data seen as essential in terms of goals to be achieved and strategies to be used.

Next comes the actual bargaining. This will involve much at-

[3]"State-by-State Roundup of Collective Bargaining Laws," *Phi Delta Kappan*, 60 (February 1979), 472–473.

the-table time by negotiators and behind-the-scenes time revising priorities, altering tactics, collecting additional data, instructing negotiators, and so on. Further, if the process bogs down, third-party intervention may occur. This stage is considered terminated when a contract is signed.

The final stage in the process is administration of the contract. The top administrators of the organization must ensure that the lower level administrators (e.g., principals, supervisors, department heads) understand and follow each provision of the contract. Further, where there are violations of the contract or disputes regarding its interpretation, the grievance procedure agreed upon must be used.

Growth of Collective Bargaining

To understand better the extent of growth of collective bargaining, the reader should have some basic understanding of how it developed in the private sector and of some of the conditions that contributed to the willingness of educational organization employees to move to this approach as a means of gaining a voice in decision making. Attention is given to these topics before turning directly to the spread of collective bargaining in education.

A Brief Look at the Private Sector

The development of collective bargaining in the private sector can be viewed as encompassing four periods. There was a period in the late 1700s and 1800s when the movement in this country was born, and all the forces of law were against the movement. In this period the workers' "combinations," or "associations," bargained by putting up signs stating the conditions under which they would work; if demands were ignored, they went on strike by simply not reporting to work. The unions were basically local and took great interest in local politics. During this period the movement was subjected to economic pressure from employers; the courts were hostile as were the legislative and executive branches of government. Leaders of the movement were on occasions jailed and physical violence was not uncommon.

The second period, beginning after the Civil War, was the formation of national unions (e.g., the National Labor Union of the late 1860s and early 1870s, Knights of Labor of the 1870s until around 1900, American Federation of Labor organized in the 1880s). The era was marked by violent strikes, and lockouts were frequently used by employers. Even though the government accepted the presence of unions, the legal balance of power rested with management. Court orders, police, and federal troops were used in efforts to contain the violence accompanying strikes.

The third period began in 1935 and extended to the late 1950s. In 1935 Congress passed the Wagner Act (National Labor Relations Act). This act legitimatized the union movement in the private sector, demanded that employers bargain with unions chosen by the workers, defined rules and regulations to cover the process, and protected workers from arbitrary discharge and discipline. It was labor's "bill of rights" and with the Taft-Hartley Act of 1947 (Labor–Management Relations Act) the national legislative foundation for collective bargaining in the private sector was set. The early years of this period also saw the organization of mass-production industries (e.g., automobile workers), which contained many unskilled and semiskilled workers. The Congress of Industrial Organizations (CIO), formed by dissident AFL leaders, led these organization efforts. By the time the AFL and CIO merged in 1955, the labor unions were at the peak of their power. The movement was international, the vast majority of the industrial blue-collar workers in the nation worked under union-negotiated contracts, the power of the national union leaders was awesome, and the workers were well disciplined, readily accepting the direction of their leaders. The ultimate weapon of labor—the strike—was used frequently and effectively. The results were great gains in wages and greatly improved working conditions.

The fourth period, beginning in the late 1950s and continuing until the present, has seen the monopolistic power of the union leadership greatly lessened and the organizing interest turn from the blue-collar worker in the private sector to workers in other sectors. More specifically, new leaders arose from the ranks to challenge the control of the established leaders, automation in the mass-production industries made employers less dependent on large numbers of unskilled and semiskilled workers, and the workers—more sophisticated than their counterparts of an earlier era—were no longer willing to follow blindly the direction of the established leadership. Also, with industrial blue-collar workers already organized, the focus turned to organizing workers in other areas. This included farm workers and workers in the public sector.

Conditions Contributing to the Willingness of Educational Employees to Organize and Bargain

Before the 1960s, local, state, and national organizations for K–12 teachers (most often the National Education Association or its affiliates) and those in higher education (generally the American Association of University Professors or its affiliates) placed considerable emphasis on professional improvement activities. Dedication to public service and/or scholarship were emphasized. Except for isolated local organizations, coercive power associated with collective action was not used as a means of trying to achieve objectives. However, educational leaders did actively lobby for economic gains for teachers and for educational improvement. Local teachers' organizations were active in attempting to influence school boards or boards of trustees to provide increased salaries and better working conditions. In instances they achieved their goals, in other instances there was partial achievement, and in still other situations the teachers were ignored.

On the state level teachers' organizations provided, at times, effective influence on the legislatures, based largely on persuasion coupled with relatively weak political influence upon individual legislators. The study by Bailey and his associates indicated that when they were well organized for political activity and had intellectual and political leadership, teachers achieved their legislative objectives.[4]

Before collective bargaining, educators, through friends in the legislature, could create some political disturbance if their demands were ignored. They were also able to obtain support from citizens' groups. Certain legislators frequently championed the educators' programs. This created a condition in which leaders in the legislative establishment were desirous of avoiding confrontation with educational interests. Nevertheless, educational interests failed to sustain enough political power to force legislative action consistently favorable to the felt needs. Various alternatives were explored during the 1950s to increase the power of educators.

One alternative was to use some of the processes identified in Chapter 1 and seek further professionalization of teaching. Both the National Education Association (NEA) and the American Association of University Professors (AAUP) took some steps in this direction. For example, the NEA created the National Committee on Teacher Education and Professional Standards. However, because of a variety of conditions the movement was toward the collective-bargaining model.

Several writers have enumerated conditions that they saw as relating to the willingness of teachers to accept the labor–management model as the primary means of achieving more control over the conditions existing in education.[5] The evidence suggests that the fol-

---

[4]Stephen K. Bailey et al., *Schoolmen in Politics* (Syracuse: Syracuse University Press, 1962).

[5]See, for example, Richard C. Williams, "Conditions Affecting Teacher Militancy," in Phillip K. Piele and Terry L. Eidell (eds.), *Social and Technological Change: Implications for Education* (Eugene, Ore.: Center for the Advanced Study of Educational Administration, University of Oregon, 1970), pp. 78–85; Frank W. Lutz, "Why Teacher Militancy," *IRS Journal*, 1 (Winter 1969), 15–27; Donald A. Myers, *Teacher Power—Professionalization and Collective Bargaining* (Lexington, Mass.: Lexington, Heath, 1973), pp. 95–100; George W. Angell, "Understanding Collective Bargaining as

lowing conditions contributed to the growth of collective bargaining in education: increased support for the "teacher union" movement from unions in the private sector, challenges to established authority by other groups, changing characteristics of teachers, desire for economic gains, and disenchantment with existing conditions.

The American Federation of Teachers (AFT), established in Chicago in 1916 and long affiliated with the AFL, was the principal mover of teacher unionism. Until the 1960s its impact outside of the Chicago area was limited. However, with support from the private-sector union leadership, the AFT locals began to challenge the established NEA units and advocate a different approach to gaining influence—use of collective bargaining. The stance of the AFT was militant when compared to the traditional NEA approaches. The breakthrough for AFT came in New York in 1961. In that district the teachers voted heavily in favor of collective bargaining and, after a bitter struggle, the AFT local, the United Federation of Teachers, was selected by the teachers as their bargaining agent. The bargaining process broke down and the following year (1962) saw the New York teachers strike—in violation of the law. Following the New York victory, the AFT, with support from the private sector and advocating use of the labor–management model, made impressive gains in other localities. This AFT pressure led the NEA to reconsider its traditional approaches, and in time it too accepted the collective-bargaining model. In sum, organized labor supported collective bargaining by teachers through its affiliate the AFT; the AFT success led NEA to a different posture. The AAUP, whose historic thrust had been somewhat parallel to NEA, felt the pressure from the AFT, and later from the NEA and some of its own local affiliates, to endorse the collective-bargaining model, which it eventually did. Thus the 1970s found the local affiliates of the three major national organizations for teachers using collective bargaining.

Obviously the success of the AFT and the altered stance of the NEA and AAUP occurred in a certain context. The late 1950s and 1960s saw numerous successful challenges to accepted authority, often by means of collective action in various forms. For example, the use of massive nonviolent demonstrations by blacks resulted in impressive gains. The young organized various protests to American foreign policy. Local and state reform groups gained control in many state houses and city halls. In other words, teachers were caught up in the fervor of this era of civil disobedience and pluralism. During this period the female–male composition of the K–12 teaching force changed.

a Constructive Process in University Leadership" in George W. Angell, Edward P. Kelley, Jr., and Associates, *Handbook of Faculty Bargaining* (San Francisco: Jossey-Bass, 1977), pp. 6–23.

By the mid-1960s the number of men teaching in elementary schools had increased significantly and men constituted a majority of the teachers in senior high schools. This has been thought significant in that the men were seen as less willing to play the subservient role that female teachers of an earlier era had accepted. In addition, the turnover rate dropped, the educational level rose, and the feeling of professionalism with accompanying controls over the conditions of education grew. It has further been asserted that the composition of the teaching force underwent changes in that more persons came from homes where unionism was accepted. As the character of the teacher was changing, education was, in the opinion of many, becoming increasingly impersonal, and the public was becoming increasingly critical. Thus it has been often suggested that the "new" teacher was less willing to accept blame for the conditions in schools when there was no feeling of power or of personal allegiance to those in power.

The foregoing is not to suggest that teachers did not hope to make economic gains through the use of collective bargaining. In fact, in one study relating to higher education faculty, the three basic reasons cited for support of unionism were all related to economics (i.e., fear of budget cuts, job security, a teacher surplus).[6] Furthermore, the history of economic achievement by private sector workers using the process of collective bargaining was evidence of its potential. However, this was not the only motivation; teachers had already achieved considerable economic gains. For example, expressed in "constant dollars" based on 1969–70 purchasing power, K–12 instructional staff salaries rose an average of about $2,300 in the 1950s and $2,500 in the 1960s.[7] Furthermore, there is evidence to suggest that collective bargaining has not resulted in the significant economic gains for teachers that some might have expected. For example, in one study, using 1969–70 and 1975–76 salary data and comparing nineteen states having no collective-bargaining laws with thirty states with such laws, it was found that teachers in the nineteen states with no such laws had averaged 40.5 percent in salary increases and those in the thirty states had averaged 36.6 percent. Furthermore, based on data from 37 colleges, it was found that the initiation of collective bargaining was not generally accompanied by "more rapid than average" salary increases.[8] Similarly, from an examination of studies covering in some way most of the 284 higher education institutions having faculty

    [6]James T. Bennett and Manuel H. Johnson, *Demographic Trends in Higher Education: Collective Bargaining and Forced Unionism* (Los Angeles: International Institute for Economic Research, 1979), p. 17.

    [7]Research Division, National Education Association, *Economic Status of the Teaching Profession,* Research Report 1971–74 (Washington, D.C.: The Association, 1971), p. 29.

    [8]"The Salary Effects of Unionism and Compulsory Bargaining Laws," *Phi Delta Kappan,* 60 (February 1979), 419.

unions in 1977, there was no convincing evidence of faculty unions having a positive impact on faculty salaries even in times of enrollment growth and financial stability.[9] Notwithstanding these studies, however, those favoring collective bargaining argue that the long-term impact favors the process and that the threat of collective bargaining has caused nonunion states to "buy off" teachers to keep them out of the movement. Thus the movement has created a climate of support for teachers generally and greatly reduced the tendency of board members to act arbitrarily.

To this point, the focus has been on teachers; yet in the 1970s, collective bargaining spread rapidly to include other educational organization employee groups (e.g., middle- and lower-level administrators, clerical workers, custodians). Presumably, some of the same conditions influencing teachers (e.g., spread of public employee unionism, increasing challenges to established authority, desire for economic gains) contributed to their willingness to organize and bargain collectively. Leadership in organizing the noninstructional or classified employees of educational organizations has been assumed by the American Federation of State, County and Municipal Employees (AFSCME), which saw its membership triple between 1964 and 1976.[10]

Spread of the Movement in Education

The Wagner Act and the Taft-Hartley Act are not applicable to the public sector. Thus as collective bargaining began to spread in the public sector, the legal framework was limited. A legal basis for collective bargaining (i.e., legislative act, executive order, court decision, attorney-general's opinion) is needed to provide recognition and protection of employee rights to organize and bargain collectively. Further, it is in effect a pronouncement of public policy. The first state legislative act was passed by the Wisconsin legislature in 1959. This act required municipalities to bargain with their employees, and in 1965 it was extended to cover state employees. In 1965 six other states (California, Connecticut, Massachusetts, Michigan, Oregon, Washington) enacted public negotiation laws.[11] The process continued and, as has been noted, by 1980 thirty-two states had collective-bargaining laws covering some or all classes of educational employees in the public sector. (This included states with so-called "meet and confer" legislation, which permits a public employer to enter into a contract but does not require it.) In a few other states there was a legal

[9] Bennett and Johnson, op. cit., pp. 19–20.

[10] Jerry Wurf, "Union Leaders and Public Sector Unions: AFSCME" in A. Lawrence Chickering (ed.), *Public Employee Unions* (Lexington, Mass.: Lexington, Heath, 1976), p. 175.

[11] "Growth of Teacher Contracts: 1966–1973," *Negotiation Research Digest,* 7 (January 1974), 16.

base for collective bargaining in the form of court decisions or attorney-generals' opinions. Some school districts in states where there is no legal basis voluntarily bargain with employee groups. Furthermore, the authors are aware of districts, located in a state where the state high court had ruled against public sector collective bargaining, in which there was bargaining by means of a "communication procedure" with teacher groups. Thus, as the 1980s began, public sector collective bargaining had spread to include some educational personnel in at least 90 percent of the states.

The movement has not been widespread in nonpublic K–12 schools; however, it has been estimated that in 1980 there were 80 nonpublic colleges and universities bargaining with the faculty.[12] In a 1980 decision, the U.S. Supreme Court held that the faculty members of Yeshiva University were "managerial employees" as defined in the Wagner Act (which is applicable to nonpublic colleges and schools) and thus not granted collective-bargaining rights by the act.[13] This created an obstacle to further spread of the movement in nonpublic higher education. However, the difficulty of distinguishing between faculties that should be "managerial" and those who should not was recognized. Therefore, it should not be concluded that the *Yeshiva* decision means that there will be no further unionization in nonpublic higher education institutions.

As mentioned before, by 1980, the movement had encompassed classified personnel and "middle managers." Our observation is that there has been a rapid growth in contracts covering various categories of classified employees and middle managers in local school districts. Between 1975 and 1979, there was a 67 percent increase in the number of school districts where some class of middle managers (e.g., principals, coordinators, supervisors) was covered by a collectively-bargained contract (from 1100 such contracts involving twenty-two states to 1838 involving twenty-eight states). Incidentally, as of 1979 there were only seven states where the laws specifically excluded public sector supervisory personnel from unionization.[14]

As of this writing, in many localities there were three or more collectively-bargained contracts that had to be administered. Such growth has not been accomplished without the employees resorting to the strike or some such work stoppage. Even though in 1980 a strike involving public sector educational employees had a legal basis in

[12]Thomas J. Flygare, "Yeshiva University: Implications for the Future of College Collective Bargaining," *Phi Delta Kappan*, 61 (May 1980), 639.
[13]*National Labor Relations Board* v. *Yeshiva University*, 444 U.S. 672, 100 Sup. Ct. 856 (1980).
[14]Bruce S. Cooper, "Collective Bargaining for School Administrators Four Years Later," *Phi Delta Kappan*, 61 (October 1979), 130–131.

only seven states,[15] strikes or other work stoppages were frequent during the 1970s. To illustrate: in 1960–61 there were 3 teacher work stoppages; in 1965–66, 18; in 1970–71, 130;[16] in 1975–76, 203; in 1979–80, 242 (involving 23 states, 201 NEA affiliates, 34 AFT locals, and 7 AAUP chapters).[17] In a 1976 Wisconsin case, where the law prohibited strikes, the U.S. Supreme Court held valid the actions of a school board that held hearings for striking teachers and then voted to terminate them.[18] Some thought this decision would greatly reduce the number of "illegal strikes"; however, there is no evidence to that effect.

Impact of Collective Bargaining in Education

Given that the growth of the movement in education was accompanied by numerous other economic, social, and political trends, it is impossible to identify changes in education that can be attributed directly to collective bargaining. However, during this period of growth there have been shifts in power balances relative to educational issues in many localities; the policy-making power of educational boards and decision-making prerogatives of administrators have been limited; the role of middle-level educational administrators has been affected; there has been a financial impact associated with collective bargaining as a process; the relationships between administrators and their subordinates has changed; the image of teachers has been altered.

Shifting Power and Power Blocs

As discussed earlier, before the advent of collective bargaining, when teachers approached state legislators and local officials, they often did so from a questionable power base. Their major resource, beyond appeal based on the status of education in the culture, was votes. This resource was not lost with bargaining; it was strengthened. Additionally, because they have "control of a valued service," the result is a more respectful audience with legislators and other officials. It is not uncommon for employee organization leaders, at

[15]"State-by-State Roundup of Collective Bargaining Laws," op cit., 473.

[16]Research Division, National Education Association, *Teacher Strikes, Work Stoppages, and Interruptions of Service*, Research Memo 1971–28 (Washington, D.C.: The Association, December 1971), p. 5.

[17]"Teachers Staged 242 Strikes in 1979–80," *Chronicle of Higher Education*, XX (July 14, 1980), 3.

[18]*Hortonville Joint School District No. 1* v. *Hortonville Education Association*, 426 U.S. 482, 96 Sup. Ct. 2308 (1976).

both state and local levels, to issue an invitation to public officials to appear before a representative group of teachers or classified employees to address issues of interest to the organization. Such invitations go unheeded at considerable risk to those invited.

Educational employee organizations, particularly the NEA and AFT, have engaged in extensive political action at all levels of government. The NEA, a strong supporter of former President Carter in both 1976 and 1980, sent more than 450 delegates and alternates to the 1980 Democratic convention and is credited with being a major force in President Carter's successful effort to create the Department of Education.[19] Candidates for state legislative bodies are endorsed and provided financial support. Subsequently, there is often an effort to secure increased state educational financial support, state statutes requiring employment of special instructional support personnel and class size maximums, and collective-bargaining laws that are more advantageous to public employees. Candidates for places on local school boards have been supported successfully. In fact, the authors are aware of some localities, in the absence of legal provisions to prohibit the practice, where teacher organization members have sought and won election to the school board with which their organization bargained. In sum, collective bargaining has resulted in greater pluralism in regard to educational affairs in many states, local school districts, and higher education institutions.

In some places, collective bargaining has resulted in a new group of power elites. Educational employee organizations, in coalition with emerging power groups in other sectors of the community and other unions, have been influential in creating a rather monolithic power group to replace the previously existing bloc. However, there exists a countervailing force to public employee-dominated blocs on economic matters, for emerging groups and other union personnel pay taxes. If the employees get too far out of line on economic issues support is lost. In fact, it has been argued that the increased educational employee power has had far more influence on "administrative procedures and governance practices" than economic benefits to the employees.[20]

One author offered a rather different perspective. He argued that the locus of power in educational affairs is shifting to three new classes of experts: (1) negotiators for governing boards, (2) the professional staffs of the unions, and (3) the professional neutrals (e.g., state pub-

[19]Beverly T. Watkins, "NEA, Now a Political Power, Plans to Use Its Clout," *Chronicle of Higher Education,* loc. cit.

[20]Michael J. Murphy and David Hoover, "Negotiations at the Crossroads: Increased Professionalization or Reinforced Bureaucracy," in Anthony M. Cresswell and Michael J. Murphy (eds.), *Education and Collective Bargaining: Readings in Policy and Research* (Berkeley: McCutchan, 1976), p. 476.

lic labor relations agency personnel, arbitrators). His basic rationale was that these experts are those most centrally involved in negotiating and administering the contracts, which define many of the conditions of work and practices in an educational organization.[21]

Limits on Board and Administrator Prerogatives

Where there is no collective-bargaining contract, so long as governing boards and administrators do not violate directives from higher authority (e.g., laws, court decisions) and stay within the tolerance limits of accepted norms, they have great freedom to act unilaterally. Employee committees may offer advice, faculty senates may pass resolutions, task forces may submit reports, and open hearings may be held. However, these inputs are advisory, and the legal authority is still vested with the governing board and its administrative employees. Collective bargaining has placed numerous limits on this authority.

In addition to salaries, welfare benefits, grievance procedures, seniority rights, and the like, contracts resulting from the collective-bargaining process have given attention to class size, number of preparations per day per teacher, length of the workday, number of and agenda for staff meetings, recruitment practices, selection criteria, basis of assignment, criteria for promotion, conditions of transfer, curriculum development processes, performance evaluation methods, reduction-in-force plans, outside employment, dues checkoff, union privileges, management rights, provisions for office space, copyrights and patents, textbook selection plans, staff development provisions, use of technology, and availability of support services. The foregoing list is merely illustrative; however, it serves to make the central point— collective-bargaining contracts frequently deal with policy and administrative matters.

To offer a specific illustration, from a National Institute of Education-commissioned study involving an analysis of 151 teacher contracts and site visits to fifteen local districts and five state capitals, it was concluded that the main impact of teacher collective bargaining was to limit the flexibility of school boards and administrators in budgetary matters and teacher transfers.[22] It was argued that when contract-mandated teacher salaries, class size limits, preparation periods, and minimum number of specialists were met, the remaining funds afforded little opportunity for board/administrator discretion. Further, when the contract makes seniority the sole or primary criterion for transfer or reduction-in-force decisions, there is difficulty in

[21] Charles W. Cheng, *Altering Collective Bargaining: Citizen Participation in Educational Decision Making,* (New York: Praeger, 1976), pp. 77–88.
[22] Lorraine McDonnell and Anthony Pascal, *Organized Teachers in American Schools,* (Santa Monica, Calif.: Rand, 1979), p. 75.

meeting externally imposed staff desegregation mandates, retaining younger teachers, and matching particular school needs with appropriate and competent staff. Also, the resulting more senior teaching force increases the salary costs.[23]

Collective-bargaining contract provisions such as the foregoing have given educational organization employees, particularly teachers, much more control over budgets and educational processes. From the point of view of teachers, this is as it should be. One of the conditions that led them to collective bargaining was the perception that they had no real control of these matters, and as professionals this control should rightly be theirs.

From the perspective of many board members and administrators the contracts negotiated in regard to items such as the foregoing have deprived them of management prerogatives; yet the public still holds them responsible. As seen by the public, the board and its administrators are responsible for what goes on in the organization; yet the contract has deprived them of the authority to carry out the responsibility.

Whether the teachers' perception or that of boards and administrators is the more valid is subject to much discussion. Nevertheless, it is obvious that much management flexibility has been taken away by the contract. For example, class size limits may fix the grouping arrangements for an elementary principal, and transfer and assignment agreements limit the options an assistant superintendent for personnel has in accommodating a declining and shifting pupil population.

In sum, what are administrative prerogatives? What are teacher prerogatives? What are the ends and means of instruction? These are no longer decisions made by boards and administrators taking into account opinions they choose to solicit. These are decisions shared with teachers and other employees by means of the bargaining process.

Influence on Middle-Level Administrators

Principals, assistant principals, coordinators, higher education institution department heads, and the like, are the immediate supervisors of teachers and other employee groups who have negotiated contracts. As such, they are the administrators with the most direct and frequent contact with those covered by the contracts and their role is affected in two ways—the carrying out of their tasks and the added responsibility of contract administration.

As has been noted, the topics covered in collectively-bargained contracts are often extensive. Unless the state statutes limit the scope

[23] Ibid.

of bargaining, it is not unusual to find that the contract will affect the manner in which each of the task areas described in Chapter 2 is carried out. State statutes often allow for bargaining about "wages, hours, and other terms and conditions of employment." The phrase *other terms and conditions of employment* has been subject to different interpretations, some so broad that all task areas may be affected. The immediate supervisor will most often be faced with a number of specific constraints when carrying out his or her duties. For example, in the previously cited NIE study, the majority of the contracts specified the length of the workday and year, guaranteed the teachers preparation periods, limited the number of different classes a teacher had to teach, restricted assignments to a teacher's area of certification, required assignments be made on the basis of seniority, limited the nonteaching duties teachers must perform, and set class size maximums. These provisions, relating to the administrative task areas of organizational structure, curriculum and instruction, and staff personnel, limited the freedom of building level administrators to make decisions about what teachers do and when they do it. Further, the majority of the contracts specified the number of teacher evaluations, length and format of classroom observations, teacher response to the evaluations, and required advance notice by principals to teachers when teacher evaluations were planned.[24]

In regard to contract administration, middle-level administrators have had to assume the principal responsibility for putting the provisions of the contract into practice. They are charged with the day-to-day interpretation of the contract. Even though this responsibility also rests, in part, with the employee organization, it is not unusual to find employee organization leadership permitting middle-level administrators to exercise considerable discretion in matters covered by the contract and then testing the validity of these actions by means of the dispute-settling mechanism (i.e., grievance procedure).

Because middle-level administrators have such a critical role in administering the contract, it is essential, even as the final touches are being put on a contract, that they become fully informed about the details of the contract and the intentions underlying the language used. This places a responsibility on the chief negotiator for the management team to offer detailed explanations of contract provisions and intent to middle-level administrators. Such administrators have a concomitant responsibility to probe for clarification until the rights and duties of both the employees covered by the contract and administrators are clear.

In addition to knowing the contract, there appear to be two keys

[24]Ibid., pp. 77–79.

to successful contract administration on the part of middle-level administrators. First, they must exhibit behavior consistent with the tenets of good human relations; there should be no display of an antiunion attitude, nor should there be subtle actions designed to undermine the spirit of the contract. Second, there must be consistency in judgments related to contract matters. This consistency must be exhibited among administrators and by the same administrator from one incident to another. Obviously, consistency in administering the contract means that under no circumstances are contract provisions to be forgotten or deals made in opposition to the language and intent of the contract.

Costs of Maintaining the Process

The budgetary impact of implementing collectively-bargained contract provisions and the economic gains of employee groups have been described. What we fear is often overlooked is the financial requirement just to maintain the process in a school district, college, or university. There are costs to both the employee organizations and the employer. Since our concern here is with the administration of educational organizations, we are confining our discussion to the costs to the educational organization. These costs, which relate to both contract negotiations and contract administration, will vary widely among educational organizations and will be determined by such variables as the state statutes governing the process, size of the organization, the number of employee groups with whom the organization bargains, the nature of the contract(s), the aggressiveness of the employee organization(s), and the skill with which the contract is administered.

Most medium and large educational organizations staff and maintain an "employee relations" unit, which is central to contract negotiations and administration. For example, in a school district of 40,000 to 50,000 pupils the unit might include two or three professionals, plus supporting clerical personnel. When a contract is in the process of being negotiated, a "management negotiating team," made up of administrators representative of different components of the organization, is often formed. The team meets with the employee organization team, and the hours involved are often long and irregular. A frequent practice, particularly in smaller organizations, is to employ an "outside negotiator" to assist the management team in the process. When there are impasses, mediators, fact finders, and/or arbitrators are usually employed. Given the legal implications of many of the items that are the subject of bargaining, there is frequent need for legal counsel. It is readily apparent that there are significant financial costs associated with maintaining employee relations staffs, providing compensatory time or extra pay to members of management negotiating teams, hiring outside negotiating and legal advice, and sharing with the employee organization the costs of impasse specialists. Also, the costs of collecting data in preparation for bargaining and recording the proceedings must be considered.

There are costs associated with keeping middle managers informed about the contract provisions and answering their queries as different situations occur during the life of the contract. Grievances are almost inevitable and if the employee organizations are aggressive and/or the middle-level managers are inept in administering the contracts, grievances will be more frequent. The time associated with settling such disputes must be translated into costs and if the fact-finding or arbitration stage is reached, the costs of these proceedings may become significant.

As previously detailed, where there is collective bargaining, strikes or work stoppages are always a possibility. If recommended procedures regarding preparing for possible work stoppages, operating during a work stoppage, and returning to "normal" after a work stoppage are followed, the costs may be considerable.[25]

In sum, it is our observation that there are significant financial costs related to collective bargaining as a process. While these costs may be difficult to identify precisely, they represent a use of resources that cannot be ignored.

Administrator–Subordinate Relations

In educational organizations where the collective-bargaining process has been implemented, the relationship between subordinates and administrators is marked by greater formality and an increased psychological distance. This may be too sweeping a generalization, and court decisions relating to equal protection and due process rights have contributed to the formalizing of the relationships. Nevertheless, anecdotal data suggest that where subordinates and administrators have bargained vigorously across the table, they have difficulty developing a relationship conducive to working cooperatively on other matters. Furthermore, the contract often contains detailed procedures and highly specific rules that must be applied. The result is often an increase in the impersonal nature of the relationship between administrators and subordinates as administrators "follow the contract" in carrying out their duties.

This state of administrator–subordinate relations may be temporary and related to the process of growth in negotiations. To illustrate, Carlton suggested that there were three attitude stages in the

---

[25] For a set of recommended procedures, see, for example, American Association of School Administrators, *Work Stoppage Strategies,* (Arlington, Va.: The Association, 1975).

process of negotiatory growth—nativity, adolescence, and maturity. He described the adolescent state in terms such as "balance of terror," "we–they," "hard-nosedness," "indignation," and "intransigence." Even though the we–they attitude does not disappear, the third stage is characterized by a spirit of accommodation, recognition of mutual interest, and integrative bargaining.[26] Thus it may be that the present relationship in many educational organizations will change as the maturity stage is reached. Parenthetically, we would suggest that a few educational organizations are still in Carlton's nativity stage, in which he characterized teachers as feeling guilty and boards and administrators as being in a state of shock.[27] Administrators still pass along anecdotes to us about the outrage of board members about the "audacity" of Ms. Jones or about Mr. Smith who, after the bargaining for the year had been completed, comes by to offer an apology for being a party to the process.

Image of Teachers

There seems to be little doubt that the traditional image of the teacher has been subject to much revision. The notion of a good teacher as a person who works quietly, patiently, selflessly, and uncomplainingly with the pupils, accepts conditions as they are, and depends upon the wisdom of superiors in major decisions concerning education may still exist in the minds of many lay citizens. However, they can find fewer living examples of their ideal than there once were.

The revised image of teachers appears to be both positive and negative. There is the image of the teacher as a professional who has a voice in the ends and means of instruction, who has expertise in matters of instruction and demands the right to use that expertise fully, who is concerned first with the classroom and courageously expresses this concern to the upper levels of the bureaucracy, who demands that the maximum number of educational dollars be related directly to instruction, who wants to assume full responsibility for planning and executing the teaching acts, and who feels fully justified in demanding that a professional salary be paid for professional services. There is the other image of the teacher who has lost sight of the high service commitment of the professions, who bargains from a position of self-interest only, who demands that seniority replace competence as a major criterion for advancement, who uses the collective power mechanism to protect the ineffective colleague, who makes unreasonable demands, who refuses to be a party to helping assure the

---

[26] Patrick W. Carlton, "Social and Attitudinal Correlates of Collective Negotiations in Education," *IRS Journal,* 1 (Winter 1969), 33–34.
[27] Ibid.

resources to meet educational demands, and who has been vindictive in the use of new-found power.

Both of the foregoing descriptions are overdrawn. Yet they do serve to emphasize that the advent of collective bargaining has resulted in teachers being viewed differently. Incidentally, in spite of the changed image of teachers there seems to be some real doubt as to whether the advent of collective bargaining has had any significant impact on what goes on in the classroom. One of the major conclusions from the NIE study to which we have referred was that "students probably experience the effects of bargaining only indirectly and occasionally."[28]

Problems and Questions Related to the Movement

The overriding and persisting question concerns the appropriateness of the collective-bargaining model for education. Assuming, based on the widespread application of the model, whether or not it is the most appropriate model, it is going to be used for the foreseeable future, there is a major problem related to the place of middle-level managers and other procedural questions to be resolved as well.

Appropriateness of the Model

We do not propose to answer such a value-laden question as whether collective bargaining is an appropriate model for education. We accept collective bargaining as a reality and see both positive and negative effects of the movement as it has been applied. Our intent here is to examine some of the pros and cons of the model and briefly mention some of the alternatives proposed to enable the reader to make a personal judgment.

Those who feel that collective bargaining is appropriate for education are likely to base their position on one or more of the following arguments. First, without collective bargaining a board–administrative team can determine unilaterally the means and ends of schooling and the conditions under which teachers and other employees will work. This is inherently unfair. Second, even though there are many mutual interests (e.g., quality schooling for students), there is a fundamental conflict between employees and employer on the basic economic issues—the educational organization employees want to maximize their rewards for services rendered and the board wants to hold the line to what they think the public is able and willing to pay. Collective bargaining is the best known means of providing parity in the resolution of this fundamental conflict. Third, the professional

28McDonnell and Pascal, op. cit., p. 88.

prerogatives of teachers are subject to erosion unless there is a structure to protect those prerogatives. Collective bargaining provides a mechanism that enables teachers to ensure that their professional standards and rights are maintained. The presence of collective bargaining reduces the probability that the services of professional teachers will be available under conditions that violate their professional standards. Fourth, experience shows it works. In support of this argument the gains of employees in the private sector are cited as are the advances made by employees in various educational organizations where there has been extensive collective-bargaining experience. Fifth, no alternative has been proposed that guarantees the teachers an equal voice in major educational decisions.

Those who oppose the imposition of the model on education often cite one or more of the following. First, because nonpublic schools are not a realistic alternative for most families, public schools have a monopoly on a critical societal service, and through collective action the employees may withhold services. Thus this mechanism gives educational organization employees the power to cripple society seriously. Put another way, the interests of clients are subordinated to narrow self-interests. Second, it is a time-consuming way to make decisions and the decisions that result from compromises are not always the most rational. Further, an outside third party (e.g., national and state organizational representatives, professional negotiators, mediators, fact finders) is imposed on the local decision-making process. Third, it creates an elaborate mechanism to govern employee–employer relationships that limits the ability of the organization to respond to changing needs and conditions. Fourth, experience has shown that outstanding performance is less likely to be rewarded; thus "just average" performance is encouraged. This last argument is most frequently advanced in relation to higher education faculties where there is no history of a single, two-axis (preparation and experience) salary schedule. Fifth, as applied to public sector teachers, there are inherent advantages in being public employees. Accordingly, their representational rights should be reduced. This is the basic thesis advanced by Lieberman, a pioneer advocate for collective bargaining for teachers. He argued that teachers in the public sector have many advantages over private sector employees, including an important role in determining who is management, gaining more from state political activity, bargaining with a management that has less incentive than private sector management to resist union demands, many rights guaranteed by law in the absence of bargaining, and self-interests, which are, in the final analysis, adverse to public interests.[29]

[29]Myron Lieberman, "Eggs That I Have Laid: Teacher Bargaining Reconsidered," *Phi Delta Kappan,* 60 (February 1979), 415–419.

Several options or alternatives in collective bargaining for teachers (which seems to be more controversial than bargaining by noninstructional or classified employees) have been proposed.[30] Myers, borrowing three alternative models from Williams and advancing another, identified four possible models—the self-employed professional model, modified hierarchical model, academic model, and academic union model.[31]

The self-employed professional model is not very practical because inherent in the model is the assumption that teachers will be self-employed and fee-charging (i.e., schooling will be provided by individual teachers on a tutorial basis). Yet the features of increased autonomy and control over licensure are seen as important to increased teacher participation. The modified hierarchical model, which has existed in some form for years, leaves the ultimate power for decision making with the board–administrative team. Teachers are included through consultation by means of membership on administrative councils, ad hoc and standing committees, and so on. The model has not provided teachers with the autonomy they want. The academic model, widely applied in higher education, divides the decisions into two broad categories: (1) academic and administrative, and (2) financial and managerial. The faculty through senate and committee structures makes major academic and administrative decisions such as those related to courses, programs, student admission and degree standards, faculty appointments, and faculty promotion and tenure. This model may be acceptable in many universities where the academic model has been long in existence.

Myers went on to describe the academic union model as follows:

> (It) . . . encompasses the characteristics of the academic model but uses collective bargaining as a coercive means of gaining and maintaining teacher authority. . . . Teachers would have the responsibility through collective bargaining for making academic decisions (such as staff selection, promotion, and evaluation; curriculum; selection of materials and supplies; instructional decisions; school organization) and would negotiate with management concerning salary and working conditions.[32]
>
> The academic union model resembles the model of authority structure that exists in most hospitals and large universities in which separate spheres of authority (dual lines of authority) have been identified. In the organizations professionals are under no obligation to take the advice of administrators concerning client care. This arrangement does

[30] See, for example, Richard C. Williams, "Alternative Models for Teacher Participation," in Piele and Eidell, op. cit., pp. 86–91; Frank Ambrosie, "Negotiations in the School System: A General Concept," *Planning and Changing*, 3 (April 1972), 25–34; Myers, op. cit., pp. 100–105; Cheng, op. cit., pp. 110–135.

[31] Myers, loc cit.

[32] Ibid., p. 102.

not preclude persons *offering* advice in any area. . . . Collective bargaining is essential for the academic union model to function effectively for teachers because it offers a form of sanction that elevates teachers to a power plane equivalent to management. Management has been reluctant historically to share its power.[33]

The proposed academic union model appears to have the potential for greatly broadening the scope of bargaining. Others, however, recognizing the public and essential nature of schooling, would move to restrict the scope of bargaining. This could be accomplished by statutes that enumerate specifically the topics subject to negotiation and prohibit bargaining on any topic not enumerated.

Cheng, among others, has proposed a "multiparty" structure for teacher bargaining. He argued that the community had a right to have a voice in educational decision making, and, as such, the bargaining process needed to be altered to provide access for community groups.[34] The general notion behind such trilateral practices seems to be that inclusion of the community in the process will provide a form of consumer restraint or countervailing force to union power. Assuming this to be the rationale, the counterargument could be that even with traditional bilateral bargaining, legal restrictions related to strikes and impasse procedures, declining enrollments, and taxpayer resistance provide more than enough constraints on the union.

Whether any of the above proposals for altering the collective-bargaining process will be adopted by educational organizations on a fairly wide scale we do not know. As with the industrial model now in wide use, we see both promise and problems. Nevertheless, we would reiterate that we believe collective bargaining in some form will continue to be used in educational organizations as one mechanism of conflict resolution.

The Place of Middle-Level Administrators

As suggested before, there is much concern about how the middle-level administrators in local school districts (e.g., principals, assistant principals) and higher education institutions (e.g., department heads), who are the primary administrators of collective-bargaining contracts, are going to be accommodated. In the 1960s two patterns relative to the place of middle-level administrators seemed to prevail—they were included as a part of the teachers' bargaining unit or they were bystanders to the whole sequence of events. As a part of an all-inclusive teachers' organization, these persons found themselves formally committed to the goals of the teacher group, goals

[33] Ibid., p. 103.
[34] Cheng, loc. cit.

that usually did not give much attention to their concerns. Thus even though they were nominally in a bargaining unit with teachers, they were still essentially left out. A few years of experience made it readily apparent to both teachers and middle managers that when bargaining becomes a formalized bilateral process with the features described previously, there are fundamental conflicts between the interests of classroom teachers and middle-level administrators. Thus the all-inclusive unit pattern began to disappear. Where middle managers were not included as a part of the teachers' bargaining unit, it could be argued that they were members of the management team. Technically this may be accurate, but the practical effect in many places was that the confrontation was seen as being between teachers and the top management team, with the middle-level administrators largely ignored. Under both patterns the results were often the same: the management prerogatives of these middle-level administrators were the subject of bargaining, their needs were given little attention, and in the end these persons lost.

At this writing, there seem to be three basic positions advocated and practiced in regard to the place of the middle-level administrators. As detailed earlier, in many places they have formed separate bargaining units and negotiated contracts on behalf of their unit membership. The basic argument for bargaining units for middle-management personnel is that this is one way they have of ensuring that their interests are fully represented and that their prerogatives do not become pawns at the table. The basic reasoning in opposition to the separate unit approach is that the management team is split, and unity is important if the industrial model of conflict resolution is used. As has been described, in the 1970s this separate unit approach, in some form, spread rather rapidly. We suspect that many middle-level administrators favor this approach, particularly those in the large urban districts, and that in the years ahead, unless there is an increase in restricting statutes, the practice will continue.

A second basic approach to providing for middle managers is to take definite steps to ensure that their interests are protected, their views are seriously considered at the top management level, and their economic benefits keep pace. This pattern exists in a number of places. In such localities, formal mechanisms have been instituted to give these persons a voice in major decisions, they are represented at the table (e.g., a principal or assistant principal is a member of the negotiating team), and management incentive programs have been agreed upon without the formality of the collective-bargaining process. The logic behind this approach is that the management team must remain intact. The difficulties come when the agreed-upon incentive programs are not fully implemented and/or the decision-making mechanisms do not seem to be providing the desired level of input. At this point the level of trust drops and interest in the separate unit pattern develops.

A third approach, which seems to hold considerable promise and has been instituted in several places, is to treat members of this large middle-level administrator group not as a large bloc, but as individuals and smaller groups depending upon role. Specifically, the idea is to classify each administrative position, regardless of how it has been traditionally viewed in the organization, or its place in the hierarchy, as either supervisory (i.e., managerial) or not. For those positions not classified as supervisory, separate bargaining units are formed and those positions classified as supervisory are included as a viable part of the management team. This trend of exempting "true" managerial employees from collective-bargaining rights is consistent with practice in the private sector, where supervisors, in the legal sense, are not provided collective-bargaining rights.

Florida, which prohibits public sector "managerial" personnel from bargaining collectively, has, in effect, taken this approach. The criteria for determining whether or not an employee is managerial are the historic relationship of the employee to the public employer and other employees and the nature of the work performed. Managerial personnel perform jobs that are not routine, clerical, or ministerial and require independent judgment relative to such areas as policies that are applicable to those covered by collectively-bargained contracts, contract negotiations and administration, and budget and personnel administration. Using the historic relationship and the nature of the job, the state agency charged with administering the Florida law may classify some public employees with similar titles differently. For example, within the state university system, department heads in some schools and colleges have been classified as "management," whereas other department heads in different schools and colleges have been classified as "nonmanagement." In sum, as illustrated by Florida, the third approach to defining the place of middle-level administrators is to classify each such administrator as either managerial or nonmanagerial and expect the managerial employees to be a part of the management team.

Three Major Procedural Questions

As the industrial union model has evolved in education, a number of procedural issues have emerged. These include: Is exclusive or multiple representation (recognition) more appropriate? What should be the scope of bargaining? Where do middle-level administrators fit? Should there be a national collective-bargaining law for public employees? Should educational organization employees be given the legal right to strike? Should the agency shop be permitted? In interest or contract disputes, should arbitration be allowed, and if so, in what form?

The question of representation has essentially been resolved in favor of exclusive representation. The questions relative to scope and middle-level administrators have been explored. There has been great interest in a national collective-bargaining statute because many believe that there should be more uniformity within the nation regarding the conditions under which public employees organize and bargain. In 1974, both the NEA and AFT were successful in getting bills introduced in the U.S. Congress; however, neither was enacted into law. At this point there seems to be little effort to enact a national public employees collective-bargaining law. The reason is a 1976 U.S. Supreme Court decision relating to the question of whether the Congress had the authority to extend the Fair Labor Standards Act provisions relative to minimum wages and maximum hours to states and their subdivisions. The high court said the Congress did not have such authority because it usurped the functions essential to a state's separate and independent existence.[35] The prevailing opinion is that any national collective-bargaining law must meet the court's standard about not infringing upon the states' integrity as independent governmental units, and to do so is a most difficult task. Thus, with any national statute facing major legal hurdles, the issues relative to the strike, agency shop, and contract dispute arbitration remain.

In only a few states is there any legal foundation for teachers or other educational organization employees to strike. Furthermore, one suspects that, exclusive of education union personnel, the preponderance of opinion is against educational organization employees having the right to strike. The basic argument for prohibiting teachers and other employees from striking is the notion that they have a monopoly over a critical public service. Yet, when compared to the sanctions notion promoted by the NEA in the 1960s,[36] the strike is "cleaner" and there is more pressure for a settlement (e.g., teachers lose pay when on strike). Further, if no strike is permitted, there is some question whether parity at the table really exists. The other side of this coin is that of public opinion, and most state statutes do not allow a board–administrative team to lock out employees.

The basic rationale for the agency shop movement, which is growing, is that all who benefit from the bargaining should share the cost of the negotiations and handling grievances. If a person can enjoy union-secured benefits without having to join the union or make a payment of support, there is no incentive to support the union and an

---

[35]*National League of Cities* v. *Usery*, 426 U.S. 833, 96 Sup. Ct. 2465 (1976).
[36]For a discussion of sanctions see T. M. Stinnett, *Professional Problems of Teachers,* 3rd ed. (New York: Macmillan, 1968), pp. 512–522.

increasing smaller percentage of those benefiting will be provided the financial support needed by the union. The counterargument is that if the union is effective in its activities, the voluntary support will be adequate. Furthermore, there is the notion of an individual's right to work without being forced to assist an employee group who may support causes and/or political candidates the individual opposes.

The movement toward interest or contract dispute arbitration, which may either be compulsory or voluntary, has been growing. It has been argued that compulsory arbitration lessens the pressure to settle a dispute because of the inevitability of arbitration and the tendency of arbitrators to "split the difference." The use of arbitration in the public sector has been opposed in that it constitutes an illegal delegation of authority. To illustrate, it has been argued that a school board cannot delegate its authority to an "outside" third party. However, several state courts have rejected this argument. Support for arbitration is found among those who believe it is a reasonable alternative to the right to strike for teachers and other public employees. In regard to the presumed tendency of arbitrators to "split the difference," which is seen as a serious barrier to reasonable final offers, there has been increased use of *final offer arbitration,* which may be either "issue by issue" or "total package." Under the final offer format, the arbitrator is required to choose either the employer's or employees' final offer, and if it is on the total package, the arbitrator cannot "split the difference" by choosing the employer's final offer on one issue and the employees' on another. In at least one state, Iowa, the law has provided the arbitrator with three offers on each issue from which to make a decision: (1) the final offer of the employer, (2) that of the employees, and (3) the recommendation of the fact finder. The basic notion is that by including the recommendation of an experienced neutral the possibility of the arbitrator being forced to choose between two extreme alternatives will be reduced. In sum, given the widespread opposition to strikes by public sector educational organization employees and the recognized need for parity at the table, we believe the trend toward contract dispute arbitration will continue, and there will be increased experimentation with some form of final offer arbitration.

ACTIVITIES/QUESTIONS FOR FURTHER STUDY

1. Determine for your state the legal framework and procedures within which collective bargaining occurs. If there is a detailed statute, become familiar with the requirements relative to who may bargain collectively, scope of bargaining, unfair labor practices, bargaining unit determination and recognition, type(s) of shop permitted, strike clauses, arbitration provisions, administrative agency, and so on. If there is no statute or if it does not detail such requirements, determine how decisions are made about such

topics as those mentioned. If you are in a state where there is no collective bargaining in educational organizations, what is the status of the movement? Have bills been introduced in the legislature dealing with such topics? If so, what were their requirements?

2. Secure from a school district or college a copy of the current collective bargaining contract and copies of contracts for earlier years (e.g., four, eight, and twelve years earlier). Analyze the contracts to determine the major changes that have occurred over time and the nature and extent of constraints placed on the middle-level administrators.

3. Invite a panel of veteran educational administrators representing different levels of the hierarchy to discuss with the class changes that have occurred with the presence of collective bargaining (e.g., how they approach the tasks described in Chapter 2, their personal leadership behavior, personal relations within the organization).

SUGGESTED READINGS

ANGELL, GEORGE W., EDWARD P. KELLEY, JR., and ASSOCIATES. *Handbook of Faculty Bargaining.* San Francisco: Jossey-Bass, Inc., Publishers, 1977.

CASTETTER, WILLIAM B. *The Personnel Function in Educational Administration,* 3rd ed. New York: Macmillan Publishing Co., Inc., 1981, Chapter 15.

CHENG, CHARLES W. *Altering Collective Bargaining: Citizen Participation in Educational Decision Making.* New York: Praeger Publishers, Inc., 1976.

"Collective Bargaining," *Phi Delta Kappan,* 63 (December 1981), 231–251.

CRESSWELL, ANTHONY M., and MICHAEL J. MURPHY (eds.). *Education and Collective Bargaining: Readings in Policy and Research.* Berkeley: McCutchan Publishing Corp., 1976.

FLYGARE, THOMAS J. *Collective Bargaining in the Public Schools.* Bloomington, Ind.: Phi Delta Kappa Educational Foundation, 1977.

HUDGINS, H. C., JR., and RICHARD S. VACCA. *Law and Education: Contemporary Issues and Court Decisions.* Charlottesville, Va.: The Michie Company, 1979, Chapter 5.

LIEBERMAN, MYRON. *Public Sector Bargaining: A Policy Reappraisal.* Lexington, Mass.: Lexington Books, D. C. Heath & Company, 1980.

McDONNELL, LORRAINE, and ANTHONY PASCAL. *Organized Teachers in American Schools.* Santa Monica, Calif.: The Rand Corporation, 1979.

PISAPIA, JOHN. "The Legal Basis of Administrator Bargaining," *NOLPE School Law Journal'* 9 (Number 1, 1980), 61–84.

Author Index

Subject Index